BRISTOL RECORD SOCIETY'S
PUBLICATIONS

General Editors: MADGE DRESSER
                 PETER FLEMING
                 ROGER LEECH

VOL. 63

THE LEDGER OF THOMAS SPEED

1681–1690

The impudent entry for 'Sir' Jahzeel Speed, flaunting a sum of over £400 appropriated by himself (f. 33.4D). Note that it is entered as a balance carried forward from the previous ledger, i.e. was already history. It also is a good example of Jahzeel's hand.

This account (f. 136.5C) is mostly in Speed's own hand, but has been closed off by the unknown person who wrote up the Ledger in 1689–90. Samuel Kekewich was his factor in Cadiz, and Isaac Heming his son-in-law and London banker. There is a picture of the Cadiz Merchant on the front cover. The shipping mark drawn in the margin of this account appears on the back cover.

THE LEDGER OF THOMAS SPEED 1681–1690

EDITED

BY

JONATHAN HARLOW

Published by
BRISTOL RECORD SOCIETY
2011

ISBN 978-0-901538-32-1

BRISTOL RECORD SOCIETY

President: The Lord Mayor of Bristol
General Editors: Madge Dresser, BA, MSc, DPhil, FR HistS.
Peter Fleming, BA, Ph.D.
Roger Leech, M.A., Ph.D., FSA, MIFA
Secretary: Jonathan Harlow
Treasurer: Gill James

The Society exists to encourage the preservation, study and publication of documents relating to the history of Bristol, and since its foundation in 1929 has published sixty-two major volumes of historic documents concerning the city. All the volumes, together with their authoritative introductions, are edited by scholars who are experts in their chosen field.

Recent volumes have included: *William Worcestre: The Topography of Medieval Bristol* (Vol. 51); *The Topography of Medieval and Early Modern Bristol* (Vols. 48 and 52); *The Diary of Sarah Fox* (Vol. 55); *The Pre-Reformation Records of All Saints'Church, Bristol* (Vols. 46, 53 and 56); *Bristol Probate Inventories* (Vols. 54, 57 and 60); *Robert Sturmy's Commercial Expedition to the Mediterranean 1457–8* (Vol. 58); *Records of Bristol Cathedral* (Vol. 59); *Bristol's Trade with Ireland and the Continent, 1503–1601* (Vol. 61); and *Westbury-on-Trym: Monastery, Minster and College* (Vol. 62).

In return for the modest subscription, members of the Society receive the volumes as they are published. The subscription for private members is £10 per annum, for UK institutions £12.50, and for overseas membership £20.

The Society acknowledges with thanks the continued support of the Universities of Bristol and of the West of England and of the Bristol Record Office.

Correspondence to the Secretary, Hardings Cottage, Swan Lane, Winterbourne, S. Glos. BS36 1RJ. Subscriptions to the Treasurer, 20 the Willows, Yate, S. Glos. BS37 5XL.

Orders for past volumes to the Bristol Record Office, 'B'BondWarehouse, Smeaton Road, Bristol, BS1 6XN. Website: http://www.bris.ac.uk/Depts/History/bristolrecordsociety

Produced for the Society by
4word Ltd
Unit 15 Bakers Park
Cater Road
Bristol BS13 7TT

CONTENTS

ACKNOWLEDGEMENTS & DEDICATION

This work is a spin-off from my doctoral thesis 'The Life & Times of Thomas Speed' and owes much to my then supervisors Madge Dresser of UWE and Jonathan Barry of Exeter University. I did most of the original transcription and the associated research in the Bristol Record Office, where the archivists are unfailingly helpful. The Council of the Bristol Record Society have been encouraging, none more so than Dr Joseph Bettey who has done so much for the history of this region. The result has greatly benefited from the wise advice of the Record Society editor Dr Peter Fleming, but I alone must be responsible for the remaining faults.

Thanks are due to Colonel High Dunsterville on behalf of the Goldney family and to the Bristol Record Office for permission to publish the facsimile images which accompany this volume, and to the Maritime Museum at Greenwich for permission to use the picture of the *Cadiz Merchant* on the cover. I should also like to thank all those at 4word for the pains they have taken in setting a very troublesome text.

My family have been not only tolerant but positively supportive. This volume is dedicated, with love, to Bertha, Cathy, Croc, Dilys, Jenny and Simon.

INTRODUCTION

1 THE DOCUMENT

Accounts do not always make interesting reading. But the Ledger of Thomas Speed gives us a unique insight into the work, the life, and the values of a successful Bristol merchant in the late 17th century.

The ledger is held in the Bristol Record Office.[1] It is catalogued as a ledger of Thomas Speed; and the naming of people like 'Isaac Heming my sonne in law' places it unmistakably as his. It belongs to the Goldney family, very likely having come into their hands when that family inherited Speed's house in Small Street around 1709, and was deposited in the Record Office in 1974..

1.1 Description

The Ledger is a single volume approximately 46 by 29 by 6 cm. It has a leather cover tooled with 'Leadger E Begun 12 december Anno Domini 1681' (see cover). [2]

The left and right hand sides of the open Ledger form a pair, and the left-hand page is numbered. Speed refers to such a double page as one 'folio'. Folios 1–184 are well preserved. Folio 185 has some minor gaps. Folio 186 is substantially impaired but can be reconstructed. No items are cross-referenced to any folio number greater than 194 and nearly all open accounts are closed off to 'Profit & Loss' (i.e. written off) or to 'Account of Balances' for posting to the next Ledger. It seems clear that the Ledger had been completed and that only a few folios are lost – most of which can be reconstructed from their counter-entries.

In each account, Debit entries are posted to the left hand page and Credit entries to the right. There may be several accounts on a page, but each account has a ruled heading right across the double page, and is closed off by the next so that there is never any confusion about which account the entries belong to. The standard entries, for which columns have been ruled, are for the year and month, the day, the narrative, the number of the folio where the counter-entry is meant to be, and £, s, & d in separate columns. The heading usually contains the year in which it was opened –

---

[1] BRO 33288 (60); also in TNA Ctalogue as NRA 21693.
[2] So presumably his fifth ledger.

though the year on the Debit side may differ from the Credit side – followed by the name of the account on at least one side, perhaps with 'Per Contra' on the other.

For reference purposes in this edition I use the folio number and the number of the account on that folio with perhaps D for Debit side and C for Credit. So the reference to Isaac Heming above will be found in f. 77.4D.

Further, in this Introduction, to save a flurry of footnotes, such references are simply bracketed in the main text, without any preliminary.

Speed's Ledger was posted in three hands. From opening until some time in the spring or early summer of 1683 it was in the stylish lettering of Jahzeel, Speed's only surviving son.[3] For the next six years it was kept in the untidy cursive script which can be identified from other documents as Speed's own. Accounts from March 1689 are in a third hand, a sort of copper-plate, which I take to be that of a clerk or book-keeper, possibly because Speed's eyesight was failing.[4] The frontispiece shows and identifies all three hands.

1.2 Importance

As accountancy, the Ledger falls easily within the established outlines of seventeenth-century practice for sole traders. But it is in other respects a unique document. First, though Bristol was clearly the second trading port of England, this is the only Bristol merchant's ledger of the period known to survive. In fact there is no other source which gives such a detailed picture of a Bristol merchant's trading over such a stretch of time. More fundamentally, the ledger supplies not only a ten-year trading history but an insight into the rationale and ethos of that trade.

Moreover, the detailed picture which it affords over nine years can be fitted into an outline of Speed's trade over forty years. In fact, Speed himself is by far the most fully documented of all the merchants and of all the Quaker leaders in the city where both so flourished in the second half of the Seventeenth Century. The historical significance of his ledger thus parallels that of John Smythe, another man of consequence, over a century earlier.[5]

The Ledger itself is indeed one of the main sources for the life of Speed the man as well as the merchant. This is not as surprising for a seventeenth-century ledger as it might be today. There was no formal distinction between business and private life. Household expenses were entered in the same account with business overheads. Nevertheless there can be few ledgers with such a story to tell: his abortive retirement, his fourth marriage, his spectacularly disappointing heir, not to mention the mystery of the sinister soap. The Ledger is an unusual human document as well as a business record.

1.3 Sources

The main sources on which this introduction is based are to be found in the notes and the brief Bibliography; but virtually all the topics discussed here are discussed and documented more fully in my thesis 'The Life & Times of Thomas Speed'.[6]

---

[3] He describes Elizabeth Milner (Appendix A, Marriage 1) as 'my sister' (f. 15.6D).
[4] It is not the hand of his son-in-law Thomas Goldney, the only member of the family who might have undertaken it. Speed bought spectacles in 1684 (f. 73.1D, last entry).
[5] J. Vane (ed.) *The Ledger of John Smythe 1538–1550*, BRS XXVIII 1975.
[6] PhD thesis, University of the West of England, 2008.

2 BACKGROUND

2.1 Bristol and its Trade

Bristol's population may have been around 15,000 in 1650 rising towards 20,000 by 1700, making it the third largest city in England after London and Norwich. Perhaps half of the adult males were freemen, with a vote in Parliamentary elections and the right to set up in business. Of these, the overseas merchants enjoyed the greatest esteem and, in repute at least, the greatest wealth.[7] Certainly they made the largest and most influential group of the hundred or so great men who were eligible for the (self-recruiting) City Council and other offices; and the Society of Merchant Venturers (SMV) which represented them was the most weighty of all the trade associations.

As elsewhere in England, merchants and other citizens aligned themselves along a range of political and religious attitudes, from high Tory High Church to Whig Dissenter. But for the most part, civic solidarity and mutual commercial interests kept all in peaceful co-existence and neighbourliness, with rare exceptions when a polarising issue forced choices or when a fanatic was elected to high civic office. Quakers were of course on the dissenting end of this spectrum but, though debarred from such office and indeed legally forbidden to worship, were in most respects integrated into the civic society.

Bristol was without question England's second port. Good access to Southern France, Portugal and Spain had made it a major importer of wines and oil and similar high value goods, still mainly in exchange for textiles. It was a principal port for Ireland where a range of manufactures was sent in exchange for butter and cheese and other primary products. It was equally well-placed for trade with the Americas, although it was not until 1698 that Bristol merchants could legitimately engage in the trafficking of slaves.

Bristol was also the distribution centre for a wide region. In an era when transport was cheaper by water than by land, Bristol had direct access to the coastline of the Bristol Channel from Lands End to St David's Head, to the Welsh borderlands on the Wye, up through the west midlands by the Severn, and to the edges of the Cotswold country via the Avon.

This very considerable hinterland, as much as the maritime links, made Bristol prosperous. As Defoe explained, Bristol merchants had[8]

> more independency of London than any other town …whatsoever exportations they make to any part of the world, they are able to bring the full returns back to their own port and dispose of it there. This is not the case in any other port in England.

That is, other outports could export full consignments or shiploads of staples but had too small a domestic market to absorb the equivalent in luxury foreign goods. So they had to dispose of the surplus in a very competitive London market or have the imports consigned to a regular London associate and get only a share of the proceeds.

---

[7] D. Sacks *The Widening Gate: Bristol and the Atlantic Economy 1450–1700* Tables 20–23 (pp 165–9).
[8] Daniel Defoe *A Tour through the whole island of Great Britain* [1724–6] abridged edn. ed P Rogers (London 1971): 361–2

A major source for Bristol's overseas trade in this period is the Society of Merchant Venturers' record of the Wharfage Fees which they levied on all imports from overseas in return for maintaining the port facilities. The SMV Wharfage Books run in a complete series from May 1654 to September 1694. They show the same details as the Port Books: consignments from named ships to named merchants by item and quantity; [9] but the surviving Port Books supply only patchy coverage. Figure 1 shows the volume of imports between 1654 and 1694 as derived from the Wharfage Books.

A good part of the wide year-to-year fluctuations is due to variations in harvests and in sailing conditions, so that trends are better shown in the three year moving average. Even these however are by no means steady. War played a great part here but not a consistent one. In particular the third Dutch War of the 1670s was largely confined to the North Sea and may have actually diverted trade to Bristol – thus the decline with the peace; whereas William III's war against France from 1688 was very bad, cutting out a major source of wine and exposing shipping to very active privateers as well as the French navy.

Unfortunately, I have not found any breakdown of this trade at its peak in the mid '70s.[10] For Bristol, as for the nation, the value of seventeenth-century trade can be estimated from Customs and Port records of shipping and consignments. Table 1 gives

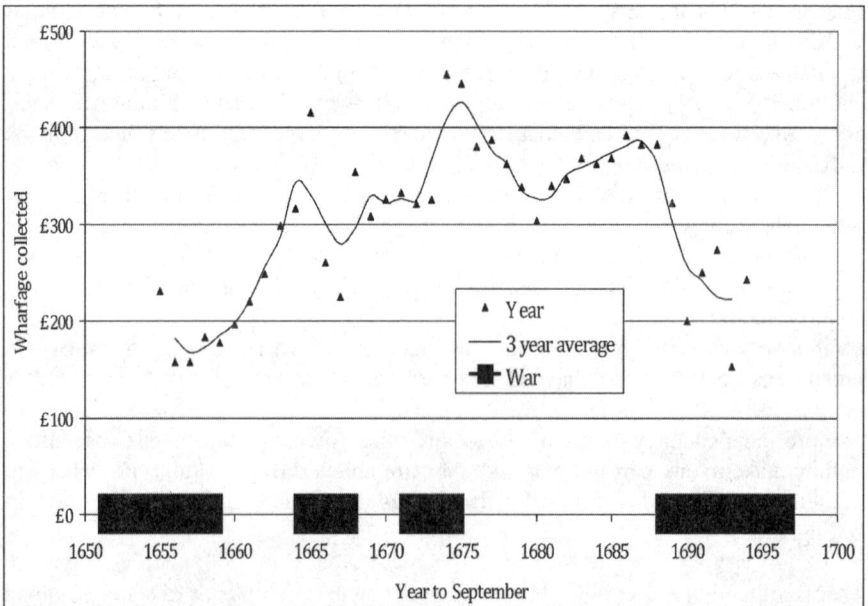

Fig. 1   Bristol Wharfage collection 1655–1694. £1 of wharfage paid represents some 30 tuns of merchandise imported

---

[9] They mostly omit the details about the vessel which are included in the Port Books

[10] McGraw *Merchants & Merchandise*. Appendix H & I summarise imports by commodity and source for 1654/5 and 1685/, showing that tobacco and sugar from the Americas made a substantial proportion at both dates but does not give values.

Table 1   Estimated Value of Bristol Overseas* Trade in 1699/1700

	Imports			Exports		
	tons	£'000	% of all	tons	£'000	% of all
North Europe	4,075	20.4	4.9%	1,183	39.6	7.3%
Nearby Europe	2,423	36.3	8.7%	3,837	70.6	13.0%
Iberia and Med	3,550	120.0	28.7%	2,195	109.8	20.2%
North America	4,660	69.3	16.6%	2,677	101.2	18.6%
West Indies	5,170	172.0	41.1%	4,700	222.3	40.9%
Total	19,878	£418.0		14,592	£543.5	

* omitting coastal trade

an analysis of Bristol's trade in 1699/1700 derived from the work of Davis and of Hussey.[11]

All these calculations are in terms of official values for Port Book purposes. Realised sales values will have been very different, and these estimates can only be indicative. They imply that the value of Bristol's import trade was about one tenth London's and a quarter of the national outport total. The export value is one eighth of London's and rather over a quarter of the outport total. These proportions are consistent with the relative customs revenues.

What comes out very strongly is the dominance of the Atlantic trade, making up virtually 60% of both import and export value. Neither London nor any other outport would have been so strongly westward-oriented. The Iberian and Mediterranean trade appears here more important than that with Nearby Europe, but at this time the import of wines from France had hardly recovered from the war, and Spanish and Portuguese wines were accordingly doing well.

2.2   Merchants

2.2.1   The seventeenth-century merchant

Overseas trade assumed a new importance in the second half of the Seventeenth Century. The English had on the whole overcome the Dutch in war and surpassed them as the leading traders in some parts of the world. Those conflicts had underlined the interdependence of colonial empire, trade and naval power. This nexus became a constant factor in a foreign policy which became more aggressive and ready to support far-flung factories and plantations with force even in times of nominal peace – 'no peace beyond the line'.[12] Domestically, small as trade was in the national economy compared with agriculture, it was obviously the most dynamic sector, it exerted a powerful employment multiplier effect and it was perceived, however illusorily, to be the quickest route to vast wealth. Trade fed the consumer market with more and more novel products

---

[11] D. Hussey, *Coastal and River Trade in Pre-Industrial England: Bristol and its Region 1680–1730* (Exeter 2000) Table 2.5; R. Davis, *The Rise of the English Shipping Industry in the Seventeenth and Eighteenth Centuries* (London 1962) 186, 200. For the methodology see Harlow 'Thomas Speed' 169–170.

[12] G. Mattingly 'No Peace beyond what Line?' *Transactions of the Royal Historical* Society (Fifth Series) (1963), 13: 145–162

and brought them within the reach of more and more consumers. Tobacco became part of the lives of even the labouring classes. The nation became trade-conscious.

Naturally this fomented interest in the figure of the merchant. There was still a view among some scholars, clerics and landed men that the merchant was at best ignoble, concerned with mean matters and contrivances; at worst a vile parasite on the gullibility or needs of others. But there were also those who praised the merchant as a paradigm, and a promoter, of just those versions of the pagan virtues which a civil society required: prudence clearly; justice and temperance in the favourable view; and fortitude in the face of Fortune. The methodical casting of accounts by the merchant was taken as a model of serious Christian self-examination. Moreover the overseas merchant was represented as a knowledgeable man, cognisant of world affairs, languages and foreign parts, skilled in calculation and ripe in practical judgement. This more positive view prevailed as trade itself was recognised as more important, and the gentry readily apprenticed their younger sons to this occupation as a respectable one in a way that brewing or building or inland wholesaling would not have been.

Correspondingly there was a positive flurry of books purporting to impart the necessary knowledge for those who would 'truly merit the generous, nay, I may say, the noble name of Merchant'.[13] But, although diaries and biographies were being written in the Seventeenth Century as never before, the aspiring merchant would find little in the way of business histories to read.[14] Even now, published studies of seventeenth-century merchants do not necessarily tell us much about their trading: being prosopographies, political analyses or biographies of great men of London, who made most of their huge fortunes in government finance.[15] There are some editions of merchants' letters and among these Roseveare's fine treatment of the London firm of Marescoe is outstanding for its setting in the context of the firm's accounts and of current prices and trading terms throughout Western Europe.[16]

There are one or two studies or memoirs of provincial merchants outside Bristol, but the information about their trading is either vague or scrappy.[17] Two previous volumes of the Bristol Record Society give a very comprehensive view of all the

[13] N. Glaisyer 'Culture of Commerce in England, 1660–1720' PhD Thesis, Cambridge 1999, 264 also n. 780.

[14] Two autobiographies of Quaker businessmen are concerned with Truth rather than trade: J. Barclay (ed.) 'Some Account of the Life of Joseph Pike' in *A Select Series, biographical, narrative epistolary & miscellaneous* 5 vols, London 1837, V 45; *The Autobiography of William Stout of Lancaster, 1665–1752* ed. J. Marshall, Manchester 1963

[15] R. Brenner *Merchants and Revolution: Commercial change, political conflict, and London's Overseas Traders 1550–1653* Princeton 1993; D. Coleman *Sir John Banks, Baronet and Businessman: a study of business, politics and society in later Stuart England* Oxford 1963; P. Gauci *The Politics of Trade: the overseas merchant in state and society 1660–1720* Oxford 2001; R. Grassby *The English Gentleman in Trade: the life and works of Sir Dudley North 1641–1691* Oxford 1994; Grassby *Business Community;* Grassby *Kinship and Capitalism;* M. Prestwich *Cranfield: Politics and Profits under the early Stuarts* Oxford 1966; R.Tawney *Business and Politics under James I: Lionel Cranfield as Merchant and Minister* Cambridge 1958.

[16] D. Hancock (ed.)*The Letters of William Freeman, London, Merchant, 1678–1685* London Record Society 36, 2002; Roseveare *Markets & Merchandise;* G. F. Steckley (ed.)*The Letters of John Paige, London Merchant 1648–1658* London Record Society 1984.

[17] J. Appleby 'Abraham Jennings of Plymouth: the commercial career of a "Western Trader", c 1602–49' *Southern History* 18 (1996) 24–42; R. Greaves *Dublin's Merchant-Quaker: Anthony Sharp and the Society of Friends, 1643–1707* Stanford 1998; Guscott *Humphrey Chetham 1580–1653: Fortune, Politics & Mercantile Culture in Seventeenth-Century England* Manchester 2003; M. Hunter & A. Gregory (eds) *An astrological diary of the seventeenth century: Samuel Jeake of Rye 1652–1699* Oxford 1988.

activities of seventeenth-century Bristol merchants – other than their costs, sales and profits. Latimer's is an institutional study of their Society, and Sacks writes more about the place of the merchants in the civic polity than their trading.[18] Studies of Sir Abraham Elton, John Whitson, Edward Colston (albeit more a London merchant than a Bristol one), Thomas Goldney I and II, and Humphrey Hooke, all tell us more of how they spent their fortunes than how they made them.[19] Thus Speed's Ledger is a unique source for the business of a Bristol merchant in this period.

2.2.2 The Merchant's trade
Traditionally the main purpose of trade and the business of the merchant was the bringing in of imports. Exports were merely the means to that end. In Chaucer's time, the merchant had been very much a one-man-show, taking his goods abroad, and bringing the proceeds in foreign merchandise back with him. But in the early modern period, foreign associates and agents ('factors') advised on markets, disposed of exports, held the proceeds, and purchased on the merchant's behalf. The merchant was freed from time-consuming travels and from the associated need to turn each export into a return cargo as quickly as possible. The bill of exchange likewise freed him from the need to purchase in the market where he sold. The merchant was thus able to participate in a great network of multilateral trade and finance. Indeed, it is not too much to say, with Price, that what a seventeenth-century merchant principally did was to manage his working capital to maintain his credit.[20] Yet both associates and bills of exchange remained essentially personal, based on the standing – credit in the wide as well as narrow sense – of the individual merchant; and what Price does not perhaps bring out is the sheer volume of written communication and the care needed to nurture the individual relationships which collectively constituted that credit.[21] Not for nothing was the term 'correspondent' first applied to a foreign business associate in this century.

3   THE LIFE OF THOMAS SPEED

3.1   Before the Ledger
3.1.1   1623–1654: a fortunate start [22]
Speed was not born to be a merchant. He was the second son of Richard Speed, master of the Almshouse at Sherborne, Dorset, a man of some but small property. In 1640,

[18] Bibliography: J. Latimer *The History of the Society of Merchant Venturers in the City of Bristol with some account of the anterior merchants' gilds* Bristol 1903; McGrath *Merchant Venturers* and *Merchants & Merchandise*; Sacks *Widening Gate*.
[19] M. Elton *Annals of the Elton Family: Bristol Merchants & Somerset Landowners* Stroud 1994; P. McGrath *John Whitson and the Merchant Community of Bristol* Bristol 1970; K. Morgan *Edward Colston and Bristol* Bristol 1999; P. Stembridge (ed.) *The Goldney Family: A Bristol Merchant Dynasty* BRS XLIX, 1998; F. Todd *Humphrey Hooke of Bristol and his family and descendants in England and America during the seventeenth century* New Haven 1938. See also Bettey, J 'Graffin Prankard, an Eighteenth-Century Bristol Merchant' *Southern History* 12 (1990) 34–47, an interesting sketch but not a business history.
[20] Price 'What did merchants do?' 278
[21] Correspondence, "together with kinship ties and the structure of credit, formed the web that held commercial society together." N Glaisyer 'Networking: trade and exchange in the eighteenth-century British empire' *HJ* 47 (2004) 454–476: 474, citing an edition of merchants' letters.
[22] For this section, see Harlow 'Thomas Speed' I.1 & 2.

xvi The Ledger of Thomas Speed 1681–1690

he went to Oxford, presumably with the intention of taking his degree and seeking a living as a minister. But by 1642 the Civil War had broken out, and Speed did not complete his degree. Although there are no records, I believe that he became a clerk in the Parliamentary forces, preaching in his spare time, came to Bristol when it was taken by Fairfax in 1645, and was then taken on as a trainee by the well-established lawyer William Yeamans.

At any rate, in the late summer of 1647, he married William's daughter, Ann. She was the widow of that Robert Yeamans who had been hanged in May 1643 as leader of a Royalist plot. Yeamans had been a member of the Society of Merchant Venturers, a Councillor from 1639 and Sheriff in 1641/2. He was thus well established as one of the mercantile elite 'the great ones amongst us, Colston, Yeomans, and their brethren'.[23] Appendix A Marriage 1 shows some of the relationships arising from this marriage.

As a result of this marriage, Speed immediately became a freeman of the City – so entitled to set up in business – and a member of the Society of Merchant Venturers. He had likewise access to the family capital, and to a network of businessmen ready to deal with him and give him credit. As an ex-army clerk he was already familiar with book-keeping, purchasing and payroll; and as to overseas trade, he could learn from his brother-in-law William, already a member of the SMV, and indeed from his wife, who was still trading as Ann Speed in 1654.

Thus this very advantageous marriage gave Speed just about all he would have had as the properly apprenticed scion of a wealthy family, and he seems to have readily embarked on his new career as merchant and as an active Merchant Venturer. In 1649/50 he became one of the ten Assistants. From then to early 1655 he was a frequent member of committees including that for revising the Society's ordinances in 1653/4. There is no information on the scope of Speed's trade in this period. But the government records show that he was involved in the transportation of horses and Irish prisoners to the Indies, and in two privateering ventures. By 1654, when the Wharfage Books begin, he was already trading at a high level. But then his family and faith began to work against him and the decade to 1664 saw a decline in his trade which is all the more dramatic against the buoyant upward trend of Bristol trade generally (Figure 2).

3.1.2   1654–1665: decline [24]

By 1654 the Speeds had their own four children: Metredone, a boy, in 1649; Theodore in 1651; Mehitabel in 1652; and Jahzeel, a boy, in 1653.[25] Meanwhile, between 1652 and 1662 all the eight step-children married or reached their majority. Each would have received the portion set aside for these events. Finally around in 1663 his wife Ann herself died, so that the last of the Yeamans property, including the New Inn where the family had lived, passed from his hands, in terms of the pre-nuptial settlement. All this would have been in itself a considerable drain on his working capital, entailing a corresponding rundown in trade. But Speed had also to cope with the consequences of becoming a Quaker.

---

[23] *The Declaration of the Mayor etc* (Bristol 1642) 1
[24] For this section, see Harlow 'Thomas Speed' I.3.
[25] Metredone (Speed's and Jahzeel's spelling in the Ledger), or Metradone, is just possibly after Metraton, an Archangel in the Talmudic tradition. Jahzeel is after the third son of Hebron, Chronicles I. 23.19.

The Quakers came to Bristol in the second half of 1654.[26] Speed was 'convinced' in the latter half of 1655. He was not alone. His brother John and many of the Yeamans also became Quakers (see Appendix A Marriage 1). The early Quaker leaders Bishop, Hollister, Pyott and Rowe were all his kinsmen and he joined this leadership group. But Speed remained the merchant, and his main contribution in these early years was helping to mind the business of the more active evangelists and publicists, such as Edward Pyott and George Bishop.

In the 1660s, Quakers broke the new Restoration laws by attending their own meetings, absenting themselves from regular parish meetings and refusing to take any oath when up before the magistrates on such charges. Speed was frequently arrested both in Bristol and in Reading He thus exposed himself to sentences of outlawry, banishment and the forfeiture of estate. What with harassment, imprisonment and anxiety on this score and the loss of Yeamans' capital, it is not surprising that by 1665 Speed's trade had fallen to its lowest point.

3.1.3 1665–1675: recovery [27]

But in 1655 Speed married again, the Quaker Martha Smith, an heiress to modest property (Appendix A Marriage 2).[28] Perhaps with this financial assistance and certainly with loans from friends, he got himself a substantial new house, backing on the Gild Hall and with cellars under it, in Small Street, which appears in the Ledger as 'House in which I live'.[29] He also began again to attend Hall at the Society of Merchant Adventurers, after a decade of absence. At the same time, he began to distance himself from the main body of Quakerism. He may well have shared the uneasiness of other first generation Friends, as the movement which had rejected all authority but the Inner Light submitted itself to the control of Fox, of London Meeting, and of Elders, and imposed its disciplines upon the freedom of members to preach, prophesy and publish – and to marry.

Marriage was the stumbling block for Speed. His second wife had died soon after giving birth to their only child, Martha. Soon Speed sought a third, Ann Sherman (Appendix A Marriage 3). But she was not a Friend, and the approval of the Bristol Meeting was so grudging as to amount to condemnation. From then on, Speed was no longer to be found among the leaders of the Bristol Quakers, and even seems to have ceased attending the fortnightly meetings for business. In successive bouts of persecution, including the most terrible of all in 1683–5, he was never again arrested; and the implication is that he was one of the Bristol Friends who 'came not to meetings and so escaped a prison'.[30] Loans to the City, to Romsey the Town Clerk, even to John Hellier , the scourge of dissenters, may help to explain his immunity (ff. 30.4, 16.6, 101.4). Yet he attended meetings for worship on occasion at least, and he was still sometimes consulted. He was aloof, but not apostate.

His withdrawal from active Quakerism probably left more time for his business. His third wife, like his second, may have brought some modest extra capital, though all

---

[26] See Harlow 'Thomas Speed' II.6.
[27] For this section, see Harlow 'Thomas Speed' I.4.
[28] The property, shared with her two sisters, has not been identified.
[29] No 18, Small Street in Leech *Topography* 158
[30] Joseph Pike, a Cork Quaker and merchant, related to Speed, made this observation on Bristol Friends after visiting in 1681.

that can be traced was a third share in a little property. Possibly he gained some business when his brother John Speed and his brother-in-law William Yeamans died – both had been trading on a greater scale than he had – or, more likely, he had acted for their families in bringing in goods consigned to them. Speed's trade rose to new heights and by the middle of the 1670s, he was clearing some 6% of all the wine imported into Bristol. It is not surprising to see his name on the SMV committee of 1676 which negotiated for the purchase of Clifton – their largest investment for the century.

3.1.4   1676–1681 Succession and semi-retirement[31]

But by this time Speed himself was in his mid fifties. It was time to consider curtailing his activity before nature forced the issue. He had three sons, all by his first marriage. The eldest, Metredone, had been a lad of great promise, sanding chemical communications to the Royal Society in his teens. He had been apprenticed to his father in 1664, but he never took his freedom and there is no mention of him in any public records after 1670. The Ledger has an account for the 'Estate of Metredone Speed' which was solemnly carried forward in 1690 (f. 22.1). In 1670 the Wharfage Books show that three shipments entered Bristol in the name of the second son Theodore. It looks as though, on the death of Metredone, Theodore was hastily drafted in to fill the succession gap. But after 1670, nothing more is heard of him either. That left just Jahzeel, the youngest. He had been apprenticed to Speed at the end of 1668, and reached his majority in 1674 but he did not marry – which usually came within a year or so of majority and freedom – and no shipments came to Bristol in his name for some time. At last, in 1678, Jahzeel was brought forward as heir presumptive, and introduced to the SMV.

The other branch of Speed's exit strategy was the building up of a country estate. In 1678 Speed had bought what he called a farm (f. 76 3D) at Clapton for perhaps £150, and later, possibly in 1680, he had purchased a much larger parcel of more or less adjoining land from the Gorges ff. 7.1, 151.1).[32] He put in hand the building of a house there, completed in January 1683 with a final payment of £280 (f.31.3). The exact location has not been identified but it was somewhere between Clapton-in-Gordano and the southern extension of modern Portishead, about 8 miles west of Bristol.

All this entered the Ledger in December 1681 as '*Estate at Clapton*' valued at £1102 (f. 38.4). At this time, he had much of the land in his own hands and was dealing in livestock, in fodder, and in dairy produce (ff. 4.5, 5.5, 5.6, 32.3, 38.3). In 1684, Speed owned two fowling pieces, such as were common for country dwellers but much less so in the city. It seems to be a fair inference that he contemplated life not so much as a country gentleman, but as what would later be termed a gentleman farmer.

By the end of 1681 when the Ledger opens, Jahzeel was keeping the Ledger, while all the imports in the first half of the 1680's were in Jahzeel's name. Speed had retired.

---

[31] For this section see Harlow 'Thomas Speed' I.5.1, 5.2.
[32] See also UBLSC Goldney papers DM1398 C.10 263

3.2 1681–1690: the Ledger story[33]

3.2.1 Fourth Marriage

But Speed's third wife Ann had died some time in 1680/81. Speed was again a widower, with his unmarried daughter Martha keeping house for him and for Jahzeel still unmarried. Perhaps this was why Speed spent much of 1682 staying with his favourite households, the Hemings in London and the Curtises in Reading. And in Reading, at the end of 1682, he married his fourth wife. Mary Lamboll was the daughter of George Lamboll, a very ancient Reading Friend: all the family seem to have been staunch Quakers. She had not been married before, probably because she had been looking after her father who had died only recently. She had then inherited some Reading leasehold property, charged with an annual maintenance for her mother Sarah, and no cash. Altogether then it was an entirely suitable, if not a glittering, match.

This marriage gave Speed the opportunity to show his contempt for the new Quaker marriage procedures which were now standard almost everywhere. But Reading Meeting was under the leadership of the Curtises, leaders of opposition to the Foxite innovations promulgated by London Meeting. The orthodox, who in Reading constituted the minority, recorded their conviction that Speed and Curtises went out of their way 'to lay waste orderly proceedings'.

3.2.2 Jahzeel!

It seems likely that all this, the absences, the courtship, and perhaps the involvement in Quaker dissident politics, distracted Speed from such oversight as he may have intended to maintain over Jahzeel's conduct of the trading business.

Having installed his new wife in the country house, Speed took a proper look at the books. What he found could not have been to his liking, and sometime between March and June 1683, Speed re-assumed responsibility for keeping the Ledger.[34] One of the first accounts he opened was devoted to Jahzeel (f. 69.2).[35] The debit entries which follow make an eloquent chronicle of wrong-doing, beginning with over £400 'money owing for which he credited himself but unduly under the title of Sir Jahzeel Speed' which Jahzeel in a positive flourish of impudence had opened and debited 'To Ballances Incognito' (f. 33.4, see frontispiece).

There were other entries for smaller sums lifted from Cash without record and several quite substantial outstanding scores for drink. But worst of all was the repeated pocketing of money received without crediting the accounts of the payers, and in one instance cash taken by Jahzeel was debited to another trader. Of course these misdoings would come to light when accounts were agreed or when debtors were asked for money they had already paid. The amounts were not huge but that was immaterial. The word would go around that Jahzeel could not be trusted. No merchant

---

[33] See Harlow 'Thomas Speed' I. 5.3, 5.5, 6.1, 6.2, 6.4

[34] Ledger entries dating from March are in his hand, but it is clear that the Ledger was posted in arrears, see 4.2.4 below.

[35] The keeping of this Jahzeel account, with items from the long past such as the cost of sending Jahzeel to Spain, served no formal accounting purpose, and Speed cannot have expected that Jahzeel would ever repay them – yet he even carried the account forward when Jahzeel was dead (f. 178.3). It was Speed's characteristic way of expressing displeasure, as the open account for Metredone's estate expressed his grief.

could succeed without trust, the personal credit on which his financial credit-rating depended. So Speed angrily wrote off the money long since spent on sending Jahzeel to lodge and learn with his factor in Spain, and took the management of the business back into his own hands. At the same time, he abandoned his farming activity, sold his agricultural stock and let out his land. But he kept the house he had built there, fenced the orchard and planted trees, making of it what would soon be thought of as a villa.

Speed may still have nourished hopes of him. For some time, Jahzeel remained in the house, still apparently able to get at the petty cash box (f. 60.2). Consignments continued to be entered in his name until 1686. In 1686/7 Jahzeel (who was never a Quaker) was senior Churchwarden for St Werburgh's. No Churchwardens' accounts were rendered that year; and it was left to Speed make up a deficit of the poor money which Jahzeel had received.[36]

In 1687 Speed sent Jahzeel off to stay with his cousin John Warren in Devon. In 1688, he was removed to the care of his step-sister Elizabeth Milner, now a widow. By 1689 the entries for his diet and for pocket money and new clothes were interspersed with those for physic and doctors' fees, and in 1690 he was sent to Bath. In March 1690, the Clerk of the Society of Merchant Venturers marked him 'sick' and at the next Hall on June 21st 'died since the last Hall'.

Jahzeel was an interesting character, obviously plausible but easy-going, and no more concerned to take trouble in concealing his peculations than in his conduct of the business. For it is also clear that under him, the management had been slack, and Speed quickly showed a healthier profit on a reduced sales volume. But his aim now was not to rebuild a business, but, in the absence of a successor, to run it down. Over the decade some £2,500 was diverted from the business into financial assets and rented properties.

3.2.3   Martha's marriage

In June 1687, Martha Speed married Thomas Goldney Junior. This marriage was eminently suitable and properly conducted 'in the way & manner of Friends'.[37] But there are indications that Speed never rated young Goldney very highly. A major dissatisfaction was the promised settlement on the bride, still outstanding when Speed made his will. In the interim, Speed hung on to the £800 dowry he had promised, though recording it as paid (f. 127.1 May 13). So, whereas Heming was eventually named as his sole executor, Goldney was only one of the trustees of a small bequest to the Quaker poor.

' Martha's marriage seems to have brought the fourth Mrs Speed a little more into the foreground. Only after it did Speed buy from his brother-in-law some of the household items from Reading that had meant home to Mary Lamboll, and, next year, pay for redecorating at Small Street and Russian leather chairs (ff. 131.1 D Oct 31, 153.1 D Sept 29, Oct 16). It seems possible that for the first few years, Mary Speed had kept the house in the country, while Martha continued to manage the Bristol house.

---

[36]   f. 69.2 D entry 14; BRO P/St W/Chw/3(b)

[37]   R. Mortimer (ed.) *Minute Book of the Men's Meeting of the Society of Friends in Bristol, 1686–1704* BRS XXX1978, 8

3.2.4   A mysterious affair

Though the Ledger reveals so much of personal life, it betrays no hint of the stormy politics of the decade: the royalist backlash after the Exclusion crisis in which Bristol Quakers suffered their worst persecution, Monmouth's rebellion, the succession of James II, the Glorious Revolution. But there is one very mysterious transaction concerning Henry Gibbs and his soap.

Henry Gibbs was a man whom Speed frequently dealt with and not infrequently lent to. In June 1682, an account was opened for 79 chests of soap deposited by Henry Gibbs (f. 51.5). Gibbs received an advance of £200, the soap was apparently sold and the proceeds, less advance, interest and commission , were paid him.

On f. 53 four merchants are debited with purchasing the soap, each entry circumstantially detailed by weight and price per hundredweight. This is the first entry for each account, and it looks as though all four were opened together and for the purpose of entering these sales, all being headed 1682. For two of them, these are the only entries, and two have further purchases in 1685 and 1689. No actual date is given for the purchases. Up to this point, all the entries are made by Jahzeel.

But the accounts remained apparently unsettled until four years later when the full amount payable is credited to each one of them with the mysterious formula 'By Proffit and Losse for the Soape per Contra received by/of **a friend**' in Speed's hand (but the emphasis is mine). The combined counter entry in Profit & Loss, in August 1686 and again in Speed's hand, sheds no more light on the matter: 'for 79 Chests of Soape sould [names] as may appeare recd per **a friend**' (f. 127.1D).

Crediting the amounts to P&L meant that they were written off. And there is no entry anywhere in the entire Ledger to indicate that any other person had in fact either paid Speed for these purchases or was owing for them. If any payment had been made, why conceal it? If not, why write off the amount rather than pressing the buyers for it? And if it was to be written off, why in such misleading terms? If, for example, Jahzeel had received and pocketed the amount, the fact would have been debited reproachfully to Jahzeel's account.

Henry Gibbs was a slightly suspicious character. He was on the 1684 list of Dangerous and Disaffected Persons to be searched for arms – as was Speed himself.[38] More significantly, Gibbs was at Lyme Regis in June 1685, just when it was made the beachhead for Monmouth's rebellion. On the 27th June, the magistrates in Bristol Quarter Sessions registered a certificate from the Mayor and four citizens of Lyme to say that Gibbs had stayed in his mother-in-law's house all the time, had no dealings with the rebels and behaved himself like a loyal subject throughout. But if, in the uneasy days after Sedgemoor, Speed entertained suspicions about Gibbs himself, they must have been soon allayed, for Speed continued to do business with him – and never reversed or disguised the entries to Gibbs's account. And it would seem that Gibbs really got the money, including £100 via Heming, Speed's London banker. So any falsification here would extend to Heming's account as well as Gibbs'.

There is little of apparent interest about the four alleged buyers of the soap: Francis Whitchurch, William Burges, Charles Herbert and Thomas Rich. Whitchurch was the most important: he would be elected to the Council in 1695 and became in turn Mayor and Alderman. He was a sugar-boiler and appears elsewhere in the Ledger as an associate of Herbert. Burges, also described in the ledger as grocer, appears nowhere

---

[38] J Maclean 'Seizure of arms in the county of Gloucester in 1684' *TBGAS* II (1877/8) 104–117.

else in the ledger or civic lists, but is very likely the one listed as a £600 man, the top rate in the Family Tax of 1696. Rich is not otherwise identifiable. None of them seems to have been a Quaker, and for what it is worth, none of them is among the Dangerous and Disaffected Persons in 1684.

However, Whitchurch and Burges bought some rice from Speed in April 1685, and the debits for these purchases come immediately after the mysterious soap purchases. Their bills were promptly settled in cash. Perhaps Speed then reminded them of the apparently long-outstanding account soap account, and had to accept their protestations of ignorance.

So, a conjectured reconstruction. In 1682, Jahzeel made some misleading entries about a transaction with Gibbs. In 1685 Speed became aware of this and suspected that the affair touched on the treasonable – it was the time of that earlier Monmouth conspiracy, the Rye House plot.[39] In some alarm, Speed wrote off the debts, throwing in the reference to 'a friend' in the (mistaken) belief that this would allay rather than arouse suspicion.

This reconstruction leaves many questions unanswered. Even if it is correct, it does not follow that Jahzeel, or any one, had actually been involved in treason. But it does provide a link from the apparently insulated world of the trader and his household to the frightening world of politics, where suspicion or prejudice or expediency could hang a man as surely as real guilt.

3.3   Speed's last years 1690–1703[40]
By 1690, when the ledger closes, Speed's trading had virtually ceased. He cleared no imports in 1691 or 1692, some consignments on behalf of his Spanish factor Samuel Kekewich in 1693 and four consignments in 1694: sugar, tobacco, ginger and oil – significantly no wine – perhaps in final settlement of outstanding balances with overseas associates.

He continued to expand and consolidate his Clevedon estate. He also purchased property in the Bristol Castle precinct and in Reading (buying old Lamboll holdings, perhaps to please his wife). Finally, in the 1700s, he acquired and then added to a considerable property in Olveston, south Gloucestershire. At his death in 1703, he left nearly £10,000 worth of real estate in town and country, to be divided, subject to an annuity for his widow, between the families of his only surviving children, the Hemings and the Goldneys.

4   ACCOUNTING

4.1   The Ledger in seventeenth-century accounting
4.1.1   Accounting Records [41]
The Ledger was an official record, producible in the civil courts as evidence of debt or discharge. It was kept by the merchant himself, or by a book-keeper acting under his direct instruction rather than by rote.

---

[39] The conspirators had links with the White Hart/Horseshoe and Mermaid clubs in Bristol; and Jahzeel was clearly a frequenter of such drinking places.

[40] See Harlow 'Thomas Speed' I. 7.4, 7.5, 7.6.

[41] See Roseveare *Markets & Merchants*; J. Price 'Directions for the Conduct of a Merchants Counting House, 1766' *Business History* 28 91986) 134–150; Yamey 'Some 17th & 18th century double-entry ledgers' and other articles.

The Ledger stood at the apex of a pyramid of accounting records. At the base were the papers which actually constituted transactions: orders (mostly in letter form), invoices and bills, receipts, notes of hand, bills, bonds, bills of lading, customs entry etc. In a well-kept office these would be filed or bound by date and type or purpose for ready location. Thus Speed referred to 'my bundle of Accts' (f. 87.5). Then there would be books of temporary record, in which the essentials of each sort of transaction would be entered more or less as they occurred. Speed refers to his Wastebook (memoranda), and books of Receipts, of Charges on Merchandises and of Petty Disbursements. From these papers and books of first entry were compiled such secondary records as the merchant found convenient. Of this kind probably are Speed's books of Accounts and of Invoices and Cashbooks, all of which as mentioned in the Ledger had numbered folios.

The key secondary record was, or should have been, the Journal in which each transaction was formally recorded in its dual aspect: account to be debited and account to be credited, the double entries from which the Ledger would be made up. Indeed the Journal and the Ledger are effectively two arrangements of the same data: the first by date and the second by the accounts to be charged. The Journal would have the more detailed narrative, and Speed's Ledger twice refers to the 'particulars' to be found there. But although he did summarise for the Ledger, it was mostly at a very petty level: he was capable of entering into the Ledger a payment for 'porteridge' separately from the tip to the porter.[42] And it seems clear that many entries were posted direct from temporary records into the Ledger without ever passing through the Journal

Today, the final outcomes of a firm's accounting system are the Balance Sheet and the Profit & Loss statement. The Balance Sheet shows all the firm's assets and its liabilities at the beginning and at the end of the trading period. The P&L statement shows the net profit arising from trading over the same period, any extraordinary gains or losses, the interest and tax paid, and how much of the eventual surplus, if any, has been paid out to the owners. To produce these summary statements in a reliable and consistent way requires some principles to be applied. For example, capital transactions should be distinguished from revenue and expenditure flows, and these flows in turn separated from investments or withdrawals by the owners; stocks must be costed; and all transactions should be consistently attributed to the period in which they took place.

Early modern treatises on accounting were well aware of the use of periodic Balance Sheets and Income statements.[43] But these were much more relevant for the enterprise with several partners or shareholders than for the sole trader or the family firm. In practice, few firms adhered to the full requirements of formal book-keeping and there was a wide variety of actual practice. Speed maintained a formal accounting system, but in a fashion which would not have permitted any useful summary of trading profit or of changes in net worth over a year or any other period.

---

[42] Compare the Marescoes who apparently transferred totals of £2000 or more at a time from the petty cash book: Roseveare *Markets & Merchandise* 13 .

[43] eg T. Browne *The Infallible, most Accurate, and most Concise Method of Merchants Accompts* London 1680; R. Dafforne *The Merchant's Mirror:or Directions for the perfect Ordering and Keeping of his Accounts* London 1684; R. Handson *Analysis or resolution of merchants accompts* London 1669; S. Monteage *Debtor and creditor made easie, or, A short instruction for the attaining the right use of accounts after the best method used by merchants* London 1682; J Vernon *The Compleat Comptinghouse* London 1678.

First, Speed did not distinguish between capital and revenue. He kept no financial stock accounts for his merchandise. For any parcel or consignment, there was one account to which costs were debited and revenues credited, so that the balance at any time showed you how much of the cost had been recovered, but not how much of the original stock remained.[44] By the time all the stock had been disposed of, this method would effectively give the same result as modern accountancy (though without attribution to the period in which the results were achieved) but intermediate reckonings would show a balance of the difference between the profit taken and the value of stock remaining. Similarly, Speed kept an account for each property which brought together its original cost, and all subsequent charges and revenues, thus hopelessly confusing capital and income: a property stood at nil in his books as soon as the net rents had covered the initial cost. So, even if he had drawn up a balance sheet at any time, say when the Ledger closed, it would not have represented his net assets.

Secondly, he used his Profit & Loss (P&L) account as a sink: if there was no meaningful account to be debited or credited as required by the double entry system, then the counter entry would be made to P&L. Thus P&L was used to write off the balance when a consignment or project was finished, which would be a profit or loss more or less as understood today, but generally as a single sum at a period much later than that in which it actually arose – more a means of closing accounts no longer active than of reckoning trading profits. P&L was charged with overhead expenses or revenues which could not be attributed to any particular consignment. It was used for household and personal expenditure, effectively the amounts withdrawn from the business, though it is sometimes not easy to tell whether a particular payment was for personal or business use. It was used for some very mysterious entries: for example cash payments of £500 and £1200 'to severals' were simply debited to P& L without any explanation or clue as to the payees or the purpose (f. 8D Jan 9, April 10). And Speed used it for what might be called Gesture Accounting, as when he debited Jahzeel with the long-sunk costs of a spell in Spain, and credited P&L; or wrote off the outstanding amounts due from Scrope when he broke with him in 1686. Although the balance of P&L was carried forward when a new folio had to be used, there is no indication that any significance was attached to the figure, and nothing was carried forward when the Ledger was closed.

Finally, Speed did not attempt to close off accounts simultaneously at any set time, so as to allow the drawing up of either a Balance Sheet or a P&L statement, or post them fully to any consistent date. Ongoing accounts were simply carried forward to a new page when there was no space to continue them. Dead accounts, on the other hand, might be left open for years – for example many Debtors brought in as balances when the ledger was opened in 1681 remained in unrequited isolation for nine years before being written off when the Ledger was closed.

Similarly, he might leave arrears of rent on property unrecorded for years before suddenly raising a single charge for the whole amount. In the end, he simply closed off the Ledger when he was running out of folios, and although several long dead

---

[44] Broadly, the proper method today would be to credit the Stock Account with the *cost* of the goods sold, debiting this to a Sales Account, from which the Gross Profit could be computed, and leaving a balance of Stock at cost among the assets. There is just one occasion on which Speed might have attempted this: the balance of the last wine account – on the badly disfigured f. 186 – is partly written off to Profit & Loss and partly carried forward to the next ledger. The first might represent the profit made on the wine sold and the second an estimate of the value of stock remaining.

accounts were closed off then, there was no particular date to which those carried forward had been posted.

4.1.2 The function of the Ledger

In all this, Speed was following the common practice of his time. Hardly any sole traders kept their books in such a way as to identify the profit made in a period of time or the net assets employed in making it. It follows that their accounts could not have fulfilled that function ascribed to them by some sociologists, as instruments in the rationalistic pursuit of maximum returns on capital.

This does not mean that Speed was not concerned to make a profit. But it demonstrates that the concept of 'profit maximisation' was not applicable: the 'bottom line' cannot have dictated decision-making when there was no bottom line.

It was not that Speed was moving about in a cloud of uncertainty which would have been dispelled by more rigorous accounting methods. A man thoroughly familiar with a business largely composed of discrete transactions rather than continuous processes would not find his books, however well-kept, told him anything he needed to know in order to make decisions.

What then was the requirement which Speed's Ledger served? It was above all to keep track of his dealings with others. As Muldrew writes,[45]

> manuals [of accounting] stressed that their value to merchants and tradesmen was not to calculate profit or gain, but to be used as a rational orderly means of keeping track of the accountant's obligations.

A credit-worthy man must not only keep, but be known to keep, a scrupulous record of his dealings. Commercial justice had not only to be done, but be seen to be done.

4.2 Speed's Accounting Practice

Thus it may be taken that the Ledger is accurate in accounts for named persons, and that adjustments are explicitly declared. That does not however mean that all interpersonal dealing were entered there. There are several cash payments to people, and sometimes for scores or hundreds of pounds, which are referenced merely to P&L. Personal accounts were only for those dealings which both parties regarded as creating future claims or extinguishing old ones.

Accounts for consignments handled on commission had also to be full and accurate. While such pure agency business was marginal for Speed, he was often in the habit of taking a share in a large consignment which he handled as a whole, charging the other partners with their share of the costs so that he had to be, and was, meticulous in keeping these accounts. With consignments on his own account there was less need to be exact; and here Speed might casually charge incidental costs to P&L rather than to the consignment concerned.

When it came to accounts which affected no-one else, Speed's book-keeping was far from exact. At the extreme, an entry would be made in one account with a proper reference to the folio where the matching counter-entry should be found – but it is not! There are one hundred and twenty such 'only twins'. Some of these are related to corrections, which have been made in the important account and simply not carried

---

[45] Muldrew *Economy of Obligation* 128

through to Speed's own. Then there are also over 150 double-entries where the amount credited does not agree with the amount debited. These are very often clearly a matter of time saving: for example, a customer is given a discount or abatement, which is correctly shown on the customer's account, but the counter entry simply shows the nominal sales value.

4.2.1   A Case Study in Cutting Corners

An account for 30 butts of sherry was opened in January 1682 (f. 45.5). The sherry was purchased in Spain by Speed's partners and colleagues John Cook & Samuel Kekewich; and shared 50/50 between himself and John Cook & Co. The consignment was fully declared – Speed paid wharfage on exactly this consignment on January 5th 1682.[46]

The wine seems to have gone off rather: the price of a Butt was lowered rapidly in only a few months, and a good deal was sold as 'corrupt' for little or nothing – three or four butts worth may have been simply poured away. Speed might well have considered that the disappointing sales were due to poor selection or cooperage at the other end, but the account scrupulously ensures that each partner gets exactly 50% of the costs, including rebates, and receives exactly 50% of the proceeds – even down to the money received for selling empty butts and iron hoops (left after throwing away wine?) to a local cooper. Cooke drew a bill on Speed for the exact amount in favour of a third merchant, which Speed met in cash.

Speed's keeping of the joint account is meticulous. But his account for his own share is a different matter (f. 45.4). It is debited, correctly, with his half of the prime costs, i.e. those sustained in Spain when the wine was purchased and despatched. It ought to have been credited with his half of the net proceeds, and as this was the lesser sum, an adverse balance of nearly £30 should have been debited to P&L. Speed saves himself an extra entry by simply entering the net proceeds as exactly the same as the prime costs, so that the account can be closed off without any posting to P&L. There can be little question of a mistake – the two accounts are on the same folio.

No less than four items debited to the joint account for Speed's own charges should also have been credited to Profit & Loss (f. 9), but are nowhere to be found there. What there is in this P&L account is an only-twin debit entry for £3.00 in respect of one hogshead of corrupt wine from this very consignment. There is no matching entry to credit either the joint consignment or Speed's share of it with this sum, and all the credits which are shown have their own properly matching counter-entry. But the main account does show a credit for £3 for a hogshead of corrupt wine sold to a merchant who did indeed pay for it – it was one of the payments received but concealed by the egregious Jahzeel. Perhaps before learning this, Speed debited the value of this item to P&L, then later entered it correctly and in full. Although he knew how such an error should properly be corrected, he knew that the entries which stood in the joint account for the wine were correct and complete, and did not take the trouble of correcting his own.[47]

---

[46] BRO SMV/7/1/1/9

[47] Crossing out is not a recommended book-keeping practice, especially if the ledger is to have evidential weight in the courts. Speed should have completed the first entry by crediting the £3.00 from P& L to the wine, then reversed both entries, debiting the wine and crediting P& L £3, with a narrative explaining the error, as he did for a different error in the joint account.

Thus the account for the joint consignment can be copied to John Cooke without a blush on the score of honesty or accountancy. But four debits in it were never actually credited to P& L; one debit was matched by a much larger credit which saved another P& L entry; and one P& L debit was neither credited to the Wine account nor reversed. As a result his P& L account lacks £29 6s 5d which should have been debited to it and £23 11s which should have been credited.

His account with Joseph Badger (f. 50.4 with n. 60) involves similar short cuts.

4.2.2   The Cash Account

The Cash account was treated with no more care than the P& L. There are frequent arithmetical mistakes in making compound entries, where two or more payments to or from different persons are lumped together in the Cash account. In one case, a single payment of £100 (as shown in the debtor account) is credited twice to Cash – within three lines of the same folio (f. 139.1 October 22, 24).

Nor was Speed's balancing of the Cash account accurate. A blatant instance was the entry showing a payment to Thomas Goldney of £800 marriage portion – which was ignored in the subtotal only a few lines below (f. 121.1C May) This may have been a deliberate error: I suppose that the payment was not made but rather put aside against the time when the Goldneys should actually fulfill their part of the marriage agreement. Nevertheless Speed's Cash balances for the next three years include £800 which has also been shown as having been paid to Goldney. Elsewhere it was probably a mere arithmetical error which cast the total Credits as exactly £100 too small (f. 68.1). Other errors were less substantial but persistent. Of the twenty-five folios for the Cash account, only nine correctly calculate the balance to be carried forward. Clearly the Ledger Cash account can have played no part as a control on the cash actually to be found on the premises, though he did keep control, via the Cash Book; as his identifying of cash lifted by Jahzeel shows.

4.2.3   Dating

Errors or shortcuts like these would have ensured that trial balances did not balance, and so provide further evidence that none was ever taken. They are not however many or significant in relation to the whole corpus of the Ledger. The most prevalent carelessness was not entering the date of the transactions, which affects some half of the entries. Even where a date is given, it is not always clear that it is the date of the transaction, and not just the date of the entry. And accounts rendered by Heming his London banker or Kekewich his main Spanish factor were simply entered up when they were received without any attempt to date them individually.

4.2.4   Posting the Ledger

The Ledger was a tertiary record and obviously made up in arrears. This should have been done regularly, daily or weekly, and from a properly kept Journal so that matching debits and credits would always be posted. The errors noted above where counter-entries are either missing or differ in amount indicate that this was not done.

The case of John Wasbrow, cooper, is instructive (f. 28.3). Specific debits dated September 1683 had been posted to his account. By March 1684, Wasbrow had died and Speed settled affairs with his widow, entering up some £17 worth of further sales to him and no less than £95 worth of cooperage work done by him, nearly all of which had been recorded only on 'noates' before then. That £95 should have included £9 worth of cooperage properly debited to the sherry account discussed above, but never individually credited to Wasbrow, although cross-referenced to his account. Some £85 worth of work, properly chargeable to specific consignments, was never assigned to them but merely bundled in a lump to P&L.

Thus the picture which emerges is of a piecemeal posting of one account or another in the Ledger from primary records which might have been sitting around for months until it was needful or handy to enter them up, and then perhaps posted only the critical entries in the accounts of other merchants, leaving counter-entries to be posted to P&L or Cash in some tidying-up session later yet. In one case, an entry which should have been dated 17 June (as the cross-entry is) is dated 17 March and brought into the end of an account which was closed in that month, implying that the Cash Account was being posted some three months in arrears (ff. 34.1, 40.1).

Something less than an orderly dealing with accumulated records is indicated also by a mistake in the Stockings account. The same consignment which had already been credited, correctly, to the ship *Rebecca*, was credited also to the *Civilia*, although the *Civilia* had already been credited, also correctly, with a different consignment. The rogue entry is not matched by a debit to the *Civilia* venture (ff. 106.1, 91.1, 101.1). Such an error could scarcely have occurred if Ledger entries had been posted properly – debit and matching credit – from a properly kept Journal. Instead it suggests rather scrappy records eked out by memory, or at any rate a haphazard method of bringing original records to Ledger. The second, and surely duplicate, credit of £100 to Cash noted above also testifies to a less than thorough posting procedure.

These same irregularities also make it clear that although there was Journal, it was by no means the only route to the Ledger as it should have been.

4.2.5   Why Double Enter?

Why did Speed bother to keep the Cash and the P&L accounts in the Ledger or use double-entry book-keeping at all? Double-entry was almost essential for keeping track when as so often there were transfers of debits or settlements between various parties. Anyhow, the double-entry system was a part of the merchant's art or mystery, and the Cash and P& L accounts were a necessary part of a full double-entry system. To keep them in a careless manner was one thing, as it might be to go out into the street with an unbrushed hat. To omit them was like going hatless altogether, a serious breach of decorum.

5   SPEED'S TRADE

5.1   Imports 1655–1694

For most of his career, the evidence for Speed's trade is the Wharfage paid by him and members of his household. This is shown, plotted against that for Bristol as a whole, in Figure 2 below. Clearly, Speed's trade did not merely mirror Bristol's. This is most striking in the late '50s and early '60s when his plunges down while Bristol's climbs. After that the movements are broadly in the same direction, peaking alike in the mid 70s; but the rates of Speed's rise to this peak and of his fall away from it are much greater than for the port as a whole.

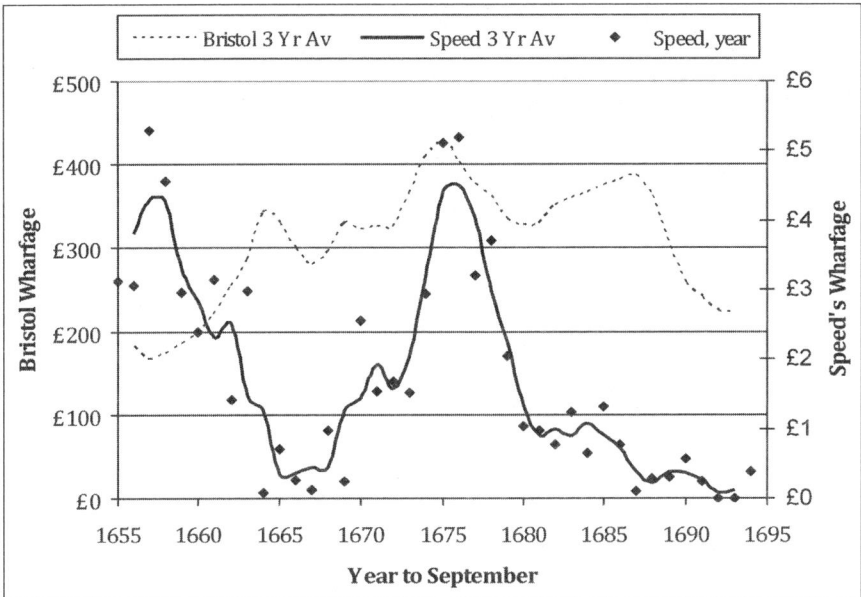

Fig. 2   Wharfage paid by Speed and for Bristol as a whole

Another way of looking at these differences is that in the late 50s Speed was paying over 2% of the entire Bristol wharfage, which makes him a major player indeed. Even when his trade regained the same absolute heights in the mid 1670s, it represented only about 1% of the whole.

Some of his associates traded at a much greater rate: Robert Yate for example paying over £4 wharfage every year for ten years; and Speed's brother-in-law William Yeamans at nearly £9 a year for 14 years. This Yeamans is up with the really great traders whose names appear on almost every page of the Wharfage books – Bullock, Bowen, Deane, and Jackson in the earlier part of the period; Crump, Davis, Dudleston, Clarke later and Elton later still; while the Popes, Michael, Richard and Charles, seem always to have been amongst the merchant magnates.[48] Speed was not quite in this class for volume, and clearly in the 1680s he was a minor figure, sinking to insignificance at around 0.1% of Bristol's trade.

These wharfage records also detail the nature of each consignment. These fall mostly into five categories: Wine, Oil, Dried Fruit, Sugar and Tobacco, and thus allow a broad estimate of wholesale value as shown in Figure 3 below. Of course, apart from being an estimate, it does not necessarily indicate the values realised by Speed as an unknown proportion may have been brought in on commission on behalf of others. In the 1680s the proportion was over 40% but that was not necessarily typical.

---

[48] I have not attempted to record entries for these merchants, but the impression left by the frequency of occurrence is overwhelming

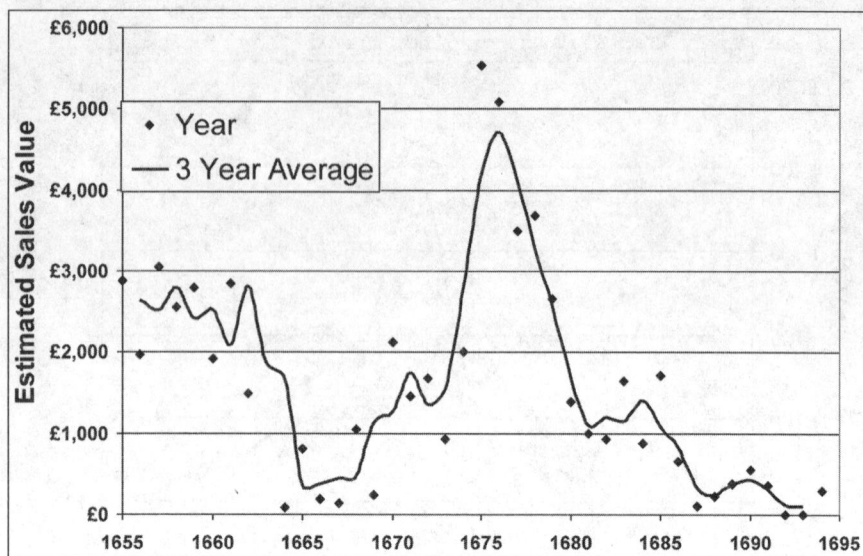

Fig. 3   Estimated Value of Speed's Imports

In fact, perhaps no decade is typical, and this is brought out by the proportions (by estimated value) of his trade as shown in Figure 4 below.

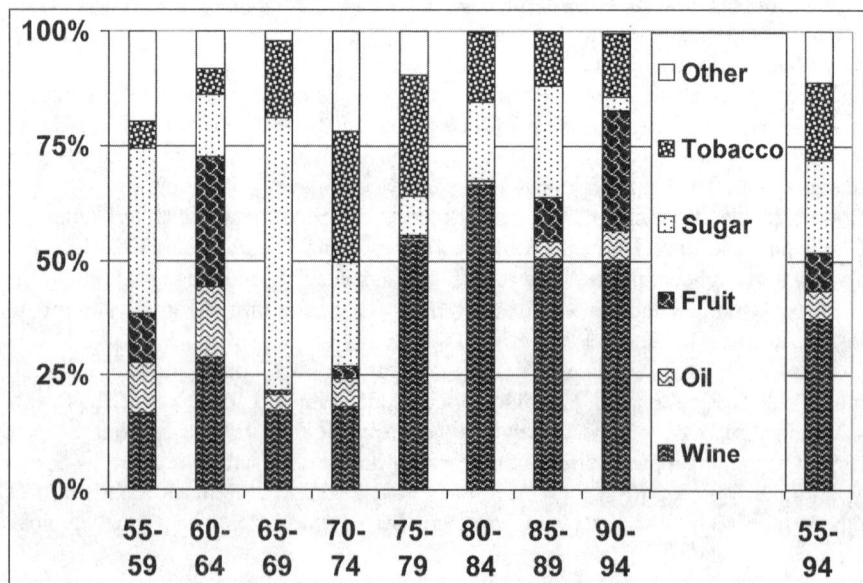

Fig. 4   Commodity Mix in Speed's Imports [49]

---

[49] For data and methodology, see Harlow 'Thomas Speed' III. 3.1.2.

Table 2   *Atlantic and Southern Europe: earlier and later periods*

	1655–74		1675–94	
	£	%	£	%
Atlantic (sugar & tobacco)	19,301	48.0%	11,345	36.6%
Europe (wine, oil & fruit)	18,192	45.3%	18,647	60.2%
Other	2,691	6.7%	982	3.2%
Total	**£40,184**		**£30,974**	

If there is any broad trend is that in the first half of his career, Speed dealt mainly with the Americas, and in the second with Southern Europe, and especially in wine.

The two trades were in some ways different.[50] The American planters needed manufactured goods, and they could pay in little else than return cargoes of sugar or tobacco. The English merchants had a protected monopoly in selling to and in buying from them. There were no problems with foreign languages, customs, or officials; the correspondents belonged to the same culture of values and expectations and there were often kinship links to work through.

It was not difficult to buy or sell sugar and tobacco. They were commodities, categorised by origin and process, but the variations were not subtle or difficult to master. It could be and often was left to the ship's master, who had delivered the English exports or the African slaves, to fill his vessel with suitable return cargoes. With competent packing they would stand transportation and keep well. Sales likewise were not a problem: surpluses on the English market could be re-exported and there was always a buyer somewhere.

But the margins on the colonial products were not good. The supply was constantly increasing; and while English traders had protected access to the English colonies, their products had to compete in London as well as in Europe. More sugar came from Brazil than from all the English sugar islands together; and tobacco grew well enough in Europe itself. Freight and duties amounted to a higher proportion of the gross margin and so increases in them were more damaging. On 22 consignments of sugar in the 1680s, mostly from Nevis, Speed made a loss of some 2% on sales. There are no complete tobacco accounts in the Ledger, an indication that Speed was not much interested in the product. [51]

Moreover there was the long sea voyage. This increased the exposure to storms and piracy, and the costs of insurance and freight. It also increased the length of time over which the return could be made.

---

[50] For the Atlantic trade, see D. Armitage & M. Braddick (eds) *The British Atlantic World, 1500–1800*, London 2002; K. Davies *The North Atlantic World in the 17th century* Minneapolis 1974; J. McCusker & K. Morgan (eds) *The Early Modern Atlantic Economy* Cambridge 2000; K. Morgan *Bristol & the Atlantic Trade in the Eighteenth Century* Cambridge 1993; I. Steele *The English Atlantic 1675–1740: an exploration of communication and community* Oxford 1986. For the Iberian: H. Fisher *The Portugal Trade: a Study of Anglo-Portuguese Commerce 1700–1770* London 1971; R. Gravil 'Trading to Spain and Portugal 1670–1700' *Business History* 10 (1968); E. Hamilton *War and Prices in Spain 1651–1800* New York 1969; H. Kamen *Spain in the later 17th century* London 1980; J. Maclachlan *Trade and Peace with Old Spain, 1667–1750* Cambridge 1940.

[51] There are seven accounts, but five open with balances from the previous Ledger, and the other two (for a total of just 6 hogsheads) were in partnership with Edward Martindale.

In southern Europe on the other hand, the English merchant had no monopoly in buying or selling. He had to deal with foreigners, directly if he used a foreign correspondent or indirectly through a resident Englishman as Speed did with Andrew Stuckey in Bordeaux and Cooke & Kekewich in Cadiz. Apart from differences in law, language and culture, neither personal attitudes nor official policies were likely to favour the outsider; and the kinship links were few and far-stretched.

Products like wine, Speed's speciality, had a much wider range of quality than sugar, and the buying took more expertise. With the best cooperage it might still travel poorly and keep badly. One whole consignment was written off entirely on arrival; and one, with an ominous charge for 63 weeks cellarage made a loss (ff. 142.2, 45.5). Of some 200–250 butts which passed through his cellars – it is difficult to be sure exactly how many – about one in ten may never have been sold for drinking. Blending or 'amendment' might be advisable.

But wine, properly handled, offered much better margins than plantation commodities, especially if disposed of among regular customers who trusted their supplier. The higher margins offered more of a buffer to variations in on-cost. Speed realised over 17% on wine sales in the 1680s. But the proper handling was important. Raisins provide a counter-example. Speed in the '80s had no regular supplier or agent of his own and no well-developed distribution channels. Of the five consignments he handled, three were from different shippers and he simply took a share in the other two, which had been organised by Thomas Strode. He made but 2½% on costs overall. Even so, it was better to make 2% two or three times a year, as was possible in trading to Spain, than once on the Atlantic run.

Putting all these factors together, the colonial products were not difficult to deal in, but they offered thin margins. To get rich on sugar or tobacco demanded large scale dealings, and exposure to whole-market risks which might mean a loss on a whole year's trading. In the European trade, well-chosen and well-handled consignments could give a better return for less investment, and with risks better spread between them.

No-one was obliged to choose either at the expense of the other. But the comparison suggests that the ease of entry into the Atlantic trade may have recommended it especially to beginners, and the scale required made it more suitable for those ready to take risks. Speed's brother John concentrated almost entirely on sugar and tobacco, and from the moment of his setting up on his own was ready to take on larger consignments than Thomas. Stepson-in-law Edward Martindale also operated mainly across the Atlantic, and in larger volume. In Speed's case there was a discernible tendency to major in Atlantic products in building or rebuilding trade and then to concentrate more and more on the Southern trade that rewarded judgement and care rather than energy and optimism.

In fact, Speed was a general trader in the first half of his career; while in the second half he might have been justly described as a wine merchant who was prepared to handle other goods. In fact over the period of the ledger his main business was stereotypically traditional: exporting textiles to import wine. Accordingly, the next sections of this Introduction focus on these two elements of his trading.

5.2   Wines
5.2.1   Wine Accounts
Speed mainly imported sherry ('Xeries') from Spain. It was usually bought by Cooke & Kekewich, later Kekewich alone, factors in Cadiz, some for Speed and some on

their own behalf with Speed as Bristol agent for them. In Bristol he did much in association with Simon Clements, Jonathan Blackwell, and Thomas Day. Clements was a relative and a Quaker, but the other two were neither. These men formed a sort of loose alliance, often bringing in wines together and then adjusting their allocations by sales among themselves. Speed would charge his commission on imports for an absent partner, e.g. Cooke & Kekewich, or even Clement sending a consignment from Spain; but not to other partners in Bristol, even when he seemed to be doing most of the work.

It is often difficult to sort out exactly what happened. The account heading itself can be misleading. Take for example 'Xeries Wine my 2/3 of 30 Butts in partnership with Simon Clement', suggesting 20 butts (f. 94.1). But in fact he sold three back to Clement, then bought six from him and then added two bought of another merchant to the same stock. The accountancy is further complicated by the rather summary treatment of the transactions between the associates, presumably mere extracts from fuller and clearer statements which they must have rendered each other. So it is not always even clear from the Ledger how much of any joint stock Speed was actually responsible for selling and how much went straight to the cellars of a partner.

This, as it were, fluidity in the accounting for wine on paper may have extended to physical stock control. One imagines a cellar with the butts of wine of a particular consignment originally standing together as a group with chalk marks on them to facilitate stock taking and stock rotation. But as the equivalent of bin ends were merged into new groups and sales were made by the butt and by the bottle, things must at times have got confused. At one point, Speed explained that two or three consignments were brought to the same account because of 'mixture of one ships wine with another, & theire being sould promiscuously as they lay in the Cellar' – probably occasioned by the unusual quantity of wines on hand at the same time, perhaps some 60 butts (f. 93. 6C). In these circumstances, the historian can hardly expect exactitude or clarity.

5.2.2 Merchandise

Sherry accounts for nearly all the direct imports. But there are also white wines and clarets, often bought in London or in Bristol; and small purchases of wines, such as Rhenish, which seem to have been used to blend with the main stocks, to enhance their flavour or extend their life.

5.2.3 Sales

Most of Speed's sales were wholesale, by the butt or hogshead. But he also sold at retail to personal customers, all named and usually in round dozens of bottles on account: he was a wine merchant, not a jug-and-bottle outlet. A widow once bought 2 bottles for cash – but he knew her name. And young Thomas Goldney occasionally took just a couple of bottles on account – trading on his relationship with Martha perhaps, if irritating her father.

The retail sales were only about 10% of the total. They were of course made at a higher price: typically a butt which sold for £20–£26 wholesale would retail at around 16s per dozen quart bottles, over £33 a butt – if it was all sold. Bottles and panniers were charged separately.

The extra margin was presumably worth the trouble. But one is struck by his regular customer list, which was short but distinguished: the Earl of Bristol, the Ladies Ann and Susan Pawlet, Sir George Strode, Sir John Drake, Dr Hungerford. There were Somerset or Dorset connections of course for most if not all of these; but these were also mostly ex-Royalists or Tories, as well as persons of some rank. There was even a single batch sold to Robert, Earl of Sunderland. Sunderland had married Ann Digby, sister of the Earl of Bristol who was Speed's main customer, and he had perhaps recommended Speed to his brother-in-law.

Was this distinguished clientele just good marketing? There may have been two other considerations. First, Speed may have been something of a snob, ready to put himself out for well-placed clients – see his interest-free loan to a bishop (f. 78.10). Certainly he was happy to enter these personages in his books without any Quakerly derogation from their full rank and title. Might there also have been an insurance aspect? Did he hope that the countenance of such men might help to avert or mitigate the penalties to which he was exposed? He seems to have written off the unpaid bill for wine supplied to the Mayor of Bristol in 1688 without a qualm (f. 155.4).

5.3   Stockings

Throughout the period covered by the ledger Speed maintained an active business in exporting worsted stockings (always spelled 'stockins'). The Ledger is the only source for this business, but it must have been going before the Ledger opened, for there is an opening balance carried forward from Ledger D. Over the period of the ledger, nearly 60,000 pairs went through his books.

The export of stockings was an important part of England's trade to Spain and Portugal.[52] In 1698 for example 1.7 million pairs of stockings were exported from England. If, as in 1668, some 60% of these went to Spain and Portugal, and rather more than half were worsted stockings, then Speed's annual average in the 80s would constitute over 1% of such a trade, putting him among the top few dozen exporters. But nearly all the information on this trade is derived from the London Port Books and other official documents. Thus the close-up of the business afforded by Speed's ledger seems especially valuable.

The business is traced through two sets of accounts: 'Stockins' which deals with purchases and 'Adventures' which deals with export consignments. The two are linked by a misleading invoicing system which needs to be ignored in determining profits.

5.3.1   Purchases

The Stocking accounts were debited with the direct costs of purchasing stockings, noting invariably the number of pairs bought and usually the price per pair. There are also charges for hotpressing (ironing) for inkle (tape, probably to tie up each dozen) and seals (tags, to relate the kind of stocking to the invoiced descriptions). These accounts show that the merchandise was bought virtually continuously through the period: there is never a month and hardly a week without an entry. One cannot imagine Jahzeel or Speed himself being constantly in attendance to check and pay for stockings – there must have been an apprentice detailed to this duty.[53]

---

[52] P. Croft, 'The Rise of the English Stocking Export Trade' *Textile History* 18 (1987) 3–16: data from pages 7 & 10.

[53] Not a clerk, as the ledger shows no payments of wages to any such person.

Nearly all the supplies came from about a dozen men, bringing in up to 180 pairs at a time.[54] These would have been manufacturers or 'hosiers' who purchased material, put it out among hand knitters and collected the finished work, paying in effect for labour. Defoe observes that this was the common pattern for spinning in these parts, as indeed it was elsewhere.[55] Most of these men are known only through their appearance in the Stocking accounts. Six of them had personal accounts in the Ledger, mostly because Speed lent or advanced them money: Richard Day, Thomas Dyer and John Massinger were all of Bristol; John Brady and John Perrie of Pensford; and Henry Britten of Bedminster (ff. 136.4, 100.2, 155.1, 20.7. 117.8, 167.3). The supply came from Somerset rather than Gloucestershire and Defoe notes it a principal industry round Wells.[56] In the relative absence of water power, knitted worsted stockings was the main if not the sole product of north-western Somerset.[57]

Among the regular suppliers was Thomas Hill, 'porter' who not only sold stockings on his own behalf, but appeared frequently as the intermediary for payments due to other suppliers. It looks as though he was trusted by other hosiers to deliver their consignments and collect their payments on their behalf. The line of communication would have been made even easier in 1687 when his son Abraham became Speed's servant (f. 131).

The prices paid cluster clearly at over 2s 3d and below 2s a pair with very few between. I take these price brackets to represent respectively full hose (above the knee) and half-hose (below the knee). Within these two broad categories, the prices at which stockings were bought vary by gradations of a farthing a pair over a range of several pence. These minor variations are not related to any recorded differences such as colour or pattern, and the basis for them is nowhere explained. I believe they are too fine to relate to any observable differences in the quality of the work. I conjecture that they were based on weight.[58] This would certainly be a consideration in the mind of the hosier, who had put out so much material to his knitters and expected it to be represented, weight-wise, in what he collected. This would make the reckoning pretty quick and straightforward: for example if a pair weighing 6oz was bought at 3s, then each half ounce per dozen would be worth a farthing per pair. Such an objective system would allow a mere apprentice to buy for Speed, and Hill to sell for other hosiers, without subjective judgments or haggling.

---

[54] Apart from one Elizabeth Dyer whose sales seldom reached double figures. She was probably a knitter rather than a dealer, allowed to sell directly to Speed rather than through a hosier as a charitable concession. She cannot be identified as a Quaker or indeed at all.
[55] Defoe *Tour of England* 261. See also S. Chapman, 'The Genesis of the British Hosiery Industry, 1600–1750' *Textile History* 3 (1972) 7–50, for the continued hand-knitting industry, despite the expansion of frame-knitting.
[56] Defoe *Tour of England* 256.
[57] R H Kinvig *The Historical Geography of the West Country Woollen Industry* (London n.d. [but said to be a reprint from the *Geographical Teacher* of 1916]) 2, 18.
[58] I found nothing in the seventeenth-century trade literature on how stockings were priced, but a customer who ordered worsted stockings from Abraham Dent in the next century specified that they should be above 6 oz. per pair: T Willan, *Abraham Dent of Kirkby Stephen: an eighteenth-century shopkeeper* (New York 1970) 93

5.3.2   Sales

Stockings were exported by the trunk-load, sent by road to London for shipping by Isaac Heming. I have not found the reason for this. There was no legal constraint, and Bristol, along with other outports, did export stockings.[59] These exports were invoiced to Kekewich in Cadiz or occasionally other merchants at nominal selling prices: 'Bristol' hose at between 2s 6d and 3s 6d, and 'Wells' at 1s 6d to 2s – presumably full and half hose respectively though I have not found Bath or Wells used elsewhere in this sense. The exported stockings were at times distinguished as Sadd or Fancy, i.e. plain/sober in colour or patterned/colourful, and some are described as Pearls, perhaps a decorative stitching. These sorts do not appear to carry a price premium or discount, but occasionally a parcel is referred to as 'Fine', 'Finest' or 'Best' and charged at a couple of pence more than others

Speed credited the Stocking account with the invoiced value which was debited an Adventure account. Then the actual value eventually realised, usually in Spanish and in English currency, was credited to the Adventure account. The result is that the financial balances as struck on the Stocking accounts bear no relation to the value of the remaining stock but only the extent to which the invoice value of the stockings exported falls short of (or exceeds) the total purchase costs of all stockings bought, whether despatched or not. Correspondingly, the 'profit' shown on the Adventure account shows only how the amount actually realised, in Spain at the current rates of exchange, exceeded or otherwise the arbitrary sterling prices under which Speed invoiced them. Neither account will identify the purchase costs of the stockings actually exported in a consignment. However I have constructed stock accounts for each type of stocking, charging them with purchases at cost and charging out exports (5.2.2) at the average cost of the stock in hand.[60] I estimate that over the period of the ledger he realised a profit of over £1,600 on sales of over £8000, an average 20%, varying between a loss of nearly 10%; and a profit of over 40% (ff. 161.3, 114.1).

5.4   Other trading

But even though he majored in these two products, Speed also traded in a wide variety of other items. The value of Stockings exported greatly exceeded that of Wine imported and much of the balance was made up of dried fruits and oil from Iberia and southern France. There were also balancing consignments of silver plate – technically illegal as an export from Spain – brought in to London where Heming would dispose of it to goldsmiths. To the plantations he sent the usual sorts of cargo –machinery and equipment, clothing, and provisions. Indeed, the range of his trade was representative of Bristol's as a whole, with the exception of shipbuilding materials and stone from the Baltic. Whether he could have done better by concentrating entirely on his main products is a question he may have considered himself. But he was a prudent man, and there was no trade, however great the demand or the profit, which might not be strangled by war. So the wise merchant kept his options open and in order to do so, his lines of communication. A fair amount of Speed's trade looks as though it may have been undertaken as much for the sake of his associates as for himself.

---

[59] McGrath *Merchant Venturers* 244, 252, 265, 268; Croft 'English Stocking Export Trade' 3.
[60] For details, see Harlow 'Thomas Speed' III.5.2.

5.5   Trading Associates

Four of Speed's main associates in Bristol were John Blackwell, Thomas Day, Henry Gibbs and Thomas Scrope.

John Blackwell, a near neighbour in Small Street, was a wine merchant (though by 1696 he was 'gent' – so probably retired).[61] His father Jonathan Blackwell was also a vintner but had moved to London and become an Alderman there. John himself was nominated to the Bristol Council by the King in 1687–88, which suggests he was a dissenter, and elected to it in 1689 which almost certainly makes him a Whig. Some half a generation younger than Speed, he died the year before him, but his son was witnessed Speed's will.

Thomas Day lived at a City property in St Nicholas street.[62] He was described by Speed as a wine cooper but in fact he seems to have been a substantial dealer, and rated at £50 pa in 1696. He never became a Councillor, and is not to be confused with Sir Thomas Day, soapboiler, who became mayor and MP; but there was probably a connection as one of Sir Thomas's sons was an executor to the other Thomas Day. Day died a couple of months after Speed and is not mentioned in his will.

Henry Gibbs has been discussed already in the context of the mysterious soap (3.2.4). He was the son and grandson of Aldermen, but himself achieved that status only for a few months of 1688 – suggesting a dissenter like Blackwell. He was a fairly active member of the Society of Merchant Venturers, though he never held any office above Warden. He dealt in wine and a variety of other goods. He was a frequent associate of Thomas Scrope, but never abandoned by Speed as Scrope was. Entries in the Ledger suggest that he was often short of cash but in a position to assist Speed in the affairs of the Clapton estate. By 1696, resident in the Castle precinct, he seems to have retired.[63]

These three were mainly associated with Speed's wine trade. Thomas Scrope was on the Atlantic side. He was a son of the old regicide Adrian Scrope, pro-Quaker Commander of the Castle garrison in 1655 when the Quakers established themselves in Bristol and the two men were for a long time very close. Two of Thomas's younger brother had been apprenticed to Speed, and he had been one of Speed's trustees in the purchase of speed's Small Street home in 1666 (and himself lived next door), and in the Sherman marriage settlement in 1668. Speed and Scrope had even shared the cost and use of Whiston's *Remembrancer* sent down from London by Heming. [64] He was also often associated, in money dealings anyway, with Henry Gibbs. But in 1683, Speed mad a complete break with him – see below 6.3.2.

Another frequent Atlantic partner was Speed's stepson-in-law Edward Martindale. (Appendix A Marriage 1). Speed also took on Edward's son Isaac as an apprentice in 1693, though his own trading was well over – but Speed was a freeman and a Merchant Venturer which Edward was not.[65] Edward was also a Quaker and, unlike Speed, an active member of the Bristol Men's Meeting.

---

[61] Ralph & Williams *Inhabitants* 223; Leech *Topography* 153
[62] Ralph & Williams *Inhabitants* 100; Leech *Topography* 143; BRO 1651/2
[63] Ralph & Williams *Inhabitants* 15; BRO 00349/9
[64] Ledger 01731D68, 0751D12. Speed called them *Avizoes*, but Whiston's name places them unmistakably: J. Price, 'Notes on some London Price Currents' *EcHR* 2nd series 7 (1954–5) 240–250:240–1
[65] BRO SMV/2/1/1/2 p548 March 20 1693/4

The other important Quaker kinsman was Isaac Heming, Speed's son-in-law (Appendix A Marriage 2), London banker (see 6.1 below), and executor. Heming was a Quaker from Reading where Speed was a frequent visitor. In London Isaac partnered John Barnard, whose son became Sir John and financial advisor to Robert Walpole.

Speed's Spanish factors were John Cooke and Samuel Kekewich at Port St Mary, Cadiz. Cooke returned to London in 1683/4 where he was occasionally involved in financial dealings with Speed. But Kekewich remained the agent both for the sale of stockings and the purchase of wine, oil and fruit. The Kekewiches are a Devon family and Samuel is a common first name, but I have found out nothing of this one. In 1693, when his own trading was done, Speed cleared five consignments of oil, wine and fruit for Samuel Kekewich who was perhaps retiring and repatriating his capital in this form.

In the '50s and the '60s Speed had been associated with fellow Quakers, his brother John, his brother-in-law William Yeamans; but then he was also associated with his brother-in-law the high Tory Robert Cann. His banker was his Quaker son-in-law but none of his principal business associates in Bristol was a Quaker. He certainly did not draw on Quaker networks for his capital. Nor indeed was he an instance of the common contemporary complaint, that Quakers dealt only with each other. Quakers generally do not seem to have figured any more prominently in his business dealings than their presence in the city would warrant, except, possibly, as recipients of small loans.

Overall, it would seem that Speed dealt with those he knew and trusted. Clearly there were ready-made links with kinsfolk and with Quakers but he does not seem to have favoured either beyond their merits as he found them: neither brother-in-law Lamboll nor son-in-law Goldney passed muster. He was in this period more closely associated with men of the dissenting or Whig community; but he was not in principle averse from dealing with Tory Anglicans – nor they with him. In this we may see reflected a city in which politico-religious differences were present and occasionally dominant, but for the most part subordinate to civic identity, connection and commerce.

5.6   Trading Capital
5.6.1   Sources
Speed started with the trading capital, as well as the connections and credit, of the established Yeamans family he married into. There was however a catch – the family capital was on loan only, and had to be returned as the step-children grew up and when his wife died. His second and third marriages all brought some property and may have played a part in relaunching his trade from the low point of the mid '60s, but there was no substantial contribution from these or his fourth marriage. For the period of the ledger, and perhaps from 1667 when he paid off debt incurred in buying his Small Street house, he was financed by the proceeds of his own trading and indeed in a position to reinvest increasingly in property.

5.6.2   Cash and credit [66]
Like other merchants, Speed bought and sold almost entirely on credit. To some extent, settlement of these dealings could be reduced by assigning the debts of others

---

[66] See Harlow 'Thomas Speed' III.6

and offsetting them against each other. Good examples in the ledger show Thomas Puxton reassigning to Speed a bond on John Williamson who drew on two of his debtors to meet it; and Speed calling on a debtor John Bradway to meet his, Speed's, obligations to Richard Wasbrow and Giles Gough (ff. 22.5, 72.2, 67.1 35.6, 70.3).

But credit, in the narrow financial sense and in the wider sense of standing and reputation, ultimately depended on due settlement in ready money.[67] Speed maintained two liquid funds: the cash he kept at his house, and the money standing to his credit with his London banker.

Isaac Heming, the trusted son-in-law, was his London banker. Apart from banking, Heming acted for him in the negotiation of foreign bills, the export of stockings to Spain, and the disposal of silver plate from Spain, all without charging commission. In effect, these were treated as equivalent to personal errands like the buying of medicines or hams. There were no bank charges, direct or indirect. Bills, whether overseas or inland, were involved in 40% of the deposits into Speed's account, and 60% of the withdrawals from it, but Heming took no premiums, commissions or discounts. But then since Speed's account was always in credit, Heming benefited from a permanent interest-free loan.[68] Speed in turn was content to leave a considerable sum in Heming's hands with no other return than a comprehensive and flexible service.

Although we cannot trust the Cash Accounts in detail, (see 4.2.2 above) if they are substantially correct, Speed might have anything from a few hundreds to over three thousand pounds in cash at home. These sums may seem surprisingly large but they were not out-of-the-way: Grassby has similar instances.[69] Speed's bank balance might also be as great. Indeed for much of the time, it was several times bigger than those deposits which the banker Edward Backwell regarded as worthy of top interest rates.[70] And clearly Cash and Bank credit were to a large extent complementary, as Figure 5 demonstrates.

The mix shifted markedly over the period. An initially large Cash balance was quickly converted into a large bank balance which was maintained for some three or four years. Then the mix shifted back slowly to an enormous preponderance of Cash which was maintained over the last three years. Two factors may account for these changes. First, the big bank balances were maintained in the period of more active trading and declined as his trade diminished. Secondly, in the early years, even before the discovery of Jahzeel's peculation, it may have seemed wise to minimise the amount of cash about the house when Speed himself was so often away.

These liquid funds required and received management. Speed had to foresee the calls and ensure that they would be met. This meant determining which amounts, due either way, were to be settled by bill on London and which in cash in Bristol; and this in turn meant negotiation. Then there were accommodations. A person who wanted

---

[67] Coin was in very short supply, all the shorter because those who could afford to hoarded it. Merchants would foregather at the great fairs of St Pauls in January and St James in June as much to settle outstanding obligations by the rapid circulation of a small amount of cash as to buy or sell.

[68] Indeed, a formal loan at interest to himself and his partner John Barnard at opening was soon merged with the general, non-interest bearing, account (f. f 69.3, 130.2).

[69] Grassby, 'Composition of Business Fortunes' 90–91.

[70] H Roseveare, *The Financial Revolution, 1660–1760* (London 1991) 20

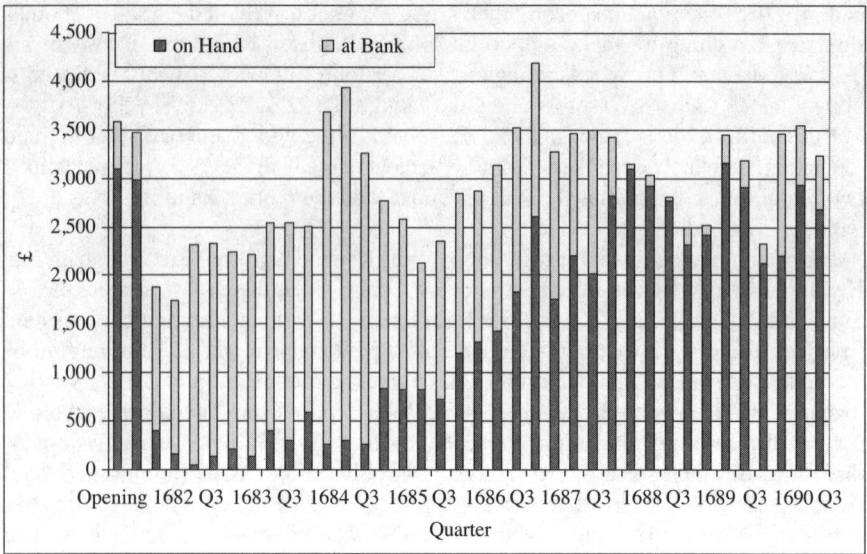

Fig. 5   Cash on Hand and at Bank at Quarter's end

to remit (or 'return') cash to London would pay it to Speed in Bristol, who would draw an equivalent bill (in effect, a cheque) in the man's favour on Heming who would then honour it in London. To remit funds the other way, the third party would pay cash into Speed's account with Heming in return for a bill drawn on Speed and honoured by him in Bristol. This process was a staple element of the domestic economy. [71] Sometimes these transactions suited both parties, but often they were favours from men with London bank accounts to men without. My analysis suggests that such transactions made up about 10% of the money paid into the account with Heming (remittance to Bristol) and 40% of the withdrawals from it (the more frequently required remittance to London). Speed did not charge for these services, though others did.[72]

The terms Cash Flow Projection and Cash Flow Management had not been invented then but Speed must have been very familiar with the process. A detailed regression analysis of his quarterly holdings shows that they were increased or reduced very exactly in line with the flows over the succeeding three months – though as prudence would dictate, more weight was given to projected payments than expected receipts.[73]

But Speed did not employ that easiest of cash-flow management techniques, the delaying of settlement. On the contrary, he was forward with payments. Nor did he press his debtors for settlement (see 6.3.2 below). In fact his Debtors at any time

---

[71] Kerridge, *Trade and banking* ch 4 & 5

[72] There was one exception where he charged Thomas Walden some ½% on his *third* substantial remittanc in a few months – in effect a warning that he was rather presuming on the favour (ff. 87.6, 90.2, 90.2).

[73] Changes in the Cash balances were as though calculated on 91% of ensuing payments out and 81% of ensuing payments (correlation coefficient r^2 0.87); and for the bank balance, 123% and 91% respectively (r^2 = 0.81) Harlow 'Thomas Speed' III. 6.1.3

exceeded his Creditors 7 or even 20 to 1.That he was nevertheless so much in overall control of his liquid funds, and so successful in avoiding embarrassment, is a tribute to his judgment and careful management.

6   LENDING [74]

Speed over this period never had to borrow, other than occasional small amounts of spending money when staying at Reading. The only exception was a mortgage on the Clapton farm held by the seller – a widow (f. 7.1). It was only £150, easily in his power to pay; but the widow presumably reckoned this as good an investment for the purchase money as she could find, and Speed obliged her. But, as a very solvent man, he did himself lend widely.

Speed's lending may be classified by nature or by status. By nature, we may distinguish Trade Debts, Financial Investments and Favours. The status of a debt varied with its documentation and its terms. At the lowest level were loans with no other documentation than the ledger entries. If Speed died, these would probably be unenforceable without the goodwill of the debtor. Next were the debts arising from a contract with a customer or tenant and those supported by a note. These too would be difficult of enforcement if there was no specific time for payment. Next was the bill, which, once accepted, had a date for settlement; and after that the bond which typically provided for a penalty in the event of non-payment on the due date and/or for interest. At the highest level was the secured bond, of which the mortgage was the chief sort.

Nature and status did not go hand in hand. One might think that interest bearing bonds or mortgages must represent financial investments, while trade debts and casual loans would be informally documented and carry no interest. But it was not so simple. If a trade debt or casual loan remained unpaid for too long, it would move up in status, be secured with more formal documentation, and eventually carry interest. This process of loan escalation has been described by Muldrew [75] and is well illustrated by Speed's loans to Nathaniel Haggatt and William Spoore, 6.2.1 and 6.2.2 below.

Nevertheless it is fairly easy to classify most of Speed's lending by looking at the origins of each loan. The breakdown between these different types of lending is estimated to be as shown in Table 3 below at three year intervals over the period of the ledger.

Table 3   Types of Lending at end of three year periods

	1681		1684		1687		1690	
	£	%	£	%	£	%	£	%
Financial	210	6%	1,086	22%	460	11%	1,920	43%
Favours	553	17%	1,116	23%	1,651	39%	925	21%
Business	2,566	77%	2,628	54%	2,119	50%	1,655	37%
Total	3,329		4,830		4,230		4,500	

[74] Harlow 'Thomas Speed' III.8
[75] Muldrew *Economy of Obligation* 175

6.1   Financial Investments

Any loan of at least £50, secured by an interest bearing bond or mortgage from the outset, and made to someone who was not a relation or regular associate, has been counted as an investment. The greater part were mortgages. Some of these were to countrymen around Bristol, but Heming occasionally fulfilled a customary function of the London banker by finding good investments. All the borrowers on bond were Bristolians. Although the bonds were for smaller amounts they might run for longer than a mortgage: good mortgages could always be re-assigned, which was why they were ideal as a temporary home for funds pending a favourable property opportunity.

6.2   Financial favours

6.2.1   Family

The two main beneficiaries of Speed's lending were cousin Nathanael Haggatt and brother-in-law Jonathan Lamboll. (Appendix A Marriages 1 and 4). Haggatt, a lawyer, owed Speed £34 when the ledger opened – no bond, no interest. It was not repaid, and the next borrowings were on bond. Interest was charged, retrospectively from the date of the loans but not until the loans had run for 4 ½ years, and further loans were made. At the end of 1687, the total, of £320, was secured by a mortgage at the maximum rate of 6% – but not much interest was paid and by the time the ledger was closed, Haggatt owed £360 odd. By the time Speed made his will, the debt had risen to £690 of which £230 was unpaid interest (technically allowing foreclosure); but Speed forgave the interest on condition the principal was paid.[76]

In 1686 Speed put £400 into Lamboll's malting business, as a partnership share not a loan. This must have been at Lamboll's suggestion, for it was geographically and occupationally remote from Speed's interests. When this proved totally unproductive, and Lamboll unable to repay it, it was converted into a mortgage at 5%. Meanwhile further money was lent him and Lamboll also owed on rents for Reading property which he was supposed to be collecting for Mary. Eventually Lamboll owed nearly £700 which was paid off, apparently by the sale of some of his own property, though not to Speed (ff. 109.5, 131.1, 147.6).

The only other important family loan was £327 outstanding on mortgage to Martha Gay (appendix A Marriage 3) at the beginning of the Ledger period, which was paid off so quickly that the question of interest did not arise. Another £115 lent her over the next few years – without interest – was simply written off in 1686. Perhaps she died (ff. 32.1, 32.2).

There were also small payments made on behalf the apprenticeships of Richard and James Speed, sons of Richard Speed mariner, deceased – great-nephews presumably. Although the word loan was not used, the Debtor balances in their names were carried forward in 1690, as was the £36 which had been advanced their father before his death (ff. 26.1, 94.7, 94.8, 117.3). But again the Will cancelled these obligations.

6.2.2   Clients

Speed frequently lent to people who regarded him as in some sense a patron (as Anthony Wood described his position among the Bristol Quakers).[77] Most of these

---

[76] ff 19.4, 138.6, 148.2. Speed's Will TNA Prob 11/484 ff. 249–252

[77] *Anthony Wood: Athenae Oxoniense: An Exact History of all the writers and bishops who have been educated in the University of Oxford, etc* 4 vols, ed. P Bliss (London 1813–20) IV c 488.

loans were small and documented with no more than 'Cash lent him' in the Ledger. The expectation was presumably that they would be repaid when the borrower was able and no doubt informal promises were made. Moreover, they could often be repaid, in part at least, by services subsequently rendered – it looks as though Speed would, rather sensibly, find occasion to get small works done by people who owed him a few pounds. Even if these debts were not paid off, Speed never enforced them. But generally a second loan made when the first was still outstanding was more likely to be supported by a note or an IOU. Constant borrowers like the Spoores, father and son, who were also tenants, were on bill/bond status from the opening of the ledger. They made some repayments and paid some interest, but in effect maintained borrowings of over £100 throughout the ledger years (ff. 30.3, 31.7, 52.6, 69.8, 151.4, 154.4, 158.5, 176.1, 176.2).

Another borrower in this category was Thomas Lutterell of Clevedon (not a tenant but a country neighbour) who owed £10 on bond before the ledger opened, and £20 with several years of unpaid interest when it closed (ff. 25.1, 97.4). Then there was John Massinger the clothier and a major supplier of stockings. Speed assisted him in legal proceedings and progressively advanced him some£200 to be paid off in Stockings: interest was never mentioned (f. 163.1). An example of a quasi-family link was the assistance given to the Taylor family. Dennis Taylor had been apprenticed to Speed's brother John. After John's death, Speed, helped the Taylors to bring in a barrel of sugar and made small loans which were written off either in the ledger period or in the Will (ff 11.1, 88.5, 179.1).

Of course we cannot know what requests for a loan Speed may have turned down. But such as they are, these loans have a benign face. Far from being a loan-shark, Speed seems to have been discharging a social obligation, what was expected of a wealthy patron, a sort of *richesse oblige*.[78]

A unique loan was afforded Peter Mewes, the Bishop of Bath & Wells: £150 lent in June 1684, to be repaid in October but £50 was still outstanding at the end of 1690, yet no interest was ever charged (f. 78.1). No other connection between the men is known. Possibly Speed found or hoped for some value from being of service to a man in high place.

6.3 Business

Most of Speed's sales were made on credit terms. But with frequent associates like Blackwell, Day, Gibbs and Scrope, there was frequent lending as well as frequent dealing; and Speed's accounts will not tell you whether the £60 a man paid today was in part settlement of the goods he had bought last week or the money he had borrowed the week before. It was simply part of the running account. But when the account ran too long one way, the outstanding amount might be upgraded to an interest-bearing loan or a bond.

The situation was further complicated when a borrower deposited goods for sale as security. The loan became in effect an advance on sales. Speed kept only the amount advanced, returning any surplus to the borrower/principal – see the mysterious soap affair, 3.2.4 above.

---

[78] C. Muldrew, 'The Culture of Reconciliation : community and the settlement of economic disputes in early modern England' *Historical Journal* 39 (1996) 915–942: 929.

The general trend of Business Credit is downward as one would expect from the cut-back in his trade, but the reductions do not seem proportionate – testimony to the long credit granted, and the longer patience with non-payment.

6.3.1   The normal course of business

Most transactions were attested primarily by a bundle of notes, memoranda, invoices and so on, and some perhaps by no original paperwork at all. Both parties would try to bring all together in their ledgers, and there was a patent will to reconcile these rather than dispute differences. 'ballance of theire acct current agreeable to theire own acct sent mee per Robt Massinger' as Speed noted (f. 111.1D December). Where they did not, the matter could be sorted by conference 'Cooperidge and cash as per severall noates of his widowes Mary Wasbrow, this day evened betwixt us as per Journal book fol 117 at large appeareth'; or 'ballance of his former acct adjusted betwixt us in Bristoll' (ff. 28.3C, 131.1D).[79] At a pinch, better write off the difference rather than quarrel e.g. 'for …errors that I can By no meanes finde, for friendship sake I here charge that wee might close all accts to this 27th day of October 1685', writing off nearly £5 (f. 85.4C).

Sometimes with larger transactions, dates were set down for payment. Even where no date was specified originally, there was an expected norm of repayment.[80] But it was a forbearing norm. and nobody was ever held to the day of promised settlement, even if stated. But when Edward Roy of Dorchester took over three years to settle an account with him, Speed charged him interest for the last 18 months – and even then Speed was left out of pocket (ff. 5.4, 44.2, 62.3). When Thomas Day, a frequent wine trade associate, allowed a trade debt incurred in April 1683 to remain unpaid for some 18 months, Speed charged interest but only for the last 9 months. In 1688, Speed lent him £100 on a deposit of gold for some three months and charged no interest. But in 1689, he lent £50 again on a deposit of gold, and charged interest for the nine months it was outstanding, though he then remitted the interest charge – it had been in effect only a gentle hint that the time for an account to remain unsettled had been passed, even between close associates (ff. 70.5, 150.5, 161.2).

Jonathan Blackwell, another wine trade associate, was also another frequent debtor. He was not usually charged interest. In fact when Blackwell actually paid interest on two occasions in 1683, Speed credited this direct to P& L, rather than to Blackwell – an indication that it had not been expected. He may have explained as much at the time – Blackwell never offered interest again. In November 1685, John Blackwell's outstanding debit was converted to two bills payable in four and seven months, but no interest was ever charged though in fact the bills were not honoured at the due date (ff. 85.4, 85.5).

6.3.2   Enforcement

Several debts which had been brought down from the previous Ledger were solemnly carried forward to the next, without a single entry in between, and with no apparent

---

[79] I believe that the so-called Account Book of Anthony Varder 1697–1713 (BRO AC/B/64) is the office copy of statements of account sent to associates for just this purpose.
[80] Or not in the Ledger. Invoices might well have carried the equivalent of today's 'Terms strictly 30 days nett' – and to as little purpose.

attempt to enforce payment. Ten years was not enough to make a debt either desperate or actionable. This was not from want of remedy: the Quaker refusal to take oaths does not seem to have hindered their going to law. Speed himself had fought and lost a claim for lord's rent by Henry Winter (ff. 38.4D March). His kinsmen Edward Martindale and William Rogers both Quakers, had actually gone to law with each other.

But he was slow to go to law for debts. Just how slow is illustrated by the case of Arthur Bramley and John Briscoe. He took legal proceedings against them in 1688 on an unpaid bond and they eventually paid up, with arrears of interest and costs, in 1689. But their bond dated from 1659. Speed had waited thirty years before taking such a step (f. 12.4). It looks as though Speed regarded the law as the appropriate arbiter of disputes over property, but that in commercial dealings he reckoned to avoid even the dispute, let alone the law-suit.

Thomas Scrope provides an instance of the ultimate sanction might be invoked. They had been close for many years, see 5.5 above. But in 1683 Speed brought together various outstanding matters in one new account (f. 75.1). The first entry is a debit of £100 'money I was to have received from him with his brother Edward Scrope, but did not receive it.' Some of Scrope's credits are treated to sceptical comments: 'which I cannot say is due'; 'for money he saith is due to him.' An outstanding loan to Scrope and Gibbs had been repaid as to the principal but short by some £70 (four years interest) as calculated by Speed. The final balance was a deficit of £93 odd. Speed simply wrote it off. No further business of any kind was done between him and Scrope, or not in the Ledger period; and Scrope is not mentioned in his will.

Scrope was still alive, so it looks like a deliberate severance. Why? Scrope had been associated with the Bristol branch of the Rye House plotters, though never charged. His son was known to be still amongst the radical Protestants plotting in Holland.[81] But if Speed decided that Scrope was a man it was impolitic to know, he should have made the break earlier, and could safely have renewed the association after the Glorious Revolution.

The tone of the final account suggests that Speed had accumulated a sense of Scrope's failure to live up to the standards of a personal relationship, rather than to the terms of a contract. His response was not to go to law, but simply to write off the amount due and sever the relationship. The language in which he did so is aggrieved, rather than aggressive. This attitude and the underlying norms will be discussed at more length below (7.3.4).

7 PORTRAIT OF A MERCHANT

7.1 Success

Over the 9 years of the ledger, Speed earned nearly £550 a year, a little over half from trading and the rest from lending and property. This is well above the £400 a year which Gregory King regarded as the norm for overseas merchants.[82] Taking into account that

---

[81] *ODNB*; Greaves *Secrets of the Kingdom* 300
[82] An estimate allowed to stand in P. Lindert & J. Williamson 'Revising England's Social Tables 1688–1912' *Explorations in Economic History* 19 (1982) 385–408

Table 4   Speed's Net Earnings and Expenditure 1681–1690 [83]

| | Income from | | | | | |
	Trading	Property	Lending	Total	Spending	Surplus
£ Net	2667	963	1255	4885	2,242	2,643
% of all income	55%	20%	26%		43%	54%

King's figures must have derived mainly from London, where earnings were much higher that in the outports, it is clear that even in these declining years, Speed was a very successful businessman. He spent nearly half of this income, and if there was nothing conspicuous about his consumption, it was at any rate very comfortable.[84]

The savings he invested, mainly in property and in mortgages. So a nominal net worth of some £11,500 when the ledger opened had become over £14,000 by the end. He was worth a little less when he died, say £12,500. Perhaps he had speculated unsuccessfully in stocks in the '90s, but the greater part of the apparent loss was very likely in debts, carried forward rather optimistically in 1690 but never realised.

Surveying the century as a whole, Grassby says that 'In Bristol estates ranged from £1,000 to £2,000; the average personalty of Merchant Venturers was £919'.[85] His examples from other provincial towns indicate that an estate of over £3,000 was unusual.[86] His citations are based on inventories at death which exclude real property. In these terms, if Speed had died in 1690, his personal estate, excluding property and discounting most of the Debts and the Stock, would been somewhere between £5,000 and £6,000. This would put him on a level with major Bristol merchants such as John Whitson or Joseph Jackson.[87] It can safely be said that Speed was a very prosperous man for the provinces.

7.2   Speed's Qualities

One factor in Speed's success was longevity. Then as now, other things being equal, wealth accumulated in the hands of the elderly, and Speed lived eighty years. This also gave him time to wind up and settle his affairs rather than be caught by death at an awkward juncture.

Speed was clearly an intelligent man and a quick study. His first marriage offered him the chance of picking up the merchant's skills, including accountancy; but it was for him to profit by it. He kept his faculties to the end: his last writings are as sharp as ever, in every sense of the word. In fact, they reveal a man of some asperity, which could have been a handicap in the commercial culture of the time, had he not kept it under control.

He was a careful trader, risk-averse and untempted by great coups. He kept large liquid balances, paid his own bills promptly, and never, to judge by the Wharfage

---

[83] Harlow 'Thomas Speed' I.6.4 & III.5 esp Table III.16
[84] Averaging nearly £300 a year up to and including 1687, the year of Martha's marrriage, then falling to about £170 a year for the last three years.
[85] Grassby *Business Community* 250 though it is not easy to relate these figures to the sources he cites
[86] Grassby *Business Community* 250–252
[87] P. McGrath, 'The Wills of Bristol Merchants in the Great Orphan Books' *TBGAS* LXVIII (1949) 91–119: 94–95. Both men were in their times Mayors, Masters of the SMV, and MPs.

Table 5   Speed's Net worth: 1681 and 1690

	end 1681	end 1690	Change
Cash	3,579	3,229	−350
Net Debtors	2,644	2,513	−131
Stock	1,862	2,465	603
Financial Investments	210	1,920	1,710
Property	3,140	3,995	855
Total	11,435	14,122	2,687

Books, traded on the scale of some of his contemporaries. This caution debarred him from great gains but it kept him out of financial trouble. Within this relatively restricted compass, he was prepared to take pains, and the apparent contrast with the short period of Jahzeel's management shows what a difference it made that a merchant should mind his business.

His care and caution, and particularly his beforehandedness in meeting liabilities must have enhanced whatever credit he had originally acquired from the Yeamans connection. Apart from paying his bills, he was ready to take back or discount unsatisfactory goods, to compromise on reckonings, to be patient with debtors and tenants, and to work in cooperation with others. If he was not casual, nor was he grasping – neither Antonio nor Shylock. These qualities owed as much to the commercial culture in which he operated as to his personality, as discussed below (7.3.4).

He seems to have been honest even in his dealings with the authorities. All the imports in the Ledger can be found in the Wharfage Books. Today we might not expect illegal dealings to enter the official accounts anyway, but Jones has shown that Bristol merchants in the sixteenth century had no such false modesty and readily entered the details of consignments shipped out clandestinely by lighter, and of bungs to Customs officers.[88] At that time, outward consignments were the most smuggled, but by the Seventeenth Century it was inward duties which were most evaded. In 1690, a number of Bristol merchants compounded for £2,700, admitting charges of substantial evasion of duty on tobacco. Nearly 40% of this total was paid by leading Quakers.[89] Speed's absence from the list is not conclusive of his innocence, for he had not dealt in tobacco on his own account since 1684; but he paid the duty then and again when clearing tobacco on commission in 1687/8 (ff. 78.4, 147.5). Perhaps he was the 'one merchant in the book you will find very honest'.[90]

7.3   Values
7.3.1   Protestant Capitalist?
This survey of Speed's business activities has brought out many ways in which he was not imbued with the Spirit of Capitalism. As a merchant, his business did not involve

[88] E. Jones, 'Illicit business: accounting for smuggling in mid-sixteenth century Bristol' *Economic History Review* 54 (2001) 17–38.
[89] Latimer *Annals* 463–4; McGrath *Merchant Venturers* 222–3; R. Mortimer, 'Quakerism in seventeenth-century Bristol' MA dissertation, University of Bristol 1946, 354–6.
[90] Colt's testimony: *Calendar of Treasury Books 1556–1696* ed. J. Reddington, London 1868, 426 – no name given.

the employment of free labour, on which Weber laid stress.[91] More importantly, his accounts did not even make that 'separation of business from personal life' which Weber regarded as allied to rational bookkeeping, and did not permit calculated profit maximisation.

We do not have Speed's diaries or his injunctions to his apprentices. But while his ledger contains several remarks expressive of his attitudes, there is not a single reference to Providence, or rendering of thanks for his good fortune – omissions all the more apparent by contrast with writings which show him to be as ready as the next man with sententious sanctimony. So far from pursuing his calling to the end, he made careful arrangements for semi-retirement when still vigorous if elderly. He was not particularly abstemious himself and allowed his son drinking money even in his disgrace. He was hardly the stereotypical Protestant or puritan businessman.[92]

7.3.2   Quakerism?

The Ledger likewise contains no hint that Speed was a Quaker, and several indications that he was not a good one. The months of the year were given their pagan names. Nobody in its pages was described as a Friend, though several were. On the other hand, the great of the land were given their worldly titles without qualification or disclaimer – if anything one might fancy that he relished having an Earl of Bristol, a Bishop of Bath & Wells, a Sir Thomas Strode and a Lady Ann Paulett on his books. There is never a reference to any donation to Quaker collections, though he not only paid his poor rates but contributed to the relief of Huguenots (f. 119.1). That he paid his rates for the militia means little: the Bristol Quakers had complained about the amount they were assessed for but had made no stand on principle. But he unblinkingly recorded that he paid his tithe on his Clevedon land while it was in his hands (f. 32. 3).

Despite some claims by Quakers themselves, it may be doubted how far there were any especially Quaker business ethics. That traders should be honest and prudent were commonplaces of commercial precept, not peculiar to Quakers. Fox made much of the Quaker's refusal to haggle over prices, as an extension of plain speaking. But this can have meant little to the wholesaler who was used to agreeing with his customers the mix of money down and money at three or six months which would suit both. Some Quakers gave up trading in goods which they considered vain or wrongful in use. Men like Stout and Pike record instances of particular deals they turned down for Truth's sake. In the absence of such record we cannot tell if Speed refrained from dealing in slaves or firearms for this reason.[93]

Early modern Quakers have been claimed as instances of a frequently observed occurrence, that minorities barred from public life or social esteem thrive the more in

---

[91] M Weber, *The Protestant Ethic and the Spirit of Capitalism* New York 2003, 21–2
[92] Perhaps the stereotype is at fault. Sommerville has argued that many Protestants disparaged the making of money ('Anti-Puritan Work Ethic' *Journal of British Studies* 20, 1981, 70–81) and Mascuch that diarists at least generally perceived themselves as 'making the family secure' rather than relentlessly pursuing either profit or salvation ('Social mobility and middling self-identity: the ethos of British autobiographers' *Social History* 22 (1995) 45–61: 55).
[93] Technically this was still a monopoly of the Royal Africa Company. Neither Speed nor any other Quaker was named to the SMV committee petitioning for entry to this trade (McGrath *Merchant Venturers* 231). But he had transported Irish prisoners to servitude on the plantations before his conversion.

those commercial fields still open to them.[94] Speed's becoming a Quaker certainly did debar him from public life, at any rate for three decades after the Restoration. This was something of a relief: the Council was a distraction and a year as sheriff or mayor a real burden. On the other hand, fines and imprisonment were not conducive to the carrying on of business. All in all, he would perhaps sooner have been exposed to the full burdens of civic office than to exile and loss of estate under the laws against non-conformity. And socially the Quakers were by no means an outcast group. Speed was kin to many of the magistracy of Bristol, he continued to associate with such people, albeit more of the dissenting persuasions, and to take his place, when he chose, in the Merchant Venturers Hall.

7.3.3 Family

Family, rather than faith, seems to have provided the framework and the dynamic of Speed's business. Family supplied, and then sapped, his trading capital. It was the deaths of his brother and brother-in-law that brought him to the peak of his trading. If he ran down his business in the later '70s, it was not because times were bad, but because he was planning to take early semi-retirement. If he switched his capital into property in his last years, this was not because rent offered better returns than trade, but because that was the best means of transmitting it to his surviving children – both daughters. Speed's business history seems to confirm the conclusion of Grassby, that the seventeenth-century business was, in the fullest sense, a family firm.[95]

7.3.4 Friendship

There has been a perception that the early modern period saw the impersonal legalistic contract become the mode of business relationships. Even Grassby, who places the businessman firmly in the household, accepts that contract became the 'organising principle' of seventeenth-century England.[96] Speed's dealings, whether as trader, lender, or landlord, seem rather to have taken place within a social context and a culture of norms and expectations which were more important than formal legal rights and obligations. The model that Speed and his associates, his creditors, his tenants and his neighbours, had reference to was Friendship.

The early modern 'friend' did not refer particularly to a person whose company you enjoyed, but to one who had a benevolent regard to your interests.[97] That was the language in which businessmen wrote to each other; and the basis on which the tenant or creditor would expect forbearance, and neighbours look for assistance whether in transmitting money to London or in borrowing. Of course the language might mask behaviour which was less than friendly, but then the language of corporate management today often masks conduct which has nothing to do with shareholder interests.

The friendship involved was not the absolute and unconditional friendship of which Montaigne wrote, but rather the 'common friendships' with which he contrasted it,

---

[94] S. Kent, 'Relative Deprivation and Resource Mobilization: a study of early Quakerism' *British Journal of Sociology* 33 (1982) 529–544

[95] Grassby *Kinship & Capitalism*, esp. 'Conclusion: Capitalism and the Life Cycle' 387–417

[96] Grassby *Kinship & Capitalism* 393.

[97] N. Tadmor, *Family and Friends in Eighteenth-Century England* (Cambridge 2001) ch 5 *passim* definition p 179

where 'a man must march with the bridle of wisdom and precaution in his hand.'[98] It was compatible with, indeed largely consisted in, a strong sense of obligations in each direction, and a conscious reckoning of how far they were being honoured or dishonoured.[99] Honour was not confined to the landed; there were many sorts of honour.[100] For those in commerce, Honour was implicated in the notion of Credit on which so much depended.[101] It was not for nothing that one spoke of a bill being 'honoured'.[102] The credit of a man was not just the financial amount for which he could be trusted: his very manhood was embodied in the notion of his solvency and, reaching back to family again, his ability to maintain his household honourably, paying his way.[103] And beyond that it was the moral credit balance he had acquired by fair dealing with others.[104] We may say of commercial honour what Donagan says of military, it 'was professional, moral, utilitarian and a force for social stability. It was pragmatic as well as idealistic.'[105]

It should hardly be surprising that the well-known and important ethic of friendship should be applied to commercial dealings. After all, those dealings were personal and conducted between persons who did not draw a barrier between the household and the firm. Friends were in a sense social capital to be invested in.[106] The language of friendship was an appropriate mean between the constant evocations of piety and religious commandment mocked in the stage Puritan and the cold legalese of contract; with enough of morality in it, and enough of obligation, to bridge that gap and to serve the purposes of a civil society. And even if it often masked real sentiment and motive, it was not merely a matter of words, but of conduct. For example it demanded that a man should not only fulfill his obligations but do so cheerfully; and call for fulfillment pleasantly and tactfully. It went with easy social intercourse: not for nothing was the coffee-shop a centre of commerce.

Friendship and the obligations of friendship, rather than legal or religious concepts, created the expectations to which men responded and against which they judged others. Cooperation rather than competition, convention rather than contract, reconciliation rather than conflict, were the norms. When these were not met, the reaction was personal reproach not litigation, as Speed showed in breaking with

---

[98] M. Montaigne Essayes trans J Florio Book I Chapter XXVII

[99] K. Swett, 'The Account between us: Honor, Reciprocity and Companionship in Male Friendship in the later Seventeenth Century' *Albion* 31 (1989) 1–30. See also S. Whyman *Sociability and Power in late-Stuart England: the cultural worlds of the Verneys 1660–1720* Oxford 2002esp. ch 1 and ch 4 showing how the unit of reckoning mutated from Venison to Visits.

[100] See the conclusions of the plenary session of the conference on 'Honour & Reputation in early-modern England' *TRHS* Sixth Series VI (1996) 247–248

[101] J. Smail, 'Credit, Risk and Honor in Eighteeenth-Century Commerce' *Journal of British Studies* 44 (2005) 439–456

[102] In print from 1706, *OED*

[103] A. Shepard, 'Manhood, Credit and Partriarchy in Early Modern England' *Past & Present* 167 (2000) 75–106

[104] P. Mathias, 'Risk, credit and kinship in early modern enterprise' in *The Early Modern Atlantic Economy* ed J McCusker & K Morgan Cambridge 2000, 15–35: 30

[105] B. Donagan, 'Web of Honour: Soldiers, Christians and Gentlemen in the English civil War' *HJ* 44 (2001) 365–389: 365

[106] Kohn 'Business Management in Pre-Industrial Europe' 12; Mathias 'Risk, credit and kinship' 29, 30

Scrope.[107] Yet in other contexts Speed was inclined to be disputatious, harshly uncompromising and self-righteous. His self-justifying pamphlet of 1690 has the same vituperative tone as those of the 1650s.[108] His last surviving letter has the same withering dismissal of the legal claims of his opponent as his first.[109] But the ethos of Friendship in business was strong enough to temper this rather harsh and unforgiving temperament.

CONCLUSION

Speed's ledger gives us not only a business history but the portrait of a successful and respected businessman: cautious, honest, and fair; observing the conventions of commercial friendship and ready to do favours; concerned above all with the interests of his family. It is a portrait he would have been happy to own.

---

[107] L. Pollock, 'Anger and the Negotitiation of Relationships in early modern England' *HJ* 47 (2004) 567–590 Muldrew 'Culture of Reconciliation' esp. 928; also *Economy of Obligation* 135–6 Shephard 'Manhood, Credit & Patriarchy' 86; Hannah 'Moral Economy of Business' 285–300: 286
[108] Reason against Rage, being some animadversions upon a scandalous libel London 1690; Christs Innocency pleaded London 1656; The Guilty-Covered Clergyman Unvailed London 1657
[109] UBLSC Goldney papers DM1398 C.11. 264 ; Dorset Record Office: D/SHS/A 227. One must add that this was his public face. Privately the man who was always so welcome in the homes of his step-daughter in Reading and his daughter in London must have been agreeable enough; and his widow, Mary, who survived him by 17 years, asked to be buried 'in the same grave that my dear husband was buried in' (TNA Family sig 56 PR11/568).

TRANSCRIPTION

The general policy has been to present the ledger as close to the original as may be intelligible to the non-specialist reader. Subject to errors in reading, the transcript is literal, EXCEPT:

Characters

Abbreviations which are no longer current are given a modern form if there is one. Thus *li* is rendered as £ or *lb.*; *et cet.* as *etc.*; *ct.* as *cwt.*; *9br* or *Nov.br* as *Nov.*; *Compay, compny, compy* all as *Co.*; and *Sa.* as *St.*

Y for thorn is always printed as *th*.

Abbreviations that have no modern form are usually expanded: eg *Exch^a* is *Exchange*; and *comission* (with contraction mark), *commission*. The expansions are not marked typographically and no attempt is made to reproduce or indicate contraction marks or superscripted characters. *Pd.* is left, where used, for *paid* ; and *recd.* for all abbreviations of *received..* Abbreviations for *what, which, with* and suchlike are expanded throughout. Pt. for part is always expanded.

Christian names have been left as abbreviated, including *Xpher* for Christopher; with the exception of *Jno* which is given as *John* throughout (the Ledger has both, apparently at random.)

Place names are modernised where there is a standard modern form (*Lixboa* beomes *Lisbon, Exon, Exeter*) but *Virginea* will not confuse anyone and rather than choose between *Jerez* and *sherry, Xerie(s)* stays

Mr. for Mister is left so, but expanded for the Master of a ship.

[?] or [conjectured reading] are used for missing or illegible text and — for spaces left in the original (often first names). [*sic*] is not used – all errors are meant to be those of the accountant, and some are annotated. Crossed out words or figures have not been transcribed but have been noted if they seem to have any interest.

Punctuation

Commas and apostrophes are used as in the original. Other stops, where given, are rendered according to today's usage, but the practice of leading the narrative across to the figures with a line of dots and dashes – not reproduced – can makes it difficult to tell when stops are intended. Figures (not sums of money) are often underlined and both figures and sums of money are often followed by a dot: no attempt has been made to reproduce these features.

Capitals in the original are reproduced as far as they are discernible (Speed's initial *M* and *m* are very alike), but *ff* is printed *F*.

Layout

The layout has been slightly simplified to save space. In the original, there are two separate columns on the left of the page for the date, which are here merged as one. Similarly there is a separate column for thousands of Ryals which has been merged here.

In the Stockings Accounts, Jahzeel used a convenient set of columns for Pairs, Shillings and Pence (per dozen) which Speed abandoned but which is adopted here throughout in these very repetitive entries. Similar space-saving tabulation has been adopted for the repetitive entries in the account for Rice (f. 95.1).

The column for references to the counter-entries in the Ledger has been retained but the references are annotated where they are incorrect or will not be found. Also, from folio 79, the Ledger provides a second column for what appear to be references to the pages of another account book, unspecified; and most though not all entries are given such a second reference. The practice suggests that, possibly as a consequence of Jahzeel's untrustworthiness, Speed may have taken to keeping duplicate accounts. But it is not easy to derive any information from the numbers given, and as they would take up space already crowded they have all been omitted.

These editorial procedures are perhaps not wholly consistent and may not have always been consistently followed. Fortunately the reader who wishes to examine the original orthography in detail may do so in the electronic images supplied on disc with this volume. The editor can at least plead that some inconsistency is fundamentally faithful to Speed's own practices; and will be happy if the outcome is an accounting document which would have been acceptable to him and intelligible to the modern reader.

THE LEDGER OF
THOMAS SPEED
1681–1690

with notes

Bristoll 1682 @				
Ballances [1]	Dr			
Richard Marsh	D			

(1)	Bristoll 1681 @				
	Per Contra	Dr	£	s	d
Jan. 4th	To Cash paid him	40	45	8	10
Oct. 30	To Ditto pd. the Towne clark	43		13	4
			46	2	2

Anno 1682				
Thomas Gibson per Contra is	Dr	£	s	d
To Proffit & Losse for money furnished Joseph Forrest being a debt due from Tho. Gibson, on John Horts & John Hardimans obligation as may appeare in folio (15) of this Leadger	105	6	2	2
To Ditto for Ballance	153	3	14	11
		9	17	1

1686				
Carpets 40 for acct. of Paul Priaulx	Dr	£	s	d
To Proffit & Losse for 9 yeares warehouse roome	105 *		9	
To Ditto for post of leters	105 *			9
To my commission for Sales at £3 per cent Ditto	105 *		12	
		1	1	9
To Paul Priaulx his acct. current for ballance	17	18	17	9
		19	19	6

Anno 1681 @				
Per Contra	Dr	£	s	d
Feb. 23 To Cash pd. him	40	1	14	1

Anno 1681 @				
	Per Contra	Dr	£	s	d
Dec. 31	To Cash pd. him	40	6	11	6
1685 March 11	To Proffit & Losse for 83 Guinies sould him at £1 1s 6d¾ per piece	105	89	9	8
Aprill 1686 14	To Cash pd. him by John Oliffe	108	50		
17	To Ditto pd. him	108	100		
			246	1	2

(2)	Bristoll 1682 @				
	Per Contra	Dr	£	s	d
July 6	To Cash pd. him	42	2	15	4

Anno 1681/2 @				
	Per Contra	Dr	£	s	d
March 15	To Cash pd. him	41	1	4	6

Anno 1683 @				
	Tho. Walden of Bristoll merchant is	Dr	£	s	d
January 25	To Cash paid lent him	68	50		
March 12	To Cash paid lent him	68	20		
	To Cash paid lent him (with the former £50) on his bond due — Aprill	68	100		
1684 June	To Cash paid Tho. Keene waggoner for carriage of 4 cwt goods	77		12	
July 19	To Cash paid him by the hands of John Bradway	77	38		
25	To Cash paid Wm. Hertly on his bill	77	50		
August 11	To Cash paid him	77	50		
	To Proffit & Losse for the intrest of the money above	73 *	3	6	10
December 3	To Xerie wine 3 butts, of John Blackwell for 6 bottles Xerie	79		8	
			312	6	10

Bristoll 1681 @				
Richard Marsh	Cr	£	s	d
By Ballances for ballance	D	45	8	10
By Proffit & Losse pd. my Father in London	8		13	4
		46	2	2

Anno 1682 @				
Thomas Gibson of Barbadoes Deceased	Cr	£	s	d
By Ballances for ballance	D	9	17	1

	Anno 1682 @				
	Carpetts for acct. of Paul Priaulx of London	Cr	£	s	d
	By Ballances for ballance	D	15	14	6
Nov. 18	By Cash recd.of John Arney for one carpet	43		13	
Jan. 8	By Hugh Parry for one Carpet	60		10	
1685 Aprill 30	By Cash recd. of John Wimpany for 2 carpets	83		18	
June 3	By Cash received of Stephen Stringer for 5 small ones & part				
	motheaten at 6d per piece.	83	1	10	
	By Proffit & Losse for 2 carpets	105 *		14	
			19	19	6

	Anno 1681 @				
	Edward Tayler of Bristoll Barber	Cr	£	s	d
	By Ballances	D	1	14	1

	Anno 1681 @				
	Humphry Corsley	Cr	£	s	d
	By Ballances	D	6	11	6
1685 March 12	By Cash recd. of him in part	108	40		
18	By Cash recd. of him	108	49	9	8
1686 Aprill	By his new acct. current for ballance carried to that acct. of				
	Debtor	117	150		
			246	1	2

Bristoll 1682 @				
Sir Thomas Walden [2]	Cr	£	s	d
By Ballances	D	2	15	4

Anno 1681/2 @				
Thomas Tayer	Cr	£	s	d
By Ballances	D	1	4	6

	Anno 1683/4				
	Tho. Walden per contra is	Cr	£	s	d
March 15	By Cash recd. of him	68	20		
April 1684 28	By Cash recd. of him in part	68	100		
June	By Cash recd. of Joane Webb on a bill of exchange	77	41	18	10
	By Cash recd. of him May 26th then omitted to bee charged	77	50		
August 6	By John Cooke for a bill on James Lapley in favour of said				
	Cooke	32	100		
	By himselfe for the 6 bottles Xerie per contra carried to that acct.	87		8	
			312	6	10

Anno 1681 @		Dr	£	s	d
	Per Contra	Dr	£	s	d
Dec. 20	To Cash paid him	40	100		
Jan. 7	To Ditto paid Charles Browne of Sheppen Mallard	40	100		
16	To Ditto pd. him	40	100		
			300		

Anno 1681 @		Dr	£	s	d
	Per Contra	Dr	£	s	d
Feb. 27	To Cash pd. him	40		14	

Anno 1688 @		Dr	£	s	d
	Fra. Ballard per Contra	Dr	£	s	d
	To Proffit & Losse because I know not of any such debt contracted by mee or any person by my order	153		8	4

Anno 1682 @		Dr	£	s	d
	Per Contra	Dr	£	s	d
July 12	To Cash pd. Mary Chambers	42		3	

	Ullage Brandy	Dr	£	s	d
	To Proffit & Losse for ballance	105	36	5	11

Anno 1688 @		Dr	£	s	d
	Sam. Hale per Contra	Dr	£	s	d
	To Proffit & Losse for ballance, because hee owed mee a great deal more to mee on an assureance made on the ship Resolution, but would not pay mee	153		13	4

Bristoll 1682 @		Dr	£	s	d
	Per Contra	Dr	£	s	d
Dec. 19	To Cash pd. William Oliffe	43		11	

Anno 1682		Dr	£	s	d
	Sugar 4 hhds 3 Kilderkins & 2 Tierces per Contra	Dr	£	s	d
	To Proffit & Losse for ballance	105	31	4	1

Anno 1682		Dr	£	s	d
	William Coles per Contra is	Dr	£	s	d
September 29	To Isaac Heming for money hee pd. him	76	4		7
	To Proffit & Losse for charges of port of leters etc.	105		1	5
			4	2	

Anno 1686		Dr	£	s	d
	Owners of the Resolution per Contra	Dr	£	s	d
	To Martha Gay for the ballance per Contra	32	10		

Anno 1681 @		Dr	£	s	d
	Per Contra	Dr	£	s	d
Dec. 30	To Cash pd. him	40	1	16	

Anno 1681 @		Dr	£	s	d
	Per Contra	Dr	£	s	d
Jan. 9	To Cash paid him in full	40	12	6	6
1682 March 29	To Wines imported on the San Mallo merchant from Oporto for 2 hhds red 5 hhds white	48	48	2	6
	To Proffit & Losse for ballance	9			2
			60	9	2

	Anno 1681 @				
	Edward Young	Cr	£	s	d
	By Ballances	D	100		
Dec. 29	By Isaac Heming for his bill	35	100		
Jan. 7	By Ditto for his bill	35	100		
			300		

	Anno 1681 @				
	John Purnell	Cr	£	s	d
	By Ballances	D		14	

	Anno 1682 @				
	Francis Ballard	Cr	£	s	d
	By Ballances	D		8	4

	Anno 1682 @				
	Good uses	Cr	£	s	d
	By Ballances	D		3	

	Anno 1682 @				
	Ullage Brandy	Cr	£	s	d
	By Ballances	D	36	5	11

	Anno 1682 @				
	Samuell Hale	Cr	£	s	d
	By Ballances for ballance	D		13	4

	Bristoll 1682 @				
	William Ollive & Company	Cr	£	s	d
	By Ballances	D		9	3
	By Proffit & Losse for ballance for what I know not	105		1	9
				11	

	Anno 1682 @				
	Sugar 4 hhds 3 Kilderkins imported on the ship Consent with two Tierces	Cr	£	s	d
	By Ballances	D	31	4	1

	Anno 1682 @				
	Wiliam Coles of London merchant	Cr	£	s	d
	By Ballances	D	4	2	

	Anno 1682 @				
	Owners of the Resolution	Cr	£	s	d
	By Ballances	D	10		

	Anno 1681 @				
	David Ronion Plomer	Cr	£	s	d
	By Ballances	D		18	1
	By Proffit & Losse for ballance	105 *		17	11
			1	16	

	Anno 1681 @				
	Alderman Ralph Olliffe	Cr	£	s	d
	By Ballances	D	7	19	8
Dec. 23	By George Pley for 4 doz of Xerie	44	4	7	
March 22	By the Earle of Bristoll for 2 doz of Xerie	37	2	1	2
1683 August 27	By Cash recd. of him	67	46	1	4
			60	9	2

(4)

Bristoll 1681 @

	Per Contra	Dr	£	s	d
Jan. 4	To Copper for 24 bottoms of 3cwt 3qr 18lb at £6 14s per Cwt	36	26	4	
1682 May 3	To Ditto for 23 bottoms of 3cwt 3qr 6lb at £6 14s per Cwt	36	25	9	8
August 14	To Ditto for 25 bottoms of 4cwt 1qr 25lb at £6 14s	36	29	19	5
1685 Aprill	To Adventure 2nd in the Owners Endeavour to Nevis and Jamaica for 7 Coolers & Yron bands brought back from Jamaica and sould him	58	20	19	
			102	12	1

Anno 1682 @

	Per Contra	Dr	£	s	d
August 3rd	To Cash pd. John Templeman [3]	42	14	10	
	To Proffit & Losse for ballance	153	10	13	
			25	3	

Anno 1682 @

	Per Contra	Dr	£	s	d
Feb. 3rd	To the House at the end of Small streete for foure yeares rent ending the 25th Dec. 1682	22	105	4	
			105	4	

Anno 1682 @

	Per Contra	Dr	£	s	d
June 27	To Cash pd. him	42	8	19	9
1685 Aprill 6	To Rice for acct. Simon Clement & Company for 1 bagge neat 3cwt 1qr 3lb at 23s	141 [4]	3	15	4
			12	15	1

Anno 1681 @

	Per Contra	Dr	£	s	d
Jan. 10	To Cash paid him lent him on his bill	40	100		
	To white wines 5 tonns hee recd. of Codner	48	2	5	
April 10	To Ditto for ½ theire cost and charges	48	55		11
	To Proffit & Loss for 3 months Intrest of £100	8	1	10	
	To Cash pd. him in full	41	29	18	5
	To wines 5 tonnes for Sweet ½ a hogshead sold him	48	3	17	6
Feb. 24	To Cash pd. him	43	30	11	6
1683 March 30	To Cash paid Wm. Gayner for poore money in Clevedon due next month for a year	66	1	2	3
August 4	To Cash paid Tho. Lutterell for making & halling hay at Clevedon 16 acres	66	3	10	8
October 13	To Cash paid Tho. Lutterell For repaireing Newlands tenement as per noate	67	4	10	6
	To Cash paid Tho. Lutterell for ½ years Lords rent 16s & poore money 15s 6d for ½ year	67	1	11	6
	To his new acct. current for ballance carried to that acct.	79	3	1	9
			237		

Bristoll 1681 @

		Cr	*£*	*s*	*d*
	Olliver Mosely	*Cr*	*£*	*s*	*d*
	By Ballances	*D*	25	9	2
Feb. 16	*By Cash recd. of him*	*40*		4	10
1682 May 11	*By Adventure in the Sarah for 6 Coolers*	*49*	20	3	3
Nov. 20	*By merchandizes in the Owners Endeavor for 6 Coolers & 2*				
	Jackes	*58*	34	16	
1685 June	*By Adventure in the Joseph to Nevis for one Copper Tach, 12*				
	Cosasha Graters, 12 Ladles, 12 Skimmers, 24 Iron sockets,				
	and setting them on, and for twine as per his noat	*98*	18	4	5
1687 Nov.	*By Cash received of him in full*	*139*	2		
	By Profitte & Losse for Ballance	*153*	1	14	5
			102	12	1

Anno 1682 @

		Cr	*£*	*s*	*d*
	Adventure in the Zant	*Cr*	*£*	*s*	*d*
	By Ballances	*D*	25	3	
			25	3	

Anno 1682 @

		Cr	*£*	*s*	*d*
	Thomas Tayler of Bristoll Schoolemaster viz. Master in Writing	*Cr*	*£*	*s*	*d*
	By Ballances	*D*	50	18	
May 11	*By Cash recd. of him*	*41*	10		
Sept. 9	*By Cash recd. of John Brown*	*42*	4		
Nov. 18	*By Ditto recd. of Tho. Hartwell*	*43*	9		
Feb. 9	*By Ditto recd. of him*	*43*	9		
1683 Aprill 13	*By Cash recd. of Andrew Ynnys by his order*	*66*	13	15	
	By Edmond Scrope for money said to bee paid him and omitted				
	to bee charged	*38*	6	10	
	By Proffit & Losse for his noat for teaching my daughter &				
	disbursements	*127*	2	1	
			105	4	

Anno 1682 @

		Cr	*£*	*s*	*d*
	Thomas Davidge	*Cr*	*£*	*s*	*d*
	By Ballances	*D*	8	19	11
1685 May 9	*By Cash recd. of him for the bagge of rice per contra*	*83*	3	15	2
			12	15	1

Anno 1681 @

		Cr	*£*	*s*	*d*
	Henry Gibbs	*Cr*	*£*	*s*	*d*
	By Ballances	*D*	3	1	9
Aprill 10	*By Wines 5 tonnes for Freight Avaridge & prisage*	*48*	15		10
	By Proffit & Loss for sundry things bought of him	*8*	6	13	2
	By Edward Burrish for a bill of 719 crownes	*49*	167		4
	By Soape 79 chests for theire neate proceeds [5]	*52*	28	9	
	By wines 5 tonns for one hogshead Sweet	*48*	6		
1683	*By land in Clevedon for the several disbursements per Contra on*				
	it	*32*	10	14	11
			237		

Anno 1683		Dr	£	s	d
	Abigall. Speed per Contra is	Dr	£	s	d
February 7	To Cash paid her	68	2		

(5)	**Bristoll 1682 @**	Dr	£	s	d
	Per Contra	Dr	£	s	d
Dec. 19	To Cash pd. weighing them etc.	43		1	6
	To Proffit & Losse for ballance	153	47		6
			47	2	

Anno 1681 @		Dr	£	s	d
	Per Contra	Dr	£	s	d
Feb. 9	To Cash pd. Edw. Macey on his bill	40	10		
21	To Ditto for Rich. Chadwell	40	6		
1682 Nov. 14	To Ditto pd. Blanch Gould on her bill	43	55	3	2
			71	3	2

Anno 1681 @		Dr	£	s	d
	Per Contra	Dr	£	s	d
Jan. 7	To Cash paid Abr. Edwards for Cloth wanting	40		4	
March 2	To Ditto pd. Tho. Scroope on his bill	40	21		
3	To Ditto pd. John Hinds on his bill	41	15		
1682 May 12	To Ditto pd. Sundryes on their bills	41	29	2	
31	To Cash pd. Thomas Hill on his bill	41	21	19	3
Sept. 13	To Ditto pd. his bill in Favour of Bernard Wilkins	42	2	17	6
25	To Cash pd. Elexander Dolman on his bill	42	47		
	To John Bubb allowed want of measure	45		7	
1684 August 12	To Cash paid his bill in favour of Lawrence Righton assign'd John Olliver	77	31	12	4
			169	2	1

Anno 1681 @		Dr	£	s	d
	Per Contra	Dr	£	s	d
Dec. 22	To Cash pd. filing a certificate & portridge of said Cloth	40			10
	To Proffit & Losse for portridge, warehouse roome, Commission etc. on the 11 Rolls per Contra as the book of Accts 25th October 1680 date	73	1	4	10
	To Edward Roy his acct. current for theire neat proceeds	44	50	13	11
			51	19	7

Anno 1682 @		Dr	£	s	d
	Per Contra	Dr	£	s	d
Aprill 20	To Cash pd. for a bull	41	2	5	
27	To Cash pd. Ed. Willis for a Pigg	41		18	
May 18	To Ditto pd. Thomas Browne for a Sow & Piggs	41	1	16	
25	To Ditto pd. for a Cow and Calfe	41	4	2	
June 1st	To Ditto pd. for a Cow & Calfe	41	4	9	3
1	To Cash pd. for 3 yoake of Oxen	42	22	15	
14	To Ditto pd. John Gore for keeping of beasts	42		2	10
Sept. 2	To Cash pd. for a Pigg	42	1		
21	To Ditto pd. for a yoake of Oxen	43	12	15	
Nov. 8	To Ditto pd. Rich. Washrough for 2 Piggs	42		16	
1683	To John Hurtnell for 4 Oxen and two Steeres	38	24	17	6
	To Robert Summers for money abated him on several cattle	17		15	
	To Proffit & Losse for ballance	153	58	5	½
			134	16	7½

Anno 1682 @		Cr	£	s	d
Abigall. Speed		Cr	£	s	d
By Ballances		D	2		

Bristoll 1682 @					
Tobacco 9 hhds imported on the Nathanaell in partnership with Ed. Martindale viz. 6 for my propper acct. & 3 Martindale		Cr	£	s	d
	By Ballances	D	31	17	6
Dec. 7	By William Davis for 2 hhds sold him	58	15	4	6
			47	2	

Anno 1681 @					
Beniamin Gould	.	Cr	£	s	d
By Ballances		D	3	2	2
By Linincloth 16 bolts for theire neate proceeds		17	68	1	
			71	3	2

Anno 1681 @					
Henry Simes		Cr	£	s	d
By Ballances		D	2	3	10
By Linincloth 10 Bolts for theire neate proceeds		35	85	8	5
1684	By Linincloth 4 packetts for theire neate proceeds	50	49	17	6
	By Lincloth 9 Bolts for theire neat proceeds	56	31	12	4
			169	2	1

Anno 1681 @					
Linincloth 11 Roles for accompt Edward Roy		Cr	£	s	d
	By Ballances	D	3	8	8
Jan. 1682 14	By Henry Glisson For 5 Roles sold him	44	25	2	10
22	By Charles Barber for 5 bolts sold him	62	23	8	1
			51	19	7

Anno 1681/2 @					
Cattle		Cr	£	s	d
	By Ballances	D	24	1	5½
March 10	By Cash recd. of John Hurtnell for 3 Heifers	40	11	10	
1682 Aprill 8	By Ro. Lysons for 9 Calves	46	6	10	
11	By Tho. Luttrell for a Colt sold him	25	4		
	By Will. Hurtnell for a Calfe	28		16	
June 12	By Ditto for a Calfe	28		12	
27	By John Ford for 3 Calfes	52	2	2	6
July 13	By Henry Priest for 3 Piggs	52	3	1	
19	By Robert Sommers for 2 Oxen sold him	17	12	5	
Sept. 6	By Barth. Bagg for a Heifer sold him	52	2	15	10
Oct. 11	By Will. Hurtnell for 2 Piggs	28	2	16	
21	By Robert Summers for 4 oxen and a Bull	17	29	10	
Dec. 22	By Will. Hurtnell for one Pigg sold him	28	1	2	
Jan. 2	By sundry acct.s for 3 burrs & a Cow	52, 60	17	0	2
1683 March 25	By John Hurtnell for 2 burrs and a Cow	38	13	16	8
31	By Cash recd. of James Horwood for surplus money for which 3 beasts attachd were sould	66	2	18	
			134	16	7½

	Anno 1689 @		£	s	d
	Cattle two Steeres bought of Richard Merrick alias Reece of Clevedon by John Hurtnell for my account are	Dr			
May 18	To Cash paid John Hurtnell to pay for said Steeres, which money said Merrick paid mee at the same time in part of rent due from him, for which hee hath credit in his acct. current in folio (92) of this booke as may appear	175	5		
	To Proffit & Loss for Ballances	180	1	5	
			6	5	

(6)	**Bristoll 1682 @**				
	Per Contra	Dr	£	s	d
	To Proffit & loss for portridge, commission etc.	9	2		
	To Maximilian. Gallop for ballance	34	81	5	9
			83	5	9

	Bartholomew Reece	Dr	£	s	d
	To Proffit & Losse for ballance	153		9	2
				9	2

	Anno 1690 @		£	s	d
	Per Contra	Cr			
Dec. 5	By Proffit & Loss for Ballance	180	8	18	11

	Jahzeel Speed & Company	Dr	£	s	d
	To Proffit & Losse for ballance	153	5	7	3
			5	7	3

	Anno 1682 @		£	s	d
	Per Contra	Dr			
	To Proffit & Loss for sundry charges on said goods	8	2	12	7
	To Christopher Williams for theire neate proceeds	7	80	14	3
			83	6	10

	Anno 1681 @		£	s	d
	Per Contra	Dr			
24	To Cash pd. him in full	40	22	2	2

	William Emblen	Dr	£	s	d
	To Proffit & Losse for ballance	153	7	16	9

(7)	**Bristoll 1681/2 @**				
	Per Contra	Dr	£	s	d
March 18	To Cash pd. them	41	1	10	
May 12	To Ditto pd. them which with the £1 10 formerly pd. them is in full for ½ a yeares Intrest ending 25 March last past	41	3		
August 5	To Cash Lent them on theire bond due on the 6th February next	42	10		
Oct. 21	To Ditto pd. ½ a yeares Intrest of £150 to Stephen Chapman ending the 29th Sept.	42	4	10	
Jan. 12	To Ditto pd. them on theire noate	43	2		
1683 August 13	To Cash paid Bridget Wallis which with the £2 foregoing is in full for ½ yeares intrest due 25th March last	66	2	10	
October 10	To Cash paid them for ½ yeares intrest ending 29 Sept. 1683	67	4	10	
1684 Aprill 3	To Cash paid them for ½ yeares intrest ending 29 March 1683	68	4	10	
July 19	To Cash lent Marie Thring on her bill	77	2		
December 17	To James Beard for ½ yeares intrest hee paid them due Sept. 29th 1684	76	4	10	
1685 July 18	To James Beard for ½ yeares intrest due & ending March 25th 1684 which hee paid them	76	4	10	

Anno 1689 @				
Wm. Ricket per contra	*Cr*	*£*	*s*	*d*
By Wm. Ricket for the 2 Steeres per contra sold to him per John				
Hurtnell	*143*	6	5	

Bristoll 1681/2 @				
Linincloth for acct. Max. Gallop	*Cr*	*£*	*s*	*d*
By Ballances	*D*	17	6	10
March 29 *By Alexander Dolman for 10 bolts*	*48*	47	18	
Aprill 6 *By Michaell Pope for 4 balets sold him*	*48*	18		11

Anno 1682 @				
Bartholomew Rees	*Cr*	*£*	*s*	*d*
By Ballances	*D*		9	2
			9	2

Anno 1682 @				
Debts Due to the Land at Redland	*Cr*	*£*	*s*	*d*
By Ballances	*D*	8	18	11

Anno 1682 @				
Mr Jahzeel Speed & Company	*Cr*	*£*	*s*	*d*
By Ballances	*D*	5	7	3
		5	7	3

Anno 1682 @				
Merchandizes in the Violet for accompt of Christopher Williams	*Cr*	*£*	*s*	*d*
By Ballances	*D*	83	6	10
		83	6	10

Anno 1682 @				
Nicholas Barnard	*Cr*	*£*	*s*	*d*
By Ballances	*D*	22	2	2

Anno 1682 @				
William Emblen	*Cr*	*£*	*s*	*d*
By Ballances	*D*	7	16	9

Bristoll 1681/2 @				
Mary Thring & Company	*Cr*	*£*	*s*	*d*
By Ballances	*D*	150		
By estate at Clapton for 5 yeares intrest of Ditto money from				
Sept. 29th 1681 to the 29th of September 1686 intrest at 6 per				
cent	*38*	45		
		195		

			£	s	d
November 25	To James Beard for ½ yeares intrest of £150 hee paid them due Sept. 29th 1685	76	4	10	
	To Marie Thring, Bridget Wallis & Sam. Thring for money lent them on bond April 1st 1686	114	20		
1686 October 28	To Proffit & Losse for intrest of the above £10 from the 4th August 1682 to 28th of Oct. 1686	127	2	10	8
	To Ditto for intrest of the above £2 lent Ma. Thring from 19th July 1684 to 28th of Oct. 1686	127		5	4
	To Ditto for intrest of the above £20 lent them & Sam. Thring from 1st of April 1686 to 28th of Oct. 1686	127		13	9
	To Ditto for charges pd. Sam. Kekewich for a certifficate of James Wallis his being alive June 1686	127		9	
November 1	To Cash pd. Edward Freeman £76 10s 00d & to themselves £- 11s 3d	129	77	1	3
1690	To Sam. Kekewich for charges in getting a certificate about James Wallis, but lost in sending	185	1	1	8
			150	1	8
	To Acct. Ballances for Ball.	193 *	44	18	4

Anno 1682 @					
	Per Contra	Dr	£	s	d
Nov. 8	To Cash pd. him	43	15		

Anno 1681 @					
	Joseph Cardrow of Dorchester	Dr	£	s	d
Jan. 30	To Cash pd. him	40	66	9	6
March 2	To Ditto pd. Nathanaell Powell on his bill	40	1	11	
1682 @ 15	To Ditto pd. Simon Hurle	41	40		
Aprill 23	To Ditto pd. him	41	40		
June 13	To Cash pd. Sam. Davis	41	28		
	To John Hollister for a bill of said Hollister on	44	20		
			196		6

Anno 1681 @					
	Martha Wright wife of Jeremiah Write of Bristoll Chirurgeon	Dr	£	s	d
Feb. 28	To Cash pd. Lent her on a silver Tankard	40	5		

Anno 1681/2 @					
	Christopher Williams of London merchant	Dr	£	s	d
March 15	To Cash pd. James Freeman	41	5		
1682 8th May	To Ditto pd. Will. Weekes on Rich. Vickris noate	41	75	14	
	To Ditto pd. port of a letter	8			4
1683 September 3	To Cash paid his bill in favour of George Weeks, assign'd him per Richd. Vickris	67	43	16	11
	To worsted stockings for his acct. for the cost and charge of 100 paire sent him to London	45	17	18	10
	To Proffit & Losse for port of letters on his acct.	9		2	10
			142	12	11

Anno 1681 @					
	Linincloth for acct. of Will. Shepard being 10 bolts	Dr	£	s	d
Jan. 31	To Cash pd. Filing a certificate	40			4
	To Proffit & Loss for portridge etc.	8	1	1	2
1682 Jan. 2nd	To Will. Sheppard for theire neat proceeds	50	38	10	4
			39	11	10

Anno 1682 @				
William Crabb	Cr	£	s	d
By Ballances	D	10		
By Account of Ballances for Ballance	193 *	5		
		15		

Anno 1683 @				
Joseph Cardro per contra	Cr	£	s	d
By Lincloth for his acct. for the neat proceeds of 22 bolts of				
Vittay	35	196		2¾
By Proffit & Losse for money over paid him	9			3¼
		196		6

Anno 1690 @				
Martha Wright per contra	Cr	£	s	d
By Acct. of Ballances for Ball	193 *	5		

Anno 1682 @				
Per Contra	Cr	£	s	d
By merchandizes in the Violet for theire neate proceeds	6	80	14	4
1683 August By Oyle 10 Jarres sould for him for theire neate proceeds	46	43	3	10
By Oyle two Cask for theire neat proceeds	19	18	14	9
		142	12	11

Anno 1682 @				
Per Contra	Cr	£	s	d
June 12 By John Sandford for 4 ballits	19	16	12	5
17 By Ditto for one bolt	19	3	12	1
Oct. 9 By John Jones for 4 bolts sold him	51	15	3	
16 By John Machen for one bolt sold him	55	4	4	4
		39	11	10

(8)	Bristoll 1681 @	Dr	£	s	d
	Proffitt & Losse				
Dec. 12	To Cash pd. myselfe at my going to London	40	3		
	To Ditto pd. Houshold expences	40	10	19	10
24	To Ditto pd. John Massinger	40		9	6
30	To Ditto pd. Edw. Penny	40		5	8
Jan. 9	To Cash pd. Joseph Drew	40	2		6
	To Ditto pd. severalls 6	40	1200		
10	To Ditto pd. severalls Houshold expences	40	7	5	2
24	To Cash pd. Walter Paine for 4 Blancketts	40		15	
Feb. 8	To Ditto pd. for 2 Truncks	40	1	15	4
10	To Ditto pd. sundryes	40	11	1	6
14	To Ditto pd. Houshold expences & for a paire of bootes	40	7	5	9
16	To Ditto pd. Matthias Warden for port charges on the Allicant merchant	40		17	
17	To Cash pd. the Towne clark & John Moore	40	2	1	6
27	To Ditto pd. Allyn Smith	40		4	9
March 7	To Jane Flower for her noate for halling	18	4		
10	To Cash pd. my selfe	40	1		
14	To Ditto pd. Houshold expences ending the 12th instant	40	4	6	6
1682 29	To John Sandford for money due to him	19	1	2	6
Aprill 6	To Ditto for his noate	19		19	2
	To Cash pd. Henry Gibbs for premio money	41		5	
7	To Ditto pd. John Goodman & the widow Ebley	41	1	8	4
10	To Henry Gibbs for sundry things bought of him	4	6	13	2
	To Cash pd. Sundryes 6	41	505	6	6
12	To Ditto pd. Joseph Jackson	41	12		
	To Ditto pd. sundryes	41	10	3	
27	To Ditto pd. Chimney money	41		8	
May 2	To Ditto pd. Elizabeth Milner	41	5		
11	To Ditto pd. Martha Speed	41	1		
19	To Cash pd. Thomas Wall for severall Bookes	41		18	8
24	To Ditto pd. John Massinger	41		5	
June 12	To Ditto pd. Rich. Paine	41	2		
	To Ditto pd. Houshold expences from the 12 Aprill	41	17	15	
	To Cash pd. John Hollister for sundry particulars	42		3	3
13	To Ditto pd. Houshold expences	42	6	10	11
15	To Ditto pd. John Yearington effor 7 12 dozen bottles	42	1	2	
20	To Ditto for a Firkin butter	42	1		10
27	To Ditto pd. John Hardiman for making of Clothes	42	1	16	
28	To Cash paid master	42	5		
August 1	To Ditto pd. Martha Speed	42	3		
10	To Ditto pd. master	42	2		
14	To Cash pd. Household expences ending this day	42	10	14	7
17	To Ditto pd. Rich. Sandford for a suite and Cloathes making	42		12	6
	To Ditto pd. George White in full of his noate	41	3	1	9
	To Ditto pd. Alexander Piott	42		14	9
26	To Cash pd. master	42		15	
30	To Ditto pd. for 3 bushells Mault	42		10	6
Sept. 3	To Ditto pd. the Towne Clarke	42	1	1	6
	To Cash pd. Robert Gibbins in full of his noate	42		13	
6	To Xerie wine for one butt	45	22		
14	To Cash pd. Houshold expences	42	9	7	1
21	To Ditto pd. her 8	42	1		
	To Ditto pd. master 3 guinnies	42	5	5	0
	To Ditto pd. Robert Lyppit in full of his noate	42		17	
Oct. 14	To Ditto pd. Houshold expences	42	9	5	6
16	To John Blackwell for wine bought of him	26	1	7	8
	To Cash pd. Rich. Paine for a hat	42	1	1	

Bristoll 1681 @

	Per Contra	Cr	£	s	d
Feb.	By lincloth for acct. of Jos. Cardrow for commission	35	4	14	
8	By Cash recd. of John Harris for a Trunck	40		10	
	By the Earle of Bristoll gave the man to drinke	37			6
Aprill 6	By Ditto for portridge etc.	37			8
	By Wines 5 tonns pd. postidge of Letters	48		10	1
	By Henry Gibbs for 3 months Intrest	4	1	10	
11	By Phi[llip Higginbottom] for 4 months intrest	17	1		8
	By Cash recd. of Nath. Haggatt for intrest	41	2	14	
12	By Ditto recd. of Ditto	41	73	5	
May 11	By Digbie for hallidge & portridge	37		1	4
25	By Cash recd. of Rob. Yate	41	100		
	By Ditto recd. of Alderman Yate [10]	41	100		
	By John Digbie for portridge of bottles	37		1	8
July 8	By Cash recd. of Mary Aldworth	42		9	
12	By Isaac Heming for a Bill of exchange	35	200		
22	By Cash recd. of Sam. Davis	42	1	13	
	By Ditto recd. of Nath. Haggatt	42	150		
	By Will. Spoore for one yeares intrest of £50	30	3		
31	By Cash recd. of Nath. Haggatt	42	50		
	By Ditto recd. of Sam. Davis	42		11	
August 26	By Sir George Strode for 2 doz white wine & 4 doz empty	24	1	9	2
Sept. 3	By John Digbie for 2 doz white wine	37	1	3	7
6	By Sir George Strode for 23 quarts of red wine	24	1	2	8
	By Anne Pawlit for 2 dozen empty bottles	48		5	7
21	By stockins for sundry Charges	55	7	2	6
	By merchandizes in the Violet for sundry Charges	6	2	12	7
	By Christopher Williams for port of a Letter	7			4
	By the Earle of Bristoll for 65 gallons Xerie	37	17	12	8
Oct. 16	By Sir George Strode for 3 doz of Xerie	24	2	14	8
	By Anne Pawlet for 2 rundletts of Xerie	48	6	18	2
25	By the Earle of Bristoll for one runlett	37	3	5	
	By Rich. Franklin for the neate proceeds of a parcell of Tobacco	56		14	7
	By Linincloth Gold for sundry charges	17	1	16	10
	By Edward Hollister for one yeares rent of a Cellar	59	2		
	By Linincloth Henry Simes for Commission etc.	35	1	18	3
	By Ditto for commission etc.	50	1	2	11
Jan. 2	By Linencloth for acct. Will. Sheppard for commission etc.	7	1	1	2
	By itselfe for ballance	9	1683	18	2
			2426	19	9

			£	s	d
19	To Cash pd. John Blackwell for 2 doz white wine	42		6	
21	To Cash Lent Nehemiah Benson	42		5	
24	To Ditto pd. David Ronion in full of his noate	42	1	2	
26	To Ditto pd. John Shuttleworth for the change of a life [9]	43	13	5	
	To Ditto pd. Rich. Codrington in full of his noate	43	2	1	
28	To Ditto pd. Jahzeel going to Wells	43		15	
30	To Ditto pd. the Towne clark	43		13	4
	To Richard Marsh recd. of him	1		13	4
Nov. 15	To Cash pd. master at sundry times	43	54	16	
	To Ditto pd. Houshold expences	43	8	2	4
	To Jahzeel Speed for ballance	33	409		2
30	To Cash pd. Rob. Bentley	43	1	10	
	To Ditto pd. John Hardiman in full of his noate	43	1		6
	To Ditto pd. making a riding shirte	43		11	6
Dec. 4	To Tho. Durbin for money abated him	47		4	5
	To Joseph Badger for money due to him on Kettles	50		9	11
8	To Cash pd. Xtian Phelps in full of her noate	43	1	12	10
13	To Ditto pd. Houshold Expences	43	9	7	3
	To Ditto pd. Robert Gibbins in full of his noate	43	1	7	
	To Ditto pd. James Biggs	43		17	
19	To Ditto pd. for Herrings sent to Wells	43		11	
	To Ditto pd. Rich. King in full of his noate	43	5	2	6
20	To Ditto pd. Mary Parsons	43		18	
21	To Ditto pd. the Cutler in full of his noate	43		14	
	To Ditto pd. John Wasbrowes men	43		2	6
			2426	19	9

(9)   Bristoll 1682 @

		Dr	£	s	d
	Proffitt & Loss				
	To itselfe for balance	8	1683	18	2
Jan. 5	To Cash pd. Rich. Sandford in full of his noate	43		15	6
	To Ditto pd. Jane Sheppard for one Firkin butter	43	1		
12	To Thomas Edwards for money hee disbursed	23	1	5	
	To Cash pd. John Cheshire for 13 doz 3 qrt 3 doz 3 pintes	43	1	15	
	To Ditto pd. Houshold expences	43	6	14	11
22	To Alexander Dolman for a wrapper	48			6
26	To Cash pd. Filing a certificate	43			4
	To Ditto pd. James Swetman in full of his noate	43	1	15	6
	To Ditto pd. Houshold Expences ending the 14th instant	43	7	11	2
	To Jos. Drew for money due to him	31	1	4	6
	To Xeries wine 30 butts f one hogshead corrupt wine	45 *	3		
Feb. 26	To Cash pd. master	43	2		11
28	To Ditto pd. keeping horses for severall monthes	43	2	4	
	To Lewis Adams for wine of him	56	1	10	6
March 15	To Cash pd. Houshold expences	66	5	16	
17	To Ditto pd. poore money	66	1	6	
	To John Hurtnell for 1 mault and maulte dust	38	6	10	3
1683	To Cash paid for a Frock for Jahzeel Speed	66		8	6
Aprill 4	To Cash paid Tho. Walden in full of his noat	66		12	
	To sundry acct.s for meat bought of them	52, 60		14	10
9	To Cash paid Robert Yate for John Broking & Company on theire bill	66	21	13	9
12	To Cash paid Jane Flowers daughter in full of her noat	66	2	2	
14	To Cash paid houshold expences	66	9	9	2¾
18	To Cash for 2 Guinnies I received	66	2	3	
	To Xeries wine 40 Butts for 12 Gallon Sack at 4s per Gallon	65	2	8	
19	To Cash for money received at my going to Reading	66	2		
	To Cash paid Alexander Doleman and John Jones in full of theire noates	66	4	12	6
27	To Cash paid Martha Speed	66	5		
May 3	To Tho. Edwards for money due to him for fees	23		4	1

Bristoll 1682 @

	Per Contra	Cr	£	s	d
	Per Contra	Cr	£	s	d
Jan. 20	By Cash recd. of Phinehas Everard	43	1	16	10
23	By Ditto recd. of Nath. Haggatt	43	100		
	By Sir John Drake for portridge of wine	63			4
	By Linincloth 10 bolts for commission etc.	56	1		6
	By John Digbie for portridge & other charges	37			10
	By Dr. Hungerford for portridge	59			6
	By Soape 79 Chest for the Intrest with charges	51	5	13	2
	By Linincloth Max. Gallop for commission etc.	6	2		
	By Cash recd. of Robert Yate	43	300		
March 17	By Linincloth for acct. of Tho. Williams for Commission etc.	47		9	5
1683 March	By Cash recd. of Peter Sanders	66	6	9	
24	By acct. of 12 hhds for acct. of Malachy Peale for sundry disbursements	36	7	14	9
	By Copper bottoms for ballance of that acct.	36	4	7	11
	By Tobacco 12 hhds on the John for cooperidge Celleridge and hallige	59		8	3
	By Ditto for my ½ of theire neat proceeds	59	3	13	7½
31	By Wm. Spoore Junior for intrest of £40 from 26th January ending at severall times	31	2	4	
	By Edward Gorges for 8 months intrest of £60	34	2	7	
Aprill 27	By Lincloth 5 bolts for acct. Max. Gallop for sundry charges	69		11	
	By Cash recd. of Wm. Spoore Senior for 6 months intrest of £10	66		6	
May 10	By William Spoore & Company for 1 yeares intrest of £50 due Aprill 21st 1683	30	3		
July 6	By Dr. Hungerford for a Pannier and portridge	59		1	
	By Wm. Spoore Junior for 3 months intrest of £40	31		12	
23	By Cash recd. of John Blackwell for intrest money	66	1	10	
	By Cash recd. of Ed. Martindale	66	200		
24	By John Earle of Bristoll for 2 dozen bottles Pannier & cover	37		5	
August	By Oyle 2 Cask for acct. Christopher Williams for severall charges on them	19		11	8
8	By John Earle of Bristoll for 3 dozen bottles Pannier & cover	37		7	2

Date	Description				
22	To Cash paid Richard Baugh	66		12	
	To Tho. Durbin for Tobacco of him	47		3	
June 18	To Cash paid John Hardiman in part of his noat	66	1		
20	To Cash paid houshold expences to the 15th instant	66	14	1	¾
July 4	To John Blackwell for 1 dozen bottles claret	26		8	
6	To Cash paid houshold expences to the 15th instant	66	9	7	1½
19	To Cash paid John Moore for cloth for Jahzeel	66	4	13	6
	To Ditto paid Richard Thomas for a Mare	66	7	7	6
	To Joseph Cardrow for money overpaid him on acct.	7			3¼
August 7	To Cash paid John Hardimans daughter for making Jahzeels clothes	66	1	2	
8	To Ditto paid John Joyner for 3 Gallons Brandy	66		10	
			1819		7¼
	To Tho. Curtis for money of him in Reading	58	90		
15	To Cash paid Joseph Drew in full of his noat	66	3	17	
	To Ditto paid houshold expenses	66	14	18	10½
16	To Cash paid Edward Martindale	67	200		
	To Ditto paid John Sandford for Gloves etc.	67		17	
27	To Ditto paid houshold expences to this 27th August	67	5	5	11
	To Ditto paid Alderman Oliffe	67	2	3	1
September 2	To Cash paid houshold expenses to this day	67	1	12	5
6	To Ditto paid John Harris for Truncks etc. bought of him	67	3	3	4
9	To Ditto paid houshold expences to this day	67	1	10	4
11	To Xeries wine, 12 Butts for 1 doz. & 8 bottles given Hugh Hodges	39	1	5	
11	To Cash paid David Roynon Plomer in full change of 3 sheets Lead etc.	67	1	5	
13	To Ditto paid houshold expences	67	2	19	9
	To Ditto delivered Jahzeel Speed	67	21	17	11
October 1	To Ditto paid the Widow Hasell[11] for an old debt	67		5	3
	To Maximilian Gollop for ballance of his acct.	34			2
13	To Cash paid houshold expences	67	9	17	7½
20	To Robert Summers for Flesh £17 18s 5d & for keeping my mare £1 17s 6d weeks	17	19	15	11
	To Ditto for money lent Jahzeel Speed at severall times	17		13	6
26	To Cash paid John Hardiman in full of his noat	67	1	7	6
27	To Samuell Davis for severall particulars as per noat	63		14	
30	To Cash paid John Moore in full of his noat	67	1	11	
November 6	To Cash paid Tho. Walden for severall goods	67	1	17	
	To Ditto paid John Hardiman	67		5	6
	To Ditto received at my departure towards London	67	2	5	
11	To Cash recd. of my servant at my going to Bath	67	2		
17	To Ditto paid houshold expences to this day	67	16	7	¾
24	To Ditto paid John Hardiman for making clothes	67	1	4	
	To Cash paid James Milward in full of his noat	67	2	6	
30	To Ditto paid Walter Hobbs in full for keeping my mare	67		8	
December 8	To Cash paid Sam. Sandford for a Rundlet	67		2	6
8	To Cash paid Jahzeel Speed for a Beaver hatt	67	2	12	6
	To Cash Jeffery Price for Tho. Wilcox for 2 groce bottles	67	2	8	
18	To Cash paid Sam. Burgess for 10 ½ bushells of Mault	67	1	15	7
	To Ditto paid Richard Sandford in full of his noat	67		12	
22	To Cash paid John Sandiford for severall things for Jahzeel	67	4	15	6
	To Ditto paid houshold expences to the 25th current	67	13	15	9
January 5	To Ditto paid Robert Gibbons in full for keeping my mare	67	1	15	
8	To Ditto paid Joseph Drew in full of his noat	67		11	6
	To Ditto paid Samuell Burgesse in full of his noat	67	1	4	6
			441	3	11¾
			2260	4	7

	By Cash recd. of John Blackwell for intrest money	66	2	3	9
15	By Lady Ann Pawlet for 7 dozen bottles 4 Panniers & covers	48		17	8
	By Tobacco 18 hhds for 112 weeks celleridge	63	5	12	
	By Tho. Puxton on bond for intrest of money	23	10	3	
	By Alderman Ralph Olliffe for ballance	3			2
September	By Oyle 10 Jarres for acct. Christopher Williams for Commision for sales etc.	46	1	5	2
	By John Earle of Bristoll for 2 Cask for Xerie & hallidge	37		8	
	By Stockins for Christopher Williams for my Commission etc.	45		7	2
	By Christopher Williams for Port of leters	7		2	10
19	By Sir George Strode for 2 doz bottles & Pannier and a box for his coat	24		5	8
	By Samuell Astry for a hogshead	49		5	
25	By Samuell Davis for 3 dozen bottles	63		6	
October 4	By Lady Susan Powlet for 6 dozen bottles & 3 Pannier & Covers	61		15	
	By adventure in the Crowne Lyon to Cadiz for ballance	25	10		4
November 8	By Cash received of mee into Cash of the £2 5s recd. per contra	67	1	10	
24	By Dr. Francis Hungerford for 2 dozen bottles & a Pannier etc.	59		5	
December 14	By Dr. Fra. Hungerford for 6 dozen bottles etc.	59		15	
			680	11	8½
14	By Samuell Davis for 4 dozen Bottles	63		8	
error	By John Blackwell for 9 weeks Celleridge at 4s 6d	-	-	-	-
18	By Cash received of Wm. Weaver for a mare sould him	67	6		
20	By Sergeant Tho. Strode for 5 dozen bottles & 2 Panniers	65		13	
20	By Lady Ann Pawlet for 6 dozen pint bottles & 2 Panniers & covers	61		9	4
29	By Cash recd. of Wm. Jackson for 4½ cwt of Lead weights	67	2	5	
January 2	By Lady Ann Pawlet for 2 dozen bottles Pannier & cover	48		5	
3	By Dr. Francis Hungerford for 2 dozen bottles Pannier etc.	59		5	
7	By George Dighton for 2 dozen bottles	60		4	
	By Samuell Davis for 2 dozen bottles	63		4	
16	By Andrew Stucky Junior for money due from him	53	41	14	
			52	7	4
			732	19	½
	By ballance carried to that acct.	73	1527	5	6½
			2260	4	7

(10)	**Bristoll 1682 @**		£	s	d
	Reynold Williams	Dr	£	s	d
	To Ballances	D	13	6	11

	Anno 1682 @				
	Nathanaell Cale Senior	Dr	£	s	d
	To ballances	D	10		

	Anno 1682 @				
	Nathanaell Cale Junior	Dr	£	s	d
	To ballances	D	5		

	Anno 1682 @				
	Sir Robert Yeamans and Capt. Edward Fox	Dr	£	s	d
	To Ballances	D	1	10	
	To Proffitt & Losse for intrest resting due for £20 formerly lent them on bond	153	3		
			4	10	

	Anno 1682 @				
	Clement Oxenbridge of London	Dr	£	s	d
	To Ballances	D	2		

	Anno 1682 @				
	Samuell Searle of Bilboa	Dr	£	s	d
	To Ballances	D	6		8

	Anno 1682 @				
	John Bush & Company merchants	Dr	£	s	d
	To Ballances	D	5	7	2

	Anno 1682 @				
	Edward Colston merchant [12]	Dr	£	s	d
	To Ballances	D	1	4	4

	Anno 1682 @				
	Robert Tyler of Bristoll Scrivener	Dr	£	s	d
	To Ballances	D	1	5	

	Anno 1682 @				
	Sotherland my meadow in Southbrind	Dr	£	s	d
	To Ballances	D	15		

(11)	**Bristoll 1682 @**		£	s	d
	Dennis Tayler Deceased	Dr	£	s	d
	To Ballances	D	2		
1684 August 9	Denis Tayler his sone Debtor to Isaac Heming for money hee paid him on my bill	90	13		
1688 Aprill 30	To Cash lent him on his Bottomree bond to furnish him to Nevis on the Neptune Sloop	141	5		
	To Adventure in Neptune for the neat proceeds of Candles 6997 lb Sugar, at 10s per cwt per acct.	143	34	19	8
January	To Proffit & Losse for money due on Bottomree for the £5 above as per his Bond	164	1	5	
1689 July 16	To Cash paid his mother for ballance per his order	168	1	5	7
			57	10	3

	Anno 1682 @				
	John Skenfield	Dr	£	s	d
	To Ballances	D	1		

	Anno 1682 @				
	John Guest	Dr	£	s	d
	To Ballances	D	3	2	

Bristoll 1682

		Cr	£	s	d
	Reynold Williams per Contra is				
	By Proffit & Losse for so much lost by his death at Olveston in				
	Gloucestershire	153	13	6	11

Anno 1690

		Cr	£	s	d
	Per Contra				
Dec. 9	By Acct. of Ballances, for Ballance	193 *	10		

Anno 1690 @

		Cr	£	s	d
	Per Contra				
Dec. 9	By Acct. of Ballances, for Ballance	193 *	5		

Anno 1688

		Cr	£	s	d
	Sir Robert Yeamans & Ed. Fox per Contra				
Aprill 28	By Cash recd. of Sir Samuell Astry by order of the Lady				
	Yeamans the widow of Sir Robert	141	4	10	
			4	10	

Anno 1688

		Cr	£	s	d
	Per Contra Creditor				
Dec. 9	By Acct. of Ballances, for Ballance	193 *	2		

Anno 1688

		Cr	£	s	d
	Samuell Searle per Contra				
	By Proffit & Losse for Ballance	153	6		8

Anno 1688

		Cr	£	s	d
	John Bush and Co.				
	By Proffit & Losse for Ballance	153	5	7	2

Anno 1688

		Cr	£	s	d
	Edward Colston per Contra is				
	By Proffit & Losse for Ballance	153	1	4	4

Anno 1688

		Cr	£	s	d
	Robert Tyler per Contra				
	By Proffit & Losse for Ballance	153	1	5	

Anno 1688

		Cr	£	s	d
	Per Contra				
	By Profit and Loss for Ballance	180	15		

Bristoll 1684

		Cr	£	s	d
	Dennis Tayler Deceased per Contra				
August 9	By Proffit &Losse abated by reason of poverty	164	2		
	By Cash recd. of his mother for my bill on Isaac Heming	77	13		
1689 Aprill	By Sugar 4 hhds for theire cost in Nevis being 7353 lb at 10s				
	per 100 lb as per his acct. laden in the Nathanael	166	36	15	3
	By Dittto for theire freight and primage in the Nathanael to				
	London £4 10s 00d per his leter Apr 26 89	166	4	10	
	By Proffit & Losse abated him the Bottomree money per contra	164	1	5	
			57	10	3

Anno 1688

		Cr	£	s	d
	John Scanfield per Contra				
	By Profit & Loss for Ballance	180	1		

Anno 1688

		Cr	£	s	d
	Per Contra				
	By Acct. of Ballances, for Ballance	193 *	3	2	

Anno 1682 @		£	s	d
John Spoore Senior	Dr			
To Ballances	D	2	8	11

Anno 1682 @		£	s	d
James Slaughter	Dr			
To Ballances	D		10	

Anno 1682 @		£	s	d
Mr Samuell Davis & Company	Dr			
To Ballances	D		18	

Anno 1682 @		£	s	d
Anne Hiscox & Company	Dr			
To Ballances	D	1	5	

Anno 1682 @		£	s	d
Henry Moore	Dr			
To Ballances	D	1		6

Anno 1682 @		£	s	d
John Garner	Dr			
To Ballances	D	2	15	

Anno 1682 @		£	s	d
Thomas Fownes	Dr			
To Ballances	D	4		

(12) **Bristoll 1682 @**

		£	s	d
Edward Biddle	Dr			
To Ballances	D	1	17	6

Anno 1682@		£	s	d
Lewis Matthew & Company	Dr			
To Ballances	D	1	6	2

Anno 1682 @		£	s	d
Thomas Grimm of Boston	Dr			
To Ballances	D	35	8	10

Anno 1682 @			£	s	d
Arthur Bramley & Company viz. John Brisgo of Marshfield		Dr			
To Ballances		D	10		
1688	To Proffit & Losse for chaarges on arresting John Brisco in Marshfield	153	1	5	6
	To Proffit & Losse for intrest of £10 lent them on theire bond 10th Sept. 1659 besydes money abated them the bond not including it	153*	10		
1689	To Proffit & Losse for intrest of £10 due March28th 1689	164		6	
	To Ditto for Ballance	180		6	
			21	17	6

Anno 1682 @		£	s	d
John Dolphin	Dr			
To Ballances	D	1		

Anno 1682 @		£	s	d
John Birkes	Dr			
To Ballances	D	70		

Anno 1682@		£	s	d
Christopher Toomer	Dr			
To Ballances	D	6	10	3

Anno 1688		£	s	d
John Spoore Senior of Gigly Hill per Contra	Cr			
By Proffit & Losse for Ballance hee dying poore	153	2	8	11

Anno 1688		£	s	d
James Slaughter per Contra is	Cr			
By Profitt & Losse for Ballance	153		10	

Anno 1690 @		£	s	d
Per Contra	Cr			
By Profit and Loss for Ballance	180		18	

Anno 1688		£	s	d
Ann Hiscox & Company	Cr			
By Profit & Losse they being dead	153	1	5	

Anno 1690		£	s	d
Per Contra	Cr			
By Profit and Loss for Ballance	180	1		6

Anno 1690 @		£	s	d
Per Contra	Cr			
By Acct. of Ballances, for Ballance	193 *	2	15	

Anno 1690		£	s	d
Per Contra	Cr			
By Profit and Loss for Ballance	180	4		

Bristoll 1688		£	s	d
Edward Biddle per Contra	Cr			
By Proffit & Losse for Ballance	153	1	17	6

Anno 1690		£	s	d
Per Contra	Cr			
By Profit and Loss for Ballance	180	1	6	2

Anno 1690 @		£	s	d
Per Contra	Cr			
By Profit and Loss for Ballance	180	35	8	10

	Anno 1688		£	s	d
	Arhtur Bramley & John Brisco of Marshfield are per Contra	Cr			
June 28	By Cash received of John Brisco for a writ & charges of arrest	141	1	5	6
October 31	By Cash received of John Brisco in part	157	10	1	
1689 May 7	By Cash recd. of John Brisco for ½ yeares intrest of £10 due March 28th 1689	162		6	
October 25	By Ditto recd. of John Brisco in full	168	10	5	
			21	17	6

Anno 1688		£	s	d
John Dolphin per Contra	Cr			
By Proffit & Losse for Ballance	153	1		

Anno 1690@		£	s	d
Per Contra	Cr			
By Acct. of Ballances, for Ballance	193 *	70		

Anno 1688		£	s	d
Christopher Toomer per Contra	Cr			
By Proffit & Losse for Ballance	153	6	10	3

			£	s	d
	Anno 1682 @				
	Stanton Jones	Dr	£	s	d
	To Ballances	D	2	18	7

			£	s	d
(13)	**Bristoll 1682 @**				
	Edward Prestwich	Dr	£	s	d
	To Ballances	D		6	8
	Anno 1682 @				
	Voyadge in the Adventure to Barbadoes	Dr	£	s	d
	To Ballances	D	27		
	Anno 1682 @				
	Indigoe one Caske for acct. Jeremiah Holwey, Arthur Plomer & myselfe	Dr	£	s	d
	To Ballances	D	15	1	2
	Anno 1682 @				
	Peter Dee	Dr	£	s	d
	To Ballances	D	1	7	
	Anno 1682 @				
	Nathanaell Milner Defunct	Dr	£	s	d
	To Ballances	D	8	7	5
	Anno 1682 @				
	John Bowen	Dr	£	s	d
	To Ballances	D	1	4	6
	Anno 1682 @				
	Mary Russett	Dr	£	s	d
	To Ballances	D		6	6
	Anno 1682 @				
	Mehetable Hemings	Dr	£	s	d
	To Ballances	D	35	8	

			£	s	d
(14)	**Bristoll 1682 @**				
	Edward Paine of Bedminster	Dr	£	s	d
	To Ballances	D	2		
	Anno 1682 @				
	Thomas Wilcox	Dr	£	s	d
	To Ballances	D	6	7	3
	Anno 1682 @				
	Thomas Lower [13] of Cornwall	Dr	£	s	d
	To Ballances	D		10	
	Anno 1682 @				
	Voyadge in the Zant to Newfoundland	Dr	£	s	d
	To Ballances	D	52	5	7
	Anno 1682 @				
	George Wallis & Company	Dr	£	s	d
	To Ballances	D	10	6	8
	Anno 1682 @				
	Thomas Scrope & Mary Aldworth on Bond	Dr	£	s	d
	To Ballances for money on bond £200 and 7 yeares intrest from January 12th 1674 to the 12th of January 1681 as may appeare in the Ledger Book No D folio 12	D	284		
	To Proffit & Losse for intrest of £200 from 12th Jan. 1681 to the 10th March 1686		61	18	
			345	18	

		Cr	£	s	d
	Anno 1688				
Stanton Jones per Contra		Cr	£	s	d
By Proffit & Losse the man dying poore		153	2	18	7
	Bristoll 1690 @				
Per Contra		Cr	£	s	d
By Profit and Loss for Ballance		180		6	8
	Anno 1688				
Voyage in the Adventure per Contra is		Cr	£	s	d
By Proffit & Losse for Ballance		153	27		
	Anno 1688				
Indigoe per Contra		Cr	£	s	d
By Proffit & Losse for Ballance		153	15	1	2
	Anno 1690 @				
Per Contra		Cr	£	s	d
By Acct. of Ballances, for Ballance		193 *	1	7	
	Anno 1690 @				
Per Contra		Cr	£	s	d
By Profit & Loss for Ballance		180	8	7	5
	Anno 1688				
John Bowen per Contra is		Cr	£	s	d
By Proffit & Losse for Ballance		153	1	4	6
	Anno 1688				
Marie Russet per Contra		Cr	£	s	d
By Proffit & Losse for Ballance		153		6	6
	Anno 1688				
Mehetabel Heming per Contra		Cr	£	s	d
By Proffit & Losse for Ballance		153	35	8	
	Bristoll 1688				
Edward Payne per Contra		Cr	£	s	d
By Proffit & Losse for Ballance		153	2		
	Anno 1688				
Tho. Wilcox per Contra		Cr	£	s	d
By Proffit & Losse for Ballance		153	6	7	3
	Anno 1690 @				
Per Contra Is		Cr	£	s	d
By Acct. of Ballances, for Ballance		193 *		10	
	Anno 1688				
Voyage in the Zant to Newfoundland		Cr	£	s	d
By Proffit & Losse for Ballance		153	52	5	7
	Anno 1690 @				
Per Contra		Cr	£	s	d
By Acct. of Ballances, for Ballance		193 *	10	6	8
	Anno 1686				
	Tho. Scrope & Company per Contra are	Cr	£	s	d
March 10	By Tho. Scrope his particular acct. current carried to his account of debt	75	345	18	

Anno 1682 @				
Habacock Turner	Dr	£	s	d
To Ballances	D	1		

Anno 1682 @				
George Hawes	Dr	£	s	d
To Ballances	D	10	8	

(15)   **Bristoll 1682 @**

Isaac Newton [14]	Dr	£	s	d
To Ballances	D	7	16	3

Anno 1682				
Richard Cabble Junir	Dr	£	s	d
To Ballances	D	10	18	

Anno 1682 @				
French wine in the Phenix	Dr	£	s	d
To Ballances	D	319		11

Anno 1682 @				
John Hort & Company	Dr	£	s	d
To Ballances	D	6	2	2

Anno 1682 @				
Adventure in the Fortune to Nevis	Dr	£	s	d
To Ballances	D	27	18	4

Anno 1682 @				
Elizabeth Milner ~ My Sister [15]	Dr	£	s	d
To Ballances	D	5		

Anno 1682 @					
	Elizabeth Milner	Dr	£	s	d
	To Ballances	D	10		
	To her acct. current for the amount immediately above written	15	5		
1688 January 22	To Cash paid her selfe	162	8		
	To Isaac Heming for my bill on him in her favor	152	12	19	9
1689 July 25	To Cash paid her as per receit	168	6	19	
January 23	To Cash paid her in full	173	7	19	10½
			50	18	7½

Anno 1682 @				
Francis Gardner	Dr	£	s	d
To Ballances	D	21	5	

Anno 1689					
	Elizabeth Milner is	Dr	£	s	d
	To the ballance of her above Account brought from that Account	15	5		
March 15	To Cash paid her in full	175	8	18	6
1690 June 12	To Ditto pd. her	181	2		
26	To Ditto pd. her in full	181	8	3	8
			24	2	2

Anno 1688				
Habacock Turner per Contra is	Cr	£	s	d
By Proffit & Losse for Ballance	153	1		

Anno 1688				
George Hawes per Contra	Cr	£	s	d
By Proffit & Losse for Ballance	153	10	8	

Bristoll 1688				
Isaac Newton per Contra is	Cr	£	s	d
By Proffit & Losse for Ballance	153	7	16	3

Anno 1685				
Richard Cabbel per Contra	Cr	£	s	d
May 11 By Cash received of William Minor for the debt per Contra by composition, on receipt of which I gave said Cabbell a discharge with his promise to pay the remainder of his debt as soone as hee should bee made able	143	3	15	10
By Acct. of Ballances, for Ballance	193 *	7	2	2
		10	18	

Anno 1688				
French wine in the Phoenix per Contra	Cr	£	s	d
By Proffit & Losse for Ballance	153	319		11

Anno 1690 @				
Per Contra	Cr	£	s	d
By Acct. of Ballances, for Ballance	193 *	6	2	2

Anno 1688				
Adventure in the Fortune to Nevis per Contra	Cr	£	s	d
By Proffit & Losse for Ballance	153	27	18	4

Anno 1682				
Elizabeth Milner	Cr	£	s	d
By her acct. current underneath per Contra	15	5		

Anno 1688				
Elizabeth Milner per Contra is	Cr	£	s	d
February By Jahzeel Speed for ¼ yeares dyet ending September 7th 1688	154	5		
By Proffit & Losse for severall things had of her as per noat	153		16	11
By Jahzeel Speed by money furnished him at severall times	154	2	18	
By Ditto for ½ yeares dyet ending March 7th 1688	154	10		
1689 Aprill 15 By Cash recd. of her	162	7		
By Jahzeel Speed for ¼ yeares dyet, & severall disbursements as per her noat	154	7	3	10
July 25 By Cash recd. of her in part	168	5		1
By Sundry acct.s for ¼ yeares dyet for Jahzeel £5 and £2 19s 10d½ other disbursements on him	154, 164	7	19	10½
By her new acct. current for ballance	15	5		
		50	18	7½

Anno 1690 @				
Per Contra	Cr	£	s	d
By Acct. of Ballances, for Ballance	193 *	21	5	

Anno 1689				
Elizabeth Milner per Contra is	Cr	£	s	d
By Sundry accounts for ¼ years dyet for Jahzeel Speed £5, money furnisht him with for his occasions £2 5s 2d and other disbursements of £0 13s 04d	154, 164	8	18	6
1690 June By Profit and Loss for Crape etc. had of her	180		18	2
By Jahzeel Speed for ¼ years dyett for him ending 7th June 1690	178	5		

(16)	**Bristoll 1682 @**		£	s	d
	Erasmus Dole [16]	Dr			
	To Ballances	D	2	12	

	Anno 1681/2 @		£	s	d
	Thomas Goldney	Dr			
	To Ballances	D	112	7	7
1683 June 23	To French wine 1 hogshead etc. for the cost & charge of 1 dozen bottles white wine	57		11	
1684 July 28	To French wine 2 hhds for 1 dozen bottles white wine at 10s & 1 doz bottles 2s -d	73, 78		12	
1685 Aprill 6	To Rice for acct. of Simon Clement & Company for 3 baggs neat 10cwt 1qr 3lb at 23s per Cwt	96	11	16	4
			125	6	11

	Anno 1682@		£	s	d
	Richard Gotley & Thomas Pope	Dr			
	To Ballances for £50 on bond and 3½ yeare intrest to the 2nd of March 1682	D	60	10	
1685	To Isaac Heming for the ballance of Tho. Popes acct. with him which I paid on acct.	100		10	7
1686 Sept. 1	To Proffit & Losse for 3½ yeares intrest from 2nd March 1682 to the 1st of Sept. 1686	127	10	10	
February	To Ditto for ½ yeares intrest of the £50 ending March 1st	127	1	10	
			73		7

	Anno 1682 @		£	s	d
	James Webb	Dr			
	To Ballances	D	56		
1687	To Proffit & Losse for 7 yeares & 1 month intrest of £50 from March 17th 1679 to Aprill 17th 1687 then due	127	21	5	
	To Proffit & Losse for intrest of £50 from 17th Aprill 87 to 28th July 1687	137		16	8
			78	1	8

	Anno 1682 @		£	s	d
	John Gagg	Dr			
	To Ballances	D	6		5

	Anno 1682 @		£	s	d
	John Romsey Esquire	Dr			
	To Ballances	D		18	

	Anno 1682 @		£	s	d
	George Silvana	Dr			
	To Ballances	D	1		

	Anno 1682 @		£	s	d
	Richard Royly of London	Dr			
	To Ballances	D	3	13	7

(17)	**Bristoll 1682 @**		£	s	d
	Adventure in the Bonnyventure	Dr			
	To Ballances	D	33	9	6

			£	s	d
	By Ditto for money furnisht , and disburst for him	178	4	5	6
	By Acct. of Ballances, for Ballance	193 *	5		
			24	2	2

Bristoll 1690 @

		Cr	£	s	d
	Per Contra				
	By Acct. of Ballances, for Ballance	193 *	2	12	

Anno 1681/2 @

		Cr	£	s	d
	Per Contra				
March 22	By Isaac Heming for a bill of Exchange	35	100		
May 23	By Cash recd. of him	41	12	6	8
1685	By Cash received for the 3 baggs rice per Contra	84	11	16	
1686 June 24	By Cash received of his sonne Thomas	108	1	3	
	By Proffit & Losse for paid short	105		1	3
			125	6	11

Anno 1683

		Cr	£	s	d
	Richard Gotley & Company per Contra are				
Aprill 18	By Cash recd. of Richard Gotley in full for intrest of £50 on bond to March 1st 1682	66	10	10	
1686 August	By Laurence Washington for his bill on mee in favor of Richard Gotley & Company	132	16		
	By Ditto for his bill on mee in favor of Joanna Pope, & assign'd to Richard Gotley	132	19		
	By Ditto for a Post ntry on his goods in the Francis & Marie paid to Richard Gotley	132		5	7
February 4	By Cash received of Richard Gotley in full	120	27	5	
			73		7

Anno 1687

		Cr	£	s	d
	James Webb per Contra is				
Aprill 16	By Cash recd. of him in full for intrest to the 17th Aprill 1687	121	27	5	
July 28	By Cash recd. of him in full	121 *	50	16	8
			78	1	8

Anno 1690 @

		Cr	£	s	d
	Per Contra				
	By Acct. of Ballances, for Ballance	193 *	6		5

Anno 1688

		Cr	£	s	d
	John Rumsey per Contra				
	By Proffit & Losse for Ballance	153		18	

Anno 1690 @

		Cr	£	s	d
	Per Contra				
	By Acct. of Ballances, for Ballance	193 *	1		

Anno 1690 @

		Cr	£	s	d
	Per Contra				
	By Acct. of Ballances, for Ballance	193 *	3	13	7

Bristoll 1682

		Cr	£	s	d
	Adventure in the Bonadventure				
	By adventure the 1st in the Dyamond Ketch to Nevis carried to that acct. of Debt because Edmond Scrope & Company do joyne the acct. of Sales of each parcell goods sent in both ships in one	18	33	9	6

Anno 1682 @				
Adventure in the Happy Entrance	Dr	£	s	d
To Ballances	D	23	9	6

Anno 1682@				
Ginger	Dr	£	s	d
To Ballances	D	20	15	11
To Profit & Losse for Ballance	153	5	16	11
		26	12	10

Anno 1681 @					
	Phillip Higginbottome	Dr	£	s	d
	To Ballances	D	50		
Feb. 8	To Cash pd. John Harris for 2 truncks and cording them	40	1	7	8
24	To Ditto pd. Porters	40			4
March 14	To Ditto pd. Francis Rottenbury	40	1	9	
Aprill 7	To Ditto pd. his wife in part of a bill of £170	41	5		
	To Isaac Heming for money hee recd. in London	35	3		
	To Proffit & loss for 4 months Intrest of £50 ending the 21st March	8	1		8
	To Cash pd. him	41	162		
	To Isaac Heming for my bill in Favor of said Heming	35 *	1		
			224	17	8

Anno 1682 @					
Lanincloth for acct. of Beniamin Gould being 16 bolts	Dr	£	s	d	
To Ballances	D			4	
To itselfe for Filing a certificate	36			4	
To Proffit & Loss for sundry charges on said cloth	8	1	16	10	
To Ben. Gould for theire neat proceeds	5	68	1		
		69	18	6	

Anno 1681 @					
	Robert Sommers	Dr	£	s	d
1682	To Ballances	D	90	17	
July 19	To Cattle for 2 oxen sold him	5	12	5	
Oct. 21	To Ditto for 4 oxen & a bull sold him	5	29	10	
			132	12	

Anno 1682 @				
Hugh Tynte Esquire [17]	Dr	£	s	d
To Ballances	D		12	5

Anno 1682 @					
	Paul Priaulx	Dr	£	s	d
	To Ballances	D	12	9	3
1686 Aprill 14	To Isaac Heming for my bill on him in favor of Paul Priaulx, for ballance of this acct.	113	6	9	
			18	18	3

(18)	**Bristoll 1681 @**				
	Elizabeth Sheward	Dr	£	s	d
	To Ballances	D	4		3

	Anno 1690 @	Cr	£	s	d
	Per Contra	Cr	£	s	d
	By Acct. of Ballances, for Ballance	193 *	23	9	6

	Anno 1682 @	Cr	£	s	d
	Per Contra	Cr	£	s	d
Oct. 9th	By Isaac Heming for the neate procees of 58 baggs Ginger	35	26	12	10

	Anno 1682 @	Cr	£	s	d
	Per Contra	Cr	£	s	d
Aprill 10	By Isaac Heming for his bill	35	170		
11	By Cash recd. of him	41	53	17	8
	By Himselfe for ballance	51	1		
			224	17	8

	Anno 1682 @	Cr	£	s	d
	Per Contra	Cr	£	s	d
Aprill 18	By Michael Pope for 2 bolts sold him	48	8	4	2
May 18	By Cash recd. of John Mahen for one bolt	41	5	3	9
July 19	By Ditto recd. of John Machen for 3 bolts	42	13	10	10
22	By John Jones for 9 bolts sold him	51	39	4	3
Sept. 14	By John Machen for one bolt sold him	55	3	15	6
			69	18	6

	Anno 1681 @	Cr	£	s	d
	Per Contra	Cr	£	s	d
Dec. 31	By Cash recd. of him	40	50		
Nov. 6	By Ditto recd. of him	43	20		
Feb. 1st	By Ditto recd. of him	43	20		
1683 October	By Cattle abated him	5		15	
	By Proffit & Losse for flesh at severall times for Flesh of him	9	17	18	5
	By Ditto for keeping my mare £1 17s 6d, & lent Jahzeel 13s 6d	9	2	11	
	By John Love for money to bee recd. of him	55	20		
	By Cash recd. of him	67	1	7	7
			132	12	

	Anno 1688	Cr	£	s	d
	Hugh Tynte per Contra	Cr	£	s	d
	By Proffit & Losse for Ballance	153		12	5

	Anno 1685/6	Cr	£	s	d
	Paul Priaulx per Contra	Cr	£	s	d
Aprill	By ballance of his acct. of Carpets brought from that acct.	1	18	17	9
	By Proffit & Losse for money to set the acct. right	105			6
			18	18	3

	Bristoll 1681 @	Cr	£	s	d
	Per Contra	Cr	£	s	d
29	By Cash recd. of her	40	3		
	By Proffit & Losse for Ballance	153	1		3
			4		3

rket.

Anno 1682 @

Mary Parsons of Portbury Widdow	Dr	£	s	d
To Ballances	D	1	15	
Jan. 12 — To Tenement in Portbury for halfe a yeares rent ending the 29th Sept.	20	1	15	
March 25 — To Ditto for ½ yeares rent ending in March Last 1682	20	1	15	
1683 — To Ditto for 1 yeares rent due 25th March 1683	20	3	10	
		8	15	

Anno 1681 @

Jeremiah Holvey	Dr	£	s	d
To Ballances	D	3	7	6

Anno 1681/2 @

Jane Flower	Dr	£	s	d
To Ballances	D	33		
March 7 — To Cash pd. her	40	4		
		37		

Anno 1682 @

Adventure in the Nathanaell	Dr	£	s	d
To Ballances for ballance	D	16	11	10

Anno 1682 @

Gold 43 pieces of 8 Deposited by Nathanaell Haggatt	Dr	£	s	d
To Ballances	D	40		

Anno 1682 @

Adventure in the Diamond to Nevis Nicholas Webber master	Dr	£	s	d
By Ballances of adventure the 1st in said ship to Nevis	D	127	5	10
To Adventure in the Bonaventure to Nevis for the cost & charges of 16 kilderkins of floure, & 10 boxes Candles sent in said ship, because Edm: Scrope & Company do joyne the acct. of sales of both ships cargoes togeather in one	17	33	9	6
To Proffit & Losse for Ballance	153	27	1	8
		187	17	

(19)   **Bristoll 1682 @**

Robert Whittle & Company of Yoarkshire Clothiers	Dr	£	s	d
To Ballances	D	7	19	2

Anno 1682 @

Adventure in the Hope of London to Barbadoes	Dr	£	s	d
To Ballances	D	15	9	9

Anno 1682 @

Kersies	Dr	£	s	d
To Ballances	D	30	7	9

Anno 1681 @

Nathanaell Haggat	Dr	£	s	d
To Ballances	D	34	3	7
Dec. 12th — To Cash lent him	40	2		
1682 Sept. 12 — To Ditto Lent him on his Bond	42	50		
1682/3 March 20 — To Cash Lent him on his Bond	66	100		
1684 July 29 — To Cash paid him	77	200		
To Wm. Godwin for 1¼ yeares intrest hee received of him	64	9		

Anno 1682 @		Cr	£	s	d
	Per Contra	Cr	£	s	d
July 8	*By Cash recd. of her*	42	1	15	
Dec. 19	*By Copyhold in Portbury*	20		17	
	By Cash recd. of her	43		18	
1683 June 23	*By Cash recd. of her*	66		12	10
	By Copiehold Tenement for her noate of disbursments	20	1	2	2
1684 May 15	*By Cash received of her sonne in full of all rent to this day*	77	3	10	
			8	15	

Anno 1682 @		Cr	£	s	d
	Per Contra	Cr	£	s	d
Dec. 23	*By Cash recd. of him*	40	3	7	6

Anno 1682 @		Cr	£	s	d
	Per Contra	Cr	£	s	d
March 7	*By Cash recd. of her*	40	16	10	
82	*By Proffitt & Loss due to her for halling*	8	4		
June 15	*By Cash recd. of her*	41	16	10	
			37		

Anno 1688		Cr	£	s	d
	Adventure in the Nathanael per Contra	Cr	£	s	d
	By Proffit & Losse for Ballance	153	16	11	10

Anno 1682 @		Cr	£	s	d
	Per Contra	Cr	£	s	d
Aprill 11	*By Cash recd. of Nath. Haggatt*	41	40		

Anno 1683		Cr	£	s	d
	Adventure in the Dyamond Ketch per Contra is	Cr	£	s	d
	By Edmond Scrope and Co. for the neat proceeds of all the goods per Contra valuing the Sugar at 10s per cwt as per acct. of sales closed November 1st 1683	33	187	17	
			187	17	

Bristoll 1684					
	Robert Whittle & Company of Yoarkshire Clothiers per Contra are	Cr	£	s	d
	By Edmond Scrope for money received by him formerly & then omitted to be charged	38	7	19	2

Anno 1688		Cr	£	s	d
	Adventure in the Hope of London	Cr	£	s	d
	By Proffit & Losse for Ballance	153	15	9	9

Anno 1688		Cr	£	s	d
	Kersies per Contra	Cr	£	s	d
	By Proffit & Losse for Ballance	153	30	7	9

Anno 1684		Cr	£	s	d
	Nathanael Haggatt per Contra is	Cr	£	s	d
July 24	*By Cash borrowed of him for my Brother John Wilmer*	77	200		
	By Proffit & Losse for money of him which was carried to that acct. in folio 9 of this book by mistake, which should have been brought to this acct.	127 *	100		
1686 Nov. 6	*By Cash received of him being the £100 lent him July 19th 1686 as per Contra*	120	100		

			£	s	d
	To Gold for money lent him on 53 pieces at the same time with the £50 and £2 above mentioned being Sept. 12th 1682 which gold hee deposited for £48 and the said £2 made £50	52	48		
	To Proffit & Losse for 4½ yeares intrest of the £48 & £2 & £50 on bond from Sept. 12th 82 to March 13th 86	127	27		
1686 July 19	To Cash paid lent him on a necklace of Pearle & severall things deposited with mee	121	100		
	To Proffit & Losse for intrest of the same 3½ months from the 26th July to 6th Nov.	127	1	15	
	To Ditto for 2 months intrest of £50 lent on the gold and £2 in silver from 13th March 86 to the 13th May 87 then[?] [18]	127		10	
			572	8	7

Anno 1682 @

	Dr	£	s	d
Thomas Shewell				
To Ballances	D		15	

Anno 1682 @

	Dr	£	s	d
William Coles of Bristoll				
To Ballances	D		7	1

Anno 1681/2 @

		Dr	£	s	d
	John Sandford				
	To Ballances	D	9	1	10
1682 June 12	To Linincloth 10 baletts Will. Shephard for 4 bolts at 1 rolls off	7	16	12	5
17	To Ditto for one bolt	7	3	12	1
Oct. 19	To Cash pd. him	42	2	11	9
1685 September 16	To Cash lent him on his Bond	84	100		
1687	To Proffit & Losse for 2 yeares intrest of £100 from 14th Sept. 1685 to 15th Sept. 1687	137	12		
	To Ditto for ½ yeares intrest from Sept. 15th 1687 to the 16th of March 1687	137	3		
1688	To Ditto for 1 yeares intrest due March 16th 1688	164	6		
1689 Sept. 16	To Ditto for ½ yeares intrest due Sept. 16th 1689	164	3		
March 16	To Ditto for ½ year's intrest due March 16th 1689	164	3		
Oct.	To Ditto for ½ year's intrest due Sept. 16th 1690	180	3		
			161	18	1

Anno 1683

		Dr	£	s	d
	Oyle 2 Cask recd. out of the ship Deborah & Sarah for acct. Christopher Williams from London				
May 18	To Cash paid John Higgenson for freight £ s d and averidge from London 12	66			
August 4	To Cash paid Robert Hauxworth for 2 lb wanting in the tare of 1 7	66			
	To Proffit & Losse for landing, halling, cooperidge & celleridge 3 8	9			
	To my Commission at £2 per cent 8	9	1	5	3
	To Christopher Williams his acct. current for theire neat proceeds	7	18	14	9
			20		

Bristoll 1682 @   *(20)*

	Dr	£	s	d
Gabriell Deane				
To Ballances	D	14	18	4

Anno 1682 @

	Dr	£	s	d
Voyadge in the Isabella to Jamaica				
To Ballances	D	78	2	
To Thomas Scrope for ¼ part cost & charges of 12 tonns beere formerly omitted to bee charged	75	15		
		93	2	

		Cr	£	s	d
	By Jonathan Lamboll for drawing Articles of partnership in Maulting trade	131	3		
	By Ditto for drawing the mortgage on his houses in Reading	131	3		
1687 error	By Proffit & Losse for money charg'd for 2 yeares intrest at £50				
May 13	By Ditto recd. of Humphrey Corsley for the 53 pieces severall sorts of Gold mentioned per Contra	127	49	15	
	By himselfe for ballance carried to his new acct. current	138	116	13	7
			572	8	7

Anno 1688

	Cr	£	s	d
Tho. Shewell per Contra				
By Proffit & Losse for Ballance	153		15	

Anno 1688

	Cr	£	s	d
William Coles per Contra				
By Proffit & Losse for Ballance	153		7	1

Anno 1681/2 @

		Cr	£	s	d
	Per Contra				
March 15	By Cash recd. of him	40	8	15	10
29	By Proffit & Losse for his Noate	8	1	2	6
Aprill 6	By Ditto for his noate	8		19	2
July 29	By Cash recd. of him	42	20	4	6
	By Max. Gallop for want of measure	34		10	2
	By Proffit & Losse for money lost out of my purse	89		5	9
1688 May 8	By Cash received of him in full for 2½ yeares intrest of £100 ending March 16th 1687	141	15		
			46	17	11
	By Acct. of Ballances for Ballance, being for £100 lent on bond and intrest to Sept. 16th 1690	193 *	115		2
			161	18	1

Anno 1683

		Cr	£	s	d
	Oyle 2 Cask per Contra is	47			
June 5	By Sundry acct.s for the 2 Cask sould Tho. Durbin & Robt. Hauxworth	28	20		
			20		

Bristoll 1688

	Cr	£	s	d
Per Contra				
By Proffit & Loss for Ballance	180 *	14	18	4

Anno 1684

	Cr	£	s	d
Voyage in the Isabella Dennis Tayler Master to Jamaica directly per Contra				
By Robert Scrope & Company for the first goods cost per Contra, the neat proceeds of which cannot credit this acct. with having received no acct. of sales, though sent in the yeare 1676				
By Acct. of Ballances, for Ballance	193 *	93	2	

	Anno 1682 @		£	s	d
	Coppyhold Tenement in Portbury	Dr			
	To Ballances	D	31	18	
July 8	To Cash pd. Mary Parsons in full of her noate	42		10	
Dec. 19	To Mary Parsons for her noate of disbursments	18		17	
1683 June 14	To Cash paid Robert Davis for Ditching the 5 acres	66		2	6
25	To Marie Parsons for her noat of disbursments	18	1	2	2
July 14	To Cash paid Wm. Spoore Junior for my part repaireing the old, & my part of a new gate	66		6	
1684 May 14	To Cash paid Marie Parsons sonne his noat of disbursments	77	1	7	
December	To Cash paid Richard Cope in full of his noat of disbursments	82	1	2	2
1685 July 29	To Cash paid Richd. Cope his noat of charges	83	1	2	
	To Richard Holbrooke for his noat of disbursments	98	1	15	8
1686 June	To Richd. Cope for his noat of disbursments to the end of the year 1685	97	1	17	
	To Arthur Hobbs for his noat of disbursments	29	2	17	7
November	To Richard Holbrook for his noat of disbursments	98		13	
1687 July 25	To Cash paid Tho. Stephens in part for thatching the house	121		8	
August 11	To Ditto paid Tho. Morrice for sparres & stretchers	121		5	
1688 July	To Richard Cope for his 2 noats of disbursments the last ending March 25th 1688	97	5	6	4
	To Proffit & Losse for 6 yeares intrest of the value of the Tenement valued in £100 [19]	153	36		
			87	9	5

	Anno 1682 @		£	s	d
	Owners of the Isabella	Dr			
	To Ballances	D	9	5	10

	Anno 1682 @		£	s	d
	William Daw	Dr			
	To Ballances	D	4		

	Anno 1681 @		£	s	d
	John Bradey	Dr			
	To Ballances for money Lent him on bond	D	10		
			10		

	Anno 1685		£	s	d
June 1685	John Brady of Pensford in the County of Somerset Hosier is	Dr			
21	To Cash paid lent him	145	2		
1686 October 9	To Cash paid lent him on his bill	120	4		
			6		

	Anno 1682 @		£	s	d
	John Hurne	Dr			
	To Ballances	D	7		1

	Bristoll 1681 @		£	s	d
(21)	Arthur Jones	Dr			
	To Ballances	D	6	3	11

	Anno 1682 @	Cr	£	s	d
	Per Contra				
	By Robert Davis for one yeares rent	51	5	5	
1683	By Mary Parsons for ½ yeares rent	18	1	15	
March 25	By Sundry accts for 2½ yeares rent	15,18,29	9	10	
1683 February 13	By Cash recd. of Wm. Spoore Senior which hee recd. of Tho.				
	Pascall for the grasse of the 2½ acres	68		4	
March 24	By Robert Davis for one yeares rent for the 5 acres & 2 acres in				
	Portburie	51	5	5	
1684 March 26	By Arthur Hobbs for 1 yeares rent ending 24th March 1683	29	2	10	
	By Marie Parsons for 1 yeares rent due 25th March 1683	18	3	10	
1685 March 26	By Arthur Hobbs for ½ yeares rent due 24th March 1683	29	2	10	
August	By Richard Holbrook for 1 yeares rent of the 5 acres, 2 acres,				
	& 2 halfe Acres	98	6		
	By Ditto for 260 Faggotts of the 2 acres at 4s 6d per ct as per				
	his noat August 18th 1685	98		11	3
1686 Aprill 16	By Richard Holbrook for 1 yeares rent due February 2 1685	98	6		
	By Richard Cope for 1½ yeares rent for the house, Barne,				
	Gardens, & Orchards due 24th of March 1685 of which hee				
	paid the first ½ yeares rent	97	5	5	
	By Arthur Hobbs for 1½ yeares rent for the house & land at				
	Gigly hill ending Sept. 29th 1686	29	3	15	
September 29	By Richard Holbrook for ½ yeares rent due Sept. 29th 1686	98	3		
March 25	By Ditto for ½ yeares rent due 25th March 1686	98	3		
1687 September	By Ditto for ½ yeares rent due part in August & part in				
	Sept.1687	98	3		
	By Arthur Hobbs for one yeares rent for Gigly hill now lowered				
	to 40s per annum due Sept. 29th 1687	125	2		
1688 Dec.	By Richard Cope for 2 yeares rent due March 24th 1687	97	7		
	By Arthur Hobbs for one yeares rent due September 29th 1688	125	2		
	By it selfe for Ballance carried to a new acct. current	160	15	9	2
			87	9	5

	Anno 1690 @	Cr	£	s	d
	Per Contra				
	By Profit & Loss for Ballance	189 *	9	5	10

	Anno 1690 @	Cr	£	s	d
	Per Contra				
	By Acct. of Ballances, for Ballance	193 *	4		

	Anno 1681 @	Cr	£	s	d
	Per Contra				
Dec. 23	By Cash recd. of him	40	2		
Aprill 6	By Ditto recd. of him	41	6		
May 27	By Ditto recd. of him	41	2		
			10		

	Anno 1685	Cr	£	s	d
	John Brady per Contra is				
August 27	By Cash recd. of him	84	2		
	By cash received of him October 30th	120	4		
			6		

	Anno 1690 @	Cr	£	s	d
	Per Contra				
	By Acct. of Ballances, for Ballance	193 *	7		1

	Bristoll 1681 @	Cr	£	s	d
	Per Contra				
Dec. 31	By Cash recd. of his wife	40	3		
August 1st	By Cash recd. of his wife	42	1		

	Anno 1682		£	s	d
	Robert Henly	Dr			
	To Ballances	D		7	1

	Anno 1681 @		£	s	d
	James Freeman Apothecary	Dr	£	s	d
	To Ballances	D	95	14	7
1683 Aprill 5	To Oyle 10 Jarres for said quantitie sold him	46	46	5	
1688 Feb. 18	To Cash paid him in full	162	8	17	
	To Proffit & Losse for ballance being so much abated	153		1	
			150	7	7

	James Freeman	Dr	£	s	d
1689 Aprill 15	To Cash paid him in full	162		10	6

	Anno 1682 @		£	s	d
	Jacob Beale	Dr	£	s	d
	To Ballances	D	1	5	

	Anno 1682 @		£	s	d
	Thomas Scrope & Company	Dr	£	s	d
	To Ballances for money Lent them on theire noat Sept. 22nd				
	1677	D	100		

	Anno 1682 @		£	s	d
	Richard Speed [21]	Dr	£	s	d
	To Ballances	D	36	17	6

	Anno 1683		£	s	d
	Adventure 2nd in the Dyamond Ketch Nicholas Webber master	Dr	£	s	d
	to Nevis				
	To acct. of Ballances for the goods sent to John Sheater &				
	Company consignd the whole cost	D	85	2	3
	To Proffit & Losse for Ballance	153	43	12	9
			128	15	

(22)	**Bristoll 1682 @**		£	s	d
	Estate of Metredone Speed [22]	Dr	£	s	d
	To Ballances	D	376	17	7

	Anno 1682 @		£	s	d
	House at the end of Small Street [23]	Dr	£	s	d
	To Ballances for the value of the house as it cost mee fitted for				
	Tenants	D	718	19	4
Oct. 24	To Cash pd. Crowne rent to Nath. King due in Sept. last	42		3	8
	To Ditto pd. Drums & Colors	43			4
1683 October 16	To Cash paid Nath. King cleark of the market for 1 yeares				
	Kings rent ending Sept. 29th	67		3	8
26	To Cash paid Richard Wasbrow for militia money	67		2	8
December 18	To Cash paid Richard Troll [24] for ½ yeares chimney money	67		7	
Aprill 2	To Cash paid for lamblack to black the house	68		4	1½
30	To Cash paid Philip Troll for ½ yeares chimney money due 25th				
	March	68		7	
October 13	To Cash paid Oziell Browne ½ charge of a lease to Edward Crofts	82		4	
November 8	To Cash paid Wm. Smart in part for painting the severall roomes	82	1	10	
March	To Cash paid Joseph Drew in full of his noat	82		15	9
1685	To Cash paid Edward Jones in full of his noat	82 *	1	10	

		4		
By *Acct. of Ballances, for Ballance*	193 *	2	3	11
		6	3	11

Anno 1690 @

		Cr	£	s	d
	Per Contra	Cr	£	s	d
	By *Acct. of Ballances, for Ballance*	193 *		7	1

Anno 1681 @

		Cr	£	s	d
	Per Contra	Cr	£	s	d
Feb. 16	By *Cash recd. of Thomas Colston*	40	20		
March 15	By *Cash recd. of him*	40	75	15	6
1683 August 20	By *Cash recd. of him*	67	46	5	
1688 Feb. 7	By *merchandise in the John to Virginea for acct. Lawrence Washington for 2 boxes of medicines sent in her by Tho. Pope, as per said Freemans noat*	160	8	17	1
			150	17	7

		Cr	£	s	d
	James Freeman	Cr	£	s	d
Aprill 9	By *Jonathan Lamboll for Pills, powders etc. as per noat*	147		10	6

Anno 1686

		Cr	£	s	d
	Jacob Beale per Contra is	Cr	£	s	d
August 28	By *Cash received of him in full*	119	1	5	

Anno 1686

		Cr	£	s	d
	Tho. Scrope and Joseph Jackson [20] *per Contra are*	Cr	£	s	d
	By *Tho. Scrope his acct. current carried to that acct.*	75	100		

Anno 1690 @

		Cr	£	s	d
	Per Contra	Cr	£	s	d
	By *Acct. of Ballances, for Ballance*	193 *	36	17	6

Anno 1683

		Cr	£	s	d
	Per Contra	Cr	£	s	d
	By *Edmund Scrope and Co. for the neat proceeds of the goods being 20 Firkins Butter, 20 boxes of candles, & 32 Kildkns Flour as per theire acct. 24th of March 1682/3, being mixd in said acct. with sales of goods out of the Owners Indeavour*	33	128	15	

Bristoll 1689

		Cr	£	s	d
	Estate of Metredone Speed per Contra	Cr	£	s	d
	By *Acct. of Ballances, for Ballance*	193 *	376	17	7

Anno 1682 @

		Cr	£	s	d
	Per Contra	Cr	£	s	d
Feb. 3d	By *Thomas Tayler for 4 yeares rent*	4	105	4	
1683 October 5	By *John Wasbrow for 33 weeks rent of the large Celar at 4s 6d per week*	28	7	8	6
	By *John Blackwell for 9 weeks Celleridge at 4s 6d per week*	26	2		6
January	By *Richard Champneys for 41 weeks Celleridge of the vault at 3s per week*	45	6	3	
June 26	By *Cash recd. of John Dessill for 1 yeares rent of the back Cellar in the Lane*	77	1	15	
1684 July 24	By *Cash received of John Yeamans for 1 years & 1/10 rent of the great upper Cellar*	77	8	16	
	By *Wiliam Smart for the money charged per Contra, which ought to have been charged to his acct. current*	26	1	10	
	By *Proffit & Losse for money I charge here only to make the ballance square with the Ballance brought per Contra from the former acct. of Ballances*	153	10	19	7½

Date	Description	Ref	£	s	d
31	To Cash paid Simon Smith for 1 yeares rent for the King ending Sept. 1684	82		5	
	To Edward Crofts for his noat of disbursments for severall particulars before his settling	96	1	9	
October 2	To Cash paid Edward Jones for work done there	84		9	1
1686 Sept. 27	To Cash paid Ed. Croft for 1 yeares rent of 2 Roomes	119	2		
October 28	To Cash paid for 1 yeares Kings rent for the house ending Sept. 29th 1686	129		2	8
1687 October 24	To Cash paid Tho. Davidge for 1 yeares Kings rent due ending 29th Sept. 1687 per receit	139		3	8
November 4	To Cash pd. Edward Jones for keeping the roofe & Gutters of the house	139		6	
1688 October 23	To Ditto pd. Edward Crofts towards the repaireing the furnace	157		10	
November 21	To Ditto pd. Ed. Jones for keeping the houses ruffe etc. to 29th of September 1688	157		6	
	To Proffit & Losse for the money per Contra, which ought not to bee there	153	132	17	
			862	15	11½

Anno 1682 @					
	Simon Clement 25 & his Father	Dr	£	s	d
	To Ballances For money resting due on bond	D	59	9	6
1689 October	To Proffit & Losse for 10 years 3 month intrest from June 24th 79 to 29th Sept. 1689	164	36	4	4
1690 October	To Ditto for 1 year's intrest ending 29th Sept. 1690 @	180	3	10	9
			99	4	7

Anno 1682 @					
	Matthew Wall of Waxford in Ireland	Dr	£	s	d
	To Ballances	D	9	14	10

Anno 1682 @					
	Tom Puxton	Dr	£	s	d
	To Ballances for 2 dozen bottles of Clarett	D	1	4	
Jan. 21	To Cash pd. Humphrey Corsely for a silver Tankard	40	7	2	6
Feb. 4	To Salt for acct. of Jahzeel Speed for one Tonne	37	2	10	
May 18	To Tobacco 6 hhds on the Victory for one hogshead weight neat 391lb at 4d per lb	25	6	9	4
July 19	To Sundry accts for 48 hogshead.s Tobacco sold him qt neat 17320 lb at 4d¼ per lb	29 25 36	306	14	
	To Salt for acct. of Jahz. Speed for 38 tonnes sold him	37	90	11	8
November 30	To Cash paid him for freight & averidge of 2 hhds Tobacco in the John	67	3	12	
			418	3	6

(23)   **Bristoll 1682 @**

	John Teage & Company	Dr	£	s	d
	To Ballances	D	2	15	11

Anno 1682 @					
	House in which I live 26	Dr	£	s	d
	To Ballances	D	656	17	9
August 10	To Cash pd. Joseph Owen	42		15	
Nov. 25	To Ditto pd. John Richardson for ½ a yeares chimney money ending the 29th Sept.	43		8	
Feb. 28	To Ditto pd. Thomas Walden for drumes etc.	43		4	
1683 July 4	To Cash paid for ½ a yeares Chimney ending 25th March last	66		8	

		£	s	d
By it selfe for ballance, being the first cost, and charges of altering, repairing, and making it fit for a Tenant carried to a new acct. current	161	718	19	4
		862	15	11½

Anno 1689				
Simon Clement & Company per Contra	Cr	£	s	d
By Acct. of Ballances, for Ballance	193 *	99	4	7

Anno 1683				
Mathew Wall per Contra is	Cr	£	s	d
September 11 By Michael Perrie for one Lanscipt Fanne sould in Jamaica	47		2	
November 8 By Cash recd. of Marie Eyles for a parcell of old silke wares etc.	67		15	
By Acct. of Ballances, for Ballance resting due	193 *	8	17	10
		9	14	10

Anno 1682 @				
Per Contra	Cr	£	s	d
Sept. 21 By Cash recd. of him	42	50		
Oct. 12 By Ditto recd. of him	42	50	3	
20 By Ditto recd. of him	42	40		
Jan. 31 By Ditto recd. of him	43	60		
1683 March 24 By Tobacco 2 hhds for freight and averidge of them in the ship John	59	3	19	
September 10 By Cash received of him	67	40		
By John Williamson for money hee gave his bond to by order of T. Puxton	72	90		
November 24 By Cash recd. of him	67	77	6	6
By Proffit and Losse freely given him for ballance	164	6	15	
		418	3	6

Bristoll 1688				
John Teage and Co. per Contra	Cr	£	s	d
By Proffit & Losse for Ballance being so much lost by John Teag's death	164 *	2	15	11

Anno 1686				
House in which I live per Contra	Cr	£	s	d
By the new Acct. current of the house in which I live	130	664	18	9

Date		Folio	£	s	d
August 24	To Cash paid Jos. Owen for whiteliming etc. 15s 6d & for keeping the house to May last	67	1	5	6
October	To Ditto paid John Guin for 2 ¾ yeares rent for the back house ending June 24th 1683	67	1	2	
25	To Ditto paid Oziell Browne for militia money	67		4	6
December 18	To Ditto pd. Philip Troll for ½ yeares Chimny money due 29th Sept. 1683	67		8	
Aprill 30	To Ditto pd. Philip Troll for ½ yeares Chimney money due 25th March 1683	68		8	
1685 Aprill 27	To Cash paid ½ yeares Chimney money	83		8	
July 23	To Cash paid the Chamberlain for 3 yeares rent of the back house ending June 25th 1686	119	1	4	
1686 August	To Cash paid David Roynon the Plomer for Plomers worke	119	1	6	
			664	18	9

Anno 1682 @		Dr	£	s	d
Tom Puxtone		D	157	10	
To Ballances for money due on Bond		9	10	3	
To Proffit & Losse for intrest with 30s abated him deducted			167	13	

Anno 1682@	Dr	£	s	d
Tom Edwards of Bristol Atturny at the Law	D	2	10	4
To Ballances				

1687

Anno 1682@	Dr	£	s	d
William Lewger of Barbadoes	D	12	10	
To Ballances				

Anno 1681@		Dr	£	s	d
Richard Godwin my servant [27]		D	18	2	11
To Ballances					
Dec. 31	To Cash pd. him	40	1	10	
Jan. 31	To Ditto pd. him	40	1		
Feb. 14	To Ditto pd. him	40		6	
1682 Aprill 8	To Ditto pd. him	41		2	6
June 10	To Ditto pd. him	41		9	11
			21	11	4

Anno 1687		Dr	£	s	d
Richard Godwin of Clapton in the County Somerset Yeoman		Dr			
August 1689 4	To Cash paid lent him on his bill	121	2		
	To Acc. of Ballances for Balance	193 *		18	4½
			2	18	4½

(24)	**Bristoll 1682@**	Dr	£	s	d
Joseph Kippin		D	12	9	10
To Ballances					

Anno 1682@		Dr	£	s	d
Joseph Speed [28]		D	20	5	
To Ballances					
Aprill 23	To Cash pd. him	41		10	
July 29	To Ditto pd. John Hort for a Bond	42	1	17	9
			22	12	9

	Anno 1683				
	Tho. Puxton per Contra	*Cr*	*£*	*s*	*d*
	By the neat proceeds of 18 hogshead Tobacco deposited for £150				
	soud Wm. Smith	*63*	136	15	
August 20	*By Cash recd. of him by the hands Edward Martindale*	*67*	30	18	
			167	13	

	Anno 1682@				
	Per Contra	*Cr*	*£*	*s*	*d*
Jan. 12	*By Proffitt and Loss for money hee disbursed*	*9*	1	5	
1683 Aprill 27	*By Cash recd. of him*	*66*	1	1	3
	By Proffit & Losse for fees as per noat	*9*		4	1
1687 Nov. error	*By estate newly purchased in Clapton for the copies of severall*				
	writings hee drew for mee, For that this money was paid him out				
	of cash, and is charged in fol (139) of this Leadger	*142*			
			2	10	4

	Anno 1688				
	William Lewger per Contra	*Cr*	*£*	*s*	*d*
	By Acct. of Ballances, for Ballance	*193 **	12	10	

	1682				
	Richard Godwin per Contra	*Cr*	*£*	*s*	*d*
	By Estate at Clapton for wages due to him and other				
	disbursments	*38*	21	11	4

	Anno 1688				
	Richard Godwin per Contra is	*Cr*	*£*	*s*	*d*
June 9	*By Cash recd. of him*	*141*	2		
1689 May	*By Estate at Clapton for his part of mooting & grubbing and 1d*				
	for weeding the new hedge	*151*		18	4½
			2	18	4½

	Bristoll 1689				
	Joseph Kippin per Contra	*Cr*	*£*	*s*	*d*
	By Acct. of Ballances, for Ballance resting due on his bond	*193 **	12	9	10

	Anno 1688				
	Joseph Speed per Contra	*Cr*	*£*	*s*	*d*
	By Proffit & Losse for the money per Contra lost by his death	*164*	22	12	9

	Anno 1682@				
	Sir George Strode [29]	Dr	£	s	d
	To Ballances	D		8	2
August 26	To sundry accts for 2 doz Xerie & 2 doz white Port with bottles	45 8	3	1	2
Sept. 6	To Cash pd. for Corkes, nutmeggs, Vinegar	42		9	8
	To Proffitt & loss pd. for 23 bottles of Red Port	8	1	2	8
Oct. 16	To sundry accts for 9 gallons of Xerie	8 42	2	16	
1683 June	To the Lady Ann Powlet for the cost of 2 doz bottles Xerie, bottles etc.	48	1	17	7
23	To French wine 1 hogshead etc. for 3 doz qts whitewine	57	1	18	
September 19	To Sundry accts for the cost & charge of 2 doz bottles Xerie sent him per Wilkins	39 9	1	15	
	To Proffitt & Loss for a Box of Tho. Walden, to send his gowne to London in	9			8
1684 August 20	To Sundry accts for the cost & charges of 4 doz white wine, & 4 doz Xerie per B Wilkins	78 79 73	6	6	6
1685 December 15	To Sundry accts for 1 doz bottles white wine & bottles, cords etc. sent to Lewston	105 97		12	4
February 24	To Sundry accts for 2 doz & 1 bottle Xerie sent him with bottles pannier cart to Lewston	103 105	2	1	8
	To Proffit & Losse for an error by omission of charging which at present I cannot find out	105		8	3
			22	17	8

	Anno 1682@				
	Elizabeth Dikes	Dr	£	s	d
	To Ballances	D		5	

	Anno 1681/2@				
	Edward Martindale [30]	Dr	£	s	d
	To Ballances	D		1	
March 22	To John Blackwell for one doz of Xerie	26	1		6
1683 Aprill 21	To Cash pd. the Towne Clark	41	1	1	6
January 7	To Cash paid him	67	20		
	To Proffit & Losse for money I left privatly with him when I went to London	105	103	5	9
			125	8	9

	Anno 1686				
	Sir George Strode Serieant at Law of Lewston in the County of Norfolk is	Dr	£	s	d
August 17	To sundry accts for severall things brought & sent him to Lewston per his order (viz)				
	To Proffit & Losse for a loafe double refined sugar weight 5¼ lb at 12d per pound	105 *		5	3
	To John Blackwell for 2 doz Xerie £1 16 3 doz white wine £1 10 00; with bottles panniers & Corkes	85	3	19	
	To Proffit & Losse for 1 qt Ollives & the Pott, & 1 doz Lemons sent at same time with sugar etc.	105		2	6
1687 June 1	To Sundry accts for 1 Pannier cont. 2 doz bottles white wine sent per Barnard Wilkins	133, 127	1	5	4
July 20	To Sundry accts for 2 Panniers cont. 4 doz Xerie with bottles etc. sent per Barnard Wilkns	137, 133	4	2	8
August 16	To Cash pd. Ed. Crofts for 12 Lemmons, & James Freeman for Capers 15d & 4s 1d	196		5	4
	To Sundry accts for 2 doz 4 bottles white wine, 12 Paniers, 2 doz 4 bottles, a sugar loafe, postage of a leter & portridge of a fardle to the waggon	133,136 137,196	1	14	7

	Anno 1682@				
	Per Contra	*Cr*	*£*	*s*	*d*
August 30	*By Cash recd. of him*	*42*	10		
1683 August 20	*By Cash recd. of him for the white wine per Contra*	*67*	1	18	
	By Ditto then recd. of him towards payment for 2 doz Xerie to bee sent him	*67*	2		
1684 December 3	*By Proffit & Losse for money received of him by my selfe in London*	*105*	6	6	6
1685 Aprill 30	*By Ditto received of him in London*	*105*	2	13	2
			22	17	8

	Anno 1688				
	Elizabeth Dikes per Contra	*Cr*	*£*	*s*	*d*
	By Profit & Loss for Ballance	*189 **		5	

	Anno 1681@				
	Per Contra	*Cr*	*£*	*s*	*d*
March 4	*By Cash recd. of him*	*40*	1		6
	By Rich. Franklin for the neat proceeds of 4 hhds Tobacco	*56*		10	5½
	By Ditto for the neate proceeds of 3 hhds neat	*56*		4	2
1683 March 24	*By Tobacco 2 hhds on the John for ½ theire neat proceeds*	*59*	3	13	7½
June 14	*By Cash recd. of him in part of a bill of exchange drawne on him*	*66*	10		
25	*By Cash recd. of him*	*66*	50		
July 4	*By Cash recd. of him*	*66*	40		
December 22	*By Cash recd. of him*	*67*	20		
			125	8	9

	Anno 1686				
	Sir George Strode is	*Cr*	*£*	*s*	*d*
August 16	*By Cash recd. of himselfe in Bristoll*	*119*	4	10	
1687 August 9	*By Cash recd. of himselfe in Bristoll*	*121*	7		
1688 August 6	*By Cash recd. of himselfe in Bristoll in full*	*141*	4	18	4
1689 August 13	*By Cash recd. of himselfe in Bristoll*	*168*	3	13	
September 17	*By Cash recd. of Bernard Wilkins*	*168*	1	13	
			21	14	4

1688 July 18	To sundry accts for 3 Panniers cont. 2 dozen of Xerie, 4 doz white wine with panniers Covers, bottles etc.	150 151,153	4	13	8
August 31	To Sundry accts for 2 doz of Xerie, 2 doz white wine, bottles & Panniers	160,169 164	3	11	
	To Tho. Goldney Junior for Fruit etc. sent him	176	1	13	
			21	14	4

(25) **Bristoll 1682@**

	Thomas Lutrell of Clevedon	Dr	£	s	d
	To Ballances for what Lent on Bond	D	10		
Aprill 11	To Cattle for a Colt sold him	5	4		
	To Proffit & Losse for the intrest of £10	89		13	
1690 June 26	To Cash pd. lent hm on his bill (for the Earl of Bristolls use) payable July 8th 1690	181	10		
			24	13	

Anno 1682@

	Edward Jones Tyler	Dr	£	s	d
	To Ballances for money Lent him on his noate	D	5		
1685 January 9	To Cash lent him on his bill when hee was under an arrest	107	2		
1687 August 6	To Ditto pd. him in part for work	121		10	
13	To Ditto paid him in full	121	1	3	
January 19	To Cash paid lent him on his bill when hee was under an arrest	140	1		
1688 August 11	To Cash paid him in part	141	1	5	
30	To Cash paid him in full	141	1	2	
			12		

Anno 1682@

	Adventure in the Martha & Sarah Thomas Whittop Master to Virginea	Dr	£	s	d
	To Ballances for ballance	D	19	10	6
May 27	To Cash pd. Thomas Hartwell for certifying	41		5	10
			19	16	4

Anno 1682@

	Tobacco sixe hhds in the Victory	Dr	£	s	d
	To Ballances	D	26	17	3
July 19	To Cash pd. weighing 4 hhds Tobacco	42		1	
	To Proffit & Losse for Ballance	164	11	1	7
			37	19	10

Anno 1682@

	William Ford [31]	Dr	£	s	d
	To Ballances for money Lent him on bond	D	10		

Anno 1682@

	Adventure in the Crowne of London	Dr	£	s	d
	To Ballances	D	53	1	4
	To Proffit & Losse for ballance	9	10		4
			63	1	8

Anno 1682

	John Cooke & Company (viz) Woolley & Keckwich intressed in one halfe (with mee) of 30 Butts of Xerie imported in equall halves twixt them & mee in the ship Olive tree Tho. Gammon Master as per their acct current closed September 30th 1682 appeareth	Dr	£	s	d
1683 November 2	To Cash paid John Bubb in full of John Cooks bill of exchange on mee in favour of said Bubb	67	109	18	6

Bristoll 1682@		Cr	£	s	d
	Per Contra				
Aprill 20	By Cash recd. of him	41	2		
May 6	By Ditto recd. of him	41	2		
1685 Aprill 30	By Cash received of Tho. Lutterell Junior in full	83	10	13	
1690 Oct. 11	By Cash recd. of Ditto	187 *	10		
			24	13	

Anno 1687	Cr	£	s	d
Edward Jones of Bristoll Tyler is				
By Proffit & Losse for work done at severall times	137	8	13	
By Proffit & Losse for work done more at severall times	104	3	7	
		12		

Anno 1688	Cr	£	s	d
Adventure in the Martha and Sarah per Contra				
By Proffit & Losse for the money per Contra being lost by the				
death of Tho. Gibbons to whom the goods were sent consigned	164	19	16	4

Anno 1682@		Cr	£	s	d
	Per Contra				
March 29	By Thomas Durbin for one hogshead sold him at 4d¹/₄ per lb	47	6	3	3
May 18	By Tho. Puxtone for one hogshead sold him at 4d per lb	22	6	10	4
July 19	By Ditto for 4 hhds sold him	22	25	6	3
			37	19	10

Anno 1688	Cr	£	s	d
William Ford per Contra is				
By Ballances for money resting due on his bond	193 *	10		

Anno 1682@	Cr	£	s	d
Per Contra				
By John Cooke & Company for the neate proceds of a parcell of				
Stockins sent him	32	63	1	8

Anno 1682	Cr	£	s	d
John Cooke & Company per Contra are				
By Xeries wine 30 Butts for theire ½ of theire neat proceeds	45	109	18	6

(26)	**Bristoll 1682@**		£	s	d
	James Holwey & Company	Dr			
	To Ballances for money Lent them on bond	D	103		

			£	s	d
	Anno 1684				
	William Smart of Bristoll Tyler and Painter [32] is	Dr			
October 6	To Cash paid him in part for painting my house at lower end Small Street	82	3		
November 8	To house at lower end of Small Street for money paid him and charg'd there by error	22	1	10	
March 7	To Cash paid him in full for painting my lower house within doors & without	82	4	7	6
1687 October 8	To Cash paid him for part painting my two Chambers, my back Chamber & forstreat chamber	139		10	
November 9	To Cash paid him in full for painting those 2 Chambers and in full of all demands	139	2		
			11	7	6

			£	s	d
	Anno 1682@				
	James Wallis [33] of Clapton	Dr			
	To Ballances for money Lent him on a dish & two Spoones Plate	D	2	3	1
Oct. 20	To Cash pd. port of a Letter	42			6
			2	3	6

			£	s	d
	Anno 1682@				
	Anne Blackwell	Dr			
	To Ballances	D		10	8

			£	s	d
	Anno 1682@				
	Henry Winter Esquire [34]	Dr			
	To Ballances	D	6		6

			£	s	d
	Anno 1682@				
	John Browne	Dr			
	To Ballances	D	5	8	

			£	s	d
	Anno 1682@				
	John Blackwell	Dr			
	To Ballances	D	49	11	4
Aprill 11	To Cash pd. lent him on his bond	41	100		
August 26	To Xeries wine 30 butts for 6 butts sold him	45	132		
Oct. 16	To Cash pd. him	42	25	2	
1683 March 30	To Xeries Wine 40 Butts for 9 Butts at £23 10s -d to pay ½ 25th July, & ½ 25th October	69	211	10	
Aprill 2	To Cash paid lent him on his bond	66	50		
May 31	To John Maine & Company for theire bill on him for 700 pieces of 8 the piece of 8 at 52½ the piece	69	153	2	6
	To French wine 1 hogshead & 1 Tierce for the Tierce Claret hee received back again	57	4		
Error	To Proffit & Losse for 9 weeks Cellerige of the great Cellar in Small Street at 4s 6d per week				
	To House at lower end of Small Street for 9 Weeks rent for the great Cellar at 4s 6d	22	2		6
			727	6	4

Bristoll 1682@

	Per Contra	Cr	£	s	d
	Per Contra	Cr	£	s	d
Aprill 8	By Cash recd. of them	41	3		
	By Walter Stephens for money due from him by composition				
	which hee undertook at 10s in the pound	53	50		
	By Profit & Loss for Balance	189 *	50		
			103		

Anno 1684

	William Smart per Contra Creditor	Cr	£	s	d
	By Proffit & Losse for money for painting per Contra	137	8	17	6
	By Proffit & Losse for money due for painting my two Chambers				
	etc.	164	2	10	
			11	7	6

Anno 1688

	James Wallis per Contra is	Cr	£	s	d
	By acct. of Ballances for Balance	193 *	2	3	7

Anno 1682@

	Per Contra	Cr	£	s	d
August 23	By Cash recd. of her	42	8	8	
	By Proffit & Losse for Ballance	164	2		
			10	8	

Anno 1688

	Henry Winter per Contra	Cr	£	s	d
	By Proffit & Losse for so much given him for my peace sake	164	6		6

Anno 1681/2@

	Per Contra	Cr	£	s	d
March 10	By John Wasbrough for money hee recd	28	5		
	By Proffit & Losse for so many shillings lost	153	8		

Anno 1681@

	Per Contra	Cr	£	s	d
Dec. 23	By Cash recd. of him	40	41	19	4
March 82 22	By Edw. Martindale for one doz Sack	24	1		6
29	By the Earle of Bristoll for 3 quarts of Xerie	37		5	4
Aprill 6	By Ditto for a rundlet qt. 12¼ gallons of Xerie	37	3	12	3
	By Ditto for a hogshead Xerie	37	16	4	6
May 11	By Ditto for 3 doz Clarrett & panniers	37	2	11	9
June 17	By Cash recd. of him	42	100		
Oct. 16	By Proffitt & Loss for wine of him 2 rundlets etc.	8	1	7	8
	By Cash recd. of him	42	25	2	
1683 June 5	By Cash recd. of him	66	120		
23	By French wine 1 hogshead & 1 Tierce for so much bought of him	57	10		
July 4	By Cash recd. of him	66	13	2	6
	By Cash recd. of Wm. Dawson by his order	66	20		
	By Proffit & Losse for 1 doz bottles Claret pints	9		3	6
23	By Cash recd. of him	66	62	18	
August 8	By Cash recd. of him	66	94		
September 25	By Cash recd. of him	67	105	15	

(27)	Bristoll 1682@				
	Humphry Little of Redland	Dr	£	s	d
	To Ballances	D		7	10

	Anno 1682@				
	Gold Deposited by Thomas Scrope	Dr	£	s	d
	To Ballances	D	53		

	Anno 1682@				
	Tobacco my ¼ part of 10 hhds in partnership with Edward Martindale & company	Dr	£	s	d
	To Ballances	D	13		5
Dec. 19	To Cash pd. weighing them	43		1	6
			13	1	11
	To Profit & Loss for Ballance	189 *	9	11	5
			22	13	4

	Anno 1682@				
	Adventure in the Comfort to Lixboa	Dr	£	s	d
	To Ballances	D	104	17	4

	Anno 1682@				
	Stephen Chapman	Dr	£	s	d
	To Ballances	D	4	18	7

	Anno 1681@				
	John Massinger	Dr	£	s	d
	To Ballances	D	10		
August 30	To Cash lent him	42	4	10	
1684 September 25	To Cash lent him on his bond	77	10		
1687 March	To Cash paid Francis Yeamans Atturny's fees for the shute of George Freeman	140		3	6
	To Ditto pd. John Pennington Serieant for Baile Fees	140		2	
1688 March 29	To Cash pd. lent him on 30 paire Bristoll hose deposited as per his noat [35]	140	3	5	
Aprill 7	To Ditto pd. lent him on 30 paire of Bristol hose	140	3	5	
12	To Ditto pd. lent him on 40 paire of hose omitted in Cashbook to bee charged that day	141	4	6	8
21	To Cash pd. lent him on 30 paire hose as per noat	141	3	5	
May 2	To Cash paid lent him on 40 paire hose as per his noat	141	4	6	8
10	To Cash paid lent him on 30 paire hose as per his noat	141	3	5	
17	To Cash paid lent him on 40 paire hose as per noat	141	4	6	8
25	To Cash paid lent him on 32 paire hose as per noat	141	3	9	4
June 1	To Cash pd. lent him on 30 paire hose as per noat	141 *	3	5	
12	To Cash pd. lent him on his noat on 30 paire hose at	141	3	5	
18	To Cash pd. lent him on 30 paire hose as per noat	141	3	5	
26	To Cash pd. lent him on 30 paire hose as per noat	141	3	5	
July 2	To Cash lent him on 33 paire hose as per noat	141	3	11	6
11	To Cash lent him on 30 paire hose as per noat	141	3	5	
			74	1	4

(28)	Bristoll 1682@				
	Thomas Sawer Hallier	Dr	£	s	d
	To Ballances	D	5	15	

			£	s	d
January	By Cash recd. of … Hulbert by his order	68	70		
	By balance of this Account, carried to his new Account in folio	59	39	4	
			727	6	4

Bristoll 1682@

		Cr	£	s	d
	Per Contra	Cr	£	s	d
Sept. 6	By Cash recd. of him	42		7	10

Anno 1690@

		Cr	£	s	d
	Gold per Contra	Cr	£	s	d
	By Tho. Scrope's Acct. current for the money per Contra	75	53		

Anno 1682@

		Cr	£	s	d
	Per Contra	Cr	£	s	d
Nov. 7	By William Davis for 3 hhds sold him at 4½ per lb	58	22	13	4

	Cr	£	s	d
Adventure in the Comfort to Lixboa is	Cr	£	s	d
By Richard Gay for the first cost & charges of a parcell of Shott sent consigned to him in the ship per Contra, of which there was never any acct. sent nor no returnes ever made before his faileing	39	104	17	4

Anno 1690

	Cr	£	s	d
Stephen Chapman per Contra	Cr	£	s	d
By Acct. of Ballances, for Ballance	193 *	4	18	7

Anno 1681@

		Cr	£	s	d
	Per Contra	Cr	£	s	d
Feb. 13	By Cash recd. of him	40	1		
25	By Ditto recd. of him	40	1		
March 1682 4	By Ditto recd. of him	40		10	
14	By Ditto recd. of him	40		10	
July 28	By Ditto recd. of him	42		10	
August 15	By Ditto recd. of him	42		10	
23	By Ditto recd. of him	42		10	
1684 Aprill 25	By Cash recd. of him in part of the £10 per Contra	68		10	
May 2	By Cash recd. of him in part of the £10 per Contra	68		10	
15	By Cash recd. of him in part of the £10 per Contra	77	1		
22	By Cash recd. of him in part	77		10	
September 28	By Cash recd. of him	77		10	
	By Cash received in full of his former obligation for ballance	77	7		
	By his new acct. current for the charges on George Freemans suite, and the severall summes paid lent him on the severall parcells of Stockins mentioned per Contra carried to that acct. of debt	155	59	11	4
			74	1	4

Bristoll 1690@

	Cr	£	s	d
Thomas Sawer per Contra	Cr	£	s	d
By Acct. of Ballances for rent due for Gastons at Redland	193 *	5	15	

Anno 1682@			
Adventure in the Francis & Marie	Dr	£	s	d
To Ballances	D	18	4	11

Anno 1681/2 @				
	John Wasbrow	Dr	£	s	d
March 1st	To Ballances	D	41	18	
10	To Cash pd him	40	15		
	To John Browne recd of him	26	5		
1683 September 25	To Xerie wines 30 Butts for 4 empty Butts & 52 Iron hoops	45	1	19	6
	To the house at lower end of Small Street for 33 weeks rent of the great Celler at 4s 6d per week	22	7	8	6
March	To Proffit & Losse for severall Cask and Iron hoopes received of mee at severall times as per particulars in Journal book fol (118)	73	17	5	
1684 29	To Cash paid his Widow in full balance of this and all other accts to this day as per her receit of 29th March 1684	68	8	8	9
			96	19	9

Anno 1682@				
	Thomas Scrope & Henry Gibbs	Dr	£	s	d
	To Ballances for £300 Lent them on bond with intrest being £28 10s ending 6th August	D	328	10	
	To Proffitt & Losse for intrest of £300 from 6th August 1682 to the 10th of March 1686 being 4½ yeares 1 month & 4 daies	127	82	10	
			411	0	0

Anno 1682@				
	William Hurtnell & John Heele Bouchers	Dr	£	s	d
	To Ballances	D	9	13	2
May 11	To Cattle for a Calfe sold him	5		16	
June 12	To Ditto for a Calfe	5		12	
Oct. 11	To Cattle for 2 Piggs sold him	5	2	16	
Dec. 22	To Ditto for one Pigg	5	1	2	
			14	19	2

Anno 1683				
	Robert Hauxworth of Bristol Grocer	Dr	£	s	d
June 5	To Oyle 2 Cask for acct. Christopher Williams for 1 Cask sould him	19	12	6	2
1685 Aprill 6	To Rice for acct. of Simon Clement & Company for 1 Bagge neat 3cwt 3qr 10lb at 23s per Cwt	96	4	9	6
July 27	To Ditto for 2 Baggs weight 3cwt 2qr 11lb & 3cwt 2qr 21lb is 7cwt 1qr 4lb Groce, 12lb neat 7cwt 0qr 16lb at 20s 6d per Cwt	96	7	7	
1687 July 19	To Reisons Solis 27 Barrills for 4 Barrills net 11cwt 0qr 21½ lb at 24s due Oct. 25th 1687	136	13	8	7¼
1689 January	To Reisons 60 Barrills & 120 ps for 8 Barrills & 16 piecess sould him at 40s & 30s per Cwt	177	60	2	6¾
			97	3	10

(29)	**Bristoll 1682@**				
	Adventure in the Blackmore to Virginea in Partnership with Ed. Martindale	Dr	£	s	d
	To Ballances	D	59	6	5

Anno 1682@				
	Adventure in the Nathanaell to Virginea	Dr	£	s	d
	To Ballances	D	21	11	2

Anno 1681@				
	Tobacco 5 hhds in the Francis & Marie to Virginea	Dr	£	s	d
	To Ballances	D	20	18	9
July 19	To Cash pd. weighing 4 hhds	42		1	
			20	19	9

		Cr	£	s	d
Anno 1690@					
	Adventure per Contra	Cr	£	s	d
	By Profit & Loss, for Ballance	189 *	18	4	9

		Cr	£	s	d
Anno 1682 @					
April 10	Per Contra	Cr	£	s	d
	By Wines 5 tonns for Cooperidge	48		10	9
1683 March 29	By Tobacco 18 hogsheads for acct Tho. Puxton for coopridge of them	63		12	
	By Proffit & Losse for Cooperidge and cash as per severall noates of his and his widowes Marie Wasbrow, this day evened betwixt us as per Journal booke fol 117 at large appeareth	73	95	17	
			96	19	9

		Cr	£	s	d
Anno 1686					
	Tho. Scrope & Henry Gibbs per Contra	Cr	£	s	d
March 10	By Tho. Scrope his particular acct. current, carried to his acct. of debt	75	411		

		Cr	£	s	d
Anno 1682@					
	Per Contra	Cr	£	s	d
	By Acct. of Ballances, for Ballance	193 *	14	19	2

		Cr	£	s	d
Anno 1683					
	Robert Hauxworth per Contra	Cr	£	s	d
August 6	By Cash recd. of him	66	12	6	2
1685 July 23	By Cash recd. of him	83	4	9	6
August 21	By Cash recd. of him	84	7	7	
1687 December 6	By Cash recd. of him	139	13	8	
1690 July 5	By Cash recd. of him	181	40		
	By his new Acct. for Balance	184	20	3	2
			97	13	10

		Cr	£	s	d
Bristoll 1690					
	Adventure per Contra	Cr	£	s	d
	By Profit & Loss for Ballance	189 *	59	6	5

		Cr	£	s	d
Anno 1690@					
	Per Contra	Cr	£	s	d
	By Profit & Loss for Ballance	189 *	21	11	2

		Cr	£	s	d
Anno 1681/2@					
	Per Contra	Cr	£	s	d
March 29	By Tho. Durbin for one hogshead sold him	47	5	15	9¾
July 19	By Thomas Puxtone for 3 hhds sold him	22	17	12	

	To Profit and Loss for Balance	189 *	9	18	10¾
			30	18	7¾

	Anno 1682@				
	John Romsey Townclark	Dr	£	s	d
	To Ballances	D	1	8	4
1682/3 March 20	To Cash Lent him on his noate	66	100		
1684 September 8	To Cash paid lent him on his noat	77	50		
			151	8	4

	Anno 1682@				
	William Woockey of Bridgewater	Dr	£	s	d
	To Ballances	D	1		

	Anno 1682@				
	Nathanaell Nappier	Dr	£	s	d
	To Ballances	D	9	16	10
1684 October	To Sundry accts for the cost & charges of 2 Panniers cont. 4 doz Xerie sent per his order by Robert White at 10s per dozen	73, 79	3	15	2
			13	12	

	Anno 1682@				
	Arthur Hobbs of Portbury at Gigly hill	Dr	£	s	d
	To ballances for one yeares rent due March 25 1681	D	2	9	6
1683 March 25	To Tenement in Portbury for one yeares rent ending 25th March 1682	20	2	10	
1684 March 26	To Ditto for 1 yeares rent ending 24th March 1683	20	2	10	
1685 March 26	To Ditto for 1 yeares rent ending 24th March 1684	20	2	10	
1686 March 26	To Ditto for 1 yeares rent due 24th March 1685	20	2	10	
September 30	To Ditto for ½ yeares rent due Sept. 29th 1686	20	1	5	
			13	14	6

(30)	**Bristoll 1682@**				
	Lawrence Washington of Virginea [37]	Dr	£	s	d
	To Ballances	D	8	1	5
1686 August 28	To Cash paid Port of 2 leters from Exeter	119		1	6
			8	2	11

	Anno 1681@				
	Abraham White of Clapton	Dr	£	s	d
	To Ballances	D		15	
Feb. 18	To Cash pd. him	40	1		
1682 Aprill 6	To Ditto pd. him	41	2	10	
14	To Ditto pd. him – Sam. Barthrams	41		5	4
May 18	To Ditto pd. him	41	2		
31	To Ditto pd. him	41		16	
August 17	To Cash pd. him	42	8	13	10
15	To John Ford for money hee recd. of said Ford	52		14	
Oct. 28	To Cash pd. his wife	43	1		
Nov. 18	To Cash pd. him	43	5	4	1
	To Ditto Lent him on his noat	43	1		
Dec. 28	To Ditto pd. his wife	43		10	
1683 Aprill 5	To Estate at Clapton for one yeares rent of the Orchard	38	1		
7	To Cash paid him	66	1		7

	By Tho. Durbin for one hogshead sold him	47	7	10	10
		30	18	7¾	

	Anno 1683@				
	John Rumsey per Contra is	Cr	£	s	d
1682/3 March 24	By Cash received of him	66	100	.	
	By Proffit & Losse for Ballance	73	1	8	4
December 10	By Cash recd. of Cousin Richard Yeamans [36] his servant	82	50		
			151	8	4

	Anno 1690@				
	Per Contra	Cr	£	s	d
	By Acct. of Ballances, for Ballance	193 *	1		

	Anno 1682@				
	Per Contra	Cr	£	s	d
Nov. 1	By Cash recd. of John Whetcombe	43	8	10	
Jan 29	By Ditto recd. of Ditto	43	1	7	
1684 Feb. 27	By Cash recd. of Robert White Fisherman	82	3	15	
			13	12	

	Anno 1684				
	Arthur Hobbs of Gigly hill in the parish of Portbury per Contra	Cr	£	s	d
March	By Proffit & Losse for his noat of Disbursments as per noat	73	2	15	
1685 August 12	By Cash receivd of James Beard for what hee left in his hands in payment of rent	84	1	10	
1686 September	By Estate at Gigly hill for his noat of disbursments added to the former which makes in the whole £5 12s 7d as per his noat, on which he hath given his receit £2 15s & £2 17s 7d	20	2	17	7
	By Proffit & Loss for money abated him by mistake in making up his account	105		3	11
	By ballance resting due for which I took his bill this 2ⁿᵈ day of October 1686 and carried to his acct. of debt	125	6	8	
			13	14	6

	Bristoll 1686				
	Lawrence Washington per Contra is	Cr	£	s	d
	By Proffit & Losse for money chargd to acct. of debt of his 26 hhds of Tobacco in the ship John part of the balance due to mee per Contra as may appeare in folio (101) of this book, in the acct. of sales of said Tobacco	127	3	15	
	By his new acct. current for the postage of the leters per Contra	132		1	6
			3	16	6
	By Profit & Loss for Ballance	189 *	4	6	5
			8	2	11

	Anno 1682@				
	Per Contra	Cr	£	s	d
August 15	By Estate at Clapton for money due to him as per his noate	38	14	13	10
	By Cash recd. of him .	42		15	
Nov. 18	By Estate at Clapton for money due to him and his wife	38	6	4	1
Aprill 6	By Ditto for money due to him, wife, & Daughter	38	6	11	11
			28	4	10

			26	8	10
To Profit and Loss for Ballance		189 *	1	16	
			28	4	10

Anno 1682@

			Dr	£	s	d
	William Spoore & Peter Collett		Dr	£	s	d
April 21	To Ballances Lent them on bond dated Aprill 21st 1682	D		50		
July 29	To Proffitt & Loss for one yeares intrest of £50 ending 21st Aprill last	8		3		
1683 May 10	To Proffit & Losse for 1 yeares intrest due 21st Aprill 1683	9		3		
1684 May 15	To Ditto for 1 yeares intrest due 21st Aprill 1684	73 *		3		
1685 May 13	To Ditto for 1 yeares intrest due 21st Aprill 1685	89 *		3		
1686 June 24	To Proffit & Losse for 1 yeares intrest due 21st Aprill 1686	105		3		
1687 July 19	To Cash pd. Wm. Spoore Senior back againe being the money £42 recd. per Contra	121		42		
1688 June	To Proffit & Losse for 2 yeares intrest of £50 ending Aprill 21st 1688	153		6		
1689 October	To Ditto for ½ yeares interest ending Oct 21st 1688	164		1	10	
	To Ditto for 1 yeares intrest ending Oct. 21st 1689	164		3		
1690 Oct.	To Ditto for 1 yeares intrest of £50 ending October 21st 1690	180		3		
				120	10	

Anno 1682@

			Dr	£	s	d
	The Chamber of Bristoll [38]		Dr	£	s	d
	To Ballances for money Lent on bond to bee on February next 1682	D		50		

Anno 1681@

			Dr	£	s	d
	Martha Smith Dayry maide [39]		Dr	£	s	d
	To Ballances	D		4		
Jan. 28	To Cash pd. her	40			10	
Aprill 8	To Ditto pd. her in full	41			18	4
				5	8	4

(31)   **Bristoll 1682@**

			Dr	£	s	d
	Desperate Debts Contracted by John Cooke in Spaine		Dr	£	s	d
	To Ballances	D		65	6	4

Anno 1682@

			Dr	£	s	d
	John Gore		Dr	£	s	d
	To Ballances	D		1	1	11
Sept. 21	To Cash Lent him on his noate	42		10		
Dec. 7	To Ditto Lent him on his bill	43		40		
1688	To Isaac Heming for money recd. of him on my bill in London	143		5		
				56	1	11
	To Acct. of Ballances for Ballance	189 *		4	15	10
				60	17	9

Anno 1682@

			Dr	£	s	d
	Joseph Drew Carpenter		Dr	£	s	d
	To Ballances [40]	D		274	16	11
Dec. 4	To Estate at Clapton for 107 lb Cheese	38		1	4	6
	To Cash pd. him in full	43		5		

Anno 1682@		Cr	£	s	d
	Per Contra	Cr	£	s	d
1683 July 29	By Cash recd. of them	42	3		
May 10	By Cash recd. of Wm. Spoore Senior for 1 yeares intrest ending Aprill 21st 1683	66	3		
1684 May 15	By Cash recd. of Wm. Spoore Senior for 1 yeares intrest ending Aprill 21st 1684	77	3		
1685 May 13	By Cash recd. of Wm. Spoore for 1 yeares intrest due Aprill 21st 1685	83	3		
1686 June 24	By Cash recd. of Wm. Spoore for 1 yeares intrest ending Aprill 21st 1686	108	3		
1687 July 14	By Cash recd. of Wm. Spoore Senior recd. of him	121	42		
19	By Cash recd. of Wm. Spoore Senior for intrest of £50 due 21st Aprill last	121	3		
1688 May 23	By Cash recd. of Wm. Spoore for 1 yeares intrest of £50 ending Aprill 21st 1688	141	3		
1689 October 31	By Cash recd. of Wm. Spoore for 1½ yeares intrest ending October 21st 1689	168	4	10	
			67	10	
	By Acct. of Ballances, for Ballance	193 *	53		
			120	10	

Anno 1682/3@		Cr	£	s	d
	Per Contra	Cr	£	s	d
March 13	By Cash recd. of Michael Pope	66	50		

Anno 1690@		Cr	£	s	d
	Martha Smith per Contra	Cr	£	s	d
	By Profit and Loss for her service	189 *	5	8	4

Bristoll 1682@		Cr	£	s	d
	Per Contra	Cr	£	s	d
Feb. 8	By John Cooke for money of Christoball [Ave?]	32	8	15	3
	By Profit and Loss for Ballance	189 *	56	11	1
			65	6	4

Anno 1682@		Cr	£	s	d
	Per Contra	Cr	£	s	d
Sept. 2	By Cash recd. of him	42	1	1	11
1683 March 17	By Ditto recd. of him	66	20		
July 26	By Cash recd. of him	66	20		
November 2	By Cash recd. of him	67	10		
1687 Aprill 6	By Proffit & Losse for 1¾ Bushells of Beanes at 3s 4d by agreement	127		5	10
1688	By Cash recd. of him for my bill per Contra on Isaac Heming	141	5		
1689	By horses 2 for a stack of Hay bought of him at Knoll at	156	4	10	
			60	17	9

Anno 1682@		Cr	£	s	d
	Per Contra	Cr	£	s	d
	By Proffitt & loss for money due to him	9	1	4	6
	By Estate at Clapton for money due to him in building the house there etc.	38	279	16	11

1686 August 5	To Cash paid lent him on his bond	*119*	4	
1688 May 3	To Cash paid lent him on his obligation	*141*	4	
		289	1	5

Anno 1682@

			£	s	d
	Adventure in the Phenix to Newingland	Dr	£	s	d
	To Ballances	D	34	11	3
	To Profit and Loss for Ballance	*189 **	3	6	9
			37	18	

Anno 1681@

			£	s	d
	Grace Keyes of Virginea	Dr	£	s	d
	To Ballance paid mending a Clock etc.	D		10	
Feb. 8	To Cash pd. John Harris for a box	*40*		1	
				11	
	To Profit and Loss for Ballance	*189 **		1	
				12	

Anno 1682@

			£	s	d
	Adventure in the Newingland merchant to Nevis	Dr	£	s	d
	To Ballances	D	29	17	11
	To Profit and Loss, for Ballance	*189 **		5	1
			30	3	

Anno 1681@

			£	s	d
	William Spoore Junior	Dr	£	s	d
	To Ballances for money Lent him on bond	D	21	4	
Jan. 26	To Cash lent him on his bond	*40*	20		
1683 March 31	To Proffit & Losse for intrest of £20 ending 20th January 1682	*9*		12	
	To Ditto for 1 yeares intrest of £20 from January 26 1681 to Jan. 26 1682	*9*	1	4	
	To Ditto for intrest of £40 from 26 January 1682 to 26 March 1683	*9*		8	
	To Proffit & Losse for 3 month intrest of £40 ending 26th June	*9*		12	
1684	To Estate at Clapton for a wayne Yoakes & Bowes sould him	*38*	3	10	
1685/6 Aprill 17	To Cash lent him on his bond	*108*	10		
1688 Feb.	To Proffit & Losse for 2½ yeares intrest of £10 ending October 16 1688	*153*	1	10	
	To my Coppiehold Tenement in Portburie for 1 yeares rent for my 2 acres and 2½ acres	*160*	3		
1689 Oct.	To Proffit & Loss for 1 yeares intrest of £10, ending Oct. 16 1689	*164*		12	
1689 Dec.	To Ditto for 2 month intrest of £10 from Oct. 17 1689 to Dec. 17 1689	*164*		2	
	To his new acct. current for ballance	*176*		7	
			63	1	

(32)   **Bristoll 1682@**

			£	s	d
	Martha Gay on Mortgage [41]	Dr	£	s	d
	To Ballances	D	327	8	
1686 July 22	To Isaac Heming for money paid lent her on her ob				
November 22	To Cash pd. Tho. Walden ½ of £10 lent her for which shee gave a bond in my name	*120 **	5		
			332	8	

		£	s	d				
1686	By his new acct. current for the first £4 per	£	s	d				
	Contra lent him	4	0	0				
	By Ditto for the 2nd £4 per Contra lent							
	him both carried to his new account of debt							
	in his acct. current	4	0	0	154	8		
						289	1	5

	Anno 1685				
	Adventure in the Phœnix to New England per Contra	Cr	£	s	d
August	By Edward Shippen of Boston in New England for the neat				
	proceeds of 4 pieces Broadcloth left with him per Wm. Loyd, as				
	per his acct. of Sales dated 14th of 6th month 1682	87	37	18	

	Anno 1683				
	Grace Keyes per Contra	Cr	£	s	d
July 31	By Cash recd. of Tho. Pope by her order	66		12	

	Anno 1683				
	Adventure in the New England merchant to Nevis	Cr	£	s	d
October 4	By Francis Rottenburie for a parcell of shooes sould him	63	2	10	
	By Edm. Scrope & Company for the neat proceeds of 14 Coyles				
	of Ropes as per acct. of Sales dated	33	27	13	
			30	3	

	Anno 1681@				
	Per Contra	Cr	£	s	d
Jan. 26	By Cash recd. of him	40		12	
1683 March 31	By Wm. Spoore Junior for money of him	66	2	8	
July 14	By Cash recd. of him	66	41		
1684 June 28	By Cash recd. of him	77	3	10	
1688 March	By my Copiehold Tenement in Porthurie for helme, Sparrs,				
	hedging, gipeing etc. per noate	160	4	1	
	By horses 2 for 1 Tonne of hay for my horses at Clapton	156	1	10	
	By his new acct. current for the £10 resting due on bond as per				
	Contra	176	10		
			63	1	

	Bristoll 1682@				
	Per Contra	Cr	£	s	d
March 29	By Cash recd. of Tom Edwards	41	327	8	
	By Acct. of Ballances, for the £5 per Contra lent her on bond	193 *	5		
			332	8	

	Anno 1681@				
	Martha Gay	Dr	£	s	d
	To Ballances	D	31	1	11
Feb. 25	To Cash Lent her	40	10		
1682 Aprill 18	To Ditto Lent her on her noate	41	3	11	4
20	To Ditto pd. her	41	70		
May 8	To Ditto Lent her	41	1		
	To Isaac Heming for money bee paid her on her bill not knowing				
1686 July 22	but that the £10 per contra might bee claymed by some other				
	person to whom shee had mortgaged her part of the ship	113	10		
			125	13	3

	Anno 1682@				
	Land at Clevedon	Dr	£	s	d
	To Ballances	D	220	11	10
Aprill 20	To Cash pd. Hugh Hodges for ½ a yeares Lords rent	41	16		
August 17	To Ditto pd. Chimney money	42	1		
Oct. 21	To Ditto pd. Tho. Luttrell for charges on the Yew	42	2	10	
1683 May 10	To Ditto pd. John Stretten for digging a ditch & Souldery money	66	1	11	9
31	To Cash paid — Burgis for Tythes	66	10		
1684 Aprill 19	To Ditto paid Tho. Smith for Drumms & colours	68	3	11	
August 4	To Henry Gibbs for severall disbursments as per particulars				
	brought from that acct.	4	10	14	11
	To Cash paid Tho. Luttrell which bee paid for cleareing the				
	Rhine etc.	77	1	9	
September 17	To Cash paid new Ditching of Insolds	77	3	4	
October 11	To Cash paid Robert Dowding & Company for 25 roape of				
	Dich more	82	16		
December 18	To Cash paid John Perrie for poore money £1 2s 9d & for				
	mending a Bridge 2s 6d	82	1	5	3
1685 May	To Cash paid John Stretton for his disbursments of Lords rent,				
	mending a [Gout?] etc.	83	1	14	6
	To Cash paid John Stretten for Souldiary money	83	9		
January 9	To John Stretton for his noat of disbursments for the poore,				
	Souldiery etc.	57	1	12	10
	To Richard Merrick for his noat of disbursments as may appeare	92	3	1	
			248	3	10

	Anno 1682@						
	John Cooke	R [42]	m	Dr	£	s	d
	To Ballances for 7934 Ryals	7934		D	210	15	6
Jan. 12	To Adventure in the Crowne from London for						
	the neat proceeds of one Trunck of Stockins	2275	17	25	63	1	8
	To Adventure in the Mauritania for the neat						
	proceeds of Stockins sent them	2815	12	60	74	15	4
Feb. 8	To Adventure on sundry ships to Cadiz for						
	the neat proceeds 12 scarlet searges	1566	11	64	41	11	11
	To acct. desperate debts for money bee						
	recovered as per his acct.	330		31	8	15	3
		15021	6		398	19	8

Anno 1682		Cr	£	s	d
Martha Gay per Contra is		Cr	£	s	d
By Proffit & Losse for the £5 upper summes of money per Contra		105	115	13	3
By owners of the ship Resolution for balance of theire acct.		3	10		
			125	13	3

Anno 1682@			Cr	£	s	d
	Per Contra		Cr	£	s	d
Oct. 31	By John Streaten for ½ a yeares rent of Insoles ending the 2nd August		57	6		
	By Cornelius Stretten for one yeares rent of an acre		62		15	
Feb. 8	By John Streaten for ½ a yeares rent of Insoles ending the 2nd Feb.		57	6		
1683 Aprill 5	By Cash recd. of — Gaynard for 1 yeares rent for the 5 acres Newlands tenement		66	3	14	6
February 21	By Cash recd. of Tho. Morgan for the Yeamoth of 9 acres		68	2	10	
26	By Ditto recd. of Wm. Perrie for the Yeamoth of 7 acres		68	1	13	6
	By John Stretten for ½ a yeares rent of Insolds due 2nd August 1683		57	6		
	By Ditto for ½ yeares rent due Feb. 2nd 1683		57	6		
1684 Feb. 27	By Cash recd. of John Thorne for 1 Reeke of Hay		82	4	10	
	By John Stretten for ½ a yeares rent of Insolds due Feb. 2nd 1684		57	6		
	By John Hartnell Junior for 1 yeares rent of Newlands Tenement ending March 1 1684		38	12		
1685 July	By Cash recd. of John Hartnell which hee received of — for a Reeke of Hay		83	6	5	
1686 Aprill 16	By Richard Merrick for 1 yeares rent for Newlands Tenement ending Feb. 1685		92	13		
	By John Stretten for ½ a yeares rent of Insolds] ending February 2 1685		57	6		
	By Ditto for ½ yeares rent due Sept. 29th 1685 & then omitted to bee charged here		57	6		
				86	8	
	By ballance carried to that acct.		116	181	15	10
				248	3	10

Anno 1682@		R	m	Cr	£	s	d
	Per Contra	R	m	Cr	£	s	d
	By Xeries wines 30 Butts for theire first cost	5242		45	139	4	11
	By Plate imported on sundry ships for the cost & charges of 600 ps. 8 recd. out of the Mexico merchant	5055	30	60	134	5	6
	By Ditto for the cost & charges of 247 pieces of 8 oute of the merchants goodwill at 51 per piece of 8	1975	33	60	52	9	9
Feb. 8	By Adventures on sundry ships to Cadiz for his commission on 500 pieces of 8	100		64	2	13	1
	By ballance carried to theire new acct. current piece of 8 at 51d	2647	11	32	70	6	5
		15021	6		398	19	8

Anno 1682@

		R	m	Dr	£	s	d
	John Cooke of St Marie Port in Spaine merchant			Dr	£	s	d
December 30	To ballance of his former acct. as per his acct. of this date brought from that acct.	2647	11	32	70	6	5
	To John Cooke, Woolley & Kekwich for balance, which they charge to mee in theire acct. dated January 26th 1683/4 the piece of 8 at 52d being the rate they drew it at per theire bill of exchange	981		69	26	11	4
		3628	11		96	17	9

Anno 1683

		R	m	Dr	£	s	d
	John Cooke of St Marie Port, now of London merchant			Dr	£	s	d
March 1684	To his acct. of Exchange sent him for ballance thereof			39	13	6	5
May 9	To Cash paid John Bubb in full of his bill on mee in favor of Henry Cornish			68	200		
	To Proffit & Losse for these errors in charging freight for Stockins in severall ships to Cadiz (viz)	R	m				
	on the Crowne overcharged for 12½ Ryals	12½					
	on the Mauritanea, stockins overcharged for 20 Ryals of plate 33	13					
	on the 2 Truncks cont. 194 doz in the Experiment overcharg'd	97					
	all making 15 Pcs of 8¼ at 52½d the piece of 8			73	3	6	8½
August 6	To Thomas Walden for his bill on James Lapley in John Cooks favor			2	100		
September 10	To Cash paid Humphrey Corseley for his bill on Alexander Rood Goldsmith in his favor			77	100		
19	To Isaac Heming for my bill on him in favor of John Cooke for ballance			76	22	5	6¾
					438	18	8¼

Anno 1684

		Dr	£	s	d
	John Cook per Contra is	Dr	£	s	d
Dec.	To Isaac Heming for money for the charges on the Baies per contra For which I valued my bill on him in favor of said Cook Oct. 4 1686	113	6	5	11

(33)   **Bristoll 1682@**

		Sugar lb	Dr	£	s	d
	Edmond Scrope & John Streater	Sugar lb	Dr	£	s	d
	To Ballances Sugar allwaies valued at 10s per Cwt [43]	24082	D	120	10	1
Jan. 12	To Adventure in the Olive branch from London to Nevis for the proceeds of 40 Caskes Flower & 3 pieces Brandy	27677	50	138	7	8
1683 June 14	To Adventure the 1st in the Owners Endeavour for the proceeds of 2 pieces Brandy and 4 Copper Taches as per acct. March 24 1682/3	22247	37	111	14	4
	To Adventure 2nd in the Diamond Ketch for the neat proceeds of 20 Firkins Butter, 20 boxes Candles, & 32 Kilderkin Flower as per same acct.	25750	21	128	15	
	To Hemmings my 1/3 49 barrils in the Owners Endeavour per acct.	2715	51	13	11	6
	To Adventure in the New England merchant for the proceeds of severall goods as per acct. dated	5530	31	27	13	

Anno 1682/3					
John Cooke per Contra is			Cr	£	s	d
January　By Xeries wine my 1/4 of 40 Butts in the Expectation in partnership with John Cooke for theire first cost & charges as per Invoyce Jan. 20th 1682/3	R	m			
	3628		58	96	7	4
By Proffit & Losse for an error of 11 Mervadees & the difference in the exchange on the 981 Ryals ballance		11	73		10	5
	3628	11		96	17	9

Anno 1683/4					
John Cooke per Contra is		Cr	£	s	d
!684　By Proffit & Losse for 3/4 parts of 54 Iron hoopes sould Marie Washrow at 4d½ per hoope, the whole £1 0s 3d the ¾ is	73 *		15	2¼
Aprill　By Xeries wine 40 Butts for 3/4 parts of theire neat proceeds	65	434	1	6
May　By Adventure in the Friston to Cadiz for carriage & Portage of a Trunck of Stockins as per his leter of 17th May 1684	64		14	10
By Ditto for Custom, freight, boathire & other charges as per his letter August 8th 1684	64	3	7	2
		438	18	8¼

Anno 1684					
John Cooke late of St Marie Port in Spaine, now of London merchant		Cr	£	s	d
October 8　By Adventure in the Andaluzia to Cadiz, for 2/3 of £9 8s 10d charges on 60 pieces Baies in partnership with him, as per his Invoyce of 13th Oct. 1684	86	6	5	11

Bristoll 1682@

Per Contra	Sugar lb	Cr	£	s	d
Jan. 2　By Sugar 4 Butts and one hogshead laden on the ship John and Elizabeth consign'd to Isaac Heming in London for theire cost as per Invoyce closed August 18th 1682 the Sugar now and allwaies valued at 10s per 100 lb	10341	60	51	14	5
By Sugar 2 Butts in the Delight for theire cost as per Invoyce Feb. 8 1681	14949	49	74	14	11
By Sugar 2 Butts & 1 hogshead in the Little Bristol for theire cost as per Invoyce Oct. 24th 1682	6158	60	30	15	9
1683 July 6　By Sugar 8 hhds in the Abra. & Isaac for theire cost & charges as per Invoyce March 24 1683	11439	46	57	4	
By Sugar 8 hhds in the New England merchant for theire cost per Invoyce May 5th 1683	12043	47	60	4	3½

	To *Adventure 1st in the Diamond Ketch for the neat proceeds of sundry goods in said ship & the Bonadventure as per acct. Nov. 1 1683*	37570	18	187	17	
	To *Adventure in the Sarah for the neat proceeds of sundry goods as per acct. of Sales closed Nov. 22nd 1683*	23579	49	117	18	
	To *Adventure 1st in the Brothers Goodwill for the neat proceeds of sundry goods as per acct. of Sales 1683*	21695	61	108	9	6
	To *Proffit & Losse for ballance of acct. of the neat proceeds formerly sent in the Isabella per Edm. Scrope as per acct. current 1683*	5458	73	27	5	7
1686 July	To *Adventure in the Owners Adventure for the neat proceeds of 40 boxes Candles & 1 hogshead Soape, as per theire acct. closed July7th 1686 sugar at 10s per 100 lbs*	21923	80	109	12	4
	To *Adventure 3rd in the Dyamond Ketch to Nevis for the neat proceeds of 2 pieces Brandy, & 20 (part of 30) boxes Candles, per acct. Sales of same date*	20029	57	100	2	5
	To *Adventure 2nd in the Brothers Goodwill for neat proceeds of 40 Cask flower, and 3 pieces Brandy, as per theire acct. closed July 7th 1686 in Nevis*	24119	65	120	11	4
October	To *Adventure in the Swallow for ½ 12153 Sugar the neat proceeds of 1240 bottles Syder, which were 2209 bottles sent in 12 hhds but 969 lost as per theire acct. closed July 31 1686 in Nevis sugar at 10s per 100*	6077	97	30	7	8
1687 May	To *Adventure 3rd in the Dyamond Ketch to Nevis for 3252 lbs Sugar the neat proceeds of 10 boxes Candles formerly omitted as per acct. Sales March 10th 1686*	3252	57	15	5	2
	To *Adventure in the Nevis merchant from Boston for 7096 lbs Sugar the neat proceeds of a parcell goods sent them per Ed. Shipppen as per acct. Sales March 10th 1686*	7096	126	35	9	4½
1688 Aprill	To *Adventure in the Joseph for the neat proceeds of a parcell goods sent in the Joseph as per theire acct. of Sales from Nevis in March 1688*	17203	98	77	4	11
		296202		1470	14	10½

	Anno 168 @				
	Adventure in the Crowne Lyon to Barbadoes	Dr	£	s	d
	To *Ballances*	D	11	15	3
	To *Profit and Loss for Ballance*	189 *	5	4	1
			16	19	1

	Anno 1681@				
	Sir Jahzeel Speed [44]	Dr	£	s	d
	To *Ballances Incognito*	D	408	10	2
Dec. 20	To *Cash pd. him*	40		10	
			409		2

	Anno 1682@				
	John Bubb And Abraham Edwards	Dr	£	s	d
	To *Ballances*	D	1	5	5

Date	Description			£	s	d
September 13	By Sugar 12 Tierces & 1 hogshead in the Dyamond Ketch for theire cost as per Invoyce July 28 1683	13231	47	66	3	
February 1684	By Sugar 2 Butts & 4 hhds in the Elizabeth & Marie to Lond. per Invoyce Nov. 29th 1683	11176	33	55	17	7
Aprill	By Sugar 2 Butts & 4 hhds in the New England merchant to Bristoll per Invoyce Feb. 13th 1683	10992	75	54	19	2
	By Sugar 2 Butts & 4 hhds in the Owners Endeavor as per Invoyce Aprill 10th 1684	10664	76	53	6	5
August 6	By Sugar 2 Butts & 8 hhds in the Dyamond Ketch John Bennet Master to London per Invoyce Aug. 6 84	18070	64	90	7	
October 6	By Sugar 1 Butt & 15 hhds in the William & Ann Capt. Combes per Invoyce Oct. 6th 1684	24624	85	123	2	5
1685 June	By Sugar 8 Butts & 4 hhds in the Rainbow Thomas Moore Master as per Invoyce March18th 1684/5	26084	99	130	8	4
	By Sugar 5 Butts &9 hhds in the Baltamoore John Browne as per Invoyce Aprill 1685	26373	99	131	17	4
November 2	By Sugar 3 Butts & 13 hhds in the Friendship of Lond. as per Invoyce Sept. 5 1685 sugar at 10s	27201	104	136		1
1687 Sept. 5	By Sugar 8 hhds in the Martha & Sarah for their cost as per Invoyce June 4th 1687 at 10s	11199	138	55	19	7½
		234544		1172	14	4
	By Account of Ballances, for Ballance	61658	193 *	298		6½
		296202		1470	14	10½

Anno 1682@					
	Per Contra		Cr	£	s	d
Nov. 20	By Edward Parsons for the neate proceeds of 10 Firkins butter	58	16	19	4

Anno 1682@					
	Per Contra		Cr	£	s	d
	By Proffitt & Loss pd. for Ballance	8	409		2

Anno 1681@					
	Per Contra		Cr	£	s	d
Jan. 4	By Cash recd. of them	40	1	5	5

			Dr	£	s	d
	Anno 1684					
	Sugar 2 Butts & 4 hhds imported to London from Nevis laden		Dr	£	s	d
	per Edm. Scrope & co. in the ship Elizabeth & Marie					
	consign'd to Isaac Heming					
January	*To Edm. Scrope & Company for theire first cost as per Invoyce*					
	Nov. 29th 1683		33	55	17	7
	To Profit and Loss for Ballance		189 *	4	14	10

(34)
Bristoll 1681@

		paire	s	d	Dr	£	s	d
	Worstead Stockins				Dr	£	s	d
	To Ballances				D	90	3	5
Dec. 17	*To Cash paid John Massinger for*	127	3	3	40	20	12	9
23	*To Ditto pd. John Bradey*	43	3	0½	40	6	10	9
24	*To Ditto pd. John Massinger*	42	3	3	40	6	16	6
31	*To Ditto pd. Dittto*	38	3	2	40	6		2
Jan. 7	*To Ditto paid John Masssinger in part*	27			40	2		
18	*To Cash pd. Ditto in full*				40	2	5	6
23	*To Ditto pd. Ditto for 3 paire*	3			40		9	6
Feb. 4	*To Ditto pd. Ditto for*	38	3	2	40	6		4
13	*To Ditto pd. Ditto for*	52	3	2	40	8	4	8
20	*To Cash pd. ditto for*	16			40	2	10	8
25	*To Ditto pd. Ditto for*	30	3	1	40	4	12	6
March 4	*To Ditto pd. Ditto for*	25			40	3	18	1
	To Ditto pd. Francis Rottenbury for hot pressing 103 paire				40		2	2
14	*To Ditto pd. John Massinger*	32	5		40	5		
18	*To Ditto pd. Ditto for*	23	3	1½	41	3	11	10
Aprill 3	*To Ditto pd. Ditto for*	23			41	3	11	10
6	*To Ditto pd. Ditto for*	45			41	7		7
	To Ditto pd. John Bradey for	43	3	½	41	6	10	9
	To Ditto pd. John Massinger for	33	3	1½	41	5	3	1½
23	*To Ditto pd. Ditto for*	24			41	3	15	
May 3	*To Ditto pd. Ditto for*	38			41	5	18	9
	To Ditto pd. John Bradey for	21	3	½	41	3	3	10
16	*To Ditto pd. John Massinger for*	35	3	1½	41	5	9	4
20	*To Cash pd. Thomas Dyer for*	8			41	1	1	4
24	*To Ditto pd. John Massinger for*	36			41	5	12	6
27	*To Ditto pd. John Bradey for*	28	3	½	41	4	5	2
June 3	*To Ditto pd. John Massinger for*	32			41	5		
10	*To Ditto pd. Ditto for*	32			41	5		
17	*To Ditto pd. John Bradey for*	11			41 45	1	13	6
23	*To Ditto pd. John Massinger for*	32	3	1½	41	5		
24	*To Ditto pd. Joseph White for*	60	3	1	41	9	5	
27	*To Ditto pd. John Massinger for*	40	3	1½	42	6	5	
	To Ditto pd. Ditto for	61			42	9	10	7
	To Ditto pd. Tho. Moreman for Carriadge of one truncke stockins				42		13	6
July 15	*To Ditto pd. Francis Rottenbury for hot pressing 171 paire*				42		3	6
28	*To Ditto pd. John Massinger for*	28			42	4	6	4
August 14	*To Ditto pd. Ditto for*	28	3	1	42	4	6	4
23	*To Ditto pd. Ditto for*	33			42	5	1	9
						276	16	6

			Dr	£	s	d
	Anno 1682@					
	Edward Gorges Esquire		Dr	£	s	d
	To Ballances for money Lent him on 50 broad Pieces of Gold		D	63	13	
1683 March 31	*To Proffit & Losse for £60 intrest from August 2 1682 to*					
	2nd Aprill 1683		9	2	7	
1684 August 2	*To Ditto for 2 yeares intrest of £60 ending the 2nd of August*					
	1684		73 *	7	4	
1686 October 28	*To Ditto for all intrest due to the 2nd of August 1686 by*					
	agreement		127	4	16	6

Anno 1684		Cr	£	s	d
	Sugar 2 Butts & 4 hhds per Contra are	Cr	£	s	d
September	By Isaac Heming for 1 / 3 £181 17s 2d the neat proceeds of 6 Butts & 12 hhds Sugar of which hee gives one acct. of Sales, so do charge this by estimate	90	60	12	5

Bristoll 1681@		Cr	£	s	d
	Per Contra	Cr	£	s	d
Dec. 31	By Cash recd. of John Massinger for 4 paire ⁴⁶	40		10	
Jan. 23	By Ditto recd. of Ditto for 4 paire	40		10	
Feb. 4	By Ditto recd. of Ditto for 4 paire	40		10	
	By themselves for ballance	54	275	6	6
			276	16	6

Anno 1683		Cr	£	s	d
	Edward Gorges per Contra is	Cr	£	s	d
Aprill 4	By Cash recd. of him	66	6		
1684 Sept. 19	By Cash recd. of him	82	4	4	
December 1	By Cash recd. of him & then returned to him the 50 broad pieces Gold	120	67	16	6
			78		6
	By Acct. of Ballances, for Ballance	193 *		12	6
			78	13	

1688 August 3	To Sundry accts for 6 bottles white wine & 6 of claret and 1 dozen bottles	*151,153*		12	6
			78	13	

	Anno 1682@				
	Maximillian Gallop	*Dr*	*£*	*s*	*d*
	To Ballances	*D*	20		4
July 22	To Alexander Dolman for money pd. Edward Young on hs bill	48	14		
	To George Pley for my bill in his Favor	44	4	7	
27	To Cash pd. him	42	41	10	5
Oct. 16	To John Sandford for what abated for want of measure	19		10	2
26	To Cash pd. him	43		18	
Jan. 31	To Xeries wine for 4 doz. bottles	59	3	4	
	To Proffitt & Loss for panniers etc.	9		2	
June 5	To Robert Yate for money paid him by said Yate per my order	39	16	13	6
			101	5	5

	Anno 1683				
	Adventure in the Cadiz merchant — Master from London to Cadiz	*Dr*	*£*	*s*	*d*
October	To Sundry accts for the cost & charges of one Trunck cont. 56 doz Bristoll and 35 doz Wells hose laden in said ship & consign'd in my sonne Hemings name to Arthur Robinson & Company merchants in St Marie Port for sales & returnes	*71,35*	162	17	2

(35)	**Bristoll 1681@**				
	Linincloth for acct. of Joseph Cardrow	*Dr*	*£*	*s*	*d*
	To Ballances	*D*		3	
Jan. 31	To Cash pd. Filing a certificate	40			4
	To John Read and John Hollister for what wanting in measure	44	1	9	8
	To Proffitt & Loss for commission etc.	8	4	14	¼
	To Joseph Cardrow his acct. current for its neat proceeds	7	196		2¾
			202	7	3

	Anno 1682@				
	Adventure on the Maidenhead To Virginea	*Dr*	*£*	*s*	*d*
	To Ballances	*D*		2	

	Anno 1682				
	Robert Richardson of London on St Marie hill there Scrivener is	*Dr*	*£*	*s*	*d*
June 17	To Isaac Heming for money lent him on a mortgage on houses & land in Branford [47] at £5 per Cent	76	150		
1686 June	To Proffit & Losse for 4 yeares intrest of £150 from June 1682 to June 1686 at 5 percent	*127 **	30		
1687	To Ditto for ½ yeares intrest due Dec. 16th 1686	127	3	15	
August	To Ditto for ½ yeares intrest due June 16th 1687	137	3	15	

	Anno 1681@				
	Linincloth for account of Henry Simes	*Dr*	*£*	*s*	*d*
	To Ballances	*D*			4
	To Sundry accts for my Commisssion & money abated	*8, 45*	1	18	9
	To Henry Simes for theire neat proceeds	5	85	8	5
			87	7	6

Anno 1682@		Cr	£	s	d
	Per Contra				
Aprill	By Linincloth 18 bolts for theire neate proceeds	6	81	5	9
1683 Aprill 27	By Lincloth 5 Bolts for theire neate proceeds	69	19	19	6
	By Proffit & Losse for Ballance	9			2
			101	5	5

Anno 1684	Cr	£	s	d
Adventure in the Cadiz merchant per Contra is				
By Adventure in the Civilia merchant for the cost & charges of the Trunck of hose per contra carried to that acct. because Arthur Robinson & Company gave theire acct. of the Sales of both Truncks in one acct.	44	162	17	2

Bristoll 1681@		Cr	£	s	d
	Per Contra				
Jan. 14	By Sundry accts for 22 Ballatts sold them at 1 Solls off the cost	44	202	7	3
			202	7	3

Anno 1690@		Cr	£	s	d
	Per Contra Creditor				
	By Profit and Loss for Ballance	189 *		2	

Anno 1682		Cr	£	s	d
	Robert Richardson on mortgage per Contra is				
December	By Isaac Heming for money recd. for ½ a yeares intrest due Dec. 1682	76	3	15	
1683 June	By Ditto for ½ a yeares intrest due June16 1683	76 *	3	15	
December	By Ditto for ½ a yeares intrest due December 1683	76 *	3	15	
1684 June	By Ditto for ½ a yeares intrest due June16 1684	90	3	15	
December	By Ditto for ½ a yeares intrest due December 1684	90	3	15	
1685 Dec.	By Isaac Heming for 1 yeares intrest due Dec. 1685	113	7	10	
1686	By Ditto for 1 yeares intrest hee received of him due Dec. 16th 1686	130	7	10	
1687 August	By Ditto recd. of him in full	130	153	15	

Anno 1681@		Cr	£	s	d
	Per Contra				
Jan. 14	By John Bubb for 12 Bolts sold him at 1 Solls off	45	87	7	6

	Anno 1683			£	s	d	Dr	£	s	d
	Sugar 2 hhds laden by Edward Parsons in the ship Crowne Lyon from Barbadoes for acct. of Martha Speed in part returnes of goods sent by her in the ship Martha & Sarah						Dr	£	s	d
July 19	To Cash paid custom fees & bills at cost			1	11	9	66			
25	To Cash paid Charles Plomer for freight and averidge			2	9	3	66			
September 28	To Cash paid weighing them					6	67	4	1	6
	To Edward Parsons for theire first cost						58	18	4	4
	To Profit and Loss, for Ballance						189 *	2	15	4½
								25	1	2½

	Anno 1681@	Dr	£	s	d
	Isaac Heming of London merchant	Dr	£	s	d
	To Ballances	D	489	8	
Dec. 29	To Edward Young for my bill in his Favor	2	100		
31	To Cash pd. Rich. Corsley on his bill	40	100		
Jan. 7	To Edward Young for my bill	2	100		
	To Cash pd. Rich. Corsley	40	150		
9	To Ditto pd. Humphry Corsley	40	150		
12	To Cash pd. Rob. Yate	40	150		
March 22	To sundry accts for severall bills in his Favor	38, 47,16	300		
1682 Aprill 1	To Cash pd. James Freeman for his bill	41	50		
6	To Ditto pd. Henry Gibbs on his bill	41	100		
10	To Phi. Higginbottom on his bill	17	170		
18	To John Hurtnell recd. of him	38	58	4	9
	To Cash pd. John Hurtnell on his bill	41	100		
May 18	To Edward Borroughes for a bill of Exchange	49	167		4
July 8	To Cash pd. Thomas Walden for his bill	42	200		
13	To Ditto pd. Will. Cheldry for his bill	42	5		
12	To Proffitt & Loss pd. on a bill his Favor	8	200		
18	To Richard Corsley for my bill of Exchange.	53	100		
	To Cash pd. sundryes for my bills	42	200		
27	To Ditto pd. John Wilmoore	42	100		
Sept. 24	To Cash pd. him	42	2		
	To Ginger for my propper acct. for the neat proceeds of 58 baggs	17	36	12	10
Oct. 11	To Cash pd. Thomas Taylor on his bill	42	150		
12	To Ditto pd. Rich. Francklin	42	49	1	6
19	To Ditto pd. Ditto on his bill	42	1	19	9
	To Richard Francklin for the neat proceeds of a parcel of Tobacco	56	3	2	2
Nov. 4	To Cash pd. John Barnard	43	1		
	To John Hurtnell for money of his hee received in London	38	5		
1683 Aprill 10	To Cash paid John Bubb for his bill in his favor	66	100		
18	To Cash paid Tho. Gammon by his order	66	1	3	
May 3	To Wm. Davis for money recd. on his bill on Ralph Swinton	58	26	10	
July 4	To Cash paid George Irish for protesting a bill of Andrew Stuckeys on Rich. Champny	66	5		
6	To Tho. Scrope for money on his bill on Hugh Horton	47	80		
	To John Wilmer for money recd. last yeare of him in London	62	60		
October 1	To Cash paid Wm. Cox for protesting Jos. Bacons Virginea bill on Sam. Corsgaine	67	5		
16	To Cash paid Wm. Rogers for which hee valued his bill on Edward Haistwell [48]	67	63		
November	To John Williamson for his bill on Richard Atkinson	72	45	17	
March 15	To Cash paid John Gandy recd. of John Budget for said Gandies acct.	68	40		
1684 May	To John Wilmer recd. of him	62	40		
			3695	9	4

	Anno 1683				
	Sugar 2 hhds per Contra are	*Cr*	*£*	*s*	*d*
September 25	By Wm. Swift for the 2 hhds weight neat 20cwt 3qr 15lb at 24s				
	per Cwt money	61	25	1	2½

	Anno 1681@				
	Per Contra	*Cr*	*£*	*s*	*d*
Jan. 14	By Edward Roy for my bill	44	30		
28	By Cash recd. of Tho. Pope £9 12s 2d & Phil. Higginbottom				
	£5	40	14	12	2
Feb. 4	By Ditto recd. of Francis Hawkins	40	2	3	
March 21	By Ditto recd. of Ditto	40	13	10	5
1682 Aprill 11	By Phillip Higginbottome for money recd. of him in part of a bill	17	3		
18	By Andrew Kirbie pd. Ben. Skinner on his bill	48	70	10	11
May 2	By Cash recd. of Robert Yate	41	100		
12	By Ditto recd. of John Browne	41	40		
27	By Adventure in the Olive branch for 40 Caske Flower 3				
	p[iece]s Brandy	50	75	14	5
June 17	By Marcellia Soape pd. Henry Gibbs bill	51	100		
24	By Cash recd. of George Tyte	41	5	1	
27	By Ditto recd. of Rich. Millard & Hugh Tynte	42	56		
July 1	By Ditto recd. of Alexander Dolman	42	100		
Nov. 8	By Ditto recd. of John Blackwell on my bill	43	80		
10	By Ditto recd. of Thomas Day on my bill	43	50		
Dec. 19	By Ditto recd. of Jos. Jackson	43	53	15	4
22	By Ditto recd. of John Blackwell	43	100		
Jan. 8	By Ditto recd. of Will. Redwood	43	19		
Feb. 8	By Ditto recd. of Tho. Day on my bill	43	22	15	
10	By Ditto recd. of John Blackwell on my bill	43	100		
1683 Aprill 10	By Cash recd. of Wm. Rogers on his bill	66	79	14	7
May 10	By Cash recd. of Sam. Sandford for his bill hee recd. in London	66	10		
July 17	By Adventure in the Civilia merchant for charges on a Trunck of				
	stockins	44	4	12	8
	By Tho. Martin paid him for 30 Cask flower	62	28	6	
August 20	By Cash recd. of Sir George Strode for which I valued my bill on				
	him	67	20		
September 22	By Cash recd. of Elizabeth Tayler for which I valued my bill on				
	him	67	18		
	By Adventure in the Cadiz merchant to Cadiz for charges on a				
	Trunck hose sent in her	34	3	19	2
October 8	By Cash recd. of Samuel Spencer blacksmith on a bill of				
	Exchange assign	67	18	4	
January	By Adventure in the Brothers Goodwill to Nevis for which hee				
	paid for 40 Cask Floure & 3 pieces Brandy	65	80	11	10
	By Cash received of Edward Grace of Winchester for which I				
	valued my bill	68	200		
February 27	By Cash recd. of John Hudson for my bill in favor of Col. Cheek	68	45		
1684	By Tho. Williams for money hee paid said Williams by bill				
	Exc.a in London	57	37	4	7
Aprill	By John Cook & Company for what hee paid John Cook on				
	theire bill of Exchange on mee	69	10	19	10
	By Andrew Stuckey for money towards payment of a bill of				
	exchange of said Stuckey	53	8	14	3

(36)	**Bristoll 1682@**				
	Tobacco 60 hhds on the Maryland merchant from Virginea	Dr	£	s	d
	To Ballances	D	364	17	7
July 19	To Cash pd. weighing 41 hhds	42		12	6
			365	10	1
	To Profit and Loss for Ballance	189 *	29	18	
			395	8	1

	Anno 1682@				
	Linincloth for acct. of Beniamin Gold	Dr	£	s	d
	To Ballances	D			4

	Anno 1681/2@				
	John Vincent	Dr	£	s	d
	To Ballances	D		1	

	Anno 1681@				
	Allyn Smith	Dr	£	s	d
	To Ballances	D	57	11	

	Anno 1682@				
	Anthony Bush	Dr	£	s	d
	To Ballances	D		7	6

	Anno 1681@				
	Tobacco 12 hhds for acct. of Malachy Peale	Dr	£	s	d
	To Ballances	D	33	8	11
Jan. 17	To Cash pd. Customary Freight & Avaridge	40	22	12	3
Feb. 4	To Ditto pd. weighing them	40		3	
	To Rich. Crump for 97lb Tobacco allowed for damage	45	1	10	9
	To Proffit and Losse for what charg'd short in the Customs	9	3	11	3
	To Ditto for halling to Cellar 6				
	To Ditto for coopridge 10				
	To Ditto for celleridge 1 4 6	9	2		6
	To Ditto for Commission at £3 per cent	9	2	2	11
	To Malachy Peale his acct. current for its neat proceeds	36	6	3	2
			71	12	9

	Anno 1681@				
	Copper for my propper acct.	Dr	£	s	d
	To Ballances	D	105	5	
August 14	To Cash pd. weighing 26 bottomes	42			6
	To Proffit & Losse for ballance	9	4	7	11
			109	13	5

	Anno 1683@				
	Malachy Peale per Contra is	Dr	£	s	d
April 18	To Cash paid Richard Gotley by his order in his leter of May				
	17th 1681	66	6	3	2

		£	s	d
By Andrew Kirby Father & Sone for 3 bills of exchange paid John Bawden & Company, who assigned them said bills for mee payable in Bourdeauxe which money should have beene charged to this acct. of Credit in Nov. 1683	64	448	9	9
By Proffit & Losse paid Tho. Martin for a Kilderkin of Flouer	73	1		
		2050	18	11
By his new acct. current carried to that acct. for ballance	76	1644	10	5
		3695	9	4

Bristoll 1682@

	Per Contra	Cr	£	s	d
March 29	By Tho. Durbin for 9 hhds sold him at 4d¼ per lb	47	63	8	11
July 19	By Thomas Puxtone for 41 hhds sold him weight neat 14896 at 4d¼ per lb	22	263	15	8
	By Tho. Durbin for 10 hhds sold him	47	68	3	6
			395	8	1

Anno 1682@

	Per Contra	Cr	£	s	d
	By itselfe carried to a new acct.	17			4

Anno 1681/2@

	Per Contra	Cr	£	s	d
March 14	By Cash recd. of him	40		1	

Anno 1681@

	Per Contra	Cr	£	s	d
Feb. 27	By Cash recd. of him	40	57	11	

Anno 1690@

		Cr	£	s	d
	Anthony Bush per Contra	189 *		7	6
	By Profit and Loss for Ballance				

Anno 1681@

	Per Contra	Cr	£	s	d
Feb. 4	By Rich. Crump for the 12 hhds per Contra sould him at 3d¾ per lb	45	71	12	9
			71	12	9

Anno 1681@

	Per Contra	Cr	£	s	d
Jan. 4	By Oliver Mosely for 24 bottomes weight 3cwt 3qr 18lb	4	26	4	
82 May 3	By Ditto for 23 bottomes weight 3cwt 3qr 6lb at £6 14s per Cwt	4	25	9	8
18	By Joseph Badger for 25 weight 4cwt 0qr 27lb at £6 14s per Cwt	50	28		4
August 14	By Oliver Mosely for 26 bottomes weight 4cwt 1qr 25lb at £6 14s	4	29	19	5
			109	13	5

Anno 1682@

		Cr	£	s	d
	Malachy Peale of Potomak river in Virginea merchant				
	By Tobacco 12 hhds imported in the ship Francis & Marie and consigned to mee for Sales and returnes for his acct.	36	6	3	2

(37)	**Bristoll 1681/2@**				
	Land at Redland	Dr	£	s	d
	To Ballances	D		19	5
Feb. 8	To Cash pd. Tho. Hopkins for ½ a yeares poore money	40		9	6
March 25	To Ditto pd. for drums & Colors	41		1	7
			1	10	6
	To Profit and Loss, for ballance	189 *	448	9	6
			450		

	Anno 1682@				
	Adventure in the Fellowship to Cadiz	Dr	£	s	d
	To Ballances	D	97	19	8

	Anno 1681@				
	Salt for acct. Speed & Company	Dr	£	s	d
	To Ballances	D	85	1	8
	To Profit and Loss, for Ballance	189 *	8		
			93	1	8

	Anno 1681@				
	Adventure in the Owners endeavour to Nevis	Dr	£	s	d
	To Ballances	D	107	6	11
Dec. 12	To Cash pd. Custome etc. of said goods	40		10	4
1683 September 11	To Michael Perrie for freight of 6 C Coolers in the Owners Endeavour to Jamaica	47		12	
	To Cash paid custom fees etc. on 17 Coppers returned, & a hogshead Sugar	82	4	13	
			113	2	3
	To Profit and Loss, for ballance	189 *	1	6	6
			114	8	9

	Anno 1681@				
	John Barwick	Dr	£	s	d
	To Ballances	D	8		

	Anno 1682@				
	Robert Scrope & Thomas Young	Dr	£	s	d
	To Ballances	D	89	14	10
	To Voyage in the Isabella to Jamaica for the first cost of sundry merchandizes laden in her consign'd them in the yeare 1676 of which no acct., but the goods received				

	Anno 1681/2@				
	John Digbie Earle of Bristoll	Dr	£	s	d
	To Ballances	D	3	19	4
March 22	To Sundry accts for 2 doz of Xerie & packing	3,8	2	1	8
29	To John Blackwell for 3 quarts of Xerie	26		5	4
Aprill 6	To Ditto for a rundlet of 12¼ gallons Xerie	26	3	12	3
	To Proffitt & loss pd. portridge etc.	8			8
May 11	To Sundry accts for a hogshead of Xerie	26,8	16	5	10
June 17	To Sundry acco.ts for 3 doz Clarrett	26,8	2	13	5
Sept. 3	To Proffitt & loss for 2 doz White Port	8	1	3	7
	To Ditto for 65 gallons Xerie in a hogshead	8	17	12	8
25	To Ditto for one rundlet Xerie qr 12 gallons & ¼	8	3	5	
Feb. 14	To sundry acco.ts for 10 doz bottles Xerie with Charges	39,37,9	8	15	
1683 July 24	To Sundry accts for 2 doz bottles Xerie sent per hors carrier	39,9	1	15	

Bristoll 1682@		*Cr*	*£*	*s*	*d*
	Per Contra				
March 30	By Cash recd. of Tom. Edwards	41	450		

Anno 1682@		*Cr*	*£*	*s*	*d*
	Per Contra				
July 18	By Richard Corsley for 411 pieces of 8 the neat proceeds of				
	one Trunck Stockins consigned to said Pim [49] Commander of				
	said ship	53	91	2	6
	By Profit and Loss, for Ballance	189 *	6	17	2
			97	19	8

Anno 1681@		*Cr*	*£*	*s*	*d*
	Per Contra				
Feb. 4	By Tho. Puxtone for 1 Tonne Salt	22	2	10	
Oct. 11	By Ditto for 38 tonnes sold him	22	90	11	8
			93	1	8

Anno 1683		*Cr*	*£*	*s*	*d*
	Adventure in the Owners Endeavour per Contra				
June 14	By Edmond Scrope & Company for the neat proceeds of 2 pieces				
	Brandy and 4 Taches as per acct. of Sales March 24th 1682/3	33	111	14	4
1684	By Cash for money of Humphry Corsley for 77 Reals & 2½				
	pieces of 8 sent per Tho. Mosse from Jamaica per Henry Dighton				
	for ballance of acct. of 1 Tache sould by him	82	2	14	5
			114	8	9

Anno 1681@		*Cr*	*£*	*s*	*d*
	Per Contra				
Jan. 18	By Cash recd. of him	40	4		
Aprill 1st	By Ditto recd. of him	41	4		
			8		

Anno 1683		*Cr*	*£*	*s*	*d*
	Robert Scrope per Contra is				
July	By Sugar 15 hogshead for the cost of 10 hogshead laden in the				
	Owners Endeavour per Invoice Aprill 12 1683	70	85	18	8
	By Acct. of Ballances, for Ballance	193 *	3	16	2
			89	14	10

Anno 1682@		*Cr*	*£*	*s*	*d*
	Per Contra				
Sept. 7	By Cash recd. of Thomas Luttrell	42	20		
Oct. 21	By Ditto recd. of Ditto	42	9	6	
26	By Ditto recd. of John Shuttleworth	42	18	18	6
	By Ditto recd. of Ditto	42	3	5	
1683 May 24	By Cash recd. of Tho. Lutterell Senior by his order	66	8	15	
1684 October 22	By Cash recd. of Edward Pryor his Bailiffe	82	30	15	6
1685 July 14	By Isaac Hemming for money hee recd. of Wm. Webb	90	5	13	
October 14	By Cash recd. of Hugh Hodges at Clevedon	84	23	18	
			120	11	4

August 8	To Sundry accts for 3 doz bottles Xerie sent per horse carrier	9,39	2	12	2
September 6	To Sundry accts for the cost & charges of 2 Cask cont. 84 5/8 Gall. Xerie at 5d & the 2 Cask	39,9	21	11	1
1684 July 16	To Sundry accts for 4 Panniers cont. 4 doz white & 4 doz claret sent per Bar.d Wilkins	73, 78	4	17	4
October 23	To Sundry accts for the cost & charges of 1 hogshead & 1 Quarter Cask of Xerie sent per Ed. Briar	79, 73	23	18	10
1685 June 26	To John Olliffe & Proffit & Losse for the cost of 6 doz Xerie sent to London per Waggen	89, 98	5	13	4
	To Proffit & Losse for former errors I cannot find out	127		8	10
			120	11	4

(38) **Bristoll 1681/2@**

			£	s	d
	Edmond Scrope of Nevis	Dr			
	To Ballances	D	47	2	4
Jan. 26	To Cash pd. Joseph Jackson for the First cost of 6 butts of wine imported on the ship Olive Tree	40	52	2	9
	To Ditto pd. Jahzeel Speed	41	7	3	9
	To Robert Whittle & Company for money formerly received of them omitted to bee charg'd	19	7	19	2
	To Thomas Taylor for money formerly recd. of him for 1/4 rent omitted to bee charg'd	4	6	10	
1684 May	To Linincloth 9 Bolts for acct. of Henry Symes for them sould him at 2s 6d off	56	32	10	1
27	To Cash paid for a permitt to ship 9 bolts Canvas in the Wm. & Ann to Nevis	77		3	8
	To Cash paid lent him for which hee gave his bill per Contra	77	50		
	To Proffit & Losse for ½ the cost of a parcell of goods formerly laden in the George to Virginea omitted to bee charg'd as per acct. given him, owned this 25th Feb. 1685	105	21	9	
			225	0	9

Anno 1681/2 @

			£	s	d
	John Hartnell Junior of Bristoll Marchant	Dr			
	To Ballances	D	118	4	9
Aprill 3	To Cash pd. lent him	41	40		
Sept. 29	To Ditto Lent him on his noate	42	12		
Jan. 8	To Xerie wine one butt for 6 quarts of wine	59		7	6
	To Cattle for 2 Breves and a Cow hee sould	5	13	16	8
	To Estate at Clapton for keeping 3 oxen 24 daies	38		17	
1683 March 24	To Cash paid him	66	9	6	7
September 11	To Cash paid lent him on his bill	67	20		
			214	11	6

Anno 1684/5

			£	s	d
	John Hartnell Junior	Dr			
	To John Gore and Co. for the remainer of his ½ of one yeares rent of Clapton as per acct.	56	19		
	To Land in Clevedon for 1 yeares rent for Newlands Tenement ending the 1st March 1684	32	12		
			31		

Bristoll 1684

	Edmond Scrope per Contra is	Cr	£	s	d
May 19th	By Proffit & Losse for the cost of the 6 Butts of Xerie per Contra charged there per error	73	52	2	9
	By Giles Gough for money paid for Candles as per the said Gough's receit May 9th 1684	65	10	13	
June	By Cash recd. of John Bubb for his bill on Tho. Elliot	77	50		
March 7	By Cash recd. of him	82	50		
	By Proffit & Losse for ½ £1 17s 5d being 1/3 of the neat proceeds of 13 hhds Tobacco in the Stephen, received of David Philips and was omitted to bee charged to his acct. of Credit in folio (216) of the Leadger booke No D as may appeare in folio (160) of the same book	105 *		18	8½
	By Adventure in the Dyamond Ketch for money hee paid custom etc. on Brandy & other Goods	57	2	11	
	By Proffit and Losse paid charges on Sugar in the Comfort	105		2	8
	By Ditto paid Ben. Moseley for a hogshead & packing a hogshead Soape	105		5	6
	By Jahzeel Speed for money paid said Speed which hee debited my Cash for	69	7	3	9
1685 February 25	By Cash received of himselfe	107	5		9
			178	18	1½
	By Acct. of Ballances, for Ballance	193 *	46	2	7½
			225		9

Anno 1681/2@

	Per Contra	Cr	£	s	d
March 22	By Isaac Heming recd. of him in London of said Hurtnell	35	100		
1682 Aprill 18	By Ditto more recd. of Ditto	35	58	4	9
1683 March 24	By Proffit & Losse for 37 Bushels Mault & 4½ bushels mault dust	9	6	10	3
	By Cattle for 2 Oxen & 4 Steeres	5	24	17	6
	By Isaac Heming for money hee received on his bill	35	5		
	By Cash recd. of him in full	68	20		
			214	11	6

Anno 1685

	John Hartnell per Contra is	Cr	£	s	d
November 10	By Cash received of him in part	107	10		
January 27	By Cash recd. of him at his house in Temple streat	107	1		
March 4	By Cash received of him in part	108	5		
June 1686	By Cash received of him Aprill 17th and then omitted to bee charg'd	108	5		
July	By Proffit & Losse for Mault as per noat	105	7	3	5
	By Ditto for Locks & other charges at Clevedon	105		3	10
Sept. 10	By Cash received of himself	119	1	15	
	By Proffit & Losse for money freely abated him	127		17	9
			31		

	Anno 1681/2@	Dr	£	s	d
	Estate at Clapton	Dr			
	To Ballances	D	1102	5	9
Jan. 7	To Cash pd. for a replevan	40		2	8
Feb. 14	To Ditto pd. sundry charges as per booke folio (88)	40	1	2	10
March 1682 25	To Ditto pd. Henry Winter for 2 yeares Lords rent end the 25th March 1682@	41	3	4	
Aprill 27	To Ditto paid Edward Willis for shooing the horses	41	4	18	1
May 11	To Ditto pd. Ditto for drums & Colors	41		10	8
25	To Ditto pd. one yeares poore money	41	1	1	4
June 24	To Ditto pd. Henry Winter for Lordsrent ending the 24th instant	41		8	
	To Ditto for a yeares Chimney money	41		6	
July 13	To Ditto pd. Abra. White	42	2		
August 15	To Abraham White for money due to him	30	14	13	10
	To Cash pd. the mowers	42	8	4	6
30	To Ditto pd. Ed. Autell	42	5		
Sept. 9	To Ditto pd. the mowers	42		12	8
22	To Cash pd. Henry Winter for ½ yeares Lords rent	42		16	
Oct. 11	To Ditto pd. Sundry Charges as per booke of Petty disbursments	42	3	4	6
12	To Ditto pd. for soldiering money	42		12	
30	To Ditto pd. for Lords rent	43		16	
Nov. 18	To Abra. White for money due to him & his Daughter	30	6	4	
25	To Cash pd. John Bullock for Hospitall money	43		7	
Dec. 13	To Ditto pd. ½ Chimney money yeare	43		6	
Jan. 6	To Ditto pd. Edw. Willis in full of his noate	43	1	5	
20	To Ditto pd. Sundry charges on said Estate	43	1	11	11
	To Cornelius Stretton for Covering of mares	62		8	
	To Jos. Drew for money due to him for building the house	31	279	16	6
March 1683 27	To Cash paid charges on a lawsuite with Henry Wynter	66	11	14	7
Aprill 5	To Cash paid Ed. Willis for one yeares poore money	66	1	18	6
	To Abraham White for his service	30	6	11	11
9	To Cash paid Samuel Bartram for charges on a law suite	66	3	15	
14	To Cash paid Henry Winter in full of all demands to this day	66	15		
July 6	To Cash paid Sundry charges on said Farme	66		13	
February 25	To Cash paid Ozziel Browne for drawing writings with James Bird	68		6	6
March 3	To Cash paid ½ a yeares Chimney money ending the 29th Sept. 1683	68		6	
1684 Aprill 3	To Cash paid John Cullimer for keeping the Tylers work in repaire for 3 yeares ending 25th of Dec. 1683	68		15	
	To Ditto paid said Culimer for whiteliming the house	68		3	9
	To Cash paid Esquire Henry Wynter in lieu of a Tierce of claret	77	4		
	To Marie Thring & Company for 5 yeares intrest of £150 from Nov. 29th 1681 to Nov. 29th 1686	7	45		
	To Richard Godwin for wages etc. omitted to be charged in the yeare of 1682	23	21	11	4
			1551	12	10

Anno 1682@		Cr	£	s	d
	Per Contra				
Aprill 27	By Cash recd. of Edward Willis for 2 yeares rent of Northmead	41	4		
May 11	By Ditto recd. of Martha Smith etc. 30th Aprill	41	22	18	9
25	By Cash recd. of Abell Adames for a Calfe	41		12	
Dec. 4	By Joseph Drew for 107 lb Cheese	31	1	4	6
	By John Hurtnell for keeping 3 oxen	38		17	
1683 Aprill 6	By Abra. White for one yeares rent of the Orchard	30	1		
July	By Cash recd. of Severalls for Butter & cheese sould in the market	66	24	18	10
October 13	By Cash recd. of Joane Daracot for for 1 hogshead sould at Clapton	67		3	
	By Estate at Clapton for the yeare 1674 for the money pd. Ozziell Browne per Contra for making the Lease twixt James Beard & mee charg'd there by error	72		6	6
	Bt Wm. Spoore Junior for a wayne Yoakes & Bows sould him	31	3	10	
	By John Gore & John Hurtnell Junior for 1 yeares rent for the farme	56	70		
	By Ballance carried to the acct. of Estate at Clapton old Farme and newly purchased of Edward Gorges & Company	151	1422	2	3
			1551	12	10

(39)	**Bristoll 1683**			Dr	£	s	d
	John Cook of St Marie Port in Spaine his acct. of Exchange	R	m				
May 19	To Cash paid Henry Gibbes on his bill at 53d per piece of 8	154		66	4	5	¼
22	To Ditto paid Ditto on his bill drawne on Richd. Vickris by him refusd	422		66	11	12	11¾
31	To Ditto paid Sir Richard Crump on his bill at 53d per piece of 8	1097		66	30	5	7½
July 4	To Cash paid George Irish for protesting 2 bills on Thomas Scrope			66		10	
17	To Cash paid his Exchange drawne in favor of Alderman Wm. Crab			66	41	5	4¼
	To Proffit & Losse for Port of leters about these bills			73		3	
					88	2	

	Anno 1683		Dr	£	s	d
	John Olliffe of Bristol Vintner is		Dr	£	s	d
January 3	To Xerie wine 40 Butts for 4 Butts sould him at £20 to pay 3rd of July next		65	80		
				80		

	Anno 16		Dr	£	s	d
	Richard Gay factor resident in the Kingdom of Portingall. late failed		Dr	£	s	d
	To Adventure in the ship Comfort to Lixboa for a parcell of shott sent consigned to him in Lixboa in the yeare 1679 of which no acct. nor any returnes ever made		27	104	17	4

	Anno 1683		Dr	£	s	d
	Robert Yate per Contra is		Dr	£	s	d
August 27	To Cash paid him		67	16	13	6
	To Henry Bainham for 1 yeares intrest of £276 hee received in trust for mee due 5th Aprill 1683		48	16	11	2
1686 October	To Proffit & Losse for 39 weeks cellridge for my Vault at lower end Small streat		127	5	17	

	Anno 1683					Dr	£	s	d
	Xeries Wine 12 Butts laden per Jno.Cook & Company in the ship Rochell Wm. Stephens Master from Cadiz		£	s	d	Dr	£	s	d
July 6	To Cash paid Custom, Fees, & Wharfage		35	16	6				
	To Cash paid Freight and averidge to John Blackwell		28	6					
	To Cash paid for a sheet of Cork				6	66	64	3	
	To Cash paid Joseph Berrie for Brokridge			5	6	68		5	6
	To John Cook & Company for theire first cost 4741 Ryals the piece of 8 at 52d as per theire acct. March 30th 1683					69	128	8	
	To Tho. Day for his noat for what he did about said wine					70	7	15	
							200	11	6
	To Profit and Loss, for Ballance					189 *	2	17	3½
							203	8	9½

	Bristoll 1683				
	John Cook his acct. of Exchange per Contra is	Cr	£	s	d
July	*By Tho. Scrope for money of him on his bill March 31st 1683*	47	20	5	
	By Ditto for money on one other bill of the same date	47	54	10	7
	By ballance carried to his particular acct. current	32	13	6	5
			88	2	

	Anno 1684				
	John Olliffe per Contra is	Cr	£	s	d
September 25	*By Cash recd. of him by my Sonne Jahzeel*	77	75	8	
	By Jahzeel Speed for ballance Scored in for wine	69	4	12	
			80		

	Anno 1684				
	Richard Gay late resident in Lixboa but failed is	Cr	£	s	d
July 9	*By Cash recd. of Charles Jones Junior for composition money at*				
	10d in the pound, with some months intrest paid by said Jones,				
	by agreement with my sonne Jahzeel for the time hee kept the				
	money in hand	77	53	5	
	By Acct. of Ballances, for Ballance	193 *	5	12	4
			104	17	4

	Anno 1683				
	Robert Yate of Bristoll merchant is	Cr	£	s	d
June 5	*By Maximelian Gallop for money paid said Gallop by my desire*	34	16	13	6
1684	*By Cash recd. of him*	68		11	6
Aprill	*By Tho. Curtis for his bill on Samuel House in Reading assign'd*				
	to said Curtis	58	16		
Dec.	*By Cash recd. of him by the hands of Wm. Mosely in November*				
	last	120	5	17	

	Anno 1683				
	Xeries Wine 12 Butts per Contra	Cr	£	s	d
July 24	*By John Earle of Bristoll for 2 doz bottles*	37	1	10	
August 8	*By Ditto for 3 doz bottles Xerie*	37	2	5	
15	*By Lady Ann Pawlet for 7 dozen qt bottles Xerie*	48	5	5	
September 6	*By John Earle of Bristoll for 2 Cask cont. 84 5/8 Gallon at 5s*	37	21	3	1½
11	*By Proffit & Losse for 20 bottles for Hugh Hodges*	9	1	5	
19	*By Sir George Strode for 2 doz bottles Xerie*	24	1	10	
	By Samuell Astry for 1 Cask cont. 66 Gallon at 5s	49	16	10	
25	*By Samuell Davis for 3 doz at 5s*	63	2	5	
October 4	*By John Bradway for 5 Butts at £24 the Butt 6 months*	70	120		
	By the Lady Susan Powlet for 6 doz bottles Xerie at 15s the				
	doz.	61	4	10	
November 8	*By Joseph Berrie for a hogshead of Lees*	62	1	4	10
	By Cash recd. of James Crofts for returnes on corrupt wines	67	7	10	10
January	*By Wm. Whitwood for 1 Butt and 3 Cask of eager Wine*	70	6	10	
31	*By Proffit & Losse for part of a Tierce*	73	4		
March 17	*By Beniamin Smith for 2 Butts of corrupt wine sould him*	50	8		
			203	8	9½

(40)	Bristoll 1681@				
	Cash	Dr	£	s	d
	To Ballances [50]	D	3090	1	10
Dec. 23	To John Blackwell recd. of him	26	41	19	4
	To John Brady recd. of him	20	2		
	To Jeremiah Holwey recd. of him	18	3	7	6
29	To Elizabeth Sheward	18	3		
31	To Worsted Stockins recd. of John Massinger	34		10	
	To Arthur Jones recd. of him	21	3		
	To Robert Sommers recd. of him	17	50		
Jan. 4	To John Bubb & Company recd. of them	33	1	4	11
18	To John Barwick recd. of him	37	4		
23	To Worstead Stockins recd. of John Massinger	34		10	
25	To John Read recd. of him	44	60		
26	To Will. Spoore recd. of him	31		12	
27	To Wines 30 Butts in the Olive tree recd. of James Crofts	45	18	3	6
28	To Isaac Heming recd. of severalls	35	14	12	2
30	To John Read recd. of him	44	6	9	6
Feb. 2nd	To John Bubb recd. of him	45	80		
4	To John Hollister recd. of him	44	40		
	To Worstead Stockins recd. of John Massinger	34		10	
	To Isaac Heming recd. of Francis Hawkins	35	2	3	
8	To Proffitt & Loss recd. of John Harris	8		10	
13	To John Massinger recd. of him	27	1		
16	To Oliver Mosely recd. of him	4		14	10
	To James Freeman recd. of Thomas Colstone	21	20		
27	To John Massinger recd. of him	27	1		
	To Allyn Smith recd. of him	36	57	11	
March 4	To John Massinger recd. of him	27		10	
	To Edward Martindale recd. of him	24	1		6
7	To Jane Flower recd. of her	18	16	10	
	To Cattele recd. of John Hurtnell	5	11	10	
14	To John Massinger recd. of him	27		10	
	To John Bubb recd. of him	45	7		
15	To John Vincent recd. of him	36		1	
	To John Sandford recd. of him	19	8	15	10
	To James Freeman recd. of him	21	75	15	6
	To Isaac Heming recd. of Francis Hawkins	35	13	10	5
			3638	2	10

	Bristoll 1681@				
	Per Contra	Cr	£	s	d
Dec. 12	By Nath. Haggatt pd. Rob. Tyler	19	2		
	By Worstead Stockins pd. Severalls	34	27	3	6
	By Proffitt & Loss pd. Houshold expences & master	8	13	19	10
	By Adventure in the Owners Endeavor pd. Custome etc.	37		10	4
20	By Ed. Young pd. him	2	100		
	By Jahzeell Speed	33		10	
22	By Linnincloth 6 Roles Ed. Roy pd. sundry charges	5			10
24	By Sundry accts pd. John Massinger	34,8	7	6	
30	By Proffitt & Loss pd. Edw. Perrin	8		5	8
30	By David Roynon pd. him	3	1	16	
31	By Rich. Corsley pd. him	31	6	11	6
	By Isaac Heming pd. Rich. Corsely	35	100		
	By Worstead Stockins pd. John Massinger	34	6		4
	By Rich. Godwin pd. him	23	1	10	
Jan. 4	By Rich. Marsh pd. him	1	45	8	10
7	By Edward Young pd. him	2	100		
	By John Linckorne	44	400		
	By Estate at Clapton pd. Repleven	38		2	8
	By Henry Simes pd. Abr. Edwards	5		4	
	By Isaac Heming pd. Humphrey Corsley	35	300		
	By Worstead Stockins pd. John Massinger	34	2		
	By Ralph Oliffe pd. him	3	12	6	6
10	By Henry Gibbs lent him	4	100		
	By Proffitt & Loss pd. severalls [51]	8	1209	5	8
12	By Isaac Heming pd. Robert Yate	35	150		
	By Edward Young pd. him	2	100		
17	By Tobacco 12 hhds pd. Freight etc.	36	22	12	3
18	By Worstead Stockins pd. John Massinger for 30 paire	34	2	15	
21	By Tho. Puxtone pd. Humphrey Corsley	22	7	2	6
24	By Nich. Barnard pd. him	6	22	2	
	By Proffitt & Loss pd. Walter Paine	8		15	
26	By Will. Spoore pd. lent him	31	20		
	By Xeries wines 30 butts pd. Customs etc.	45	97	5	4
	By Edmond Scrope pd. Jos. Jackson	38	52	2	9
27	By Martha Speed pd. her	46	1		
28	By Martha Smith pd. her	30		10	
30	By Joseph Cardrow pd. him	7	66	9	6
31	By Rich. Godwin pd. him	29	1		
	By sundry accts pd. F[il]ing certificates	7,35			8
Feb. 4	By Tobacco 12 hhds pd. weighing them	37		3	
	By Stockins pd. John Massinger	34	6		4
8	By Land at Readland pd. poore money	37		9	6
	By Grace Keyes pd. Jos. Harris	31		1	
	By Sundry accts pd. Jos. Harris	17,8	3	3	
9	By Xeries wines pd. Tho. Gammon	45	60	18	6
	By Benj. Gould pd. Edward Macey	5	10		
	By Martha Speed pd. her	46	1		
	By Proffitt & Loss pd. sundryes	8	11	1	6
13	By Worstead Stockins pd. John Massinger	34	8	4	8
	By Rich. Godwin pd. James Biggs	23		6	
	By Proffitt & Loss pd. severalls	8	8	2	9
17	By Ditto pd. sundry persons	8	2	1	6
18	By Abr. White pd. him	30	1		
21	By Worstead Stockins pd. John Massinger	34	7	3	2
	By Ben. Gould pd. Rich. Chadwell	5	6		
23	By Ed. Tayler pd. him	1	1	14	
	By Phill. Higginbottome pd. the Porters	17			4

(41)   ***Bristoll 1682@***

	Cash	Dr	£	s	d
	To itselfe for ballance	40	453	12	11
March 30	To sundry accompts recd. of Tom. Edwards	32, 37	777	8	
Aprill 1st	To John Barwick recd. of him	37	4		
6	To John Bradey recd. of him	20	6		
8	To James Holwey recd. of him	26	3		
	To Sundry accts recd. of Nath. Haggatt	8, 18	42	14	
11	To Phill. Higginbottom recd. of him	17	53	17	8
	To Proffitt & loss recd. of Nath. Haggatt	8	73	5	
20	To Thomas Lutrell recd. of him	25	2		
	To John Hollister recd. of him	44	40		
27	To Estate at Clapton recd. of Ed. Willis	38	4		
May 2nd	To Isaac Heming red of Robert Yate	35	100		
6	To Thomas Lutrell recd. of him	25	2		
12	To Thomas Taylor recd. of him	4	10		
	To Estate at Clapton recd. of Martha Smith	38	22	18	9
	To Isaac Heming reiid of John Browne	35	40		
18	To Linincloth Ben. Gould recd. of John Machen	17	5	3	
23	To Thomas Goldney recd. of him	16	12	6	9
25	To Cattle recd. of Abell Adams	5		12	
	To Proffitt & loss recd. of Rob. Yate	8	100		
27	To Edward Willis recd. of him	20	2		
31	To John Bradey recd. of him	49		18	
June 2	To Anth. Wood & co. recd. of them	49	50		
12	To John Hollister recd. of him	44	30		
	To Proffitt & Losse recd. of Yate	8	100		
15	To Jane Flower recd. of her	18	16	10	
26	To Isaac Heming recd. of George Tyte	35	5	1	
	To John Hollister recd. of him	44	5	9	5
			1962	16	6

25	By Martha Gay lent her	32	10		
27	By John. Purnell pd. him	2		14	
	By Proffitt & Loss pd. Allyn Smith	8		4	9
28	By Martha Write Lent her	7	5		
March 1st	By John Washrow pd. him	28	15		
	By merchandizes Mar. Sarah pd. permitt	46		2	2
2	By Henry Simes pd. Tho. Scroope	5	21		
	By Jos. Cardrow pd. Nath. Powell	7	1	11	
4	By Wors. Stockins pd. Jos. Massinger	34	3	18	1
7	By Jane Flower pd. her	18	4		
	By Stockins pd. Fran. Rottenbury	34		2	2
10	By Proffitt & Loss pd. my selfe	8	1		
14	By Phillip Higginbottome pd. Hotpressing	17	1	9	
	By Stockins pd. John Massinger	34	5		
	By Proffitt & Loss pd. Houshold expences	8	4	6	6
	By Estate at Clapton pd. sundry persons	38	1	2	10
17	By Stockins pd. John Bradey	34	1	13	6
	By itselfe for ballance	41	453	12	11
			3638	2	10

Bristoll 1681/2 @

	Per Contra	Cr	£	s	d
March 15	By Tho. Tayer pd. him	2	1	5	6
	By Jos. Cardrew pd. Simon Hurle	7	40		
	By Christopher Williams pd. James Freeman	7	5		
18	By Marie Thring pd. her	7	1	10	
	By Stockins pd. John Massinger	34	5		
25	By Land at Redland pd. Tho. Hopkins	37		1	7
	By Estate at Clapton pd. Henry Winter	38	3	4	
Aprill 3	By Isaac Heming pd. James Freeman	35	50		
	By John Hurtnell lent him	38	40		
	By 4 bolts of cloth for Tho. Williams pd. Filing a certificate	47			4
	By Worstead stockins pd. John Massinger for 23 paire	34	3	11	10
6	By sundry accts pd. Henry Gibbs	35, 8	100	5	
	By stockins pd. severalls	34	13	11	5
	By Abraham White pd. him	30	2	10	
7	By Proffit & Loss pd. sundryes	8	1	8	4
	By Phillip Higginbottome pd. his wife	17	5		
	By Martha Smith pd. her	30		18	4
	By Rich. Godwin pd. him	28		2	6
10	By Wines 5 tonns pd. custome etc.	48	25	14	4
	By Henry Gibbs pd. him	4	29	18	5
11	By Phill. Higginbottome pd. him	17	162		
	By Proffit & loss pd. Severalls 53#	8	500		
	By Ditto pd. Master	8	2		
	By sundry accts pd. John Blackwell	8, 26	103	6	6
12	By Proffitt & loss pd. Jos. Jackson	8	12		
	By Ditto pd. Houshold Expences	8	7	4	
	By Ditto pd. Sundryes	8	2	19	
	By Edmond Scrope pd. Speed 52	38	7	3	9
14	By Abr. White pd. for him	30		5	4
15	By Stockins pd. John Massinger	34	5	3	1
18	By Linincloth for acct. Tho. Williams pd. portridge	47			4
	By Martha Gay Lent her	32	3	11	4
	By Isaac Heming pd. John Hurtnell	35	100		
20	By Cattle pd. for a Bull	5	2	5	
	By Estate at Clevedon pd. Hugh Hodges	32		16	
	By Martha Gay pd. her	32	70		
21	By Edw. Martindale pd. him	24	1	1	6
	By Jos. Speed pd. him	24		10	

                               Bristoll 1682@

	Cash	Dr	£	s	d
	To itselfe for balllance	41	169	7	7
July 1st	To Isaac Heming recd. of severalls	35	156		
	To Robert Davis recd. of him	51	5	5	
4	To John Ford recd. of him	52		16	3
8	To Mary Parsons recd. of her	18	1	15	
	To Proffitt & loss recd. of Mary Aldworth	8		9	
14	To John Blackwell recd. of him	26	100		
	To Rich. Crump recd. of him	45	70	2	
19	To Linincloth Ben. Gold recd. of John Machen	17	13	10	10
	To Proffitt & loss recd. of severalls	8	151	13	
27	To Alexander Dolman recd. of him	48	33		
	To Mich. Pope recd. of him	48	18		9
28	To John Massinger recd. of him	27		10	
29	To John Jones recd. of him	51	39		
	To Will. Spoore recd. of him	30	3		

			£	s	d
25	By Stockins pd. John Massinger	34	3	15	
	By Jos. Cardrew pd. him	7	40		
	By sundry accts pd. Edw. Willis	38, 5	5	16	1
May 1st	By Proffitt & loss pd. Chimney money	8		8	
2	By Ditto pd. Eliz. Milner	8	5		
3	By Henry Simes pd. him	5	15		
	By Stockins pd. severalls	34	9	2	7
6	By Christopher Williams pd. him	7	75	14	
	By Martha Gay lent her	32	1		
	By Sugar 2 butts pd. custome	49	17	6	2
	By Edward Willis pd	49		18	
11	By Estate at Clapton pd. Ed. Willis	38		10	8
	By Proffitt & Loss pd. Martha Speed	8	1		
	By the Adventure in the Sarah pd. Thomas Tayer for 13 Chests				
	of Soape	49	46	3	7
	By Ditto pd. custome etc.	49	2	8	9
	By Mary Thring pd. them	7	3		
	By Henry Simes pd. severalls	5	29	2	
	By Stockins pd. John Massinger	34	5	9	4
	By Abra. White pd. him	30	2		
	By Cattle pd. Tho. Browne	5	1	16	
20	By Proffitt & Loss pd. Thomas Wall	8		18	8
	By Stockins pd. Tho. Dyer	34	1	1	4
24	By sundry accts pd. John Massinger	34, 8	5	17	6
25	By Cattle pd. for a Cow	5	4	2	
	By Estate at Clapton pd. one yeares poore money	38	1	1	4
27	By Adventure in the Martha & Sarah pd. Tho. Hartwell	25		5	10
	By Stockins pd. John Bradey	34	4	5	2
31	By Henry Simes pd. Thomas Hill	5	21	19	3
	By Cattle pd. for a cowe & Calfe	5	4	9	3
June 1st	By Abr. White pd. him	30		16	
10	By Worstead Stockins pd. John Massinger	34	10		
	By Phill. Higginbottom pd. sundryes	51		11	1
	By Rich. Godwin pd. him	23		9	11
12	By Proffitt & Loss pd. Richard Paine	8	2		
	By Ditto pd. Houshold Expences	8	17	15	
	By Soape pd. Henry Gibbs	51	100		
13	By Jos. Cardrew pd. Sam. Davis	7	28		
23	By Sundry accts pd. Severalls for stockins	34	14	5	
24	By Estate at Clapton pd. Severalls	38		14	
	By itselfe for ballance	42	169	7	7
			1962	16	6

Bristoll 1682@

	Per Contra	Cr	£	s	d
June 26	By John Hollister & Proffitt & loss pd. him	44, 8	1	4	8
27	By Thomas Davidge pd. him	4	8	19	9
	By Worstead Stockins pd. John Massinger	34	6	5	
July 6	By Linincloth Hen. Simes pd. Filing a certificate	50			7
	By Tho. Walden pd. him	2	2	15	
	By Tenement in Portbury pd. Mary Parsons	20		10	
8	By Isaac Heming pd. sundryes	35	205		
12	By Good Uses & Mary Chambers	2		3	
13	By Worstead Stockins pd. Sundryes	34	10	4	1
	By Estate at Clapton pd. Abra. White	38	2		
	By Proffitt & Loss pd. Houshold expences	8	6	10	11
14	By Rich. Washrow pd. him	15	38	5	4
15	By Proffitt & loss pd. for 12 doz bottles	8	1	2	
	By Stockins pd. Rottenberry	34		3	6
	By Rich. Corsely pd. him	53	8	17	6

	To Jo. Sporford 53 recd. of him	19	20	4	6
31	To Proffitt & loss recd. of sundryes	8	50	11	
August 3rd	To Arthur Jones recd. of him	21	1		
15	To John Massinger recd. of him	27		10	
	To Anth. Wood & co. recd. of him	49	57	17	
	To Alexander Dolman recd. of him	48		18	
	To Walter Stephens recd. of him	53	51	1	
	To Abr. White recd. of him	30		15	
23	To John Massinger recd. of him	27		10	
	To Anne Blackwell recd. of him	26		8	8
30	To Sir George Strode recd. of him	24	10		
Sept. 2nd	To John Gore recd. of him	31	1	1	11
7	To Humphrey Little recd. of Will. Dawson	27		7	10
9	To John Digbie recd. of Tho. Luttrell	37	20		
	To Barth. Bagg recd. of him	52	2	15	10
	To Thomas Taylor recd. of John Browne	4	4		
16	To John Machen recd. of him	55	3	15	6
21	To Tho. Puxtone recd. of him	22	50		
Oct. 11	To Tho. Durban recd. of him	47	75	5	
	To Tho. Puxtone recd. of him	22	50	3	
14	To Michael Pope recd. of him	48	8	4	
16	To John Machen recd. of him	55	4	4	4
	To John Blackwell recd. of him	26	25	2	
20	To Tho. Puxtone recd. of him	22	40		
21	To Earle of Bristoll recd. of Thomas Luttrell	37	9	6	
26	To Robt. Lysons recd. of him	46	6	10	
	To the Earle of Bristoll recd. of him	37	22	3	6
	To Proffitt & Loss recd. of Robert Yate	9	300		
			1579	3	6

Date	Description				
	By Sundry accts pd. weighing Tobacco	36,25,29		14	6
20	By Proffitt & loss pd. for a Firkin of butter	8	1		10
22	By Isaac Heming pd. sundryes on their bills	35	200		
27	By Ditto pd. John Wilmore	35	100		
	By Proffitt & Loss pd. John Hardiman	8	1	16	
	By Max. Gallop pd. him	34	41	10	5
28	By Stockins pd. John Massinger	34	4	6	4
	By Proffitt & Loss pd. Master	8	5		
29	By Will. Shephard pd. him	50	20		
	By Joseph Speed pd. for a Bend	24	1	17	9
August 1st	By Proffitt & loss pd. Martha Speed	8	3		
5	By Adventure in the John Frigatt pd. John Templeman	4	14	10	
	By Mary Thring & Company lent them on theire bond	7	10		
10	By Proffitt & Loss pd. Master	8	2		
	By House in which I live pd. Jos. Owen	23		15	
14	By Stockins pd. John Massinger	34	4	6	4
	By Proffitt & loss pd. Houshold expences	8	10	14	7
	By Cattle pd. for 3 Yoake of Oxen	5	22	15	
	By Copper pd. weighng 26 bottomes	36			6
	By Proffit & Loss pd. sundryes	8	4	9	
	By Land at Clevdon pd. Chimney money	32		1	
	By Abraham White pd. him	30	8	13	10
	By Stockins pd. John Massinger	34	5	1	9
26	By Proffitt & Loss pd. Master & John Hurtnell	8	1	5	6
	By Stockins pd. sundryes	54	7	4	11
30	By Estate at Clapton pd. sundryes	38	13	4	6
	By John Massinger Lent him	27	4	10	
Sept. 2nd	By William Pleydall Lent him	46	1		
	By Cattle pd. John Gore	5		2	10
6	By Proffitt & Losse pd. the Towne Clark	8	1	1	6
	By George Strode for Corkes, wine etc.	24		9	8
9	By Proffitt & Loss pd. Robert Gibbins	8		13	
	By Estate at Clapton pd. John Dorracut	38		12	8
12	By Sundry accts pd. Nathanaell Haggatt	19, 52	98		
13	By Henry Simes pd. his bill	5	2	17	6
14	By Stockins pd. Severalls	54	6	4	2
	By Proffitt & Loss pd. Houshold expences	8	9	7	1
21	By Cattle pd. for a Pigg	5	1		
	By Profitt & Loss pd. severalls	8	6	5	
	By John Gore Lent him	31	10		
22	By Estate at Clapton pd. Lords rent	38		16	
24	by Isaac Heming pd. him	35	2		
25	By Henry Simes pd. Dolman	5	47		
28	By Proffitt & Loss pd. Rob. Lippit	8		17	
	By Adventure in the Martha & Sarah pd. for 6 Firkins Butter	55	4	18	6
29	By John Hurtnell Lent him	38	12		
	By Stockins pd. John Massinger	54	4	9	5
Oct. 3rd	By Linincloth for acct. Thomas Williams pd. Carriage	47		10	
	By Stockins pd. Joseph White	54	3	14	
11	By Clapton for sundry Charges pd	38	3	4	6
	By Isaac Heming pd. Thomas Tayler	35	150		
12	By Proffitt & loss pd. Houshold Expences	8	9	5	6
	By Sundry accts pd. Richard Francklin	35, 56	50	10	2
	By Estate at Clapton for pd. soldering money	38		12	
	By Stockins pd. John Massinger	54	5	7	11
16	By John Blackwell pd. him	26	25	2	
	By Proffitt & Loss pd. Richard Paine	8	1	1	
	By Stockins pd. Thomas Browne for 24 paire	54	1	2	
	By Sir George Strode for 2 panniers & covers	24		1	4

(43)	Bristoll 1682@	Dr	£	s	d
	Cash				
	To itselfe for ballance	42	306	4	2
	To Thomas Williams recd. of him	57	20		
Nov. 1st	To Sir Nath. Nappier recd. of John Whetcombe	29	8	10	
	To Anne Pawlett recd. of Bernard Wilkins	48	6	18	
4	To John Streaten recd. of him	57	6		
6	To Robert Summers recd. of him	17	20		
8	To Alex. Dolman recd. of him	48	4		
	To Isaac Heming recd. of John Blackwell	35	80		
10	To Isaac Heming recd. of Thomas Day	35	50		
	To Thomas Tayler recd. of Tho. Hartwell	4	9		
18	To Carpetts recd. of John Arney	1		13	
26	To John Jones recd. of him	51	15	3	
	To Thomas Durbin recd. of him	47	75	10	
Dec. 19	To Mary Parsons recd. of her	18		18	
	To Isaac Heming recd. of Jos. Jackson	35	53	15	4
21	To Edward Hollister recd. of him	59	1	10	
22	To Isaac Heming recd. of John Blackwell	35	100		
Jan. 8	To Ditto recd. of Will. Redwood	35	19		
12	To John Pitts recd. of him	55	44	10	
20	To Cornelius Stretten recd. of him	62		7	
	To Proffit & loss recd. of Phineas Everard	9	1	16	10
23	To Ditto recd. of Nath. Haggatt	9	100		
	To Alexander Dolman recd. of him	48	57	3	
26	To Sir John Drake recd. of him	63	5	5	
29	To Sir Nath. Nappier recd. of him	29	1	7	
	To Tho. Longman recd. of him	58	20		
31	To Abra. Sanders recd. of him	59	19	11	
	To Tho. Puxtone recd. of him	22	60		
Feb. 1st	To Rob. Summers recd. of ima	17	20		
8	To Isaac Heming recd. of Thom. Day	35	22	15	
9	To Tho. Tayler recd. of him	4	9		
10	To Isa. Heming recd. of John Blackwell	35	100		
	To Anne Pawlett recd. of her	48		17	7
	To Charles Barber recd. of him	62	23	8	
March 6	To Lewis Adams recd. of him	56	44	9	6
7	To Thomas Longman recd. of him	58	2	7	6
			1309	18	11

			£	s	D
19	By Proffitt & Loss pd. John Blackwell	8		6	
	By Isaac Heming pd. Richard Francklin	35	1	19	9
	By merchandizes in the Martha & Sarah pd. George Popley	55	9	18	
	By John Sandford pd. him	19	2	11	9
20	By James Wallis pd. port of a Letter	26			6
	By Land at Clevedon pd. Thomas Luttrell	32		2	10
	By Mary Thring & co. pd. Stephen Chapman	7	4	10	
	By Nehemiah Benson Lent him	8		5	
	By House end Small Street pd. Nathanaell King	22		3	8
	By Proffitt & Loss pd. David Ronion	8	1	2	
	By William Spoore Lent him	52	10		
	By Cattle pd. Richard Wasbrow for 2 Piggs	5		16	
	By itselfe for ballance	43	306	4	2
			1579	3	6

Bristoll 1682@

	Per Contra	Cr	£	s	D
Oct. 26	By Stockins pd. Sundryes	54	16	12	6
	By Proffitt & loss pd. John Shuttleworth	8	13	5	
	By Ditto pd. Rich. Codrington, delivered master, Jahzeel & the Towne Clark	8	3	9	4
	By Abraham White pd. his wife	30	1		
	By merchandises in the Martha & Sarah pd. butter	55	3	9	5
	By Ditto pd. for Bacon	55	3	17	3
	By Linincloth 10 bolts pd. for straw	56		6	1
	By Linincloth 32 bolts pd. for straw	56		13	10
	By Rich. Marsh pd. the Towne Clark	1		13	4
30	By Estate at Clapton pd. Lords Rent	38		16	
Nov. 3d	By Stockins pd. John Massinger	54	8	9	7
	By merchandises in the Martha & Sarah pd. sundryes	55	5	2	9
	By Isaac Heming pd. John Barnard	35	1		
	By Tho. Williams pd. port of a Letter	57			9
	By Linincloth James Gould pd. Filing a certificate	56			4
	By Worstead Stockins pd. severalls	54	18	11	2
	By Cattle pd. for a Yoake of oxen	5	12	15	
9	By 30 butts wine pd. Jos. Berry	45		10	
10	By Stockins pd. Sundryes	54	30	7	
12	By Thomas Curtis pd. William Coleman	58	100		
14	By Worstead Stockins pd. Sundryes	54	33	11	6
	By Ben. Gould pd. his wife	5	55	3	2
15	By Profitt & Loss pd. Sundryes	8	62	18	4
18	By Abr. White pd. him	30	6	4	1
	By Will. Crabb pd. him	7	15		
20	By Worstead Stockins pd. Jos. Pinny	54	3	8	
	By merchandizes pd. Custome etc.	55	1	2	7
	By Sugar 2 hhds pd. Custome etc.	58	3	14	9
	By merchandizes in the Owners endeavour pd. Custome etc.	58	3	14	9
	By House in which I live pd. 1/2 a yeares Chimney money	23		8	
	By Worstead Stockins pd. sundryes	54	33	12	5
	By Estate at Clapton pd. John Bullock	36		7	
Dec. 4	By Proffitt & Loss pd. severalls	8	3	1	6
	By Stockins pd. John Massinger	54	5	7	11
5	By Stockins pd. Francis Rottenbury	54		6	4
6	By William Sheppard pd. Henry Combes	50	5	1	9
7	By John Gore paid him	31	40		
8	By Proffitt & Loss pd. Sundryes	8	18	17	7
13	By Stockins pd. sundryes	54	35		6
	By Jos. Badger pd. him	50	3	15	4
	By Estate at Clapton pd. Chimney money	38		6	
19	By Will. Olive pd. him	3		11	
	By sundry accts pd. weighing a parcell Tobacco	27, 5		3	

(44)	**Bristoll 1681@**				
	George Pley of Weymouth	Dr	£	s	d
Dec. 23	To Ralph Oliffe for 4 doz bottles new Xerie at 6s 4d per gallon				
	with bottles and pannier	3	4	7	

	Anno 1681@				
	Edward Roy of Dorchester	Dr	£	s	d
Jan. 14	To Isaac Heming for my bill in his Favor	35	30		
	To Henry Glisson for money unreceived of him on his failing for				
	which hee hath sued said Glisson at the law	44	25	2	10
	To Proffit & Losse for interest of the said £30 advanced to him	73	2	13	5
1685 March 3	To Cash paid him in full	108	2	9	
			60	5	3

20	By Proffitt & loss pd. sundryes	8	1	12	

21	By Tobacco 3 hhds pd. Custome etc.	59	7	16	6
	By Worstead Stockins pd. Sundryes	54	23	6	2
	By Abra. White pd. his wife	30		10	
	By Proffitt & loss pd. the Coopers	8		2	6
	By Will. Sheppard pd. him	50	5		
	By Stockins pd. Sundryes	54	30	14	
	By Proffitt & loss pd. Sundryes	9	1	15	6
	By Estate at Clapton pd. Ed. Willis	38	1	5	
Jan. 11	By Stockins pd. Jos. Pinn for 60 paire	54		17	
12	By Mary Thring & Company pd. them	7	2		
13	By Worstead Stockins pd. severalls	54	19	8	10
15	By Xerie wine one butt pd. John Cheshire	59	3	8	4
	By Proffitt & loss pd. Sundryes	9	8	9	11
20	By Estate at Clapton pd. sundry charges	38	1	11	11
	By Stockins pd. John Massinger	54	6	9	6
25	By John Wilmore pd. John Bush	62	60		
	By James Gould pd. Maxi. Gallop	62	41	4	
26	By Max. Gallop pd. him	34		18	
	By Stockins pd. John Massinger	54	6		
	By Will. Sheppard pd. him	50	7	8	7¼
	By Proffitt & loss pd. Filing a certificate	9			4
31	By sundry accts pd. for 5 panniers	34, 63		4	8
	By merchandizes in the Sarah pd. Ed. Tayler	55	2	19	
Feb. 1st	By Stockins pd. Sundryes	54	16	17	9
	By Adventure in the Rochell pd. custome etc.	63	3	17	
	By Proffitt & loss pd. James Swetman	9	1	15	6
14	By Stockins pd. Sundryes	54	8	14	1
	By the House in small street pd. drumes & Colors	22			4
	By John Digbie pd. for 5 panniers	37		4	2
	By Anne Pawlett for a pannier	48			8
	By Proffitt & loss pd. Houshold expences	9	7	11	2
	By Stockins pd. Sundryes	54	5	19	4
22	By Doctor Hungerford pd. for panniers & covers	59		2	6
25	By Jos. Drew pd. him	31	5		
	By Hen. Gibbs pd. him	4	30	11	6
	By Proffitt & loss pd. Sundryes	9	4	4	11
28	By the house in which I live pd. Tho. Walden	23		4	
	By Stockins pd. severalls	54	8	11	2
March 5	By Tobacco 18 hhds pd. weighing them	63		4	6
	By Stockins pd. Sundryes	54	16	13	10
	By Linincloth for James Gould abated in measure	56		1	8
	By itselfe for ballance	66	413	9	11
			1309	18	11

Bristoll 1682@

		Cr	£	s	d
	Per Contra				
July 22	By Max. Gallop for my bill in said Gallops Favor	34	4	7	

	Anno 1681				
	Edward Roy of Dorchester merchant per Contra	Cr	£	s	d
1685 July	By Lincloth 11 Rolls of Canvas for theire neate proceeds	5	50	13	10
	By Lincloth for his acct. for 1 Roll Hallcloth sould John Jones	99	9	9	
			60	2	10
	By Profit and Loss for Ballance	189		2	5
			60	5	3

Anno 1681@		Dr	£	s	d
	Henry Glisson Junior	Dr	£	s	d
Jan. 14	To *Linincloth* for acct. of Edward Roy for 5 bolts sould him at 6 deniers off	5	25	2	10

Anno 1681@		Dr	£	s	d
	John Linckhorne	Dr	£	s	d
Jan. 7	To Cash paid him	40	400		

Anno 1681@		Dr	£	s	d
	John Hollister	Dr	£	s	d
Jan. 14	To *Linincloth* for acct. Jos. Cardrow for 14 bolts at one Solls of	35	135	9	5
1682 June 26	To Cash pd. him for what wanting in measure	42	1	1	5
			136	10	10

Anno 1681@		Dr	£	s	d
	John Read	Dr	£	s	d
Jan. 4	To *Linincloth* for acct. of Jos. Cardrow for 8 bolts sold him at 1 Solls off	35	66	17	9

Anno 1683		Dr	£	s	d
	Adventure in the ship *Civilia merchant* of Lond. Capt. Bradyl to Cadiz £ s d	Dr	£	s	d
	To Worsted stockins for 1 Trunck cont.				
	68 doz Bristol hose at 3s 6d 142 16				
	To Ditto for 28 doz Wells hose at 2s a paire 33 12	71	176	8	
	To Isaac Heming for charges consigning them				
	to Art. Robinson & Company 4 12 8	35	4	12	8
	To Adventure in the Cadiz merchant to Cadiz for the cost & charges of one Trunck cont. 56 doz Bristol & 38 doz Wells hose, consign'd to Ar. Robinson & Company, brought hither because they give one acct. of Sales of both Truncks	34	162	17	2
			343	17	10

(45)	*Bristoll 1681@*	Dr	£	s	d
	John Bubb of Bristoll Linindraper	Dr	£	s	d
Jan. 14	To *Lininclothfor* acct. of Henry Simes for 10 bolts sold him at 1 soll off	35	87	7	6
1686 July 23	To *Lincloth* for acct. Wm. Brice for 4 Rolls Canvas cont. 448 @ at 8s 10d½ per @	117	19	17	6
1688 October 18	To Sailecloth 20 pieces sould him at 44s per piece to pay at demand	150	44		
			151	5	

Anno 1681@		Dr	£	s	d
	Alderman Rich. Crump	Dr	£	s	d
Feb. 4	To Tobacco 12 hhds Malachy Peale for 4585lb neat at 3d¾	36	71	12	9

Anno 1683		Dr	£	s	d
	Worsted stockins for acct. of Xpher Williams of Lond. merchant	Dr	£	s	d
August 27	To Cash paid John England for 100 paire at 3s 6d per paire	67	17	10	
September 6	To Cash paid John Harris for a Trunck box to pack them in	67		1	8
	To Proffitt & Losse for Portridge to the Carrier	9			2
	To Ditto for my Commission for buying at £2 per cent	9		7	
			17	18	10

Anno 1682				
Henry Glisson per Contra	Cr	£	s	d
By Edward Roy, for the money per Contra, lost, by his Failing	44	25	2	10

Anno 1690@				
John Linckhorn per Contra	Cr	£	s	d
By Profit and Loss for Ballance	189 *	400		

Anno 1681@					
	Per Contra	Cr	£	s	d
	By Linincloth per Contra for money abated for want of measure	35	1	1	5
Feb. 4th	By Cash recd. of him	40	40		
1682 Aprill 20	By Ditto recd. of him	41	40		
June 12	By Ditto recd. of him	41	30		
26	By Ditto recd. of him	41	5	9	5
	By Joseph Cardro for his bill given Joseph Cardro for ballance	7	20		
			136	10	10

Anno 1681@					
	Per Contra	Cr	£	s	d
Jan. 25	By Cash recd. of him	40	60		
30	By Ditto recd. of him	40	6	9	6
	By Lining cloth per Contra for what wanting in measure	35		8	3
			66	17	9

Anno 1684				
Adventures in the ships Civilia merchant & Cadiz merchant per Contra	Cr	£	s	d
By Arthur Robinson & Company for the neat proceeds of the 2 Truncks of stockin per Contra, as per theire acct. of Sales dated January 17th 1684 being 12m 787½ Ryals plate is 1598 pieces of 8 3 Ryals & ½ the piece of 8 at 4s 4d	61	319	4	
By Profit and Loss for Ballance	189 *	24	13	10
	343	17	10	

Bristoll 1681@					
	Per Contra	Cr	£	s	d
Feb. 2d	By Cash recd. of him	40	80		
14	By Ditto recd. of him	40	7		
	By Linncloth per Contra for money abated him	35			6
	By Henry Simes for money allowed him want of measure	5		7	
1686 Oct. 9	By Cash received of him	120	19	17	6
1688 Feb. 6	By Cash recd. of him in full	157	44		
			151	5	

Anno 1682@					
	Per Contra	Cr	£	s	d
July 14	By Cash recd. of him	42	70	2	
	By Tobacco 12 hhds Malachy Peale for damage allowed him	36	1	10	9

Anno 1683				
Worsted stockins per Contra	Cr	£	s	d
By Xpher Williams his acct. current for the cost of the stockins per Contra	7	17	18	10

	1683				
	Xeries Wine my ½ of 30 Butts imported from Cadiz in the ship Olive tree in partnership with John Cooke & Company & by them laden	Dr	£	s	d
	To Xerie wine 30 Butts for the ½ of theire first cost, charg'd to that acct. by error	45	139	4	11

	Anno 1681@				
	Xeries Wine 30 Butts imported on the Olive tree from Cadiz in Equall halfes Betweene myselfe & Mr John Cooke & Company	Dr	£	s	d
Jan. 26	To Cash paid Custome, Fees , bills etc. of said wine	40	97	5	4
Feb. 9	To Ditto pd. Thomas Gammon for Freight, Avaridge etc.	40	60	18	6
Nov. 9	To Ditto pd. Joseph Berry	43		10	
10	To Wines 5 tonns for one hogshead of Sweet	48	7	10	
	To John Cooke for theire First cost	32	139	4	11
March 6	To Lewis Adams for money abated him	56	1		
1683 27	To Cash given Joseph Berrie for Brokridge	66		8	
Aprill 6	To Thomas Day for money due to him	70	6	15	6
	To Proffit & Losse for hallidge to Celler	9 *		15	
	To Ditto for 63 weeks celleridge	9 *	11		6
	To John Wasbrow for cooperidge as per noate	28 54	9	14	
	To Proffit & Losse for Cork, Bungcloth & candles at several times	9 *		6	2
	To Ditto for my Commission at £2 per cent	9 *	8	9	4
			343	17	3
	To sundry accts for theire neate proceeds viz)				
	To John Cooke & Company for their ½ £109 18s 6d				
	To Xeries Wine my ½ of 30 Butts for ½ £109 18s 6d	25 45	219	17	
			563	14	3

	Anno 1683				
	Richard Champneys of Bristoll merchant	Dr	£	s	d
	To Andrew Stuckey Junior for a part of the ship Humility as per said Stuckeys advice in his letter to mee	53	73		
January	To the house at the Lower end of Small Streat for 41 weeks of Celleridge in the vault there from the 5th of February to the 19th Nov. 1683 at 3s per week	22	6	3	
1687 July	To Malaga wines 4 Butts for 1 Butt sould him payable at the faire	134	31		
	To Profit and Loss for rent of the Lower vault omitted to be charged	189 *	8	8	
			118	11	

	Anno 1682				
	James Jacob & Richard Sandford of Bristoll joint in distilling strong waters	Dr	£	s	d
February	To Wines 30 Butts twixt John Cooke & Company & my selfe for 1 hogshead & a qt corrupt wine	45	3		

(46)	Bristoll 1681@				
	Martha Speed	Dr	£	s	d
Jan. 27	To Cash pd. her	40	1		
Feb. 10	To Ditto pd. her	40	1		
1683 September 22	To Cash paid her	67	1		
24	To Cash paid her	67	2	2	
November 22	To Cash paid Tho. Walden for severall things for her	67		12	
March 17	To Cash paid her	68		10	
1684 Aprill 16	To Cash paid her	68		10	
21	To Cash paid her	68	4		
22	To Cash paid her	68	2		

Anno 1683				
Xeries Wine my half of 30 Butts per Contra	Cr	£	s	d
By Xerie Wines 30 Butts for my ½ of theire neate proceeds	45	139	4	11

Anno 1681@					
	Per Contra	Cr	£	s	d
Jan. 27	By Cash recd. of James Crofts for allowance on said Wine	40	18	3	6
1682 August 26	By John Blackwell for 6 butts sold him at £22 per butt	26	132		
	By Sir George Strode for 2 dozen bottles 6 botte	24	1	12	
Sept. 6	By Anne Pawlet for 6 gallons	48	1	12	
	By Proffitt & Loss for one but for my owne use	8	22		
24	By John Pitts for 2 butts sold him	55	44	10	
Oct. 11	By Lewis Adams for 2 butts	56	47		
	By John Pitts for 2 butts sold him	55	45		
	By Xeries wine for one butt I take to my selfe	59	20	10	
	By Peter Rosewell for Lees sold him charg'd at nothing because good for nothing, cast away	60			
Feb. 16	By Edward Jones for 2 butts sold him	64	18		
	By James Jacobs & Company for one hogshead & a qt of corrupt for the still	45	3		
March 22	By John Whitwood for 6 butts corrupts & 1 butt Lees	70	29	9	
1683 Aprill 5	By Thomas Day for 3 butts sold him abating for 6 gallons wanting	70	39	13	4
September 25	By John Wasbrow for 4 Empty butts & 52 Yron hoops	28	1	19	6
	By my halfe of Xeries Wine 30 butts for ½ theire first cost, charg'd by error per Contra, which should have been charg'd in that account	45	139	4	11
			563	14	3

Anno 1683					
	Richard Champnyes per Contra is	Cr	£	s	d
September 10	By Cash receivd of John Joyner by his order	67	70		
13	By Cash recd. of him	67	3		
1684 Aprill 4	By Cash receivd of him	68	6	3	
1687 Sept. 5	By Cash recd. of him in full	139	31		
1689 June 25	By Cash recd. of him	162	8	8	
			118	11	

Anno 1682				
James Jacob & Company per Contra	Cr	£	s	d
By Jahzeel Speed for money hee received of them but brought it not into Cash	69	3		

Bristoll 1685				
Martha Speed per Contra	Cr	£	s	d
By her selfe for ballance	109	21	4	

Date			£	s	d
May 27	To Cash paid her	77	2		
June 9	To Cash paid her	77	2		
November 11	To Cash paid her	82	1		
1685 June 20	To Cash paid her	144	2		
	To Cash paid her	83	1	10	
			21	4	

Anno 1682@

Date	William Pleydall	Dr	£	s	d
Sept. 2d	To Cash pd. Lent him	42	1		
1684 September 17	To Cash paid him	82		5	
1686 September 30	To Cash paid lent to him	119		2	6
1687 February 25	To Cash paid him in part	140	1		
March 1	To Cash paid him in full	140		12	
			2	19	6

Anno 1683

Oyle 10 Jarres recd. out of the ship Ann Tho. Thorp Master from London for acct. of Christopher Williams of Lond. merchant

Date		£	s	d	Dr	£	s	d
March 31	To Cash paid portridge into the warehouse		1	6	66			
Aprill 5	To Ditto pd. Landing it		1	6	66			
9	To Cash paid Tho. Thorpe for freight & averidge		1	13	66			
	To Proffit & Losse for hallidge to Celler		1	6	9			
	To Ditto for Celleridge			5	9	2	2	6
	To Commission in Proffit & Losse at £2 per Cent				9		18	8
	To Christopher Williams his acct. current for its neat proceeds				7	43	3	10
						46	5	

Anno 1681/2@

Marthandinces [55] on the Martha & Sarah for acct. of Barthlomew Rees of Barbadoes merchant

Date		Dr	£	s	d
March 1st	To Cash pd. a permitt for shipping said goods undermentioned	40		2	2

Anno 1682@

Robert Lysons of Bristoll Bucher

Date		Dr	£	s	d
Aprill 8	To Cattle for 9 Calves sold him	5	6	10	

Anno 1683

Sugar 8 hhds on the Abraham & Isaac John Jones Master from Nevis

Date		£	s	d	Dr	£	s	d
July 6	To Edmund Scrope & Company for theire cost & charges as per Invoyce March 24 1683				33	57	4	
	To Cash paid custom fees & bills	4	17					
	To Cash paid Wm. Dunning for freight & averidge	9	8		66			
September 28	To Cash paid weighing them	0	2		67	14	7	
						71	11	

(47)   Bristoll 1681/2@

Date	Tho. Scrope of Bristoll merchant his acct. of exchange	Dr	£	s	d
	To his particular acct. current for the 2 bills per Contra charg'd there by error	75	100		
1683 July 6	To John Cooke his acct. of exchange for 2 bills on him, the one for £20 5s the other for £54 10s 7d	39	74	15	7
			174	15	7
	To Profit and Loss for Ballance	189 *	5	4	5
			180		

Anno 1687		Cr	£	s	d
William Plydall per Contra is					
By Proffit & Losse for the money lent him, & the money due for					
work as per his noate		137	2	19	6
			2	19	6

	Anno 1683@	Cr	£	s	d
Aprill 5th	Per Contra	21	46	5	
	By James Freeman for the 10 Jarrs per Contra sold him				

	Anno 1690@	Cr	£	s	d
	Merchandizes per Contra	189 *		2	2
	By Profit and Loss for Ballance				

	Anno 1682@	Cr	£	s	d
Oct. 26	Per Contra	42	6	10	6
	By Cash recd. of him				

	Anno 1683	Cr	£	s	d
September 25	Sugar 8 hhds per Contra are	61	71	3	
	By Wm. Swift for the 8 hhds sould him				
	By Proffit and Loss for Ballance	189 *		8	
			71	11	

	Bristoll 1681/2@	Cr	£	s	d
	Thomas Scrope				
March 22	By Isaac Heming for 2 bills of Exchange in his Favor	35	100		
1683 July 6	By Ditto for money hee recd. on his bill of exchange on Hugh				
	Horton in London	35	80		
			180		

Anno 1683

	Sugar 12 Tierces & 1 hogshead imported in the Dyamond Ketch John Bennet Master from Nevis	Dr	£	s	d
September 13	To Edmond Scrope & Company for theire 1st cost 13231 lb sugar at 10s per Cwt, as per Invoyce　£ s d	33	66	3	
	To Cash paid custom fees bills & wharfage　5 18 6	67			
24	To Cash paid John Bennet for freight & averidge　12 14 3	67			
27	To Cash paid weighing them　2 3	67	18	15	
			84	18	
	To Profit and Loss, for Ballance	189 *	5	2	6
			90		6

Anno 1683

	Michael Perrie of Bristoll Marriner	Dr	£	s	d
September 11	To merchandizes in the Owners Endeavour for 1 Copper still, 1 pewter worme 2 Copper Taches & 1 Copper Cooler sould in Jamaica as per acct. May 1st 1683	58	43	2	10
	To Matthew Wall for 1 Fan sould there as per same acct.	22		2	
	To Sugar 15 hhds in the Owners Endeavour for sugar wanting in 1 hogshead laden by him	70	1	1	3
			44	6	1

Anno 1682@

	Thomas Durbin of Bristoll	Dr	£	s	d
March 29	To Sundry accts for 11 hhds of Tobacco sold him at 4d¼ per lb	29,25,36	75	8	
July 19	To Sundry accts for 11 hhds of Tobacco sold him at 4d¼ per lb	29,36	75	14	5
1683 May 31	To Oyle 1 Cask for acct. Christopher Williams for 1 Cask sould him	19	7	13	6
			158	15	11

Anno 1682@

	Per Contra	Dr	£	s	d
Aprill 3rd	To Cash pd. Filing a Certificate	41			4
18	To Ditto pd. Portridge	41			4
Oct. 3	To Ditto pd. Carriage of said Cloth from Dorchester	42		10	
	To Ditto pd. Dolman for want of measure	48		1	10
March 17	To Proffitt & Loss for Commission etc.	9		9	5
	To Thomas Williams his acct. current for its neat proceeds	57	17	12	10
			18	14	9

Anno 1683

	Sugar 8 hhds in the New England mercht Francis Plomer Master from Nevis	Dr	£	s	d
July 6	To Edm. Scrope & Company for theire cost & charges per Invoyce May 5th 1683　£ s d	33	60	4	3
	To Cash paid custom, fees, bills & wharfage　5 8 8				
	To Ditto paid Francis Plomer for freight and averidge　10 6	66			
September 28	To Cash paid weighing them　2	67	15	16	8
			76		11
	To Profit and Loss, for Ballance	189 *	6	9	1
			82	10	

(48)　　　**Bristoll 1681/2@**

	Alexander Dolman	Dr	£	s	d
March 29	To Linincloth 10 bolts for account of Max. Gallop for said 10 sold him	6	47	18	
Oct. 3d	To Linincloth 4 bolts for acct. Tho. Williams for said 4 sold him	47	18	14	9
26	To Linincloth 1 bolts for acct. James Gold & Compy for said 10 bolts	56	43		7

	Anno 1683				
	Sugar 12 Tierces & 1 hogshead per Contra	*Cr*	*£*	*s*	*d*
September 25	By *Wm. Swift* for the Tierces & 1 hogshead sould him weight				
	neat 87cwt 3qr 9lb at 20s 6d	*61*	90		6

	Anno 1683				
	Michael Perrie per Contra	*Cr*	*£*	*s*	*d*
September 11	By Sugar 15 hhds for the first cost of 5 laden in the Owners				
	Endeavour in Jamaica	*70*	41	8	8
	By sundry accts for freight of 10 Coolers from Nevis to Jamaica	*37, 49*	1		
October 1	By Cash recd. of him in 8 light pieces of 8 towards ballance of his				
	acct.	*67*	1	8	5
	By Sugar 15 hhds for money lost on the pieces of 8	*70*		9	
			44	6	1

	Anno 1682@				
	Per Contra	*Cr*	*£*	*s*	*d*
Oct. 11	By Cash recd. of him	*42*	75	5	
Nov. 26	By Ditto recd. of him	*43*	75	10	
Dec. 4	By Proffitt & Loss for money abated him	*8*		4	5
	By Proffit & Losse for Tobacco had of him	*9*		3	
1683 August 4	By Cash recd. of him	*66*	7	13	6
			158	15	11

	Anno 1682@				
	Linincloth 4 Bolts for acct. of Thomas Williams	*Cr*	*£*	*s*	*d*
Oct. 3rd	By Alexander Dolman for said Cloth sold him at one Solls off	*48*	18	14	9

	Anno 1683				
	Sugar 8 hhds per Contra are	*Cr*	*£*	*s*	*d*
September 25	By *Wm. Swift* for the 8 hhds neat 80cwt 1qr 26lb at 20s 6d per				
	Cwt at 3 months	*61*	82	10	

	Bristoll 1682@				
	Per Contra	*Cr*	*£*	*s*	*d*
July 22	By Max. Gallop for money hee pd. Edw. Young	*34*	14		
27	By Cash recd. of him	*42*	33		
August 15	By Ditto recd. of him	*42*		18	
	By Ditto recd. of him	*43*	4		

1683 July 17	To *Lincloth for acct. James Gould for 4 bolts Vittry sould him*	*56*	21	17	4
25	To *Ditto for an Invoyce of 12 Bolts Vittry sould him 1s 3d off*				
	Invoyce	*56*	62		1
			193	10	9

Anno 1686					
	Alexander Doleman of Bristoll Linindraper is	*Dr*	*£*	*s*	*d*
July 31	To *Nicholas Baber for money hee received of him by my order*	*103*	36	15	

Anno 1682@					
	Per Contra	*Dr*	*£*	*s*	*d*
Aprill 18	To *Isaac Heming pd. Ben.. Skinner on his bill*	*35*	70	10	11

Anno 1683					
	Alexander Caduggan of Bristoll Vintner is	*Dr*	*£*	*s*	*d*
September 13	To *Xeries wine 40 Butts for 7 Butts at £24 per Butt at 6*				
	months	*65*	168		
1689 November	To *Xeries wine 23 Butts for 5 Butts at £29 per Butt payable at*				
	3 payments as per Journall	*169*	145		
			313		

Anno 1682@					
	Per Contra	*Dr*	*£*	*s*	*d*
	To *sundry accts for theire cost & Charges*	*8, 48, 41, 28, 4*	112	6	11
	To *Henry Gibbs for one hogshead of sweet*	*4*	6		
			118	6	11

Anno 1682					
	Henry Bainham of Yate in the County of Glocester Gent. [56] *is*	*Dr*	*£*	*s*	*d*
Aprill 4th	To *Proffit & Losse for money lent him on a mortgage £276* [57]	*73*	276		
1683 Aprill 5	To *Ditto for one yeares intrest due this day*	*73*	16	11	2
1684 Aprill 20	To *Ditto for one yeares intrest due April 5th 1684*	*73*	16	11	2
1685 Aprill 4	To *Ditto for one yeares intrest due April 5th 1685*	*89*	16	11	2
			325	13	6

Date	Description	fol	£	s	d
Nov. 8	By sundry accts for want of measure etc.	47,56,9		12	4
Jan. 23	By Cash recd. of him	43	57	3	
1683 November 2	By Cash recd. of him	67	82		
	By Lincloth for acct. James Gould abated him for want of measure and damage	56	1	9	6
January 21	By Cash received of him for ballance	68		7	11
			193	10	9

Anno 1686

Date	Description	fol	£	s	d
	Alexander Doleman per Contra is	Cr	£	s	d
August 5	By Proffit & Losse for his noat for severall goods bought of him by my wife	105	17	8	
	By Cash received of him in full	119	19	7	
1689 Dec. 21					
			36	15	

Anno 1682@

Date	Description	fol	£	s	d
	Andrew Kirbie of Bordeaux Merchant	Cr	£	s	d
Aprill 10	To wines 5 tonns for theire cost	48	70	10	11

Anno 1684

Date	Description	fol	£	s	d
	Alexander Caduggan per Contra	Cr	£	s	d
Aprill 22	By Cash recd. of him	68	100		
July 24	By Cash recd. of him	77	27		
	By Jahzeel Speed received by him in full as per his receit	122	41		
1689 Jan. 10	By Cash recd. of him December 21st in part	173	40		
10	By Ditto recd. of him in part	173	5		
1690 April 14	By Ditto received of him per the Hands of Edw. Martindale Junior	175	50		
June 26	By Cash recd. of him	181	48	18	6
	By Xeries wines 23 Butts, for money abated him on 5 Butts sold him	169	1	1	6
			313		

Anno 1681@

Date	Description	fol	£	s	d
	Wines imported on the San Mallo merchant from Oporto	Cr	£	s	d
March 29	By Ralphe Olliffe for 2 hhds Red & 5 of White at £27 10s per tonne	3	48	2	6
	By Henry Gibbs for what he recd. of Codner	4	2	5	
1682 Aprill 10	By Ditto for ½ theire cost & charges	4	55		11
Nov. 10	By Xeries wines 30 butts for one hogshead Sweet	45	7	10	
	By Henry Gibbs for ½ a hogshead sweet	4	3	17	6
	By Proffit & Losse for ballance	73	1	11	
			118	6	11

Anno 1683

Date	Description	fol	£	s	d
	Henry Bainham per Contra is	Cr	£	s	d
	By Robert Yate for money hee paid him for 1 yeares intrest due Aprill 5 83	39	16	11	2
1685 Aprill 30	By Cash received of my Cosen Nath. Haggatt	83	307	15	
			324	6	2
	By Profit and Losse for Ballance	189 *	1	7	4
			325	13	6

Anno 1681@					
	Michael Pope of Bristoll Linindraper	Dr	£	s	d
Aprill 6th	To Linincloth Max. Gallop for 4 bolts sold him at 1s 6d off	6	18		9
18	To Linincloth 2 bolts for acct. of Benj. Gold for said Cloth sold him	17	8	4	
1688 Aprill	To Samuel Kekewich for Simon Clements bill for 160 pieces of 8 assign'd in my favor piece of 8 52d	148	34	13	4
			60	18	1

Anno 1682@					
	Anne Pawlet Lady	Dr	£	s	d
Sept. 6	To Sundry accts for 2 doz of Xerie	45, 8	1	17	7
Oct. 16	To Proffitt & Loss for 2 rundletts qt 24 Gallon 3 qt & a pinte with charges	8	6	18	2
	To sundry accts for one doz Xerie	59, 43		17	8
1683 August 15	To sundry accts for 7 doz bottles Xerie with bottles etc.	9, 39	6	2	8
January 2	To sundry accts for 2 doz bottles Xerie with bottles etc. sent per Bernard Wilkins	70, 9	1	17	
March 20	To Proffitt & Losse for 4 doz bottles of Xerie panniers etc.	73	3	10	
1684 August 13	To sundry accts for the cost & charges of 2 doz white & 2 doz Claret sent per B. Wilkins	73, 78	2	8	8
27	To sundry accts for 5 Panniers containing 10 doz bottles of Xerie sent at twice per B. Wilkins	73, 79	9	7	
			32	18	9

(49)	Bristoll 1682@				
	Edward Burrish of London Linindraper	Dr	£	s	d
Aprill 10	To Henry Gibbs for a bill Exchange of 719 crownes	4	167		4

Anno 1682@					
	Anthony Wood & Mr. Phanateren of Bristoll Sugarbakers	Dr	£	s	d
May 3d	To Sugar 2 butts & six hogshead for said sugar sold them at 23s 11d per Cwt	49	107	17	7
1682/3 Mar. 17	To Sugar 2 butts one hogshead for said sugar sold them at 22s per Cwt	70 58	42	7	6
			150	5	1

Anno 1682@					
	Per Contra	Dr	£	s	d
May 8	To Cash pd. custom Fees etc. of said sugar	41	17	6	2
Jan. 2	To Edmond Scrope & Company for theire cost	33	74	14	11
			92	01	1
	To Profit and Loss for Ballance	189 *	15	16	6
			107	17	7

Anno 1682@					
	Edward Willis of Clapton	Dr	£	s	d
May 11	To Cash Lent him	41		18	

Anno 1682@					
	Per Contra	Dr	£	s	d
May 11	To Oliver Moseley for 6 Copper Coolers	4	20	3	3
	To Rich. Wasbrow for 30 boxes Candles	50	38	5	4
	To Cash pd. Tho. Tayer for 13 Chests of Soape & Custome & Fees	41	48	12	4
1683 September 11	To Michael Perrie for freight of 4 Coolers in owners Endeavour from Nevis to Jamaica	47		8	
	To Cash paid Sir John Knight for freight of said goods	67	6	12	
			114	00	11
	To Profit and Loss for Ballance	189 *	3	17	1
			117	18	

	Anno 1682@				
	Per Contra	Cr	£	s	d
July 27	By Cash recd. of him	42	18		9
Oct. 4	By Cash recd. of him	42	8	4	
1688 May 22	By Cash recd. of him in full	141	34	13	4
			60	18	1

	Anno 1682@				
	Per Contra	Cr	£	s	d
Nov. 1st	By Cash recd. of Bernard Wilkins	43	6	18	
Feb. 21	By Ditto recd. of Ditto	43		17	8
	By Sir George Strode for the cost & charges of the 2 doz Xeries per Contra	24	1	17	7
1683 August 27	By Cash recd. of Bernard Wilkins	67	6	2	8
February 26	By Cash recd. of Bernard Wilkins	68	1	17	
1684 June 5	By Cash recd. of Bernard Wilkins	77	3	10	
October 4	By Cash recd. of Bernard Wilkins	82	11	15	1
	By Proffitt and Losse for ballance	89			9
			32	18	9

	Bristoll 1682@				
	Per Contra	Cr	£	s	d
May 18	By Isaac Heming for money hee recd. on the bill per Contra	35	167		4

	Anno 1682@				
	Per Contra	Cr	£	s	d
June 2d	By Cash recd. of them	41	50		
August 15	By Ditto recd. of them	42	57	18	
1683 August 13	By Cash recd. of Anthony Wood	66	42	7	1
			150	5	1

	Anno 1682@				
	Sugar 2 butts & 16 hhds imported in the Delight from Nevis	Cr	£	s	d
May 3d	By Anth. Wood & Company sold them at 23s 6d per Cwt	49	107	17	7

	Anno 1682@				
	Per Contra	Cr	£	s	d
May 31	By Cash recd. of him	41		18	

	Anno 1682@				
	Adventure in the Sarah to Nevis John Snow Commander	Cr	£	s	d
	By Edm. Scrope and Co. for the neat proceeds of the goods per Contra as per acct. of Sales closed Nov. 22th 1683, sugar at 10s per Cwt	33	117	18	

Anno 1683						
	Samuell Astry Esquire is	Dr	£	s	d	
September 19	To Xeries wine 12 Butts for 1 hogshead cont. 66 Gall. at 5s	39	16	10		
	To Proffit & Losse for the hogshead	9		5		
	£ s d					
1684 August 22	To Xeries wine 2 Butts of John					
	Blackwell for 1 hogshead containing 60					
	Gall. at 5s 4d 16 0 0	79				
	To Proffit & Losse for the Cask					
	cooperidge and halling to the Rainbow 00 05 0	73	16	5		
September 12	To Ditto wines for 10 doz bottles sent					
	per Tobias Luton to Robert Winter in					
	London per his order of 3rd Sept.					
	1684 at 16s per doz 8 00 00	79				
	To Proffit & Losse for 10 doz bottles					
	£1 & 3 panniers corks & portridge 4s 1 04 00	73	9	4		

(50)	Bristoll 1682@				
	Per Contra	Dr	£	s	d
July 14	To Cash paid him	42	38	5	4
1684 Aprill 22	To Cash paid him selfe in full	68	22	19	9
November	To John Bradway for money of him on my noat	70	32	19	2
1688 June	To Anthony Owen recd. of him in part	111	19	6	9
21	To Cash paid him in full as per receit	141	6	15	5
			120	6	5

Anno 1683					
	Maximelian Gollop of Dorchester in the County of Dorset mercht.	Dr	£	s	d
January 31	To Proffit & Losse for 4 doz bottles of Xerie & the bottles sent him per Carrier	73	3	4	

Anno 1682@					
	Linincloth 4 packets for acct. of Henry Simes	Dr	£	s	d
July 6	To Cash pd. Filing a certificate & portridge of one	42			7
	To Walter Stephens for money abated him	53			6
	To Proffitt & Loss for sundry charges on said Cloth	8	1	2	11
	To Henry Simes for theire neat proceeds	5	49	17	6
			51	1	6

Anno 1682@					
	Joseph Badger of Bristoll Brasier	Dr	£	s	d
May 18	To Copper for 25 bottomes sold him at £6 14s weight 4cwt 0qr 27lb	36	28	8	4
Dec. 13	To Cash pd. him in full	43	3	15	4
1685 Aprill	To Adventure in the Owners Endeavour to Nevis for 10 Coolers with Iron bands sent him	58	29	14	2
	To Proffit & Losse for money paid him & wrong charg'd in Cash 60	89	2	9	4
			64	7	2

Anno 1682@					
	Adventure in the Olive branch of London Jonathan Francis Master for Nevis consigned to Edm. Scrope & Company	Dr	£	s	d
May 27	To Isaac Heming for 40 Kilderkin Flower 3 pieces Brandy	35	75	14	5
	To Profit and Loss for Balance	189 *	82 61	13	3
			158	7	8

Anno 1683					
	Samuell Astry per Contra	*Cr*	*£*	*s*	*d*
October 13	By Cash recd. of him	67	16	15	
1684 September	By Cash recd. of him	77	16	5	
	By Cash recd. of his servant	82	9	4	

Bristoll 1682@					
	Richard Washrow	*Cr*	*£*	*s*	*d*
May 11	By Adventure in the Sarah to Nevis for 30 boxes of Candles	49	38	5	4
Aprill 22	By Adventure 3 in the Dyamond Ketch to Nevis for 20 boxes of Candles	57	22	19	11
September 5	By Adventure in the Owners Adventure to Nevis for 20 boxes of Candles	80	32	19	2
1688 May	By Adventure in the Neptune Sloope to Nevis for 20 boxes Candles cont. 128 Doz 10 at 3s 10d [59]	143	26	2	
			120	6	5

Anno 1683					
	Max. Gollop per Contra is	*Cr*	*£*	*s*	*d*
	By James Gould for the 4 doz bottles Xerie per Contra	62	3	4	

Anno 1682@					
	Per Contra	*Cr*	*£*	*s*	*d*
July 19	By Walter Stephens for the 4 packets Dowlas per Contra	53	51	1	6

Anno 1682@					
	Per Contra	*Cr*	*£*	*s*	*d*
Nov. 20	By merchandizes in the Owners endeavour for sundry goods bought of him	58	31	13	9
	By Proffitt & loss pd. for change of Kettles	8		9	11
1685 June	By what recd. of him in 3 Copper Taches sent in the Ship Joseph to Nevis	98	32	3	6
			64	7	2

Anno 1682@					
	Per Contra	*Cr*	*£*	*s*	*d*
	By Edmond Scrope & Compn for the neate proceeds of goods per Contra	33	138	7	8

Anno 1682@				
William Shepard of Dorchester merchant	Dr	£	s	d
July 29 To Cash pd. him	42	20		
Dec. 6 To Ditto pd. Henry Combes	43	5	1	9
28 To Ditto pd. Peter Rouswell	43	5		
Jan. 26 To Cash pd. him	43	7	8	7¼
To Bartholmew Bagg recd. of him	52	1		
		38	10	4¼

Anno 1683/4				
Beniamin Smith of the Citie of Bristoll distiller is	Dr	£	s	d
March 17 To Xeries Wines 12 Butts for 2 Butts of corrupt wines sould him	39	8		
1689 Feb. To Xeries Wines 23 Butts for 2 Casks of Lees Sold him	169	6		
		14		

(51)   **Bristoll 1682@**

Phillip Higginbottome	Dr	£	s	d
June 6 To Cash pd. Sundryes ~ out off: To	41		11	1
To Himselfe for ballance	17	1		
		1	11	1

Anno 1682				
Herrings my 1/3 of 49 Barrills in the Ship Owners Endeavour Michael Perrie Master to Nevis consign'd to Edmond Scrope & Company	Dr	£	s	d
To Tho. Scrope for theire cost & charges in Bristoll, being laden in partnership betwixt us, & consign'd as above				
To Tho. Scrope for my 1/3 of theire cost & charges in Bristoll	47 ⁶²	14	6	9

Anno 1682@				
John Jones	Dr	£	s	d
July 22 To Linincloth for acct. of Ben. Gold for 9 bolts	17	39	4	3
Oct. 9 To Linincloth 10 bolts for Will. Sheppard for 4 bolts sold him	7	15	3	
		54	7	3

Anno 1682				
Tho. Cooke & Nicholas Cary of London in Exchange Ally Goldsmiths	Dr	£	s	d
To Isaac Heming for money lent them £ s d				
on theire bond at £5 per Cent 400 0 0	76			
To Intrest at this £400 charg'd to				
Proffit & Losse 11 0 0	89			
December 14 To Isaac Heming for money lent them more on theire bond with the £411				
before mentioned, at £5 per Cent 189 0 0	76	600		
To Proffit & Losse for 6 month intrest of the £600	89	15		
		615		

Anno 1682@				
Marcellia Soape 79 Chests deposited by Henry Gibbs ⁶³	Dr	£	s	d
June 12 To Cash pd. Henry Gibbs	41	100		
17 To Isaac Heming for my bill in Favour of Gibbs	35	100		
To Proffitt & loss for Intrest of £200 & other charges	9	5	13	2
To Henry Gibbs for theire neate proceeds	4	28	9	
		234	2	2

Anno 1682@				
Robert Davis Yeoman	Dr	£	s	d
To Coppyhold Tenement in Portbury for one yeares rent ending the 24th March ending 1681@	20	5	5	
March 24 To Ditto for one yeares rent ending the 25th March 1682	20	5	5	

Anno 1682@		Cr	£	s	d
Per Contra					
By Linincloth for 10 bolts theire neate proceeds		7	38	10	4¼

Anno 1683/4		Cr	£	s	d
Beniamin Smith per Contra is		Cr	£	s	d
March 20	By Cash recd. of him	68	8		
1690 March 28	By Cash Received of him	175	6	00	00
			14		

Bristoll 1690@

		Cr	£	s	d
Philip Higginbottom per Contra		Cr	£	s	d
By Acct. of Ballances, for Ballance		193 *	1	11	1

Anno 1682		Cr	£	s	d
Herrings per Contra are		Cr	£	s	d
By Edm. Scrope for my 1/3 of theire neate proceeds as per acct.					
of sales dated		33	13	11	6
By Profit and Loss for Ballance		189 *		15	3
			14	6	9

Anno 1682@		Cr	£	s	d
Per Contra		Cr	£	s	d
July 29	By Cash recd. of him	42	39	4	3
Nov. 26	By Ditto recd. of him	43	15	3	
			54	7	3

Anno 1683		Cr	£	s	d
Tho. Cooke & Nicholas Cary per Contra		Cr	£	s	d
June	By Isaac Heming for money he received of them for intrest ½				
	yeare and the principall	76	615		

Anno 1682@		Cr	£	s	d
Per Contra		Cr	£	s	d
By Sundry accts for 79 Chests sold them at 43s per Cwt		53	234	2	2

Anno 1682@		Cr	£	s	d
Per Contra		Cr	£	s	d
July 1st	By Cash recd. of him	42	5	5	
1683 June 14	By Cash recd. of him	66	5	5	
1684 June 7	By Cash recd. of him in full of all rent	77	5	5	
			15	15	

1683	To Coppiehold Tenement in Portburie for one yeares rent due the 24th day of March 1683 for the 5 acres & 2 acres in Portburie	20	5	5
			15	15

Anno 1683

	Dr	£	s	d
Tikeing 12 pieces for acct. Robert Symes recd. per Horse Carrier	Dr	£	s	d
To Proffit & Losse for Portridge & £ s d				
Warehousroome 2				
To Ditto for Commission at £2 per Cent 6 7	*		8	7
To acct. current of Robert Symes for its				
neat proceeds 16 3 5	51	16	3	5
		16	12	

Anno 1684

	Dr	£	s	d
Robert Simes of Cerne in the County of Dorset merchant	Dr	£	s	d
To Cash paid his bill in favor of Bernard Wilkins	77	16	3	5

(52)   **Bristoll 1682@**

		Dr	£	s	d
	Gould 53 Pieces deposited by Nath. Haggatt	Dr	£	s	d
Sept. 12	To Cash pd. Lent said Haggatt on said Gold	42	48		

Anno 1682@

		Dr	£	s	d
	Barthlomew Bagg	Dr	£	s	d
Sept. 6	To Cattle for a Heifer sold him	5	2	15	10
Jan. 2	To Ditto for 2 bucces sold him	5	8	12	
			11	7	10

Anno 1684

	Dr	£	s	d
Tho. Dike of Bristoll Upholsterer is	Dr	£	s	d
To Tikeing 12 pieces for acct. of Robert Simes for 12 pieces sould				
him viz. 4 pieces at £1 13s 2 pieces at £1 8s 6 pieces at £1 4s				
per piece	51	16	12	

Anno 1682@

		Dr	£	s	d
	John Ford of Bristoll Boutcher Senior	Dr	£	s	d
June 27	To Cattle for 3 Calfes sould him	5	2	2	6

Anno 1682@

		Dr	£	s	d
	Henry Priest of Bristoll Boutcher	Dr	£	s	d
July 13	To Cattle for 3 Piggs sold him	5	3	1	

Anno 1682@

		Dr	£	s	d
	William Spoore Senior	Dr	£	s	d
Oct. 25	To Cash Lent him on his bill payable with intrest the 26th Aprill next	42	10		
1683 July 25	To Cash lent him on his bill	66	5		
February 13	To Cash paid lent him on his bill payable 13th May next	68	10		
1684 June 5	To Proffit & Losse for intrest of £5 to this day	73		3	6
1685 August	To Cash lent him on his bill	84	5		
January 25	To Cash lent him more for which hee hath given his bill wiith the foregoing £5 in one	107	5		
November 18	Wm. Spoore Senior is Debr		35	3	6

		Cr	£	s	d
	Anno 1684				
	Tikeing 12 pieces per Contra is	Cr	£	s	d
Aprill	*By Thomas Dyke for the 12 pieces sould him*	52	16	12	

		Cr	£	s	d
	Anno 1684				
	Robert Symes per Contra is	Cr	£	s	d
	By Tikeing 12 pieces for its neat proceeds as per acct. of Sales	51	16	3	5

Bristoll 1687

		Cr	£	s	d
	Gould 53 pieces viz) ten 22s pieces broad Gold of which one was	Cr	£	s	d
	light wanting about ⁸/₄, 14 20s piecess broad Gold, 1 piece old				
	gold valued at 20s / 12 halfe 20s pieces/ eight Guinies, six halfe				
	Guinies, and 2 five shilling pieces per Contra are				
	By Nathanael Haggatt for the money per Contra lent to him on				
	said 53 pieces of Gould, which were afterwards sould to				
	Humphry Corsley	19	48		

		Cr	£	s	d
	Anno 1682@				
	Per Contra	Cr	£	s	d
Sept. 7	*By Cash recd. of him*	42	2	15	10
Jan. 26	*By William Sheppard recd. of him*	50	1		
1683 Aprill 7	*By Cash recd. of him*	66	7	2	2
	By Proffit & Losse for meat at severall times	9		9	10
			11	7	10

		Cr	£	s	d
	Anno 1684				
	Tho. Dike per Contra is	Cr	£	s	d
June	*By Cash recd. of him*	77	16	12	

		Cr	£	s	d
	Anno 1682@				
	Per Contra	Cr	£	s	d
July 4	*By Cash recd. of him*	42		16	3
August 15	*By Abraham White for money hee recd*	30		14	
	By Jahzeel Speed for money hee recd. of him & spent it	122 *		12	3
			2	2	6

		Cr	£	s	d
	Anno 1682				
	Henry Priest per Contra is	Cr	£	s	d
	By Jahzeel Speed for money hee receivd of him and kept it &				
	spent it	122	3	1	

		Cr	£	s	d
	Anno 1683				
	William Spoore Senior per Contra	Cr	£	s	d
Aprill 27	*By Cash received of him*	66	10		
February 13	*By Cash received of him*	68	5		
1684 May 15	*By Cash recd. of him in part of his bill for £10*	77	5		
June 5	*By Cash recd. of him for intrest*	77		3	6
	By Cash received of him in full of his bill	77	5		
	By ballance resting due on his bill this eighteenth of November				
	1685 carried to the acct.	52	10		
	Wm. Spoore Senior per Contra		35	3	6

			£	s	d
	To money due on his bill for ballance of the above and due with intrest May 19th 1686	52	10		
	To Proffit & Losse for ½ yeares intrest due May 19th	105		6	
1687 July	To Ditto for intrest of said £10 to the 19th July 1687	137		12	
March 8	To Cash pd. lent him on his bill 27th instant	140	2		
			12	18	

(53)   **Bristoll 1682@**

		Dr	£	s	d
	Francis Whitchurch [64]	51	58	9	
	To Soape deposited per Henry Gibbs for 20 Chests				
1685 Aprill 6	To Rice for acct. of Simon Clement & Company for 2 baggs neat 6 3 17 at 23s	96	7	18	9
1689 January	To Reisons 60 Barrils & 120 piecess for 8 Barrils and 16 piecess sould him	177	59	1	½
			125	8	9½

Anno 1682@

		Dr	£	s	d
	William Burges of Bristoll Grocer	51	60	2	10
	To Soape deposited per Henry Gibbs for 20 Chests				
1685 Aprill 6	To Rice for acct. of Simon Clement & Company for 2 baggs neat 6cwt 2qr 22lb at 23s per Cwt	96	7	14	
1688 January	To Reisons Solis 32 Barrils for 8 barrills neat 21cwt 1qr 14lb at 22s per Cwt due Aprill 1st by contract	158	23	10	
			91	6	10

Anno 1682@

		Dr	£	s	d
	Charles Herbert	51	58	15	6
	To Soape deposited per Henry Gibbs for 20 Chests				

Anno 1682@

		Dr	£	s	d
	Thomas Rich	51	56	14	10
	To Soape deposited per Henry Gibbs for 19 Chests				

Anno 1682@

		Dr	£	s	d
	Richard Corsley of Bristoll Goldsmith	37	91	2	6
	To Worstead Stockins one trunck for 411 7/8 pieces of 8 at				
July 18	To Cash pd. him	42	8	17	6
			100		

Anno 1683

		Dr	£	s	d
	Andrew Stuckey Junior resident in the Kingdom of France in Rochell merchant				
Journall Fol 106	To Proffit & Losse for an error in an old acct. not now to bee found being committed some yeare since but by him acknowledged per his leter Oct. 30th 1683	9	41	14	
October 2	To Cash paid Jahzeel Speed disburs'd on a Certificate of marriage St. Nicklus	67		7	6
	To Isaac Heming for money made good to him to pay part of a bill of Exchange valued by him on said Heming & Company to salve his reputation, they having not effects in theire hands, which said Stuckey approves of in his leter to mee Feb. 26 1684	35	8	14	3
1684	To Cash paid ½ the reckoning on his arbitration at the Rose twice	77		2	6
June	To Cash paid port of a leter to him	77		2	
Sept. 2	To Cash paid ½ the reckoning on his arbitration at the 3 Cranes	77			9
25	To Cash paid postage of a Packet to him	77		3	
	To proffit & Losse for postage of severall leters & packets to, & from him about his own business	73	1	5	3
	To Ditto paid for a Release to Richard Champney and ½ reckoning at last meeting	73		1	0

June 24	By Cash recd. of him for ½ yeares intrest of £10 ending May 19th last past	108		6	
1687 May 26	By Ditto recd. of him in part	121	8		
July 19	By Cash recd. of him in full	121	2	12	
1688 May 23	By Cash received of him in full	141	2		
			12	18	

Bristoll 1685

			Cr	£	s	d
	Francis Whitchurch		127	58	9	
	By Proffit & Losse for the Soape per Contra received by a friend	144 65	7	18	8	
	By Cash recd. of him					
	By Proffit & Losse for					
1690 June 25	By Cash recd. of him in full	181	59	01	1½	
			125	8	9½	

Anno 1685

			Cr	£	s	d
	William Burgis per Contra		127	60	2	10
	By Proffit & Losse for the Soape per Contra received of a friend		83	7	14	
Aprill	By Cash recd. of him for 2 baggs rice		162	10		
1689 May 25	By Cash recd. of Wm. Lewis of his order in part		162	13	10	
31	By Cash recd. of him in full			91	6	10

Anno 1682

		Cr	£	s	d
	Charles Herbert per Contra is				
	By Proffit & Losse received of him by a friend	127	58	15	6

Anno 1682

		Cr	£	s	d
	Tho. Rich per Contra is				
	By Proffit & Losse for the money for the Soape received of him by a friend	127	56	14	10

Anno 1682@

		Cr	£	s	d
	Per Contra				
July 18	By Isaac Heming for his bill	35	100		

Anno 1683

		Cr	£	s	d
	Andrew Stuckey Junior per Contra				
	By Richard Champneys for a part of the ship Humility as per advice	45	73		
1684 September	By Cash recd. of Richard Champneys by an award on an arbitration	77	30	4	6
			103	4	6

			£	s	d
October 29	To Cash paid Daniel Guillin for charges in procuring a Certificate of — Nicholas's marriage	82	1		6
	To Ballance carried forward to his new acct. current	55	49	13	8
			103	4	6

Anno 1682@

		Dr	£	s	d
	Walter Stephens of Bristoll Linindraper	Dr	£	s	d
July 19	To Linincloth Henry Simes for 4 bolts sold him Dowlas	50	51	1	6
			51	1	6

Anno 1684

		Dr	£	s	d
	Walter Stephens of Bristoll Linindraper To James Holway & — Moxon for money bee undertook to pay to them by composition made at 10s in the pound	Dr	£	s	d
		26	50		

(54) Bristoll 1682@

		paire	s	d		Dr	£	s	d
	Worstead Stockins					Dr	£	s	d
	To it selfe for ballance					34	275	6	6
August 28	To Cash pd. Jos. White for	20	3	1		42	3	1	8
	To Ditto pd. John Massinger for	27				42	4	3	3
Sept. 14	To Cash pd. Joel Pinn for	09	2	10		42	1	5	6
	To Ditto pd. John Massinger for	32	3	1		42	4	18	8
29	To Ditto pd. Ditto for	29				42	4	9	5
	To Ditto pd. Joseph White for	24				42	3	14	
Oct. 12	To Ditto pd. John Massinger for	35				42	5	7	11
16	To Cash pd. Tho. Browne for	24		22		42	1	2	
26	To Ditto pd. John Massinger for	30	3	1		43	4	12	6
	To Ditto pd. Anth. Harris for	160	1	6		43	12		
Nov. 3d	To Ditto pd. John Massinger for	55				43	8	9	7
6	To Ditto pd. Joseph White for	40				43	6	3	4
7	To Ditto pd. Joseph George for	120	1	4		43	8		
8	to Ditto pd. John Day for	31	2	10		43	4	7	10
	To Ditto pd. John Ashman for	240		17		43	17		
10	To Ditto pd. Francis Rottenbury for Hot pressing of 488 paire					43		10	
	To Ditto pd. Anth. Harris for	50		18½		43	3	17	
10	To Ditto pd. Will. Spurbock	120		18		43	9		
14	To Ditto pd. Thomas Hill for	120		16		43	8		
	To Ditto pd. John Shuter for	48				43	7	8	
	To Ditto pd. for a doz Carnation Tape					43		8	
	To Ditto pd. John Massinger for	24				43	3	14	
	To Ditto pd. Frances Rottenbury					43		14	10
	To Ditto pd. Thomas Hill for	160		20		43	13	6	8
20	To Ditto pd. Ditto for	24	2	10		43	3	8	
25	To Ditto pd. Anthony Harris for	80		18		43	6		
	To Ditto pd. John Massinger for	47	3	1		43	7	4	11
	To Ditto pd. Jos. White for	24				43	3	14	
	To Ditto pd. Thomas Hill for	200		20		43	16	13	4
Dec. 4	To Ditto pd. John Massinger for	35				43	5	7	11
	To Ditto pd. Frances Rottenbury					43		6	4
	To Ditto pd. John Massinger for	41	3	1		43	6	6	5
	To Ditto pd. Ditto for	37				43	5	14	1
	To Ditto pd. Thomas Hill	160		20		43	13	6	8
	To Ditto pd. Andrew Creed for	80		20		43	6	13	4

	Anno 1682@				
	Per Contra	*Cr*	*£*	*s*	*d*
August 15	By Cash recd. of him	*42*	51	1	
	By Linincloth 4 packetts for money abated	*50*			6
			51	1	6

	Anno 1684				
	Walter Stephens per Contra is	*Cr*	*£*	*s*	*d*
October 4	By Cash received of him	*82*	25		
1689 June 21	By Cash recd. of him in full, the remainer being lost by a slight as				
	I am told	*162*	13		
			38		
	By Acct. of Ballances, for Ballance	*193 **	12		
			50		

	Bristoll 1682@				
	Per Contra	*Cr*	*£*	*s*	*d*
	By Worstead Stockins 2 Truncks for 960 paire at 3s 6d per				
	paire	*55*	168		
Jan. 12	By Adventure in the Mauretania 394 paire at 3s 6d'/₂	*60*	69	15	5
	By Adventure in the Rochell for 40 doz Bristol & 78 doz Wells	*63*	185	14	
			423	9	5
	By ballance carried to that acct.	*71*	304	4	3
			727	13	8

Date	Description				Fol.	£	s	d
	To Ditto pd. John Ashman for	40		18	43	3		
22	To Ditto pd. John Day for	17	3		43	2	11	
	To Ditto pd. John Massinger	43			43	6	12	7
28	To Ditto pd. Jos. White for	50			43	7	18	4
	To Ditto pd. an overplus of money to said White				43		4	
30	To Ditto pd. John Massinger for	39			43	6	0	3
						512	1	10
Jan 4	To Ditto pd. Thomas Hill for	180		20	43	15		
	To Ditto pd. Anth. Harris for	200		18	43	15		
	To Ditto pd. Francis Rottenbury				43		14	
11	To Ditto pd. Joell Pinie for	6	2	10	43		17	
13	To Ditto pd. John Massinger for	26	3	1	43	4		2
	To Ditto pd. Jos. White for	70			43	11	1	8
	To Ditto pd. John Day for	29			43	4	7	
20	To Ditto pd. John Massinger for	43			43	6	9	6
26	To Ditto pd. Ditto for 39 paire	39			43	6		3
Feb 1	To Ditto pd. Tho. Browne for	24	3	1	43	3	14	
2	To Ditto pd. John Day for	16			43	2	8	
3	To Ditto pd. Jos. White for	36	3	2	43	5	14	
	To Ditto pd. John Massinger for	33			43	5	1	9
12	To Ditto pd. Ditto	37			43	5	14	1
14	To Ditto pd. John Day for	20			43	3		
20	To Ditto pd. John Massinger for	28			43	4	6	4
21	To Ditto pd. John Day for	11			43	1	13	
28	To Ditto pd. John Massinger for	38			43	5	17	2
March 2d	To Ditto pd. John Day for	18			43	2	14	
7	T Ditto pd. for 100 paire Wells & 62 Bristol	162			43	16	13	10
13	To Ditto pd. for	88			66	13	5	6
17	To Ditto pd. John Massinger for	35			66	5	7	11
1683 March 26	To Cash paid John Massinger for	33	3		66	4	19	
27	To Cash paid John Ashman for	80	1	4	66	5	6	8
30	To Ditto paid John Ashman for	120	1	4	66	8		
Aprill 2	To Cash paid Tho. Hill for	48	1	4	66	3	13	8
	To Ditto paid him for	12	2	9	66	1	13	
	To Ditto paid him for	26	2	10	66	3	4	
4	To Ditto paid John Massinger for	40	3		66	6		
9	To Cash paid John Massinger for	35	3		66	5	5	
14	To Cash paid Tho. Hill for	20	2	10	66	2	16	8
18	To Cash paid Francis Rottenburie for hot pressing 491 paire				66		10	2
	To Cash paid John Perrie for	19		2 8	66	2	10	8
19	To Cash paid John Massinger for	39	3		66	5	17	
27	To Ditto paid John Massinger for	48	2	11	66	7		
May 4	To Cash paid Tho. Hill for	13	2	10	66	1	16	10
	To Ditto paid Joell Piney for	7	2	9	66		18	8
	To Ditto paid John Massinger for 28 paire	28	2	11	66	4	1	8
11	To Cash paid John Massinger for	40	2	11	66	5	16	8
	To Ditto paid Joel Pinn for	9	2	8	66	1	4	
18	To Ditto paid John Day for	7	2	10	66		19	10
19	To Ditto paid John Massinger for	34	2	11	66	4	19	2
						727	13	8

(55)	**Bristoll 1682@**							
	John Machen				Dr	£	s	d
Sept. 14	To Linincloth for Ben.Gold for one bolt sold him				17	3	15	6
Oct.	To Linincloth for William Sheppard for one bolt sold him				7	4	4	4
						7	19	10

Bristoll 1682@

		Cr	£	s	d
	Per Contra				
	By Cash recd. of him	42	3	15	6
Oct. 16	By Ditto recd. of him	42	4	4	4
			7	19	10

	Anno 1682@				
	Merchandizes in the Martha & Sarah to Barbadoes	Dr	£	s	d
Sept. 28	To Cash pd. for 6 Firkins Butter	42	4	18	6
Oct. 19	To Ditto pd. George Popley for his noate for shooes	42	9	18	
28	To Ditto pd. Jane Sheppard for 4 Firkins Butter	43	3	9	5
30	To Ditto pd. for 7 Flitches Bacon	43	3	17	3
Nov. 4	To Ditto pd. Thomas Bolton etc. for a Flitch & a halfe of Bacon	43		18	1
	To Ditto pd. Rich. Wasbrow 4 boxes candles William Rogers for 16 paire shoes	43	4	4	8
20	To Ditto pd. sundry charges on said goods	43	1	2	7
Jan. 31	To Ditto pd. Edward Taylor for a hogshead of Biskett	43	2	19	
			31	7	6

	Anno 1682				
	Andrew Stuckey Junior of Rochell merchant	Dr	£	s	d
1686 Oct.	To Calfskins 36 dozen laden per his order in the Ship and to himselfe consigned	85	43	10	3
	To Cash paid port of a leter to him	119		1	
	To Cash paid John England for 30 paire Stockins, sent to him in the ship — to Rochele	120	4	17	6
			8	8	9
	To acct. of Ballances, for Ballance	193 *	1	4	11
			49	13	10

	Anno 1682@				
	Worstead Stockins two Truncks Laden aboard the Agreement of Corke Jarvis Hurst Master for Cadiz	Dr	£	s	d
Sept. 21	To Stockins for 960 paire at 3s 6d per paire	54	168		
	To Proffitt & Loss pd. Charges on said Stockins	8	7	2	6
			175	2	6
	To Ditto for Ballance	189 *	8	7	3
			183	9	9

	Anno 1682@				
	John Pitts	Dr	£	s	d
Sept. 24	To Xeries Wine 30 butts for 2 butts sold him	45	44	10	
Nov. 10	To Ditto for 2 butts sold him	45	45		
			89	10	

	Anno 1683				
	John Love of Bristoll Grocer is	Dr	£	s	d
August 27	To Sugar 15 hhds in the Owners Endeavour from Jamaica wt neat 108cwt 2qr 22lb at 24s per Cwt	70	130	8	9
October	To Robert Summers for money drawne on him & by him accepted to bee paid	17	20		
1685 Aprill 6	To Rice for acct. Simon Clement & Company for 3 baggs neat 10cwt 2qr 16lb at 23s per Cwt	96	12	4	9
August 22	To French wine 6 hhds for 2 doz qt bottles of claret at 9s 6d	94			
	To Proffit & Losse for 2 doz empty bottles at 2s per doz	89	1	3	
1687 May 9	To Cash paid him for his bill of Exchange assign'd mee, payable in London	121	100		
July 19	To Reisons Solis 27 Barrills for 4 Barrills weight neat 10cwt 3qr 10lb at 24s due Oct. 25th next	136	13		1½
November 7	To Reisons Solis 65 Barrills for 6 Barrills neat 16cwt 0qr 18lb at 24s due Feb. 7th	145	19	7	10¼
1689 February	To Reisons 60 Barrills & 120 pcs for 8 Barrils & 16 pieces sould him	177	59	3	1¼
			355	7	7

Anno 1685				
Merchandines in the Martha & Sarah per Contra	Cr	£	s	d
By Adventure the 2nd in Ditto Ship to Barbadoes for the cost &				
charges of the good per Contra, carryed to that acct., because				
Edward Parsons to whom they were consign'd, doest render an				
acct. of both Adventures in one	60	31	7	6

Anno 1684				
Andrew Stuckey Junior of Rochel in France merchant is	Cr	£	s	d
By ballance of his former acct. current sent him per Post	53	49	13	8

Anno 1682@				
Per Contra	Cr	£	s	d
By Arthur Robinson & Company for theire neate proceeds	61	183	9	9

Anno 1682@					
	Per Contra	Cr	£	s	d
Jan. 12	By Cash recd. of him	43	44	10	
March 1683 26	By Cash recd. of him	66	43	5	
	By Jahzeel Speed for money hee had Spent in potts of wine on				
	Score in said Pitts his house	122	1	15	
			89	10	

Anno 1683					
	John Love per Contra is	Cr	£	s	d
December 18	By Cash recd. of him	67	20		
February 14	By Cash recd. of him	68	125		6
	By Proffit & Losse for ballance abated	89	5	8	9
1685 Aprill	By Cash received of him for 2 baggs of rice	83	12	4	9
1686 Dec. 28	By Cash recd. of him for the wine per Contra	120	1	3	
1687 June 10	By Isaac Heming for money of Ralph Swinson on the bill per				
	Contra	130	100		
November 30	By Cash received of him	139	13		1
February 24	By Cash received of him	140	19	7	6
1690 June 26	By Cash recd. of David Phillips on his bill	181	59	3	
			355	7	7

(56)	**Bristoll 1682@**				
	Lewis Adams of Bristoll Vintner	Dr	£	s	d
Oct. 11	To Xeries wines 30 butts for 2 butts sold him	45	47		
1683 September 19	To Xeries wine 40 Butts for 5 Butts sould him at £24 5s per Butt at 6 moths	65	120		
1688 January 1	To Xeries Wine 23 Butts for 10 Butts sould him at £26 per Butt payable one half the 1st of Aprill other ½ the 1st of July next	150	260		
1689 March 14	To Ditto for one Butt sold him at £34 payable April 14th 1690	169	34		
1690 Octobr 8	To wines my ½ of 20 Butts for ½ the amountant of 9 Butts of Xerie & 1 hogshead Tent sold him and John Wimpenny Jointly the Xerie at £33 per Butt and the Tent at £18 to be pd. for ½ on the 7th Dec. & ½ on 25th Jan. next as per Bills	186	157	10	
			618	10	

	Anno 1682@				
	Per Contra	Dr	£	s	d
Oct. 28	To Cash pd. for straw etc.	43		6	1
Jan 22	To Alexander Dolman for want of measure	48		10	
	To Proffitt & loss for comission portridge etc.	9	1		6
	To James Gould for theirre neat proceeds	62	41	4	
			43		7

	Anno 1683				
	John Gore of Bristoll Grasier & John Hurtnell Junior merchant of same Citie	Dr	£	s	d
September 29	To Estate at Clapton for ½ yeares rent for the farme due 1st August £ 35 s 0 d 0				
March 22	To Ditto for the other ½ yeares rent due 20th March following 35 0 0	38	70		

	Anno 1682@				
	Richard Francklin	Dr	£	s	d
Oct. 12	To Cash pd. him for the neate proceeds of a parcell of Tobacco	42	1	8	8
	To sundry accts for the neate proceeds of seaven hds Tobacco	24,57,8	1	13	6
			3	2	2

	Anno 1682@				
	Linincloth 32 bolts for acct. of Mr James Gould	Dr	£	s	d
Oct. 28	To Cash for straw etc.	43		13	10
Nov. 4	To Ditto pd. Filing a certificate	43			4
March 12	To Ditto allowed Sanders for what wanting in measure	43		1	8
1683 January	To Alexander Dolman for money abated for short measure and damage	48	1	9	6
	To John Sanders for 1 Bolt damnified return'd & sent him per Carrier to Dorchester £ s d	57	4	8	4½
	To Proffit & Losse for Portridge & warehouseroome 16 00				
	To Ditto for my Commission at £2 per Cent 3 7 5½	73	4	3	5½
	To James Gould his acct. current for its neat proceeds	62	157	17	6
			168	14	8

	Bristoll 1682/3@				
	Per Contra	*Cr*	*£*	*s*	*d*
March 6	*By sundry accts recd. of him in full*	*45,43,,9*	47		
1684 Aprill 22	*By Cash recd. of him in part*	*68*	60		
June 26	*By Cash recd. of him*	*77*	25		
August 8	*By Cash recd. of him*	*77*	24		
	By Jahzeel Speed for wine hee drank of his at severall times as				
	per his noate	*69*	11		
1689 Aprill 29	*By Cash received of him in part*	*162*	50		
August 5	*By Cash received of him in part*	*160*	50		
September 28	*By Cash recd. of him*	*168*	50		
December 24	*By Cash received of him in part*	*173*	80		
February 20	*By Ditto recd. of him in full*	*175*	30		
1690 June 18	*By the Lady Ann Powlett , for 4 doz quarts of Xerie sent her*	*155*	4	8	4
July 4	*By John Earl of Bristoll, for a Rundlett and 2 quart bottles of*				
	Xerie sent him per Esaw. White	*150*	4	11	4
24	*By Cash recd. of him in full*	*181*	25	00	4
			461	00	
	By Acct. of Ballances, for Ballance	*193 **	157	10	
			618	10	

	Anno 1682@				
	Linincloth 10 bolts for acct. of of James Gould & Max. Gallop	*Cr*	*£*	*s*	*d*
Oct. 26	*By Alexander Dolman for said 10 bolts sold him at the cost*	*48*	43		7

	Anno 1684				
	John Gore & Company per Contra are	*Cr*	*£*	*s*	*d*
June 10	*By Cash recd. of John Gore in part*	*77*	30		
October 22	*By Cash recd. of John Hurtnell in part*	*82*	16		
	By Cash then recd. of John Gore	*82*	4	5	
	By Proffit & Losse received on acct. of John Gore wth what hee				
	hath paid is £35	*89*		15	
	By John Hurtnell Junior for the remainder of his ½ of the rent				
	per Contra	*38*	19		
			70		

	Anno 1682@				
	Per Contra	*Cr*	*£*	*s*	*d*
Oct. 25	*By Isaac Heming for the neate proceeds of a parcell Tobacco*	*35*	3	2	2

	Anno 1682@				
	Per Contra	*Cr*	*£*	*s*	*d*
Nov. 10	*By John Sanders sold him 9 bolts at 6 deniers off the cost*	*57*	49	4	8
1683 July 17	*By sundry accts for an Invoyce of 11 Bolts sould Alex. Dolman*				
	& John Sanders at 1s off	*48, 57*	57	9	11
25	*By Alexander Doleman for 12 Bolts sould him at 1s 3d off the*				
	Invoyce	*48*	62		1
			168	14	8

	Anno 1683/4				
	Lincloth 9 Bolts recd. per Horse Carrier for acct. of Henry Simes	Dr	£	s	d
March 12	To Cash paid fileing the Certificate in the Custom house	68			6
	£ s d				
	To Proffit & Losse for portridge &				
	warehouse roome 4 6	73			
	To Ditto for my Commission at £2 per				
	Cent 12 9	73		17	3
	To Henry Symes his acct. current for its neat proceeds	5	31	12	4
			32	10	1

(57)	**Bristoll 1682@**				
	John Streaten of Clevedon Yeoman	Dr	£	s	d
Oct. 3rd	To Land Clevedon for ½ a yeares rent of 14 acres ending the				
	2nd August	32	6		
Feb. 8	To Ditto for ½ a yeares rent ending the 2nd Feb. instant	32	6		
1683	To Ditto for ½ yeares rent due the 2nd August 1683	32	6		
	To Ditto for ½ yeares rentrest due February 2nd 1683	32	6		
1684 Feb. 2	To Ditto for ½ yeares rent due Feb. 2nd 1684	32	6		
1685 Jan. 9	To Ditto for ½ yeares rent due Sept. 29th 1685	32	6		
	To Cash paid him for his noat of disbursements , Lords rent etc.	107	1	12	10
1686 Aprill 16	To Land in Clevedon for ½ a yeares rent for Insolds ending 2nd				
	February 1685	32	6		
January 11	To Ditto for ½ a yeares rent of Insolds ending 29th of September				
	1686	116	6		
1687 June 7	To Ditto for ½ yeares rent due Feb. 2nd 1686	116	6		
September 29	To Ditto for ½ yeares rent due Sept. 29th 1687	116	6		
1688 July	To Ditto for ½ yeares rent due March 1st 1687	116	6		
	To Ditto for ½ yeares rent due August 2nd 1688	116	6		
1689	To Ditto for ½ yeares rent due March 1st 1688	116	6		
	To Ditto for ½ yeares rent due Sept. 1689	116	6		
			85	12	10

	Anno 1682@				
	John Sanders Linincloth draper	Dr	£	s	d
Nov. 10	To Linincloth for acct. James Gold for 9 bolts sold him at 6				
	deniers	56	49	4	8
1683 July 17	To Ditto for 7 bolts of Wittry sould him	56	35	12	7½
			84	17	3½

	Anno 1684	Cr	£	s	d
	Lincloth 9 Bolts per Contra are	Cr	£	s	d
May	By Edmond Scrope for theire value sent him at 2s 6d off the Invoyce	38	32	10	1

	Bristoll 1682@				
	Per Contra	Cr	£	s	d
Nov. 4	By Cash recd. of him	43	6		
1683 May 10	By Cash recd. of him	66	6		
November 8	By Cash recd. of him	67	6		
	By Henry Gibbes for ½ yeares rent paid him in 16s Lords rent heee paid & £5 4s	79	6		
1684 May 14	By Cash recd. of John Stretton	83	6		
1685 Januy 9	By Cash reecd of John Streatten for ½ yeares rent for Insolds ending 29th Sept. 1685	107	6		
	By Land in Clevedon for John Strettens noat of disbursements for the poore etc.	32	1	12	10
Aprill 22	By Ditto for ½ yeares Lords rent for both Tenements to Sept. 1685 & £2 abated him out of his rent	116		18	
May 22	By Cash received of him for ½ yeares rent ending the 25th March last	108	5	2	
1686 January 13	By Cash received of him for ½ yeares rent due Sept. 29th 1686 abating him 1s 4d½	120	6		
1687 July 28	By Cash received of him for ½ yeares rent due Feb. 2nd 1686	121 *	6		
December 24	By Cash received of him in part for ½ yeares rent due Sept. 29th 1687	140	4		
March 21	By Ditto recd. of him in money £1 19s 00d & 1s allowed for powder & shott is in full for ½ yeares rent ending September 29th 1687	140	2		
1688 August 16	By Cash rec in part for ½ yeares rent due February 2nd 1687	141	4		
	By Ditto Received of him in full for 1 yeares Intrest id est rent ending Feb. 2nd 1687	157	2		
1689 May 11	By Cash received of him in part of ½ yeares rent due Nov. 29th 1688	162	5	4	
	By Land at Clevedon for his noat of disbursment for ½ yeares Lords rent	116		16	
November 16	By Cash recd. of him in part	168	3	10	
	By Acct. of Ballances, for Ballance	193 *	8	10	
			85	12	10

	Anno 1682/3@				
	Per Contra	Cr	£	s	d
1683 March 12	By Cash recd. of him	66	49	4	8
February 6	By Cash received of the Widow Sanders	68	31	1	
	By James Gould for money allowed for want of measure on one bolt	62		3	3
	By Ditto for 1 Bolt of damnifyed cloth received back, and return'd to James Gould	56	4	8	4½
			84	17	3½

	Anno 1684				
	Hugh Hodges of Sherborne in the County of Dorset Counsellor at law	Dr	£	s	d
Aprill 22	To sundry accts for 2 doz bottles white wine, bottles, pannier etc.	73	1	2	8
	To Profit and Loss, for Ballance	189 *		2	4
			1	5	

	Anno 1682@				
	Per Contra	Dr	£	s	d
Nov. 4	To Cash pd. port of a Letter from him	43			9
	To Proffit & Losse for port of severall leters	73		7	6
	To Isaac Heming for money paid him per bill of Exchange in London	35	37	4	7
			37	12	10

	Anno 1684				
	Adventure 3rd in the Dyamond Ketch John Bennet master to Nevis consignd to John Streater & Edmond Scrope merchants there	Dr	£	s	d
Aprill	To Cash paid Henry Gibbes for 2 pieces cont. 238 Galls of Brandy at 3s 3d per Gal	68	38	15	
	To sundry accts for 30 boxes cont. 179 doz 11 at 3s 6d per dozen £ s d	65,50	33	13	½
26	To Cash paid custom, fees & bills 2 6 6	38			
	To Ditto paid John Bennet for fraight 4	68	6	6	6
May 9	To Cash paid Rich. Washbrow		78	14	6½
	To Profit and Loss for Ballance	· 189 *	36	13	½
			115	7	7

	Anno 1690@				
	Thomas Gibbons per Contra is	Dr	£	s	d
	To Acct. of Ballances, for Ballance	193 *		4	2

	Anno 1683				
	French Wine 1 hogshead white & 1 Tierce Claret bought of John Blackwell	Dr	£	s	d
June 23	To John Blackwell for said hogshead & tierce bought of him	26	10		

(58)	**Bristoll 1682@**				
	Thomas Curtis	Dr	£	s	d
Nov. 10	To Cash pd. Tho. Coleman on his bill	43	100		
1684 Aprill 27	To Robert Yate for money hee recd. of Samuell House by a bill of exchange assign'd per said Yate	39	16		
1685 November 21	To Cash paid lent his wife in Bristol	107	3		
1688 October 22	To Cash paid Wm. Richards for 7 Casks Butter, with charges of Cooperidge etc.	157	7	15	6
November 20	To Cash paid Edward Lloyd for a parcell of wine as per noat	157	3	3	
	To his new acct. current for ballance, carried to that acct.	169	14	1	6
			144		

		Anno 1684				
	Hugh Hodges per Contra is	*Cr*	*£*	*s*	*d*
Aprill 19	By Cash recd. of him	68	1	5	

		Anno 1682@				
	Thomas Williams of Merleaux merchant	*Cr*	*£*	*s*	*d*
Oct. 31	To Cash recd. of John Machen	43	20		
	By Lincloth for his acct. for the neat proceeds of 4 Bolts Canvas	47	17	12	10
			37	12	10

		Anno 1686				
	Adventure 3rd in the Dyamond Ketch per Contra is	*Cr*	*£*	*s*	*d*
	By Edmond Scrope & Company for the neat proceeds of the two				
	pieces Brandy 20 of the boxes of Candles per Contra, as per				
	theire acct. of Sales closed July 7th 1686, being 20029 lb Sugar				
	at 10s per Cwt	33	100	2	5
1687 May	By Ditto for 3252lb Sugar per neat proceeds of 10 boxes				
	Candles omitted in theire former acct. of Sales as per acct. of				
	Sales March 10th 1686	33	15	5	2
			115	7	7

		Anno 1682@				
	Thomas Gibbins of Virginea merchant	*Cr*	*£*	*s*	*d*
	By Richard Francklin for the neate proceeds of 3 hhds Tobacco	56		4	2

		Anno 1683				
	Port wine 1 hogshead & 1 Tierce per Contra	*Cr*	*£*	*s*	*d*
June 23	By Sir George Strode for 3 doz bottles, & the bottles etc.	24	1	18	
	By Tho. Goldney for 1 doz bottles	16		11	
July 4	By Sam. Davis for 3 doz bottles & bottles	63	1	13	
6	By Doctor Francis Hungerford for 2 doz bottles and bottles etc.	59	1	4	
September 3	By Samuel Davis for 1 doz bottles wine & the bottles	63		11	
	By John Blackwell for the Tierce of Claret return'd to him which				
	hee received back	26	4		
			9	17	
	By Profit and Loss, for Ballance	189 *		3	
			10		

		Bristoll 1683				
	Thomas Curtis per Contra is	*Cr*	*£*	*s*	*d*
July	By Cash recd. of Ben. Cole [66] for which I valued my bill on				
	Thomas Curtis	66	10		
	By Proffit & Losse paid by my order in Reading	9	90		
January 31	By Cash recd. of Ben. Cole for which I valued my bill on him	68	8		
	By Proffit & Losse recd. of him in Reading	153	11		
	By Isaac Heming for money hee paid said Heming in London	152	25		
			144		

Anno 1682@				
Thomas Longman of Bristoll Grocer	Dr	£	s	d
Nov. 20 To sugar 2 hhds for said sugar sold him at 23s per Cwt	58	22	7	6

Anno 1682				
Xeries Wine my ¼ part of 40 Buttts imported in the ship	Dr	£	s	d
Expectation in partnership with John Cooke				
January To John Cooke for theire first cost as per Invoyce Jan. 20th				
1682/3 appears	32	96	7	4
To Profit and Loss, for Ballance	189 *	48	6	6
		144	33	30

Anno 1682@				
Edward Parsons of Barbadoes merchant	Dr	£	s	d
Nov. 20 To Adventure in the Crown Lyon for the neate proceeds 40				
Firkins butter	33	16	19	4
1685 To Adventures 1st & 2nd in the ship Martha & Sarah to				
Barbadoes for the neat proceeds of sundry merchandizes sent				
consign'd to him as per his acct. of sales closed June 1685 may				
appeare	60	90		1
		106	19	5
To Profit and Loss, for Ballance	189 *			3½
		106	19	8½

Anno 1682@				
Sugar 2 hhds imported on the Crowne Lyon for acct. of Martha	Dr	£	s	d
Speed				
Nov. 20 To Cash pd. Custome, Fees & Freight etc.	43	3	14	9
To Edward Parsons for theire First cost	58	17	13	11
		21	8	8
To Profit and Loss for Ballance	189 *		18	10
		22	7	6

Anno 1682@				
Adventure 2nd in the Owners endeavour for Nevis And Jamaica	Dr	£	s	d
Nov. 20 To Sundry accts for goods & charges	4,50,43	70	4	6
To Profit and Loss, for Ballance	189 *	34	9	3
		104	13	9

Anno 1682				
William Davis of Bristoll	Dr	£	s	d
Sept. 7 To Sundry accts for 5 hhds Tobacco sold him	27, 5	37	1	9

Anno 1683				
William Rishton of Bristoll Linindraper	Dr	£	s	d
Aprill 27 To Lincloth 5 bolts acct. Max. Gallop for theire value sould him	69	20	10	9

Anno 1682@				
	Per Contra	Cr	£	s	d
Jan. 29	By Cash recd. of him	43	20		
March 8	By Ditto recd. of him	43	2	7	6
			22	7	6

Anno 1683/4				
	Xeries Wine my ¼ of 40 Butts per Contra	Cr	£	s	d
	By Xeries wine 40 Butts for my ¼ part of theire neat proceeds	65	144	13	10

Anno 1682@				
	Per Contra	Cr	£	s	d
Nov. 20	By Sugar 2 hhds for theire first cost in her 1st voyage to Barbadoes	58	17	13	11
1683	By Sugar 2 hhds in the Crowned Lyon her 2nd voyage to Barbadoes for theire 1st cost as per Invoyce dated 3rd moth 26th 1683	35	18	4	4
1683/4	By Sugar 4 hhds in the Restauration for theire cost there as per Invoyce March 1st 1683/4	75	40	10	10
1684	By Sugar 2 hhds in the Olive tree for theire cost & charges per Invoyce 5th month 9th 1684	79	17	13	7½
	By Sugar 1 hogshead 1 Kilderkin & 1 Firkin in the Olive tree for theire cost & charges as per Invoyce 13th June 1685	92	12	17	
			106	19	8½

Anno 1682@				
	Per Contra	Cr	£	s	d
Nov. 20	By Thomas Longman for said 2 hhds sold him	58	22	7	6

Anno 1683				
	Adventure in the Owners Endeavour per Contra	Cr	£	s	d
September	By Michael Perrie for 1 Worme, 1 Copper Still, 2 Taches & 1 Cooler sould in Jamaica as per his acct. of sales	47	43	2	10
	By Bethell Walter for 1 hogshead Sugar from Jamaica laden per Thomas Mosse	92	10	17	9
1685 Aprill	By sundry accts for 17 Copper Coolers returned, & sold to Oliver Mosely & Jos. Badger	50, 4	50	13	2
			104	13	9

Anno 1683				
	William Davis per Contra	Cr	£	s	d
May 3	By Cash received of him	66	10	11	
	By Isaac Heming for his bill on Ralph Swinton	35	26	10	
			37	1	
	By Profit & Loss, for Ballance	189 *			9
			37	1	9

Anno 1683				
	William Rishton per Contra	Cr	£	s	d
Aprill 27	By Lincloth 5 bolts for acct. Max. Gallop for money abated him	69			3
	By Cash recd. of him	66	20	10	6
			20	10	9

(59)	Bristoll 1682@				Dr	£	s	d
	Tobacco 2 hhds imported on the John in partnership with Edw. Martindale							
Dec. 19	To Cash pd. Custome, Fees, weighing etc.				43	7	16	6
	To Abraham Sanders for money abated him	£	s	d 6	59			
	To Tho. Puxton for freight and averidge	3	19		22			
	To Proffit & Losse for cooperidge 2s Celleridge 5s 9d hallidge 6d		8	3	9	4	7	9
1683 March 24	To Ed. Martindale for his ½ of theire neat proceeds	3	13	7½	24			
	To Proffit & Losse for my ½ of its neat proceeds	3	13	7½	9	7	7	3
						19	11	6

	Anno 1682@	Dr	£	s	d
	Abraham Sanders				
Dec. 21	To Tobacco 2 hhds for said hhds sold him	59	19	11	6

	Anno 1683	Dr	£	s	d
	James Twivord of Bristoll mercer is ~~to sundry accts~~				
January 28	To Xeries wine 1 butt out of 40 for 3½ dozen Bottles Xerie	70	2	16	
	To Proffit & Losse for 3½ doz bottles	73		7	
			3	3	

	Anno 1682@	Dr	£	s	d
	Doctor Hungerford of Reading				
Dec. 30	To Xerie wine one butt for 6 doz bottles with panniers etc.	59	5	14	
	To Ditto for 2 doz for himselfe & 4 doz for Winchcombe	43, 9, 59	5	11	
July 6	To sundry accts for 2 doz bottles white wine, bottles etc.	9, 57	1	5	
November 24	To sundry accts for 2 doz bottles Xerie, with bottles & Panniers etc.	65,9	1	17	
December 14	To sundry accts for 6 doz bottles Xerie sent Sir Henry Winchcomb	70, 9	5	11	
January 3	To sundry accts for 2 doz bottles Xerie, bottles etc. sent per Roger Redbourne	70, 9	1	17	
31	Tp Proffit & Losse for 4 doz bottles Xerie, bottles etc. sent per Roger Redbourne	73	3	10	
1684 Aprill 4	To Ditto for 2 doz bottles of Xerie & the bottles sent per Thobias Lewtons waggon	73	1	13	
June 26	To John Blackwell for 2 doz Xerie for himself, 6 doz for Sir H. Winchcombe, panniers etc.	59	8	3	6
July 10	To sundry accts for 4 Panniers cont. 12 doz bottles white & claret, with bottles, Panniers etc.	73, 78	6	18	6
September 25	To sundry accts for 6 Panniers cont. 8 doz Xerie with bottles Panniers etc.	73, 79	7	9	
			49	9	

	Anno 1682@	Dr	£	s	d
	Edward Hollister of Bristoll Cooper				
Dec. 21	To Proffit & loss for one yeares rent of the Cellar in Rosemary Lane	8	2		

	Anno 1682@	Dr	£	s	d
	Xeries wine one butt				
	To Xeries wine 30 butts for said butt	45	20	10	
Jan. 15	To Cash pd. John Cheshire for 41 dozen empty bottles	43	3	8	4

Bristoll 1682@		Cr	£	s	d
	Per Contra	Cr	£	s	d
Dec. 21	By Abraham Sanders for said Tobacco sold him	59	19	11	6

Anno 1682@		Cr	£	s	d
	Per Contra	Cr	£	s	d
Jan. 31	By Cash recd. of him	43	19	11	
1683 March 24	By Tobacco 2 hhds for money abated	59			6
			19	11	6

Anno 1684		Cr	£	s	d
	James Twiford per Contra is	Cr	£	s	d
Aprill 25	By Cash recd. of him in full	68	3	3	

Anno 1683		Cr	£	s	d
	Doctor Francis Hungerford per Contra is	Cr	£	s	d
January 16	By Cash received of Tho. Hungerford his nephew	67	9	5	
	By Proffit & Losse for money I recd. of him at twice in Reading	11 [67]	11	5	
1684 Aprill 7	By Cash recd. of Tho. Hungerford	68	3	14	
November	By Jonathan Lamboll for money hee paid him by my order	87	24	4	
	By Proffit & Losse for ballance	73 *	1	1	
			49	9	

Anno 1682@		Cr	£	s	d
	Per Contra	Cr	£	s	d
Dec. 21	By Cash recd. of him	43	1	10	
1683 March 26	By Cash recd. of him	66		10	
			2		

Anno 1682@		Cr	£	s	d
	Per Contra	Cr	£	s	d
Dec. 30	By Doctor Hungerford for 18 gallons with charges	59	5	14	
Jan. 8	By John Hartnell for six quarts	38		7	6
26	By Sam. Davis for 2 doz bottles	63	1	12	

			23	18	4
	To Profit and Loss, for Ballance	189 *	7	10	2
			31	8	6

	Anno 1683/4				
	John Blackwell of Bristoll Vintner is	Dr	£	s	d
March	To ballance of his former acct., brought from that accont	26	39	4	
	To Wines Xeries 20 Butts for 9 Butts sould him at £19 10s per Butt, abating £1 6s 0d for ullage, payable ½ 25th June, & ½ 25th Sept. by his bills £ s d	76	174	4	
1684	To Andrew Kirby Father & Sonne for 530 1/3 Ecu ⁶⁸ the cost & charges in Bourdeaux of 8 tonns wine in the Successe Samuell Greening which I spared him at the first cost, hee to runne the Risgo, & pay theire cost there the Ecu at 55½ 122 12 10	64			
	To Proffit & Losse for the Post of leters about these wines 3 9	73	122	16	7
	To Xeries Wines 10 Butts for ½ 446¾ pieces 8 the first cost of 10 Butts Xerie I spared to him on the ship Agreement laden by John Mayne the piece of 8 at 4s 6d 50 5 2¼	70			
Aprill	To Ditto for ½ port of leters about these wines 5 9	70			
	To Ditto paid £53 1s 2d custom, freight, etc. his ½ is 26 10 7	70	77	1	6
8	To Ditto for my other halfe sould him payable by his bill Oct. 8th	70	112		
	To Proffit & Losse for money he abated by consent on the severall parcells wine per Contra	73		11	6
			525	17	7

(60)

	Bristoll 1682@				
	Thomas Wedmore & John Ford	Dr	£	s	d
Jan. 2	To Cattle for a bucc & a Cow sold them	5	8	10	

	Anno 1683				
	George Dighton of Bristoll Brewer is	Dr	£	s	d
January 7	To sundry accts for 2 doz bottles of Xerie at 16s & 2 doz bottles empty	70, 9	1	16	
1684 June 21	To Cash lent him on his bond, being money wanting in his sonns Cash	77	58	14	6
			60	10	6

	Anno 1682@				
	Sugar 4 Butts and one hogshead imported on the John & Elizabeth to London consigned to Isaac Heming there	Dr	£	s	d
Jan. 2d	To Edmond Scrope & John Streater for theire cost	33	51	14	5
	To Isaac Heming for custom & other charges	76	13	11	2
			65	5	7
	To Profit and Loss, for Ballance	189 *		10	11
			65	16	6

31	By Max. Gallop for 4 doz	34	3	4	
	By Sir John Drake for 6 doz	63	5	2	
Feb. 8	By John Whitwood for 1 doz	64		14	
14	By John Digby for 10 doz	37	8	10	
	By Ann Pawlet for one doz	48		17	
22	By Dr. Hungerford for 6 doz	59	5	8	
	By James		31	8	6

Anno 1683/4

		Cr	£	s	d
	John Blackwell per Contra is	Cr	£	s	d
March 15	By Cash received of him paid John Gandy	68	20		
1684 Aprill 15	By Cash recd. of him	68	11	13	
17	By Cash recd. of him	68		17	10
22	By Hugh Hodges for 2 doz bottles white wine, Pannier, bottles etc.	57	1	2	6
	By Proffit & Losse for 12 Gals Xerie out of one of my Butts sould him at 4s	73	2	8	
June 26	By Dr. Fra. Hungerford for 8 doz bottles Xerie at 6s with panniers etc.	59	8	3	
July 24	By Cash recd. of him	77	100		
	By Xerie wine 2 Butts bought of him at £25 per Butt	79	50		
	By French wine 2 hhds for 1 hogshead bought of him at	78	6	10	
	By Proffit & Losse for 2 Galls Xerie for my own use	73		8	
August 21	By Cash recd. of him	77	119	16	6
September	By sundry accts for 1 hogshead of Claret bought of him at	79, 80	6		
November 18	By Cash recd. of him	82	87		
	By Ballance carried to his new acct. current	85	111	18	9
			525	17	7

Bristoll 1683

		Cr	£	s	d
	Tho. Wedmor & John Ford per Contra are	Cr	£	s	d
Aprill 7	By Cash recd. of Tho. Wedmor	66	4		
	By Proffit & Losse for meat of him	9		5	
1684 June	By Cash recd. of John Ford	77	4	5	
			8	10	

Anno 1684

		Cr	£	s	d
	George Dighton per Contra is	Cr	£	s	d
July	By Cash received of him in June past then omitted to bee charged	77	1	12	
August 2	By Cash recd. of him	77	58	14	6
			60	6	6
	By Profit and Loss for Ballance	189 *		4	
			60	10	

Anno 1682

		Cr	£	s	d
	Sugar 4 Butts	Cr	£	s	d
January	By Isaac Heming for theire neat proceeds as per acct.	76	65	16	6

	Anno 1682@				
	Sugar 2 butts & one hhd imported on the Little Bristoll from Nevis	Dr	£	s	d
Jan. 2nd	To Edmond Scrope & company for theire cost	33	30	15	9
1682/3 March 20	To Cash pd. Custome, Fees, bills etc.	66	7	6	4
			38	2	1
	To Profit and Loss, for Ballance	189 *	4	5	5
			42	7	6

	Anno 1682@				
	Peter Roswell	Dr	£	s	d
Jan. 6	To Xeries wine 30 butts for Lees sold him	45		12	
1683 January 25	To Cash lent him on his noate with 6 pieces of Plate	68	8		
			8	12	

	Anno 1682				
	Hugh Parry	Dr	£	s	d
Jan. 6	To Carpetts for 1 Carpett sold him	1	00	10	

	Anno 1682				
	Adventure in the ship Experiment of London Wm. Maddison Master to Cadiz	Dr	£	s	d
	To Worsted Stockins for 2 Truncks sent in said ship consign'd to John Cooke & Company containing viz. 113 doz cont. 1356 paire at 3s 6d per paire Bristoll hose	74	237	6	
	To Ditto for 81 doz 972 paire Wells hose of 3 sorts at 2s per paire	74	97	4	
	To Isaac Heming for charges on said 2 Truncks of hose custom etc.	76	8		
	To Ditto paid assureance	90	4	7	6
			346	17	6

	Anno 1682@				
	Adventure in the Mauretania Thomas Morlay Master to Cadiz from London	Dr	£	s	d
Jan. 12	To Stockins for one trunck quantity 394 paire at 3s 6½d	54	69	15	5
	To Profit and Loss for Ballance	189 *	4	19	11
			74	15	4

	Anno 1683				
	Adventure in the Martha & Sarah Wm. Needs Master to Barbadoes for acct. of Martha Speed to sundry accts is consignd to Edward Parsons	Dr	£	s	d
November 2	To Cash-paid George Poply for 3 paire plaine & 6 paire french falls	67	1	1	
6	To Ditto paid Tho. Walden for severall merchandizes as per Journall appears	67	44	17	
	To Ditto paid custom fees bills etc.	67		13	4½
	To Adventure 1st in Ditto ship for the cost & charges of sundry merchand then sent in her for Ditto and consigned as above as per particulars	55	31	7	6
			77	18	10½
	To Profit and Loss for Ballance	189 *	12	1	2½
			90		1

(61)	**Bristoll 1682**				
	Plate imported in sundry Ships from Cadiz To John Cooke & Company for the cost & charges of 847	Dr	£	s	d
	pieces of 8	32	186	15	
	To Arthur Robinson & co. for 5160 Ryals	61	137	1	3

Anno 1682/3@		Cr	£	s	d
	Per Contra				
March 17	By Anth. Wood & Company for said hhds sold them at 22s per				
	Cwt to pay at the Faire next	49	42	7	6

Anno 1684		Cr	£	s	d
	Peter Rouswell per Contra is				
	By Proffit & Losse for the Lees per Contra				
	By Ditto for 12 pints French wine at 3d per pint and				
1685 November 25	By Cash recd. of his daughter on giving up the 6 pieces plate per				
	Contra	107	8		
	By Profit and Loss, for Ballance	189 *		12	
			8	12	

Anno 1682		Cr	£	s	d
	Hugh Parry per Contra				
	By Jahzeel Speed for money or wine of him	69 *		10	

Anno 1683		Cr	£	s	d
	Adventure in the Experiment per Contra is				
	By John Cooke & Company for theire neat proceeds as per acct.				
	sales 26 Jan. 1683/4	69	335	18	
	By Profit & Loss, for Ballance	189 *	10	19	6
			346	17	6

Anno 1682@		Cr	£	s	d
	Per Contra				
Jan. 12	By John Cooke & Company for the neate proceeds of the				
	Stockins per Contra	32	74	15	4

Anno 1685		Cr	£	s	d
	Adventures in the Martha & Sarah per Contra				
	By Edward Parsons for the neat proceeds of all the Goods per				
	Contra as per his acct. of sales closed June 1685	58	90		1

Bristoll 1682		Cr	£	s	d
	Plate in Sundry Ships from Cadiz per Contra				
	By Isaac Heming for money of Tho. Cooke goldsmith for 1 bagge				
	cont. 648 pieces of 8 recd. from Arthur Robinson & Company				
	being 5160 Ryals plate as per said Hemings acct. closed				
	February 24th 1682	76	141	8	7

To Ditto for 1747 Ryals plate sent to Isaac Heming in London for ballance		61	46	15	1
To Proffit & Losse for ballance		73	7	1	5
			377	12	11

Anno 1683					
	William Swift of Worcester merchant	Dr	£	s	d
September 25	To sundry accts for 17 hhds & 12 Tierces Nevis sugar weight neat 237cwt 2qr 26lb at 20s 6d per Cwt to pay for them Dec. 29th next	46,47	243	13	6
	To Sugar 2 hhds for acct. Martha Speed strain'd weight neat 20cwt 3qr 1lb at 24s money	35	25	1	2½
			268	14	8½

Anno 1683					
	The Lady Susan Powlet of Hinton St-George in the County of Somerset Widow	Dr	£	s	d
October 4	To sundry accts for 6 doz bottles Xerie in 3 Panniers sent her by William Baker the Crewkerne Carrier	9, 39	5	5	
December 20	To sundry accts for 6 doz bottles cont. 9 Gall. Xerie with Panniers and covers sent her to London by Tho. Cambourne's waggon	70, 67, 9	2	17	9
			8	2	9

Anno 1682@						
	Arthur Robinson & Company of Puerto Sa[nta Maria]	R	m	Dr	£	s	d
Jan. 12	To Worstead Stockins 2 Truncks laden in the Agreement of Corke for theire neat proceeds	6907	25	55	183	9	9
	To Proffit & Losse for the sterling ballance			73		6	7
		6907	25		183	16	4

Anno 1684						
	Arthur Robinson & Company of St Marie Port merchants	R	m	Dr	£	s	d
	To Adventures in the ships Cadiz merchant and Civilia merchant for the neat proceeds of 121 doz Bristoll, & 63 doz Wells hose, as per theire acct. of sales, closed Jan. 25th 1685 the piece of 8 at 4s 4d	12787	17	44	319	4	
	To Profit and Loss for an error in the Sterling Account per contra occasioned by Misvaluing the Spanish money			189 *	29	15	3½
	Ryals plate	12787	17		348	19	3½

By *Ditto for mony I recd. of Tho. Cooke and paid in to said Heming for 1747 Ryals & 25 Maravedis plate imported from said Robinson & Company as per said Hemings acct. mentioning 43 Guinnies & 8s in silver, closed May 13th 1683*	*76*	46	15	1
By *Isaac Heming received of Tho. Cooke for 600, part of the 847 pieces of 8 per Contra*	*76*	135	11	
By *Isaac Heming for what recd. of Tho. Cooke for the remaining 247 pieces of 8 out of 847 pieces per Contra*	*76*	53	18	3
		377	12	11

	Anno 1683				
	William Swift per Contra is	*Cr*	*£*	*s*	*d*
September 28	By *Cash received of him for the 2 hhds per Contra strain'd sugar*	*67*	25	1	
	By *Ditto recd. of him in part for the 17 hhds & 12 Tierces*	*67*		13	
February 6	By *Cash recd. of Arthur Hart*	*68*	143		
March 20	By *Cash recd. of Tho. Walden by a bill assign'd by Arthur Hart*	*68*	100		
	By *Proffit & Losse for ballance abated him*	*73*			8½
			268	14	8½

	Anno 1684				
	The Lady Susanna Powlet per Contra is	*Cr*	*£*	*s*	*d*
May 22	By *Cash recd. of Francis Vincont. for her acct.*	*77*	8	2	9

Anno 1682@						
Per Contra	*R*	*m*	*Cr*	*£*	*s*	*d*
By *Plate for 5160 Ryals in the Adventure Frigat*	5160		*61*	137	1	3
By *Plate for Gold sent per the ship — to London*	1747	25	*61*	46	15	1
	6907	25		183	16	4

	Anno 1684						
	Arthur Robinson & Company per Contra are			*Cr*	*£*	*s*	*d*
March	By *Isaac Heming for theire bill in his favor for 1000 pieces of 8 the pieces of 8 at 4s 5d as per said Hemings acct. February 1683*	*R* 8000	*m*	*76*	220	16	8
1686 May	By *Ditto for money of Tho. Shepheard on theire bill for 318 pieces of 8 2 Ryals*	2576	17	*90*	70	5	7
December	By *Isaac Heming for 1304 Ryals plate recd. of them per Samuel Kekewich and shipd. home by him in the Angel & sould per said Heming amounting to*	1204		*113*	33	15	1
	By *Ditto for 98 pieces 8 per the James Galley soud Wm. Atwill & Company per Isaac Heming weight 84½ oz received of them per Samuel Kekewich at 5s 2¼d per oz*	813	174	*130*	21	13	10
		12698	21		346	11	2
	By *Profit and Loss for Ballance*	88	30	*189 **	2	8	1½
	Ryals plate	12767	17		348	19	3½

Anno 1682				
Adventure in the Brothers Goodwill from London to Nevis	Dr	£	s	d
Jan. 12 To sundry accts for 36 Caskes of Flower & 3 pieces Brandy	62	71	2	4
To Isaac Heming for freight paid the master in London	76	5	2	6
To Profit and Loss for Ballance	189 *	32	4	8
		108	9	6

Anno 1683				
John Browne of Bristoll merchant & Factor	Dr	£	s	d
To Profit and Loss for rent of the Lower house	189 *	6		

(62)

Anno 1683				
Tho. Martin per Contra is	Dr	£	s	d
To Isaac Heming for money of him	35	28	6	

Anno 1682				
Robert East per Contra is	Dr	£	s	d
January 12 By Isaac Heming for money paid him in London, which should have been charged before, but was omitted	76	42	16	4

Anno 1682@				
Charles Barber of Bristoll Linindraper	Dr	£	s	d
Jan. 22 To Linincloth 5 bolts for Ed. Roy for said Cloth sold him	5	23	8	

Anno 1683							
Adventure in the Ship Agreement Wm. Fisher Master to Cadiz				Dr	£	s	d
October 4 To Worsted Stockins for 54 doz Bristoll & 32 doz Wells hose in a Trunck laden in said ship & consign'd to John Maine Supra Cargo on said ship for sales & returnes	£	s	d	71	150	9	4
13 To Cash paid custom Fees bill etc.	2	14		67			
To Isaac Heming paid Assureance of £150 to Cadiz	2	12	6	67	5	6	6
					155	15	10
To Profit and Loss, for Ballance				189 *	5	00	
					156		10

Anno 1682@				
Cornelius Stretton of Clevedon Yeoman	Dr	£	s	d
Jan. 17 To Land at Clevedon for one yeares rent	32	15		
1689 To Ditto for one year's rent of Newlands ending March 2nd 1689	116	8		
		8	15	

Anno 1682@				
John Wilmore of London Silkeman	Dr	£	s	d
Jan. 24 To Cash pd. John Bush on his bill	43	60		
1683 July 25 To Cash paid lent him	66	200		
September 25 To Cash paid John Gandy Junior of Bristolll, for money of John Budget per said Gandys order	67	60		
January 31 To Cash paid Edmond Greene by his order and £7 to himselfe	68	67		
1684 July 29 To Cash paid himselfe in Bristoll	77	100		
December To Isaac Heming for money recd. of him by my order	76	20		
1685 August 4 To Proffit & Losse for ballance omitted to bee charged	105		10	5½
		507	10	5½

Anno 1683		Cr	£	s	d
Adventure per Contra is					
By Edm. Scrope & Company for the neat proceeds of the goods					
per Contra as per acct. of Sales Anno 1682		33, 100	108	9	6

	Anno 1683	Cr	£	s	d
	John Browne per Contra				
October 8	By Cash recd. of him on acct. of rent for the lower house in Small				
	Street	67	6		

	Bristoll 1682@	Cr	£	s	d
	Thomas Martin of London				
Jan. 12	By Adventure in the Brothers goodwill for 36 Caskes Flower	61	28	6	

	Anno 1682@	Cr	£	s	d
	Robert East of London Brandy Seller				
Jan. 12	By Adventure in the Brothers goodwill for 3 pieces Brandy	61	42	16	4

	Anno 1682@	Cr	£	s	d
	Per Contra				
Feb. 24	By Cash recd. of him	43	23	8	

	Anno 1684	Cr	£	s	d
	Adventure in the Ship Agreement per Contra is				
Aprill	By John Mayne for the neat proceeds of a parcell of Stockins per				
	Contra as per his acct. of Feb. 15th 1683	69	156		10

	Anno 1682@	Cr	£	s	d
	Per Contra				
Jan. 20	By Estate at Clevedon for Covering of mares	38		8	
22	By Cash recd. of him	43		7	
1690 Sept. 20	By Ditto recd. of him	187 *	5		
	By Acct. of Ballances, for Ballance	193 *	3		
			8	15	

	Anno 1683	Cr	£	s	d
	John Wilmer per Contra is				
	By Isaac Heming for money hee paid him	35	60		
July 27	By Cash recd. of him by severall hands	66	200		
January 31	By Cash recd. of him at twice	68	17		
February 4	By Cash recd. of Nath. Berrow by his order	68	50		
1684	By Isaac Heming received of him	35	40		
	By Proffit & Losse for money I received of him in London in				
	part of the £60 per Contra	73	20		
July 5	By Cash recd. of John Blackwell for whichI valued my bill on				
	John Wilmer	77	100		
November 2	By Cash recd. of Wm. Yates on his bill	82	20		
1685 August 4	By Proffit & Losse for a cheese wt 28lb less 2 oz at 4½d per lb				
	& sent in to my sonne Heming	89		10	5½
			507	10	5½

	Anno 1682@				
	James Gould	Dr	£	s	d
Jan. 25	To Cash pd. Maximilian Gallop per his order	43	41	4	
1683 Aprill 12	To Cash paid Geo. Evered on his bill in favor of John Weare	66	46		
January 25	To Cash paid Max. Gollop by his order of 23rd Jan. 1683	68	40		
February 20	To Cash paid Christopher Hurlstone on his bill	68	50		
	To John Sanders for money abated him for want of measure on a bolt cloth	57		3	3
	To Maximilian Gollop for 4 doz bottles Xerie chargd here by his consent	50	3	4	
	To Proffit & Losse for 4 doz bottles Ditto sent himselfe	73	3	4	
March 4	To Cash paid Christopher Hurlston on his bill in his favor	68	15	6	3
			199	1	6

	Anno 1683				
	Joseph Berrie of Bristoll (Quondam Vintner) now Winebroker is	Dr	£	s	d
November 8	To sundry accts for 1 Butt & 8 Gall. & 18 Gallons of Lees	39, 65	4	8	6
	To Xeries wine 20 Butts in the Expectation for 1 Butt of ordinary wine	76	8	10	
1688 Nov. 1	To Cash paid him in a panne of Butter amounting to	236 ⁶⁹		5	
January 18	To Cash paid him in full	157	4		
			17	3	6

(63)	Bristoll 1682@				
	Sir John Drake and William his Brother succeeding him at Ash	Dr	£	s	d
Jan. 31	To sundry accts for 6 doz Xeries	59, 9	5	2	4
	To Cash pd. for 3 panniers	43		2	8
1684 August 28	To Xeries wine 2 Butts for 3 Panniers £ s d containing 6 doz of Xerie at 16s per doz 4 16	79			
	To Proffit & Losse for 6 doz best bottles Corks etc. 12 0 To Ditto for 3 Panniers, covers & portridge 3 6	73	5	12	6
November 28	To sundry accts for 3 Panniers cont. 6 doz Xerie with bottles & panniers	73, 79	5	13	
December 11	To sundry accts for 2 Panniers cont. 4 doz at 16s £3 4s 00d 4 doz bottles, 2 Panniers etc. 10s 10d all	73,79	3	14	10
			20	5	4

	Anno 1682@				
	Samuell Davis of Bristoll merchant	Dr	£	s	d
Jan. 26	To Xeries one butt for 2 doz bottles Sack	59	1	12	
1683 July 4	To Port Wine 1 hogshead etc. for 3 doz bottles white wine & bottles	57	1	13	
September 3	To Ditto for 1 doz bottles same wine & the bottles	57		11	
25	To sundry accts for 3 doz bottles Xerie at 15s per doz & bottles	9, 39	2	11	
October 27	To Sugar 10 hhds bought of John Browne for the ½ of them in partnership with mee	65	50	6	9
December 14	To sundry accts for 4 doz bottles Xerie, & the bottles at 16s per doz wine & 2s bottles	70, 9	3	12	
January 7	To sundry accts for 2 doz bottles Xerie at 16s & 2 doz bottles at 2s	70,9	1	16	
			62	1	9

	Anno 1683				
	Francis Rattenburie of Bristoll Hotpresser is	Dr	£	s	d
October 4	To Adventure in the New England merchant to Nevis for a parcell shooes sould him	31	2	10	
March 17	To Worsted Stockins for 3 paire burnt in the hot-pressing them	74		4	6
			2	14	6

	Anno 1682@	Cr	£	s	d
	Per Contra	Cr	£	s	d
Feb. 8	by Linincloth 10 bolts for theire neat proceeds	56	41	4	
	By Lincloth 32 Bolts for theire neat proceeds	56	157	17	6
			199	1	6

	Anno 1683	Cr	£	s	d
	Joseph Berrie per Contra is	Cr	£	s	d
November 8	By Cash received of him in part	67	1	1	6
	By Cash recd. of him	68	8	10	
1684 Aprill 7	By Cash recd. of Wm. Whitwood by his order	68	3	7	
	By Profit and Loss, for Ballance	189 *	4	5	
			17	3	6

	Bristoll 1682@	Cr	£	s	d
	Per Contra	Cr	£	s	d
Jan 26	By Cash recd. of John Warren	43	5	5	
1684 October 4	By Henry Gibbes for money paid by Wm. Drake to John Burridge in Lyme for his acct.	79	5	12	6
December	By Ditto for money pd. by him to John Burrridge in Lyme as per receit	79	5	13	
January	By Cash recd. of John Warren for his acct.	82	3	14	10
			20	5	4

	Anno 1683	Cr	£	s	d
	Samuell Davis per Contra is	Cr	£	s	d
Aprill 13	By Cash recd. of him	66	1	12	
October	By Proffit & Losse for Plates, a Brish, & Westphalia Ham as per noat	9		14	
November 2	By Cash received of him	67	54	7	9
	By ballance carried to his new acct. current underneath	63	5	8	
			62	1	9

	Anno 1683	Cr	£	s	d
	Fra. Rattenburie per Contra is	Cr	£	s	d
October 8	By Cash recd. of him	67		9	6
March 17	By Cash recd. of him	68	2	5	
			2	14	6

Anno 1683

	Samuel Davis of Bristoll merchant	Dr	£	s	d
	To ballance of his acct. current as above £ s d	63	5	8	
1684 June 7	To Wine 2 hhds for 3 doz white 3 doz				
	claret at 9s per doz 2 14	78			
	To Proffit & Losse for 6 doz bottle &				
	Corks 12 9	73	3	9	0
1685	To Sugars 10 hhds in partnership for ½ charges on them when				
	sent to Rotterdam	65		13	4
	To Ditto for ½ £2 12s 00d hee recd. for returnes on the				
	debentur in Custom house	65	1	6	
18	To Cash paid Joseph Davis in full	83	29		
September 7	To Cash paid him in full by his Brother Joseph	84	14		
October 16	To wines 6 hhds & Proffit & Losse for 2 doz white wine & 1	105,			
	doz claret at 9s 6d & the bottles	97	1	14	6
December	To Ditto for 2 doz bottles Claret wine & the bottles at 9s 6d	105,			
	wine & 2s per doz bottles	97	1	3	
	To Ditto for 3 doz bottles white wine delivered Joseph in	105,			
	December with the bottles	97	1	14	6
	To Proffit & Losse for money abated in the 6 hhds Rhenish				
	bought per Contra	127 *		2	8
			58	11	

Anno 1682/3

	Adventure in the Rochell Will. Stephens master for Cadiz	Dr	£	s	d
	To Worstead Stockins for 40 doz Bristoll & 78 doz Wells	54	185	14	
Feb. 3d	To Cash pd. Custom Fees etc.	43	3	17	
	To Isaac Heming paid assureance	90	3	3	
			192	11	

Anno 1682/3@

	Tobacco 18 hhds deposited per Thomas Puxtone	Dr	£	s	d
March 5	To Cash paid weighing them	43		4	6
1683 August	To John Wasbrow for cooperidge as per his noat	28		12	
	To Proffit & Losse for 112 weeks celleridge	9	5	12	
	To Thomas Puxton his acct. on bond for theire neat proceeds	23	136	15	
			143	3	6

Anno 1683

	John Cooper Senior of Yarmouth merchant is	Dr	£	s	d
July	To Cash delivered John Spanton Master of the Content Ketch per				
	his order May 28th 1683	66	31		
March 17	To Cash paid Adam Coombs on his bill	68	30		
1684	To Proffit & Losse paid port of leters at severall times	73		3	3
April 5	To Isaac Heming for my bill on him for ballance in favor of said				
	John Cooper	76	12		
			73	3	3

Anno 1683

	William Prichard & Herbert Vaughan of the Cittie of Bristoll Gent.	Dr	£	s	d
October 1	To Proffit & Losse for money lent them on theire bond dated				
	Oct. 1st due Jan. 2nd	73	50		
1684 Aprill	To Ditto for ½ yeares intrest due 2nd of Aprill 1684	73	1	10	
October	To Ditto for ½ yeares yeares intrest due 2nd October 1684	73	1	10	
1685	To Ditto for ½ yeares intrest due Aprill 2nd 1685	89	1	10	
1686 Aprill	To Ditto for 1 yeares intrest due Aprill 2nd 1686	105	3		
October 2	To Ditto for ½ yeares intrest due September 2 1686	105 *	1	10	
			59		

Anno 1684					
	Samuel Davis per Contra is	*Cr*	*£*	*s*	*d*
September 25	*By Cash recd. of him*	*77*	8	17	
1685	*By Sugar 10 hhds in partnership to Rotterdam for his*				
	disbursements on them in custom house etc.	*65*		5	6
May	*By Xeries Wine 30 Butts for the cost & charge 1 hogshead & 1*				
	Aum Rhenish in Rotterdam	*94*	11	6	6
July	*By Ditto for 3 hhds bought of him here 1 at £5 10s & 2 at £7*				
	each	*94*	19	10	
August 19	*By Xeries wine in sundry ships for one other hogshead of Rhenish*	*101*	7		
Sept. 3	*By Ditto for one other hogshead*	*101*	7		
	By Proffit & Losse for 1 dozen pint bottles of Mum at	*105*		3	
1686 Sept. 10	*By Cash received of his wife after his decease*	*119*	4	9	
			58	11	

Anno 1683					
	Adventure in the Rochell to Cadiz per Contra	*Cr*	*£*	*s*	*d*
Aprill 27	*By John Maine and William Stephens for theire neate proceeds*	*69*	159	2	9
	By Profit and Loss, for Ballance	*189 **	33	8	3
			192	11	

Anno 1682/3@					
	Per Contra	*Cr*	*£*	*s*	*d*
March 5	*By Will. Smith for said Tobacco sold him*	*65*	143	3	6

Anno 1683					
	John Cooper per Contra is	*Cr*	*£*	*s*	*d*
	By Fish North sea Codd recd. out of the Content Ketch John				
	Spanton Master for its neat proceeds as per acct. sent him	*72*	73	3	3

Anno 1684					
	Wm. Prichard & Herbert Vaughan per Contra are	*Cr*	*£*	*s*	*d*
September 25	*By Cash recd. of Wm. Prichard for ½ yeares intrest due Aprill*				
	2nd 1684	*77*	1	10	
1685 Aprill 18	*By Cash received of Wm. Prichard*	*83*	2	5	
1686 October 2	*By Cash received of Wm. Prichard in part*	*119*	50		
14	*By Cash received of Wm. Prichard in full*	*120*	5	5	
			59		

(64)	**Bristoll 1682@**			Dr	£	s	d
	Adventures on sundry Ships to Cadiz			Dr	£	s	d
Feb. 8	To John Cooke for his comission on a bill of 500 pieces of 8			32	2	13	1
	To Proffit & Losse for ballance			73 *	38	18	10
					41	11	11

	Anno 1683						
	Andrew Kirby Father & Sone merchants resident in Bordeauxe			Dr	£	s	d
May 7	To Isaac Heming for money of him remitted them per bill of						
	Exchange to Bordeauxe for a tryalll of the benefit of remittance [70]			90	113	5	7
	To Profit and Loss, for what gotten by Exchange			189 *	1	15	4
					115		11

	Anno 1683						
	Andrew Kirby Father & Sone merchants in Bordeauxe			Dr	£	s	d
November	To Isaac Heming for money paid John	Livres	Sous				
	Bawden & Company for theire bill assign'd						
	them for mee on Fra. Malartie in						
	Bourdeaux for 1100 Ecu Turnois at 54						
	d the French Ecu at 2 Usance	3300	35	246	18	6½
	To Ditto for money pd. said Bawden &						
	Company for theire bill assign'd them for						
	600 Ecu at 53 d the Ecu & 6s over on						
	said Malartie at 2 Usance	1800	35	134	7	6
	To Ditto for money pd. said Bawden &						
	Company for theire bill assign'd them for						
	300 Ecu Turnois on said Malartie at 2						
	Usance	900	35	67	3	9
1685 Aprill 14	To Isaac Heming for his bill on mee for						
	31Ecu 8 Sou in favor of George Toriano of						
	Lond. merchant is 93 livre 8 sous 00 denier	93	8	90	7	6	7
		6093	8		455	16	4½
	To Profit and Loss for what gained by Exchange		*	12	6	6½
					468	2	11

	Anno 1684						
	Sugar 2 Butts & 8 hhds in the Dyamond Ketch from Nevis to			Dr	£	s	d
	London John Bennet master, laden per John Streater &						
	Company Consignd Isa. Hemming						
	To Edm. Scrope & John Streater for theire cost & charges in						
	Nevis per Invoyce August 6th 1684 being 18070 lb sugar at						
	10s per 100 lb is			33	90	7	

	Anno 1682@						
	John Whitwood of Bedminster Aledraper			Dr	£	s	d
Feb. 8th	To Xeries wine one butt for one doz of bottles			59		14	

	Anno 1682@						
	Edward Jones of Bristoll merchant			Dr	£	s	d
Feb. 16	To Xeries wine 30 butts for 2 butts sold him payable in twelve months			45	18		

	Anno 1683						
	William Godwin of Nailsey in the County of Somerset Yeoman			Dr	£	s	d
September 26	To Cash paid lent him on his mortgage in Cosen Haggatts name			67	100		
1684	To Proffit & Losse for ½ yeares intrest due the 27th March						
	1684			73	3		
1685 March 27	To Ditto for 1 yeares intrest due 27th March 1685			105	6		
1686 March	To Ditto for 1 yeares intrest due 27th March 1686			105	6		
1687 Sept. 27	To Ditto for ½ yeares intrest due Sept. 27th 1687			137	3		

Bristoll 1682@						
	Per Contra		Cr	£	s	d
Feb. 8	By John Cooke for the neate proceeds of 12 scarlett Searges		32	41	11	11

Anno 1683					
	Andrew Kirby Father & Sonne per Contra	Cr	£	s	d
September	By Isaac Heming for money on theire bill drawne by them on				
	John Bellamy of London in my favor	76	115		11

Anno 1684							
	Andrew Kirby Father & Sone per Contra are			Cr	£	s	d
Aprill	By Isaac Heming for theire bill of 1500	Livres	Sous				
	Ecus drawn by them on John Bellamy in my						
	favor & recd. per the said Heming the Ecu						
	at 55¼ d	4500		76	345	6	3
	By John Blackwell for 530 Ecu 1 Livre 6						
	Denier the cost and charges in Bordeauxe of						
	eight tons wine laden in the ship Success						
	Samuell Greening master the Ecu at 55½ d	1591		59	122	12	10
	By Proffit & Losse for 2 livre 8 sou the cost						
	of 6 boxes of Prunellas laden in said ship as						
	per Invoyce of both may appeare	2	8	73		3	10
		6093	8		468	2	11

Anno 1684					
	Sugar 2 Butts & 4 hhds per Contra	Cr	£	s	d
March	By Isaac Heming for the neat proceeds of the 2 Butts & 8 hhds				
	per contra as per Leter and acct. from him 25th March 1685	90	76	11	3
	By Profit and Loss, for Ballance	189 *	13	15	9
			90	7	

Anno 1690					
	Per Contra	Cr	£	s	d
	By Profit and Loss, for Ballance	189 *		14	

Anno 1683					
	Edward Jones per Contra	Cr	£	s	d
October 13	By Cash received of him	67	18		

Anno 1684					
	Wm. Godwin per Contra is	Cr	£	s	d
June	By Cash recd. of Cosen Nathanaell Haggatt which he recd. of				
	William Godwin	77	3		
1686 June 4	By Cash received of Wm. Godwin for ½ yeares intrest due 27th				
	March 1686	108	3		
October 2	By Cash recd. of him for ½ a yeares intrest due Septemb 27th				
	1686	168	3		

1688 September 27	To Ditto for 1 yeares intrest due Sept. 27th 1688	153	6		
	To Ditto for 1 yeares intrest omitted to be chargd ½ in the yeare 83 & ½ in the yeare 1686	164	6		
			130		

Anno 1684

		Dr	£	s	d
	Adventure in the Ship Friston Capt. Wm. Gutheridge from London to Cadiz				
May	To sundry accts for the cost & charges of one Trunck Stockins sent to Lond. & ship'd by John Cooke in said ship consign'd to said Cooke & Samuell Kekewich, viz				
	To worsted Stockins for 600 paire Bristoll , & 596 Wells hose, at severall prices	74	153	2	
			£	s	d
	To John Cooke for carriage & portage hee paid in London			14	10	32
	To Proffit & Losse for the Trunck and a Cord			14	10	73
	To John Cooke for custom, Fees etc. per his leter August 8th 1684	3	7	2	32

			£	s	d
			4	16	10
			157	18	10
	To Profit and Loss, for Ballance	189 *	3	8	3
			161	7	1

---

(65)   **Bristoll 1682/3@**

	William Smith of Bristoll Tobacconist	Dr	£	s	d
March 5	To Tobacco18 hhds for 7636 lb neat at 4½d per lb	63	143	3	6
			143	3	6
	To Profit and Loss, for Ballance	189 *		8	6
			143	12	

Anno 1683

	Sugar 10 hhds Sundried bought of John Browne which hee bought of Philip Bifford	Dr	£	s	d
October 8	To Cash paid John Browne for them weiging 94cwt 20lb at 21s per cwt & ½ a guiny over	67	99	8	3¾
	To Ditto paid him for Brokridge, Coopridge, halling & weighing them	67	1	5	2
January	To Cash paid shipping them in the Marie Ketch for Lond. and Rotterdam	68		1	10
March 8	To Cash paid Joseph Davies for charges hee was at in shipping them	68		5	10
	To Proffit & Losse paid halling 4 hhds to Sam. Davis house, & the 10 hhds from his & my Celler to the Key	89		3	6
	To Ditto for what paid the Widow Wasbrow for hooping them before ship'd	89		10	
	To Samuel Davis for his disbursments in cleareing them for Rotterdam	63		5	6
	To Profit and Loss, for Ballance	189 *	1	4	3¼
			103	4	5

		£	s	d
	By *Nath. Haggatt for 1½ yeares intrest pd. him from*			
	m Sept. 26th 1683 to March 27th 85 1½ yeares	19	9	
	By *Proffit & Losse recd. of him for ½ yeares intrest in Aprill*			
	1687 but omitted to bee charged	137	3	
1687 January 7	By *Cash recd. of him for ½ yeares intrest ending September 27th*			
	1687	140	3	
1688 March 14	By *Cash recd. of him for 1 yeares intrest ending September 27th*			
	1688	162	6	
	By *his new acct. current for ballance resting due Sept. 27th 1688*	166	100	
		130		

Anno 1684				
	Adventure in the Friston per Contra is	Cr	£	s	d
October 24	By *John Cooke & Samuel Kekewich for the neat proceeds of the*			
	Trunck of stockins per Contra 6512 Ryals plate is 774½ pieces			
	of 8 the piece of 8 at 4s 2d as per theire acct. of sales Oct. 1684	88	161	7	1

Bristoll 1683				
	William Smith per Contra is	Cr	£	s	d
July 24	By *Cash recd. of him*	66	100	
Oct. 20	By *Ditto recd. of him*	67	43	12
		143	12	

Anno 1683				
	Sugar 10 hhds per Contra are	Cr	£	s	d
October 27	By *Samuell Davis for ½ theire cost & charges*	63	50	6	9
1684 June 7	By *Cash recd. of Samuell Davis for ½ theire neat proceeds sould*				
	by his brother Isaac Davis in Rotterdam	77	50	5	
	By *Samuel Davis for ½ the charges per contra on the Sugar when*				
	ship'd out	63		13	4
	By *Ditto for ½ £2 12s 00d recd. on the debentur at custom*				
	house for returns on the sugar	63	1	6	
	By *Proffit & Losse for t'other halfe of the charges per Contra*	89		13	4
		103	4	5

		Dr	£	s	d
	Anno 1683				
	Seargant Thomas Strode of London his house in Shire Lane there	Dr	£	s	d
	To sundry accts for 5 doz bottles Xerie sent him in 2 Panniers per Thomas Cambornes Waggon, with the charge of the bottles Panniers etc.	(70) 67, 9	4	13	6
1684 December	To sundry accts for 1 Cask cont. 24 Galls Xerie sent him per Waggon to London at 5s 4d per Gall	73,79	6	13	9
1686 December 23	To sundry accts for 1 Rundlet Xerie sent him per Tobias Lutons waggon	126, 127	3	19	6
			15	6	9

		Dr	£	s	d
	Anno 1683				
	Adventure the 2nd in the Ship Brothers Goodwill from London Wm. Winter Master to Nevis is	Dr	£	s	d
January	To Isaac Heming for the cost & charge of 40 Kilderkins floure, & 3 pieces Brandy laden in her & sent consign'd to Edm. Scrope & John Streater, as per particulars in Journall fol. (107) may appeare	35	80	11	10
	To Profit and Loss, for ballance	189 *	39	9	6
			120	11	4

Anno 1682/3@

					Dr	£	s	d
	Xeries wine 40 Butts imported in the Expectation from Cadiz for acct. of him & myselfe viz. ¾ for Cooke & one for selfe				Dr	£	s	d
March 17	To Cash pd. Custome, Freight etc.				66	193		8
1683 August 15	To Cash paid brokridge of 5 Butts to Joseph Berrie				66	1	5	
October 1	To Ditto paid Jos. Berrie for brokridge				67	2	10	
		£	s	d				
	To Proffit & Losse for hallidge etc.	1						
	To Ditto for 45 weeks Celleridge	7	17	6				
	To Ditto for Cooperidge as per noat	8	6	4				
	To Ditto for Cork, Bungcloth & Candles etc.		7	8				
	To Ditto for port of leters at severall times		5	6				
	To my Commission at £2 per cent	16	3	9	73	34		9
	To sundry accounts for theire neat proceeds viz.							
	To acct. current of John Cooke for his ¾ parts	434	1	6	32			
	To Xeries wines ¼ part of 40 Butts for my ¼ part	144	13	10	58	578	15	4
						809	11	9

		Dr	£	s	d
	Anno 1683				
	Peter Kekewich of London Haberdasher of Small wares	Dr	£	s	d
February 18	To Cash paid Sir Tho. Earle by his order	68	50		
Aprill	To Cash paid Spent per Jahzeel Speed at the Taverne at severall times & paid Attorneys Fees	68		4	11
			50	4	11

		Dr	£	s	d
	Anno 1683				
	Giles Gough of Bristoll Soapboyler	Dr	£	s	d
May 9	To Edmond Scrope for the cost of 10 boxes Candles as per his receit May 9th 1684	38	10	13	
1684 November	To John Bradway for money of him on my noat	70	28	4	2
			38	17	2

	Anno 1684				
	Sergeant Tho. Strode per Contra is	Cr	£	s	d
August 11	By Cash recd. of him	77	4	13	6
February 7	By Isaac Heming for money of Hugh Strode by his order	76	6	13	9
1686 January 24	By Ditto received of his Bro. Hugh Strode by his order	130	3	19	6
			15	6	9

	Anno 1686				
	Adventure in the Brothers Goodwill per Contra	Cr	£	s	d
	By Edmond Scrope & Company for the neat proceeds of the 40 Casks Flower and 3 ps Brandy per Contra, being 24119 lb sugar at 10s per 100lb as per theire account of Sales from Nevis closed July 7th 1686	33	120	11	4

	Anno 1682/3@				
	Per Contra	Cr	£	s	d
March 16	By Cash recd. of James Crofts for Allowance of 3 butts	66	3	13	1
1683 29	By John Blackwell for 9 butts sold him at £23 10s per butt	26	211	10	
	By Proffit & Losse for 12 Galls sent to Reading	9	2	8	
August 10	By John Bradway for 5 Butts sould him at £24 per Butt	70	120		
September 13	By Alexander Caduggan for 7 Butts at £24 per Butt at 6 month time	48	168		
19	By Lewis Addams for 5 Butts sould him at £24 5s per Butt at 6 month time	56	120		
October 4	By John Bradway for 3 Butts at £24 per Butt to pay at 6 months	70	72		
November 8	By Joseph Berrie for 1 Butt and 18 Gall. Lees	62	3	3	8
24	By Dr. Hungerford for part of a Butt sould him	59	1	12	
	By Xeries Wine one Butt the part of 5 remaining of the 40	70	21		
January 3	By John Olliff for 4 Butts at £20 per Butt to pay at 6 months	39	80		
31	By Proffit & Losse for 1/3 of a Butt for my own acct.	73	5		
	By Ditto for 5 Empty Butts of John Wasbrow	73	1	5	
			809	11	9

	Anno 1683				
	Peter Kekewich per Contra is	Cr	£	s	d
February 8	By Cash recd. of Sicely by his order	68	30		
	By Cash recd. of James Lawhorne by his order	68	5		
March 8	By Cash recd. of John Weare	68	15		
	By Acct. of Ballances, for Ballance	193 *		4	11
			50	4	11

	Anno 1684				
	Giles Gough per Contra is	Cr	£	s	d
Aprill	By Adventure 3rd in the Dyamond Ketch to Nevis for 10 boxes Candles	57	10	13	
September 4	By Adventure in the Owners Adventure to Nevis for 20 boxes Candles	80	28	4	2
			38	17	2

(66)	**Bristoll 1683**	Dr	£	s	d
	Cash				
	To it selfe for ballance	43	413	9	11
March 13	To John Sanders recd. of him	57	49	4	8
	To Chamber of the Cittie recd. of Mich. Pope	30	50		
16	To Xeries wines 40 butts recd. of James Crofts	65	3	13	1
17	To John Gore recd. of him	31	20		
1683 March	To Proffitt & Loss recd. of Peter Sanders	9	6	9	
24	To John Rumsey recd. of him	29	100		
26	To John Pitts recd. of him	55	43	5	
	To Edward Hollister	59		10	
30	To Cattle recd. of James Horwood	5	2	18	
31	To Wm. Spoore Junior recd. of him	31	2	8	
Aprill 4	To Edward Gorges recd. of him	34	6		
5	To Land at Clevedon received of — Gaynor for ½ yeares rent	32	3	14	6
7	To Bartholmew Bagg recd. of him	52	7	2	2
	To Tho. Wedmor & Company recd. of Tho. Wedmor	60	4		
10	To Isaac Heming recd. of William Rogers on his bill	35	79	14	7
13	To Tho.Tayler recd. of Andrew Ynnys	4	13	15	
	To Samuell Davis recd. of him	63	1	12	
18	To Richard Gotley & Company recd. of Richard Gotley	16	10	10	
27	To Wm. Spoore Senior recd. of him	52	10		
	To Proffit & Losse recd. of him	09		6	
	To Wm. Rishton recd. of him	58	20	10	6
	To Tho. Edward recd. of him	23	1	1	3
30	To John Maine & Company recd. of Sam. Plomer	69	5	12	
May 3	To William Davis recd. of him	58	10	11	
10	To John Stretten recd. of him	57	6		
	To Isaac Heming recd. of Sam. Sandford	35	10		
	To Wm. Spoore & Company recd. of Wm. Spoore Senior	30	3		
24	To John Earle of Bristoll received of Tho. Lutterell	37	8	15	
June 5	To John Blackwell for money recd. of him	26	120		
14	To Robert Davis recd. of him	51	5	5	
	To Edward Martindale recd. of him	24	10		
23	To Marie Parsons recd. of her	18		12	10
25	To Ed. Martindale recd. of him	24	50		
July 3	To Fish for acct. of John Cooper for money of Widow Sandford & Marie Sweet	72	2	2	8
4	To John Blackwell recd. of himselfe and Wm. Dawson by his order	26	33	2	6
	To Edward Martindale recd. of him	24	40		
6	To John Gore recd. of him	31	20		
	To Estate at Clapton for money for Butter & Cheese	38	24	18	10
14	To Wm. Spoore Junior recd. of him	31	41		
	To Fish for acct. of John Cooper recd. of severalls	72	1		
			1242	3	6
23	To John Blackwell recd. of him	26	62	18	
24	To Proffit & Losse recd. of Ed. Martindale £200 & John Blackwell £1 10s	9	201	10	
24	To Wm. Smith recd. of him	65	100		
27	To John Wilmer recd. of him	62	200		
August 2	To Grace Keyes recd. of Tho. Pope	31		12	
3	To Tho. Curtis recd. of Ben. Cole	58	10		
4	To Tho. Durbin recd. of him	47	7	13	6
	To Fish for acct. of John Cooper recd. of Widow Sandford Marie Sweet & others	72	10	6	6
6	To Robert Hauxworth recd. of him	28	12	6	7
8	To sundry accts recd. of John Blackwell	9, 26	96	3	9
13	To Anthony Wood & Company recd. of Anthony Wood	49	42	7	3
	To Fish for acct. John Cooper for 2 Couple	72	4		
			1986	5	1

Bristoll 1683

	Per Contra	Cr	£	s	d
March 13	By Stockins pd. John Massinger	54	8	6	6
	By Ditto pd. John Brady for 16 paire	54	2	8	
	By Ditto pd. John Perry	54	2	11	
15	By Proffitt & loss pd. Houshold expences	9	5	16	
17	By Stockins pd. John Massinger	54	5	7	11
	By Proffitt & Loss pd. poore money	9	1	6	
	By Xeries wine 40 butts pd.sundry charges	65	193		8½
20	By Nath.Haggatt Lent him	19	100		
	By John Romsey Town clark Lent him	29	100		
1683 March	By Sugar 2 butts pd. Custome etc.	60	7	6	4
24	By Proffit & Losse paid for a Frock for Jabzeel	9		8	6
	By John Hurtnell paid him	38	9	6	7
26	By Worsted Stockins paid John Massinger for 33 paire	54	4	19	
27	By Xerie wines 30 Butts paid Joseph Berrie	45		8	
	By Estate at Clapton paid sundry charges in law [71]	38	11	14	7
30	By Worsted Stockins paid John Ashman for 2 parcells containing 200 paire	54	13	6	8
	By Henry Gibbes paid Wm. Gainer	4	1	2	3
31	By Oyle 10 Jarres paid portridge into warehouse	46		1	6
Aprill 2	By John Blackwell paid lent him	26	50		
	By Worsted Stockins paid severalls for 4 parcells	54	14	10	8
4	By Proffit & Losse paid Tho. Walden	9		12	
5	By Estate at Clapton pd. Edward Willis	38	1	18	6
	By Oyle 10 Jarres pd. Landing them	46		1	6
7	By Abraham White paid him	30	1		7
9	By Worsted Stockins paid John Massinger for 35 paire	54	5	5	
	By Estate at Clapton paid Samuel Barthrum	38	3	15	
	By Proffit & Losse paid Robert Yate on John Brooking & Company theire bill	9	21	13	9
	By Oyle 10 Jarres for acct. of Christopher Williams paid the Master for freight	46	1	13	
11	By Isaac Heming paid John Bubb	35	100		
12	By James Gould paid George Evered	62	46		
	By Proffit & Losse paid Jane Flowers daughter	9	2	2	
14	By Worsted Stockins paid Tho. Hill Fra. Rottenberrie & John Perry	54	5	17	6
	By Estate at Clapton paid Henry Winter in full [16]	38	15		
	By Proffit & Losse paid houshold expences and 2 Guinies I received	9	11	12	2¾
18	By Malachy Peale paid Richard Gotley	36	6	3	2
	By Isaac Heming paid Tho. Gammon per his order	35	1	3	
19	By Proffit & Losse paid severalls	9	11	12	6
27	By worsted stockins paid John Massinger for 2 several parcells both 87 paire	54	12	17	
May 4	By Worsted Stockins Thomas Hill, Joel Pinny & John Massinger	54	6	17	2
10	By Land at Clevedon paid John Stretton	32	1	11	9
11	By Worsted Stockins paid John Massinger, Joel Pinny & John Day	54	8		6
18	By Oyle 2 Cask for Christopher Williams paid John Higgenson for freight	19		12	
19	By Worsted Stockins paid John Massinger	54	4	19	2
	By Proffit & Losse paid Richard Baugh	9		12	
22	By John Cooke his acct. of Exchange paid his 2 bills to Henry Gibbes	39	15	18	
			818	17	6¼
25	By Worsted Stockins paid John Massinger & John Perry	71	6	19	5
31	By Land at Clevedon paid — Burgesse for money	32		10	

(67)		**Bristoll 1683**	Dr	£	s	d
		Cash is				
August 15		To ballance of that acct. from folio	66	523	7	11
	20	To Tho. Puxton on bond for money of him	23	30	18	
		To Fish for acct. of John Cooper recd. of severalls for severall parcels	72	9	4	
		To sundry accts recd. of Sir George Strode	24, 35	23	18	
		To James Freeman recd. of him	21	46	5	

Date	Description	Ref	£	s	d
31	By John Cooke for his acct. of Exch paid Sir Richard Crump on his bill	39	30	5	7
June 8	By Worsted Stockins paid severalls for 5 parcells & given Tho. Hill	71	22	17	1
14	By Tenement in Portbury paid Robert Davis	20		2	6
	By Proffit & Losse paid John Hardiman £1 & houshold expences £14 1s 0¾ d is	9	15	1	¾
20	By Tho. Day paid cleaning the 2 Cellars	70		2	6
	By Worsted Stockins paid John White & John Massinger for 3 parcells	71	36	4	
25	By Worsted Stockins paid John Massinger & Fra. Rottenburie	71	4	12	9
July 4	By Ditto paid John Massinger, Ant. Harris & Joel Pinny for 3 parcells	71	11	16	2
	By sundry accts paid George Irish	39, 35		15	
	By house in which I live paid ½ yeares Chimny money	23		8	
6	By Worsted Stockins paid Jos. White, John Brady & Thomas Hill for 3 parcells	71	22	10	6
	By John Cooper paid John Spanton	63	31		
	By Xeries wine 12 Butts paid custom, freight etc.	39	64	3	
	By sundry accts paid charges on 16 hds Sugar	46, 47	29	19	6
	By Estate at Clapton paid sundry charges	38		13	½
	By Fish for acct. of John Cooper paid sundry charges on it	72	1	10	6
	By Proffit & Losse paid houshold expences	9	9	7	1½
13	By Worsted Stockins paid John Perrie & John Massinger	71	6	9	7
	By Copie hold Tenement in Portburie paid Wm. Spoore	20		6	
17	By John Cooke his acct. of Exchange paid Alderman Wm. Crabb	39	41	5	4½
19	By Worsted Stockins paid John White & Thomas Hill	71	17	13	8
	By Proffit & Losse paid John Moore £4 13s 6d & Rich. Thomas for my mare £7 7s 6d	9	12	1	
	By Sugar 2 hhds in the Crowne Lyon for charges on them	35	1	11	9
	By Worsted Stockins paid Tho. Hill, John Perrie, Joel Pinny & John Massinger	71	15	11	4
25	By Worsted Stockins paid John Brady	71		14	2
	By John Wilmer paid lent him	62	200		
	By Wm. Spoore Senior paid lent him	52	5		
	By Sugar 2 hhds paid Charles Plomer for freight & averidge	35	2	9	3
August 4	By Henry Gibbes paid Tho. Lutterell	4	3	10	8
	By Oyle 2 Cask for Christopher Williams for charges paid on them	19		1	7
	By Worsted Stockins paid John Massinger	71	5	16	8
7	By Worsted Stockins paid Tho. Hill	71	8	14	
	By Proffit & Losse paid John Hardiman £1 2s & John Joyner 10s is	9	1	12	
13	By Marie Thring & Company paid Bridget Wallis	7	2	10	
	By Sugar 15 hhds from Jamaica paid custom etc.	70	6	19	
14	By Worsted Stockins paid John Perrie	71	2	15	
15	By Proffit & Losse paid Jos. Drew & houshold expences	9	18	15	10½
	By Xeries wines 40 Butts paid John Perrie	65	1	5	
			1462	17	2
	By ballance carried to that account	67	523	7	11
			1986	5	1

Bristoll 1683

Date	Description	Cr	£	s	d
	Cash is				
August 16	By Proffit & Losse paid Ed. Martindale £200 & John Sandford 17s	9	200	17	
	By Worsted Stockins paid John Massinger & Fra.s Rottenburie	71	5	12	7
24	By house in which I live paid Jos. Owen £1 5s 6d & John Gwin for rent £1 2s	23	2	7	6

Date					
27	To Alderman Ralph Olliffe recd. of him	3	46	1	4
	To Fish for acct. of John Cooper recd. of severalls	72	2	11	
	To the Lady Ann Powlet recd. of Barnard Wilkins	48	6	2	8
29	To Fish for acct. of John Cooper recd. of severalls	72	13	12	
September 10	To Fish for acct. of John Cooper recd. of severalls	72	11	18	3
	To Richard Champneys recd. of himselfe & John Joyner	45	73		
	To William Whitwood recd. of him	70	29	9	
	To Tho. Puxton recd. of him	22	40		
19	To Fish for acct. of John Cooper for 6½ couple of large Codd	72		13	
22	To Isaac Heming recd. of Elizabeth Tayler for which I valued my bill	35	18		
25	To John Blackwell recd. of him	26	105	15	
	To Fish for acct. of John Cooper for ¼ Cwt & 5 couple large Codd	72	1	13	6
28	To Ditto for money of John Hollister for 1 Couple	72		2	
	To Wm. Swift recd. of him	61	25	14	
October 1	To Michael Perrie recd. of him	47	1	8	5
	To Fish for acct. of John Cooper recd. of severalls	72		4	
8	To Fish for acct. John Cooper for severall parcells Fish	72	2	9	3
	To John Browne recd. of him	61	6		
	To Fra. Rattenburie recd. of him	63		9	6
	To Isaac Heming recd. of Sam. Spencer	35	18	4	
13	To Edward Jones recd. of him	64	18		
	To Estate at Clapton recd. of Joane Daracot	38		3	
16	To Sam. Astry recd. of him	49	16	15	
20	To Fish for acct. John Cooper recd. of Jer. Holvey	72		6	
	To Robert Summers recd. of him	17	1	7	6
	To William Smith received of him	65	43	12	
	To John Williamson received of James Fisher per his order	72	60		
27	To Fish for acct. John Cooper recd. of severalls for 1½ Cwt large Codd	72	5	8	
November 2	To Alexander Doleman recd. of him	48	82		
	To Fish for acct. John Cooper recd. for 5 Fish	72		5	
	To Samuell Davis recd. of him	63	54	7	9
	To John Gore recd. of him	31	10		
			1329	4	1
8	To Proffit & Losse received of my selfe	9	1	10	
	To Xeries Wine 12 Butts recd. of James Crofts	39	7	10	10
	To Matthew Wall recd. of Joane Eyles	22		15	
	To Joseph Berrie recd. of him	62	1	1	6
	To John Stretten recd. of him	57	6		
	To Fish for acct. John Cooper recd. of severalls	72		10	
24	To Ditto for money of John Godwin	72	1	17	6
	To Tho. Puxton recd. of him	22	77	6	6
December 1	To Fish for acct. John Cooper recd. for 3 Couple	72		6	
	To Xeries Wine 1 Butt recd. of the Widow Aldworth	70		11	
18	To Proffit & Losse recd. of Wm. Weaver	9	6		
	To John Love recd. of him	55	20		
22	To Ed. Martindale recd. of him	24	20		
29	To Proffit & Losse recd. of William Jackson	9	2	5	
January 8	To Fish for acct. of John Cooper for 1 Cwt of Colefish recd. of James Wallis	72	2	5	
16	To Dr. Fra. Hungerford received of Tho. Hungerford	59	9	5	
	To Xeries wine one Butt for money of Ditto	70		9	
			1486	16	5

	By Worsted Stockins paid John Massinger	71	4	10	5
27	By Worsted stockins for acct. of Christopher Williams paid John England	45	17	10	
	By Robert Yate paid him	39	16	13	6
	By Proffit Losse paid houshold expences and Alderman Olliffe	9	7	9	
	By Sugar 15 hhds in the Owners Endeavour paid weighing them	70		3	9
30	By Worsted Stockins paid Tho. Hill & John Brady	71	11	5	4
September 2	By Proffit & Losse paid houshold expences	9	1	12	5
	By Christopher Williams paid George Weeks	7	43	16	11
3	By Fish for acct. John Cooper paid delivering severall parcells	72		3	10
6	By sundry accts paid John Harris	9, 45	3	5	
	By Worsted Stockins paid John Perrie & John Massinger	71	7	17	11
	By Proffit & Losse paid houshold expences	9	1	10	4
11	By Cash paid alloud for monies delivered Jahzeel at severall times without my order	67	21	7	11
	By Proffit & Losse paid David Roynon & houshold expences	67	4	4	9
	By Adventure in the Sarah to Nevis paid Sir John Knight for freight	49	6	12	
	By John Hurtnell paid lent him on his bill	38	20		
	By Sugar 15 hhds paid freight & averidge	70	19	13	9
	By Sugar 12 Tierces & 1 hogshead paid custom etc.	47	5	18	6
13	By Fish for acct. John Cooper for taking up pickle & delivery of fish	72		1	1
15	By Worsted Stockins paid John Massinger & Jos. White	71	11	5	5
22	By Martha Speed paid her at twice	46	3	2	
	By Worsted Stockins paid John Massinger, John Perrie & Tho. Hill	71	15	16	8
24	By Sugar 12 Tierces & 1 hogshead paid freight & averidge	47	12	14	3
25	By John Wilmer paid John Gandy Junior	62	60		
28	By sundry accts paid weighin 19 hhds & 12 Tierces Sugar	46, 47, 35		6	9
	By John Godwin paid lent him on his mortgage	64	100		
October 1	By Worsted Stockins paid John Massinger	71	3	10	
	By Xeries wine 40 Butts paid Joseph Berrie	65	2	10	
	By Proffit & Losse paid the Widow Hasell	9		5	3
	By Isaac Hemming paid Wm. Cox	35		5	
2	By Andrew Stucky paid Jahzeel Speed	53		7	6
6	By Worsted Stockins paid John Perrie, John Massinger & Fra.s Rottenburie	71	8	9	6½
8	By Sugar 10 hhds of John Browne paid him for theire cost & charges	65	100	13	5¾
10	By Worsted Stockins paid Joseph White & John Massinger	71	20	9	
	By Marie Thring & Company paid them	7	4	10	
13	By Henry Gibbes paid Tho. Lutterell	4	4	10	6
	By Proffit & Losse paid houshold expences	9	9	17	7½
	By Adventure in the Agreement to Cadiz paid custom etc.	62	2	14	
			764		5¾
16	By Isaac Heming paid Wm. Rogers	35	63		
	By House at lower end Small Streat paid Nath. King	22		3	8
	By Worsted Stockins paid John Brady	71	2	11	
25	By Ditto paid Tho. Hill for 34 paire & John Massinger for 44 paire	71	11	11	10
	By house in which I live, & house at lower end of Small Streate paid militia money	22, 23		7	2
	By Proffit & Losse paid John Hardiman	9	1	7	6
30	By Ditto paid John Moore in full of his noat	9	1	11	
31	By Henry Gibbes paid Tho. Lutterell	4	1	11	6
November 2	By John Cooke & Company paid John Bubb	25	109	18	6
	By Adventure 2nd in the Martha & Sarah paid George Popley	60	1	1	

(68)		Bristoll 1683		£	s	d
		Cash is	Dr			
		To ballance of that acct.	67	256	11	2
		To Fish for acct. of John Cooper for money of Ann Hort chargeable August 29th last	72	2	7	6
	January 21	To Ditto for money of Wm. Smith for 1 Cwt of Colefish	72	2	5	
		To Alexander Doleman recd. of him	48		7	11
		To Proffit & Losse received for 8 Bottles of Wine	73		10	8
	28	To Isaac Heming for money of Edward Grace on my bill in his favour	35	200		
	31	To John Wilmer received of him and Nath. Berrow at severall times	62	67		
	February 1	To Thomas Curtis recd. of Ben. Cole	58	8		
		To Fish for acct. of John Cooper recd. of Sir Wm. Poole	72	1	4	
		To John Blackwell recd. of John Hulbert	26	70		
	6	To sundry accts. recd. of Peter Kekewich	70, 73	1	18	
		To John Sanders received of his Widow	57	31	1	
		To Wm. Swift recd. of Arthur Hart	61	143		
	8	To Fish for acct. of John Cooper recd. of John Duddlestone	72	2	15	
		To Peter Kekewich recd. of Cicely —	65	30		

	By Worsted Stockins paid John Massinger	71	4	10	5
6	By Adventure 2nd in the Martha & Sarah paid Tho. Walden	60	44	17	
	By Proffit & Losse paid severalls	9	4	7	6
8	By Adventure in the Martha & Sarah	60		13	4½
	By John Williamson paid him	72	15	17	
12	By Proffit & Losse paid mee and houshold expences	9	18	7	¾
	By Worsted Stockins paid John Perrie & John Massinger for 3 parcells	71	12	8	9
17	By Fish for acct. John Cooper abated Marie Earle	72		7	
22	By Martha Speed paid Tho. Walden	46		12	
	By Worsted Stockins paid Tho. Hill, John Perrie, John Gray, Jos. White & John Massinger	71	25	19	7
24	By Proffit & Losse paid John Hardiman & James Milward	9	3	10	
30	By Worsted Stockins paid Thomas Hill & John Massinger	71	4	6	8
	By Proffit & Losse paid Walter Hobbs	9		8	
	By Thomas Puxton paid him	22	3	12	
December 7	By Worsted Stockins paid Tho. Hill, John Perrie, & John Massinger	71	8	16	5
	By Proffit & Losse paid severalls	9	5	3	
14	By Worsted Stockins paid Gabriell Knight & Tho. Hill	71	11	12	3
17	By Ditto paid Joseph White John Massinger & John Day for severall parcels	71	13	5	4
18	By Proffit & Losse paid Sam. Burgesse & Richard Sandiford	9	2	7	7
	By sundry accts paid Philip Troll	23, 22		15	
20	By Seargant Tho. Strode paid for a permitt at custom house	65			6
	By Lady Ann Pawlet for a permitt at custom house	61			6
22	By Worsted Stockins paid John Perrie, Tho. Browning & John Massinger	71	18	9	3
	By Proffit & Losse paid John Sandford & houshold expences	9	18	11	3
January 3	By Worsted Stockins paid Jos. White & John Massinger	71	11	9	5½
5	By Proffit & Losse paid Robert Gibbons	9	1	15	
7	By Ed. Martindale paid him	24	20		
8	By Fish for acct. of John Cooper paid sundry charges	72		1	7
	By Proffit & Losse paid Joseph Drew and Samuell Burgesse	9	1	16	
12	By Worsted Stockins paid John Perry, John Massinger, & Tho. Hill	71	19	2	1½
			1230	5	3
	By ballance carried to that acct.	68	256	11	2
			1486	16	5

Bristoll 1683

	Cash per Contra is	Cr	£	s	d
January 18	By Worsted Stockins paid Gabriell Knight	74	4	16	
23	By Proffit & Losse paid houshold expences	73	12	1	3
	By Worsted Stockins paid John Day, John Perrie, Gabriell Knight & John Massinger	74	12	18	5
25	By Proffit & Losse paid for 2 Blankets	73		17	
	By James Gould paid Max. Gallop	62	40		
	By Tho. Walden paid lent him	2	50		
	By Peter Rossewell paid lent him	60	8		
	By Proffit & Losse paid John Cheshire	73	8	5	
31	By Worsted Stockins paid Joseph White & John Ruddock	74	16	11	1
	By John Wilmer paid Edmond Greene & himselfe at our last faire	62	67		
Ferbruary 3	By Worsted Stockins paid John Perrie Wm. Thiery & Tho. Hill	74	18	4	3
	By Proffit & Losse paid houshold expences & a draught of Faggots	73	3	8	11
6	By Ditto paid James Deane	73		11	10½
	By Worsted stockins paid Tho. Hill for 96 paire	74	11	16	

13	To Coppie hold Tenement in Portburie recd. of Wm. Spoore	20		4	
	To Wm. Spoore Senior recd. of him	52	5		
	To Proffit & Losse recd. of Ditto	73		2	
14	To John Love recd. of him	55	125		
18	To Peter Kekewich recd. of James Lawhorne	65	5		
	To John Bradway recd. of him	70	120		
21	To Fish for acct. of John Cooper recd. of severalls for ½ Cwt & 6 couple	72	2	12	
	To Land at Clevedon recd. of Tho. Morgan	32	2	10	
26	To the Lady Ann Powlet recd. of Bernard Wilkins	48	1	17	
	To Land at Clevedon recd. of Wm. Perrie	32	1	13	6
27	To Isaac Heming recd. of John Hudson	35	45		
March 4	To Proffit & Losse recd. of Frances Hallidge for 4 dozen bottles Xerie	73	3	4	
8	To Peter Kekewich for money of John Weare	65	15		
15	To Tho. Walden recd. of him	2	20		
	To John Blackwell recd. of him	59	20		
17	To Francis Rottenburie recd. of him	63	2	5	
20	To Beniamin Smith received of him	50	8		
	To Wm. Swift recd. of Tho. Walden	61	100		
24	To John Hurtnell recd. of him	38	20		
	To Fish for acct. John Cooper recd. of John Godwin	72	2	10	
1684 Aprill 4	To Richard Champneys recd. of him	45	6	3	
7	To sundry accts recd. of Tho. Hungerford	59, 73	4	8	
	To Xeries wines 20 Butts recd. of James Crofts	76	1	17	4
	To Joseph Berrie recd. of him	62	8	10	
			1337	16	1
15	To John Mayne recd. of him	69	52	1	
	To John Blackwell recd. of him in 2 summes	59	12	10	10
22	To Alexander Caduggan recd. of him	48	100		
	To Lewis Addams recd. of him	56	60		
	To Hugh Hodges received of him	57	1	5	
23	To sundry accts recd. of Wm. Whitwood	(62) 70	9	17	
25	To John Massinger for money of him in part	27		10	
28	To Tho. Walden recd. of him	2	100		
May 2	To John Massinger recd. of him	27		10	
	To James Twiford recd. of him chargeable Aprill 25th but then by error omitted	59	3	3	
5	To Robert Yate received of him	39		11	6
			1678	4	5

Date		Folio	£	s	d
7	By Abigall. Speed paid her	4	2		
	By Sugar 10 hhds paid shipping them	65		1	10
9	By Worsted Stockins paid John Massinger & Tho. Browning	74	28	15	10
13	By Wm..oore Senior paid lent him	52	10		
14	By Worsted Stockins paid John Davis, Thomas Hill, John Day, Jos. White & John Massinger	74	37	18	6
18	By Peter Kekewich paid Sir Tho. Earle	65	50		
20	By James Gould paid Christopher Hurlstone	62	50		
	By Worsted Stockins paid Gabriell Knight	73	3		
	By Estate at Clapton paid Ozziel Browne for drawing a Lease with James Beard	38		6	6
	By Ditto paid Chimney money for ½ a yeare to John Fry	38		6	
March 3	By Proffit & Losse paid David Dorvill for a Case of bottles	73		16	
4	By Worsted Stockins paid John Massinger, John Perrie & Joseph White	74	24	2	7½
	By Proffit & Losse paid Samuell Burgesse	73	1	7	6
	By James Gould paiid Christopher Hurlstone on his bill	62	15	6	3
8	By Sugar 10 hhds paid Joseph Davis	65		5	10
	By Proffit & Losse paid my selfe, Joseph Drew & houshold expences	73	13	18	10
12	By Tho. Walden paid lent him	2	20		
	By Lincloth for acct. Henry Symes 9 bolts paid fileing a Certificate	56			6
15	By Isaac Heming paid John Gandy Junior	35	40		
	By Worsted Stockins paid John Massinger	74	3	2	4
17	By Proffit & Losse paid John Gandy	73		3	6
	By Worsted Stockins paid Fra. Rottenburie & John Day	74	6		5
	By Martha Speed paid her	46		10	
	By John Cooper paid Adam Combes	63	30		
	By Worsted Stockins paid Richard Moone & John Massinger	74	20	12	6
20	By Proffit & Losse paid John Hort	73	2	9	6
	By Worsted Stockins paid Eliza. Dyer, John Perrie & Joseph White	74	12	18	1½
24	By Tho. Walden paid lent him on his bond	2	100		
	By Proffit & Losse paid my wife & Tho. Moreman	73	2	7	6
27	By Worsted Stockins paid John Ruddock	74	12	1	8
	By Xeries wines 12 Butts paid Joseph Berrie	39		5	6
	By Proffit & Losse paid James Swetnham	73		12	
			743	19	½
29	By Worsted Stockins paid John Massinger for 25 paire	74	3	10	10
	By John Wasbrow paid his Widow in full	28	8	8	9
	By Proffit & Losse paid Sam. Burges & Peter Sanders	72	2	3	4
1684 Aprill 2	By the house at lower end of Small Streat paid for Lamblack etc.	22		4	1½
3	By Estate at Clapton paid John Culimer for 3 yeares keeping the house & whiteliming	38		18	9
	By Marie Thring & Bridget Wallis paid them	7	4	10	
	By Worsted Stockins paid Tho. Hill & John Massinger	74	12	12	8
	By Xeries wines 20 Butts paid custom, fees & bills	76	59	14	9
	By Proffit & Losse paid my wife & houshold expences	73	14	11	5
10	By Xeries wine 20 Butts for money paid Robert Alexander	76	40		
	By Worsted Stockins paid Tho. Hill & John Massinger	74	3	13	2
	By Proffit & Losse paid John Batchelor for holland	73	1	5	4
	By Xeries wine 20 Butts given Joseph Berrie	76		10	
	By Martha Speed paid her	46		10	
17	By Worsted Stockins paid Joseph White & John Massinger	74	12	18	1
	By Proffit & Losse paid Henry Matthewes & Henry Gibbes for a hatt & cloth	73	5	15	
19	By Land at Clevedon paid Tho. Smith for Drums & colours	32		3	11
	By Martha Speed paid her at twice	46	6		

(69)	**Anno 1683**				
	Xeries Wine 40 Butts imported in the Ship Expectation for accts (viz) ¾ parts of John Cook merchant resident in Port St Marie in Spaine and ¼ part for my propper acct.	Dr	£	s	d
	To itself for ballance	65	211	10	

	Anno 1682				
	Jahzeel Speed is	Dr	£	s	d
1684	To Proffit & Losse for money owing for which hee credited himself by Proffit and Losse but unduly under the title of Sir Jahzeel Speed in folio (33) of this Leadger	105	409		2
	To John Mayne for ballance of his acct. and recd. of him	69		8	3
September 6	To Cash paid him	77		5	
	To John Olliffe for ballance of his acct. Spent in wine and pd. said Olliffe	39	4	12	
	To Cash delivered him	145		10	
	To Cash paid John Matthews for his beaver	84	2	1	
	To Isaac Heming for money of him in London	90	3		
	To Cash hee paid Wm. Richstone for what I know not	107	6	15	
December 5	To Ditto paid Louis Vintner in full for wine drunk in his house	107	1	11	
9	To Ditto paid John Blackwell in my absence for old scores of wine	107	19	13	7
	To Ditto paid John Hardiman	107	1	10	
	To Ditto paid said Hardiman more	107	1	1	
January	To Cash for money wanting in Cash at my returne from London	107	13	11	
	To Cash paid left in his hands to pay the poore of St Walbourgs parish	107	4		
	To Edmond Scrope for money hee took out of Cash and charg'd to acct. of said Scrope	38	7	3	9
	To James Jacob & Company for money hee recd. of them for a hogshead decayd wine & kept the money	45	3		
	To Louis Adams for money of him in Potts of wine drunk there as per his noate	56	11		

22	By *Adventure 3rd in the Dyamond Ketch to Nevis paid Henry*			
	Gibbes for 2 pieces Brandy	57	38	15	
23	By *Proffit & Losse recd. out of Cash*	73	3	10	
24	By *Worsted Stockins paid John Perrie & John Massinger*	74	9	19	9
26	By *Proffit & Losse paid houshold expences*	73	7	8	3½
	By *Adventure 3rd in the Dyamond Ketch paid John Bennet*	57	4		
	By *Xeries wines 10 Butts paid charges on them*	70	51	2	8
	By *Sugar 2 Butts & 4 hhds paid charges on them*	75	4	16	7
	By *Peter Kekewich paid severall charges on his buisnesse with*				
	Noah Wall	65		4	11
30	By *sundry accts paid Philip Troll for ½ yeares Chimney money*	22, 23		15	
	By *Proffit & Losse paid John Hardiman*	73		18	
May 1	By *Worsted Stockins paid Joseph White & John Massinger*	74	10	18	6
2	By *Proffit & Losse paid my wife & Joane etc.*	73	1	13	8
	By *Sugar 2 Butts & 4 hhds in the New England merchant paid*				
	Fra. Plomer	75	10	18	
9	By *Richard Wasbrow paid him in full*	50	22	19	9
	By *Worsted Stockins paid Fra. Rottenburie in full for*				
	hotpressing	74		8	
	By *John Cooke paid his bill of Exchange to John Bubb*	32	200		
10	By *Worsted Stockins paid John Massinger at twice for 32 paire*	74	4	8	
	By *Proffit & Losse paid Wm. Fisher*	73		8	
	By *Worsted Stockins paid Tho. Hill & John Perrie for 98 paire*	74	12	5	
			1206	18	3½
	By *ballance carried to that acct. of debt*	77	471	6	1½
			1678	4	5

Bristoll 1683

	Xeries wines 40 Butts per Contra is	Cr	£	s	d
March 30	By *John Blackwell for 9 Butts sould him at £23 per Butt*	26	211	10	

Anno 1685/6

	Jahzeel Speed per Contra is	Cr	£	s	d
March 20	By *Cash recd. of Robert Webb for poore's money*	108		17	4
	By *Ballance carried to that acct.*	122	492	16	5
			493	13	9

			£	s	d
	To Proffit & Losse for money short in Cash in Henry Dightons absence found at his returne with which said Dighton chargeth mee in folio (3) of Cashbook No E	105	4		
	To Ditto paid Richard Baugh for old Scores as per Cashbook folio (24) chargd per Henry Dighton	105		12	
			493	13	9

Anno 1683

	Isaac Heming & John Barnard of London merchants in partnership on bond	Dr	£	s	d
May 10	To Isaac Heming his acct. current for money hee & John Barnard took of mee at intrest at £4 per Cent per Annum as per theire bond, and said Isaac's acct. closed May 13th 1683 may appeare	90	400		
1685 November 10	To Proffit & Losse for 2 1/2 yeares of the £400 ending November 10th 1685	105	40		
1686 Nov. 10	To Ditto for 1 yeares intrest of £400 due 10th November 1686	127	16		
1687 Nov. 10	To Ditto for 1 yeares intrest of £400 ending 10th November 1687	137	16		

Anno 1683@

	Linincloth 5 bolts for acct. of Max. Gallop		£	s	d	Dr	£	s	d
Aprill 27	To Proffit & Losse for fileing a Certificate				4				
	To Ditto for portridge & Warehouse roome			2	6				
	To Ditto for my Commission at £2 per Cent		8	2		9		11	
	To William Rishton for money abated him					58			3
	To Maximilian Gallop for theire neat proceeds carried to his acct. current					34	19	19	6
							20	10	9

Anno 1683

	John Maine of the Pill & William Stephens of Bristoll Marriner	Dr	£	s	d
April 27	To Adventure in the Ship Rochell to Cadiz for neat proceeds of 40 doz Bristoll, and 77 doz Wells hose sould by them there as per theire acct.	63	159	2	9

Anno 1683

	John Cooke, Wm. Woolley, & Samuel Kekewich mercht in St Marie Port in Spaine		R	m	Dr	£	s	d
	To Adventure in the Experiment to Cadiz for the proceeds of 2 Truncks Stockins sent them, as per acct. of sales dated 26th Jan. 1683/4 piece of 8 at 52d		12402	17	60	335	18	
	To Isaac Heming for theire bill hee paid valued on mee for		406		35	10	19	10
			12808	17		346	17	10

	Anno 1684				
	Isaac Heming & John Barnard per Contra	*Cr*	*£*	*s*	*d*
May 10	*By Isaac Heming for 1 yeares intrest of the £400 lent them per*				
	Contra due May 10th 1684	*90*	*16*		
1685 May 10	*By Ditto for 1 yeares intrest at £4 per Cent due 10th of May*				
	1685	*90*	*16*		
	By Ditto for ½ yeares intrest due 10th of November 1685	*90*	*8*		
1686 Nov. 10	*By Ditto for 1 yeares intrest due 10th of November 1686*	*113*	*16*		
	By Isaac Heming for his acct. current for ballance of this acct.	*130*	*416*		

	Anno 1683				
	Lincloth 5 Bolts per Contra	*Cr*	*£*	*s*	*d*
Aprill 27	*By William Rishton for said 5 Bolts sould him*	*58*	*20*	*10⁷²*	*9*

	Anno 1683				
	John Maine & William Stephens per Contra	*Cr*	*£*	*s*	*d*
Aprill 30	*By Cash recd. of Sam. Plomer for 25 pcs of 8 3/8 at 53d the*				
	piece of 8	*66*	*5*	*12*	
May 31	*By John Blackwell for theire bill on him of 700 pcs of 8 the piece*				
	of 8 at 52½d	*26*	*153*	*2*	*6*
	By Jahzeel Speed for full balance paid him	*69*		*8*	*3*
			159	*2*	*9*

	Anno 1683					
	John Cooke & Company per Contra are	*Cr*	*£*		*s*	*d*
	By Xeries Wine 12 Butts in the Ship	*R*	*m*			
March	*Rochell for theire first cost as per acct. March*					
	30th 1683 4741 the piece of 8 in this whole					
	acct. at 52d	*4741*	*39*	*128*	*8*	
	By John Cooke his particular acct. for					
	ballance of that acct. charg'd to my debt per					
	his order as per theire acct. closed Jan. 26th					
	1683/4	*981*	*32*	*26*	*11*	*4*
	By Xeries Wine 20 Butts for theire first cost					
	in the Expectation, as per Invoyce 26th					
	January 1684 the piece of 8 at 52d	*7086*	*17*	*76*	*191*	*18*	*6*
		12808	*17*		*346*	*17*	*10*

Anno 1684				
John Mayne of the Pill and Bristoll merchant supra Cargo in the Ship Agreement to Cadiz	Dr	£	s	d
To *Adventure in the Agreement to Cadiz* for the R m				
Aprill neat proceeds of one Trunck of Stockins sent				
consign'd to him, as per acct. of Sales 15th Feb.				
1683 5574	62	156		10

Anno 1684				
William Spoore Junior & Wm. Spoore Senior of Portburie in County Somerset	Dr	£	s	d
June 5 To Cash lent them on theire bond payable Dec. 5th next £40	77	40		
1685 June 5 To Proffit & Losse for 1 yeares intrest due June 5th 1685	105	2	8	
1686 June 5 To Ditto for 1 yeares intrest due June 5th 1686	127	2	8	
1688 Jan. To Proffit & Losse for 2 1/2 yeares intrest due Dec. 5th 1688	153	6		
1689 Oct. To Ditto for 1/2 yeares intrest of £40 ending June 5th 1689	164	1	4	
Dec. To Ditto for 6 moths & 12 daies intrest of £40 from June 5th to Dec. 17	164	1	5	6
1690 To Ditto for one year's intrest ending Dec. 17th 1690 @	180	2	8	
		55	13	6

(70)	**Bristoll 1682/3@**				
	William Whitwood of Bristoll Distiller	Dr	£	s	d
March 22	To Xeries wine 30 butts for 7 butts corrupt viz. 1 Butt Lees & 6 lesse 16 Gall. wine	45	29	9	
1683 January 3	To Xeries wine 12 Butts for one Butt & 3 Cask of eager wine sould him	39	6	10	
			35	19	

Anno 1683					
Sugar 15 hhds recd. out of Owners Endeavour Michael Perrie Master from Jamaica laden (viz) 10 hhds per Robert Scrope merchant in part returnes of goods formerly sent, & 5 by said Perrie in part returnes of goods sent by him hence, & taken in per him from Edm. Scrope & Company in Nevis for my acct.		Dr	£	s	d
July To Robert Scrope for the cost & charges of 10 hhds as per Invoyce Aprill 12th 1683		37	85	18	9
To Michael Perrie for 1st cost of 5 hhds laden by him, as per Invoyce in his acct. of 1st May 1683 £ s d		47	41	8	8
August 13 To Cash paid custom fees & bills 6 19		66			
To Cash paid John Richardson for freight and avridge 19 13 9		67			
To Cash paid weighing them when sould 3 9		67			
To Michael Perrie for money lost on the pieces of 8 recd. of him 9		47	27	5	6
			154	12	11

Anno 1683					
John Bradway of Bristoll Vintner		Dr	£	s	d
August 10	To Xeries wine 40 Butts in partnership with John Cooke for 5 Butts sould at £24	65	120		
October 4	To sundry accts for 8 Butts Xerie sould him at £24 per Butt 6 months	39, 65	192		
1684 March 25	To Xeries Wine 20 Butts in the Expectation for 9 Butts at £20 per Butt to pay 1/2 the 24th June next, & 1/2 24th Sept., as per his bills	76	180		
			492		

	Anno 1684			Cr	£	s	d
	John Mayne per Contra is			Cr	£	s	d
Aprill	By *Proffit & Losse* for 6lb of *Choccolatte* as	R	m				
	per his acct.		36	73	1		10
	By *Xeries Wines* 10 Butts recd. out of the						
	Agreement as per said acct.		3678	70	102	19	
Ryals 1860	By Cash recd. of him in 232¾ pieces of 8						
	sould Richard Corsley at 4s 5d¾ the piece		1860	68	52	1	
					156		10

	Anno 1685		Cr	£	s	d
	William Spoore Junior & Senior per Contra are		Cr	£	s	d
November 21	By Cash recd. of Wm. Spoore for 1 yeares intrest ending June 5th					
	1685		107	2	8	
	By *Wm. Spoore Junior* for intrest of the £40 resting due Dec.					
	17th 1689		176	10	17	6
				13	5	6
	By *Acct. of Ballances*, for Ballance		194 *	42	8	0
				55	13	6

	Bristoll 1683		Cr	£	s	d
	William Whitwood per Contra is		Cr	£	s	d
September 10	By Cash recd. of him		67	29	9	
1684 Aprill 23	By Cash recd. of him in full		68	6	10	
				35	19	

	Anno 1683		Cr	£	s	d
	Sugar 15 hhds per Contra		Cr	£	s	d
August 27	By John Love for said Sugar weight neat 108cwt 2qr 22lb at					
	24s per Cwt to allow discount		55	130	8	9
	By Michael Perrie for 136 lb Sugar wanting in one of the 5 hhds					
	laden by him		47	1	1	3
				131	10	
	To Profit and Loss, for Balance		189 *	23	2	11
				154	12	11

	Anno 1683		Cr	£	s	d
	John Bradway per Contra is		Cr	£	s	d
February 18	By Cash recd. of him		68	120		
1684 May 28	By Cash received of him in part		77	100		
	By Cash received of him in part		77	40		
July 5	By Ditto recd. of him in part		77	14		
24	By Cash received of him per Tho. Walden		77	38		
September 26	By Cash recd. of him		77	90		
November	By Richard Wasbrow paid him on my noat		50	32	19	
1684/5	By Giles Gough for money paid him on my noat		65	28	4	
March 24	By Cash recd. of him		82	28	17	
				492		

Anno 1688		Dr	£	s	d
	John Bradway of Bristoll Vintner is	Dr			
January 8	To Xeries wine 23 Butts for 8 Butts at £26 5s payable ½		210		
	Aprill 8th & tother ½ July 8th next	150			

Anno 1683@		Dr	£	s	d
	Thomas Day of Bristoll Cooper	Dr			
Aprill 5	To Xeries wines 30 butts for 3 butts sold him	45	39	15	9
June 18	To Cash paid cleaning the 2 lower Cellars	66		2	6
	To Proffit & Losse for intrest of £32 10s	73	1	10	
1684 Sept. 1	To Cash paid him	77	7	15	
1685 January 2	To Isaac Heming for 2 bills on him in his favor, 1 for £13 6s 7d: tother for £93 12s 9d is	90	106	19	4
	To Ditto for money he drew per bill on him in favor of Wm. Denne Grocer	90	23		
	To Proffit & Losse for ballance	105			2
			179	2	9

Anno 1683		Dr	£	s	d
	Xeries Wine 1 Butt part of 5 Butts remaining of 40 Butts	Dr			
	To Xeries Wine 40 Butts for the value of this Butt	65	21		
	To Profit & Loss, for Ballance	189 *	6		
			27		

Anno 1683/4					Dr	£	s	d
	Xeries Wine 10 Butts in the Ship Agreement from Cadiz Wm. Fisher Master laden by John Mayne Supra Cargo in Cadiz				Dr			
Aprill	To John Mayne for theire first cost as per acct.				69	102	19	
	To the Widow Wasbrow for cooperidge as per noat				75	1	2	
		£	s	d	68			
26	To Cash paid custom fees & bills	33	12	8	68	51	2	8
	To Ditto paid Wm. Fisher for freight	17	10	0		155	3	8
					189 *	34	3	10¼
	To Profit and Loss, for Ballance					189	7	6¼

(71)	**Bristoll 1683**				Dr	£	s	d
	Worsted Stockins				Dr			
May 25	To acct. of themselves for ballance brought from that acct.				54	304	4	3
		paire	s	d				
	To Cash paid John Massinger for	32	2	11	66	4	13	4
31	To Ditto paid John Perrie for	17	2	9	66	2	6	1
June 8	To Cash given Tho. Hill				66		2	6
	To Cash paid Tho. Browning for	120	1	5½	66	8	15	
	To Ditto paid John Day for	22	2	8	66	2	18	8

Anno 1689		Cr	£	s	d
	John Bradway per Contra is				
July 29	By Cash recd. of him in part	168	50		
September 25	By Cash recd. of him	168	30		
November 20	By Cash recd. of him	168	30		
February 3	By Cash recd. of him in part	173	40		
1690 April	By Henry Parsons for money pd. him per my order	145	40		
June 17	By Cash recd. of him per the Hands of Henry Parsons	181	20		
			210		

Anno 1683@		Cr	£	s	d
	Per Contra				
Aprill 6	By Xeries wine 30 butts for his noate of Charges	45	6	15	6
	By Xeries wines 12 Butts for his noat of disbursments on them	39	7	15	
1684 Sept.	By Cash recd. of him	77	34		
	By Proffit & Losse for money forgiven him	105		12	9
1685 Nov.	By Wines in sundry ships from Cadiz for his noat for work etc.	101	23		
January 6	By Cash received of him	107	107		
			179	2	9

Anno 1683		Cr	£	s	d
	Xeries wine 1 Butt per Contra is				
December 1	By Cash received of Widow Aldworth for 2 Gall. 1/8 at 5s 4d	67		11	
14	By Dr. Francis Hungerford for 6 doz bottles at 16s per dozen	59	4	16	
	By Samuell Davis for 4 doz at 16s per dozen	63	3	4	
20	By Seargeant Tho. Strode for 5 doz bottles at 16s	65	4		
	By the Lady Susan Pawlet for 6 doz Pinte bottles at 9 Gall. at 5s 4d per Gallon	61	2	8	
	By the Lady Ann Pawlet for 2 doz bottles at 16s per doz	48	1	12	
	By Dr. Francis Hungerford for 2 doz bottles at 16s	59	1	12	
January 7	By George Dighton for 2 doz bottles at 16s	60	1	12	
	By Samuell Davis for 2 doz bottles at 16s	63	1	12	
16	By Cash recd. of Tho. Hungerford for 6 quart bottles	67		9	
	By James Twivord for 3 1/2 doz bottles at 16s	59	2	16	
31	By Proffit & Losse for 1 doz bottles sent to London	73		16	
February 6	By Cash recd. of Peter Kekewich for 2 doz bottles of Xerie	68	1	12	
			27		

Anno 1684		Cr	£	s	d
	Xeries Wine 10 Butts per Contra are				
	By John Blackwell				
April	By the Widow Washrow for 16 Iron hoops at 4½ per hoope	75		6	
	By John Blackwell for ½ theire fist cost in Spaine, custom, freight etc. in Bristoll	59	77	1	6¼
	By Ditto for my ½ sould him payable Oct. 8th next as per his bill	59	112		
			189	7	6¼

Bristoll 1683		Cr	£	s	d
	Worsted Stockins per Contra				
July 17	By Adventure in the ship Civilia merchant to Cadiz for 1 Trunck cont. 68 doz Bristoll, & 28 doz Wells hose at 3s 6d and 2s per paire	44	176	8	
October	By Adventure in the Cadiz merchant from London to Cadiz for 56 doz Bristoll hose Bristoll hose at 3s 6d & 18 doz Wells hose & 2s 1d & 14 doz ditto at 2s per paire	34	158	18	

Date	Description							
	To Ditto paid John Massinger for	46	2	11	66	6	14	2
	To Ditto paid John Brady for	18	2	10	66	2	11	
14	To Ditto paid John Perrie for	13	2	9	66	1	15	9
16	To Ditto paid John Massinger for	30	2	11	66	4	7	6
23	To Ditto paid Joseph White for	60	2	11½	66	8	17	6
	To Ditto paid Jos. White for	153	3		66	22	19	
25	To Ditto paid John Massinger for	28	2	11	66	4	1	8
July 3	To Ditto paid Fra. Rottenburie for hotpressing 536 paire				66		11	1
4	To Ditto paid John Massinger for	34	2	11	66	4	19	2
	To Ditto paid Anthony Harris for	80	1	5	66	5	13	
	To Ditto paid Joel Pinny for	9	2	8	66	1	4	
6	To Ditto paid Joseph White for	76	3		66	11	8	
	To Ditto paid John Brady for	15	2	10	66	2	2	6
	To Ditto paid Tho. Hill for	120	1	6	66	9		
13	To Ditto paid John Perrie for	10	2	9	66	1	7	6
14	To Ditto paid John Massinger for	35	2	11	66	5	2	1
17	To Cash paid Jos. White for	64	3		66	9	12	
	To Ditto paid Tho. Hill for	20	2	10	66	2	16	8
	To Ditto paid Tho. Hill for	72	1	5½	66	5	5	
21	To Ditto paid Ditto for	32	2	10	66	4	10	8
23	To Ditto paid John Perrie for	20	2	9	66	2	15	
	To Ditto paid Joel Piny for	14	2	8	66	1	17	4
	To Ditto paid John Massinger for	44	2	11	66	6	8	4
25	To Cash paid John Brady for	5	2	10	66		14	2
August 4	To Ditto paid John Massinger for	40	2	11	66	5	16	8
7	To Ditto paid Tho. Hill for	116	1	6	66	8	14	
13	To Ditto paid John Perrie for	20	2	9	66	2	19	
16	To Cash paid John Massinger for	35	2	11	67	5	2	1
	To Ditto paid Fran. Rottenburie for hotpressing 500 paire				67		10	6
24	To Ditto paid John Massinger for	31	2	11	67	4	10	5
30	To Ditto paid Tho. Hill for	120	1	6	67	9		
September 1	To Ditto paid John Brady for	16	2	10	67	2	5	4
8	To Ditto paid John Perrie for	15	2	9	67	2	1	3
	To Ditto paid John Massinger for	40	2	11	67	5	16	8
15	To Cash paid John Massinger for	31	2	11	67	4	10	5
19	To Ditto paid Jos. White for	45	3		67	6	15	
						507	14	3
22	To Cash paid Tho. Hill for	120		18	67	9		
	To Ditto paid John Massinger for	28	2	11	67	4	1	8
24	To Ditto paid John Perrie for	20	2	9	67	2	15	
October 1	To Ditto paid John Massinger for	24	2	11	67	3	10	
6	To Cash paid John Perrie for	20	2	9	67	2	15	
	To Ditto paid John Massinger for	36	2	11	67	5	5	
8	To Ditto paid Fra. Rottenburie for hotpressing 458 paire				67		9	6½
10	To Cash paid Joseph White for	104	2	11¾	67	15	9	10
12	To Cash paid John Massinger for	34	2	11	67	4	19	2
20	To Cash paid John Brady for	18	2	10	67	2	11	
	To Cash paid Tho. Hill for	34	2	9	67	4	13	6
27	To Ditto paid John Massinger for	44	2	11	67	6	18	4
November 2	To Ditto paid John Massinger for	31	2	11	67	4	10	5
12	To Ditto paid John Massinger for	27	2	11	67	3	18	9
	To Ditto paid John Perrie for	30	2	9	67	4	2	6
17	To Ditto paid John Massinger for	30	2	11	67	4	7	6
22	To Ditto paid Tho. Hill for	120	1	6	67	9		
24	To Ditto paid John Perrie for	32	2	9	67	4	8	
	To Ditto paid John Day for	13	2	9	67	1	15	9
	To Ditto paid Joseph White for	47	2	11¾	67	7		
	To Ditto paid John Massinger for	26	2	11	67	3	15	10
30	To Ditto paid Tho. Hill for	5	2	9	67		13	9
	To Ditto paid John Massinger for	25	2	11	67	3	12	10

By Adventure in the Agreement to Cadiz for 54 2/3 doz Bristoll, & 32 doz Wells hose	62	150	9	4
		485	15	4
By ballance carried to that acct.	74	214	7	1½
		700	2	5½

December 7	To Ditto paid Tho. Hill for	24	2	9	*67*	3	6	
	To Ditto paid John Perrie for	20	2	9	*67*	2	15	
8	To Ditto paid John Massinger for	19	2	11	*67*	2	15	5
14	To Ditto paid Gabriell Knight for	19	2	9	*67*	2	12	3
	To Ditto paid Tho. Hill for Tho. Browning for	120	1	6	*67*	9		
17	To Cash paid Joseph White for	48	2	11¾	*67*	7	3	
	To Ditto paid John Massinger for	32	2	10	*67*	4	7	6
18	To Ditto paid John Day for	13	2	8	*67*	1	14	10
21	To Ditto paid John Perrie for	37	2	9	*67*	5	1	9
22	To Ditto paid Tho. Browning for	120	1	6	*67*	9		
	To Ditto paid John Massinger for	30	2	11	*67*	4	7	6
January 3	To Cash paid Joseph White for	50	2	11¾	*67*	7	8	11½
5	To Ditto paid John Massinger for	28	2	10½	*67*	4		6
12	To Ditto paid John Perrie for	24	2	9	*67*	3	6	
	To Ditto paid John Massinger for	23	2	10½	*67*	3	6	1½
	To Ditto paid Tho. Hill for	100	2	6	*67*	12	10	
						700	2	5½

(72) **Bristoll 1683**

	Fish NorthSea Codd being a parcell received out of the Content Ketch of Yarmouth John Spanton Master for acct. of John Cooper Senior of same place merchant	£	s	d	Dr	£	s	d
July 6	To Cash paid for landing, housing		13	10				
	To Ditto paid Richard Wasbrow for 12½ busheles Salt		16	8	*66*			
	To Cash paid for delivery per Porters at severall times, & clearing the brine		3	10	*67*			
September 13	To Ditto paid taking up Pickle & delivery of severall parcells of fish		1	1	*67*			
November 17	To Ditto paid abated Marie Earle on a parcell of fish			7				
January	To Ditto paid sundry charges in delivery of part of it		1	7	*67*			
	To Proffit & Losse for 22 Weeks Celleridge		2	10	*73*			
	To Ditto for charges in taking up the Pickle			6	*73*			
	To Ditto for halling to Cellar			8	*73*	5	2	6
	To my Commission for Sales & remittance of money at £3 per Cent				*73*	2	8	2
						7	10	8
	To John Cooper his acct. current for the neat proceeds				*63*	73	3	3
						80	13	11

Bristoll 1683				
	Fish per Contra is	Cr	£	s	d
July 3	By Cash received of the widow Sandford for ¼ Cwt & 5 fish large Cod , ¼ Cwt small Cod	66	1	12	8
	By Ditto received of Marie Sweet for ¼ cwt small Codd	66		10	
17	By Ditto recd. of severalls for 10 Couple	66	1		
August 4	By Cash recd. of severalls for 7 Couple	66		14	
	By Ditto recd. of the Widow Sandford for 1cwt large & 1 Cwt smaller Codfish	66	6	5	
	By Ditto recd. of Marie Sweet for ½ cwt large & ½ smaller Codd	66	3	7	6
13	By Ditto for 2 Couple of severalls	66		4	
20	By Cash recd. of severalls for 33 fishes large Codd	67	1	13	
	By Ditto recd. of Widow Sandford in full for the fish sould her the 4th instant	67		5	
	By Ditto recd. of Ann Hort for 1cwt of small Codd	67	2	15	
	By Ditto recd. of severalls for 5 Couple	67		10	
23	By Ditto recd. of the Widow Grubb for ½ cwt small Cod	67	1	7	6
	By Ditto recd. of Marie Sweet for ¼ Cwt large & ¼ Cwt small Codd	67	1	13	6
	By Ditto recd. of Geo. Dighton for ¼ larger Cod	67	1		
27	By Ditto recd. of the Widow Grubb for ¼ Cwt large Codd ¼ cwt small cod, & ¼ cwt Colefish	67	2	5	9
	By Ditto recd. of John Freaks for 3 couple of large codd	67		6	
29	By Ditto recd. of — Gardner for ½ cwt large, & ½ Cwt small Codd	67	3	7	6
	By Ditto recd. of John Chance for 1¼ cwt & 1 couple sould him	67	5		
	By Ditto recd. of severalls for 8½ Couple large Codd	67		17	
	By Ditto recd. of the Widow Sandford for ½ cwt large & ½ cwt small Codd	67	3	7	6
	By Ditto recd. of Marie Earle for ¼ cwt of large Codd	67	1		
September 10	By Cash recd. of severalls for 17 Couple large Codd	67	1	15	3
	By Ditto recd. of John Chance for 2 cwt & 1 Fish large Codd & 1 cwt Colefish	67	10	5	
19	By ditto recd. of severalls for 6½ Couple large Codd	67		13	
25	By Cash recd. of Marie Earle for a qtr Cwt of large Codd	67	1	3	6
	By Ditto recd. of severalls for 5 Couple large Codd	67		10	
28	By Cash recd. of John Hollister for 1 couple of fish	67		2	
October 1	By Cash recd. of severalls for 2 Couple large Codd	67		4	
8	By Cash recd. of John Browne for ¼ Cwt & of Marie Earle for ¼ Cwt large Codd	67	2	7	3
10	By Ditto recd. of John Gandy for 1 couple	67		2	
20	By Cash recd. of Jer. Holwey for 3 Couple large Cod	67		6	

Anno 1683		Dr	£	s	d
	John Williamson of Bristoll Sugarbaker is				
October 27	To Tho. Puxton for money on bond due to said Puxton, & by order of said Puxton transferred to bee paid by his bond to Ma. Speed [73]	22	90		
November 11	To Cash paid him	67	15	17	
			105	17	

Anno 1683/4		Dr	£	s	d
	Estate at Clapton let to rent to James Beard for 3 yeares				
March 1685	To Cash charg'd to Estate at Clapton by Error there brought from that acct.	38		6	6
	To Cash paid Katherine Winter for ½ yeares reserved rent	107		16	
	To James Beard for money abated him on 2½ yeares rent to the 1st Sept. 1686	76	8	10	
	To Ditto for his noat of Disbursments for the yeares 1684 & 1685	76	24		
	To Cash paid Ozziel Browne for my part of the Covenants with Edward Jacob	120		6	
1687 Aprill 1	To Cash paid Ann Smith for 3 Locks & nailes	102		5	4
23	To Marie Beard for her noat of disbursments	125	2	16	2
	To Marie Beard for money abated her on the last ½ yeares rent by agreement	125	2	10	
	To Ditto for 15s 4d abated her out of the charges of the Administration etc.	125		15	4
July 29	To Cash paid John Cullimer in part	121		5	
August 22	To Ditto paid Tho. Walden for a Sparre to make a Ladder	139		5	
September 17	To Cash paid Tho. Godwin for paving part of the Court	139		12	6
	To Ditto paid Henry Skydmore for bringing the Ladder from the Pill	139		2	
	To Estate at Clapton the old Farm, & what I newly purchased, for the money per Contra which I received of the Trustees for the land I sould them in Clapton being charg'd there by error	151	170		
			211	9	10
	To Proffit & Losse for ballance	164	49	10	2
			361		

Anno 1683		Dr	£	s	d
	Frances Beckford of London Widow on a Mortgage is				
	To Isaac Heming for money paid lent her on £ s d				
December 18	a Mortgage of the manor of Yate, to John				
	Cook & Isaac Heming in trust £1500 1500	90			
1684 June	To Proffit & Losse for ½ yeares intrest £45 45	89	1545		

27	By Ditto recd. of severalls for 1½ cwt large Codd	67	5	8	
November 2	By Cash recd. of severalls for 5 large Codd	67		5	
8	By Cash recd. of severalls for 5 couple large Codd	67		10	
24	By Cash recd. of John Godwin for ½ cwt large Codd	67	1	17	6
December 1	By Cash recd. of Wm. Rogers & Tho. Day for 3 Couple	67		6	
January 8	By Cash recd. of James Wallis for 1 Cwt of Colefish	67	2	5	
	By Cash recd. 29th August of Ann Hort for ¼ cwt large and ¼ small Codd omitted then to bee chargd	68	2	7	6
21	By Cash recd. of Wm. Smith for 1 cwt of Colefish for the ship Factor	68	2	5	
February 1	By Ditto recd. of Sir Wm. Poole for 12 Couple	68	1	4	
8	By Ditto recd. of John Duddlestone for 1 cwt of small Codd	68	2	15	
March 21	By Ditto recd. of Wm. King & John Ollife for ½ cwt & 6 couple large Codd	68	2	12	
25	By Ditto recd. of John Godwin for ¾ cwt of large Codd	68	2	10	
			80	13	11

Anno 1683@					
	Per Contra	Cr	£	s	d
Oct. 20	By Cash recd. of him	67	60		
November	By Isaac Heming for his bill on Richard Atkinson recd. by said Heming	35	45	17	
			105	17	

Anno 1683/4					
	Estate at Clapton in the County of Somerset per Contra is	Cr	£	s	d
1684 September 1	By James Beard for ½ yeares Rent due by lease for the farme (which I let to him from the 1st of March 1683, for 3 yeares) due the 1st of September 1684	76	31		
March 1	By Ditto for ½ yeares intrest due March 1st 1684 as by Lease may appeare	76	31		
1685 September 1	By Ditto for ½ yeares rent due Sept. 1 1685, as by Lease may appeare	76	32		
March 1	By Ditto for ½ yeares rent due March 1st 1685 as may appeare	76	32		
1686 September 1	By Ditto for ½ yeares rent due Sept. 1 1686 as may appeare	76	32	10	
March 1	By Marie Beard for ½ yeares rent for the farme ending March 1st 1686	125	32	10	
1687 Sept. 1	By Cash recd. of Sir John Smyth, John Piggot & Edward Gorges for 3 closes in Clapton (viz) my oxlease, 2 acres Leemead, & 2 acres in Normead value £8 10s 00d per Annum at 20 yeares purchase	139	170		
			361		

Anno 1684					
	Frances Beckford per Contra is	Cr	£	s	d
June	By Isaac Heming recd. of him	90	1545		

(73)	**Bristoll 1683**	Dr	£	s	d
	Proffit and Losse is				
	To ballance brought from that acct.	9	1527	5	6½
January 23	To Cash paid houshold expences to this 23th	68	12	1	3
25	To Cash paid for 2 Blankets	68		17	
25	To Cash paid John Cheshire for bottles	68	8	5	
31	To Xeries wines 1 Butt for 1 doz qt bottles Xerie sent to London	70		16	
	To sundry accts for 1/3 of a Butt & part of a Tierce Xerie	65, 39	9		
February 3	To Cash paid houshold expences to this day 3rd Feb.	68	3	7	
	To Ditto paid postage of a leter & a draught of Faggotts	68		1	11
6	To Cash paid James Deane for my part charges on a Butt of Xerie	68		11	10½
March 3	To Cash paid David Dorvill for a Duch Case of bottles	68		16	
4	To Cash paid Samuell Burgesse for Mault & a cheese in full	68	1	7	6
8	To Cash paid Joseph Drew for 6 stockin boards	68		11	
	To Cash paid my selfe	68	2	10	
	To Ditto paid houshold expences to the 7th instant	68	10	17	10
17	To Cash paid John Gandy in full of all accts	68		3	6
20	To Wm. Swift for ballance abated him	61			8½
22	To Cash paid John Hort for 1½ Bend of Leather for Joseph Speed	68	2	9	6
	To Ditto delivered my wife	68	1		
	To Ditto paid Tho; Moreman for Carriage of a Cask Floure & Cask Canary	68	1	7	6
27	To Cash paid James Swetnham in full of his noat	68		12	
	To John Washrow for cooperidge & Cask as per severall noates	28	95	17	
29	To Cash paid Samuell Burges for 6 Bushels of Mault	68		19	6
	To Ditto paid Peter Sanders for ½ yeares arreares to the poore for Mathias Aldington	68	1	3	10
Aprill 4	To Ditto paid houshold expences to the 7th instant	68	12	12	11
	To Ditto paid for a piece of Kenting & a piece of muzling	68	1	18	6
	To John Cook for ballance of his Sterling acct.	32		10	5
10	To John Mayne for the Cost of 6lb of choccolattee bought in Spaine	69	1		2
	To Cash paid John Bachelaure for Holland	68	1	5	4
	To Xeries wines 40 Butts for 5 Butts empty sould John Washrow	65	1	5	
17	To Cash paid John Matthews for a Hatt for Jahzeel	68		10	
19	To Ditto paid Henry Gibbes for ½ piece of Dowlas	68	5	5	
23	To Cash received out of Cash	68	3	10	
26	To Cash paid houshold expences to this 1st of May	68	7	8	3½
30	To Cash paid John Hardiman in full of his noat	68		18	
1684 May 2	To Ditto paid my wife 30s & 3s to Joane for a cheese & for paper 8d	68	1	13	8
	To Isaac Heming for money paid Tho. Martin for a Cask of flower	35	1		
	To Arthur Hobbs for his noat of disbursments	29	2	15	10
			1723	14	7
	To Edmond Scrope for the first cost of 6 Butts of Xerie	38	52	2	9
	To Andrew Stucky for 2 Livers 8 Sous the cost of 6 boxes Prunellars	64		3	10
12	To Cash paid Wm. Fisher	68		8	
	Proffit & Losse Dr. to Cash paid John Harris in full to this day	77	3	1	10
26	To Cash paid John Ford in full	77	1	15	8
June	To Cash paid houshold expences	77	18	9	5
	To Cash paid John Seward for a Mare bought of him	77	9	10	

Bristoll 1683/4				
Proffit & Losse per Contra is	Cr	£	s	d
January By Fish for acct. of John Cooper for 22 Weeks Celleridge	72	2	10	
28 By Cash recd. for 8 bottles of Xerie	68		10	8
By James Twivord for 3½ doz bottles	59		7	
By Dr. Fra. Hungerford for 4 doz botttles Xerie	59	3	10	
31 By Max. Gallop for 4 doz bottles Xerie, bottles etc.	50	3	4	
February 6 By Cash recd. of Peter Kekewich for 2 doz bottles, Pannier etc.	68		6	
13 By Cash recd. of Wm. Spoore Sonne for the interest of £5	68		2	
By James Gould for 4 doz bottles of Xerie sent him with bottles etc.	62	3	4	
27 By Lincloth for acct. James Goud for portridge, warehouse room and Commission	56	4	3	5½
March 4 By Cash : recd. of Frances Hallidge for 4 doz bottles Xerie	68	3	4	
20 By the Lady Ann Pawlet for 4 doz bottles Xerie pannier etc.	48	3	10	
By Fish for acct. of John Cooper for severall charges	72	2	16	8
By John Cooper Senir for Port of leters	63		3	3
By Tho. Williams paid port of severall leters	57		7	6
By Edm. Scrope & Company for ballance of the neat proceeds of sundry goods formerly sent in the Isabella to Nevis consign'd to Edm. Scrope Sugar at 10s per Cwt	33	27	5	7
By John Washrow for hoops Iron & Cask received at severall times	28	17	5	
1684 Aprill 4 By Dr. Fra. Hungerford for 2 doz bottles Xerie	59	1	13	
By John Cooke his acct. of Exca for port of leters	39		3	
7 By Cash recd. of Tho. Hungerford for 10 bottles Xerie	68		14	
15 By Xeries wine 40 Butts for hallidge, Celleridge, Cooperidge and other charges as per particulars	65	34		9
22 By Hugh Hodges for portridge of a pannier of bottles	57			2
May By Adventure in the Friston to Cadiz for a Trunck & cord	64		14	10
By John Blackwell for Port of leters to & from Bordeauxe	59		3	9
By Wm. Spoore Senior for intrest money	52		3	6
By Charles Plomer & Company for ½ yeares intrest of £150	78	4	10	
June 10 By Samuell Davis for 6 doz bottles & Corks	63		12	9
By Dr. Hungerford for 12 doz empty bottles 4 Panniers etc.	59	1	10	6
By Henry Bainham for money paid lent him on a mortgage Aprill 4th 1682	48	276		
By Ditto for 2 yeares intrest due Aprill 5th 1684	48	33	2	4
By Wm. Godwin for ½ yeares intrest of £100	64	3		
By Tho. Goldney for 1 doz bottles & Corks	16		2	
By John Cooke for 15¼ pieces of 8 overcharg'd on freight of 3 parcells Stockins	32	3	6	8½
By John Earle of Bristoll for 8 doz Cost bottles 2s 2d¼ Panniers etc.	37	1	1	4
August By Sir George Strode for 8 doz bottles, & 4 Panniers etc.	24	1	2	6
By the Lady Ann Pawlet for 4 doz bottle & 2 Panniers	48		10	8
By John Blackwell for money hee abated on severall parcells of mine	59		11	6
23 By Sir Samuell Astry for 1 hogshead & Cooperidge	49		5	
By the Lady Ann Pawlet for 10 doz bottle, & 5 Panniers	48	1	7	
By Tho. Day for intrest money	70	1	10	
By Lincloth for acct. of Henry Simes for charges on 9 bolts cloth	56		17	3
September 12 By Sir Sam. Astry for 10 doz bottles & 3 Panniers & covers	49	1	4	
By Wm. Drake for 6 doz bottles & panniers	63		16	6
		441	12	2
25 By Dr. Hungerford for 8 doz bottles 17s 4d & 3 Panniers & covers 3s 8d	59	1	1	
By Wm. Prichard & Company for money lent them on theire bond	63	50		
By Ditto for ½ yeares intrest due Aprill 2nd 1684	63	1	10	

Date	Description		£	s	d
14	To Cash paid houshold expences	77	5	3	
	To Dr. Francis Hungerford for money received of him at twice in Reading	59	11	5	
	To John Blackwell for one Rundlet cont. 12 Gall. Xerie at 4s	59	2	8	
July 5	To Cash paid houshold expences	77	4	16	11
	To John Wilmer for money I formerly received of him in London	62	20		
	To Wine 2 hhds for 1 doz bottles given Cosen Haggatt	78		9	
	To Wines on the St Malo merchant for ballance	48	1	11	
17	To Cash paid houshold expences	77	10	12	9
	To John Blackwell for 2 Gallons Xerie at	59		8	
August 26	To Cash paid John Cheshire in full for bottles etc.	77	8		
September	To John Rumsey for ballance of his acct.	29	1	8	4
8	To Cash paid Alexander Doleman in full of his noat	77	8	13	
18	To Cash paid houshold expences	77	26	7	1
23	To Cash paid John Hurtnell for severall parcels of Mault	82	5	18	2
November 3	To Cash paid houshold expences to this 3rd November	82	36	9	3
December 6	To Cash paid Martha Speed	82	1	17	
	To Ditto paid Anthony Dell in full of his noat	82		10	9
12	To Cash paid Richard Sandford for Jahzeel	82	1		
14	To Ditto paid Dennis Pitts in full of his noat	82		10	1
January 6	To Cash paid Richard Champneys for 1 yeares poore money	82	3	5	
17	To Cash paid George White for freeze for Jahzeel	82		16	
	To Xeries wine 3 Butts for 2 doz bottles sent Phil. Ward	79	1	12	
	To John Blackwell for 2 dox Xerie & bottles sent to Reading	85	2	1	
	To Isaac Heming for ½ £1 2s 6d paid James Whiston for the weekly avizoes [74]	76		11	3
	To Ditto for money paid Wm. Russell in London	76	20		
	To Ditto for 2 Protests 9s charges on stockins 17s 10d Port leters 9s 10 & 2 Keggs sturgeon £2	76	3	16	8
	To Ditto for charges on Sugar, his wives charge to Bristol, his to Reading £5 14s and money of him £6 8d	76	11	17	8
	To Ditto for carriage 2 Truncks hose 12s money of him in London £3 and a firkin Butter £1 5s 0d in all	76	4	17	
	To Ditto paid myTayler £1 16s 0d charges shipping hose £1 16s 11d & money of him in London £5 in all	76	8	12	11
	To Ditto paid for a petticoat £4 Specticles 2s & money of him in London £2 in all	76	6	2	
			296	10	4
			2020	4	11

Bristoll 1683/4

		paire	s	d		Dr	£	s	d
	Worstead Stockins are					Dr	£	s	d
January	To ballance brought from that acct.					71	214	7	1½
18	To Cash paid Gabriell Knight for	36	2	8		68	4	16	
23	To Ditto paid John Day for	8	2	8		68	1	1	4
25	To Ditto paid John Perrie for	33	2	7½		68	4	6	6
26	To Ditto paid Gabriell Knight for	16	2	7		68	2	1	4
28	To Ditto paid John Massinger for	38	2	10½		68	5	9	3
31	To Ditto paid Joseph White for	48	2	11¾		68	6	11	1
	To Ditto paid John Rudduck for	80	2	6		68	10		
February 3	To Ditto paid John Perrie for	21	2	7		68	2	14	3
	To Ditto paid Wm. Thiery for	44	2	6		68	5	10	
	To Ditto paid Tho. Hill for	80	2	6		68	10		
6	To Ditto paid Tho. Hill for	48	2	6					
	and	48	2	5		68	11	16	
9	To Ditto paid John Massinger for	55	2	10		68	7	15	10
	To Ditto paid Tho. Browning for	200		15		68	12	10	

			£	s	d
	By Andrew Stucky for Postage of severall leters & Packets to & from himselfe	53	1	5	3
October 23	By John Earle of Bristoll for 1 hogshead & 1 Qter Cask to put Xerie in	37		9	6
	By Adventure in the Joseph to Cork & Cadiz for 23 Guinies delivered Simon Clements to buy Butter in Cork, which produced there as per his acct. Oct. 18th 1684	85	26	9	
	By Wm. Drake for 6 doz bottles & 3 Panniers & Covers	63		17	
	By Sir Nath. Napier for 4 doz bottles 8s 8d & 2 Panniers, covers etc. 2s 6d	29		11	2
December	By Sgt Tho. Strode for a Qutr Cask, Certificate & hallidge	65		5	9
	By Philip Frowde for 2 doz bottles, 2 Panniers & covers & ½ a Certifficate	85		10	6
	By Doctor Hungerford for 10 doz bottles, 4 Panniers & Covers etc.	87	1	8	2
	By Xeries wine 3 Butts for ballance of that acct.	79	25	08	
11	By Wm. Drake for 4 doz bottles 2 Panniers & covers etc.	63		10	10
	By Wm. Prichard & Company for ½ yeares intrest 2nd October last	63	1	10	
	By Jonathan Lamboll for money lent him on his bond in Reading	87	40		
	By John Blackwell for Celleridge of my 2 vaults in Small Streat	85	13	7	
	By Lincloth 11 Bolts, for acct. of Edward Roy for charges in them	5	1	4	10
	By Edward Roy for intrest of money	44	2	13	5
	By Arthur Robinson & Company for ballance	61		6	7
	By Isaac Heming for money of David Barrett £50 of John Hurtnell £50 of Jos. Tily £3 4s 6d	76	103	4	6
	By Plate received out of severall ships for ballance of that acct.	61	7	1	5
	By Isaac Heming for money hee recd. of James Deane	76	10		
	By Ditto for money hee recd. of Robert Payne in London	76	50		
	By Ditto for money I paid him in London	76	54	12	6
	By Ditto for money of Allyn Smith in London	76	2	6	6
	By Ditto for ½ yeares intrest of Robert Richardson	76 *	3	15	
	By Isaac Heming for the neat proceeds of 4 hhds Tobacco	76	17	12	6
	By Ditto. of one for the neat proceeds of 1 hogshead Tobacco	76	3		7
	By Ditto recd. of Paris Slaughter on 2 bills of Exchange one for £150 tother for £100	76	250		
	By Ditto for a parcell of old books I sould in London	76	6		
			677	1	
			1118	13	2
	By Ballance carried to that acct.	89	901	11	9
			2020	4	11

	Bristoll 1683/4				
	Worstead Stockins are	Cr	£	s	d
January	By Francis Rottenburie for 3 paire burnt in hotpressing them	63		4	6
	By Adventure in the Experiment to Cadiz for 2 Truncks containing 1356 paire Bristoll hose at 3s 6d per paire, and 972 paire Wells hose at 2s	60	334	10	
1684 May	By Adventure in the Friston of London to Cadiz for 600 paire Bristoll, & 596 paire Wells sent in one Trunck No 5 to John Cooke to bee sent to Cadiz to himselfe & Sam. Kekewich	64	153	2	
June 24	By Adventure in the ship Agreement Wm. Fisher master to Cadiz & the Straights for 1 Trunck containing 672 paire Bristoll hose at 3s per paire consign'd to said Wm. Fisher	78	100	16	
	By Ditto for 1 Trunck laden in said ship cont. 668 paire Bristoll hose, 220 paire best Wells hose, & 160 paire ordinary Wells hose, consign'd to John Cooke & Samuel Kekewich merchants in St Marie Port, the Bristoll hose at 3s the best Wells at 22d, the other at 20d	78	133	14	

	To Ditto paid Tho. Browning for	120		17	68	8	10	
14	To Ditto paid John Perrie for	35	2	7	68	4	10	5
	To Ditto paid Tho. Hill for	360		13	68	19	10	
	To Ditto paid John Day for	16	2	7	68	2	1	4
16	To Ditto paid Joseph White for	53	2	11	68	7	14	7
	To Ditto paid John Massinger for	29	2	10	68	4	2	2
20	To Cash paid Gabriell Knight for	24	2	6	68	3		
29	To Cash paid John Massinger for	47	2	10	68	6	13	2
March 4	To Cash paid John Perrie for	50	2	7	68	6	9	2
6	To Ditto paid Joseph White for	51	2	10½	68	7	6	7½
	To Ditto paid John Massinger for	26	2	10	68	3	13	8
15	To Cash paid John Massinger for	22	2	10	68	3	2	4
17	To Ditto paid Fra. Rottenburie for hotpressing 2179 paire at ¼ per paire				68	2	5	5
	To Ditto paid John Day for	30	2	6	68	3	15	
	To Ditto paid Richard Moone for	320		12½	68			
	and 8s 4d over				68	17	1	8
19	To Ditto paid John Massinger for	25	2	10	68	3	10	10
22	To Ditto paid Elizabeth Dyer for	6	2	6	68		12	6
	To Ditto paid John Perrie for	43	2	7	68	5	10	6
	To Ditto paid Joseph White for	47	2	10½	68	6	15	1½
27	To Ditto paid John Rudduck for	100	2	5	68	12	1	8
29	To Ditto paid John Massinger for	25	2	10	68	3	10	10
Aprill 4	To Ditto paid Tho. Hill for	58	2	6	68	7	5	
	To Ditto paid John Massinger for	38	2	10	68	5	7	8
10	To Ditto paid Tho. Hill for	10	2	6	68	1	5	
	To Ditto paid John Massinger for	17	2	10	68	2	8	2
17	To Ditto paid Joseph White for	61	2	10	68	8	12	10
	To Ditto paid John Massinger for	31	2	9	68	4	5	3
						459	19	7½
24	To Cash paid John Perrie for	47	2	6½	68	6		
25	To Ditto paid John Massinger for	29	2	9	68	3	19	9
May 1	To Ditto paid Joseph White for	48	2	10	68	6	16	
2	To Ditto paid John Massinger for	30	2	9	68	4	2	6
9	To Ditto paid Fra. Rottenburie in full for hotpressing stockins				68		8	
10	To Ditto paid John Massinger for	32	2	9	68	4	8	
12	To Ditto paid Tho. Hill for	37	2	6	68	4	12	6
	To Cash paid John Perrie for 61	61	2	6	77	7	12	6
15	To Ditto paid Joseph White for	54	2	9	77	7	8	6
	To Ditto paid John Massinger for	24	2	9	77	3	6	
21	To Ditto paid John Massinger for	26	2	8	77	3	9	4
	To Ditto paid John Massinger for	44	2	9		6	1	
26	To Ditto paid John Perrie for	67	2	6½	77			
	and 2s 6½ paid short last at 2s 6d½				77	8	12	10
June 5	To Ditto paid Tho. Hill for	145	2	6	77	18	2	6
7	To Ditto paid John Perrie for	67	2	6½	77	8	10	3
13	To Ditto paid Elizabeth Dyer for	18	2	6	77	2	5	
	To Ditto paid John Massinger for	30	2	8	77	4		
	To Ditto paid John Brady for	23	2	6	77	2	17	6
	To Ditto paid Ed. Iffe for Fra. Rottenburie in full for pressing stockins				77		7	9
	To Ditto paid John Massinger for	26	2	8	77	3	9	4
14	To Ditto paid Tho. Hill for	51	2	6	77	6	7	6
	To Ditto paid John Massinger for	29	2	8	77	3	17	4
26	To Ditto paid Elizabeth Dyer for	10	2	6	77	1	5	
28	To Ditto paid John Massinger for	19	2	8	77	2	10	9
	To Ditto paid John Perrie for	26	2	6½	77	3	8	9
	To Ditto paid Joseph White for	97	2	9	77	13	5	9
30	To Ditto paid John Brady for	22	2	6	77	2	15	

By Adventure 2nd in the Rachel to Cadiz, for 1 Trunck cont. *768 paire Bristoll at 3s 180 best Wells at 2s & 200 paire ordinary at 1s 6d per paire is*	*79*	148		
By Adventure in the John Frigat to Cadiz for 1 Trunck containng 864 paire at 3s	*80*	129	12	
		999	18	6

Date						£	s	d
July 5	To Ditto paid John Massinger for	30	2	8	77	4		
	To Ditto paid Ed. Iffe for Fra. Rottenburie for hot pressing 264 paire				77		5	6
10	To Ditto paid John Perrie for	46	2	6¼	77	5	16	
	To Ditto paid John Massinger for	27	2	8	77	3	12	
17	To Ditto paid John Brady for	22			77	2	14	6
	To Ditto paid John Massinger for	27	2	8	77	3	12	
24	To Ditto paid John Perrie for	55	2	6¼	77	6	19	6
	To Ditto paid John Massinger for	28	2	8	77	3	14	8
25	To Ditto paid John Brady for	19	2	6	77	2	7	
August 1	To Ditto paid John Massinger for	24	2	8	77	3	4	
2	To Ditto paid Joseph White for	39	2	8	77	5	4	
11	To Ditto paid John Massinger for	23	2	8	77	3	1	4
	To Ditto paid John Brady for	23	2	6	77	2	17	
12	To Ditto paid John Massinger for	22	2	8	77	2	18	8
23	To Ditto paid John Massinger for	37	2	8	77	4	18	8
	To Ditto paid Joseph White for	36	2	8·	77	4	16	
30	To Ditto paid John Massinger for	22	2	8	77	2	18	8
						662	18	5½
	To Ballance carried to that acct.				81	337		½
						999	18	6

(75)   **Bristoll 1683**

		Dr	£	s	d
Thomas Scrope [75] per Contra is					
To Proffit & Losse for money I was to have received of him with his brother Edmond Scrope but did not receive it as per his acct.		127	100		
To himselfe & Joseph Jackson for money lent them on theire noat Sept. 22nd 1677		21	100		
To Proffit & Losse for the freight of 6 tons in the Dove formerly made good to his acct. in Leadger No D & againe included in the £22 12s 6d per Contra by error		127	16	10	
To Ditto for money charg'd short on a parcell Pitch & Resin in Leadger No D fol 28		127		11	10
To Ditto for 1/3 of neat proceeds of Paper in the Isabella from Rochell as per his acct.		127	43	11	3
To Ditto for neat proceeds of severall small Casks of Brandy as per his acct.		127	23	8	5
To Ditto for money due to mee on the Isabella's booke as per his acct.		127		9	6
To Ditto for ¾ parts cost & charges of Wines etc. on the Tho. & Francis per his acct.		127	83	3	4
To Ditto for money paid David Philip & Robt. Bond in part setting out ships per Contra		127	15	17	10
To Tho. Scrope & Company viz. Marie Aldworth for £200 principal & 12 yeares & 2 moneths lesse 3 daies intrest from the 12th of Jany 1674 to 10th March 1686		14	345	18	
To Tho. Scrope & Henry Gibbes for £300 principal on bond & 6 yeares 7 moneths & 4 daies intrest from 5th Jan. 1680 to 10th March 1686		28	411		
To Isaac Heming for ½ £1 2s 6d paid James Whiston for the weekly printed Avizoes per agreement		76		11	3
To Proffit & Losse for ½ 15s paid more by Isaac Heming for printed Avizoes		89		7	6
To Gold deposited by Tho. Scrope for Ballance of that Account		27	53		
			1194	8	11

Bristoll 1683				
Thomas Scrope of Bristoll merchant is	*Cr*	*£*	*s*	*d*
By Acct. of Ballances brought from folio (176) in Leadger book				
No D which should have been brought sooner into this book, by				
mistake omitted	224	427	6	2¼
By Tho. Scrope his acct. of Exchange with John Cooke for money				
charg'd there by error	47	100		
By Herrings my 1/3 of 49 barrills theire cost & charges sent in				
the Owners Endeavour to Nevis	51	14	6	9
By voyage in the Isabella to Jamaica for ¼ cost & charges of 12				
tonns of beere	20	15		
By Proffit & Losse for my part of Andrew Kirbies bill for the				
Isabella's wine from Bourdeaux	127	47		8
By Ditto for my part of charges on the Corne buisness In July				
1675 as per his acct.	127	2	8	
By Ditto for my part of charges on the Isabella's wines which I				
canot say is due	127	13	3	8
By Ditto for a Reame of Paper	127		6	6
By Ditto for ¼ 17 Gall. french wine to Wm. Willett	127		14	10½
By Ditto for money he saith is due to him on the Isabella's booke	127	4		1
By Ditto for ¾ parts of a hogshead wine on the Tho. & Francis	127	5	5	
By ¼ partt 12 tonns of beere in the Isabella to Jamaica	127	15		
By ¼ part cost of Pease on the Isabella to the Madera	127	5	18	2
By Ditto for money due on the Isabella's wine from the Madera				
to Jamaica	127	5	12	
By Ditto for money charg'd short on an Iron Pott	127		1	10
By Ditto for 1/8 setting out the Isabella to Nevis	127	8	11	1
By Ditto for 1/8 setting out the Isabella to Cadiz	127	22	3	4
By Ditto for 1/8 charges in port there	127	2	5	1½
By Ditto for freight & Prisage of wine in the Dove	127	22	12	6
By Ditto for Prizage of wine in the Isabella from Cadiz	127	8	10	
By Ditto for money charg'd short on the Stockholme voyage	127	1	7	4
By Ditto for 1/8 setting out the Isabella that voyage	127	4	7	4
By Ditto for 4 Gall. 7/8 french wine at 3s per Gall. by				
agreement made with him	127		14	7½
By Ditto for 1/8 setting out the ship Isabella to Nevis	127	18	16	8
By Ditto for 1/8 of Edmund Scropes bill from Ireland	127	4	17	1
By 1/8 of his bill from Nevis	127	2	7	1

	Anno 1684				
	Marie Wasbrow the Widow of John Wasbrow of Bristoll Cooper deceased	Dr	£	s	d
Aprill	*To Xeries wine 10 Butts in the Agreement for 16 Iron hoopes at 4d 1/2 per hoope*	70		6	
	To Isaac Heming for Racking Tooles bee bought for her husband with baggs, Cock & Boarer	76	2	7	
	To Ditto for a new racking boarer in lieu of one broken	90		5	6
1686 March 27	*To Cash paid her in part*	108	20		
	To Proffit & Losse, a parcell of Butts, Iron hoops & hhds since 29th March 1684	127	6	18	11
January 3	*To Cash paid her in full to this day as per her receit*	120	2	5	6
			32	2	11

	Anno 1684				
	Sugar 2 Butts & 4 hhds imported in the Ship New England merchant from Nevis	Dr	£	s	d
Aprill	*To Edmond Scrope & Company for theire first cost 10992 lb Sugar at 10s per Cwt as per Invoyce of 13th February 1683*	33	54	19	2
26	*To Cash paid custome fees & bills* £ s d 4 16 7	68			
May 3	*To Cash paid Francis Plomer for freight & averidge* 10 18	68			
21	*To Cash paid for a permitt to ship them in the Gift of Bredhemson for London* 1 8	77	15	16	3
			70	15	5

	Anno 1684				
	Sugar 4 hhds in the Ship Restauration from Barbadoes James Porter Master laden per Edward Parsons in part returne of goods sent him in the Ship Martha & Sarah	Dr	£	s	d
	To Edward Parsons for theire first cost as per Invoyce 1st March 1683/4	58	40	10	10½
May	*To Cash paid for a permitt to ship them in the Comfort* £ s d 0 0 4	77			
	To Ditto paid custom fees & bills 2 17 6	77			
June 30	*To Cash paid James Porter for freight & averidge* 5 4	77	8	1	10
			48	12	8½

	By Ditto for one piece of cloth	127		10	
1686 March 10	By Cash recd. of Henry Gibbes by consent of Robert Yate & Tho. Edwards	120	340	10	
	By Proffit & Losse for freight of a parcell of Ginger in baggs to Hambrow in the Anna Maria, and 16 cwt of Copper plates home	127	7		
			1100	15	10¾
	By Profit and Loss for Ballances,	189 *	93	13	1¼
			1194	8	11

Anno 1684

		Cr	£	s	d
	Marie Wasbrow per Contra is	Cr	£	s	d
Aprill	By Xeries wine 10 Butts in the Agreement from Cadiz for cooperidge as per noat	70	1	2	
	By merchandizes for Lawrence Washington in the John for a brandy Cask	124		3	6
1686 January 3	By Proffit & Losse for money due to her on her severall noates besydes the two foregoing, for hooping, racking wines etc. to this 3rd day of January 1686	127	30	17	5
			32	2	11

Anno 1684

		Cr	£	s	d
	Sugar 2 Butts & 4 hhds per Contra	Cr	£	s	d
	By Isaac Heming for 1/3 of £181 17s 2d the neat proceeds of 6 Butts & 12 hhds Sugar, of which hee gives one acct. of sales togeather, so do here charge it by estimate	90	60	12	4½
	By Proffit and Loss, for Ballance	189 *	10	3	½
			70	15	5

Anno 1684

		Cr	£	s	d
	Sugar 4 hhds per Contra	Cr	£	s	d
	By Isaac Heming for theire neat proceeds	90	42	9	7
	By Proffit and Loss, for Ballance	189 *	6	3	1½
			48	12	8½

(76)

Anno 1684		Dr	£	s	d
	Xeries Wines 20 Butts imported from Cadiz in the Ship Expectation of Bristoll Robert Alexander Master laden per John Cooke & Company				
	To John Cooke Woolley & Kekewich for theire first cost 7086½ Ryals As per Invoyce of Jan. 26th 1683/4 may appeare the piece of 8 at 52d	69	191	18	6
Aprill 4	To Cash paid custom fees & bills	68	59	14	9
10	To Ditto paid Robert Alexander for freight, prisage, & averidge	68	40		
	To Cash paid Joseph Berrie for Brokridge	68		10	
			292	3	3
	To Profit and Loss, for Ballance	189 *	73	15	7
			365	18	10

Anno 1684		Dr	£	s	d
	Sugar 2 Butts & 4 hhds imported in the Owners Endeavour Michaell Perrie Master from Nevis laden per Edm. Scrope & John Streater, sent hence to London				
May	To Edmond Scrope & John Streater for theire first cost being 10664 lb as per Invoyce of 10th Aprill 1684 at 10s per Cwt the Sugar	33	53	6	5
	To Profit and Loss, for Ballance	189 *	7	5	11½
			60	12	4½

Anno 1684		Dr	£	s	d
	James Beard of Clapton Yeoman my Tenent in the farme there				
May 21	To Cash lent him on his bill	77	10		
Seeptember 1	To Estate at Clapton for ½ yeares rent of my farm there let to him for 3 yeares by Lease, due the 1st day of September 1684 as may appeare	72	31		
March 1	To Ditto for ½ yeares rent due 1st day of March 1684 as may appeare	72	31		
1685 Sept.	To Ditto for ½ yeares rent due 1st day of September 1685 as may appeare	72	32		
March 1	To Ditto for ½ yeares rent due 1st day of March 1685 as may appeare	72	32		
1686 September 1	To Ditto for ½ yeares rent due 1st day of September 1686 as may appeare	72	32	10	
	To Proffit & Losse for 2 yeares & 4 months intrest of £10 from the 21th May 1684 to the 21st Sept. 86	105	1	8	
			169	18	

Anno 1684		Dr	£	s	d
	Isaac Heming my Sonne in law of London merchant is				
	To his former acct. Current for ballance brought from that acct.	35	1644	10	5
	To Andrew Kirby Father & Sonne for theire bill on John Bellamy of 1500 Ecu at 55¼ per Ecu	64	345	6	3
	To Sgt Tho. Strode recd. of Hugh Strode per his order, as per advice 12th month 7th 1684	65	6	13	9
	To Plate in sundry ships for money recd. of Tho. Cook for a bagg pieces of 8 from Arthur Robinson & Company, which with the following summe shoud have been formerly charg'd as per his acct. Oct. 1682	61	141	8	7

Anno 1684

		Cr	£	s	d
	Xeries Wines 20 Butts in the Expectation per Contra				
March 25	By John Bradway for 9 Butts at £20 per Butt to pay ½ 24th June & ½ 24th Sept.	70	180		
	By Joseph Berrie for 1 Butt of ordinary sack	62	8	10	
	By John Blackwell for 9 Butts lesse 7½ Gall. for ullage at £19 10s per Butt	59	174	4	
	By Cash recd. of James Crofts for returnes on 2 Butts of Xerie	68	1	17	4
June 10	By Cash recd. for returne of one Butt ½ Custome	77	1	7	6
			365	18	10

Anno 1684

	Cr	£	s	d
Sugar 2 Butts & 4 hhds per Contra				
By Isaac Heming for the 1/3 of £181 17s 2d the neat proceeds of 6 Butts 12 hhds Sugar of which hee gives one acct. of sales togeather, so do here charge this by estimate	90	60	12	4½

Anno 1684

		Cr	£	s	d
	James Beard per Contra				
February 7	By Cash recd. of him in part of rent	82	13	10	
1685 Sept. 29	By Cash received of him in part for rent for the farme at Clapton	84	10	10	
	By Ditto received for 1 yeares intrest of £10 due May 21th 1685	84		12	
January 14	By Cash received of him in part for rent	107	10	10	
1686 June 7	By Cash received of him in part for rent	108	16		
19	By Cash received of him in part for rent	108	2		
	By Ditto received of him for 1 yeares intrest of £10 due May 21 1686	108		12	
	By Marie Thring & Company for ½ yeares intrest of £150 hee paid them Dec. 17th 1684	7	4	10	
	By Ditto for another ½ yeares intrest hee paid them July 18th 1685	7	4	10	
	By Ditto for another ½ yeares intrest hee paid them Nov. 25th 1685	7	4	10	
	By Estate at Clapton by money abated him by on the first yeares rent of the 3 yeares	72	2		
	By Ditto for money abated him on the 2nd of the 3 yeares rent	72	4		
	By Ditto for money abated him on ½ yeeares rent of the 3rd yeare ending Sept. 1 1686	72	2	10	
	By Ditto for his noat of Disbursments agreed on betwixt us	72	24		
	By ballance resting due at the time of his death carried to acct. of his widow Mary Beard	125	70	4	
			169	18	

Anno 1684

		Cr	£	s	d
	Isaac Heming per Contra is				
	By Robert East for money paid him for 3 Pieces Brandy, which shoud have beeen charged on the 12th January 1682 sent in the Brothers Goodwill from London	62	42	16	4
June	By Cash recd. of John Bubb for my bill on said Heming	77	100		
September 19	By John Cooke for my bill in favor of said Cooke	32	22	5	6
	By John Cooper for my bill in favor of said Cooper which should have been charg'd Aprill 5	63	12		
October 31	By Cash recd. of Samuell Spencer BlackSmith on his bill	82	16	4	
	By John Wilmer for money paid him Dec. 1684	82	20		

To Ditto for money I paid him 43 Guinnies & 8 in silver, recd. of Tho. Cook for a parcell Gold from Robinson & Company	61	46	15	1
To Arthur Robinson & Company for theire bill for 1000 pieces of 8 in his favor per his acct. Feb. 1683	61	220	16	8
To John Cooke & Samuel Kekewich for money of Wm. Atwell & Company for 800 pieces of 8	88	181	13	6
To Proffit & Losse for money of David Barret in London Feb. 2nd 1681, which with divers other summes should have been formerly charg'd as per his own account, but were then omitted because of my absence in London, Caversham & Reading	73	50		
To Ditto for money of John Hurtnell Junior in London, Feb. 26 81 as per his acct.	73	50		
To Ditto for money received of Joseph Tily	73	3	4	6
To Plate in severall ships for what hee recd. of Tho. Cook for 600 pieces of 8	61	135	11	
To Proffit & Losse for money recd. on a Virginea bill	73 *	5	12	
To Plate out of severall ships recd. of Tho. Cook for 247 pieces of 8 recd. from Spaine	61	53	18	3
To Proffit & Losse for what hee recd. of mee in Lond for 45 Guinnies	73 *	48	7	6
To Ditto for money hee recd. of James Deane for his halfe of a Butt of Xerie	73	10		
To Robert Richardson for ½ yeares intrest of £150 in Dec. 1682 as per his acct.	35	3	15	
To Proffit & Losse for money hee recd. of Robert Payne as per his acct. Jan. 5th 1682	73	50		
To Sugar 4 Butts & 1 hogshead sould in London for theire neat proceeds	60	65	16	6
To Proffit & Losse for money of mee in London	73	54	12	6
To Ditto for money on a bill recd. of Henry Cornish as per his acct. closed May 13th 1683	73 *	200		
To Ditto for money of Allyn Smith for Xerie sack sould him	73	2	6	6
To Tho. Cook & Company for ½ yeares intrest of £600 recd. of them with the Principall	51	615		
To Proffit & Losse for the neat proceeds of 4 hhds Tobacco in the Concord	73	17	12	6
To Ditto for the neat proceeds one hogshead Tobacco per Capt. Purvis	73	3		7
To Andrew Kirby Father & Sonne for theire bill on John Bellamy as per acct. Sept. 1683	64	115		11
To Proffit & Losse for 2 bills on Paris Slaughter, 1st for £150 the other for £100 per acct. Nov. 1683	73	250		
To Ditto for money hee recd. for a parcell old books I sould on London	73	6		
		4327	1	11

	Bristoll 1684	Dr	£	s	d
	Cash is				
May	To ballance brought from that acct.	68	471	6	1½
15	To Wm. Spoore Senior & Company recd. of him	30	3		
	To Wm. Spoore Senior recd. of him in part of his bill	52	5		

By *Adventure in the ship Andaluzia to Cadiz for money hee paid for 2/3 parts of 60 pieces Baies shipd. in her for Cadiz*	86	155	10	10
By *sundry accts fro what paid James Whiston for weekly Avizoes, which with many other summes following in this accct ought sooner to have been charg'd, but through my absence were omitted*	75, 73	1	2	6
By *Proffit & Losse paid Wm. Russell in London*	73	20		
By *Ditto for 2 Protests 9s charge on stockins 17s 10d Port of leters 9s 10d & 2 Keggs sturgeon £2 in all*	73	3	16	8
By *Ditto for charges in selling sugar 3s his wives charge to Bristoll £5 to Reading 14s and money of him in London £6 8d*	73	11	17	8
By *Ditto for carriage 2 Trunck hose 12s money of him in London £3 & for a firkin butter £1 5s 0d all*	73	4	17	
By *Ditto paid my Tayler £1 16s charges shipping hose £1 16s 11d and money of him in London £5 in all*	73	8	12	11
By *Ditto paid for a Petticoat £4 Spectacles 2s and money of him £2 in London*	73	6	2	
By *Marie Wasbrow for racking Tools for her husband*	75	2	7	
By *Proffit & Losse paid Tho. Cox for severall small parcells of wine*	89	5	11	9
By *Adventure in the Brothers Goodwill to Nevis for fraight of Floure & Brandy*	61	5	2	6
By *Proffit & Losse paid Philip Higgenbottom on Jahzeels bill*	89	1		
By *Ditto paid for a hatt for mee*	89	2	11	
By *Tho. Cook & Nicholas Cary lent them on theire bond*	51	400		
By *Proffit & Losse for money of him £3 5s chest drawers, & £3 10s & £4 6s & of Robert Paine £5*	89 *	16	1	
By *Robert Richardson for money lent him on a mortgage*	35	150		
By *Proffit & Losse for a ham 6s 6d & money of Jos. Tily £3 4s 6d*	89	3	11	
By *Adventure in the Agreement to Cadiz for assurance money*	62	2	12	6
By *Proffit & Losse for a Ham 8s 5d & Port of leters £1 19s 6d*	89	2	7	11
By *Ditto paid Tho. Curtis £1 Cleark of Crowne £1 0s 6d for a book 10s to myselfe £5 to Robert Payne per bill £4*	89	11	10	6
By *Ditto for Abraham Beeles bill for charges on Stockins in the Agreement of Cork*	89	5	1	9
By *Ditto for carriage of a Trunck of stockins, and Port of letters*	89	1	5	3
By *Wm. Coles for money paid him for his part of a Cask of Indigo*	3	4		7
By *Proffit & Losse of him in £3 & 8 Guinnies*	89	11	12	
By *Ditto for charges of a journey to Bristoll £3 15s for Printed Avizoes 15s & pd. Robert Payne £1*	89	5	10	
By *Adventure in the Experiment from London to Cadiz for charges on 2 Truncks stockins*	60	8		
By *Proffit & Losse paid carriage of a box 3s 2d & paid Joseph Tily in Exchange for Guinnies £6 9s*	89	6	12	2
By *Sugar 4 Butts in the John & Elizabeth for custom & other charges*	60	13	11	2
By *Proffit & Losse for money of him £4 & 45 Guinnies £48 7s 6d*	89	52	7	6
By *Ditto for money of him at severall times*	89	4	3	2
By *Tho. Cook & Nicholas Cary paid them*	51	189		
		1329	4	2
By *himselfe for ballance carried to his new acct. current*	90	2997	17	9
		4327	1	11

Bristoll 1684

			Cr	£	s	d
	Cash per Contra is					
May 14	By *Andrew Stuckey Junior paid ½ his reckoning on his arbitration with Richd. Champneys*		53		1	6½
	By *my Tenement in Portburie paid Marie Parsons sonne*		20	1	7	

	To Marie Parsons recd. of her sonne	18	3	10	
	To John Massinger recd. of him in part	27	1		
22	To John Massinger recd. of him in part	27		10	
	To the Lady Susan Pawlet recd. of Francis Vincent	61	8	2	9
28	To John Bradway recd. of him in part	70	40		
	To John Massinger recd. of him	27		10	
June 5	To the Lady Ann Pawlet recd. of Bernard Wilkins	48	3	10	
	To Wm. Spoore Senior recd. of him	52		3	6
	To Wm. Spoore Junior recd. of him	31	3	10	
	To Wm. Spoore Senior recd. of him in full of his bill	52	5		
7	To Edmond Scrope recd. of John Bubb	38	50		
	To Robert Davis recd. of him	51	5	5	
	To Sugar 10 hhds bought of John Browne recd. of Samuell Davis	65	50	5	
	To Isaac Heming recd. of John Bubb	76	100		
	To John Bradway recd. of him	70	100		
	To Tho. Dike recd. of him	52	16	12	
	To Tho. Walden recd. of him May 26th then omitted to bee charg'd	2	50		
	To Ditto recd. of Joane Webb on a bill Exca	2	41	18	10
	To John Ford & Tho. Wedmore recd. of John Ford	60	4	5	
	To House at the lower end of Small Streat recd. of John Dessill	22	1	15	
26	To Lewis Addams recd. of him	56	25		
July 5	To John Bradway recd. of him	70	14		
	To George Dighton recd. of him	60	1	12	
	To John Wilmer recd. of John Blackwell for my bill on him	62	100		
	To Xeries wines 20 Butts recd. of Eusolius Brook returnes on a Butt Xerie	76	1	7	6
12	To John Gore & Company recd. of John Gore	56	30		
	To Wm. Godwin recd. of him for ½ yeares intrest per hands of Cousin Nath. Haggatt	64	3		
	To George Maison recd. of him in full	79	27	12	
24	To John Bradway recd. of him	70	38		
	To Alex. Caduggan recd. of him	48	27		
	To Nathanael Haggatt recd. of him	19	200		
	To John Blackwell recd. of him	59	100		
	To the house at the lower end of Small Streat received of John Yeamans	22	8	16	
			1541	10	8½
August 2	To George Dighton received of him	60	58	14	6
8	To Lewis Addams recd. of him	56	24		
9	To Dennis Tayler recd. of his mother	11	13		
	To Richard Gay recd. of Charles Jones	39	53	5	
11	To Sergt Tho. Strode recd. of him	65	4	13	6
	To John Earle of Bristoll recd. of Ditto Sgt Tho. Strode	79	50		
	To Ditto for money of James Gaskoine deposited in my hands	79	200		
21	To John Blackwell recd. of him	59	119	19	6
September	To Tho. Day recd. of him	70	34		
	To Sir Samuel Astry received of him	49	16	5	
	To Andrew Stucky Junior recd. of Richard Champneys	53	30	4	6
	To John Mayne recd. of him	80	2		
25	To John Olliffe recd. of him	39	75	8	
	To Samuel Davis recd. of him	63	8	17	
	To John Massinger recd. of him	27	7		
	To Wm. Prichard & Company recd. of Wm. Prichard	63	1	10	
26	To John Bradway received of him	70	90		
			2330	7	8½

15	By Worsted stockins paid Joseph White & John Massinger for 78 paire	74	10	14	6
21	By James Beard lent him on his bill	76	10		
	By Worsted stockins paid John Massinger for 26 paire	74	3	9	4
	By Sugar 2 Butts & 4 hhds in the New England merchant paid for a permitt	75		1	8
	By worsted stockins paid John Massinger for 44 paire	74	6	1	
	By Proffit & Losse paid John Harris	73	3	1	10
26	By Proffit & Losse paid John Ford	73	1	15	8
	By Worsted Stockins paid John Perrie	74	8	12	10
	By Sugar 4 hhds in the Restauration paid for a permitt	75			4
	By Estate at Clapton paid Henry Wynter	38	4		
27	By Edmond Scrope paid for a permitt to ship 9 bolts Canvas	38		3	8
	By Martha Speed paid her	46	2		
June 5	By Worsted Stockins paid Tho. Hill	74	18	2	6
	By Wm. Spoore Junior & Senior lent them on theire bond	69	40		
	By Peter Mewes Bishop etc. lent him in his bond	78	150		
7	By Edm. Scrope paid lent him	38	50		
	By Worsted Stockins paid John Perrie and Elizabeth Dyer	74	10	15	3
	By Tho. Walden paid Tho. Keene	2		12	
	By Worsted Stockins paid John Massinger, John Brady & Fra. Rottenburie	74	7	5	3
	By Charles Plomer & Company lent them on theire bond	78	150		
	By Profitt & Losse paid houshold expences	73	18	9	5
	By Sugar 4 hhds in the Restauration paid custom etc.	75	2	17	6
	By Proffit & Losse paid John Seward for a mare	73	9	10	
	By Worsted Stockins paid John Massinger & Tho. Hill	74	9	16	10
	By Tobacco 4 hhds in the Francis & Marie paid custom etc.	78	12	7	1
	By Profitt & Losse paid houshold expences	73	5	3	
	By Worsted Stockins paid John Massinger for 29 paire	74	3	17	4
	By George Dighton paid lent him on his bond	60	58	14	6
	By Andrew Stuckey Junior paid port of a leter	53		2	
26	By Robert Symes paid Bernard Wilkins	51	16	3	5
	By Worsted Stockins paid Elizabeth Dyer	74	1	5	
28	By Adventure 2nd in the Agreement to Cadiz paid Tho. Morgan for 30 Firkins Butter	78	29	17	6
	By Worsted Stockins paid John Massinger, John Perrie & Jos. White	74	19	5	3
30	By Sugar 4 hhds in the Restauration paid James Porter	75	5	4	
	By Adventure 2nd in the Agreement to Cadiz paid custom of Stockins etc.	78	5	8	1
	By Worsted Stockins paid John Brady for 22 paire	74	2	15	
July 5	By Worsted Stockins paid John Massinger & Wm. Iffe	74	4	5	6
	By Profitt & Losse paid houshold expences	73	4	16	11
9	By Martha Speed paid her	46	2		
10	By Worsted Stockins paid John Perrie for 46 paire at 2s 6d¹/₂ & John Massinger 27 paire at 2s 8d	74	9	8	
17	By Ditto paid John Brady & John Massinger	74	6	6	6
19	By Profitt & Losse paid houshold expences	73	10	12	9
	By Marie Thring paid lent her on her bill	7	2		
			718	9	11¹/₂
	By Tho. Walden paid him	2	38		
24	By Worsted Stockins paid John Perrie & John Massinger	74	10	14	2
	By Henry Gibbes paid lent him on his noat	79	50		
28	By Tho. Walden paid Wm. Hartley	2	50		
	By Worsted Stockins paid John Brady for 19 paire	74	2	7	
29	By Nathanael Haggatt paid him by his servant Wm. Phelps	19	200		
	By John Wilmer paid him	62	100		
August 1	By Tobacco 4 hhds paid weighing them	78		1	
	By Worsted Stockins paid John Massinger for 24 paire	74	3	4	

(78)	**Bristoll 1684**				
	Peter Mewes Bishop of Bath & Wells	Dr	£	s	d
June 5	To Cash lent him on his bond payable 20th Oct. next	77	150		

2	By Stockins paid Joseph White for 39 paire	74	5	4	
4	By Land at Clevedon paid Tho. Lutterell	32	1	9	
5	By Tobacco 4 hhds paid Wm. Nicklus for freight etc.	78	5	4	
8	By John Earle of Bristoll paid John Shuttleworth	79	80		
11	By Worsted Stockins paid John Massinger & John Brady	74	5	18	4
	By Tho. Walden paid him	2	50		
12	By Henry Simes paid John Olliver on his bill	5	31	12	
14	By John Earle of Bristoll paid John Shuttleworth	79	70		
	By Worsted Stockins paid John Massinger	74	2	18	8
21	By Ditto paid Joseph White for 36 paire	74	4	16	
	By Ditto paid John Perrie for 50 paire	81	6	6	
	By E. Bristoll paid John Shuttleworth	79	50		
23	By Adventure 2nd in the Rachell to Cadiz paid for 20 Firkins Butter	79	21	11	1
	By Worsted Stockins paid John Massinger for 37 paire, & 22 paire at twice	74	7	17	4
26	By Proffit & Losse paid John Cheshire	73	8		
	By John Earle of Bristoll paid John Shuttleworth in 2 summes (viz) £50 & £25	79	75		
	By Tho. Day paid him	70	7	15	
September 2	By Andrew Stucky paid at the 3 Cranes	53			9
3	By Stockins paid Joseph White for 32 paire	81	4	5	4
	By John Mayne paid lent him	80	2		
5	By Adventure in the John Frigat paid John Seward	80	2	8	2
6	By Worsted Stockins paid James Davis & John Massinger	81	4	11	2
	By John Earle of Bristoll paid John Shuttleworth	79	75		
	By Jahzeel Speed paid him	69		5	
8	By John Rumsey paid lent him	29	50		
	By Proffit & Losse paid Alexander Doleman	73	8	13	
10	By John Cooke paid Humphrey Corsley	32	100		
17	By Estate at Clevedon paid ditching Insolds	32	3	4	
19	By Worsted Stockins paid John Massinger & John Perrie for 3 parcells	81	17		4
25	By sundry accts paid John Massinger £10 lent, and And. Stuckey for port of a leter 3s	27, 53	10	3	
26	By Adventure in the Owners Adventure paid Richard Baily	80	21	2	6
	By Worsted Stockins paid Elizabeth Dyer & Joel Pinnie for 104 paire	81	13		
	By ballance carried to that acct.	82	412	6	11½
			2330	7	8[½]

Bristoll 1685

		Cr	£	s	d
	Peter Mewes late Bishop of Bath and Wells now of Winchester per Contra				
November 27	By Isaac Heming for money I recd. of the Bishop, and paid Heming in London as per receit	90	50		
1686 March 8	By Ditto for money hee received by his order in London, as per his leter March 8th 1686	130	50		
			100		
	By Acct. of Ballances, for Ballancee	194 *	50		
			150		

Anno 1684					
	Adventure 2nd in the Ship Agreement Wm. Fisher Master to Cadiz & the Straights	Dr	£	s	d
	To sundry accts being the cost & charges of 1Trunck of Stockins & 30 Firkins butter laden in said ship, consign'd to Wm. Fisher for sales as per Invoyce & bill lading viz.				
	To Worsted Stockins for 56 doz being £ s d				
June 27	672 paire fine Bristoll hose at 3s per				
	paire 100 16	74			
28	To Cash paid Tho. Morgan for 30				
	Firkins Butter ship'd in her 29 17 6	77			
	To Ditto paid custom etc. of the				
	Stockins & Butter 2 5 5	77	132	18	11
	To Worsted Stockins for one Trunck laden in said ship consign'd to John Cooke & Samuell Kekewich merchants in St Marie Port, for sales & returnes containing viz £ s d				
	64 doz fine Bristoll hose is 768 paire				
	at 3s per paire 115 4	74			
	15 doz and 2 scores finest Wells hose				
	cont. 220 paire at 22d per paire 20 3 4	74			
	8 scores ordinary Wells hose with a X				
	on the Inkle of each score at 20d 13 6 8	74			
	To Cash pd. custom etc. of the Stockins 3 2 8	77	151	16	8
			284	15	7
	To Profit and Loss for Ballance	189 *	60	14	7½
			345	10	2½

Anno 1684					
	Charles Plomer & Isaac Taylor of Bristoll merchants, & Wm. Minor of the same Citie Cordwynder, are £ s d	Dr	£	s	d
June 6	To Cash paid lent them on theire bond				
	payable Dec. 7th next 150	77			
	To Proffit & Losse for ½ yeares intrest				
	then due for the same 4 10	73	154	10	
	To Ditto for 7 month intrest	105	5	4	6

Anno 1684					
	Tobacco 4 hdds laden per Lawrence Washington in the Ship Francis and Marie Wm. Nicklus Master in part ballance of a former acct. £ s d	Dr	£	s	d
June	To Cash paid custom fees & bills 12 7 1	77			
August 1	To Ditto paid weighing them 1	77			
5	To Ditto paid Wm. Nicklus for freight				
	& averidge 5 4	77	17	12	1
	To Profit and Loss, for Ballance	189 *	10		7
			27	12	8

Anno 1684					
	Wine 2 hhds 1 White & t'other red of JB being 2 hhds I had of John Blackwell on a bargaine by agreement are	Dr	£	s	d
August	To John Blackwell for one other hogshead of whitewine bought of				
	him	59	6	10	
	To Profit and Loss for Ballance	189 *	10	17	9
			27 [76]	7	9

Anno 1674				
Adventures in the Agreement per Contra	Cr	£	s	d
By William Fisher for 6008¾ Ryals plate the neat proceeds of said stockins and Butter per contra, being 751 pieces of 8 ¾ of Ryal the piece of 8 at 4s 6d as per his acct. closed in Venice 1684	87	169	2	10½
By John Cooke & Samuel Kekewich for 6512 Ryals plate being 814 pieces of 8 the neat proceeds of the Trunck hose consign'd them, as per acct. sales Oct. 24th the piece of 8 at 52d	88	176	7	4
		345	10	2½

Anno 1685					
	Charles Plomer & Company per Contra	Cr	£	s	d
January 6	By Cash received of them	107	150		
	By Ditto received of them for 13 months intrest	107	9	14	6

Anno 1684					
	Tobacco 4 hhds per Contra	Cr	£	s	d
July 9	By George Maison for theire value weight neat 1673 lb at 4d per lb to abate 5s on the 4 hhds	79	27	12	8

Anno 1684					
	Wine 2 hhds per Contra	Cr	£	s	d
June 7	By Samuel Davis for 3 doz white & 3 doz red at 9s per doz	63	3	6	9
	By Proffit & Losse for 1 doz given my Cosen Haggatt	73		9	
10	By Dr. Francis Hungerford for 12 doz ½ each for him & Sir H Winchcombe at 9s	59	5	8	
July 28	By Tho. Goldney for 1 doz bottles at 10s per doz	16		10	
	By John Earle of Bristoll for 4 doz white and 4 doz Claret at 9s 6d	37	3	16	
August 20	By Sir George Strode for 4 doz bottles at 10s	24	2		
	By the Lady Ann Pawlet for 2 doz white & 2 doz Claret at 9s 6d	48	1	18	
			17	7	9

Anno 1684/5		Dr	£	s	d
	John Kent Junior of Reading Clothier [77]	Dr	£	s	d
Aprill 10	To Cash paid him on his bill of Exchange in favor of Peter Zinsano	83	1		

(79)	**Bristoll 1684**				
	George Maison of Bristoll Soapmaker is	Dr	£	s	d
July 9	To Tobacco 4 hhds out of the Francis & Marie weight 1673 lb at 4d per lb abating 5s on all	78	27	12	8
1689 December	To Xeries wine 23 Butts for one hogshead of Canary sould him	169	16	10	
			44	2	8

Anno 1684		Dr	£	s	d
	Xeries Wine 3 Butts bought of John Blackwell	Dr	£	s	d
July	To John Blackwell for theire first cost at £25 per Butt	59	50		
November	To John Blackwell for one other Butt of Xerie bought of him at	85	25		
	To Proffit & Losse for ballance	73	25	8	

Anno 1684		Dr	£	s	d
	John Earle of Bristoll is on acct. of money lent him, and money by him depossited in my hands to bee paid to John Shuttleworth for the Sea-wall	Dr	£	s	d
August 8	To Cash paid lent him to John Shuttleworth by his order	77	80		
12	To Cash paid John Shuttleworth	77	70		
22	To Cash paid John Shuttleworth	77	50		
26	To Cash paid John Shuttleworth	77	50		
	To Cash lent him which I paid John Shuttleworth	77	25		
September 6	To Cash more paid Matthew Barber on John Shuttleworth's receit	77	75		
			350		

Anno 1684		Dr	£	s	d
	Sugar 2 hhds out of the Olive tree from Barbadoes laden per Ed. Parsons for acct. of Martha Speed in part returns of goods sent in the Martha & Sarah £ s d	Dr	£	s	d
November 3	To Cash paid custom freight etc. 3 11 6	82	3	11	6
	To Edward Parsons for theire 1st cost in Barbadoes as per Invoyce 9 of 5th month 84	58	17	13	7½
			21	5	1½

		Cr	£	s	d
	Anno 1685				
	John Kent per Contra	Cr	£	s	d
	By *Proffit & Losse recd. of him in Reading*	105	1		

		Cr	£	s	d
	Bristoll 1684				
	George Maison per Contra is	Cr	£	s	d
June	By *Cash recd. of him*	77	27	12	8
1689 *Jan. 11*	By *Cash recd. of him in full*	173	16	10	
			44	2	8

		Cr	£	s	d
	Anno 1684				
	Xeries wine 2 Butts per Contra are	Cr	£	s	d
August 20	By *Sir George Strode for 4 doz bottles at 16s per doz*	24	3	4	
23	By *Sir Samuell Astry for 1 hogshead containing 60 Gall. at 5s 4d per Gallon*	49	16		
27	By *the Lady Ann Pawlet for 10 doz bottles at 16s per doz*	48	8		
September 12	By *Sir Sam. Astry for 10 doz sent to Robert Wintour in London at 16s per dozen*	49	8		
	By *Wm. Drake for 6 doz sent to Ash per Henry Stover at 16s per doz*	63	4	16	
October 25	By *Dr. Fra. Hungerford for 6 doz bottles for Sir H Winchcomb & 2 doz for selfe at 16s*	59	6	8	
23	By *John Earle of Bristoll for 1 hogshead and 1 Quarter Cask containing 88 Gall. at 5s 4d per Gallon*	37	23	9	4
November 28	By *Wm. Drake for 6doz bottles at 16s per doz*	63	4	16	
December 3	By *Sir Nath. Nappier for 4 doz at 16s sent him per Robert White*	29	3	4	
	By *Tho. Walden for 6 bottles*	2		8	
	By *Marie Aldworth for 2 Gall. at 5s 4d*	80		10	8
	By *Philip Frowde for 3 doz bottles at 16s*	85	2	8	
	By *Sgt Tho. Strode for 1 Cask cont. 24 Galls at 5s 4d per Gallon*	65	6	8	
	By *Dr. Fra. Hungerford for 10 doz bottles at 16s*	87	8		
	By *Wm. Drake for 4 doz bottles at 16s*	63	3	4	
	By *Proffit & Losse for 2 doz sent per Waggon to Phil. Ward*	73	1	12	
			100	8	

		Cr	£	s	d
	Anno 1684				
	John Earle of Bristoll on loane etc. per Contra	Cr	£	s	d
August 11	By *Cash recd. of Sgt Tho. Strode by order of his Brother Sir George for his acct.*	77	50		
	By *Ditto recd. of James Gasguine his servant to bee paid John Shuttleworth for the use of the work of the Sea-wall as per advice from his Countesse*	77	200		
October 22	By *himselfe for ballance for which hee hath given his bond dated September 10th 1684*	80	100		
			350		

		Cr	£	s	d
	Anno 1684/5				
	Sugar 2 hhds per Contra	Cr	£	s	d
March	By *Charles Herbert & Company for theire value sould them*	93	18	3	
	By *Profit and Loss, for Ballance*	189 *	3	2	1½
			21	5	1½

	Anno 1684	Dr	£	s	d
	Henry Gibbes per Contra is	Dr	£	s	d
July	To John Stretten for ½ yeares rent hee recd. of him for Insolds in Clevedon allowing 16s hee paid for Lords rent	57	5	4	
24	To Cash paid lent him on his obligation due on demand	77	50		
October 4	To Wm. Drake for money paid John Burrage in Lime for his acct.	63	5	12	6
December 15	To Ditto for money paid said Burridge per Wm. Drake in Lyme as per receit	63	5	13	
1685 March 2	To Cash paid himselfe	108	25		
June 15	To Cash paid himselfe in full	108	5	18	6
1686 March 15	To Cash paid him in full	121 *	13	6	
1687 July 23	To Cash pd. lent him	121	50		
January 14	To Cash pd. lent him on his bill & 20 pieces of Hollands Duck	140	40		
1688 June 8	To Cash pd. him in full for a hogshead whitewine	141 *	7		
			207	14	

	Anno 1684	Dr	£	s	d
	Adventure in the Ship Rachell Wm. Berkin Master to Cadiz	Dr	£	s	d
August 3	To Cash paid Abraham Hill the widow Shepheards servant for 20 Firkins of Butter laden in said ship, & consign'd with other goods following ¼ John Maine Supra Cargo on said ship for sales & returnes, neat 1478 lb at 3d'½	77	21	11	1
	To Worsted Stockins for 1 Trunck laden & consign'd as above viz £ s d				
	64 doz fine Bristoll hose at 3s per paire being 768 paire 115 4 0				
	15 doz in 180 paire best Wells hose at 2s per paire 18 00 00				
	10 score 200 paire ordinary Wells at 1s 6d per paire 15 00 00	74	148		
September	To John Mayne for ½ cost of 8 Cask bread 8cwt 2 17 in halves twixt us 3 5 7½				
	To Ditto for ½ 20 boxes strong waters at 6s per case twixt us 3 00 00				
	To Ditto for ½ charges on bottles for 25 dozs claret etc. 2 09 6	80	8	15	1½
	To John Mayne for custom & other charges paid for my stockins & butter	80	3	7	3
	To John Blackwell for ½ a hogshead claret laden in 25 doz bottles twixt John Mayne and my selfe in equall halves	59	3		
	To Worsted Stockins for 6 paire fine wove hose at 3s per paire put in John Maynes Trunck and consign'd to him	81		18	
	To John Mayne for ½ of 18 doz Syder in 1 hogshead laden in Ditto ship in equall halves twixt us, bought of Wm. Rogers	80	2	14	
			188	5	5½
	To Profit and Loss, for Ballance	189 *	6	6	3½
			194	11	9

(80)	**Bristoll 1684**	Dr	£	s	d
	Adventure in the John Frigat to Cadiz John Seward master and Supra Cargo is	Dr	£	s	d
August 30	To Worsted Stockins for one Trunck cont. 72 dozen fine Bristoll hose in 864 paire laden in said ship, & consign'd to said John Seward for Sales & returnes at 3s per paire	74	129	12	
September 5	To Cash paid John Seward for custom & other charges	77	2	8	2
	To Profit & Loss, for Ballance	190 *	10	14	2
			142	14	4

	Anno 1684	Dr	£	s	d
	Marie Aldworth of Bristoll Widow my Sister in law [78]	Dr	£	s	d
December	To Xeries wines 3 Butts for 2 Gall. Xerie at 5s 4d	79		10	8

	Anno 1684				
	Henry Gibbes of Bristoll Merchant is	Cr	£	s	d
	By ballance of his former acct. current brought from that acct.	4	3	1	9
October 31	BY Cash received of him	82	20		
1685 June 16	By Brandy 3 pieces bought of him wt neat 30cwt 3qr 27lb is				
	433 7/8 Gallons at 3s 4d	103	72	6	3
1686 March	By French wine 4 hhds for ½ cost & charges of 4 hhds				
	whitewine in the ship — from Bordeauxe, as per his acct. closed	133	13	6	
1687 August 1	By Cash recd. of Joseph Burgesse on his bill	121	50		
	By Xeries wine my ½ of 20 Butts for 6 Galls madera wine at 4s				
	per Gall	134	1	4	
	By French wine 3 Tierces & 3 hhds for 1 hhd Cognac wine at	151	7		
			166	18	
	By his new acct. current carried to that acct.	151	40	16	
			207	14	00

	Anno 1684/5				
	Adventure in the Rachell to Cadiz per Contra is	Cr	£	s	d
March	By John Mayne for the neat proceeds of the Butter, Stockins &				
	other goods per Contra, amounting to 7793 Ryals plate, is 389				
	1/8 pieces of 8 at 55d as per his acct. closed in Cadiz February				
	7th 1684/5 may appeare	93	194	11	9

	Bristoll 1684				
	Adventure in the John Frigat per Contra is	Cr	£	s	d
December	By Cash for 3 Bills of Exchange received of John Seward on the				
	3 person undernam'd viz				
18	By Cash received of Edward Thurston in full of a bill on him	82	27	10	5
	By Ditto received of Richard Lane in full of a bill on him	82	23	9	11
January 17	By Ditto received of Giles Merrick in full of a bill on him	82	91	14	
			142	14	4

	Anno 1690@				
	Marie Aldworth per Contra	Cr	£	s	d
	By Acct. of Ballances, for Ballance	194 *		10	8

Anno 1684

		Dr	£	s	d
	John Mayne of the Pill merchant as intrusted is				
September 27	To John Cheshire for 25 doz bottles bought to put claret in which hee left for mee to pay	80	2	10	
	To John Blackwell for 1/2 a hogshead claret bought of him which I paid for	59	3		
	To Cash for what paid him 4th currrent	77	2		
30	To Cash paid him	82	2		
October 1	To Cash paid him for balance	82	4	12	4
29	To Cash paid Wm. Rogers for 18 doz Syder in 1 hogshead in halves betwixt us shipd. in the Rachell for Cadiz	82	5	8	
			19	1	4

Anno 1684

		Dr	£	s	d
	John Earle of Bristoll is				
	To ballance of his acct. on loane for which hee hath given mee his bond payable with interest on the 11th day of March 1684	79	100		
1685 Aprill 3	To Proffit & Losse for ½ yeares intrest due 11th March 1684	89	3		
October 14	To Ditto for ½ yeares intrest due 11th of September 1685	89	3		
1686 Aprill	To Ditto for ½ yeares intrest due 11th of March 1685	105	3		
	To Ditto for 30 daies intrest to the 21st Aprill 1686	105		10	4
June 7	To Cash paid John Blackwell in full of his noat for wine per the Earle's order of May 16th	108	21	17	
			131	7	4

Anno 1684

		Dr	£	s	d
	John Cheshire of Bristoll Glazier is				
	To Proffit & Losse paid him but by error chargd to acct. Proffit & Losse	127 *	2	10	

Anno 1684

		Dr	£	s	d
	Adventure in the Owners Adventure Daniel Greening master to Nevis is Debtor to Sundry accts being the cost and charges of Sundry merchandizes laden in said ship, consignd to John Streater and Edmond Scrope merchants (viz)				
September 5	To Richard Wasbrow for 20 boxes of Candles 125 doz & 10 Candles at 5d	50	32	19	2
	To Giles Gough for 20 boxes cont. 107 ½ doz Candles at 5d	65	28	4	2
26	To Cash paid Richard Baily for 30 Cernes cont. 7cwt 1qr 4lb Alicant Soape in a hogshead at 58s	77	21	2	6
November 3	To Cash paid custom etc. on Soape & Candles	82	5	17	6
	To Profit and Loss for Ballance	190 *	21	9	0
			109	12	4

Anno 1684

		Dr	£	s	d
	John Hardiman Senior of Bristoll Taylor is				
November 13	To Cash paid lent him on his noat	82	1	10	
1687 November 21	To Cash paid lent him on his bond	139	5		
1688 August 1	To Cash paid him in part	141	2		
September 15	To Cash paid him in part	141	1		
21	To Cash pd. him in full	141	1	8	
February 28	To Cash paid lent him on his bill and a doposite	162	3		
1689 Nov. 2	To Cash paid him in full	168		11	
February 5	To Cash paid lent him on his obligation	173	2		
			16	9	

	Anno 1684		Cr	£	s	d
	John Mayne					
	By sundry accts for goods, & charges on them, bought & ship'd in equal halves twixt us in the ship Rachell now bound to Cadiz viz	£ s d				
September 27	By ½ £6 11s 3d paid David Phillips for 8cwt 2qr 17lb Bisket iin 8 Cask	3 05 7½				
	By Adventure the 2nd in Ditto ship to Cadiz for said bread & ½ 20 Cases strong waters	3 00 00				
	By Ditto for ½ charges on said goods bottles etc.	2 09 6				
	By Ditto for charges on a parcel Butter & stockins for my acct. paid for mee	3 7 3	79	12	2	4
	By Cash recd. of him		77	2		
	By Cash recd. of him for his ½ of the hogshead Syder per Contra		82	2	14	
	By Adventure in the Rachell to Cadiz for my ½ of the 18 doz Syder per Contra		79	2	14	
				19	1	4

	Anno 1685		Cr	£	s	d
	John Earle of Bristoll per Contra is					
Aprill 3	By Cash recd. of Hugh Hodges at Clevedon for 1/2 yeares intrest due March 11 1684		83	3		
October 14	By Cash recd. of Hugh Hodges at Clevedon for 1/2 yeares intrest due Sept. 11th		84	3		
Aprill 21	By Cash received of his steward Fisher at Clevedon Court		108	103		
1686 Oct. 14	By Cash received per my sonne Jahzeel of Serjeant Hodges at Clevedon Court		120	21	18	11
	By Proffit and Losse for ballance for so much abated		164		8	5
				131	7	4

	Anno 1684		Cr	£	s	d
	John Cheshire per Contra is					
September 27	By John Mayne for 25 doz glasse bottles for Claret		80	2	10	

	Anno 1686		Cr	£	s	d
	Adventure in the Owners Adventure to Nevis per Contra					
	By Edmond Scrope & Company for the neat proceeds of the 40 boxes Candles, & hogshead of Soape per Contra, as per theire acct. of sales received in August 1686 being 21923 lb Sugar at 10s per 100 lb		33	109	12	4

	Anno 1684/5		Cr	£	s	d
	John Hardiman per Contra					
March 17	By Cash recd. of him		82	1	10	
November	By Cash received of him in part by work done		139	2	10	
1688 Sept. 21	By sundry accts for work done etc. for my sonne Jahzeel and selfe		154 153	6	18	
1689 Nov. 18	By sundry accts for money due to him as per his noat		154			
			164	3	11	
				14	9	
	By Acct. of Ballances, for Ballance		194 *	2		
				16	9	

(81)	*Bristoll 1684*				Dr	£	s	d
	Worsted Stockins are							
		paire	*s*	*d*				
August 22	To Cash paid John Perrie for	50	2	6¼	77	6	6	
September 3	To Cash paid Joseph White for	32	2	8	77	4	5	4
5	To Cash paid James Davis for wove							
	hose	6	2	10	77		16	6
	To Ditto paid John Massinger for	28	2	8	77	3	14	8
18	To Ditto paid John Massinger for	54	2	8	77	7	4	
19	To Ditto paid John Perrie for	48	2	6¼	77	5	8	4
25	To Ditto paid John Massinger for	33	2	8	77	4	8	
26	To Ditto paid Elizabeth Dyer for	6	2	6	77		15	
	To Ditto paid Joell Pinne for	98	2	6	77	12	5	
29	To Ditto paid John Perrie for	61	2	5	82	7	7	6
30	To Ditto paid Joseph White for	190	2	8	82	27	6	8
October 1	To Ditto paid Fra. Rottenburie for hotpressing 486 paire				82		10	1
	To Ditto paid John Massinger for	38	2	8	82	5	1	4
9	To Ditto paid John Massinger for	35	2	8	82	4	13	4
11	To Ditto paid John Perrie for	59	2	6¼	82	7	8	8
13	To Ditto paid Tho. Hill for	63	2	5	82	7	12	3
	To Ditto paid Tho. Hill for Wells hose	80	1	6	82	6		
17	To Ditto paid Tho. Hill for Wells hose	40	1	5	82	2	16	9
	To Ditto paid Eliza. Dyer for	3	2	6	82		7	6
	To Ditto paid John Massinger for	39	2	8	82	5	4	
	To Ditto paid George Bond for	12	2	10	82	1	14	
24	To Cash paid John Perrie for	40	2	6¼	82	5		10
	To Ditto paid John Massinger for	28	2	8	82	3	14	8
	To Ditto paid Edward Iffe for hotpressing — paire				82		7	6
25	To Ditto paid Joseph White for	65	2	8	82	8	13	4
30	To Ditto paid John Massinger for	22	2	8	82	2	18	8
November 3	To Ditto paid Tho. Hill for	50	2	6	82	6	05	
8	To Ditto paid John Perrie for	54	2	6½	82	6	17	6
	To Ditto paid John Massinger for	33	2	8	82	4	8	
10	To Ditto paid Joell Pinne for	18	2	6	82	2	5	
11	To Ditto paid Tho. Hill for	100		17	82	7	1	8
14	To Ditto paid Elizabeth Dyer for	7	2	6	82		17	6
	To Ditto paid John Massinger for	26	2	8	82	3	9	4
19	To Ditto paid Tho. Hill for	70	2	6	82	8	15	
20	To Ditto paid Wm. Maston for	60		15½	82	3	17	6
	To Ditto paid John Bradway for	53	2	6	82	6	12	6
21	To Ditto paid John Perrie for	65	2	6½	82	8	5	6
22	To Ditto paid John Massinger for	26	2	8	82	3	9	4
27	To Ditto paid Joseph White for	98	2	8	82	13	1	4
	To Ditto paid Ed. Iffe for hotpressing — paire				82		11	6
						217	16	7
	To Cash paid Tho. Hill for	60	2	4	82	7	2	6
29	To Ditto paid John Massinger for	28	2	8	82	3	14	8
December 2	To Ditto paid Tho. Browning for	120	1	6	82	9		
	To Ditto paid Joel Pinne for	25	2	6	82	3	2	6
4	To Ditto paid John Perrie for	107	2	6½	82	13	12	
6	To Ditto paid John Massinger for	31	2	8	82	4	2	8
11	To Ditto paid Joel Pinne for	20	2	6	82	2	10	
	To Ditto paid John Perrie for	26	2	6½	82	3	6	1
12	To Ditto paid Tho. Hill for	116	2	6	82	14	10	
	To Ditto paid John Massinger for	38	2	8	82	5	1	4
18	To Ditto paid Jos. White for	60	2	8	82	8		
	To Ditto paid John Massinger for	33	2	8	82	4	8	
20	To Ditto paid John Perrie for	53	2	6½	82	6	14	8½

	Bristoll 1684				
	Worsted Stockins per Contra are Creditors	*Cr*	*£*	*s*	*d*
August 30	*By Ballance brought from that acct.*	*74*	*337*		*½*
	By Adventure 2nd in the Rachell to Cadiz for 6 paire fine wove hose at 3s	*79*		*18*	
October 28	*By Adventure in the ship Joseph to Cadiz for 73 doz fine Bristoll hose and 124 paire fine Wells hose laden in one Trunck in said ship*	*85*	*143*		*4*
November 28	*By Adventure in the ship Wellcom to Cadiz for one Trunck cont. 648 paire Bristoll, & 160 paire of Wells hose laden in said ship*	*86*	*113*	*4*	
January	*By Adventure in the Beniamin to Cadiz for one Trunck cont. 588 paire of Bristoll hose, & 380 paire Wells hose sent in said ship from London*	*86*	*127*	*6*	*4*
			721	*8*	*8½*

Date	Description					£	s	d
	To Ditto paid Ed. Iffe for hotpressing				82	1		
	To Ditto paid Joel Pinne for	20	2	6½	82	2	11	10
	To Ditto paid Tho. Hill for	146			82	8	15	8
23	To Ditto paid Tho. Hill for	120	1	6	82	9		
24	To Ditto paid John Massinger for	28	2	8	82	3	14	8
January 8	To Ditto paid John Perrie for	40	2	6½	82	5	1	8
	To Ditto paid Jos. White for	38	2	8	82	4	16	
10	To Ditto paid John Massinger for	21	2	8	82	2	16	
13	To Ditto paid Joell Pinne for	7	2	6¾	82		18	
15	To Ditto paid Tho. Hill for	120		18	82	9		
17	To Ditto paid Joseph White for	60	2	8	82	8		
	To Ditto paid John Massinger for	30	2	8	82	4		
	To Ditto paid Ed. Iffe for hotpressing				82	1	3	8
	To Ditto paid Tho. Hill for	60	2	6	82	6	15	
	To Ditto paid John Perrie for	66	2	6½	82	8	7	9
	To Ditto paid Tho. Hill for 142 paire viz	120		16				
		16	2	6				
		6	2	5	82	10	14	6
	To Ditto paid John Massinger for	26	2	8	82	3	9	4
	To Ditto paid Tho. Hill for	140	2	4½	82	16	12	6
	To Ditto paid Joel Pinne for	20	2	6	82	2	10	
	To Ditto paid Edward Boner for	20	2	6	82	2	7	
	To Ditto paid John Massinger for	33	2	8	82	4	8	
February 2	To Ditto paid John Perrie for	71	2	6½	82	9		5
	To Ditto paid Jos. White for	38	2	8	82	5	1	4
	To Ditto paid Tho. Hill for	28	2	6	82	3	10	
	To Ditto paid John Massinger for	34	2	8	82	4	10	6
7	To Ditto paid John Day for	12	2	4	82	1	8	00
9	To Ditto paid Marie Dyer for	9	1	6	82		12	6
	To Ditto paid John Massinger for	33	2	8	82	4	8	
						447	13	4½
	To ballance carried to that acct.				91	273	15	4
						721	8	8½

(82)	**Bristoll 1684**				
	Cash is	Dr	£	s	d
	To ballance of acct. brought from	77	412	6	11
October 4	To Walter Stephens recd. of him	53	25		
	To Ann Pawlet recd. of Bernard Wilkins	48	11	15	
14	To Edward Gorges recd. of him by the hands of his servant	34	4	4	
	To Sir Samuel Astry recd. of his man	49	9	4	
22	To the Earle of Bristoll recd. of Ed. Pryor	37	30	15	6
	To John Gore & John Hurtnell recd. of them	56	20	5	
	To John Mayne recd. of him for ½ hogshead Syder	80	2	14	
31	To Henry Gibbes recd. of him	79	20		
	To Isaac Heming recd. of Samuell Spencer	76	16	4	
Nov. 18	To John Blackwell recd. of him	59	87		
December 2	To John Wilmot recd. of Wm. Yates	62	20		
10	To John Rumsey received of him	29	50		
18	To Adventure in the John Frigat recd. of Edward Thurston	80	27	10	5
20	To Ditto recd. of Richard Lane	80	23	9	11
	To John Blackwell recd. of him	85	40		
January 6	To Philip Frowde recd. of him	85	2	18	6
7	To Adventure in the John Frigat received of Giles Merrick	80	91	14	
	To Wm. Drake recd. of John Warren	63	3	14	10
	To John Blackwell recd. of him	85	40		
	To Adventure in the Owners Endeavour recd. of Humphrey Corsley	37	2	14	5
February 2	To Isaac Heming for money recd. for my 3 bills on him, for £130,£300,& £100	90	530		

Bristoll 1684					
	Cash per Contra is	Cr	£	s	d
September 29	By Worsted Stockins paid John Perrie	81	7	7	6
30	By John Mayne paid him	80	2		
October 1	By Worsted Stockins paid John Massinger, Joseph White, & Francis Rottenburie	81	32	18	1
6	By John Mayne paid him in full	80	4	12	8
	By Wm. Smart paid him	26	3		
11	By Worsted Stockins paid John Massinger, John Perrie & Tho. Hill	81	25	14	3
13	By Land at Clevedon paid Robert Dowding	32		16	8
	By house at lower end of Small Streat paid Oziel Browne	22		4	
	By Proffit & Losse paid houshold expences which should have been charg'd Sept. 18	73	26	7	1
17	By Worsted Stockins paid Tho. Hill & Elizabeth Dyer	81	3	4	3
	By Ditto paid John Massinger & George Bond	81	6	18	
	By Wm. Plydall paid him	46		5	
23	By Proffit & Losse paid John Hurtnell for mault	73	5	18	2
24	By Worsted Stockins paid John Perrie, John Massinger, Ed. Iffe & Joseph White	81	17	16	4
29	By Andrew Stucky paid Daniell Guillim	53	1		6
30	By John Mayne paid Wm. Rogers for 18 doz Syder	80	5	8	
	By Adventure in the Joseph to Cadiz for custom etc. on a Trunck of Stockins	85	2	15	10
November 3	By Worsted Stockins paid John Massinger	81	2	18	8
	By Proffit & Losse paid houshold expences	73	36	9	3

	To Ditto recd. of Simon Hurle for my bill on him	90	100		
7	To James Beard recd. of him	76	13	10	
	To Isaac Heming for money of Tho. Walden for my 3 bills of £100 each	90	300		
	To Ditto for money of John Watson for my bill in his favor	90	100		
21	To Richard Merrick recd. of him	92		1	
27	To Sir Natha. Nappier recd. of Robert White	29	3	15	
	To Estate of Land in Clevedon recd. of John Thorne	32	4	10	
March 6	To Isaac Heming recd. of Tho. Day	90	86	7	
7	To Edmond Scrope recd. of him	38	50		
17	To John Mayne recd. of Humphry Corsley for 61 pieces of 8	93	13	15	10
	To John Hardiman recd. of him	80	1	10	
	To Proffit & Losse recd. of Edward Harvord	89	2	5	
	To John Bradway recd. of him	70	28	17	
			2176	1	4

	By *Adventure in the Owners Endeavour* [79] *to Nevis paid custom etc.*	80	5	17	6
	By *Sugar 2 hhds in the Olive tree from Barbadoes for custom etc.*	79	3	11	6
6	By *Stockins paid Tho. Hill, John Perrie & John Massinger*	81	17	10	3
8	By *house at the lower end of Small Streat paid Wm. Smart & Joseph Drew*	22	2	5	9
10	By *Worsted Stockins paid Joel Pinne, Tho. Hill, Eliza. Dyer & John Massinger*	81	13	13	6
	By *Martha Speed paid her*	46	1		
	By *John Hardiman paid lent him*	80	1	10	
19	By *Worsted Stockins paid Tho. Hill, Wm. Masters, John Brady & John Perrie*	81	27	10	6
	By *Ditto paid John Massinger, Jos. White, Ed. Iffe, & Tho. Hill*	81	24	4	8
29	By *Ditto paid John Massinger, Tho. Browning, & Joel Pinne*	81	15	17	2
December 4	By *Ditto paid John Perrie & John Massinger*	81	17	14	8
6	By *Copiehold Tenement in Portburie paid Richard Cope*	20	1	2	2
	By *Proffit & Losse paid Martha Speed £1 17s & Anthony Dell 10s 9d*	73	2	7	9
11, 12	By *Worsted Stockins paid Joel Pinne, John Perrie, Tho. Hill & John Massinger*	81	25	7	5
14	By *Proffit & Losse paid Richard Sandford & Dennis Pitts*	73	1	10	1
18	By *Worsted Stockins paid Jos. White & John Massinger*	81	12	8	
	By *Land at Clevedon paid John Perrie*	32	1	5	3
20	By *Worsted Stockins paid John Perrie, Wm. Iffe* [80]*, Joel Pinne & Tho. Hill*	81	19	2	2½
	By *Calfskins for acct. of Andrew Stuckey paid John Hort*	85	37	7	6
23, 24	By *Worsted Stockins paid Tho. Hill, John Massinger, & John Perrie*	81	17	15	4
January 6	By *Proffit & Losse paid Richard Champneys*	73	3	5	
8	By *Worsted Stockins paid Joseph White*	81	4	16	
	By *Sugar 1 Butt & 15 hhds paid Adam Combes*	85	30	12	
10, 13	By *Worsted Stockins paid John Massinger, Joel Pinne & Tho. Hill*	81	12	14	
15, 17	By *ditto paid Jos. White, John Massinger & Ed. Iffe*	81	13	3	
			499	5	5½
17	By *Proffit & Losse paid George White*	73		16	
	By *Worsted Stockins paid Tho. Hill*	81	6	15	
	By *Proffit & Losse paid Robert Gibbons*	89	3	4	6
	By *Worsted Stockins paid John Perrie £8 7s 9d & Tho. Hill £10 14s 6d*	81	19	2	3
	By *Proffit & Losse paid houshold expences*	89	20		8
	By *Worsted Stockins paid John Massinger £3 9s 4d to Tho. Hill £16 12s 6d, to Joel Pinne £2 10s 0d*	81	22	1	10
	By *Proffit & Losse pd. John Cheshire*	89	2	12	9
	By *Tho. Walden lent him pd. George Bent & John Mandeville*	87	100		
	By *Worsted Stockins paid Edward Boner*	81	2	7	
	By *Adventure in the Wellcom to Cadiz paid custom etc. of Stockins*	86	2	9	3
	By *Sugar 1 Butt 15 hhds paid custom etc.*	85	11		10
	By *Proffit & Losse paid charges on a Butt Xerie*	89	5	3	2
	By *Calfskins for Andrew Stuckey paid charges on them*	85	6	2	9
	By *Xeries Wine 20 Butts in the Expectation paid custom etc.*	87	65	11	3
	By *Worsted Stockins paid John Massinger*	81	4	8	
February 6	By *Ditto paid John Perrie £9 0s 5d Jos. White £5 1s 4d Tho. Hill £3 10s 00d John Massinger £4 10s 6d*	81	22	2	3
9	By *Ditto paid John Day £1 8s 0d Marie Dyer 12s 6d John Massinger £4 8s 0d*	81	6	8	6
	By *Adventure in the Owners Endeavour paid custom etc.*	37	4	13	
	By *Ralph Grant paid lent him on a mortgage*	88	300		

(83)	**Bristoll 1684/5**				
	Cash is	Dr	£	s	d
Aprill 2	To Ballances brought from that acct.	82	895	8	9½
3	To John Earle of Bristoll for money of Hugh Hodges at Clevedon	80	3		
13	To John Blackwell recd. of him per the hands of Ed. Lloyd	85	25		
18	To William Prichard recd. of him	63	2	5	
24	To Daniel Griffith recd. of him for a bagge of Rice	95	4	5	2
30	To Thomas Lutterell recd. of him	25	10	13	
	To Carpets for acct. Paul Priaulx recd. of John Wimpany	1		18	
	To Tho. Jordan for money of him per Simon Clement	95	11	18	
	To Henry Baynham for money of Cosen Nath. Haggatt	48	307	15	
May 2	To John Curtis recd. of Tho. Callowhill	95	8	5	3
	To Rice for acct. of Simon Clement recd. of severalls for 1 bagge divided	96	3	15	2
5	To Xeries wine 30 Butts recd. of James Crofts for returnes on 2 Butts	94	1	16	4
7	To Wines 14 Butts for acct. of Simon Clement for recd. of Ed. Haggatt, custom etc.	97	5	2	6
9	To Richard Holbrook recd. of his wife in part	98	1	10	
	To Tho. Davidge recd. of him	4	3	15	
11	To Richard Cabbel recd. of Wm. Minor for his composition	15	3	15	10
13	To Wm. Spoore & Company recd. of Wm. Spoore	30	3		
	To Richard Haines Junior recd. of Sir Richard Crump	98	40	1	
14	To John Stretten recd. of him for ½ yeares rent of Insolds	57	6		
	To Prisage Wine recd. of William Lansdown	96	73	10	4
25	To Isaac Heming for money of Tho. Day for my bill on him	90	55	9	4
29	To Tho. Walden recd. of Nath. Pinny in full of his bond and intrest	87	102		

			£	s	d
	By *Proffit & Losse paid houshold expences*	91	12	18	8
16, 19	By *Worsted Stockins paid Wm. Iffe #, Tho. Hill, Andrew Creed & John Perrie*	91	29	11	4
20	By *Ditto pd. John Massinger, Tho. Hill and Joseph White*	91	12	11	10
21	By *Proffit & Losse paid Tobias Luton*	89	1	9	
27	By *Worsted Stockins paid Joel Pinne £2 8s 4d John Massinger £4 13s 4d Ed. Iffe 8s 9d, in all*	91	7	10	5
March	By *Proffit & Losse paid Robert White 6d & houshold expences £8 3s 11d*	89	8	4	5
2	By *Adventure in the Joseph paid Simon Clements bill to Tho. Callowhill*	85	1	10	
4	By *Martha Linch paid her covenant money*	92		1	
5	By *Worsted Stockins paid John Massinger & £4 13s 00d & Jos. White £6 2s 8d*	91	10	15	8
	By *Proffit & Losse paid Hump. Corsley £7 9s 00d, & John Moore £2 7s 3d*	89	9	16	3
7	By *Worsted Stockins paid John Perrie*	81	8	8	10
	By *Wm. Smart paid him in full*	26	4	7	6
14	By *Worsted Stockins paid Tho. Hill £3 12s 00d & John Massinger £4 13s 4d*	81	8	5	4
	By *Elizabeth Taylor paid lent her*	88		10	
18	By *Worsted Stockins paid John Massinger, Joel Pinne, John Perrie & Joseph White*	91	18	3	8
	By *Proffit & Losse paid John Hardiman*	89	2	16	
27	By *Worsted Stockins paid Tho. Hill, John Massinger Andrew Creed, & Jos. White in all*	91	33	17	4
31	By *House at lower end of Small Streate paid Symon Smith*	22		5	
	By *Worsted Stockins paid John Perrie for 42 paire*	91	5	5	10
			1280	12	6½
	By *ballance caried to that acct. of debt*	83	895	8	9½
			2176	1	4

Bristoll 1685

			£	s	d
	Cash per Contra is	Cr			
Aprill 4	By *Worsted Stockins paid John Massinger for 40 paire*	91	5	6	8
	By *Isaac Heming paid John Gandy Junior*	90	31		
	By *Worsted Stockins paid Jos. White, Henry Britten & Tho. Hill*	91	17	11	6
7	By *Sugar 1 Butt & 15 hhds paid weighing them*	85		4	7
9, 10	By *Worsted Stockins paid John Day, Jos. White & John Massinger*	91	12	1	2
	By *John Kent Junior paid Peter Zinsano*	78	1		
13	By *Worsted Stockins paid John Perrie*	91	4	8	2
	by *Xeries wine 2 Butts bought of Edward Loyd paid him in part*	94	20		
16, 17	By *Worsted Stockins paid Tho. Hill, Joel Pinne & John Massinger, in all*	91	11	13	11
	By *Ditto paid John Perry & Joseph White*	91	12	2	3
22	By *Proffit & Losse paid Tho. Browne £1 1s 0d & Jane Flower £6 9s6d*	89	7	10	6
24	By *Edward Lloyd paid him in part*	95	4		
25	By *Worsted Stockins paid Tho. Hill for 25 paire*	91	2	18	4
	By *Tho. Lutterell & Company paid lent them*	97	20		
27	By *Proffit & Losse paid Ed. Iffe*	89		6	
	By *House in which I live paid Chimny money*	23		8	
	By *Stockins paid Tho. Walden*	91		7	
29	By *Simon Clement paid lent him*	86	11	18	
	By *Worsted Stockins paid John Perry & John Ruddock*	91	7	14	4
May 1, 2	By *Ditto Paid John Day, Henry Britten, John Massinger, & Joseph White at twice*	91	18	17	7
7	By *Henry Davis & Company paid Henry Davis in part*	97	50		
	By *Adventure in the Swallow to Nevis paid Wm. Rogers*	97	31	16	

June 3	To *Carpets for acct. Paul Priaulx recd. of Stephen Stringer*	*1*	1	10	
	To *Joseph Badger recd. of him*	*50 **	29	8	11
	To *sundry accts for money received of severalls for 33 Baggs of*	*95,92,*			
	rice as per Journall books particculars	*53,55*	133	12	10
	To *Elizabeth Taylor received of her*	*88*		10	
	To *Charles Herbert & Company recd. of Charles Herbert*	*93*	44		
July 23	To *Ditto & Company recd. of Charles Herbert*	*93*	50		
	To *Robert Hauxworth recd. of him*	*28*	4	9	6
	To *Isaac Heming recd. of John Bubb for my bill*	*90*	100		
29	To *Richard Cope recd. of him*	*97*	1	15	
	To *John Mayne recd. of him*	*93*	16		
	To *Simon Hall received of him*	*95*	3	19	
	To *Land at Clevedon recd. of John Hurtnell which hee recd. for*				
	a Reek bay	*32*	6	5	
			1960	13	11½

Date	Description	Folio	£	s	d
	By Worsted Stockins paid Tho. Hill for 100 paire	91	6	17	6
	By Proffit & Losse paid household expences to 2nd May	89	20	7	11
9	By Worsted Stockins paid John Massinger & Andrew Creed	81	11	9	
15	By Land at Clevedon paid John Stretten	32	1	14	6
	By Worsted Stockins paid Tho. Hill	91	4	11	9
	By Proffit & Losse paid James Swetenham & for a firkin of Butter	89	2	7	9
	By Worsted Stockins paid John Massinger for 42 paire	91	5	12	
	By William King paid him	96	85		
16	By Worsted Stockins paid John Brady's man, Tho. Hill & John Perrie	91	27	16	1
21	By Simon Clement paid him 21th £40 1s 00d & 23th £50 both is	86	90	1	
22	By Worsted Stockins paid John Massinger for 47 paire	91	6	5	4
25	By Ditto paid John Day & Joseph White	91	10	5	8
26, 27	By Ditto paid John Harris in full for Truncks	91	4		
28	By Ditto paid John Massinger for 45 paire	91	6		
	By Ditto paid Edward Iff in full	91		8	6
	By Ditto paid John Rudduck for 35 paire	91	4	6	9
	By Proffit & Losse paid given Sarah Maycock	89		10	
	By Xeries wine 20 Butts in the Expectation paid freight & averidge	87	33	6	8
30	By James Speed paid Richard Miller towards binding him an apprentice	94	6		
June 1	By Worsted Stockins paid Joseph White & Andrew Creed	91	13		
	By Adventure in the Joseph to Nevis paid Joseph Badger	98	32	3	6
	By Edward Lloyd paid him in full	95	2	18	6
	By Worsted Stockins paid John Perrie for 80 paire	91	10		
5	By Ditto paid John Massinger for 38 paire	91	5	1	4
6	By Ditto paid John Day, Tho. Hill & William Thyers	91	23	7	2
	By Adventure in the Joseph paid Wm. Jefferies for fraight	98	0	10	
9	By John Shuttleworth paid putting his Sonne aboard the Joseph	93		4	
			685	9	8
12	By Worsted Stockins paid John Massinger for 32 paire	91	4	5	4
	By Henry Davis & Company paid Henry Davis	97	64	8	
	By Proffit & Loss paid Ann Clement	89		17	
15	By Simon Clement paid him	86	40		
	By Worsted Stockins paid John Day & Edward Iffe	91	4	15	8
	By Martha Speed paid her	46	2		
16	By Worsted Stockins paid John Massinger	91	5	9	4
20	By Richard Haynes paid Tho. Callowhill	98	35		
27	By Joane Daracot paid her	98	2	15	
	By Isaac Heming paid Elizabeth Taylor	90	20		
29	By Xeries wine 30 Butts paid custom fees etc.	94	89		
	By Proffit & Losse paid John Cheshire	89	2	18	
	By Xeries wine 14 Butts paid Custom etc.	97	41	16	
	By Rice 50 Baggs paid custom fees , & petty charges	96	13	8	7
	By Olives 14 Jarres paid custom etc.	96		2	3
	By Wine 6 hhds in the Angel Gabriell paid custom etc.	94	7	16	
	By sundry accts paid custom etc. on 13 Butts & 13 hhds in the Rainbow & Baltamoore	99	68	13	10½
July 3	By Worsted Stockins paid Elizabeth Massinger	91	3	12	
4	By Tho. Walden paid him	87	3		
7	By Proffit & Losse paid John Sandford	89		11	
11	By John Mayne paid lent him	93	16		
	By Worsted Stockins paid John Massingers sister for 36 paire	91	4	16	
13	By Ditto paid John Rudduck, John Perrie, Henry Britten & John Day	91	23	14	7
15	By Estate at Clevedon paid John Stretten	32		9	
17	By Jahzeel Speed delivered him	69		10	

(84)	Bristoll 1685					
	Cash is	Dr	£	s	d
July 29	To ballance brought from that acct.	83	705	17	7½
August	To Edward Croft received of him for 1/2 yeares rent of the house hee lives in	96	18		
	To Isaac Heming recd. of Richard Stubbs for my two bills on him	90	57	4	
	To Tho. Goldney receid of him for 3 baggs of rice	16	11	16	
	To Arthur Hobbs recd. of him per the hands of James Beard	29	1	10	
	To Isaac Heming for money of John Bubb for my bill on him	90	100		
	To Ditto for money of Tho. Walden for my bill on said Heming	90	120		
18	To Richard Holbrook for money of him	98	2	5	
21	To Charles Herbert & Company recd. of Fra.s Whitchurch				
	To Robert Hauxworth received of him	28	7	7	
22	To Thomas Longman recd. of him	95	8		
27	To Isaac Heming recd. of Thomas Walden for my bill on him	90	334	7	4
	To John Brady recd. of him	20	2		
	To Tho. Walden recd. of him	87	1	8	9
	To Lady Ann Pawlet recd. of Bernard Wilkins	100	7	18	4
September 29	To James Beard recd. of him	76	11	2	
	To Henry Howard & Comp.y recd. of Oziel Browne for ½ years intrest £100	92	3		
October 14	To John Earle of Bristoll for what recd. of Hugh Hodges in full of his acct. of wine	37	23	18	
	To Ditto on bond for ½ yeares intrest of £100 due Sept. 11th past	80	3		
26	To Stephen Stringer recd. of him	103	72		
	To John Winpenny recd. of him	101	72		
November 5	To Edward Woodhouse & Company recd. of Edward Woodhouse in part	103	140	5	
			1702	19	

18	By Worsted Stockins paid Elizabeth Massinger	91	3	17	4
	By Samuel Davis paid Joseph Davis	63	29		
20	By John Oliffe paid him	98	15	4	
	By Proffit &Losse paid Roger Addams	89	2	4	6
	By Worsted Stockins paid John Brady	91	4	13	9
21	By John Brady paid lent him	20	2		
	By WorstedStockins paid Tho. Hill	91	4	1	10
22	By Martha Speed paid her	46	1	10	
23	By Worsted Stockins paid John Rudduck, Joseph White, &				
	John Perrie	91	23	7	11½
24	By Proffit & Losse paid Joseph Drew & Joseph Owen in full	89	2	12	
25	By Worsted Stockins paid John Massinger for 38 paire	102	5	1	4
27	By Proffit & Losse paid Robert Summers for keeping my mare	89		11	
29	By Tenement in Portburie paid Richard Cope	20	1	2	
	By Worsted Stockins paid Andrew Creed, Tho. Browning &				
	Joel Pinne	102	18	3	4
			1254	16	4
	By ballance carried to that acct.	84	705	17	7½
			1960	13	11½

Bristoll 1685

		Cr	£	s	d
	Cash per Contra is				
August 1	By Worsted Stockins paid John Perrie & Henry Britten	102	14	2	6
	By Jahzeel Speed paid John Matthew for his Beaver	69	2	1	
3	By Worsted Stockins paid Joseph White & John Day	122	8	19	11
	By Robert Dowding & Company paid lent them on theire bond	100	100		
5	By Worsted Stockins paid John Massinger	102	5	12	
6	By Proffit & Losse paid John Hardiman	89	1		
	By Ed. Crofts paid him for ½ yeares rent of 2 Chambers, & his				
	noat of disbursments	96	2	9	
	By Proffit & Losse paid David Phillips	89.		7	
	By Ditto paid for 22½ lb Butter	89		10	3
	By Worsted Stockins paid John Brady, Joseph White & John				
	Massinger	102	18	5	6
12	By Sugar in the Rainbow & Baltamoore paid Gilbert Cale for				
	weighing them	99		11	9
	By Worsted Stockins paid Ed. Iffe, Joseph White & Tho. Hill	102	19	11	5
	By Wm. Spoore Senior lent him on his bill	52	5		
	By Worsted Stockins paid Robert Webb, Tho. Hill & John				
	Massinger	102	12	9	4
22	Ditto paid John Perrie & Tho. Hill	84	11	4	
	By Isaac Heming paid Elizabeth Tayler on his bill	90	5		
27	By Worsted Stockins paid Tho. Hill & Wm. Thiery	102	6	2	6
	By Proffit & Losse paid Jahzeel & Martha at going to London	89	2		
	By Worsted Stockins paid John Massinger and John Day	102	6		6
	By Proffit & Losse paid John Sandford in full	89	1	1	9
29	By Worsted Stockins paid John Perrie, Jos. White, & John				
	Brady, & Tho. Hill	102	17	4	4
September 1	By Ditto paid Andrew Creed, John Rudduck, John Massinger				
	& Henry Britton	102	16	13	8
	By Ditto paid Edward Iffe in full for hot pressing	102		11	
7	By Samuel Davis paid his Brother Joseph in full	63	14		
	By Worsted Stockins paid Wm. Thiery & John Massinger	102	7	5	9
14	By Xeries wine paid Joseph Berry	101	1		
16	By Worsted Stockins paid Anthony Palmer for 41 paire	102	5		
	By John Sandford for money lent him on bond	19	100		
17	By Worsted Stockins paid Joseph White for 40 paire	102	5	6	8
	By Adventure in the Olive branch paid in three summs to John				
	Mayne	100	37	14	6
18	By Worsted Stockins paid Henry Britton for 50 pair	102	6	5	
19	By Ditto paid John Massinger, John Perrie & Tho. Hill	102	14	18	

25	By Ditto paid Tho. Browning, Wm. Thiery & Henry Britton	102	16	5	10
26	By Ditto paid John Massinger, John Perrie & John Bradys servant	102	16	16	4
28	By Proffit & Losse paid houshold expences, & to Tho. Walden	89	52	9	8
30	By Worsted Stockns paid Joseph White for 54 paire at 2s 8d	102	7	4	
October 2	By Xeries wine 10 Butts in the Expectation paid custom etc.	93	34	16	8
	By Worsted Stockins paid Tho. Hill for 64 paire	102	8		
	By house at the lower end of Small Streat paid Edward Jones in full	22		9	1
3	By Joane Daracot & Martha Linch paid them in full to the 29th Sept.	98, 92	1	6	3
	By Worsted Stockins paid Anthony Palmer for 40 paire	102	4	16	8
	By Adventure in the Dilligence to Cadiz paid Tho. Mansill for 40 hydes	103	27	15	
7	By merchandizes for L. Washington in the Francis & Marie paid John Matthews	104		10	
	By Proffit & Losse paid said Matthews	89		4	
			619		7
	By Worsted Stockins paid John Perrie & Tho. Hill	102	10		
8	By Wine in the Angell Gabriell for money paid John Batchelor for frieght etc.	94	4	4	
	By Stockins paid James Woollen & Wm. Thiery	102	8	1	
10	By Ditto paid Tho. Hill & John Massinger	102	15	16	10
	By merchandizes in the Fra. & Marie for sundry accts paid Tho. Walden and custom & other charges on them	104	11	16	4
12	By Stockins paid Tho. Hill for 3 parcels at severall prices	102	9	2	6
	By merchandizes in the Fra. & Marie for sundry accts paid Wm. Rogers for 6 dozen shoes	104	8	8	
	By Stockins paid John Day for 18 paire	102	2	3	6
13	By Ditto paid Edward Iffe in full for hot pressing	102	1	2	6
	By merchandizes in the Fra. & Marie for L. Washington pd. for a parcell shoes	104	1	16	6
	By merchandizes in said ship for my account and pd. Ditto for 4 doz plaine & ½ doz Fals	104	5	19	
14	By Stockins paid John Perrie, John Rudduck & Tho. Hill	102	11	12	6
16	By Stockins paid Henry Britten	102	5	5	
	By Xeries wine paid Joseph Berrie	101	1		
17	By Stockins paid Jos. White, John Massinger & John Brady	102	13	17	8
	By merchandizes in the Fra. & Marie for L. Washington pd. Jerom Churchy	104	3	10	
	By Proffit & Losse paid Edmond Driver	89		7	
21	By Stockins paid Tho. Hill for 158 paire	102	9	17	6
	By merchandizes for Law. Washington paid Walter Payne	104	7	16	6
	By Proffit & Losse paid Ditto	89		1	6
	By Stockins paid John Perrie, Tho. Hill & Jos. White	102	16		8
23	By Sugar in the Rainbow and Baltamoore paid Robert Bodenham	99	1	10	
24	By Proffit & Losse paid Edward Tyler	89		6	6
	By merchandizes for Law. Washington paid Philip Higgenbottom	104	2	3	
	By Proffit & Losse paid Ditto	89	1	10	
	By Worsted Stockins paid John Massinger, & Wm. Thiery	102	8	19	1
26	By Stockins paid Tho. Hill for 72 paire	102	9		
	By Wine in sundry ships from Cadiz paid Joseph Berrie	101	1		
	By Stockins paid Robert Webb & John Brady	102	2	13	
	By Proffit & Losse paid Abraham Hill for 2 Tubbs Butter	89	1	19	
	By merchandizes for L. Washington & friend paid John Blackley	104	3	4	
	By Stockins paid Ant. Palmer, John Rudduck, James Woollen, John Masssinger, Tho. Hill & Elizabeth Dyer	102	22	10	

(85)	**Bristoll 1684**				
	Adventure in the ship Joseph Wm. Jefferies Master bound to Cadiz but first to Cork in Ireland and consignd to Simon Clement Supra Cargo on said ship for sales and returnes	Dr	£	s	d
October	*To Worsted Stockins for 1 Trunck laden in that ship cont. viz*				
	72 doz is 864 paire fine Bristoll hose at 3s per paire 129 12 00	81			
	1 doz finest at 3s 5d per paire 2 01 00	81			
	10 1/3 doz is 5 score & 2 doz is 124 paire 11 07 04	81	143		4
30	*To Cash paid custom etc. on said stockins* 2 15 10	82	2	15	10
	To sundry accts for my 3/5 parts of 30 Cask of Butter laden by him in Cork in partnership betwixt us as per his leter of Nov. 18th 1684 from Cork	73, 86	27	19	2
March 2	*To Cash paid Tho. Callowhill on Simon Clements bill from Cadiz*	82	1	10	
			175	5	4
	To Profit and Loss, for Ballance	190 *	34	9	
			209	14	4

	Anno 1684				
	Calfskins 36 dozen bought of John Hort & ship'd in the ship Three Brothers of Yarmouth John Spry Master for acct. of Andrew Stucky Junior merchant & consignd to himselfe in Rochell by his order	Dr	£	s	d
December 20	*To Cash paid John Hort for 36 dozen weight . . . at 6d¹/₂ per pound*	82	37	7	6
	To Ditto paid custom & other charges	82	6	2	9
			43	10	3

	Anno 1684				
	Philip Frowde of London Postmaster General is	Dr	£	s	d
December	*To sundry accts for 1 Pannier cont. 3 doz bottles Xerie sent per waggon at 16s per dozen*	73, 79	2	18	6
1690 Sept. 26	*To sundry accounts for Cost & Charges of 2 panniers cont. 3 doz Xerie at 20s per doz*	186, 180187	3	8	6
			6	7	

	Anno 1684				
	John Blackwell of Bristoll Vintner is	Dr	£	s	d
December	*To ballance of his former acct. current brought from*	59	111	18	9
	To Proffit & Losse for 45 weeks Celleridge for my Lower vault in Small Streat, from the 14th February 1683 to the 23th Dec. 1684 at 3s 6d per week	73	6	15	
	To Ditto for 37 weeks in my vault under my house from 10th Aprill to 23rd Dec. 1684 at 4s	73	7	8	

31	By merchandizes for Law. Washington paid John Edwards	104	2	18	6
	By Stockins paid John Perrie & Tho. Hill	106	15	2	6
	By sundry accts paid Matthew Morgan	104,105, 93	1	15	9
November 2	By merchandizes for Law. Washington paid Tho. Case for 2 doz Spoones	104		5	
	By sundry accts paid Fra.s Ballard, Wm. Window, John Brady, & John Days servant	104, 105,106	9	9	5
			851	4	10
	By ballance carried to that acct.	107	851	14	2
			1702	19	

Bristoll 1684/5

	Adventure in the Joseph to Cadiz per Contra	Cr	£	s	d
March	By Simon Clement for his bill per Contra paid Tho. Callowhill chargd per error	86	1	10	
	By Ditto for the neat proceeds of the Trunck of Stockins per Contra amounting to 799 1/8 pces of 8 the piecce of 8 at 53d as per his account of sales	86	176	9	5
	By Ditto for my 3/5 part of the neat proceeds of the 30 Cask Butter per contra amounting to 143¾ piecees of 8 the piece of 8 at 53d as per same acct.	86	31	14	11
			209	14	4

Anno 1684

	Calfskins 36 dozen for acct. of Andrew Stuckey Junior	Cr	£	s	d
	By Andrew Stuckey his acct. current for the cost & charges of the Calfskins per Contra	55	43	10	3

Anno 1684

	Philip Frowde per Contra is	Cr	£	s	d
December	By Cash recd. of Tho. Cale by his order	82	2	18	6
1690 Oct. 24	By Ditto, received of William Dickinson, on Stephen Lilly's bill	187 *	3	8	6
			6	7	00

Anno 1684

	John Blackwell per Contra is	Cr	£	s	d
December 20	By Cash received of him	82	40		
	By Xerie wine 3 Butts for 1 Butt of him at	79	25		
	By Proffit & Losse for 2 doz bottle Xerie £1 16s 00d & 2 doz bottles & a Pannier 5s	73	2	1	
January 31	By Cash recd. of him	82	40		
March	By Henry Howard & Company paid them by my order	92	100		
Aprill 1685 13	By Cash recd. of him per the hands of Edward Lloyd	83	25		

			£	s	d
February	To John Mayne for his bill on him from Daniel Whetham for 500 pieces of 8 in favor of Isaac Heming the piece of 8 at 53d as per bill	93	110	8	4
1685 October 28	To Xeries wine in sundry ships from Cadiz for 10 Butts sould him at £23 18s per Butt, lesse 15 Galls ½ 1/8 for ullage of the 10 Butts	101	231	17	6
	To French wine 6 hhds in the Angell Gabriell from Bourdeaux for 2 hhds Sweet lesse 23 ¾ Galls for ullage at £26 per tonne is	94	10	8	6
	To Proffit & Losse for 29 weeks Celleridge of the lower vault in Small Streat	89 *	5	1	6
			483	17	7

Anno 1685

	John Blackwell of Bristoll Vintner	Dr	£	s	d
		£ s d			
November	To Ballance of his former acct. for which I have taken his two bills one Billl for £114 10s payable 28th March next	114 10 0			
	The other bill for £114 10s payable 28th July next	114 10 00	85	229		
1686 Aprill 3	To Xeries wine 6 Butts for said wine sould him payable per bill August 25th next		113	163	10	
	To Proffit & Losse for money remaining on acct. Jos. Baughs redemption at Leghorne		105	1	6	7
				393	16	7

Anno 1684

	Sugar 1 Butt & 15 hhds laden by John Streater & Edm. Scrope in the Wm. & Ann from Nevis	Dr	£	s	d
		£ s d			
January 8	To Cash paid Adam Combes Master for freight & averidge	30 12	82	30	12	
	To Edm. Scrope & John Streater for theire first cost 24624 lb of Sugar at 10s per 100lb as per Invoyce Oct. 6th 1684		33	123	2	5
	To Cash paid custom fees etc.		82	11		10
Aprill 4	To Cash paid weighing them		83		4	7
				164	19	10

(86)   Bristoll 1684

	Simon Clement of Bristoll merchant is	Dr	£	s	d
March 2	To Adventure in the Joseph paid Tho. Callowhill on his bill charg'd there by error R m	85	1	10	2
	To Ditto for the neat proceeds of one Trunck of Stockins sould in Cadiz by him amounting to 799 1/8 pieces of 8 the piece of 8 at 53d as per his acct. of sales closed in Cadiz Feb. 23th 1684/5 and is 6393	85	176	9	5
	To Ditto for my 3/5 of 30 Cask of Butter its neat proceeds as per same acct. amounting to 143¾ pieces of 8 the piece of 8 at 53d 1150	85	31	14	11
			209	14	6

		Cr	£	s	d
	By *Xeries wine 10 Butts in the Rachell for 5 tonns freight from Cadiz at £3 12s per tonne*	93	18		
	By *Proffit & Losse for severall qts & pints of wine and other errors that I can by no meanes finde, for friendship sake I here charge that wee might close all accts to this 27th day of October 1685*	89	4	16	7
November 6	By *Ballance for which I have taken his two bills carried to his new acct. current*	85	229		
			483	17	7

Anno 1686

		Cr	£	s	d
	John Blackwell per Contra is				
May 21	By *John Miles Senior for 2 doz bottles Xerie, with bottles, Pannier & Cover*	114	2	1	
June 7	By *Cash received of him in part*	108	21	17	
16	By *the Lady Ann Pawlet for 2 doz quart bottles of Xerie £2 bottles & cover 1s*	100	2	1	
July 27	By *Isaac Heming for money on John Pococks bill asssign'd mee on Tho. Wootin in London*	113	50		
August	By *Sir George Strode for 2 doz bottles Sack & bottles, & 3 doz Whitewine & bottles, & 3 Panniers*	24	3	19	
	By *the Lady Ann Pawlet for 4 doz qt bottles Xerie & bottles & Panniers*	100	4	2	
16	By *Cash received of him in part*	119	100		
October 9	By *Cash received of him*	120	100		
November 29	By *Cash recd. of him in part*	120	100		
December 3	By *Cash recd. of him in full*	120	9		
	By *Proffit & Losse for severall small parcels of wine recd. of him*	127		16	7
			393	16	7

Anno 1685

		Cr	£	s	d
	Sugar 1 Butt & 15 hhds per Contra				
March 24	By *Charles Herbert and Company for theire value sould them*	93	149	4	
	By *Profit & Loss, for Ballance*	190 *	15	15	10
			164	19	10

Bristoll 1684

		Cr	£	s	d
	Simon Clement per Contra is				
November	By *Adventure in the ship Joseph to Cork & Cadiz for ballance of my 3/5 parts of 30 Cask of Butter laden in said ship in partnership betwixt us* R m	85	1	10	2
March	By *Xeries wine my 2/3 of 10114 Ryals is 1264¼ pieces of 8 the cost & charges of them laden by him in the Joseph the piece of 8 at 53d is sterling £279 4s 10d my 2/3 is* 6743	94	186	3	2
May	By *ballance of this Spanish acct. carried to his new acct. current 99 7/8 pieces of 8 at 53d per piece of 8* 799	86	22	1	2
			209	14	6

Anno 1685				
		Dr	£	s	d

		Dr	£	s	d
May 2	Simon Clement is				
	To ballance of his Spanish acct. 799 Ryals plate is 99 7/8 pieces of 8 at 53d the piece of 8	86	22	1	2
	To Xeries wine 30 Butts for 3 Butts sould him at £15 per Butt	94	45		
	To Olives 14 Jarres for 3 Jarres delivered himself Tho. Callowhill & Tho. Jordan	96		16	6
	To Tho. Harris for 9 Jarres sould him, for which Simon Clement recd. the money	96	2	9	6
	To Cash paid lent him per the hands of Tho. Jordan	83	11	18	
21	To Cash paid him which I recd. of Sir Richard Crump on his bill from Cadiz	83	40	1	
	To Ditto paid him in part	83	50		
June 15	To Cash paid him	83	40		
	To Xeries wine 14 Butts in the Joseph for custom freight and other charges on 11 Butts for his propper acct.	97	61	8	3
	To Isaac Heming for my bill on him in his favor August 20th as per receit	90	60		
	To sundry accts for 6 bottles claret and the bottles at 9s 6d wine & 1s bottles	89, 94		5	6
	To sundry accts for 1 doz bottles claret & bottles	89, 94		11	6
	To Cash paid him in full ballance of all accts Nov. 13th 1685 as per receit	107	6	2	10
			340	14	3

Anno 1684				

		Dr	£	s	d
	Adventure in the ship Andaluzia Capt. John Jacobs from London is debitor to sundry accts being the cost & charges of 2/3 parts of 3 Bales cont. 60 pieces white Colchester Baies laden for my acct. in partnership with John Cooke of London merchant, and goe consign'd to said John Cooke & Samuel Kekewich merchant in St Marie Port the other 1/3 being for acct. of said Cooke as per bill lading (viz)	Dr	£	s	d
October 8	To Isaac Heming for 2/3 of first cost of 40 Crownes at 18d per ell, and 6d per Bay, & 20 Cutts at 17d ½ per ell, & 6d per Bay as per John Cooks acct.	76	155	10	10
	To John Cooke for 2/3 of £9 8s 10d charges on said Baies as per acct. Oct. 13th 1684	32	6	5	11
			165	16	9
	To Profit and Loss, for Ballance	190 *	26	12	3
			188	9	

Anno 1684				

		Dr	£	s	d
	Adventure in the ship Wellcom of Bristoll Philip Freke Master bound to Cadiz in Spaine	Dr	£	s	d
October 25	To acct. of Worsted Stockins for one Trunck containing as underneath laden in said ship, consign'd to John Cook & Samuell Kekewich merchants in St Marie Port viz				
	54 dozen fine Bristoll hose is 648 Paire at 3s per paire £ 97 s 04 d 00	81	113	4	
	13½ doz fine Wells hose at 2s per paire being 160 paire 16 00 00				
	To Cash paid custom Fees etc. for the stockins	82	2	9	3
			115	13	3
	To Profit and Loss, for Ballance	190 *	17	11	1½
			133	4	4½

Anno 1685		Cr	£	s	d
	Simon Clement per Contra is	Cr	£	s	d
May	By Xeries wine 30 Butts for 1/3 of theire first cost bought of him by agreement at £9 sterling per Butt	94	90		
	By Ditto for 6 Butts Xerie bought of him 4 at £17 & 2 at £14 per Butt	94	96		
	By Richard Haines for money recd. of Sir Richard Crump on a bill of Exchange	98	40	1	
	By Olives 14 Jarres on the Joseph for theire neat proceeds	96	2	14	
	By Rice 50 Baggs for the neat proceeds of his 34 Baggs	96	109	9	7
	By Proffitt and Loss for 8 yards ¼ ½ at 5s 7d per yd	105	2	6	8
	By Ditto for Halladge which hee paid	105		3	
			340	14	3

Anno 1684/5		Cr	£	s	d
	Adventure in the Andaluzia per Contra	Cr	£	s	d
March	By John Cook & Samuel Kekewich for the neat proceeds of the Baies per Contra amounting to 6892 Ryals plate is 861½ pieces of 8 the piece of 8 at 52d as per theire acct. closed March 20th 1684/5	88	188	9	

Anno 1684/5		Cr	£	s	d
	Adventure in the ship Wellcom per Contra	Cr	£	s	d
March 20	By John Cook & Samuel Kekewich for the neat proceeds of the trunck of hose per Contra, as per theire acct. of sales of 20th March 1685 is 609 pieces of 8 at 52d ½ the piece of 8	88	133	4	4½

Anno 1684

		£	s	d	Dr	£	s	d
	Adventure in the ship Beniamin of London John Paine Master bound to Cadiz in Spaine is To sundry accts being the cost & charges of one Trunck of worsted hose & 20 pieces Dyed Baies laden in said ship, & consign'd to John Cook & Samuell Kekewich in St Marie Port for sales & returnes viz							
December	*To Isaac Heming for money hee paid for 20 pieces Colchester Baies to Tho. Worrell dyer, white 10 of them at 18d per ell, & 10 at 17½ d, £76 18s 4d, & 7s the piece dying in all is*	83	18	04	*90*			
	To Ditto for custom, packing, charges in shipping etc.	4	00	00	*90*	87	18	4
	To Worsted Stockins for 49 doz is 588 paire Bristoll hose at 3s 1d per paire	90	13	00	*81*			
	To Ditto for 25 doz is 300 paire best Wells at 2s per paire	30	00	00	*81*			
	To Ditto for 80 paire ordinary Wells hose at 1s 8d	6	13	04	*81*			
	To Isaac Heming paid custom, carriage etc. of said Trunck	3	08	11	*90*			
	To Ditto for premium of assureance £200	4	01	00	*90*	134	16	3
						222	14	7
	To Profit and Loss, for Ballance				*190 **	16	1	11½
						238	16	6½

(87) **Bristoll 1684**

		Dr	£	s	d
	Jonathan Lamboll of Reading Maultster is				
November	*To Doct. Francis Hungerford for money hee recd. of him on my bill*	*59*	24	4	
	To Proffit & Losse for money lent him on his bond in Reading payable the 24th day of June next ensuing without intrest	*73*	40		
1685 June	*To John Miles for money received of him by my order*	*114*	2	1	
1685 Sept.	*To Proffit & Losse for money of Thomas Curtis by my order*	*105*		17	
22	*To Isaac Heming for money of him in London on my bill on said Heming*	*113*	50		
	To houses in Fryer Streat for ¼ yeares rent hee received of severall Tenants whose names and rents are recited in the Wastbook November 3rd 1686 due the 24th of June 1686 as per his acct.	*129*	11	3	6
	To Ditto for ¼ yeares rent recd. of same Tenants due 29th Sept. 1686	*129*	11	3	6
	To Dr. Hungerford for money hee recd. of him in Reading	*87*	1	2	11
	To Proffit & Losse for money I left with him to pay Dr. Hungerford	*127 **		4	
			140	15	11

Anno 1684

		Dr	£	s	d
	Doctor Francis Hungerford of Reading Physician				
December	*To sundry accts for 4 Panniers and 10 dos bottles Xerie £8 bottles, Panniers at £1 8s 2d is*	*73, 79*	9	8	2
1685 June 12	*To sundry accts for 10 Doz Xerie, bottles & Panniers sent Sir H Winchcomb*	*89, 94*	9	15	8
July 23	*To sundry accts for 10 dozen Xerie, Bottles & Panniers sent himselfe*	*89, 94*	9	15	8

	Anno 1685	Cr	£	s	d
	Adventure in the ship Beniamin per Contra				
September	*By John Cook & Company for the neat proceeds of the stockins per Contra being 654¾ pieces of 8 as per theire acct. sales dated July 17th 1685 the piece of 8 at 50d*	88	136	8	1½
December	*By Ditto for the neat proceeds of the 20 ps Baies per Contra as per acct. of sale Novem.r 1685 485 7/8 pieces of 8 the piece of 8 at 4s 2d*	88	101	4	7
	By Samuel Kekewich for 45 Ryals overcharg'd on landing the Baies	111	1	3	10
			238	16	6½

	Bristoll 1684	Cr	£	s	d
	Jonathan Lambolt per Contra				
November 1685	*By Proffit & Losse for money recd. of him in London 20 Guinnies and £2 14s silver*	73 *	24	4	
	By Maulting trade in partnership with said Jonathan Lambolt, for the £40 per Contra which hee doth put into our joint stock for that trade, in part of £400 hee is to have of mee being 2/3 parts of £600 wee are to imploy for our joint benefit in that trade	109	40		
1686 June	*By Proffit & Losse for 2000 of fossetts the bagge and charges*	105	1		8
	By Ditto for what hee paid Dr. Hungerford recd. of Tho. Moreman	127			6
	By Houses in Fryer Streat for 4s pd. Bussells hearth money, & 5s 6d for mending Wm. Spotts Chimney	129 *		9	6
September	*By Sarah Lamboll my monther in law for ¼ yeares Annuity due June 24th 1686 paid her*	129	6		
	By Ditto paid her for ¼ yeares Annuity due September 29th 1686	129	6		
	By Bethsuah Wastfield [81] paid Thomas Curtis for her use by my order	124	5		
	By his acct. of Debt on mortgage for the £50 per contra recd. of Isaac Heming	109	50		
	By his new acct. current carried to that acct. of debt	131	8	1	3
			140	15	11

	Anno 1684	Cr	£	s	d
	Doctor Fra. Hungerford per Contra is				
December 19	*By Proffit & Losse recd. of him in Reading my selfe*	73 *	9	8	
	By Isaac Heming for money hee received on Dr. Hungerfords bill in London	90	17	11	4
1686	*By Jonathan Lamboll for money hee received of him*	87	1	2	11
March 9	*By Cash received of him by the hands of Tho. Hungerford*	120	2	5	
1687 Aprill 30	*By Ditto received of Tho. Hungerford*	121	2	1	2

Date	Description		£	s	d
1686 June 4	To sundry accts for ½ doz pints & 1 doz qt bottles Whitewine, pannier, cover & bottles	116,105	1	2	11
February 4	To sundry accts for 2 doz bottles Xerie, bottles & Pannier sent per Tho. Mooreman	132,127	2	1	6
1687	To Proffit & Losse for 2 paire of Stirrupps sent him with the wine	127		3	6
Aprill	To sundry accts for 2 doz bottles Xerie, the bottles, pannier etc.	132,127	2	1	2
August 11	To sundry accts for 1 doz Xerie, 1 doz Whitewine, bottles pannier etc. sent per John Edwards	133,137	1	13	2
December 27	To sundry accts for 2 do Xerie bottles Pannier & portridge sent per Tobias Luton	137	2	1	2
1688 August 23	To sundry accts for 2 doz. Xerie 1 doz at 16s & 1 doz at 18s with bottles & a Pannier	150,153	1	19	2
1689 June 15	To sundry accts for 1 doz qts & 1 doz pints Xerie, with bottles Pannier etc. sent per Tho. Mooreman	150,164	2	1	8
			42	3	9

Anno 1684

Date	Description		£	s	d
	William Fisher of Bristoll Marriner Master of the ship Agreement To Adventure the 2nd in the ship Agreement to Cadiz for the neat proceeds of 56 doz Bristoll hose, & 30 Firkins Butter, consign'd to him in said ship for sales and returnes 6008¾ Ryal plate being 701¾ pieces of 8 Ryals the piece of 8 at 4s 6d	Dr	£	s	d
		78	169	2	10½

Anno 1684

Date	Description		£	s	d
	Xeries Wine 20 Butts laden per Samuel Kekewich in the ship Expectation Robert Alexander Master from Cadiz	Dr	£	s	d
January	To John Cook & Samuel Kekewich for theire first cost 6262½ Ryals plate is 78¾ pieces of8 & ¼ a Real, the piece of 8 at 4s 4d as per theire Invoice Dec. 31 1684	88	169	12	2
	To Cash paid custom fees & Prisage	82	65	11	3
	To Cash paid Freight & averidge to Robert Alexander	83	33	6	8
			268	10	1

Anno 1685

Date	Description		£	s	d
	Edward Shippen of Boston in New England merchant is	Dr	£	s	d
August	To Adventure in the Phoenix to New England Wm. Lloyd Master, for the neat proceeds of 4 pieces Broadcloth left with him the said Lloyd for sales as per his acct. from Boston of the sales thereof received from him 1685	31	37	18	

Anno 1684

Date	Description		£	s	d
	Thomas Walden is	Dr	£	s	d
	To ballance of his former accct current for 6 bottles of Xerie etc.	2		8	
January 26/27	To Cash lent him paid George Bent £50 & to John Mandevill £50 by his order	82	100		
1685 May 29	To Proffit & Losse for 4 months intrest due 27th of May 1685	89	2	1	
July 4	To Cash paid him	83	3		
	To Proffit & Losse for Premio remitting money to London	89	1	17	5
	To wines 6 hhds in the Angell Gabriell & Proffit & Losse for eight qrt bottles claret & the bottles	(89), 94		7	8
October 1686	To Ditto for 6 qt bottles whitewine & 21 qrt bottles claret & the bottles	(89), 94	1	5	10
November 27	To Cash paid lent him on his noat	120	5		
1689 May 6	To Tho. Day for 1 doz bottles claret and the bottles	161		14	
			114	13	11

			£	s	d
	By *Proffit & Losse for money abated him*	127	2		2
August 31	By *Cash recd. of Tho. Hungerford by his order*	139	1	13	2
February 11	By *Cash recd. of Tho. Hungerford in full*	140	2	1	2
1688 Sept. 5	By *Cash recd. of Tho. Hungerford in full*	141	1	19	2
1689 August 23	By *Cash recd. of Tho. Hungerford*	168	2	1	8
			42	3	9

Anno 1684					
William Fisher per Contra is		Cr	£	s	d
By *John Brooking & Company for 700 Pieces of 8 delivered*					
them at 4s 6d per piece of 8		88	168	15	
By *Profit and Loss for Ballance*		190 *		7	10½
			169	2	10½

Anno 1684/5					
Xeries Wine 20 Butts per Contra are		Cr	£	s	d
By *Xeries wine in sundry ships for the cost & Charges on the 10*					
Butts per contra carried to that acct. to avoyd confusion in Sales		101	268	10	1

Anno 1686					
Edward Shippen per Contra is		Cr	£	s	d
By *Adventure in the ship — for sundry merchandizes laden in*					
the said ship in Boston for my acct., & consigned to John Streater					
& Edmond Scrope merchants in Nevis, as per his Invoyce &					
acct. current sent mee bearing date Sept. 14th 1686 recorded in					
my book of Invoyces No E folio 11 & my bundle of accts may					
appear		126	37	13	5
By *Profit and Loss, for Ballance*		190 *		4	7
			37	18	

Anno 1685					
Tho. Walden per Contra is		Cr	£	s	d
May 29	By *Cash received of Nath. Pinny in full of his bond and intrest*	83	102		
July 4	By *Proffit & Losse for money formerly borrrowed of him by my*				
	sonne Jahzeel	89	3		
	By *Ditto for 1 doz Inkle*	89		8	
August	By *Ditto for 1 doz Inkle*	89		7	10
	By *Ditto for Tape and Twine*	89			10
	By *Cash recd. of him*	84	1	8	9
	By *Profit & Losse for 1 doz Inkle*	105		7	
November 10	By *Cash received of him*	107	1	7	6
1687 June 1	By *Cash recd. of him in full*	121	5		
1689 May 8	By *Cash recd. of himselfe*	162		14	
			114	13	11

(88)	**Bristoll 1684**						
	John Cooke now resident in or near London & Samuel Kekewich resident in St Marie Port in Spaine, Merchants and Factors in partnership for sales and returnes of goods			Dr	£	s	d
November	To Adventure in the ship Friston Capt. Gutheridge to Cadiz, for the neat proceeds of one Trunck of hose as per theire acct. Oct. 24th 1684 valuing the piece of 8 (being 778 pieces of 8 & 1 Ryal plate) at 52d	R 6226	m	64	168	11	10
March	To Adventure in the Agreement Capt. Wm. Fisher from Bristoll for the neat proceeds of one Trunck of hose as per theire acct. closed October 24th 1684 the piece of 8 being 814 pieces of 8	6512	17	78	176	7	4
20	To Adventure in the ship Wellcom for the neat proceeds of a Trunck of Hoses as per theire acct. closed March 20th 1684/5 pieces of 8 609 at 52d ½ per piece of 8	4877	17	86	133	4	4½
	To Adventure in the Andaluzia for the neat proceeds fo 2/3 parts of 60 pieces Baies in partnership with John Cooke being 861½ pieces of 8 the piece of of 8 at 52d½ as per theire acct. closed March 20th 1684/5	6892	17	86	188	9	
	To Ballance carried to theire Credit in theire new acct. current	3252	17	88	88	6	8
		27761	17				

	Anno 1685						
	John Cooke & Samuel Kekewich merchants in St Marie Port are			Dr	£	s	d
Sept.	To Adventure in the Beniamin for the neat proceeds of a Trunck Stockins, as per theire acct. of sales July 17th 1685 654 pieces of 8 3/4 the piece of 8 at 50d	R 5235	m	86	136	8	1½
December	To Adventure 2nd in the Mauritanea for the neat proceeds of a Trunck Stockins 1021 pieces of 8 as per acct. of sales Novem.br 1685 the piece of 8 at 4s 2d	8168		93	212	14	2
	To Adventure in the Beniamin for the neat proceeds of 20 pieces dyed Baies 485 7/8 pieces of 8 the piece at 4s 2d as per acct. sales November 1685	3887		86	101	4	7
	To Adventure in partnership in the Cesar for ½ 7351 Ryals plate 17Mervides is 459 3/8 pieces of 8 25Mervides piece of 8 at 4s 2d as per acct. sales of the Trunck Stockins	3675	25	100	95	14	5
	To Adventure in the Merchants Goodwill for the neat proceeds of a Trunck hose 925¼ pieces of 8 the piece of 8 at 4s 2d as per acct. sales November 1685	7402		97	192	15	4
	To Adventure in the Civilia Merchant for 950 1/8 pieces of 8 the neat proceeds of a Trunck of hose as per acct. of Sales November 1685 the piece of 8 at 4s 2d	7601		101	197	19	4
		35968	25				

Bristoll 1684

		R	m	Cr	£	s	d
	John Cooke & Samuel Kekewich per Contra are			Cr	£	s	d
November	By Isaac Heming for money hee recd. of Wm. Atwell & Adrian Courtenay for 800 pieces of 8 in the Merchants Goodwill at 5s 3¼d the oz as per his acct. Nov. 1684	6741	17	76	181	13	6
March 1685	By Xeries wine 20 Butts in the Expectation for theire first cost 782 3/4 pieces of 8 & ½ a Real, the piece of 8 at 4s 4d as per theire Invoyce of 31st Oct. 1684	6262	17	87	169	12	2
	By Isaac Heming & Company for money of Henry Finch on theire bill for piece of 8 at 53d	3254	17	90	88	6	8
	By Plate in sundry ships for the cost & charges of 500 pieces of 8 in the James to Is. Heming	4274		92	112	10	
	By Isaac Heming for money of Tho. Lambert on Robt. Wilmets bill for 250 pieces of 8 & charge	2034		90	54	13	9
	By Plate for one bundle wrought Silver, & 311½ pieces of 8 in the Britton as per Invoyce sent to Lond.	5194	17	92	140	13	4
		27761	17				

Anno 1685

		R	m	Cr	£	s	d
	John Cooke and Samuel Kekewich are			Cr	£	s	d
May	By Ballance of theire former acct. current agreeing with theire acct.	3254	17	88	88	6	8
October	By Plate out of severall ships for 2 Cakes silver in the Saphire 53m 4½ at 72½	4030		92	103	9	
December	By Ditto for the cost & charges 3 Cakes silver in the Unity 710 7/8 pieces of 8 the piece of 8 at 4s 2d as per Invoyce Nov. 5th 1685	5687		92	148	1	10
	By Ditto for the cost & charges of 2 baggs cont. No 1 650 pieces of 8 No 2 600 pieces of 8, and one bundle cont. 43 marks 6 oz wrought plate in the Crowne Capt. Dorrill of which were wanting in the baggs No 1 139 pieces of 8 all by Invoyce Nov. 1685 6728¼ pieces of 8 at 4s the piece	13462		92	336	11	
	By Isaac Heming for 1/2 theire bill of £113 3s 4d for 2094½ Ryals plate on William Windham at 52d½ the piece of 8 at 4s 4d lesse 2s 10d on the whole	2094	17	90	56	11	8
		28528	·		733		2
	By Ballance carryed to theire new acct. current conformeable to theire own acct. current sent mee per Robert Massinger in the Dilligence closed December 1685 as may appeare	7440	25	111	193	15	
		35968	25				

	Anno 1684	Dr	£	s	d
	John Broking (now resident in London) but in partnership with Parker & Holditch merchants factors in Leghorne	Dr	£	s	d
October 23	To William Fisher for 750 pieces of 8 received of him out of the ship Agreement of Bristoll the piece of 8 at 4s 6d as per theire acct. of sales	78	168	15	
	To Profit and Loss, for Ballance	190 *	5	19	6
			174	14	6

	Anno 1684	Dr	£	s	d
	Ralph Grant of Bristoll Brewer is	Dr	£	s	d
February 4	To Cash lent him on a mortgage on his Land in Coningsburie alias Coomsberrie in the County of Somerset & Certaine houses over against the Almeshouse beyond Redcliffe hill, made to Cos. Nath. Haggatt, & Cosen Thomas Walden in trust for mee as may appeare, to pay intrest after the £ s d rate of £5 10s 00d per Cent 300 00 00	82	300		
1685 February 5	To Proffit & Losse for 1 yeares intrest due 5th February 1685	105 *	16	10	
1687 August 4	To Ditto for intrest due 4th August 1687	137	24	15	
		.	341	5	

	Anno 1684/5	Dr	£	s	d
	Elizabeth Tayler of Bristoll widow	Dr	£	s	d
March 14	To Cash paid lent her on her receit & obligation in receit book	82		10	00
1686 July 22	To Cash paid lent her	119		5	
August 7	To Cash paid lent her	119		5	
September 4	To Cash paid her	119	1		
October 2	To Cash paid her	119	7		
			9		
	To Profit & Loss, for Ballance	190 *		16	11
			9	16	11

(89)	**Bristoll 1684**	Dr	£	s	d
	Proffit & Losse is	Dr	£	s	d
	To Ballance brought from that acct.	73	901	11	9
	To Isaac Heming paid Tho. Cox for severall parcells of wine	76	5	11	9
	To Ditto paid Philip Higgenbottom and for a hatt for mee	76	3	11	
	To Isaac Heming for a Westphalia Ham & money paid Jos. Tily	76	3	11	
	To Ditto for a ham 8s 6d, & port of leters £1 9s 6d	76	2	7	11
	To Ditto pd. Tho. Curtis £1, Cleark Crowne £1 0s 6d a book 10s to myselfe £5 to Robt. Payne £4	76	11	10	6
	To Ditto for money to Abraham Beele £5 1s 9d carriage a Trunck 16s & port of leters 9s 3d	76	6	7	
	To Ditto for 3 & 8 Guinnies	76	11	12	
	To Ditto for charges to Bristol £3 15s printed Avizoes 15s & paid Robt. Payne £1	76	5	10	
	To Ditto paid carriage of a box 3s 2d & to Jos. Tily £6 9s	76	6	12	2
	To Ditto for money of him in silver £4 & 45 Guinnies	76	52	7	6
	To Ditto for money of him	76	1	3	2
	To Ditto for 2 silver spoones	90		18	
	To Ditto for fraight Gold 9s 9d Racking Leather 8s 6d Port of leters £1 17s 10d	90	2	16	1
	To Ditto for expences to Reading £1 1s 6d Coach earnest 10s & to the Tayler 3s	90 *	1	14	6
	To Ditto for Alice's Coate, carriage of Truncks, and money of him at severall times	90	12	8	2
	To Ditto for money of him, pd. the French master, bottles & wine and money of him	90	10	18	
	To Ditto for money paid Charles Reynoldson for wine	90	1	12	5

Anno 1684		Cr	£	s	d
	John Broking & Company per Contra				
December	By Isaac Heming for money hee received for the neat proceeds of the				
	750 pieces of 8 per Contra sould by them in Leghorne & remitted				
	to mee in London by theire bill of Exchange on said Broking in				
	my favor as per theire acct. closed in Leghorne October 23th 1684	90	174	14	6

Anno 1686		Cr	£	s	d
	Ralph Grant per Contra is				
July 14	By Cash received of himselfe	119	16	10	
1687 August 4	By Cash received of John Hawkins by his order in full	121	324	15	
			341	5	

Anno 1685		Cr	£	s	d
	Elizabeth Taylor per Contra				
June 27	By Cash recd. of her	83		10	
	By acct. of Sugar one Butt For acct. of Eliz. Tailor for it's neat				
	proceeds	103	9	06	11
			9	16	11

Bristoll 1684

		Cr	£	s	d
	Proffit & Losse is				
	By Tho. Cook & Company for intrest money	51	11		
	By Tho. Scrope for ½ 15s paid per Isaac Heming for printed Avizoes	75		7	6
	By Tho. Cook & Company for 6 months intrest of £600	51	15		
	By Frances Beckford for ½ yeares intrest of £1500	72	45		
	By Isaac Heming for 20 Guinnies delivered him	90	21	11	3
	By Ditto for money 7 Guinnies I paid him, & 2s 6d hee recd. of John Wilmer	90	8	2	6
	By Isaac Heming for money hee recd. of mine of John Haggatt in London February 1681	90	150		
	By John Harris for 2 cases sould him	92		4	
1685 March	By Henry Bainham for 1 yeares intrest of £276 due 5th Aprill 1685	48	16	11	2
	By Cash recd. of Edward Harvord for 10 weeks celleridge	82	2	5	
	By Sugar 10 hhds of John Browne for halling them at severall times	65		3	6
	By Ditto for hooping them before ship'd	65		10	
May	By John Earle of Bristoll for ½ yeares intrest of £100	80	3		
	By Edward Crofts for ¼ yeares rent of the house in Small Streat	96	9		
	By Tho. Walden for 4 months intrest of £100	87	2		
	By Wm. Prichard & Company for ½ yeares intrest of £50 ending Aprill 2nd 1685	63	1	10	
	By adventure in the Merchants Goodwill for a Trunck	97		18	
	By Tho. Lutterell for the intrest of £10	25		13	
	By John Earle of Sunderland for halling 3 Panniers, & port of leters	99		1	

Date		Folio	£	s	d
	To Ditto paid for a Ham 5s 6d to Tho. Curtis £30 charge on a Chest 5s 2d port leters £1 9s 2d	90	32	3	8
	To Ditto paid Sam. Davis for an Iron Chest £5 1s 9d & money of him in London £6	90	11	1	9
	To Ditto to losse on Guinnies 4s 2d a Correll [82] £7 10s Butter £1 3s & pd. Richard d Haynes 2 4 6	90	11	1	8
	To Ditto for Brokeridge 9s a book 3s 6d a firkin Butter £1 4s sugar £3 8s port leters £1 17s 5d	90	7	1	11
	To Ditto pd. Tho. Cox £27 9s 9d for a ham 7s 10d	90	27	17	7
	To Ditto pd. charges on Trunck hose 1 1 3 Phil. Ward 5 7 6 money of him £6 port leters & Trunck £1 10s	90	13	18	9
	To Ditto for money of him £3 10s for butter £1 10s for a looking Glasse 3 15 in all	90	8	15	
	To Cash paid Robert Gibbons in full for keeping my mare	89	3	4	6
	To Cash paid houshold expences ending Dec. 30th	82	20	0	8
January	To Cash paid John Cheshire for Bottles	82	2	12	9
	To Cash paid severall charges on a Butt of Xerie	82	5	3	2
	To Isaac Heming for 23 Guinies of him in London	90	24	15	11
	To Ditto for a Choccolat pot, Coffee pot etc. & £20 to John Wilmer	90	20	13	8
	To Ditto for a Case for Iron Chest 5s & port of leters to 9th March 1684 £2 3s	90	2	8	
	To Cash paid houshold expences	82	12	18	8
	To Cash paid Tobias Luton for carriage of goods	82	1	9	
February 27	To Cash paid Robert White 6d & houshold expences £8 3s 11d	82	8	4	5
March 5	To Ditto paid Humphry Corsley for a Tankard	82	7	9	
	To Ditto paid John Moore for cloth, & in full of all acct.s	82	2	7	3
18	To Ditto paid John Hardiman in full of his noat	82	2	16	
	To John Love for ballance	55	5	8	9
Aprill 20	To Olives 14 Jarres for acct. Simon Clement for 1 Jarre	96		5	6
22	To Cash paid Tho. Browne in full of his noat	83	1	1	
	To Cash paid Jane Flower in full of her noat for halling	83	6	9	6
			1284	11	
25	To Cash paid Edward Iffe in full	83		6	
May 7	To Cash paid houshold expences	83	20	7	11
	To Joane Darracot for 1 yeares wages due June 24th 1685	98	2	15	
	To Martha Linch for ¼ yeares wages due June 30th being ¼ of 45s	92		11	3
15	To Cash paid James Swetnham in full	83		12	
	To Ditto paid for a Firkin & a Pott of Butter	83	1	15	9
28	To Cash paid given Sarah Maycock for her necessity	83		10	
	To Sugar 10 hhds in partnership with Sam. Davis for ½ the charges on them	65		13	4
	To Cash paid Ann Clement for 20 Panniers	83		17	
	To John Wilmer for a Cheese bought in London & sent in to Isaac Heming	62		10	5
June 29	To Cash paid John Cheshire for 30 doz bottles	83	2	18	
	To Tho. Walden for money formerly borrowed of him	87	3		
	To Cash paid John Sandford in full	83		11	
	To Cash paid Roger Addams in full for Mault	83	2	4	6
	To Tho. Walden for 2 doz Inkle & tape	87		16	8
	To the Lady Ann Pawlet for ballance	48			9
	To John Gore & Company recd. of John Gore on acct. for keeping my horses	56		15	
July 24	To Cash paid Joseph Drew in full	83	1	1	
	To Ditto paid Joseph Owen in full for work and keeping the house	83	1	11	
	To Ditto paid Robert Summers in full	83		11	
	To Cash paid John Hardiman in full	84	1		

By John Earle of Bristoll for port of 2 leters to & from Isaac Heming	37			6
By Joseph Badger for money paid him & wrong charg'd	50	2	9	4
By Edward Lloyd for halling, cooperidge & other charges on 2 Butts Xerie	95		4	
By Xeries wine 14 Butts for acct. Simon Clement for Celleridge & halling	97		15	3
By Adventure in the Cesar to Cadiz, for a Trunck, cord, matting etc.	100		17	
By Xeries wine 14 Butts for acct. Simon Clement for Cooperidge & commission	97	4	10	
By Rice 50 Baggs for odd pence abated & my Commission	96	4	5	3
By Tho. Walden for Premium for remittance of money to London	87	1	17	5
By the Lady Ann Powlet for 4 doz bottles, 2 panniers etc.	100		11	2
By Dr. Fra. Hungerford for 10 doz bottles, panniers etc.	87	1	5	8
By Ditto for 10 doz bottles, Panniers etc.	87	1	5	8
By the Lady Ann Powlet for 4 doz bottles, & 2 Panniers	100		11	2
By Sir Wm. Drake for 6 doz bottles, 3 Panniers & Covers	100		16	9
By sundry accts for 16 2/3 doz bottles at 2s per dozen	99,55 94,95 87	1	13	4
By Simon Clement for 6 bottles	86		1	
October By John Earle of Bristoll for 1/2 yeares intrest of £100 due Sept. 11th past	80	3		
By Tho. Walden for 3 doz bottles	87		6	
By Tho. Day for 2 doz bottles at 2s	94		4	
By Henry Howard & Company for 1/2 yeares intrest of £100	92	3		
By Simon Clement for 1 doz bottles for Claret	86		2	
		315	2	5
By Ballance carried to that acct.	105	1092	14	1
		1407	16	6

			£	s	d
August 6	To Cash paid David Phillips for Drums & Colours	84		7	
	To Tho. Jordan for his severall small goods as per his noat	95	1	1	7
	To Ed. Croft for the rent of 2 Chambers for ½ yeare reserved ending 24 June 1685	96	1		
	To Cash paid for 22½ lb butter	84		10	3
	To Cash paid Martha and Jahzeel at theire going to London	84	2		
	To Ditto paid John Sandford in full	84	1	1	9
	To John Sandford lost by him for ballance of his acct.	19		5	9
September 28	To Cash paid houshold expences £52 2s 8d & houshold, Tho. Walden 7s	84	52	9	8
	To Ditto paid for a Barnstable oven	84 *		5	6
	To Cash paid John Matthew for dressing severall hatts	84	4		
	To John Blackwell for severall small parcells wine & errors that I cannot finde out	85	4	16	7
	To John Jones for severall parcells of Linnin etc. as per noat of particulars	99	13	10	10
	To Cash paid Edward Driver for Carridge & portridge of goods to the Fra. & Marie	84		7	
	To Ditto paid Walter Payne for mending an old chayre	84		1	6
	To Ditto paid Ed. Tyler for shooing my Mare	84		6	6
	To Ditto for paid Philip Higgenbottom for 1cwt of Cheese	84	1	10	
			123	5	6
			1407	16	6

(90)	**Bristoll 1684**				
	Isaac Heming is	Dr	£	s	d
	To ballance of his former acct. current	76	2997	17	9
	To Isaac Heming & Company for ½ yeares intrest of £400 due May 10th 1684	69	16		
June 14	To Frances Beckford recd. of her for principall and intrest	72	1545		
July 15	To Robert Richardson for money of him for ½ yeares intrest of £150 due June 1684	35	3	15	
September 29	To sundry accts for the neat proceeds of 6 Butts & 12 hhds Sugar consign'd him	33, 75, 76	181	17	2
	To Sugar 4 hhds in the Restauration for the neat proceeds sent in the Comfort	75	42	9	7
	To Proffit & Losse for 20 Guinnies delivered him as per his acct. closed Nov. 20th 1684	89	21	11	3
	To Ditto for money I paid him in London £8 & 2s 6d of John Wilmer for Exchange 100 Guinnies	89	8	2	6
December	To John Broking & Company for money recd. of said Broking on theire bill	88	174	14	6
	To Robert Richardson for ½ yeares intrest of £150 ending Dec. 1684	35	3	15	
	To Proffit & Losse for money of John Haggatt which hee received by a bill in London from his Bro. Nathanaell Haggatt as per his acct. sent mee Feb. 1681	89	150		
	To Ditto for ballance of errors committed, in acct. with him for 3 yeares past , which I cannot find out but do ballance this acct. with his acct. current sent mee closed March 10th 1684/5 as may appear per the same	89 *	9	8	6
			5145	2	9

Bristoll 1684

		Cr	£	s	d
	Isaac Heming per Contra is				
	By Proffit & Losse for 2 Silver Spoones	89		18	
	By Adventure in the Rachell to Cadiz for assurance money	63	3		
	By Proffit & Losse paid freight of Gold 9s 9d, for racking Leathers, 8s 6d port leters £1 17s 10d	89	2	16	1
	By Andrew Kirby Father & Sonne for money paid Jaques Gonsailes for his bill in theire favor	64	113	5	7
	By Isaac Heming & John Barnard for money they took at intrest at £4 per Cent on theire bond for which they stand debited	69	400		
	By Proffit & Losse pd. for Alice' Coate £2 8s money of him £9 4s 8d, carriage & port leters 15s 6d	89	12	8	2
	By Ditto for money of him £4 pd. the French master £3 bottles hampior & wine £2 7s & money of him £2	89	10	18	
	By Ditto for money paid Charles Reynoldson for wine	89	1	12	5
	By Marie Wasbrow for a racking bearer	75		5	6
	By Proffit & Losse for a ham 9s 4d pd. Tho. Curtis £30 charge on a Chest 5s 2d Port leters £1 9s 2d	89	32	3	8
	By Ditto pid Samuel Davis on my bill £5 1s 9d & money of him in London £6	89	11	1	9
	By Frances Beckford for money lent her on a mortgage	72	1500		
	By Proffit & Losse for losse on Guinnies 4s 2d a Corrall [21] £7 10s Butter £1 3s & pd. Richard Haynes £2 4s 6d	89	11	4	8
	By Ditto paid Brokeridge 9s for a book 3s 6d for Butter £1 4s James Deane Sugar £3 8s Port leters £1 17s 5d in all	89	7	1	11
	By Ditto paid Tho. Cox £27 9s 9d & for a ham 7s 10d	89	27	17	7
	By Dennis Tayler paid him on my bill	11	13		
	By Proffit & Losse for charge Trunck hose £1 1s 3d Phil. Ward £5 7s 6d, money of him £6 Port leters & of a Truncke £1 10s in all	89	13	18	9
	By Ditto for money of him £3 10s a firkin Butter £1 10s & a Looking Glasse £3 15s in all	89	8	15	
February 2	By Cash recd. of Peter Sanders, for my Bill on him in his favor	82	130		
	By Ditto recd. of Samuel Davis, for my bill on him in his favor	82	300		
4	By Ditto for money of Jacob Beele for my 2 bills on him in his favor	82	100		

	Anno 1684				
	Isaac Heming of London Merchant & Company	Dr	£	s	d
March 9	To ballance of theire last acct. current of 9th March 1684	90	1804	19	10
	To John Cook & Samuel Kekewich for money recd. of Henry Finch on theire bill	88	88	6	8
	To Arthur Robinson & Company for theire bill on Tho. Shepheard for 2576½ Ryals	61	70	5	7
	To Sugar 2 Butts & 8 hhds in the Dyamond Ketch from Nevis for theire neat proceeds	64	76	11	3
1685 Aprill 4	To Cash paid John Gandy Junior for so much hee recd. of John Budget for said Gandy's acct.	83	31		
	To John Cook & Samuel Kekewich for Robt. Wilmets bill on Tho. Lambart for 250 pieces of 8	88	54	13	9
July 9	To John Earle of Bristoll recd. of Wm. Webb by his order in London	37	5	13	4
	To Robert Earle of Sunderland recd. of his Countesse in London on my bill	99	9	12	8
	To Cash paid Elizabeth Tayler on his bill of Exchange in his favor	83	20		
	To Adventure in partnership for ½ cost & charges of a Trunck of stockins in the Cesar Capt. Wm. Maddison to Cadiz for acct. of my selfe and his wife	100	75	3	7
	To Plate in severall ship from Cadiz for 278 oz wrought plate in the Britton which 278 oz at 4s 8d per oz	92	64	17	4
	To Ditto for 800½ pieces of 8 weight 692½ oz at 5s 2d per oz as per leter Oct. 8th 1685	92	178	17	11
October	To Plate out of severall ships for 2 Cakes silver sould weight 395½ oz at 5s 3d	92	103	9	
	To Cash paid Elizabeth Tayler on his bill	84	5		
	To Peter Bishop of Winchester for money recd. of mee which I recd. of him in London as per his receit	78	50		
	To Proffit & Losse for 100 Guinnies hee recd. by my consignement in a Trunck hose	105 *	107	10	
	To Exchange in partnership for ½ £200 remitted by bill per Sam. Kekewich & Company on Joseph Herne	99	100		

			£	s	d
	By Cash recd. of Simon Hurle for which I valued my bill on him	82	100		
7	By Ditto recd. of Tho. Walden for which I valued my 3 bills in his favor	82	300		
	By Ditto recd. of John Watson for which I valued my bill in his favor	82	100		
	By Proffit & Losse for 23 Guinnies of him in London as per acct. closed March 1684	89	24	15	11
	By Adventure in the Beniamin to Cadiz paid Tho. Worrell for 10 pieces Baies & charge Custom etc.	86	87	18	4
	By Proffit & Losse for Choccolate pot etc. 13s 8d & paid John Wilmer £20	89	20	13	8
	By Adventure in the Beniamin for custom etc. of Trunck hose £2 14s 2d, carriage of ditto 14s 9d	86	3	8	11
	By ditto for premium of assureance of £200 on her goods to Cadiz	86	4	1	
	By Proffit & Losse for a Looking Glasse £5 12s 6d & a bottle of Oyle 6s	89 *	5	18	6
	By Ditto for a Case for my Iron Chest	89		5	
	By Ditto for port of leters to 9th march 1684	89	2	3	
			3249	19	10
	By Ballance resting due as per his acct. closed March 9th 1684 carried to that acct.	90	1804	19	10
			5145	2	9

	Anno 1684/5				
	Isaac Heming & Company, being John Barnard merchant per Contra	Cr	£	s	d
March 6	By Cash received of Tho. Day for which I valued my 2 bills	82	86	7	
	By Adventure in the Mauritania to Cadiz for charges on a Trunck hose in her	93	4	19	6
	By Port Wines 6 hhds in the Angell Gabriell from Bourdeauxe for Tho. Arundells bill 77 Ecu 5sous 6 denier at 56d	94	18	3	8
1685	By Adventure in the Mercants Goodwill to Cadiz for charges on a Trunck of hose	97	4	5	2
Aprill	By Andrew Kirby Father & Sonne for theire bill paid George Toriano	64	7	6	7
	By Cash for money of Tho. Day for my bill on him in favor of Wm. Denn	83	55	9	4
	By Exchange to Spaine in partnership for ½ £205 4s 2d pd. for a bill 1000 pieces of 8 at 49d¼	99	102	12	1
	By Adventure in partnership in the Cesar to Cadiz for charges on a Trunck of hose	100	4	4	6
	By Cash recd. of John Bubb for which I valued my bill on him in his favor	83	100		
August	By Simon Clement for my bill on him in his favor	86	60		
	By Exchange to Spaine for ½ a bill of Exchange of Sir Ben. Newland for 1000 pieces of 8 at 49d 7/8 sent Cook & Kekewich	99	103	18	1½
September	By Adventure in the Civillia Merchant for Cadiz for the charges on a Trunck of stockins	101	4	19	7
	By Cash recd. of Richard Stubbs for my two bills on him	84	57	4	
	By Cash recd. of John Bubb for my bill in his favor on said Heming	84	100		
	By Ditto received of Tho. Walden for my bill on him in favor of said Walding	84	120		
	By Cash received of Tho. Walden for my bill on him in his favor	84	334	7	4
	By Proffit & Losse for 40 papers powder £1 10s & 40 papers more £1	105	2	10	
	By Jahzeel Speed paid him in London	69	3		
	By Martha Speed paid her in London	46	5		
	By Proffit & Losse for port of leters to the 29th Sept. 1685	105	2	3	6

			£	s	d
	To John Cook & Sam. Kekewich for ½ £113 3s 4d theire bill of Exchange on Wm Windham for acct. in equall halves betwixt mee and his wife Mehetabel	88	56	11	8
	To Exchange to Spaine in partnership for ½ £211 4s 5d recd. of Wm. Atwill & Company for the neat proceeds of 950 pieces of 8 sent per Cook & Kekewich in the Unity in part of 2 bills sent m/y	99	105	12	2½
December	To Plate out of sundry ships from Spaine, received of Wm. Atwill & Company for 1111 pieces of 8, and a bundle Plate in the Crowne, and 3 Cakes silver in the Unity as per acct.	92	468	6	
	To himselfe & John Barnard for 1½ yeares intrest of £400 ending Nov. 10 1685	69	24		
	To Matthew Walter & Company for John Bubbs bill assign'd by him on Tho. Lane	103	20		
	To Exchange acct. for ½ neat 88¾ pieces of 8 per the Ruby weight 77¼ onz at 5s 2d¼ per onz	99	9	18	1
	To Doctor Hungerford for money received on his bill in London	87	17	11	4
	To Proffit & Losse for 2 Guinnies delivered him when I came out of London	105	2	3	
	To Adventure in partnership in the Wellcom to Cadiz for ½ the cost and charge of a Trunck of stockins sent twixt my wife and his etc.	110	73	4	3
			3623	7	5½

---

(91)   ***Bristoll 1684***

	Worsted Stockins are	Paire	s	d	Dr	£	s	d
13	To Cash paid Tho. Hill for	200	1	5	82	14	3	4
February 16	To Ditto paid Edward Iffe for hot pressing to this day				82		13	4
20	To Ditto paid Andrew Creed for	120	1	4	82	8		
	To Ditto paid Andrew Creed for	53	2	6¼	82	6	14	8
	To Ditto paid John Massinger for	30	2	8	82	4		
21	To Ditto paid Tho. Hill for	25	2	6	82	3	2	6
	To Ditto paid Joseph White for	41	2	8	82	5	9	4
27	To Ditto paid Joel Pinne for	20	2	5	82	2	8	4
	To Ditto paid John Massinger for	35	2	8	82	4	13	4
	To Ditto paid Edward Iffe in for hot pressing 418 paire 5d per score				82		8	9
March 5	To Ditto paid John Massinger for	35	2	8	82	4	13	
	To Ditto paid Joseph White for	46	2	8	82	6	2	8
7	To Ditto paid John Perrie for	67	2	6¼	82	8	8	10
14	To Ditto paid Tho. Hill for	29	2	5¾	82	3	12	
	To Ditto paid John Massinger for	35	2	8	82	4	13	4
18	To Ditto paid John Massinger for	40	2	8	82	5	7	
21	To Ditto paid Joel Pinne for	12	2	5	82	1	9	
	To Ditto paid John Perrie for	47	2	6¼	82	5	18	6
1685	To Ditto paid Joseph White for	41	2	8	82	5	9	2
27	To Ditto paid Tho. Hill for	200	1	4	82	13	6	8
	To Ditto paid John Massinger for	40	2	8	82	5	6	8
28	To Ditto paid Andrew Creed for	132	1	4	82	8	16	
	To Ditto paid Joseph White for	48	2	8	82	6	8	
Aprill 2	To Ditto paid John Perrie for	42	2	6¼	82	5	5	10
4	To Ditto paid John Massinger for	40	2	8	83	5	6	8
	To Ditto paid Joseph White for	54	2	8	83	7	4	
	To Ditto paid Henry Britton for	60	2	4½	83	7	2	6

	By Ditto paid to Philip Ward per my order	105	5	7	6
October	By Martha Speed paid her in London	109	2		
2	By Maulting trade in partnership with Jonathan Lamboll pd. said Lamboll on my bill	109	100		
14	By Ditto paid said Lamboll on my Bill on same acct.	109	100		
	By Adventure in the Rebeckah to Cadiz paid for 40 ps Baies, dying 20 £7 packing etc.	109	165	12	4
November 16	By Maulting trade in partnership with Jonathan Lamboll pd. said Lamboll on my bill	109	100		
	By Tho. Day Wine Cooper for money pd. on said Day's bill in favor of Wm. Denne	70	23		
	By Adventure in the Rebeckah paid charges on a Trunck of stockins	109	5	4	5
	By Cash recd. of John Hartnell by his order	107	2	14	3
	By Cash recd. of Sir John Smith for which Jahzeel valued a bill on said Hemming	107	100		
	By Adventure in the Rebeckah to Cadiz paid Premio of assurance for £200 thither	109	3	1	
	By Proffit & Losse recd. of him in London £2, & of another time & times £11	105	13		
	By sundry accts for Premio of assurance of £300 on Goods in the Welcom to Cadiz	110	6	1	
	By sundry accts for Premio of assurance of £200 on Goods in the Betty to Cadiz	110, 111	5	11	6
	By Tho. Day for 2 bills drawne on him in favor of said Day £13 6s 7d/ £93 12s 9d	70	106	19	4
			1915	1	8
	By ballance carried to his acct. of debt in a new acct.	100	1708	5	9
			3623	7	5

Bristoll 1684/5

	Worsted Stockins per Contra	Cr	£	s	d
March	By Ballance brought from that acct.	81	273	15	4
	By Adventure 2nd in the Mauritania to Cadiz for one Trunck laden in her cont. 1116 paire Bristoll hose at 3s per paire and 212 paire Wells hose at 2s	93	188	12	
May 30	By Adventure in the Merchants Goodwill to Cadiz for 82 doz Bristoll hose is 984 paire at 3s 1d & 260 paire Wells hose at 1s 11d per paire	97	176	12	4
June	By Adventure in partnership in the ship Cesar to Cadiz for 960 paire Bristoll & 244 paire Wells hose laden in her the Bristoll hose at 2s 8d & the Wells at 1s 5d	100	145	5	8
August	By Adventure in the ship Civilia merchant to Cadiz for one Trunck laden in cont. 768 Bristoll, & 648 paire Wells hose the Bristoll at 2s 9d the Wells 1s 8d	101	159	12	
			943	17	4

	To Ditto paid Tho. Hill for	26	2	6	83	3	5	
7	To Ditto paid John Day for	20	2	6¼	83	2	9	2
9	To Ditto paid Joseph White for	40	2	8	83	5	6	8
10	To Ditto paid John Massinger for	32	2	8	83	4	5	4
13	To Ditto paid John Perrie for	35	2	6¼	83	4	8	2
16	To Ditto paid Tho. Hill for	13	2	5¾	83	1	12	6
	To Ditto paid Joel Pinne for	37	2	5	83	4	9	5
17	To Ditto paid John Massinger for	42	2	8	83	5	12	
18	To Ditto paid John Perrie for	39	2	6¼	83	4	18	3
	To Ditto paid Joseph White for	54	2	8	83	7	4	
24	To Ditto paid John Massinger for	30	2	8	83 *	4		
25	To Ditto paid Tho. Hill for	25	2	8	83	2	18	4
27	To Ditto paid Tho. Walden for 1 doz of Inkle to bind stockins				83		7	
29	To Ditto paid John Perry for	31	2	6	83	3	17	6
30	To Ditto paid John Ruddock for	31	2	5¾	83	3	16	10
May 1	To Ditto paid John Day for	14	2	6	83	1	15	
						214	8	7
	To Ditto paid Henry Britten for	36	2	5¾	83	4	9	3
2	To Ditto paid John Massinger for	28	2	8	83	3	14	8
	To Ditto paid Joseph White for	49	2	8	83	6	10	8
	To Ditto paid Jos. White for	18	2	8	83	2	8	
7	To Ditto paid Tho. Hill for	100	1	4½	83	6	17	6
	To Ditto paid John Massinger for	39	2	8	83	5	4	
9	To Ditto paid Andrew Creed for	100	1	3	83	6	5	
15	To Ditto paid Tho. Hill for	37	2	5¾	83	4	11	9
	To Ditto paid John Massinger for	42	2	8	83	5	12	
16	To Ditto paid John Brady's man in part for	40			83	8		
21	To Ditto paid Tho. Hill for	120		12	83	6		
	To Ditto paid Ditto for	105	1	4	83	7		
	To Ditto paid John Perrie for	54	2	6¼	83	6	16	1
22	To Ditto paid John Massinger for	47	2	8	83	6	5	4
25	To Ditto paid John Day for	14	2	6	83	1	15	
26	To Ditto paid Joseph White for	64	2	8	83	8	10	8
27	To Ditto paid John Harris in full for Truncks to pack stockins in				83	4		
28	To Ditto paid John Massinger for	45	2	8	83	6		
	To Ditto paid Ed. Iffe for hot pressing stockins to this day				83		8	6
	To Ditto paid John Rudduck for	35	2	5¾	83	4	6	9
June 1	To Ditto paid Joseph White for	60	2	8	83	8		
	To Ditto paid Andrew Creed for	78	1	3½	83	5		9
	To Ditto paid John Perrie for	80	2	6	83	10		
3	To Ditto paid John Day for	14	2	6	83	1	15	
5	To Ditto paid John Massinger for	38	2	8	83	5	1	4
6	To Ditto paid Tho. Hill for	74	2	5¾	83	9	3	6
	To Ditto paid Tho. Hill for	135	1	4	83	9		
	To Ditto paid Wm. Thyery for	38	2	4	83	4	8	8
9	To Ditto paid John Massinger for	32	2	8	83	4	5	4
16	To Ditto paid John Day for	38	2	4	83	4	8	8
	To Ditto paid Ed. Iffe for hot pressing stockins to this day				83		7	
26	To Ditto paid John Massinger for	41	2	8	83	5	9	4
July 3	To Ditto paid Elizabeth Massinger for	27	2	8	83	3	12	
11	To Ditto paid Elizabeth Massinger for	36	2	8	83	4	16	
13	To Ditto paid John Ruddock for	49	2	5¾	83	6	1	6
	To Ditto paid John Perrie for	41	2	6	83	5	2	6
15	To Ditto paid Henry Britten for	92	2	5¾	83	11	8	1
17	To Ditto paid John Day for	21	2	5	83	1	2	6
18	To Ditto paid Elizabeth Massinger for	29	2	8	83	3	17	4
21	To Ditto paid John Brady for (£8 being formerly paid)	105	2	5	83	4	13	9
	To Ditto paid Tho. Hill for	33	2	5¾	83	4	1	10

22	To Ditto paid John Rudduck for	26	2	5¼	83	3	4	5½
23	To Ditto paid Joseph White for	73	2	8	83	9	14	8
	To Ditto paid John Perrie for	85	2	6	83	10	12	6
						454	10	5
	To ballance carried to that acct.				102	489	6	10½
					.	943	17	4

(92)   Bristoll 1684

			£	s	d
	Richard Merick alias Reece of Clevedon in the County of Somerset Yeoman is	Dr			
January 18	To Cash paid him for his noat of disbursments	107	3	1	
Aprill 1686 16	To Land at Clevedon for — yeares rent for New Lands Tenement in Clevedon, due 2nd February 1685 now past	32	13		
	To Proffit & Losse for poore money by mistake hee paid , when paid by John Stretten before, & was afterwards allowed it	105 *		15	6
November	To Land at Clevedon for ½ yeares rent due 29th Sept. 1686 for Newlands Tenement	116	6	10	
1687 August	To Ditto for ½ yeares rent due March 1st 1686	116	6	10	
	To Ditto for 1 yeares rent due March 1st 1687	116	13		
1689 June	To Ditto for 1 yeares rent due March 1st 1688	116	13		
			55	16	6

			£	s	d
	Anno 1684				
	Bethel Walter of Bristol Grocer is	Dr			
January	To Adventure in the Owners Endeavour to Nevis & Jamaica for 1 hogshead Nevis sugar imported from Jamaica weight neat 7cwt 3qr 3 lb at 23s per Cwt	58	10	17	9
1685 Aprill	To Rice for acct. Simon Clement & Company for 1 Baggs neat 3cwt 2qr 10lb at 28s per Cwt	96	4	2	6
			15	00	3

					£	s	d
	Anno 1684/5						
	Plate imported in severall ships for my propper acct.				Dr			
	To John Cook & Sam. Kekewich for the cost &	R	m				
March	charges of 500 pieces of 8 laden in the ship James Capt. Roberts consign'd to Isaac Heming in London the piece of 8 at 4s 6d	4275			88	112	10	
1685 May	To Ditto acct. for one Bundle of wrought silver and 311½ pieces of 8 sent in the ship Britton Capt.Ford consign'd to Isaac Heming as per Invoyce May 85	5194	17		88	140	13	4
October	To Ditto for 2 Cakes Silver in the Saphire friggat as per Invouce Sept. 17th containing 53m 4½ fine ware at 72½ Ryals with charges 503¾ pieces of 8 at 4s 2d	4030			88	103	9	

	Bristoll 1684				
	Richard Merrick alias Reece per Contra	*Cr*	*£*	*s*	*d*
February	By Cash recd. of him in part of payment of ½ yeares rent when hee took it	82		1	
1685 *January 18*	By Cash received of him for ½ a yeares rent of Newlands Tenement ending September 29th 1685	107	6	10	
1686 *July 24*	By Land at Clevedon for his noat of disbursments per Contra	32	3	1	
	By Cash received of him with the noat of disbursments in full for ½ yeares rent Feb. 2nd				
	By Land at Clevedon for poores money £1 3s 3d militia money 1s 4d	116	1	4	7
	By Proffit & Losse abated him freely	105		2	11
	By Cash received of him	119	5	4	5
	By Ditto recd. of him which is in full for the yeares rent, and the poores money twice paid	119		12	7
February 2	By Cash recd. of him for ½ yeares rent due September 29th 1686 in part	120	5	13	
	By sundry accts for ½ yeares Lords rent 16s and abated him 1s	116,127		17	
1687 August	By sundry accts for ½ yeares Lords rent 16s for mending sea wall 2s and abated him 2s 6d in all	116,137	1		6
	By Cash recd. of him for ½ a yeares rent due March 1st 1686, with said disbursmentns is in full	139	5	9	6
March 14	By Ditto recd. of him in part for ½ yeares rent due Sept. 29th 1687	140	3	10	
1688 Feb. 11	By Cash recd. of him in part	162	4	10	6
16	By Ditto recd. of him in part	162		9	6
1689 May 18	By Cash recd. of him in part	162	5		
October 10	By Land at Clevedon for his 2 noates of Disbursments	116	6	19	
	By ballance carried to his new acct.	174	5	11	
			55	16	6

	Anno 1685				
	Bethel Walter per Contra	*Cr*	*£*	*s*	*d*
Aprill	By Cash recd. of him for a bagge of Rice	83	4	2	6
November 10	By Cash received of him in part per the hands of Tho. Hill	107	10		
			14	2	6
	By Profit and Loss, for Ballance	190 *		17	9
			15		3

	Anno 1685				
	Plate in severall ships from Cadiz per Contra	*Cr*	*£*	*s*	*d*
October	By Isaac Heming for the 800½ pieces of 8 per Contra, 11 pieces paid fraight weight 692½ oz at 5s 2d per oz	90	178	17	11
	By Ditto for the wrought silver per Contra weight 278 oz at 4s 8d per oz	90	64	17	4
December	By Ditto for 2 Cakes silver in the Saphire weight 395½ oz at 5s 3d per oz is	90	103	9	
	By Ditto for £468 0s 6ds received of Wm. Atwell & Company for 111 pieces of 8 & one Bundle wrought plate in the Crowne, and 3 Cakes silver in the Unity as per said Atwills account	90	468	6	
1686 Aprill 1	By Ditto for the 100 pieces of 8 in the Hanniball per Contra sould Wm. Atwill & Company	111 [83]	223	9	3

			£	s	d
December	To Ditto for the cost of 3 Cakes silver in the Unity Capt. Tucker weight 75 marks oz 4 Ryals with charges is 710 7/8 pieces of 8 the piece of 8 at 4s 2d	5687	88	148	1	10
	To Ditto for the cost of 1250 ps of 8 & 43 marks 6 oz wrought plate in the Crowne in all 1682¼ pieces of 8 of [?] wanting in one bagge 139 pieces of 8 the piece of 8 at 4s as per Invoyce 9 1685	13462	88	336	11	
February 1686	To Ditto for 1000 pieces of 8 with charges laden in the ship Hannibal is 1069 pieces of 8 the piece of 8 at 4s 2d the piece of 8 is	8557	111	222	16	7
December	To John Cook & Company for 1000 pieces of 8 in the James Galley the piece of 8 at 4s 2d	8425 17	173 111	219	8	3
				1283	10	

Anno 1684

		Dr	£	s	d
	John Harris of Bristoll Trunckmaker is				
March 23	To Proffit & Losse for 2 Deale cases sould him cost 10s in London	89		4	

Anno 1685

		Dr	£	s	d
	Sugar 1 hogshead 1 Kilderkin, & 1 Firkin, laden per Edward Parsons in the ship Olive tree James Porter Master in Barbadoes				
October	To Edward Parsons for theire cost & charges as per Invoyce June 1685	58	12	17	5
	To Cash paid James Porter for freight & averidge	84 *	2	6	6
			15	3	11

Anno 1684

					Dr	£	s	d
	Henry Howard of St Martins in the fields, John Thorowgood of Linregis merchant, & George Hart of the Citie of Bristoll merchant on bond							
March 18	To John Blackwell for money paid them by my order on theire bond payable wiith intrest Sept. 19th 1685	£ 100	s 00	d 00	85			
	To Proffit & Losse for ½ yeares intrest due Sept. 19th	3	00	00	89	103		
1686	To Ditto for ½ yeares intrest due March 19th 1685				105	3		
	To Ditto for ½ yeares intrest due September 19th 1686				127	3		
	To Ditto for ½ yeares intrest due March 19th 1686				137	3		
1687 Sept.	To Ditto for ½ yeares intrest due September 19th 1687				137	3		
	To Ditto for ½ yeares intrest due March 19th 1687				153 *	3		
1688 Sept. 19	To Ditto for ½ yeares intrest ending September 19th 1688				153	3		
March 18	To Ditto for ½ yeares intrest ending March 18th 1688				164	3		
						124		

Anno 1684/5

		Dr	£	s	d
	Martha Linch of Tockinton my maid-servant is				
March 4	To Cash gave her covenant money in part of a Quarters wages to come at 45s per annum, and shee came to my house to begin her time of service March 30th 1685	82		1	
1685 Sept. 3	To Cash paid her for ¼ yeares wages ending 29th September past	84		10	3
January 6	To Cash paid her for ¼ yeares wages ending 25th Dec. 1685	107		11	3
March 13	To Cash paid her for ¼ yeares wages ending 30th instant	108		11	3
			1	13	9

December	By Isaac Heming for 1000 pieces of 8 per the James Galley sould Wm. Atwill & Company weight 877¼ oz at 5s 2d¼ per oz, deducting £2 8s 6d for freight & charges	*130*	225	2	2
			1264	1	8
	By ballance carried to a new acct. current	*143*	19	8	4
			1283	10	

Anno 1690@					
	Per Contra	*Cr*	£	s	d
	By Profit and Loss, for Ballance	*190 ***		4	

Anno 1686					
	Sugar 3 Cask per Contra	*Cr*	£	s	d
March 25	By Edward Thornhull for theire value, weight neat 14cwt 1qr 25lb, at 21s per Cwt	*114*	15	3	11

Anno 1685					
	Henry Howard & Company per Contra	*Cr*	£	s	d
October 8	By Cash received by the hands of Ozziel Browne for ½ yeares intrest ending Sept. 19th	*84*	3		
June 23	By Cash received of Ozziel Browne for ½ yeares intrest ending March 19th 1685	*108*	3		
1686 Nov. 10	By Cash received of Ozziel Browne for ½ yeares intrest ending Sept. 19th 1686	*120*	3		
1687 August 22	By Cash received of Oz. Browne for ½ yeares intrest due March 18th 1686	*139*	3		
November 5	By Cash received of Oz. Browne for ½ yeares intrest due Sept. 18th 1687	*139*	3		
1688 March 28	By Cash received of Ozziel Browne for ½ yeares intrest due 18th March 1687	*140*	3		
September 19	By Ditto recd. of Ozziel Browne for ½ yeares intrest due September 19th 1688	*141*	3		
1689 March 28	By Cash recd. of Ozziel Browne for ½ yeares intrest due March 18th 1688	*162*	3		
	By theire new acct. current for ballance carried to that acct.	*163*	100		
			124		

Anno 1685					
	Martha Linch per Contra	*Cr*	£	s	d
June	By Proffit & Losse for ¼ yeares wages due 30th June 1685	*89*		11	3
1686 March	By Proffit & Losse for ½ yeares wages due March 30th 1686	*105*	1	2	6
			1	13	9

(93)	**Bristoll 1684/5**				
	Adventure 2nd in the ship Mauritania Capt. Tho. Morsley to Cadiz	Dr	£	s	d
March	To the cost & charges of one Trunck of Worsted Stockins laden in her, & consign'd to John Cooke & Samuell Kekewich merchants in St Marie Port for sales & returnes (viz)				
	To Worsted stockins for 93 dozen is £ s d				
	1116 paire at 3s per paire 167 8 00	91			
	To Ditto for 10 score & 1 doz is 17				
	2/3 doz is 212 paire fine Wells hose				
	at 2s per paire 21 04 00	91	188	12	
	To Isaac Heming for carriage to London, custom and other				
	charges as per his leter of 21th Aprill 1685 will appeare	90	4	19	6
			193	11	6
	To Profit and Loss, for Ballance	190 *	19	2	8
			212	14	2

	Anno 1684/5				
	Charles Herbert of Bristoll Grocer, Jonathan Alline merchant and Tho. Day Soapboyler & Company intressed in a Sugar work are	Dr	£	s	d
March 24	To sundry accts for 1 Butt & 17 hhds sugar sould them due June 24th	8579	167	7	
			167	7	

	Anno 1685				
	William Rogers of Bristol merchant is	Dr	£	s	d
November 7	To Wines out of sundry ships from Cadiz, for 3 Butts & part of a Butt of Lees sould him to pay on demand	101	10	10	
1687 Aprill 6	To Marie Beard for 12 Cheeses weight 1cwt 1lb at 19s per Cwt	125		19	2
			11	9	2

	Anno 1684/5				
	John Mayne of the Pill neare St Georges Merchant	Dr	£	s	d
	To Adventure 2nd in the ship Rachell to Cadiz for R m				
	the neat proceeds of a Trunck of stockins, Butter &				
	other merchandizes soud for mee in Cadiz as per his				
	acct. closed Feb. 7th 1684/5 amounting to 849				
	1/8 pieces of 8 the piece of 8 at 55d 7093	79	194	11	9
	To Proffit & Losse for ballance	89 *	10	17	7
			205	9	4

	Anno 1685				
	John Mayne merchant	Dr	£	s	d
July 7	To Cash paid lent him on his bond	83	16		

	Anno 1684/5				
	Xeries Wine 10 Butts laden per John Mayne in the ship Rachell Wm. Birkins Master from Cadiz R m	Dr	£	s	d
March	To John Mayne for theire first cost 410 pieces of				
	8 the piece of 8 at 53d as per his acct. Feb. 7th				
	1684/5 3280	93	90	10	10
	To Cash paid custom prisage etc.	84	34	16	8
	To John Blackwell for the freight of them which I heare make				
	good to him per desire of John Mayne, said Blackwell being the				
	owner of the ship at £3 12s 0d per tonnes per agreement made				
	twixt Mayne & Blackwell	85	18		
			143	7	6

Bristoll 1684/5 1685		Cr	£	s	d
	Adventure 2nd in the Mauritanea per Contra	Cr	£	s	d
December	By John Cook & Samuel Kekewich for the neat proceeds of the				
	Trunck of stockins per Contra 1021 pieces of 8 being 8168				
	Ryals plate the piece of 8 at 4s 2d as per theire acct. of sales of				
	November 1685	88	212	14	2

Anno 1685		Cr	£	s	d
	Charles Herbert & Company per Contra	Cr	£	s	d
July 11	By Cash received of Charles Herbert	83	44		
23	By Cash recd. of Charles Herbert	83	50		
August 21	By Cash recd. of Francis Whitchurch	84	73	7	
			167	7	

Anno 1686		Cr	£	s	d
	William Rogers per Contra is	Cr	£	s	d
August 6	By Cash received of him	119	10	10	
1687 Aprill 18	By Ditto recd. of his wife	121		19	2
			11	9	2

Anno 1684/5				Cr	£	s	d
	John Mayne per Contra			Cr	£	s	d
March 17	By Cash recd. of Humphry Corsley for 61	R	m				
	pieces of 8 recd. of said Mayne being in Spanish						
	money	488		82	13	15	10
	By Xeries wine 10 Butts in the Rachell for						
	410 pieces of 8 theire cost the piece of 8 at 53d	3280		93	90	10	10
	By John Blackwell for his bill of Exchange for						
	500 pieces of 8 on him in favor of Isaac						
	Heming by my order, the piece of 8 at 53d	4000		85	110	8	4
	By Proffit & Losse for a Rove of Potatoes &						
	3 pound of choccolate	26		89 *		14	4
					205	9	4

Anno 1685		Cr	£	s	d
	John Mayne per Contra is	Cr	£	s	d
July 29	By Cash recd. of him	83	16		

Anno 1685		Cr	£	s	d
	Xeries Wine 10 Butts per Contra	Cr	£	s	d
	By Xeries wine out of sundry ships from Cadiz for the cost and				
	charges of the 10 Butts per Contra carried hence to that acct. to				
	avoyd confusion in accts by mixture of one ships wine with				
	another, & theire being sould promiscuously as they lay in the				
	Cellar	101	143	7	6

		Dr	£	s	d
	Anno 1685				
	John Shuttleworth Secretary to the Earle of Bristoll	Dr	£	s	d
June 9	To Cash paid for a boat & 2 men to render his Sonne aboard the ship Joseph by night when bound to Ireland	83		4	
	To Cash paid for a knife comb etc. to Mathew Worgan	84		1	4
1689	George his sonne is debtor to Cash pd. James Freemans noat when sick of the small pox	168		4	
	To Cash pd. severall other disbursments on his nurse etc.	168		19	8
			1	8	

		Dr	£	s	d
(94)	**Bristoll 1684/5**				
	Xeries Wine my 2/3 of 30 Butts in partnership with Simon Clement & by him laden in the ship Joseph Wm. Jefferies Master from Cadiz in part returnes of goods sent in her are	Dr	£	s	d
March 1685	To Simon Clement for 2/3 of 10114 Ryals plate theire cost & charges in Spaine, is 1264¼ pieces of 8 the piece of 8 at 53d £279 4s 10d of which 2/3 is	86	186	3	2¾
	To Ditto for the other 1/3 of said 30 Butts bought of him at £9 per Butt	86	90		
May 19	To Ditto for 6 Butts bought of him (viz) 4 at £17 and 2 at £14 per Butt	86	96		
	To Edward Lloyd for 2 Butts bought of him at £20 per Butt	95	40		
	To Henry Davis & Company owners for freight & averidge of 30 Butts at £3 10s 10d per Butt	97	53	2	6
	To Prisage wine 4 Butts for the Prisage of 30 Butts at 7s per Butt	96	10	10	
	To Samuel Davis for the cost & charge of 1 hogshead & 1 Aum Rhenish from Rotterdam	63	11	6	6
	To Ditto for 3 hhds Rhenish bought of him; 1 at £5 10s & 2 at £7 each is	63	19	10	
	To Cash paid custom fees, bills & wharfage of 30 Butts in the Joseph	83	89	3	10
			595	16	¾

		Dr	£	s	d
	Anno 1685				
	Thomas Day of Bristoll Soapmaker is	Dr	£	s	d
August	To Tobacco 26 hhds in the John for acct. of Lawrence Washington for said Tobacco sould him as it lay aboard the ship, hee to pay all manner of charges, and to take them at 400lb neat each hogshead at 3d per pound as per his contract under hand and obligation in the same	101	130		
	To Wine 6 hhds in the Angell Gabriell £ s d for 2 doz bottles Claret at 9s 6d 19	94			
	To Proffit & Losse for 2 doz bottles at 2s 4	89	1	3	
1686 Dec. 6	To Tobacco 26 hhds in the Fra. & Marie and the John for 16 hhds soud him weight neat 6694 lb at 7d¼ per lb to pay for them 25thJan. for acct. Lawrence Washington	126	201	11	
1687 Dec. 30	To Tobacco 4 hhds for Law. Washington for them weight neat 1638 lb at 6d½ to pay in 3 month	147	44	7	3
1688 May 8	To Cash paid him in full	141	45	17	6
	To Proffit & Losse for 5 pints wine for Ullage to the 2 Butts per Contra	137		2	6
			423		3

		Dr	£	s	d
	Anno 1685				
	William Dawson of Redland (late of Bristoll) Hopmerchant is	Dr	£	s	d
	To French wines 6 hhds for 2 doz £ s d				
August 24	qrt bottles Claret at 9s 6d 00 19 00	94			
	To Proffit & Losse for 2 doz bottles at				
	2s per doz 00 04 00	89	1	3	
November 10	To same acct. for 1 doz Whtie wine & 1 doz Claret with bottles	94, 105	1	3	
			2	6	

Anno 1689		Cr	£	s	d
	John Shuttleworth & George his Sone per Contra are	Cr	£	s	d
December 6	By Cash received of George Shuttleworth in part	168	1	3	8
	To Profit and Loss, for Ballance	190 *		4	4
			1	8	

Bristoll 1685		Cr	£	s	d
	Xeries Wine 30 Butts per Contra are	Cr	£	s	d
May 2	By Simon Clement for 2 Butts sould him at £15 per Butt	86	45		
5	By Cash recd. of James Croft for returnes on 2 Butts	83	1	16	4
	By Edward Lloyd for 15 Gall. Xerie to Ullage 2 Butts	95	2	12	8
	By the Lady Ann Powlet for 4 doz bottles at 17s per doz	100	3	8	
	By Dr. Fra. Hungerford for 10 doz bottles sent Sir H. Winchcomb	87	8	10	
	By Ditto for 10 doz bottles sent himselfe	87	8	10	
	By the Lady Ann Pawlet for 4 doz bottles	100	3	8	
	By Sir Wm. Drake for 6 doz bottles	100	5	2	
			78	7	
	By Ballance carried to that acct.	101	516	9	¾
			595	16	¾

Anno 1685		Cr	£	s	d
	Tho. Day per Contra is	Cr	£	s	d
December 8	By Cash received of him	107	130		
March 12	By Cash recd. of him in full	108	1	3	
1686 February	By Simon Clement and co. paid them by my order	133	100		
March 3	By Cash recd. of him in full	120	101	11	
1687 Feb. 19	By wines of severall sorts bought of severalls for 2 Butts of Malaga at £23 per Butt	149	46		
1688 May 8	By Cash recd. of him in full for the Tobacco	141	44	7	3
			423	1	3

Anno 1686		Cr	£	s	d
	Wm. Dawson per Contra	Cr	£	s	d
July 5	By Cash received of his Sonne William in full	119	2	6	

Anno 1685				
Xeries Wine 2 Butts bought of Edward Lloyd Wm. Rogers's overseer	Dr	£	s	d
Aprill 13 *To Cash paid him in part by the hands of John Blackwell*	83	20		

Anno 1686				
Welthian Ruther my Maidservant per Contra is	Dr	£	s	d
October 13 *To Cash paid her for ½ yeares wages due 13thOcto.br 1686*	120	1	5	
1687 November 23 *To Cash paid her in part of wages*	139		10	
December 27 *To Cash paid her in full for 1 yeares wages ending October 13th 1687*	140	2		
1688 May 12 *To Cash pd. her for ½ yeares wages ending Aprill 13th 1688*	141	1	5	
1689 July 8 *To Cash pd. Edward Pruet for her Poll*	168		2	
1690 June 28 *To Ditto pd. John Duddlestone and. . . Rainstrope for her Poll*	181		1	
		5	3	

Anno 1685				
Port Wines [84] *2 hhds white 2 hhds Claret & 2 hhds of Sweet laden per Tho. Arundell in the ship Angell Gabriell Tho. Templeman Master for mee*	Dr	£	s	d
March *To Isaac Heming for Tho. Arundells bill on mee in his favor 77 Ecu & 5sous at 56d per Ecu drawne per said Arundell on mee in his favor for theire cost*	90	18	3	8
To Cash paid custom, fees, bill & wharfage	83	7	16	
To Cash paid John Batchelor for freight, prisage and avridge	84	4	4	
		30	3	8

Anno 1685				
James Speed Sonne of Richard Speed Marriner deceased	Dr	£	s	d
May 30 *To Cash paid Richard Miller his uncle towards the binding him an apprentice to — Tucker an Apothecary in Redcliffe streat*	83	6		

Anno 1687				
Richard Speed the Sonne of Richard Speed, & Bro. of James Servant to Caleb Shuter	Dr	£	s	d
May 24 *To Cash paid Christian Richards for a firkin of Butter hee carried to Barbados in the Joseph*	121		17	1
1688 July 3 *To Cash delivered Caleb Suter to buy an Adventure for him in Ireland*	141	2	3	
To Cash pd. John Curtis for 7 weeks schooling	141		3	6
		3	3	7

(95)	**Bristoll 1685**				
	Sundry accts are Debitors to Rice 50 Baggs imported in the ship Joseph Wm. Jefferies master from Cadiz for acct. of Simon Clement & Richd. Hains merchant	Dr	£	s	d
Aprill 6	*Thomas Burgis of Bristol Grocer is Debtor for* [85] *one Bagge neat 3ct 2qr 17lb at 23s per Cwt*	96	4	3	11
6	*Tho. Jordan: 3 Baggs neat 10ct 1qr 11lb at 23s per Cwt*	96	11	18	
6	*James Attwood: 1 Bagge neat 3ct 2qr 13lb at 23s per Cwt*	96	4	3	2
	Onisipherus Tindall: 1 Bagge neat 3ct 2qr 15lb at 23s	96	4	3	7
6	*Charles Herbert: 2 Baggs neat 7ct 0qr 6lb at 23s*	96	8	2	3
6	*Simon Hall: 1 Bagge 3ct 1qr 22lb at 23s*	96	3	19	3
6	*Henry Parsons: 3 Baggs neat 10ct 2qr 14lb at 23s per Cwt*	96	12	4	4

Anno 1685				
Xeries Wine 2 Butts per Contra are	Cr	£	s	d
By Edward Lloyd for the money per Contra, which hee recd. of John Blackwell	95	20		

Anno 1686				
Welthian Ruther my servant maid is	Cr	£	s	d
October By Proffit & Losse for ½ yeares wages from 13th of Aprill 1686 to 13th Oct. 1686	127 *	1	5	
By Account of Ballances for Ballance	194 *	3	18	
		5	3	

Anno 1685				
Wine 6 hhds per Contra are	Cr	£	s	d
By John Jones for 10 doz qrt bottles claret at 9s 6d per doz	99	4	14	6
August 22 By John Love for 2 doz bottles Claret at 9s 6d per doz	55		19	
24 By William Dawson for 2 doz qrt bottles Claret at 9s 6d per doz	94		19	
September 15 By Thomas Jordan for 2 doz qrt Bottles White wine at 9s 6d	95		19	
By Tho. Walden for 8 bottles of Claret at 9s 6d per doz is	87		6	4
By Simon Clement for 6 bottles Claret	86		4	6
By Tho. Walden for 21 bottles Claret & 6 bottles Whitewine	87	1	1	4½
By Tho. Jordan for 1 doz White & 1 doz Claret with bottles	95	1	3	
By Tho. Day for 0 doz White & 2 doz Claret at 9s 6d	94		19	
By John Blackwell for 2 hhds Sweet less 23¾ Gall. at £26 per tonne	85	10	8	6
By Simon Clement for 1 doz bottles Claret	86		9	6
By Wm. Dawson for 1 doz White & 1 doz Claret at 9s 6d	94		19	
By ballance carried to that acct.	97	7		11½
		30	3	8

Anno 1690@				
Per Contra	Cr	£	s	d
By Acct. of Ballances, for Ballance	194 *	6		

Anno 1690@				
Per Contra	Cr	£	s	d
By Acct. of Ballances, for Ballance	194 *	3	3	7

Sundry accts per Contra buyers of the Rice per Contra are	Cr	£	s	d
Tho. Burgis: [86] By Cash received of him	83	4	3	11
Tho. Jordan: By Cash per the hands of Simon Clement	83	11	18	
James Attwood: By Cash received of him	83	4	3	
Onisiphorus Tindal: By Cash recd. of him	83	4	3	
Charles Herbert: By Cash recd. of him	83	8	2	
Simon Hall: By Cash recd. of him	83	3	19	
Henry Parsons by Cash received of him	83	12	4	3
Samuel Hollister: By Cash recd. of him	83	4	5	4
Tho. Tyler: By Cash recd. of him	83	4	2	6
Charles Towke: By Cash recd. of him	83	8	7	6

			£	s	d
6	Samuel Hollister: 1 Bagge neat 3ct 2qr 24lb at 23s	96	4	5	5
6	Tho. Tyler: 1 Bagge neat 3ct 2qr 10lb at 23s	96	4	2	6
6	Charles Towke: 2 Baggs neat 7ct 1qr 4lb at 23s	96	8	7	7
6	John Curtis: 2 Baggs neat 7ct 0qr 21lb at 23s	96	8	5	3
6	Robert Bartly: 2 Baggs neat 7ct 0qr 10lb at 23s	96	8	3	
6	Dawbeny Buckler: 1 Bagge neat 3ct 1qr 25lb at 23s	96	3	18	8
6	Marie Wade Widow: 1 Bagge neat 3ct 2qr 10lb at 23s	96	4	2	6
6	Isaac Crump: 1 Bagge neat 3ct 0qr 20lb at 23s	96	3	13	
6	Tho. Longman: 2 Baggs neat 6ct 3qr 23lb at 23s	96	8		
6	Daniel Griffeth: 1 bagge neat 3ct 2qr 23lb at 23s	96	4	5	2
6	Thomas Tayer: 2 baggs neat 6ct 1qr 24lb at 23s per Cwt	96	7	6	4
6	Elizabeth Beaton Widow: 2 baggs neat 7ct 0qr 11lb at 23s	96	8	3	3
6	Matthew Walter: 1 bagge neat 3ct 1qr 8lb at 23s	96	3	16	4
6	Edward Chetwine: 2 baggs neat 7ct 2qr 26lb at 23s	96	8	12	
	William Vaughan: 1 bagge neat 3ct 3qr 6lb at 23s	96	4	7	6

			£	s	d
	Anno 1688				
	Onesiphorus Tyndall of Bristoll Grocer is	Dr			
January	To Reisons Solis 32 Barrills for 8 Barrils neat 21ct 2qr 4d at	158			
	22s per Cwt due Aprill 1st		23	13	9

			£	s	d
	Anno 1685				
	Thomas Jordan of Bristoll Grocer is	Dr			
	£ s d				
September 15	To French wine 6 hhds for 2 doz				
	bottles White wine at 9s 6d 19	94			
	To Proffit & Losse for 2 doz bottles at				
	2s per doz 4	89			
	To French wine 6 hhds for 1 doz				
	White & 1 doz Claret with bottles 1 3	94	2	6	
November	To fruite 9 Barrils & 27 pieces weight neat as per Journall at				
	30s & 20s per Cwt to pay in 4 month	110	55	11	2
1687 July 19	To Reisons Solis 27 barrills for 4 barrills weight neat 10ct 3qr				
	22lb at 24s due Oct. 25th 1687	136	13	2	8½
November 7	To Reisons 65 barrills for 6 barrills neat 16cwt 26¾ lb at 24s				
	due Feb. 7th	145	19	9	8¾
			90	9	7¼

			£	s	d
	Anno 1685				
	Edward Lloyd of Bristoll Mannager of Wm. Rogers his Syder	Dr			
	Cellars				
Aprill 13	To Xeries wine 2 Butts for money hee received of John Blackwell				
	charg'd to said wines by mistake	94	20		
24	To Cash paid him in part	83	4		
	To sundry accts for freight custom & other charges on 2 Butts				
	Xerie in the Joseph	89,97	10	8	10
	To Xeries wine 30 Butts for 15 Gall. sack to Ullage the 2 Butts	94	2	12	8
	To Cash paid him in full	83	2	18	6
			40		

			£	s	d
(96)	**Bristoll 1685**				
	Rice 50 Baggs imported in the ship Joseph Wm. Jefferies Master	Dr			
	for acct. of Simon Clement of Bristoll merchant , and Richard				
	Haines Junior of London merchant				
	To Cash paid custom fees, bills & £ s d				
	wharfage 12 1 04				
	To Ditto paid charges in Hungroad,				
	mending baggs, portridge into Celler,				
	weighing to the Grocers, and halling,				
	& Celleridge 1 17 3	83	13	18	7
	To Henry Davis & Company owners of the Joseph for freight of				
	6 Tonns rice at £3 10s	97	21		

John Curtis: By Cash recd. of Tho. Callowhill by his order	83	8	5	3
Robert Bartly: By Cash recd. of him	83	8	2	6
Dawbenny Buckler: By Cash recd. of him	83	3	18	6
Marie Wade: By Cash recd. of her	83	4	2	6
Isaac Crump: By Cash recd. of him	83	3	13	
Tho. Longman: By Cash recd. of him	84	8		
Daniel Griffeth: By Cash recd. of him	83	4	5	2
Tho. Tayer is Creditor: By Cash recd. of him	83	7	6	3
Elizabeth Beaton: By Cash recd. of her	83	8	3	
Matthew Walter: By Cash recd. of him	83	3	16	4
Edward Chetwin: By Cash recd. of him	83	8	12	
William Vaughan: By Cash recd. of him	83	4	7	4

	Anno 1689				
	Onesipherus Tyndell per Contra	*Cr*	*£*	*s*	*d*
June 1	By Cash recd. of him at twice in full	*162*	23	13	9

	Anno 1685				
	Thomas Jordan per Contra	*Cr*	*£*	*s*	*d*
	By Proffit & Losse for his noat for severall particculars of him as per noat	*89*	1	1	7
1686 July 12	By Cash received of him	*119*	56	15	
1687 March 23	By Cash received of him	*140*	19	9	6
	By Profit and Loss, for an error committed per Contra but not to be found out [87]	*190 **	13	3	6¼
			90	9	7¼

	Anno 1685				
	Edward Lloyd per Contra is	*Cr*	*£*	*s*	*d*
Aprill 6	By Xeries wine my 2/3 of 30 Butts for 2 Butts bought of him at £20 per butt	*94*	40		

	Bristoll 1685				
	Rice per Contra is	*Cr*	*£*	*s*	*d*
	By Cash recd. of severalls for one bagge divided twixt Giles Gough etc. weight 3ct 1qr 7lb	*83*	3	16	
	By Robert Hauxworth for 1 bagge weight neat 3ct 3qr 16lb	*28*	4	9	6
	By sundry accts for 33 baggs sould severalls	*959253*	133	12	10
	By Thomas Goldny for 3 baggs	*16*	11	16	
	By Tho. Jordan for 3 baggs	*95*	11	18	
	By Simon Hall for 1 bagge	*95*	3	19	
	By John Curtis for 2 baggs	*95*	8	5	
	By Tho. Longman for 2 baggs	*95*	8		
	By Tho. Davidge for 1 bagge	*4*	3	15	

	Description	£	s	d	Fol	£	s	d
	To Ditto for Averidge of said rice				97		19	6
	To Proffit & Losse for abatement of odd pence on the money		4	10				
	To Ditto for my Commission at £2 per Cent	4	0	5	89	4	5	3
	To Simon Clement for the neat proceeds of 34 Baggs for his acct.	109	9	7	86			
	To Richard Haines for the neat proceeds of 16 Baggs for his acct.	51	10	5	98	161		
						201	3	4

Anno 1685

	Description	Dr	£	s	d
	Olives 14 Jarrs received out of the ship Joseph from Cadiz for the acct. of Simon Clement merchant	Dr	£	s	d
Aprill	To Cash paid Custom etc.	83		2	3
	To Proffit & Losse for halling, portridge & Celleridge	89 *		1	10
	To Henry Davis & Company for freight & averidge	97		12	2
	To Proffit & Losse for my Commission at £2 per Cent	89 *		1	3
	To Simon Clement his acct. current for theire neat proceeds	86	2	14	
			3	11	6

Anno 1685

	Description	Dr	£	s	d
	Thomas Harris of Bristoll Apothecary is	Dr	£	s	d
Aprill 20	To Olives 14 Jarres for acct. Simon Clement for 9 Jarres sould and delivered him at 5s 6d per Jarre	96	2	9	6

Anno 1685

Description	Dr	£	s	d
Prisage Wine 4 Butts out of the ship Joseph from Cadiz To Wm. King Custom house Surveyor & Prisage master, for said foure Butts which were to bee taken, valued by agreement at	Dr	£	s	d
	96	85		

Anno 1685

Description	Dr	£	s	d
William Kinge of Bristoll Surveyor of the Customs & Prisage master	Dr	£	s	d
To Cash paid him by the hands of Wm. Lansdon in the custom house	83	73	10	4
To Ditto paid himselfe in full	83	11	9	8
		85		

Anno 1685

	Description	Dr	£	s	d
	Edward Crofts of Bristoll Merchant is	Dr	£	s	d
May 25	To Proffit & Losse for ¼ yeares rent of the house in which hee now liveth (let to him at £36 per Annum) ending March 21 1684/5	89	9		
	To Cash paid him for ½ yeares rent of 2 Chambers ending March 21	84	1		
August 5	To Ditto paid him for his noat of disbursments on the house	84	1	9	
	To Proffit & Losse for ¼ rent due 24th of June 1685	89 *	9		
1686 June 30	To Proffit & Losse for 1 yeares rent due 24th of this instant June 1686	105	36		
January	To John Cook & Sam. Kekewich for theire bill on him for 80 pieces of 8 at 53d per piece of 8	111	17	13	4
1687 June 24	To Proffit & Losse for 1 yeares rent due June 24th 1687	153	36		
1688 June 28	To Ditto for 1 yeares rent due June 24th 1688	153	36		
	To Cash paid him for 2 reserved roomes in my house ending June 24th 1688	157	2		

			£	s	d	
	By Daniel Griffith for 1 bagge	95	4	5		
	By Robert Hauxworth 2 large baggs weight neat 7cwt 0qr 20lb					
	at 20s 6d per Cwt	28	7	7		
			201	3	4	

Anno 1685					
	Olives 14 Jarrs per Contra are	Cr	£	s	d
Aprill 20	By Thomas Harris for 9 Jarres sould him at 5s 6d per Jarre	96	2	9	6
	By Simon Clement for 3 Jarres delird himselfe, T Callowhill &				
	T Jordan	86		16	6
	By Proffit & Losse for 1 Jarre taken to my selfe	89		5	6
	By acct. of kindnesse for 1 Jarre Si. Clement gave my wife				
			3	11	6

Anno 1685					
	Tho. Harris per Contra	Cr	£	s	d
	By Simon Clement for money paid him	86	2	9	6

Anno 1685					
	Prisage Wine per Contra	Cr	£	s	d
May	By Cash recd. of Wm. Lansdoune in part of the money per				
	Contra	83	73	10	4
	By sundry accts for the				
	By wines my 2/3 parts of 30 Butts in the Joseph, for their				
	prisage	94	10	10	
			84		4
	By Profit and Loss, for Ballance	190 *		19	8
			85		

Anno 1685					
	William King per Contra is	Cr	£	s	d
Aprill	By Prisage wine 4 Butts in the Joseph from Cadiz for money due				
	to him for said 4 Buttts by agreement	96	85		

Anno 1685					
	Edward Croft per Contra is	Cr	£	s	d
June	By Proffit & Losse for ½ yeares rent of 2 Chambers reserved in				
	his now dwelling house	89	1		
	By house at the lower end of Small Streat in which bee now liveth				
	for his noat of disbursments	22	1	9	
August 6	By Cash received of him for ½ years rent of the house bee now				
	lives in at the lower end of Small Streat, ending 24th June 1685				
	let at £36 per annum	84	18		
1686 August 12	By Cash recd. of him in part for 1 yeares rent due June 24th 1686	119 *	20		
September 27	By Cash recd. of him in full for that yeares rent	119	12		
February 16	By Cash recdd of him in full of the bill of Exchange per Contra	120	17	13	4
1687 Sept. 21	By Cash recd. of him in part for 1 yeares rent due June 24th 1687	139	2	11	
	By Tho. Goldney recd. his noat for money by his order	96	16	9	
	By Isaac Heming for money of Edward Tayler on a bill assign'd				
	by Edward Crofts	143	15		
1688 August 15	By Cash recd. of him in part of 1 yeares rent	141	20		

March 9	To Cash paid lent him on his bill	162	20		
	To Proffit & Losse for ½ yeares rent due December 22th 1688	164	18		
1689	To Ditto for ½ yeares rent due 24th June 1689	164	18		
December	To house at Lower End of Small Street, for ½ years rent due Dec. 21th 1689	161	18		
			222	2	4

---

(97)	**Bristoll 1685**				
	Adventure in the ship Merchants Goodwill Beniamin Morley Master bound to Cadiz in Spaine, consigned to John Cooke & Samuel Kekewich merchants in St Marie Port	Dr	£	s	d
May	To Worsted stockins for one Trunck containing viz				
	82 doz is 984 paire fine Bristoll hose £ s d				
	at 3s 1d per paire 151 14 00				
	10 score, & 5 doz fine Wells hose is				
	260 paire at 1s 11d 24 18 04	91	176	12	4
	To Isaac Heming for custom, carriage				
	to London etc. 4 5 02	90			
	To Proffit & Losse for the Trunck cord etc. 18 00	89	5	3	2
			181	15	6
	To Profit and Loss, for Ballance	190 *	13	3	8
			194	18	2

	Anno 1685				
	Xeries Wine 14 Butts imported in the ship Joseph Wm. Jefferies Master from Cadiz, for acct. of Simon Clement	Dr	£	s	d
	To Cash paid custom, fees, bills and wharfage	83	41	16	6
	To Proffit & Losse for Celleridge of 11 Butts until disposed of	89		7	6
	To Ditto for halling & halfe double halling from Cellar to Cellar	89		7	9
	To Henry Davis and company for freight & averidge at £3 10s 10d per ton.	97	24	15	10
	To Prisage wine for the Prisage of 14 Butts at 7s per Butt	96 *	4	18	
	To Proffit & Losse paid cooperidge of 11 Butts	89	3		
	To Ditto for ½ Commission of £150	89	1	10	
			76	15	7

	Anno 1684				
	Richard Cope of Portburie in the County of Somerset Blacksmith	Dr	£	s	d
March 24	To my Copiehold Tenement in Portburie for ½ yeares rent of my house, barne, Paddock of Land, Gardens & orchard there ending March 24th 1684 88	20	1	15	
1685 March 24	To Ditto for 1 yeares rent due for said house etc. ending March 24th 1685	20	3	10	
1686 March 24	To Ditto for 1 yeares rent due March 24th 1686	20	3	10	
1687 March 24	To Ditto for 1 yeares rent due March 24th 1686	20	3	10	
1689	To Ditto for 2 yeares rent due March 24th 1688	160	7		
			19	5	

Date	Description	Ref	£	s	d
October 23	By Cash received of him in full for 1 yeares rent ending June 24th 1688	157	16		
1689 Aprill 11	By Cash recd. of him in full of the money lent him per Contra	162	20		
May 15	By Cash recd. of him for ½ yeares rent due December 22th 1688	162	18		
October	By house at lower end of Small Streat £1 for ½ yeare for 2 rooms and 11s 3d aid money	161	1	11	3
	By Proffit & Losse for 3 Grose of Corks	164		5	3
14	By Cash recd. of his Daughter in full for ½ yeares rent due June 24th 1689	168	16	3	6
March 13	By Ditto recd. of him in full for ½ yeares rent due Dec. 21th 1689	175	15	15	
	By house at the lower end of Small Streat £1 for the rent of two rooms and £1 5s 00d disbursments	161	2	5	
	By Proffit & Losse for severall omissions of Creditt which should have been given him formerly at our severall evenings for rent	191 *	8		
			222	[2]	[4]

Bristoll 1685

Date	Description	Cr	£	s	d
	Adventure in the Ship Merchants Goodwill per Contra	Cr	£	s	d
December	By John Cooke & Samuel Kekewich for the neat proceeds of the Trunck of stockins per Contra being 7402 Ryals plate is 925¼ pieces of 8 the piece of 8 st 4s 2d as per acct. sales Nov. 1685	88	192	15	4
	By Samuel Kekewich for what overcharged on the Trunck of stockins per acct. closed Sept. 2nd 1687 appeares	111	2	3	10
			194	19	2

Anno 1685

Date	Description	Cr	£	s	d
	Xeries Wine 14 Butts per Contra	Cr	£	s	d
	By Cash recd. of Edward Haggatt for custom, freight etc. of one Pipe of Tent	83	5	2	6
	By 6 Butts hee sould to my selfe	95	10	4	10
	By 4 Butts & 1 Ullage hogshead delivered to himselfe				
	By Ballance carried to Simon Clement his acct. current	86	61	8	3
			76	15	7

Anno 1685

Date	Description	Cr	£	s	d
	Richard Cope per Contra is	Cr	£	s	d
July 29	By Cash recd. of him for ½ yeares rent of the house & Land in Portburie ending March 24th 84	83	1	15	
1686 June 24	By Cash recd. of him with his noat of disbursements for 1 yeares rent due March 24th 1685	108	1	13	
	By my Copiehold Tenement in Portburie for his noat of disbursments to the end of the yeare 1685	20	1	17	
1687 June 4	By Cash recd. of him	121		15	
13	By Cash recd. of him	141		18	
1688 July	By Tenement in Portburie for his two noats of disbursments with said money in full to March 25th 1688	20	5	6	4
1690 May 15	By Cash recd. of him	181	1		
	By Acct. of Ballances, for Ballance	194 *	6		8
			19	5	

	Anno 1685				
	Thomas Luttrell & Richard Prestoll of Clifdon [89] Yeomen	Dr	£	s	d
Aprill 25	To Cash lent them on theire bond payable Oct. 27th with intrest	83	20		
	To Proffit & Losse for ½ yeares intrest then also due	89 *		12	
1686 Aprill 26	To Proffit & Losse for ½ yeares intrest due Aprill 26th 1686	105		12	
1687 Aprill 26	To Ditto for 1 yeares intrest ending Aprill 26th 1687	153 *	1	4	
1688 October 26	To Ditto for 1½ yeares intrest ending October 26th 1688	153 *	1	16	
1689 October 16	To Ditto for 1 yeares intrest ending October 26th 1689	164	1	4	
1690 April	To Ditto for halfe years intrest ending April 26th 1690	164		12	
Oct.	To Ditto for ½ yeares intrest ending Oct. 26th 1690	180		12	
			26	12	

	Anno 1685				
	Henry Davis of Bristoll Hatter, & Co. owners of the ship Joseph	Dr	£	s	d
May 7	To Cash paid them in part	83	50		
	To Cash paid Henry Davis in full	83	64	8	
			114	8	

	Anno				
	Wines 6 hhds out of the Angell Gabriell from Bordeauxe	Dr	£	s	d
	To Ballance brought from that acct.	94	7		11½
	To Profit and Loss for Ballance	190 *	4	14	½
			11	15	

	Anno 1685				
	Adventure in the ship Swallow George Ayres master to Nevis	Dr	£	s	d
May 7	To Cash paid Wm. Rogers for ½ of 12 hhds cont. 192 dozen 5 bottles of Syder at 6d per doz aboard & ½ the freight of said Syder laden in said ship, & consign'd to John Streater & Company merchants there	83	31	16	

	Bristoll 1685				
	Richard Holbrook of Portburie in the County of Somerset Yeoman	Dr	£	s	d
Aprill 30	To my Copihold Tenement in Portburie for 1 yeares rent of the five acres, two acres, & two halfe acres in Portburie all let to hiim at £6 per annum for 7 yeares as per Covenant, the yeare ending in February 1684	20	6		
	To Ditto for 260 Faggotts at 4s 6d per Cwt as per his own noat given August 18th 85	20		11	3
1686 Aprill 16	To Ditto for 1 yeares rent of the Land aforesaid due 2 Feb. 1685	20	6		
November	To Ditto for ½ yeares rent ending 29th of September 1686	20	3		
March 25	To Ditto for ½ yeares rent due 25th March 1686	20	3		
1687 Sept.r	To Ditto for ½ yeares rent due February 2nd	20	3		
			21	11	3

Anno 1687		Cr	£	s	d
	Tho. Lutterell & Company per Contra	Cr	£	s	d
August 12	By Cash recd. of Tho. Lutterell for 2 yeares intrest ending Aprill 26th 1687	121	2	8	
	By Acct. of Ballances for Ballance	194 *	24	4	
			26	12	

Anno 1685		Cr	£	s	d
	Henry Davis & Company are	Cr	£	s	d
	By sundry accts for the freight & averidge of 44 Butts Wine in the ship Joseph from Cadiz at £3 10s 10d per tonne	94, 97	77	18	4
	By rice 50 baggs for Simon Clement & Co. for freight & averidge of 6 tons by agreement at £3 10s per tonne, and 19s 6d averidge	96	21	19	6
	By Olives for freight & averidge of 14 Jarres	96		12	2
	By Profit and Loss for Ballance	190 *	13	18	
			114	8	

Anno 1685		Cr	£	s	d
	Wine 6 hhds per Contra	Cr	£	s	d
November 7	By John Olliffe for 1 hogshead of White wine sould him	98	6	10	6
	By Sir George Strode for 1 doz bottles White wine	24		9	6
	By Sam. Davis for 2 doz bottles White wine & 1 doz bottles claret at 9s 6d	63	1	8	6
	By Ditto for 2 doz claret with etc. at 9s 6d	63		19	
	By Ditto for 3 doz White wine per order of his brother Joseph and the bottles	63	1	8	6
	By Richard Haynes for 2 doz bottles white wine at 9s 6d	111		19	
			11	15	

Anno 1685		Cr	£	s	d
	Adventure in the Swallow per Contra is	Cr	£	s	d
October 1	By Edmond Scrope & Company for ½ the neat proceeds of 1340 Bottles instead of 2309, there being 969 bottle said to bee left us as per theire acct. of sales dated July 31th 1686 may appear the ½ in sugar being 6077 lb at 10s per 100	33	30	7	8
	By Profit & Loss, for Ballance	190 *	1	8	4
			31	16	

Bristoll 1685		Cr	£	s	d
	Richard Holbrook of Portburie per Contra is	Cr	£	s	d
May 9	By Cash recd. of his wife in part	83	1	10	
August 18	By Cash received of himselfe in part for 1 yeares rent due March 24 1684	84	2	5	
	By Copie hold Tenement in Portburie for his noat of disbursments	20	1	15	8
1686 July 7	By Cash received of him in part for 1 yeares rent due March 1685	119	1	10	3
August 6	By Cash recd. of him in part for 1 yeares rent due at same time	119	2		
November 13	By Cash recd. of him in part	120	2		
	By Coppiehold Tenement for his noat of Disbursments given in the 14th Nov. 1686	20		13	
March 19	By Cash received of him in part	121	2		
1687 July 16	By Cash received of Susan Copie for his acct.	121	1	10	
	By Proffit & Losse for money hee saith his wife told him shee paid mee but neither I nor my servants do know any such thing, nor hath hee any receit for it	137		18	
February 21	By Cash of Capt. Samuel Gorges	140	3		
	By Acct. of Ballances, for Ballance	194 *	2	9	4
			21	11	3

	Anno 1685			
	Richard Haines of London Junio merchant Sonne of Richard Haines hatter	Dr	£	s	d
	To Simon Clement for the money per Contra being his money	86	40	1	
June 27	To Cash paid Tho. Callowhill per his order in part proceeds of 16 baggs of rice	83	35		
November 19	To Cash paid Simon Clement for ballance by his order, November 12th 1685	107	16	10	5
			91	11	5

	Anno 1685			
	Adventure in the ship Joseph Wm. Jeffferies Master to Nevis	Dr	£	s	d
June 1	To Cash paid Joseph Badger for 3 Copper Taches weight 468 lb laden in said ship & consign'd to John Streater & Company there at 16d¹/2 per pound	83	32	3	6
6	To Cash paid Wm. Jefferies for fraight	83		10	
	To Oliver Mosely for 1 Copper Tach, 12 Cosatha Graters, 12 ladles, & 12 skimmers, and 24 Iron sockets & setting them on as per his noat	4	18	4	5
			50	17	11
	To Profit and Loss for Ballance	190 *	26	7	
			77	4	11

	Anno 1685			
	Joane Darracot of Barnstable my maidservant	Dr	£	s	d
June 27	To Cash paid her in full for one yeares wages ending June 24th 1685	83	2	15	
October 2	To Cash paid her for ¹/4 yeares wages ending Sept. 29th 1685	84		15	
January	To Cash paid her ¹/4 yeares wages ending 25th Dec. 1685	107		15	
1686 June 25	To Cash paid her for ¹/2 yeares wages ending 24th June 1686	108	1	10	
October 13	To Cash paid her for ¹/4 wages due 29th Sept. 1686	120		15	
1687 Dec. 27	To Cash paid her for 1¹/4 yeares wages ending 25th of Dec. 1687	140	3	15	
January	To Cash paid lent her	157	2		
1688 March 7	To Cash paid her in full of all wages to the 25th of March 1689	162	3	15	
			16		

	Anno 1685			
	John Olliffe per Contra is	Dr	£	s	d
June 20	To Cash paid himselfe	83	15	4	
August 10 13	To Xeries wine in sundry ships for 14 Butts sould him, 8 at £25 10s per Butt, & 6 at £26 per Butt to pay ¹/2 the 10th November, & ¹/2 the 10th February as per his Bills given	101	360		
November 7	To Wines 6 hhds in the Angel Gabriel from Bourdeaux for 1 hogshead whitewine	94	6	10	6
			381	14	6

	Anno 1685			
	Henry Whitehead of Bristoll Distiller is	Dr	£	s	d
November 7	To Brandy 3 pieces for theire value sent him weight neat 30ct 3qr 27 lb at 3s 7d¹/2d per Gallon being 433 7/8 Gallons in all	103	78	12	9

(99)	**Bristoll 1685**			
	Robert Earle of Sunderland is	Dr	£	s	d
	To John Olliffe for 10 doz bottles Xerie sack sent to London per Tho. Moormans Waggon by John £ s d				
June 12	Shuttleworths order 8 07 02				

Anno 1685				
Richard Haines per Contra is	Cr	£	s	d
May By Cash recd. of Sir Richard Crump on a bill drawn on him per				
Simon Clement in favor of said Haines, but only used his name,				
but the money was said Clements	83	40	1	
By Rice 50 Baggs for neat proceeds of 16 Baggs for his acct.	96	51	10	5
		91	11	5

Anno 1688				
Adventure in the ship Joseph to Nevis per Contra	Cr	£	s	d
Aprill By Edm. Scrope & John Streater for 17203 lb Sugar the neat				
proceeds of the goods per Contra as per theire acct. of sales March				
1687 the sugar at 10s per Ct	33	77	4	11

Anno 1685				
Joan Darrracot per Contra	Cr	£	s	d
June 27 By Proffit & Losse for 1 yeares wages due 24th this instant June	89	2	15	
1688 Jan. 26 By Cash recd. of her the £2 lent her per Contra	157	2		
By Proffit & Losse for severall yeares wages	164 *	11	5	
		16		

Anno 1685				
John Olliffe of Bristoll Vintner is	Cr	£	s	d
June 12 By Robert Earle of Sunderland for 10 doz bottles Xerie, with				
bottles, Panniers & covers	99	9	11	8
26 By John Earle of Bristoll for 6 doz Xerie, bottles, Panniers &				
covers	37	5	12	10
March 22 By Cash received of him per Simon Clement	108	50		
1686 Aprill 14 By Cash received of him by Humphry Corsley	108	50		
August 7 By Humphry Corsley received of him by my order	117	86	10	
September 8 By Cash received of him by the hands of Joseph Davis	119	80		
December 8 By Cash received of him by the hands of Humphry Corsley	120	100		
		381	14	6

Anno 1685				
Henry Whitehead per Contra is	Cr	£	s	d
February 1 By Cash recd. of — Hawes per his order	107	40		
5 By Cash received of him in part	107	34		
By Jahzeel Speed for money hee received of him for ballance and				
never brought it to acct. of Cash but kept it to himselfe	122	4	12	9
		78	12	9

Bristoll 1685				
Robert Earle of Sunderland per Contra	Cr	£	s	d
July 14 By Isaac Heming for money received of his Countesse in London	90	9	12	8

		£	s	d				
	To Ditto for 10 doz bottles, & 3 Panniers & covers & permit	1	04	06	98	9	11	8
	To Proffit & Losse for halling to the Waggon, & port of leters	0	01	00	89		1	
						9	12	8

Anno 1685

		Dr	£	s	d
	Sugar 8 Butts & 4 hhds imported from Nevis in the Rainbow Tho. Moore Master	Dr	£	s	d
June	To Edmond Scrope & John Streater for 26084lb theire contents at 10s per Cwt as per Invoyce	33	130	8	4
	To Cash paid custom fees bills & wharfage as per particulars fol (121)	83	34	12	3
			165		7

Anno 1685

		Dr	£	s	d
	Sugar 5 Butts & 9 hhds imported from Nevis in the ship Baltamoore James Browne Master	Dr	£	s	d
June	To Edm. Scrope & John Streater for 26273lb theire contents at 10s per Cwt, as per Invoyce Aprill 85	33	131	17	4
	To Cash paid custom, fees, bills & wharfage as per particulars fol 121	83	34	1	7½
	To Sugar 8 Butts & 4 hhds in the Rainbow for theire cost & charges brought from	99	165		7
	To Cash paid weighing the 26 Cask	84		11	9
	To Cash paid Robert Bodenham in full for Celleridge of said sugar	84	1	10	
			333	1	3½
	To Profit and Loss, for Ballance	190 *	20	6	6½
			353	7	10

Anno 1685

		Dr	£	s	d
	Exchange to and from St Marie Port in Spaine in partnership with Isaac Hemming, negotiated with John Cooke & Samuel Kekewich merchants there	Dr	£	s	d
July	To Isaac Heming for ½ £205 04s 2d paid Lionell Horne for his bill 1000 pieces of 8 sent to said Cook & Kekewich at 49d¼ the piece of 8 as per his leters of 27th July, & 4th August 1685	90	102	12	1
August	To Ditto for ½ £207 16s 3d for another bill of 1000 pieces of 8 at 49 7/8d per piece of 8 of Sir Beniamin Newland, sent to St Marie Port in favor of said Cook & Kekewich	90	103	18	1½
	To Proffit & Losse for ballance this 22th Feb. 1685	105	8	10	1
			215		3½

Anno 1685

		Dr	£	s	d
	Linnin one Bale of Hallcloth left with mee for sales by Edward Roy of Dorchester Merchant for his acct. charg'd by him to mee to bee 94½ @ 23 solls per @ is	Dr	£	s	d
July	To acct. current of Edward Roy for the cloth its value sould per Contra	44	9	9	

Anno 1685

		Dr	£	s	d
	John Jones of Bristoll Linnindraper is	Dr	£	s	d
August	To Lincloth for acct. of Edward Roy for 1 Roll of Hallcloth 94½ @ ½ cost per Invoyce 23d per @ at 3d per @ off is	99	9	9	
	To Wine 6 hhds for 10 doz bottles claret at 9s 6d per doz £ 4 s 14 d 6	94			
	To Proffit & Losse for the 10 doz bottles at 2s per doz 1	89	5	14	6

Anno 1685		Cr	£	s	d
Sugar 8 Buttts & 4 hhds per Contra are		Cr	£	s	d
By Sugar 5 Butts & 9 hhds in the Baltamoore from Nevis imported thence at the same time, for the cost & charges of the sugar per Contra, which I carry thither to avoyd confusion in accts because both parcells were sould at the same time, to the same persons, & the charges of weighing, Celleridge etc. were paid on both parcells togeather		99	165		7

Anno 1685		Cr	£	s	d
	Sugar 13 Butts & 13 hhds in the Ships per Contra are	Cr	£	s	d
August	By Matthew Walter & Elizabeth Beaton for said sugar weight 321 cwt 1qr 2lb at 22s per Cwt	147	353	7	10

Anno 1685		Cr	£	s	d
	Exchange to & from St Marie Port in partnership per Contra	Cr	£	s	d
October	By Isaac Heming for ½ £200 bill sent per John Cook & Sam. Kekewich, drawne per John Frere, on Joseph Herne for [w]ith charges 7330½ Ryals plate at 52d¾ per piece of 8	90	100		
	By Ditto for ½ £211 4s 5d recd. of Wm. Atwill & Company for the neat proceeds of 950 pieces of 8 sent per Ditto merchants in the ship Unity Capt. Tucker in part of the money remitted per Contra	90	105	12	2½
February	By Ditto for ½ £19 16s 2d the neat proceeds of 88¾ piecesof 8 per the Ruby weight 77¼ oz at 5s 2d¼ per oz being sent for ballance of this acct. per John Cooke & Samuel Kekewich	90	9	18	1
			215		3½

Anno 1685		Cr	£	s	d
	Lincloth per Contra is	Cr	£	s	d
August	By John Jones for the Roll of Hallcloth 94½ @ at 2s 0d per @ 3d off Invoyce	99	9	9	

Anno 1685		Cr	£	s	d
	John Jones per Contra is	Cr	£	s	d
Aprill	By Proffit & Losse for Linnin, Stuffe and other particulars as per noat	89	12	13	6
October	By Ditto for 3 yds muzling & 2 yds Barras as per his acct. 4½ yds Crape	89		17	4
	By sundry accts for severalls parcell of Linnin and other goods as per his noat of particulars	104	23	8	8
			36	19	6

			£	s	d
October 4	To Cash paid him in full as per receit Oct. 4th 1686 then omitted to bee charg'd in Cash				
	To Proffit & Losse for what hee abated	105 *		1	
	To Cash paid him October 4th last in full	119	21	15	
			36	19	6

(100)   **Bristoll 1685**

		Dr	£	s	d
	Adventure in partnership with my Daughter Heming of London in the ship Cesar Capt. William Maddison to Cadiz, consign'd to John Cooke & Samuel Kekewich Merchants resident in St Marie Port in equal halves	Dr	£	s	d
	To one Trunck of worsted stockins cont. viz) £ s d				
	80 dozen is 960 paire fine Bristol hose at 2s				
	8d per paire 128 00 00	91			
	12 doz & 5 score is 244 paire fine Wells				
	hose at 1s 5d per pair 17 05 08	91	145	5	8
	To Proffit & Losse for a Trunck, cord & matting 17 00	89		17	
	To Isaac Heming for custom £3 06s 00d, charge shipping 4s 9d & carridge from Bristol	90	4	4	6
			150	7	2
	To Profit & Loss, for Ballance	190 *	20	10	9
			150	17	11

                              Anno 1685

		Dr	£	s	d
	Thomas Dyer of Bristoll hosier is	Dr	£	s	d
November 7	To Cash lent his wife on a score of hose	107	2		

                              Anno 1685

		Dr	£	s	d
	Isaac Heming & Company Merchants in London	Dr	£	s	d
January	To Ballance of theire former acct. current brought from that acct.	90	1708	5	9

                              Anno 1685

		Dr	£	s	d
	Adventure in the ship Olive Branch Capt. Edward Dowding to Cadiz	Dr	£	s	d
	To sundry accts being the cost & charges of sundry merchandizes laden in said ship & consign'd to John Mayne Supra Cargo on said ship (viz)				
August	To Worsted stockins for 45 doz Bristoll hose in a Trunck 540 paire at 2s 9d per paire	102	74	5	
	To Ditto for 40 doz Wells hose is 480 paire at 1s 6d per paire is	102	36		
	To Cash for 30 Guinnies delivered John Mayne to buy Butter in Cork	84	32	5	
	To Ditto paid him for ½ 20 Cases strong waters & charges on them	84	3	6	6
	To Ditto paid him for custom of the stockins etc.	84	2	3	
	To Proffit & Losse paid for a Trunck for the stockins				
			147	19	6
	To Profit and Loss, for Ballance	190 *	37	1	9
			185	1	3

                              Anno 1685

		Dr	£	s	d
	Lady Ann Powlet of Chartmark in the County of Dorset	Dr	£	s	d
June 10	To sundry accts for 4 doz bottles Xerie, bottles & Panniers sent per B. Wilkins	94,89	3	19	2

Bristoll 1685		Cr	£	s	d
	Adventure in partnership per Contra is				
July	By Isaac Heming for ½ the cost and charges of the Trunck of stockins per Contra	90	75	3	7
December	By John Cook & Samuel Kekewich for my ½ of the neat proceeds of the Trunck of stockins per Contra 3675 Ryals 25 Mervedis is 459 3/8 pieces of 8 as per acct. of sales November 1685 the piece of 8 at 4s 2d is	88	95	14	5
			170	17	11

Anno 1685					
	Thomas Dyer per Contra is	Cr	£	s	d
November 25	By Cash received of Elizabeth his wife	107	2		

Anno 1685					
	Isaac Hemming & John Barnard	Cr	£	s	d
December	By Adventure in the Popley Frigate to Cadiz, for charge on a Trunck of stockins	110	5	7	10
	By Proffitt & Losse for 6 Guinnies & 21s Silver, £7 10s paid Tho. Cox £1 5s a Kegge sturgeon 1 & Rd Russell £1	105	10	15	1
	By Maulting trade paid Jonathan Lamboll on my bill	109	60		
February 19	By Tho. Pope & R Gotley for ballance of Tho. Popes acct.	10		10	7
	By Proffit & Loss pd. port leters, Jahzeels shooes, brokridge pieces of 8, carridge Trunck, protest Earle, & procuration	105	2	18	6
	By ballance carried to theire acct. of debt in a new acct. current	113	1628	13	9

Anno 1685					
	Adventure in the Olive branch per Contra is	Cr	£	s	d
December	By John Mayne for the neat proceeds of the Goods per Contra as per John Mayne his acct. of Sales closed in Malaga November 1st 1685 being 6773 Ryals plate is 846 5/8 pieces of 8 the piece of 8 at 52d½ is	111	185	1	3

Anno 1685					
	Lady Ann Powlet per Contra	Cr	£	s	d
August	By Cash recd. of Bernard Wilkins	84	7	18	4
March 9	By Cash received of Bernard Wilkins	108	2	1	6

			£	s	d
July 22	To sundry accts for 4 doz bottles Xerie, bottles & Panniers sent per Wilkins	94,89	3	19	2
February 3	To sundry accts for 2 doz bottles Xerie, bottles, Pannier etc. sent per Bernard Wilkins	103,105	2	1	6
1686 June 16	To sundry accts for 2 doz bottles Xerie, bottles, Pannier & cover & portridge etc.	85,105	2	1	6
August	To John Blackwell for 4 doz qt bottles Xerie the bottles & covers	85	4	2	
October	To Proffit & Losse for what was abated by John Blackwell when paid 8d per Gall	105		8	
6	To sundry accts for 6 doz bottle Xerie, bottles Panniers & Covers etc.	126,127	6	4	
1687 May 18	To sundry accts for 4 doz bottles Xerie sent her by Francis Edwards by her order	133,127	4	2	6
July 26	To sundry accts for 4 doz 10 bottles Xerie, 1 doz 2 bottles whitewine, with bottles Panniers & covers	133,137	5	14	8
February 27	To sundry accts for 2 dozen of Xerie sent her per Fra. Edwards	133,137	2	1	4
1688 June 20	To sundry accts for 4 doz bottles Xerie, the bottles, Panniers, covers etc. by Fra. Edwards	111,153	4	2	3
			38	16	1

	Anno 1685				
	Sir William Drake of Ash in the Parish of Musburie in the County of Devon	Dr	£	s	d
June 12	To Xeries wines in sundry ships, & Proffit & Losse for 6 doz bottles Xerie, 6 doz bottles, and 3 Panniers sent him per Henry Stover	94,89	5	18	9

	Anno 1685				
	Robert Dowding of Bristoll Roapmaker & Samuel Price of the same Citie merchant	Dr	£	s	d
August 3	To Cash lent them on theire bond payable February 4th	84	100		
1686 August 4	To Proffit & Losse for 1 yeares due August 4th 1686	137	6		
1687 August 4	To Ditto for 1 yeares intrest due August 4th 1687	137	6		
1688 August 4	To Ditto for 1 yeares intrest due August 4th 1688	153	6		
February	To Ditto for ½ yeares intrest due February 4th 1688	164	3		
1689 August 4	To Proffit & Losse for ½ yeares intrest due August 4th 1689	164	3		
February 4	To Ditto for 1½ yeares intrest due February 4th 1689	164	3		
1690 Oct.	To Ditto for ½ years intrest due August 4th 1690	180	3		
			130		

(101)	**Bristoll 1685**				
	Adventure 2nd in the ship Civillia merchant Capt. John Braddyl to Cadiz	Dr	£	s	d
	To sundry accts for one Trunck of Bristoll & Wells hose laden in said ship & consign'd to John Cooke & Samuel Kekewich merchants for sales etc. viz				
	To Worsted stockins for 64 doz Bristoll hose is 768 paire at 2s 9d per paire is	91	105	12	
	To Ditto for 54 doz is 648 paire fine Wells hose at 1s 8d per paire is	91	54		
	To Proffit & Losse for a Trunck cord & matting	105		15	
	To Isaac Heming for carriage to London, custom & other charges	90	4	19	7
			165	6	7
	To Profit and Loss, for Ballance	190 *	32	12	9
			197	19	4

	Anno 1685				
	Tobacco 26 hhds for acct. Lawrence Washington & his friend imported from Potomak river in Virginea in the ship John Edmund Watts Master	Dr	£	s	d
August	Tobacco 20 hhds for his own acct. to Proffit & Losse for my Commission for sales at £2½ per Cent	127	2	10	

			s	d
1686 Nov. 3	By Cash recd. of Bernard Wilkins for the 10 doz bottles Xerie per Contra	120	10	14	
August 9	By Cash recd. of Christopher Parker by her order	121	9	17	
1687 March 6	By Cash recd. of Francis Edwards	140	2	1	4
July 26	By Cash recd. of Francis Edwards	141 *	4	2	3
	By Proffit & Losse for money which wee do not remember was ever received	158	2	1	8
			38	16	1

Anno 1685				
	Sir William Drake per Contra is	Cr	£	s	d
January 26	By Cash received of John Warren per his order	107	5	18	9

Anno 1686				
	Robert Dowding & Company per Contra	Cr	£	s	d
October 16	By Cash received of Ozziel Browne for 1 yeares intrest due August 4th 1686	120	6		
1687 Jan. 27	By Cash recd. of Ozziel Browne for 1 yeares intrest due August 4th 1687	140	6		
1688 August	By Cash recd. of Ditto for 1 yeares intrest due August 4th 1688	168	6		
1690 March	By Cash recd. of Ditto for 1 year's intrest due August 4th 1689	175	6		
			24		
	By Acct. of Ballances, for Ballance	194 *	106		
			130		

Bristoll 1685@				
	Per Contra	Cr	£	s	d
	By John Cook and Sam. Kekewich for 950 1/8 pieces of 8 being the neat proceeds of the Trunck of Stockins per Contra as per acct. of Sales closed November 1685, the piece of 8 at 4s 2d	88	197	19	4

Anno 1685				
	Tobacco 26 for Lawrence Washington & his friend per Contra	Cr	£	s	d
August	By Thomas Day for 20 hhds sould him at 3d per lb cleare of all charges unsight and unseene and to take them at 400 lbs neat one with the other	94	100		

To Ditto for 300 lb Tobacco due to mee on a former acct. charg'd to this acct. by his order at 3d per lb being the price these 20 hhds were sould at	127	3	15	
To Lawrence Washington his acct. current for theire neat proceeds	132	93	15	
		100	00	
Tobacco 6 hhds for acct. of his friend whose name I know not				
To Proffit & Losse for my Commission for Sales	127		15	
To Lawrence Washington his acct. current for theire neat proceeds	132	29	5	
		30		

Anno 1685

			Dr	£	s	d
	Xeries Wine imported from Cadiz in sundry ships viz. the Expectation, the Rachell and the Joseph brought here together for methods sake					
	To Xeries Wine 2/3 of 30 Butts in the Joseph in partnership with Simon Clement for ballance		94	516	9	¾
	To Xeries Wine 20 Butts in the Expectation for theire cost & charges		87	268	10	
August	To Cash paid Joseph Berry in part for Brokridge		84	1		
	To Xeries Wine 10 Butts in the Rachell for theire cost & charges		93	143	7	6
October 16	To Cash paid Joseph Berrie for Brokridge		84	1		
26	To Cash paid Joseph Berrie		84	1		
	To Tho. Day Wine Cooper for his noat for work etc.		70	23		
	To Samuel Davis for 2 hhds of Rhenish wine		63	14		
				968	6	6¾
	To Profit and Loss, for Ballance		190 *	475	5	11¼
				1443	12	6

Anno 1685

		Dr	£	s	d
	John Hellier Attorney at the Law [91] is				
January 27	To Cash paid lent him on his noat	107	20		
1687 June 4	To Cash paid lent him on his noat	121	15		
			35	00	00

Anno 1685

		Dr	£	s	d
	John Winpenny of Bristoll Vintner is				
October	To Xeries Wine out of sundry ships from Cadiz for 9 Butts the ½ f 18 Butts sould him & Stephen Stringer at £24 per Butt payable 1/3 money, 1/3 at 3 months, and 1/3 at 3 months after as per his bills	161	216		
1690 Oct. 8	To Wines my ½ of 20 Butts for ½ the amountant of 9 Butts Xerie at 33s per Butt and one hogshead Tent at 18s sold him and Lewis Adams to be pd. for ½ on 7th Dec. next, and ½ 25th Jan. next as per his bills	186	157	10	
			373	10	

(102)   **Bristoll 1685**

		paire	s	d	Dr	£	s	d
	Worsted Stockins are				Dr	£	s	d
July 24	To Cash paid John Massinger for	38	2	8	83	5	1	4
29	To Cash paid Andrew Creed and Tho. Browning	220	1	4	83	14	13	4
	To Ditto paid Joel Pinne for	30	2	4	83	3	10	
August 1	To Ditto paid Henry Britten for	65	2	6	84	8	2	6
	To Ditto paid John Perrie for	48	2	6	84	6		
	To Ditto paid Joseph White for	52	2	8	84	6	18	8
	To Ditto paid John Day for	17	2	5	84	2	1	5
5	To Ditto paid John Massinger for	42	2	8	84	5	12	
	To Ditto paid Edward Iffe in full for hotpressing stockins				84 *	1	7	4
8	To Ditto paid John Brady for	42	2	5	84	5	1	6
	To Ditto paid Joseph White for	69	2	8	84	9	4	

			£	s	d
	Tobacco 6 hhds for his friend whose name I know not [90] per Contra				
	By Thomas Day for 6 hhds sould him unsight and unseene cleare of all charges and to take them at 400 lbs neat at 3d per lb	94	30		

		Cr	£	s	d
	Anno 1685				
	Xeries Wine out of sundry ships per Contra	Cr	£	s	d
August 10, 13	By John Olliffe for 14 Butts 8 at £25 10s & 6 at £26 per Butt	98	357		
	By Edward Woodhouse & Company for 11 Butts sould them at £25 10s per Butt	103	280	10	
September	By Nicholas Baker for 5 Butts sould him at £25 10s per Butt	103	127	10	
October	By John Winpenny for 9 the ½ of 18 Butts sould him and Stephen Stringer at £24 per Butt	101	216		
	By Stephen Stringer for 9 the ½ of 18 Butts sould him and John Winpenny	103	216		
28	By John Blackwell for 10 Butts lesse 15 5/8 for Ullage at £23 10s per Butt	85	231	17	6
	By William Rogers for 3 Butts & part of a Butt of Lees soud Wm. Rogers	93	10	10	
	By Cash recd. of Sir Wm. Poole for returnes	107	2	10	
	By Tho. Day Wine Cooper for 14 Gall. Rhenish wine hee had of mee	114	1	15	
			1443	12	6

		Cr	£	s	d
	Anno 1685				
	John Hellier per Contra is	Cr	£	s	d
March 18	By Cash received of him	108	20		
1687 July 12	By Cash recd. of him	121	15		
			35	00	00

		Cr	£	s	d
	Anno 1685				
	John Winpenny per Contra is	Cr	£	s	d
October 26	By Cash recd. of him	84	72		
January 30	By Cash recd. of him	107	72		
July 7	By Cash received of him in full	119	72		
			216		
	By acct. of Ballnces, for Ballance	194 *	157	10	
			373	10	

		Cr	£	s	d
	Bristoll 1685				
	Bristoll Stockins & Wells per Contra are	Cr	£	s	d
August	By Ballance brought from that acct.	91	489	6	10½
	By Adventure in the ship Olive branch to Cadiz for one Trunck cont. 540 paire Bristoll hose, and 480 paire Wells hose	100	110	5	
			599	11	10½

	To Ditto paid John Massinger for	30	2	8	84	4		
15	To Ditto paid Edward Iffe in full for hotpressing stockins				84		11	9
17	To Ditto paid Joseph White for	160	2	8	84	8		
18	To Ditto paid Tho. Hill for	40	1	6	84	3		
	To Ditto paid Tho. Hill for	120	1	4	84	8		
20	To Ditto paid Robert Webb for two Truncks				84	1	3	
	To Ditto paid Tho. Hill for	50	2	6	84	6	5	
	To Ditto paid John Massinger for	38	2	8	84	5	1	4
22	To Ditto paid John Perrie for	47	2	6	84	5	17	6
24	To Ditto paid Tho. Hill for	43	2	5¾	84	5	6	6
27	To Ditto paid Tho. Hill for	20	2	6	84	2	10	
	To Ditto paid Wm. Thiery for	30	2	5	84	3	12	6
28	To Ditto paid John Massinger for	27	2	8	84	3	12	
	To Ditto paid John Day for	20	2	5	84	2	8	6
	To Ditto paid John Perrie for	23	2	6	84	2	17	6
	To Ditto paid Joseph White for	46	2	8	84	6	2	8
	To Ditto paid John Brady for	40	2	5	84	4	10	8
	To Ditto paid Tho. Hill for	27	2	6	84	3	7	6
September 1	To Ditto paid Andrew Creed for	32	1	4	84	2	2	8
3	To Ditto paid John Rudduck for	30	2	5¾	84	3	14	4
	To Ditto paid John Massinger for	40	2	8	84	5	6	8
4	To Ditto paid Henry Britten for	44	2	6	84	5	10	
5	To Ditto paid Edward Iff for hotpressing to this day				84		11	
12	To Ditto paid William Thiery for	25	2	5	84	3		5
13	To Ditto paid John Massinger for	32	2	8	84	4	5	4
	To Ditto paid Anthony Palmer for	41	2	5	84	5		
	To Ditto paid Jos. White for	40	2	8	84	5	6	8
18	To Ditto paid Henry Britten for	50	2	6	84	6	5	
	To Ditto paid John Perry for	40	2	6	84	5		
23	To Ditto paid Tho. Hill for	28	2	6	84	3	10	
25	To Ditto paid Tho. Browning for	19	2	6	84	2	7	6
						195	18	1
	To Cash paid Tho. Browning for Wells	40	1	4	84	2	13	4
	To Ditto paid Wm. Thiery for	30	2	5	84	3	12	6
	To Ditto paid Henry Britten for	60	2	6	84	7	12	6
26	To Ditto paid John Massinger for	38	2	8	84	5	1	4
	To Ditto paid John Perrie for	54	2	6	84	6	15	
	To Ditto pd. John Bradys servant for	45	2	5	84	5		
30	To Ditto paid Joseph White for	54	2	8	84	7	4	
	To Ditto paid Tho. Hill for	64	2	6	84	8		
September 6	To Ditto paid Anthony Palmer for	40	2	5	84	4	16	8
7	To Ditto paid John Perrie for	50	2	6	84	6	5	
	To Ditto paid Tho. Hill for	30	2	6	84	3	15	
8	To Ditto paid James Woollen for	18	2	6	84	2	5	
	To Ditto paid Wm. Thiery for	48	2	5	84	5	16	
10	To Ditto paid Tho. Hill for	79	2	6	84	9	17	
	To Ditto paid John Massinger for	41	2	8	84	5	9	4
	To Ditto paid Tho. Hill for	60	1	4	84			
12	To Ditto paid Ditto for	58	1	3	84			
	To Ditto paid Ditto for	12	2	6	84	9	2	6
	To Ditto paid John Day for	18	2	5	84	2	3	6
13	To Ditto paid Edward Iff in full for hotpressing				84	1	2	6
14	To Ditto paid John Perrie for	54	2	6	84	6	15	
	To Ditto paid John Rudduck for	21	2	6	84	2	12	6
	To Ditto paid Tho. Hill for	18	2	6	84	2	5	
16	To Ditto paid Henry Britten for	42	2	6	84	5	5	
17	To Ditto paid Joseph White for	42	2	8	84	5	12	
	To Ditto paid John Massinger for	31	2	8	84	4	2	8
	To Ditto paid John Brady for	34	2	5	84	4	3	
21	To Ditto paid Tho. Hill for	158	1	3	84	9	17	6

October 10	To Ditto paid John Perrie for	37	2	6				
	and	15	2	4	84	6	7	6
	To Ditto paid Tho. Hill for	20	2	6	84	2	10	
	To Ditto paid Jos. White for	49	2	8				
	&	5	2	6	84	7	3	2
24	To Ditto paid John Massinger for	44	2	8	84	5	17	4
	To Ditto paid Wm. Thiery for	27	2	4	84	3	1	
26	To Ditto paid Tho. Hill for	72	2	6	84	9		
27	To Ditto paid Robert Webb for a Trunck				84		13	
28	To Ditto paid John Bradys servant for	19	2	5	84	2		
29	To Ditto paid Anthony Palmer for	38	2	5	84	4	13	
	To Ditto paid John Rudduck for	38	2	6	84	4	15	
	To Ditto paid James Woollen for	23	2	6	84	2	17	·6
30	To Ditto paid John Massinger for	40	2	8	84	5	6	8
	To Ditto paid Tho. Hill for	36	2	6	84	4	10	
	To Ditto paid Eliza. Dyer for	3	2	6	84		7	6
						392	3	7
	To ballance carryed to that acct.				106	207	8	3½
						599	11	10½

(103)   Bristoll 1685

		Dr	£	s	d
	Edward Woodhouse of Bristoll Vintner & Wm. Higgs Wine Cooper				
August 20	To Xeries wines in sundry ships for 11 Butts sould them at £25 10s per Butt to bee paid ½ the 20th of November, & ½ 20th Feb. as per theire bills	101	280	10	
Aprill 1686 17	To Cash paid him in full	108	4		
			284	10	

Anno 1685

		Dr	£	s	d
	Simon Clement of Bristoll merchant				
January 8	To Cash paid lent him payable on demand	107	10		
1686/7 March 24	To Cash paid himselfe	121	8	10	
1688 May	To Proffit & Losse for 47 weeks celleridge of my vault from Feb. 1st 86 to Dec. 19th 87 at 3s	137	7	1	
	To Adventure in the Tygre to Cadiz for neat proceeds of Trunck hose per acct. Aprill 2nd 1688	144	80	16	¾
	To Xeries wine 23 Butts for 21 pieces of 8 an error on 6 Butts, & 5s 9d overcharg'd in averidge	150	4	16	9
July 20	To sundry accts for 1 doz Claret, 1 doz whitewine at 10s pr doz and 2 doz bottles	151, 153	1	4	
August 28	To sundry accts for 1 doz whitewine delivered Charles Jones by his order	151, 153		12	6
	To sundry accts for 6 bottles whitewine and the bottles	151, 153		6	
1689 Aprill 22	To Cash for bad money return'd to him being part of the £30 said to bee received per Contra	162		17	6
	To ballance carried to his acct.	166	5		11¼
			119	4	9

Anno 1685

		Dr	£	s	d
	Nicholas Baker of Bristoll Vintner is				
September	To Xeries Wine out of severall ships from Cadiz for five Butts soud him at £25 10s per Butt payable as per Contract & bills	101	127	10	
1686 August 5	To Cash paid him for ballance which hee overpaid per Contra	119	3		
1687 M	To Malaga Wines 4 Butts for 1 Butt sould him payable July 25th	134	31		
			161	10	

Bristoll 1685				
Edward Woodhouse & Company	*Cr*	£	*s*	*d*
November 5 By Cash recd. of Edward Woodhouse in part	84	140	5	
25 By Cash received of Edward Woodhouse in part	107	12		
January 14 By Cash received of Edward Woodhouse	107	126	5	
February 3 By the Lady Ann Pawlet for 2 doz bottles Xerie and the bottles	100	2		
24 By Sir Geo. Strode for 2 doz & 1 bottles Xerie & the bottles	24	2		
By Profit and Loss for Ballance		2		
		284	10	

Anno 1686				
Simon Clement per Contra	*Cr*	£	*s*	*d*
May By Cash received of him	108	4		
21 By Ditto received of him in full	108	6		
1686/7 March 24 By Proffit & Losse for 2 Quarter Cask Xerie bought of him at	127	8	10	
1687 Nov. By Adventure in the Tygre to Cadiz for custom & other charges on 2 Truncks hose	144	7	5	6
By Ditto for charges of custom etc. hee paid on a Trunck of stockins consign'd to himself	144	1	16	6
1688 May By Xeries wines 23 Butts for the cost of 6 Butts in the Tygre being 278¼ pieces of 8 at 52d	150	60	5	9
August By Proffit & Losse for 2 doz & 1 bottle Xerie at 4s 6d per Gallon	153	1	7	
By Cash received of him in part good and part bad money	162	30		
		119	4	9

Anno 1685				
Nicholas Baker per Contra is	*Cr*	£	*s*	*d*
January 16 By Cash received of him in part by the hands of Tho. Hill	107	50		
February 22 By Cash received of him per Robert Massinger	107	13	15	
March 24 By Cash received of him in part by Tho. Hill	108	30		
1686 July 31 By Alexander Dolman for paid him by my order, but by mistake £3 too much	48	36	15	
1687 Dec. 13 By Cash recd. of him in part	140	15		
January 23 By Cash recd. of him in full	140	16		
		161	10	

Anno 1685		Dr	£	s	d
	Brandy Three Pieces received of Henry Gibbs are	Dr	£	s	d
June 16	To Henry Gibbs for theire value cont. neat 433 7/8 Gallons at 3s 4d per Gallon	79	72	6	3
	To Proffit & Losse for halling, cooperidge, weighing & Celleridge from the 16th of June to the 7th of November, being first halled to a Cellar in the Marsh, thence to my Vault, and thence to the Backhall, & one of the pieced new hoop'd	105	1		9
			73	15	3
	To Profit and Loss, for Ballance	190 *	4	17	6
			78	12	9

Anno 1685		Dr	£	s	d
	Stephen Stringer of Bristoll Vintner is	Dr	£	s	d
October	To Xeries wine out of severall ships from Cadiz for 9 the ½ of 18 Butts sould him & John Winpenny at £24 per Butt payable money at 3 months & at 6 months as per Contract & bills	101	216		
			216		

Anno 1686		Dr	£	s	d
	Francis Whitchurch, & Charles Herbert & Company of Bristoll Sugar bakers	Dr	£	s	d
August	To Sugar 1 Butt for Elizabeth Tayler out of the Olive branch from Nevis soud them	103	15	17	8

Anno 1685		Dr	£	s	d
	Matthew Walter of Bristoll Grocer & Eliza. Beaton Widow Grocer	Dr	£	s	d
August	To Sugars in the Ships Rainbow and Baltamoore from Nevis Thirteene Butts & Thirteene hhds 321 cwt 1 qr 2lb neat at 22s per Cwt.	99	353	7	10
	To Proffit & Losse for what they gave mee in sugar, for intrest money	105	1		
	To Cash paid Mathew Walter in full as per his receit for the foregoing intrest & Sugar per Contra	119		19	
			355	6	10

Anno 1685		Dr	£	s	d
	Adventure in the ship Dilligence to Cadiz John Seward Commander	Dr	£	s	d
October	To Cash paid — Mancell for 40 hides ship'd in said ship and consign'd to Robert Massinger Supra Cargo on her weighing 9cwt 2qr 2lb is 1126 lb sable at 6d¹/₄ per pound is	84	27	15	
	To Cash paid Robert Massinger for custom & other Charges	84 *	1	2	6
	To Proffit & Losse	105	3		
			31	17	6

Anno 1686		Dr	£	s	d
	Sugar 1 Butt recd. out of the ship —. from Nevis for acct. of Elizabeth Tayler, laden per — Lloyd there as per his leter	Dr	£	s	d
August	To Cash paid Tho. Walden for custom, Fees, Freight etc. as per noat	119	6	10	3
	To Cash paid weighing at the Backhall	119			6
	To Eliz. Taylor, for the neat proceeds	88	9	6	11
			15	17	8

Anno 1685		Cr	£	s	d
	Brandy Three pieces per Contra are	Cr	£	s	d
November 7	By Henry Whitwood for the 3 pieces soud him weight neat 30ct 3qr 27lb being 433 7/8 Gallons soud him at 3s 7d½ per Gallon	98	78	12	9

Anno 1685		Cr	£	s	d
	Stephen Stringer per Contra is	Cr	£	s	d
October 26	By Cash received of him	84	72		
February 9	By Cash recd. of him	107	72		
1686 June 17	By Cash received of him in full	108	72		
			216		

Anno 1686		Cr	£	s	d
	Francis Whitchurch & Company	Cr	£	s	d
September	By Cash recd. of Fra. Whitchurch	119	15	17	8

Anno 1685		Cr	£	s	d
	Matthew Walter & Company per Contra are	Cr	£	s	d
December 2	By Cash received of Matthew Walter in part	107	65		
	By Ditto received of Matthew Walter per Simon Clement	107	30		
	By Isaac Heming for John Bubbs bill assign'd to said Heming on Tho. Lane	90	20		
February 13	By Cash received of them per Edward Martindale for mee	107	100		
March 21	By Cash received of Elizabeth Beaton in part	108	21		
22	By Cash recd. of Matthew Walter in part	108	25		
Aprill 17	By Cash recd. of Elizabeth Beaton by Simon Clement	108	20		
21	By Cash recd. of them per Simon Clement	108	14		
	By Cash received of them per Simon Clement	108	20		
August 5	By Humphrey Corsley for money hee received of the Widow Beaton	117	38	7	10
17	By Proffit & Losse for a Sugar Loaf weight 5¼ lb at 11d per lb is	105		4	9
	By Ditto for 2 Sugar loaves more, and 2 quarters of powder sugar as per Mat. Walters noat	105	1	14	3
			355	6	10

Anno 1685		Cr	£	s	d
	Adventure in the Dilligence per Contra is	Cr	£	s	d
February	By Robert Massinger for the neat proceeds of the 40 hydes per Contra 1224 Ryals plate is 153 pieces of 8 the piece of 8 at 4s 2d	109	31	17	6

Anno 1686		Cr	£	s	d
	Sugar 1 Butt per Contra is	Cr	£	s	d
August	By Fra. Whitchurch & Company Sugarbakers for the Butt sould them weight Groce 20cwt 0qr 7lb, tare 1cwt 1qr 14lb at 17d per lb is	103	15	17	8

(104)	**Bristoll 1685**	Dr	£	s	d
	Merchandizes sundry laden in the ship Francis & Marie Wm. Nicklus Master bound to Patomack river in Virginea for acct. Lawrence Washington merchant, and his namelesse friend	Dr	£	s	d
October 7	To Cash paid John Matthews for a french hatt & hatband with silver Buckles	84		10	
	To Cash paid custom fees & bills for the merchandizes in proportion	84		10	2
	To Cash paid George Poply for 1 doz plaine shooes, and 3 paire of French falls for his own use	84	1	16	6
20	To Cash paid Jerom Churchy for pieces Brecknock Cottens	84	3	11	
	To John Jones for 40 Ells of fine sheeting Linnin at 21d per Ell	99	3	10	
	To Cash paid Walter Payne for a £ s d Rugg 11s 11				
	To Ditto paid for a paire Blankets 10 6				
	To Ditto for 1 doz Russia Leather Chaires at 5s 6d 3 6 0				
	To Ditto for matts & Cords 1 6	84	4	9	
	To Ditto pd. Philip Higgenbottom for 3 doz hoes & ½ doz Axes as per particulars	84	2	3	
	To Cash paid John Blackley for a large Chest clamp	84		17	
Nov.	To Ditto paid Matthew Morgan for 2 paire Sheep Sheeres	84		2	8
	To Ditto paid Tho. Case for 2 doz Spoones	84		5	
	To Ditto paid Fra. Ballard for Nails & Stocklocks as per noat	84	2	7	6
	To Ditto paid Wm. Window for 1 dozen best Irish hose	84		14	
	To Proffit & Losse for a Plowshare & Coulter of John Edwards weight 28lb at 3d½ as per noat	127		8	2
	To Ditto for 2 parcells blew Linnin bought of John Jones as per noat & book of Invoyces	127	1	10	4
	To Ditto for portridge hallidge & lyteridge to the ship	127		8	
	To Ditto for a barrill & packing 2s 6d	127		2	6
	To my Commission at £2 per Cent	127		9	2
			23	14	
October	Merchandizes in the same ship for his Friend by his order				
	To Cash paid for theire proportion of custom fees & bills	84		8	2
	To Cash paid Walter Payne for 1 doz Russia Leather Chaires & matts & Cover	84	3	7	6
	To Cash paid John Blackley for 2 Table boards matts & cords	84	2	8	
	To Cash paid John Edwards for a paire of Cartwheels, axeltree & Linchpin	84	2	11	
	To Proffit & Losse for portridge hallidge & lyteridge aboard	127		4	4
	To Ditto for my Commission at £2 per Cent	127		3	6
			9	2	6

	Anno 1685	Dr	£	s	d
	Merchandizes in the ship Francis & Marie Wm. Nicklus Master bound to Patomak river in Virginea, for my propper acct., and consign'd to Lawrence Washington merchant at Upper Machoduck there, are	Dr	£	s	d
October 10	To Cash paid Tho. Walden for 6 lb white, 6 lb coloured thred, 12 Groce Buttons, and 4 11/16 oz Silk as per Invoyce and his noat	84	3	4	6
	To Cash paid theire proportion of custom fees bills etc.	84		13	6
	To Cash paid Wm. Rogers for 3 doz plaine & 3 doz french falls at 28s	84	8	8	
	To Cash paid George Popley for 4 doz plaine shooes, and ½ doz fr falls	84	5	19	
	To John Jones for 20 Ells Sheeting Canvas at 15d¼, ½ piece broad dowlas at £4 6s 6d, 115 Ells Canvas at 11d¼, 1 piece Searge at £1 8s 6d, 1 Groce silke buttons, with Silk and thred in all amounting to as per noat of particulars	99	14	1	7

Bristoll

	Cr	£	s	d
Merchandizes per Contra are				
By Lawrence Washington his acct. current for the cost & charges				
of the goods per Contra, carried to that acct.	132	23	14	
Merchandizes in the ship Francis & Marie for account of				
Lawrence Washington's Friend, sent by his order per Contra				
By Lawrence Washington for the cost & charges of the said goods	132	9	2	6

Anno 1685	Cr	£	s	d
Merchandizes per Contra are				
By Lawrence Washington his acct. current for the Cost &				
Charges of the goods per Contra charg'd by agreement betwixt us				
to his acct. of debt, hee having the Tobacco made good to his acct.				
which came in the John & Francis & Marie	132	42	3	1¼

		£	s	d
To Ditto for 2 pieces Searges at 27s 6d, 3 pieces Glazd Callacoes at 12s 6d 49¼ parcels Coloured Linnin at 6d per yd is in all as per noat of particulars	99	5	17	1½
To Proffit & Losse for assureance money my Commission and a Virginea hogshead & packing the, goods in, packing them etc. all which I did advance on the severall commodities sent in the Invoyce	127	3	19	4¾
		42	3	1¼

Anno 1685				
Sugar 3 Butts & 13 hhds laden in Nevis by John Streater & Company in the ship Friendship of London Richd. Young Master consign'd to Isaac Heming mer	Dr	£	s	d
November 2 To Edmond Scrope & John Streater for the first cost of Ditto sugar in Nevis 27201 lb sugar, as per theire Invoyce Sept. 5th 1685 the sugar at 10s Sterling per Cwt	33	136		1

Anno 1685				
James Symonds Junior of Yarmouth merchant is	Dr	£	s	d
January 26 To Cash paid John Wayland on his bill valued on mee	107	24	19	6
To Proffit & Losse for port of leters about the foregoing bill	105			6
		25		

(105)	**Bristoll 1685**				
	Proffit & Losse is	Dr	£	s	d
October	To Ballance brought from that acct.	89	1092	14	1
28	To Cash paid Abraham Hill for 2 Tubbs of Butter	84	1	19	
November 2	To Ditto paid Matthew Morgan for a Cheddar Cheese	84	1	11	9
	To Tho. Walden for 1 doz Inkle	87		7	
	To Simon Clement for 8¼ yds ½ of Plush	96	2	6	8
	To Ditto for Hallidge hee paid	96		3	
	To Isaac Heming for 80 papers powder at twice	90	2	10	
	To Ditto paid port leters to the 29th Sept. 1685 as per acct.	90	2	3	6
	To Isaac Heming paid Philip Ward of the Crowne Office	90	5	7	6
7	To Cash paid Roger Addams in full for Mault	107	3	13	
	To Tho. Day for money abated him	70		12	9
	To Cash paid George White in full of his noat	106	3	10	
9	To Cash paid George Hayne Upholsterer in full of his noat	107	1	12	6
	To Ditto paid George Deighton for 2 Cask beere	107		6	6
January 5	To Cash paid Edward Jones in full	107		9	
	To Cash paid Ben. Baily for freight etc. of a Cask of Fruit	107		5	
	To Cash paid port of leters	107	1	8	10
8	To Ditto paid houshold expences to this day	107	20	16	8
February 5	To Cash paid houshold expences to the 5th instant	107	12	4	3
	To Isaac Heming recd. of him in London in Dec. last	90	13		
	To Edm. Scrope for charges on sugar in the Comfort & on a hogshead of sugar	38		8	2
	To Sir George Strode for money recd. of him in London Dec. 1684 & forgot to bee charg'd	24	6	6	6
	To Isaac Heming for 6 Guinnies & 21s in Silver recd. on London	100	7	10	
	To Isaac Heming for money hee paid Tho. Cox for mee	100	1	5	
	To Ditto for a Kegge of Sturgeon	100	1		
	To Ditto paid Richard Russell for 40 papers powder	100	1		
	To Isaac Heming for port of leters 39s 3d, brokridge of ½ 2000 pieces of 8 a paire of shooes for Jahzeel 4s carriage of my Trunck 4s 9d protest of Joseph Earles bill 1s 6d procuration against Robinson 5s in all	100	2	18	6
March 1686	To Martha Linch for 1/2 yeares wages due March 30th 1686	92	1	2	6
	To Marie Speed my wife for 68 Guinnies received of her	113	73	2	
	To John Kent Junior for money of him at Reading	78	1		

Anno 1686		Cr	£	s	d
	Sugar 3 Butts & 13 hhds per Contra are				
	By Isaac Heming for theire neat proceeds as per his acct. closed				
	Sept. 29th 1686	113	103	3	1
	By Profit and Loss, for Ballance	190 *	32	17	
			136	0	1

Anno 1685		Cr	£	s	d
	James Symonds Junior per Contra is				
January 11	By Cash received of Thomas Jones Junior of Llandavenny in				
	Wales on his bill of Exchange drawne by Abraham Barrington	107	25		

Bristoll 1685		Cr	£	s	d
	Proffitt & Losse is				
November	By Wm. Dawson for 2 doz bottles	94		4	
	By Wm. Spoore Junior & Senior for 1 yeares intrest of £40 due				
	June 5th 1685	69	2	8	
	By Adventure in the Civilia merchant to Cadiz for a Trunck				
	cord etc.	101		15	
	By Isaac Heming & Company for 2½ yeares intrest of £400				
	ending Nov. 10th 1685	69	40		
	By Charles Plomer & Company recd. of them for intrest	78	5	4	6
	By Adventure in partnership in the Wellcom to Cadiz for a				
	Trunck Cord etc.	110		14	
	By James Symones Junior for port of leters	104			6
	By John Mayne for ballance	111		2	7
	By Jahzeel Speed for ballance of his acct. wrongfullly charg'd to				
	this acct. fol. 33 of this book	69	409		2
	By Exchange to and from St Marie Port for ballance of that				
	acct.	99	8	10	1
	By Edmond Scrope for ½ cost of a parcell goods in the George to				
	Virginea omitted to bee charg'd	38	21	9	
	By John Mayne for port of leters	111			3
	By the Lady Ann Powlet for a pannier, cover etc.	100		1	6
	By Sir George Strode for a Pannier cover etc.	24		1	6
	By Ditto for 1 doz bottles, pannier & cover for whitewine sent				
	him	24		2	10
	By Samuel Davis for 3 doz bottles	63		6	
	By Ditto for 5 doz bottle delivered with wine at twice	63		10	
	By Richard Haynes for 2 doz bottles	111		4	
	By Isaac Heming for 2 Guinnies delivered him when I came out				
	of London	90	2	3	
1686 Aprill	By Humphry Corsley for 83 Guinnies sould him	1	89	9	8
	By Wm. Godwin for the intrest of £100 2 yeares due March				
	27th 1686	64	12		
	By Worsted stockins for one Trunck in the Lumbley Castle	114		14	
	By Tho. Day Wine Cooper for ballance	70			2
	By John Earle of Bristoll for ½ yeares intrest of £100	80	3		
	By Cash recd. of the Widow Hibbert for poore money by my				
	daughter Martha	108	1	6	

Date	Description	Fol.	£	s	d
Aprill 2	To Cash paid John Cheshire in full	108		6	15
	To Isaac Heming received of him at severall times	113	12	9	
17	To Cash paid postage of a leter	108			3
	To Cash paid Tho. Isay for 12 sacks Coale	108		6	
	To Ditto paid houshold expences	108	1		
	To Ditto paid for 1½ bushell of oates	108		3	
			1283	6	11
	To Cash paid Sweeping the chimnyes & a draught of Faggotts	108		4	8
	To Cash paid houshold expences & postage of a leter	108	1		3
29	To Cash paid Joseph Drew	108		1	
May 1	To Cash paid port 3 leters	108			8
5	To Cash paid Jahzeel £1 4s 6d household expences 10s keeping Nicholas Warrens horse 6s 7d & paid Francis Yeamans clark 2s 6d & port of 2 leters 5d	108	2	4	
6	To Cash paid port of a leter 1d a peck ¼ beanes 11d¼ 2 bushells oates 3s 9d	108		4	9¼
10	To Ditto for paid port of a leter	108			2
	To Ditto paid houshold expences 10s 6d, & 12 sacks Cole 6s	108		16	6
14	To Ditto paid Martha Speed 10s port of 2 leters 4d, & Wm. Plydall 5s	108		15	4
18	To Cash paid for houshold expences & port of a leter	108		10	2
21	To Cash paid Wm. Plydall in full	108		5	
	To Paul Priaulx	17			6
	To Wm. Olliffe for ballance	3		1	9
	To Ann Challoner widow for keeping my black & Bay mare to May 27	114	6	18	6
June 1	To Cash paid Jane Flower in full for halling to this day	108	2	1	2
	To Jonathan Lamboll for 2000 of Fossets & a bagge sent from Reading	87	1		8
16	To Cash paid for a flitch of Bacon	108		9	4
	To Cash paid Tho. Goldney for severall particulars	108 *		11	6
	To Cash paid Tho. Palmer, Charles Stubbs etc. for reliefe of French Protestants	119	1	10	
	To Cash paid Abraham Pretty & Richard Cope for building at Portburie	119	1	1	
	To John Hartnell for Mault May 1685 to June 1686	38	7	3	5
	To Ditto for lock & charges at Clevedon	38		3	10
	To Richard Merrick abated him	92		2	11
	To Martha Gay for ballance of her acct.	32	115	13	3
	To Samuel Davis for 1 doz pint bottles of Mum	63		3	
	To Alexander Doleman for severall goods bought of him as per noat	48	17	8	
July	To Cash paid Abraham Hill for a Firkin Butter to send to London	119		16	6
9	To Cash paid Joane for 1½ dozen Butter	119		8	9
	To Cash paid Wm. Clark for 8 doz pints & 5 doz quart bottles	119	1	1	6
14	To what paid out of Cash for houshold expences	119	31	6	4½
	To Cash paid John Hardiman in full of his noat	119		10	
22	To Cash paid Thomas Bourne for my part of charges on the stable	119		4	6
August 5	To Ditto paid George Cabbell for mending the Pump	119		3	
	To Ditto paid for a permitt for a box stockins	119			6
	To Mathew Walter & Company for a Sugar loafe 5lb	103		4	9¾
	To Sir George Strode for money of him in London	24	2	13	2
	To Mathew Walter & Company for severall small parcells Sugar	103	1	14	3
	To Tho. Goldney for ballance of his acct.	16		1	3
	To Arthur Hobbs abated him	29		3	11
	To John Wilmer abated him on a mare sould him	117	2		

Month	Description	Fol.	£	s	d
May	By John Miles for port of a leter	114			2
	By Thomas Lutterell & Company for ½ yeares intrest of £20 due Aprill 26 86	97		12	
	By Adventure in the Friston for a Trunck cord etc.	116		16	
	By Tho. Gibson for money furnishd John Hort & John Hardiman for Joseph Forest	1	6	2	2
	By Ullage Brandy for ballance	2	36	5	11
	By Sugar in the Consent for ballance	3	31	4	1
	By Wm. Coles for ballance	3		1	5
	By Brandy 3 pieces for halling, cooperidge & other charges	103	1	9	
June	By Jonathan Lamboll for money of Tho. Curtis	87		17	3
	By Dr. Fra. Hungerford for 9 qrt bottles & port leters	87		1	10
	By John Earle of Bristoll for 40 Daies intrest of £100	80		13	4
	By the Lady Ann Powlet for portridge & port of leters	100			6
	By sundry acct.rs for the cost & charges of 2000 Fossetts from Reading for T. Day, & John Jaine	114, 116	1	2	
	By Henry Howard & Company for ½ yeares intrest of £100	92	3		
	By Wm. Spoore Senior & Company for 1 yeares intrest of £50 due Aprill 21th 1686	30	3		
	By Wm. Spoore Senior for ½ yeares intrest of £10 due may 19th 1686	52		6	
	By Jahzeel Speed for money taken out of Cash in absence of Henry Deighton	69	4		
	By Ditto paid Richard Baugh for old scores	69		12	
	By John Blackwell for money resting due on acct. of Joseph Baughs redemption	85	1	6	7
	By Jahzeel Speed for money hee took up of Robt. Summers at severall times	122		13	6
	By Ditto paid Alderman Olliffe for potts of wine	122	2	3	1
	By Ditto paid John Sandford	122		17	
			693	11	7
	By Jahzeel Speed for money pd. Lewis Addams for pots of wine in Feb. 1682	122	1	10	6
	Bu Ditto for money hee received privatly out of Cash of Hen. Deighton without my knowledge	122	21	7	11
	By Ditto for severall couple of North Sea Codd, which hee took up money for, & kept it	122	1	12	
	By Edward Croft for 1 yeares rent of the house in which hee liveth	96	36		
	By Jahzeel Speed for money hee received & took out of Cash at severall times	122	21		
	By Adventure in the ship Malaga merchant to Malaga for a Truncke etc.	122		11	
	By Wines 6 Butts in partnership for severall charges on them	116		10	8
	By Wm. Prichard & Company for 1 yeares intrest of £50 due Aprill 2nd 1686	63	3		
	By John Wilmer for ballance	62		10	5½
	By Sir George Strode for ballance of his acct.	24		8	3
	By Edward Martindale for money left with him at my departure for London	24	103	5	9
	By Adventure in the Adventurers delight for a Trunck cord & matting	123		11	
	By Mathew Walter & Company for intrest money	103	1		
	By Oyles 10 pipes for acct. of John Cooke & company for halling & portridge	117		6	5
	By James Beard for 2 yeares 4 months intrest of £10 ending Sept. 21st 1686	76	1	8	
	By Sir George Strode for 1 quart Olives & 1 dozen Lemons & the Pott for the Olives	24		2	6
	By John Wilmer for my young Bay mare sould him at	117	17		

To Cash paid James Freeman for Olives & a Pott for Sir George Strode				119		1	3
					262	1	1½
					1485	7	½

(106)   **Bristoll 1685**

	Worsted Stockins are To	paire	s	d	Dr	£	s	d
October 31	To Cash paid John Perrie for	45	2	4				
	To Ditto paid Ditto for	34	2	6	84	9	10	
	To Ditto paid Tho. Hill for	45	2	6	84	5	12	6
November 6	To Ditto paid John Brady for (part paid before)	19	2	5	84		6	
	To Ditto paid John Day's servant for	31	2	5	84	3	14	11
	To Ditto paid Joseph White for	45	2	8	107	6		
7	To Ditto paid Andrew Creed for	212		15	107	13	5	
	To Ditto paid (and 2d over) for	7	2	4	107		16	6
	To Ditto paid James Woollen for	21	2	6	107	2	12	6
	To Ditto paid John Massinger for	33	2	8	107	4	8	
14	To Ditto paid John Massinger for	34	2	8	107	4	10	8
	To Ditto paid James Wollen for	16	2	6	107	2		
18	To Ditto paid Edward Iffe for hot pressing in full				107	1	14	4
	To Ditto paid Tho. Hill for	42	2	6	107			
	To Ditto paid him for	50	2	4	107	11	1	8
	To Ditto paid Tho. Hill for	69	2	6	107	8	12	6
19	To Ditto paid John Lukins for	42	2	3	107	4	14	6
21	To Ditto paid James Wollen for	30	2	6	107	3	15	
	To Ditto paid John Perry for	38	2	6	107	4	15	
	To Ditto paid John Massinger for	44	2	8	107	5	17	4
	To Ditto paid Tho. Hill for	60	2	6	107	7	10	
	To Ditto paid Joseph White for	113	2	8	107	15	1	2
23	To Ditto paid Wm. Thiery for	29	2	4	107	3	8	
	To Ditto paid Anthony Palmer for	40	2	5	107	4	17	
	To Ditto paid John Ruddock for	50	2	5	107	6	1	10
	To Ditto paid John Brady for	60	2	6	107	7	10	
28	To Ditto paid John Perry for fancies	43	2	4	107			
	To Ditto paid Ditto for sadds	32	2	6	107	9		4
	To Ditto paid Tho. Hill for	98	2	6	107	12	5	
	To Ditto paid Joseph White for	63	2	8	107	8		
	To Ditto paid John Massinger for	52	2	8	107	6	18	8
December 1	To Ditto paid John Day for	23	2	5	107	2	15	7
5	To Ditto paid John Brady for	22	2	6	107			
	To Ditto paid him for	20	2	4	107	5	2	8
	To Ditto paid Joseph White for	60	2	8	107	7	10	
	To Ditto paid Anthony Palmer for	45	2	6	107	5	12	6
	To Ditto paid Robert Webb Trunckmaker in full				107	1	18	
	To Ditto paid John Massinger for	36	2	8	107	4	16	
	To Ditto paid James Wollen for	21	2	6	107	2	12	6
	To Ditto paid Tho. Hill for	34	2	4	107	3	19	6
	To Ditto paid Tho. Hill for	20	2	5	107	2	8	4
						210	13	6
	To Cash paid Tho. Hill for Wells hose, less 8s	232	1	3	107	14	2	
	To Ditto paid Tho. Hill for	34	2	6	107	4	5	
8	To Ditto paid John Rudduck for	50	2	6	107	6	5	
8	To Ditto paid Tho. Hill for	34	2	5	107	4	2	2
	To Ditto paid John Perry for	65	2	6	107	8	2	6

			£	s	d
	By the Lady Ann Powlet for money John Blackwell abated mee on 4 doz Xerie	100		8	
	By Adventure in the Dilligence to Cadiz for ballance of that acct.	103	3		
			213	10	5½
			907	2	½
	By ballance carried to that acct.	127	578	5	
			1485	7	½

Bristoll 1685

		Cr	£	s	d
	Stockins per Contra are				
November	By Ballance of the former acct.	102	207	8	3½
	By Adventure in the Civilia merchant to Cadiz for 1 Trunck cont. 1332 paire fine Bristoll hose, and 120 paire fine Wells hose, the one at 2s 9d tother at 1s 6d per paire [92]	109	192	3	
	By Adventure in partnership in the Wellcom to Cadiz, for one Trunck cont. 88 dozen is 1056 paire fine Bristoll hose at 2s 8d per paire	110	140	16	
December	By Adventure in the Wellcom for my own acct. for one Trunck laden in her cont. 54 doz fine Bristoll sadds, 14 doz Bristoll fancies is 816 paire at 2s 9d per paire	110	112		
	By Ditto for 12 doz fine Wells sadds & 7 doz Wells fancy colours is 228 paire laden in same Trunck in same ship, at 1s 6d per paire is	110	17	2	
	By Adventure in the Rebeckah Capt. Pulman to Cadiz for 1 Trunck cont. 1332 paire fine Bristoll hose at 2s 9d per paire, and 120 paire Wells hose at 1s 6d per paire is	109	192	3	
	By Adventure in the Popley Frigat to Cadiz for one Trunck cont. 840 pair Bristoll hose at 2s 9d, and 528 paire Wells fancies, and 96 paire sadd Wells at 1s 6d per paire in all	110	162	6	
			1023	18	3½

					Folio	£	s	d
9	To Ditto paid Edward Iffe in full for hot pressing				107	1	4	2
11	To Ditto paid Tho. Hill for	35	2	4	107	4	2	
12	To Cash paid Jonathan Abram for	58	2	6	107	7	5	
	To Ditto paid James Wollen for	28	2	6	107	3	10	9
	To Ditto paid Joseph White for	62	2	8	107	8	5	4
	To Ditto paid John Massinger for	43	2	8	107	5	15	
16	To Ditto paid Tho. Hill for	57	2	6	107	7	2	2
19	To Cash paid Jonathan Abram for	45	2	6	107	5	12	6
	To Ditto paid Tho. Hill for	31	2	5	107	3	14	11
	To Ditto paid Ditto for	25	2	4	107	2	18	4
	To Ditto paid Tho. Hill for sadds	31	2	6	107			
	To Ditto paid Ditto for Fancies	44	2	5	107	9	3	10
	To Ditto paid John Brady for	29	2	6	107	3	12	6
21	To Ditto paid Robert Webb in full for one Trinck				107		13	
23	To Ditto paid John Webb for	18	2	5	107	2	3	7
	To Ditto paid John Perry for fancies	40	2	4	107			
	To Ditto paid him for sadds	75	2	6	107			
	To Ditto paid John Rudduck for	60	2	5	107	14	1	
	To Ditto paid him for	28	2	20	107	10	6	
	To Ditto paid Henry Britten for	55	2	6	107	6	17	6
	To Ditto paid John Massinger for	81	2	8	107	10	16	4
24	To Ditto paid James Wollen for	37	2	6	107	4	12	6
	To Ditto paid Tho. Hill for	50	2	6	107	7	5	
	To Ditto paid Ditto for	40	2	4	107	4	13	4
	To Ditto paid Ditto for	39	2	5	107	4	14	4
	To Ditto paid Edward Iffe in full for hot pressing				107	1		7
26	To Ditto paid Joseph White for sadds	49	2	8	107			
	To Ditto paid him for Fancies	32	2	6	107	10	10	8
January 2	To Ditto paid Anthony Palmer for	75	2	6	107	9	7	6
	To Ditto paid John Massinger for	20	2	8	107	2	13	4
6	To Ditto paid Tho. Hill for	30	2	6	107	3	15	
	To Ditto paid Tho. Walden for 2 dozen Inkle				107		13	6
7	To Cash paid Joel Pinns wife for	11	2	4	107	1	6	
8	To Ditto paid Jonathan Abram for	40	2	6	107	5		
	To Ditto paid Tho. Hill for	480		13	107			
	To Ditto paid him for	120		16	107	34		
9	To Ditto paid John Massinger for	38	2	8	107	5	1	4
	To Ditto paid John Brady for	19	2	6	107	2	7	6
	To Ditto paid Wm. Thiery for	26	2	4	107	3		8
	To Ditto paid Ed. Iffe in full for hotpressing stockins				107	1	10	2
	To Ditto paid Henry Britten for sadds	29	2	6	107			
	To Ditto paid him for Fancies	82	2	5	107	13	10	8
	To Ditto paid James Wollen for	40	2	6	107	5		
	To ballance of this acct. carried to that acct. of debt				112	549	2	1½
						1023	18	3½

(107)   Bristoll 1685

		Dr	£	s	d
	Cash is				
November	To ballance brought from that acct.	84	851	14	2
10	To John Hurtnell Junior received of him	38	10		
	To Tho. Walden received of him	87	1	7	6
	To Bethel Walter received of him per Tho. Hill	92	10		
13	To Isaac Heming recd. of John Hurtnell Junior per his order	90	2	14	3
21	To Wm. Spoore Junior & Senior recd. of Wm. Spoore Junior for intrest	69	2	8	
25	To Edward Woodhouse recd. of him in part	103	12		
	To Tho. Dyer received of his wife	100	2		
	To Peter Roswell recd. of him per the hands of his daughter	60	8		
December 2	To Matthew Walter & Company recd. of Martha Walter	103	65		
5	To Isaac Heming received of Sir John Smith on my bill on him	90	100		
8	To Tho. Day Soapmaker recd. of him	94	130		

Bristoll 1685

		Cr	£	s	d
	Cash per Contra is				
November 5	By *Stockins paid Joseph White and Andrew Creed*	*106*	20	1	6
	By *Tho. Dyer lent his wife on a score of hose*	*100*	2		
	By *Proffit & Losse paid Roger Addams in full for mault*	*105*	3	13	
	By *Stockins paid James Wollen & John Massinger*	*106*	7		6
	By *Fruite in the Olive branch for custom & other charges on 9 barrells & 27 frails*	*110*	4		2
14	By *Stockins paid John Massinger, James Wollen, & Edward Iffe*	*106*	8	5	
18	By *Proffit & Losse paid George White in full*	*105*	3	10	
	By *Stockins paid Tho. Hill and John Lukins*	*106*	24	8	8
19	By *Richard Haynes paid Simon Clement by his order in full*	*98*	16	10	5
21	By *Thomas Curtis paid lent his wife*	*58*	3		
	By *Stockins paid James Wollen, John Perrie, John Massinger Tho. Hill & Jos. White*	*106*	36	18	6

January 6	To Tho. Day Wine Cooper recd. of him	70	107		
	To Charles Plomer & Company received of them	78	159	14	6
	To Wines out of sundry ships from Cadiz recd. of Sir Wm. Poole	101	2	10	
9	To John Stretten recd. of him	57	6		
	To John Mayne recd. of him	111	4	3	
11	To James Symonds Junior recd. of Tho. Jones	104	25		
14	To James Beard recd. of him	76	10	10	
	To Edward Woodhouse recd. of him	103	126	5	
16	To Nicholas Baker recd. of him in part	103	50		
	To Richard Merrick recd. of him	92	6	10	
	To John Mayne for money of Joseph Earle	111	131	5	
26	To John Warren received of him to keepe for him	111	27		
	To Sir Wm. Drake received of said Warren	100	5	18	
27	To John Hurtnell Junior recd. of him	38	1		
28	To Matthew Walter & company recd. of Matthew Walter	103	30		
30	To John Wimpenny received of him	101	72		
Feb. 1	To Henry Whithead received of — Hawes per his order	98	40		
5	To Ditto received of him	98	34		
9	To Stephen Stringer recd. of him	103	72		
13	To Matthew Walter & Company received of them	103	100		
20	To John Mayne received of his wife	111	2	16	
22	To Nicholas Baker recd. of him	103	13	15	
25	To Edmond Scrope received of him	38	5		9
			2227	11	2

Date	Description	Ref	£	s	d
23	By Ditto paid Wm. Thiery, Anthony Palmer, John Rudduck, and John Brady	106	21	16	10
28	By Ditto paid John Perry, Tho. Hill, Jos. White, John Massinger and John Day	106	37	7	7
December 1	By Martha Speed paid her	109	2	8	
	By Jahzeel Speed paid Wm. Richstone	69	6	15	
5	By Stockins paid John Brady for 22 paire at	106	5	2	8
	By Jahzeel Speed paid Lewis Addams	69	1	11	
	By Stockins paid Jos. White, Anthony Palmer, Robt. Webb Trunckmaker	106	15		6
	By Martha Speed paid her	109	1	8	
	By Stockins paid John Massinger, James Wollen, Tho. Hill	106	13	16	4
	By Ditto paid Tho. Hill, and John Rudduck	106	24	12	
8	By Ditto paid Tho. Hill, & John Perry	106	12	4	8
	By Proffit & Losse paid George Rayne in full	105	1	12	6
9	By Jahzeel Speed paid John Blackwell	69	19	13	7
	By Stockins paid Ed. Iffe in full	106	1	4	2
	By Proffit & Losse paid George Dighton	105		6	6
11	By Stockins paid Tho. Hill	106	4	2	
	By Estate at Clapton paid Katherine Winter	72		16	
12	By Stockins paid Jonathan Abram, James Wollen, Jos. White, & John Massinger for	106	24	16	1
16	By Ditto paid Tho. Hill ,& Jonathan Abram	106	28	11	9
19,21	By Ditto paid John Brady, Robert Webb, John Webb, & John Perry	105	20	10	1
	By Ditto paid John Rudduck, Henry Britten, John Massinger, & James Wollen	106	32	12	4
24,26	By Ditto paid TTho. Hill, Edward Iffe, & Joseph White	106	28	3	11
January 2	By Stockins paid Anthony Palmer & John Massinger	106	12		10
	By Proffit & Losse paid Edward Jones in full	105		9	
6	By Stockins paid Tho. Hill	106	3	15	
	By Proffit & Losse paid Beniamin Baily	105		5	6
	By Stockins paid Tho. Walden	106		13	6
	By Joane Darracot paid her for ¼ wages	98		15	
	By Martha Linch paid her for ¼ wages	92		11	3
	By Jahzeel Speed paid John Hardiman	69	2	11	
	By Simon Clement paid him in full Nov. 13th past then omitted to be charg'd	86	6	2	10
7	By Stockins paid Joel Pinns wife & Jonathan Abram	106	6	6	
	By Simon Clement paid lent him	103	10		
	By Proffit & Losse paid port of leters & houshold expences	105	22	5	6
	By sundry accounts paid charges on 2 Trunck Stockins in the Welcome to Cadiz	110	5	17	10
	By Stockins paid Tho. Hill, John Massinger, John Brady & Wm. Thiery	106	44	9	6
			550	2	
	By Jahzeel Speed for money wanting in Cash	69	13	11	
	By John Stretten paid his noat of disbursements	57	1	12	10
	By Jahzeel Speed left in his hands to pay the poore	69	4		
	By Stockins paid Wm. alias Edward Iffe in full	106	1	10	2
	By Fruite in the Olive tree paid Arthur Harts sonne	110	8	18	6
	By Edward Jones paid lent him on his bill	25	2		
	By Stockins paid Henry Britten & James Wollen	106	18	10	8
14	By Ditto paid Tho. Hill for 3 parcells	112	15	11	8
16	By Ditto paid Anthony Palmer, John Massinger & Joseph White	112	24	17	8
	By Ditto paid John Perrie	112	8	4	
	By Richard Merrick paid his noat of disbursments	92	3	1	
19,20	By Stockins paid Tho. Walden, Tho. Hill & John Massinger	112	9	6	
	By Ditto paid John Day & Jos. White	112	14	16	1

(108)	**Bristoll 1685/6**				
	Cash is	Dr	£	s	d
February 27	To ballance in Folio (107)	107	1193	7	3
March 4	To John Hartnell Junior received of him in part	38	5		
9	To the Lady Ann Pawlet recd. of Bernard Wilkins	100	2	1	6
12	To Humphry Corsley recd. of him	1	40		
	To Tho. Day Soapmaker recd. of him	94	1	3	
18	To Humphry Corsley recd. of him	1	49	9	8
	To John Hellier recd. of him	101	20		
20	To Jahzeel Speed recd. of Robert Webb	69		17	4
21	To Matthew Walter & Company recd. of Eliza. Beaton by Simon Clement	103	21		
22	To John Olliffe recd. of him per Simon Clement	98	50		
	To Matthew Walter & Company recd. of Matthew Walter	103	25		
24	To Nicholas Baker recd. of him per Tho. Hill	103	30		
Aprill 14	To John Olliffe recd. of him per the hands of Humphry Corsley	98	50		
16	To Isaac Heming recd. of Tho. Day, £54 & Sir Samuel Astry £300	113	354		
17	To Matthew Walter & Company recd. of Eliza. Beaton per Simon Clement	103	20		
21	To John Earle of Bristoll recd. of him in full	80	103		
	To Simon Clement received of him	103	6		
	To Matthew Walter & Company recd. of them per Simon Clement	103	14		
May 15	To Proffit & Losse recd. of the Widow Hibbert	105	1	6	
	To Thomas Day borrowed and received of him	114	20		

			£	s	d
25	By Wm. Spoore Senior paid lent him	52	5		
26	By James Symonds Junior paid John Wayland on his bill	104	24	19	6
27	By Stockins paid Jonathan Abram	112	6	11	6
	By John Hellier paid lent him on his noat	101	20		
28	By Stockins paid John Perrie	112	21	9	4
29	By Adventure in the Betty paid Ozziel Browne for Premio of assureance	110	3	18	
Feb. 1	By Stockins paid Tho. Hill, John Massinger & Robert Webb	112	21	19	7
5	By Ditto paid Anthony Palmer, Andrew Creed, Jonathan Abram & Elizabeth Dyer	112	18	17	10
	By Robert Massinger paid lent him	109	16		
	By Stockins paid Elizabeth Dyer	112	3	2	10
	By Proffit & Losse paid houshold expences	105	12	4	3
8	By Stockins paid John Massinger, Wm. Thiery & John Rudduck	112	16	1	9
10	By Stockins paid Tho. Hill & Joseph White	112	16	4	9
11, 12	By Ditto paid John Perrie, Joane White, Ed. Iffe & Tho. Hill	112	24	13	8
13	By Ditto paid John Day, John Massinger & Anthony Palmer	112	14	10	9
15, 17	By Stockins paid Tho. Walden, Henry Britten, Tho. Hill & John Brady	112	15	16	1
20	By Ditto paid Jonathan Abram, John Massinger & Joseph White	112	27	1	5
	By Ditto paid Tho. Hill for 3 parcells	112	16	6	11
22	By Ditto paid Robert Massinger for wine in part at twice	109	23	15	
24	By Ditto paid Robert Webbs wife for a Trunck	112		13	
25	By Isaac Heming paid Edmond Scrope for his bill	113	20		
	By Stockins paid Jonathan Abram & James Wollen	112	8	14	2
27	By Ditto paid Henry Britten for 33 paire fancies, & 26 paire sadds	112	7	1	6
	By Robert Massinger paid him in full	109	7	7	6
	By Stockins paid John Massinger	112	5	12	
			1034	3	11
	By Ballance carried to that acct. of debt	108	1193	07	3
			2227	11	2

Bristoll 1685/6

	Cash per Contra is	Cr	£	s	d
March 1	By Stockins paid John Day for 31 paire	112	3	15	
2	By Proffit & Losse paid John Cheshire	105	6	15	
	By Henry Gibbes paid him	79	25		
	By Stockins paid John Perrie for 30 paire	112	3	12	6
3	By Edward Roy paid him in full	44	2	9	
4	By Stockins paid Wm. Thiery & Tho. Hill	112	19	17	6
6	By Ditto paid Wm. Turley & John Massinger	112	9	4	
8	By Ditto paid Joseph White, Ed. Iffe & Tho. Hill	112	13	11	7
	By Wine 6 Butts in the Dilligence paid John Seward for freight etc.	113	7	3	8
10,	By Stockins paid Tho. Hill & John Massinger	112	7	5	1
12	By Ditto paid John Brady & Tho. Hill	112	13	19	11
13	By Stockins paid John Day for 21 paire	112	2	10	3
	By Martha Linch paid her for ¼ yeares wages	92		11	3
	By Stockins paid Joseph White & Tho. Hill	112	27	12	8½
	By Ditto paid Jona. Abram, Anthony Palmer & Tho. Hill	112	14	2	10
18	By Ditto paid Tho. Hill, John Perry & Jonathan Abram	112	15	4	6
20	By Ditto paid Robert Webb, Elizabeth Dyer & John Massinger	112	6	17	1
25	By Ditto paid John Day, Tho. Hill & Joseph White	115	13	2	11
27	By Stockins paid John Brady & Tho. Hill	115	15	11	7½
	By Marie Wasbrow paid her in part	75	20		
31	By Stockins paid John Massinger, Edward Iffe & Tho. Hill	115	10	19	2
Aprill 1	By Ditto paid Tho. Hill & Anthony Perry for John Perry	115	15	3	7
2	By Ditto paid John Rudduck, Henry Britten & John Lukins	115	17	19	3

	To Matthew Walter & Company recd. of them per Simon Clement	103	20		
22	To Simon Clement received of him	103	4		
	To John Streatten received of him	57	5	2	
June 4	To Wm. Godwin recd. of him for ½ yeares intrest of £100	64	3		
	To John Blackwell received of him	88	21	17	
	To John Hartnell Junior received of him in part	38	5		
7	To James Beard recd. of him in part for rent	76	16		
17	To Stephen Stringer received of him	103	72		
19	To John Cooke & Sam. Kekewich received of Charles Stubbs on theire bill	111	88	5	10
	To James Beard received of him	76	2	12	
	To Richard Haines received in full	111	1	3	
23	To Tho. Day Wine Cooper recd. of him	114	1	2	
	To Henry Howard & Company recd. of Ozziel Browne	92	3		
24	To sundry accts recd. of Wm. Spoore Senior for intrest money	52, 30	3	6	
	To Richard Cope received of him	97	1	13	
	To Tho. Goldney recd. of his Sonne Thomas	16	1	3	
			2255	8	7

9	By Ditto paid Elizabeth Dyer & Anthony Palmer	115	6	5	9
	By Marie Thring & Company lent them on theire bond	114	20		
10	By Stockins paid Joseph White, John Massinger & Jonathan Abram	115	17	4	5
	By Ditto paid James Wollen & Tho. Hill	115	6	8	11
14, 16	By Stockins paid John Perrie & John Massinger	115	12	2	10
	By Tho. Day Wine Cooper paid him in full	114	20	17	1
	By Humphry Corsley paid him by John Olliffe	1	50		
17	By Wm. Spoore Junior paid lent him	31	10		
	By Edward Woodhouse paid him in full	103	4		
	By Stockins paid Wm. Turley for 17 paire	115	1	19	8
	By Proffit & Losse paid port of a leter	105			3
21	By Stockins paid John Day	115	1	6	4
	By Proffit & Losse paid for a draught fagots I say 12 sacks cole	105		6	
22	By Stockins paid Eliza. Dyer, Jos. White, John Rudduck & James Wollen	115	16	9	6½
	By Proffit & Losse paid houshold expences £1 & a bushell & ½ oates 3s	105	1	3	
23	By Stockins paid John Brady & John Massinger	115	7		8
26	By Ditto paid Edward Iffe & Jonathan Abram	115	5	8	7
27	By Proffit & Losse paid sweeping Chimnys, houshold expences, a draught fagots, & port of a leter	105	1	4	11
29	By Stockins paid John Lukins, Henry Britten, James Wollen, and Joseph White	115	22	17	
	By Proffit & Losse paid Joseph Drew	105		1	
May 1	By Ditto paid port of a leter	105			3
	By Stockins paid John Massinger, Anthony Palmer, John Perry, & John Day	115	19	17	9
	By Proffit & Losse paid port 2 leters 5d	105			5
4	By Stockins paid Joseph White for 40 paire sadds & 13 paire Pearles	115	6	5	
5	By Proffit & Losse paid Jahzeel £1 4s 6d, houshold expences 10s keeping Nich Warrens horse 6s 7d, paid Fra. Yeaman cleark 2s 6d & port 2 leters	105	2	4	2
	By Stockins paid Elizabeth Dyer	115	1	4	
	By Humphry Corsley for money paid him Aprill 17th	1	100		
			606	15	11½
6	By Stockins paid John Massinger, John Ruddck & Joane White	108	13	7	10
8	By Ditto paid Jonathan Abram & John Perry	108	9	8	7
	By Proffit & Losse paid port of a leter 1d a peck ¼ beanes & 2 bushells Oates 3s 9d	105		4	9¼
	By Stockins paid Anthony Palmer, James Wollen, Henry Britten, & John Brady	115	16	6	10
10	By Proffit & Losse paid port of a leter	105			2
	By Stockins paid Joseph White	115	6	16	
11	By Proffit & Losse paid houshold expences 10s 6d & 12 sacks Cole 6s	105		16	6
	By Stockins paid John Massinger	115	5	4	
	By Proffit & Losse paid Martha Speed	105		10	
	By Stockins paid James Wollen, John Perry, & Henry Britten	115	19	19	6
15	By Proffit & Losse paid Port of a leter & Wm. Plydal	105		5	4
18	By Ditto paid houshold expences & port of a leter	105		10	2
	By Thomas Day paid him	114	20		
21	By Stockins paid Henry Britten	115	4	19	1
	By Proffit & Losse paid Wm. Plydall in full	105		5	
	By Stockins paid John Day & John Lukins	115	6	13	9
	By Ditto paid Jonathan Abram & John Massinger	115	10	14	10
22	By Ditto paid Elizabeth Dyer, Joseph White and John Brady	115	13	9	7
	By Ditto paid Tho. Hill for 3 parcells	115	12	4	2
25	By Ditto paid Tho. Walden & John Massinger	115	6	2	8

(109)	**Bristoll 1685**				
	Martha Speed my daughter is	Dr	£	s	d
September	To ballance of a former acct. brought from that acct.	46	21	4	
	To Isaac Heming for money of him in London	90	5		
	To Ditto recd. more then of him in London	90	2		
December 2	To Cash paid her by her Bro. Jahzeel in my absence	107	2	8	
5	To Cash paid her by her Brother	107	1	8	
			32		

	Anno 1685				
	Adventure in the ship Rebeckah of London Capt. Tho. Pulman to Cadiz, consign'd to John Cooke & Samuell Kekewich merchant in St Marie Port	Dr	£	s	d
October 31	To Isaac Heming for 40 pieces white Colchester Baies, for dying 20, pd. custom, packing etc.	90	165	12	4
	To Ditto for charges of carriage of the Trunck to London custom & other charges	90	5	4	5
	To Stockins for 1 Trunck cont. 1332 fine Bristoll hose at 2s 9d per paire	106	183	3	
	To Ditto for 120 paire Wells hose at 1s 6d per paire	106	9		
	To Isaac Heming for charge of assureance of £200 to Cadiz	90	3	1	
	To Profit and Loss, for Ballance	190 *	58	14	6
			424	15	3

	Anno 1685				
	Robert Massinger of Bristoll merchant is	Dr	£	s	d
February 5	To Cash paid lent him payable on demand	107	16		
	To Adventure in the Dilligence to Cadiz for the neat proceeds of 40 Tannd hydes as per his acct. closed Dec. 24th 1685 1224 Ryals is 153 pieces of 8 at 4s 2d the piece of 8	103	31	17	6

28	By Ann Challenor paid her in part	114	2		
31	By Ditto paid her in full	114	4	18	6
June 1	By Stockins paid Jonathan Abram & John Perrie	115	11	13	1
	By Proffit & Losse paid Jane Flower in full	105	2	1	2
	By Stockins paid Tho. Walden, Eliza. Dyer, John Rudduck & Anthony Palmer	115	4	18	6
7	By Stockins paid Elizabeth Dyer	115	2	6	4
	By John Earle of Bristoll paid John Blackwell per his order	80	21	17	
8	By Stockins paid Tho. Walden, Henry Britten, & John Day	115	6	19	10
10	By Ditto paid Joane White, John Lukins, & James Wollen	115	12	10	6
	By sundry accts paid Richard Miller	117	10		
	By Stockins paid John Massinger, Henry Britten, Wm. Thiery & Tho. Hill [93]	115	20	16	1
14, 15	By Ditto paid Joseph White & John Perry	115	12	19	3½
19	By Henry Gibbes paid him in full	115	5	18	6
	By Stockins paid for 3 Bedcoards	118		3	
	By Proffit & Losse paid for a Flitch of Bacon	105		9	4
	By Stockins paid Robert Webb & Jonathan Abram	118	5	18	10
	By Ditto paid Anthony Palmer, John Massinger & Peter Hinton	118	9	11	6
21	By Ditto paid Joseph White	118	5	15	9
25	By Joane Darracot paid her	98	1	10	
	By Oyles 10 Pipes in the Betty from Cadiz pd, custom, fees, freight etc.	117	22	19	7
26	By Wine 1 Butt in Ditto ship, pd. custom, coynage, Prisage, freight etc.	116	10	15	1
	By Stockins paid John Brady & Jonathan Abram	118	11	9	1
			940	5	7
	By Ballance carried to that acct.	119	1315	3	
			2255	8	7

Bristoll 1690@					
Per Contra is		Cr	£	s	d
By Profit & Loss for Ballance		190 *	32	00	00

Anno 1686					
Adventure in the Rebecca per Contra		Cr	£	s	d
By John Cook & Sam. Kekewich for 579¼ pieces of 8 the neat proceeds of 29 pieces Baies as per acct. Sept. 2nd 1686		111	123	2	4
By Ditto for 713 pieces of 8 the neat proceeds of part of the Trunck of Stockins per Contra Nov. 3d		111	151	14	
By Ditto for 413¼ pieces of 8 the neat proceeds of the remainer of the stockins per acct. Sept. 2nd 1686		111	87	16	10
By Samuel Kekewich for neat proceeds of 11 pieces dyed Baies per acct. closed Oct. 21th 1687		111	62	2	1
			424	15	3

Anno 1685					
Robert Massinger per Contra is		Cr	£	s	d
February	By Wines 6 Butts in the Dilligence for the cost of 4 Butts in Spaine as per Invoyce December 24th 1685 by him laden in returne of the hydes per Contra	113	36	9	8
	By Ditto for 2 Butts bought of him a remnant in a small caske at	113	42	10	

			£	s	d
20	To Cash paid him in part	107	10		
22	To Ditto paid him per Nicholas Baker at the Rose	107	13	15	
27	To Cash paid him in full	107	7	7	6
			79		

	Anno 1685				
	Maulting trade in partnership with Jonathan Lamboll in Reading	Dr	£	s	d
October 2	To Isaac Heming for money hee paid Jonathan Lamboll on my bill in part of £400 hee was oblidg'd to put into the stock with £200 of said Jonathan Lamboll	90	100		
14	To Ditto for £100 more hee paid him per my order in part of the said £400	90	100		
November 16	To Ditto for £100 more hee paid him by my order in part of the said £400	90	100		
	To Jonathan Lamboll for money formerly lent him, and now by him paid in to our joint stock of trade in partnership for my acct. in said trade	87	40		
Feb. 19	To Isaac Heming for money hee paid Jonathan Lamboll on my bill in full of the £400 above mentioned	100	60		
			400		

	Anno 1686				
	Jonathan Lamboll of Reading Maultster is	Dr	£	s	d
September 29	To sundry accts for £450 lent him on a mortgage of all those his houses in Fryer Streat in the Towne of Reading at £5 per Cent intrest per Annum as per the Deed of mortgage may appeare (viz)				
	To Maulting trade in partnership with himselfe for principall money left in his hands at the dissolution of our partnership, which was my share of the stock wee put in to £ s d drive the said trade 400	109			
	To his acct. current for money hee received of Isaac Heming in London by my order to make up the summe aforesaid 50	87	450		
1687 March 25	To Proffit & Losse for ½ yeares intrest of £450 due 25th March 1687	127	11	5	
September 29	To Ditto for ½ yeares intrest of the £450 due Sept. 29th 1687	137	11	5	
1688 March 25	To Ditto for ½ yeares intrest of £450 due March 25th 1688	137	11	5	
June 24	To Ditto for ¼ yeares intrest due 24th of June 1688	137	5	12	6
1689 June 25	To Ditto for 1 yeares intrest from June 24th 1688 to June 24th 1689 of £450	164	22	10	
	To Ditto for 7 months intrest of £450 from the 24th June 1689 to 25th Jan. 1689	164	13	2	6
			525	00	

(110)	Bristoll 1685				
	Fruite 9 Barrills & 27 frailes laden by John Mayne in the ship Olive branch of Bristoll Edward Dowding master from Malaga	Dr	£	s	d
November 7	To Cash paid custom Fees etc.	107	4		2
	To Ditto paid Arthur Harts sonne for freight & averidge	107	8	18	6
	To John Mayne for its first cost 1821 Ryals plate is pieces of 8 227 5/8 at 52d½	111	49	15	10
			62	14	6

	Anno 1685				
	Adventure in the ship Wellcom of Bristoll Philip Freake Master to Cadiz in partnership betwixt Marie Speed my Wife, and Mehetabel Heming & children in equal halves	Dr	£	s	d
December	To Stockins for one Trunck cont. 88 doz is 1056 paire laden in said ship and consignd for said accts to John Cooke & Samuel Kekewich merchants in St Marie Port at 2s 8d per paire	106	140	16	

		Cr	£	s	d
	By Profit and Loss, for Ballance	190 *			4
			79	00	

	Anno 1686				
	Maulting trade in partnership with Jonathan Lamboll per Contra is	Cr	£	s	d
	By Jonathan Lamboll his acct. of Debt on Mortgage, for the money per Contra lent him on the dissolution of our partnership on the 29th day of September 1686 without any proffit to mee, resting satisfyed with my principall money put into the stock in our maulting trade	109	400		
			400		

	Anno 1687				
	Jonathan Lamboll on Mortgage per Contra is	Cr	£	s	d
September 29	By his particular acct. current for 1 yeares intrest of £450 ending Sept. 29th 1687	131	22	10	
1688 June 24	By ¾ yeares intrest of £450 ending June 24th 1688 carried to his acct. current in 2 particular summes (viz) by ½ yeares intrest due 25th March 1688 & ¼ yeares intrest being £5 12s 6d due June 24th 1688 & makes up the summe now charg'd	147	16	17	6
1689 June 24	By his acct. current for 1 yeares intrest of £450 from the 24th June 1688 to the 24th June 1689	147	22	10	
	By his acct. current for ½ yeares intrest from 24th June 1689 to 25th 10ber 1689	147	11	5	
	By Ditto for 1 months intrest of £450 from 25th Dec. 1689 to 25th Jan. 1689	147	1	17	6
			75	00	00
	By his Acct. Current for Ballance	147	450	00	00
			525	00	00

	Bristoll 1685				
	Fruite per Contra is	Cr	£	s	d
November	By Thomas Jordan for said fruite sould him at 30s per Cwt reisons solis, and 20s per Cwt the frailes to pay in 4 months	95	55	11	2
	By Profit and Loss for Ballance	190 *	7	3	4
			62	14	6

	Anno 1685				
	Adventure in the Wellcom per Contra	Cr	£	s	d
February	By Isaac Heming for ½ the cost and charges of the Trunck of Stockins per Contra	90	73	4	3
	By Mary Speed my Wife for her ½ the cost and charges of said Trunck	113	73	4	3
			146	8	6

		£	s	d
To Cash paid custom, hallidge, portridge, Lyteridge etc.	107	2	18	2
To Proffit & Losse for a Trunck cord and matting	105		14	
To Isaac Heming for Premio assureance of £100 on Goods for this acct. to Cadiz	90	2		4
		146	8	6

Anno 1685

		Dr	£	s	d
Adventure 2nd in the ship Wellcom Philip Freake Mr to Cadiz for my propper acct.		Dr	£	s	d
December To Stockins for one Trunck laden in said cont. (viz) £ s d					
59 dozen fine Bristoll sadd colour)					
14 doz Ditto fine fancy coloured)					
73 doz is 876 paire at 2s 9d 120 9					
12 doz fine sad Wells hose)					
7 doz ditto fancy colours)					
19 doz is 342 paire at 1s 6d 17 2	106		137	11	
To Cash paid custom & other charges	107		2	19	8
To Isaac Heming for Premio of assurance of £200 assured on these goods to Cadiz	90		4		8
To Samuel Kekewich for charges on the Trunck of stockins per Contra sould being 863 Rys 29 Mervidees, and is 107 7/8 pieces of 8 the piece of 8 at 51d the piece of 8 as per his acct. of said charges closed September 1686 may appeare	111		23		10
			167	12	2
To Profit and Loss, for Ballance	190 *		23	1	4
			190	13	6 ·

Anno 1685

		Dr	£	s	d
Adventure in the Popley Frigat of London Robert Wood commander bound to Cadiz, and goe consign'd to John Cook & Samuel Kekewich merchants		Dr	£	s	d
December To Stockins for one Trunck cont. 840 paire Bristoll hose at 2s 9d per paire, and 528 paire fancy coulerd Wells hose, and 96 paire sadd Wells, in all 624 paire at 1s 6d per paire	106		162	6	
To Iasaac Heming for custom & other charges in London	100		5	7	10
			167	13	10
To Profit and Loss, for Ballance	190 *		42	18	11
			210	12	9

Anno 1685

		Dr	£	s	d
Adventure in the ship Betty Tho. Bagge Master to Cadiz consign'd to John Mayne		Dr	£	s	d
To Stockins for one Trunck, cont. 65 dozen £ s d					
January is 780 paire of fine Bristoll hose at 2s 9d per paire 107 05 00					
48 doz Fancy coloured Wells hose)					
5 doz Wells sadd coloured hose)					
53 doz is 636 paire at 1s 6d 47 14 00	112		154	19	
To Isaac Heming for 1/2 5 11s 6d premio of assurance of £200, on said goods	90		2	15	9
To Cash paid custom & other charges	168		3	14	9
To Samuel Kekewich for charges			161	9	6
To Profit and Loss for Ballance	190 *		27	9	1
			188	18	7

Anno 1685

		Dr	£	s	d
Adventure in the ship Betty Tho. Bagg Master, consign'd to John Cooke and Samuel Kekewich merchants in St Marie Port		Dr	£	s	d
January To Cash paid Ozziel Brown for Premio of assurance of £150	107		3	18	
To Stockins for one Trunck cont. 1104 paire of Bristoll hose viz					

Anno 1685				
Adventure in the Wellcom per Contra *By John Cooke & Sam. Kekewich 915 2/8 pieces of 8 the neat* *proceeds of the Trunck of stockins per Contra as per theire acct. of* *sales dated Nov. 30th 1686 the piece of 8 at 4s 2d the piece of 8*	*Cr*	*£*	*s*	*d*
	111	190	13	6

Anno 1686				
Adventure in the Popley Frigat per Contra	*Cr*	*£*	*s*	*d*
Aprill 26 *By John Cooke & Sam. Kekewich for the neat proceeds of the* *Trunck of stockins per Contra being 8088½ Ryals plate is* *1011 pieces of 8 & ½ Ryal the piece of 8 4s 3d as per theire* *acct. of sales Aprill 26th 1686*	*111*	210	12	9

Anno 1686				
Adventure in ship Betty to Cadiz consign'd to John Mayne per *Contra*	*Cr*	*£*	*s*	*d*
May *By John Mayne for 1675 Ryals plate is 209 3/8 pieces of 8* *being the neat proceeds of 40 doz Wells hose sould in Cadiz, as* *per his acct. of sales, the piece of 8 at 4s 5d*	*111*	46	4	7
By Ditto for 5270 Rys plate, which is 658¾ pieces of 8 which *by agreement hee made mee good for 65 dozs fine Bristoll hose at* *9¾ pieces of 8 per dozen , and 5 doz Wells hose at 5ps of 8 per* *dozen , which hee left in the hands of Samuel Kekewich merchant* *in St Marie Port as his owne, and now are all for his acct., the* *piece of 8 at 4s 4d*	*111*	142	14	
		188	18	7

Anno 1687				
Adventure in the ship Betty per Contra is	*Cr*	*£*	*s*	*d*
By Samuel Kekewich for the neat proceeds of part of the Trunck *of stockins as per his acct. of sales closed Oct. 14th 1687 being* *6965 Ryals is 870 pieces of 8 5/8 at 51d Aprill 26th 1686*	*111*	185		2

	£	s	d				
30 doz is 360 paire fancy coloured)							
62 doz is 784 paire sadd coloured)							
92 doz is 1104 paire at 2s 9d	151	16	00				
15 doz 10paire Wells fancy coloured)							
4 1/2 doz of Wells sadd coloured)							
19 1/3 doz is 244 paire at 22d	18	6		112	160	2	
To Cash paid custom & other charges				119	3	14	9
To Samuel Kekewich for charges in Spaine on the stockins as per his acct. of Charges closed Sept. 1686 1057 Ryals 23 Mervedis, is 132 pieces of 8 1/8 23 mervedis at 51d				111	28	1	10
To Profit and Loss, for Ballance				190 *	49	19	7
					245	16	2

(111)   Bristoll 1685

		Dr	£	s	d
	John Cooke and Samuel Kekewich merchants in St Marie Port my Factors in Spaine are				
December	To ballance of theire acct. current agreeable to theire own acct. sent mee per Robert Massinger closed Dec. 1685	R 7440 m 25	88 193	15	
1686 Aprill	To Adventure in the Popley Frigat for the neat proceeds of a Trunck of stockins sent in her as per theire acct. sales Aprill 26th 1686 being 1011 pieces of 8 & ½ Ryals the piece of 8 at 4s 2d	8088 17	110 210	12	9
September	To John Mayne for his bill in my favor on Sa. Kekewich for 100 pieces of 8 at 51d the piece of 8 which bill Sam. Kekweich did accept to charge to my credit as per his leter of Oct. 28th 1686	800	125 21	5	
November 30	To Adventure in the Rebecca for the neat proceeds of 20 white & 9 pieces black Baies as per acct. of sales closed Sept. 2nd 1686 5791 pieces of 8 at 51d	4635	109 123	2	4
	To Ditto for neat proceeds of 73 doz 1 paire Bristoll, & 10 doz Wells hose as per theire acct. closed Sept. 2nd 1686 being 713 pieces of 8 7/8 at 51d the piece of 8	5711	109 151	14	
	To Ditto for the neat proceeds of 37 doz 11 paire Bristoll hose, the remainer of the Trunck in the Rebecca 413 3/8 pieces of 8 at 51d as per acct. sales closed Nov. 30th 1686	3307	109 87	16	10
	To Adventure in the Wellcom for neat proceeds of 73 doz Bristoll & 19 doz Wells hose, being 915 2/8 pieces of 8 at 50d as per acct. sales closed Nov. 30th 1686	7322	110 190	13	6
	To Adventure in the Beniamin for what overcharg'd on landing Baies per acct.	45	86 1	3	10
	To Adventure in the Merchants Goodwill overcharg'd on a Truck stockins per accct closed Sept. 2nd 1686	82 18	97 2	3	,10
	To Proffit & Losse for what overcharg'd on Ennys his bill as per same acct.	20	137	10	8
	To Adventure in the Rebecca for neat proceeds 11 pieces dyed Baies as per acct. Sept. 26th 1686	2338 25	109 62	2	1
	To Proffit & Losse for ½ neat proceeds of a Trunck hose per the Wellcom as per the same acct.	3403 8	137 85	17	10
	To Adventure in the Betty for part neat proceeds of Trunck stockins per acct. Oct. 14th 1687	6965	110 185		2

By Ditto his acct. of time for the value of 19 Doz Bristoll, & 9 dozen Wells hoses at 10½ pieces of 8 the Bristoll, & 7 pieces of 8 the Wells, as per his leter August 4th 1687 amounting to 286 1/8 pieces of 8 at 51d as may appeare	143	60	16	
		245	16	2

Bristoll 1686

		R	m	Cr	£	s	d
	John Cooke & Samuel Kekewich per Contra are						
	By Plate in sundry ships from Cadiz for						
February	1000 pieces of 8 in the Hannibal with charges the piece of 8 at 4s 2d as per theire Invoyce may appeare	8557		92	222	16	7
Aprill	By Isaac Heming for money on theire bill drawne per Richard Enys on Richard Richards for 500 pieces of 8 at 4s 5d the piece of 8 as may appeare per the bill	4000		113	110	8	4
	By Xeries wine 1 Butt laden in the Betty for its costs and charges being 40 pieces of 8 at 54d	320		116	9		
June 19	By Cash recd. of Charles Stubbs on theire bill for 403 5/8 pieces of 8 at 54d is	3229		108	88	5	10
	By Isaac Heming for money hee recd. on theire bill drawne per Robert Isaacson on Robert Jonson, assign'd to mee, & by mee to him being 246 2/8 pieces of 8 at 53d	1971		113	54	10	4
August 17	By Ditto for 4274 Ryals plate for 500 pieces of 8 sent in the Crowne sould by Isaac Heming weight 4434¼ oz at 5s 3d per oz as per his leter August 17th 1686	4274		113	112	16	3
December	By Plate in sundry ships from Cadiz for cost & charges 1000 pieces of 8 in the James Gally the piece of 8 at 4s 2d as per Invoyce closed Nov. 6th 1686	8425	17	173	219	8	3
January 13	By Scarbrow Chapman for Simon Clements bill for money of them 400 pieces of 8 at 53d	3200		132	88	6	8
	By Michael White for Simon Clements bill on him for 200 pieces of 8 of them at 53d	1600		132	44	3	4
	By Edward Crofts for theire bill on him for 80 pieces of 8 furnish'd him at 53d	640		96	17	13	4
	By Charles Stubbs for theire bill on him for 372¾ pieces of 8 in my favor at 52d½	2982		133	81	10	9¼
	By Adventure in the Wellcom for charges on a Trunck hose per acct. Sept. 1686	863	29	110	23		10
	By Adventure in the Betty for charges on a Trunck stockins per acct. Sept. 1686	1057	23	110	28	1	10
	By Adventure in the Lumbly Castle for charges on Trunck hose per acct. same date	1238		114	32	18	1
	By Proffit & Losse for charges on Charles Stubbs his bill, Ennys bill & Jonsons bill	126	6	137	3	6	11
	By Ditto for ½ cost & charge of 300 pieces of 8 in the James Galley per acct. Oct. 21th 86	1263	26	137	33	12	4
	By Ditto pd. charges on Charles Stubbs his last bill per same acct.	30		137		15	11¼
	By Marie Speed for ½ losse on 20 doz hose to Pedro Sanche on Pragmatica per same acct.	55	00 94	113	1	9	2¾

To *Adventure in the Lumbly Castle* for part proceeds of *Trunck hose* as per acct. same date	478		*114*	12	13	11
To *Adventure in the Friston* for neat proceeds of *Trunck hose* per acct. sales of same date	6822	17	*116*	181	4	2
To *Adventure in the Spanish merchant* for neat proceeds *Trunck hose* per acct. of same date	4819	17	*131*	128		4
	62278	25				

Anno 1685			Dr	£	s	d
	John Mayne of the Pill merchant is		*Dr*	*£*	*s*	*d*
December	To *Adventure in the Olive branch* to *Cadiz* for the neat proceeds of 41 *Cask of Butter*, and the ½ of 10 *Cases* strong water sent consign'd to him in said ship for sales and returns as per his acct. closed R m November 1st 1685 the piece of 8 at 52½ d 6773	100	*185*	1	3
	To *Proffit & Losse* for ballance	105			2	7
				185	3	10

Anno 1685			Dr	£	s	d
	John Mayne merchant is		*Dr*	*£*	*s*	*d*
February 4	To *Isaac Heming* for ½ £5 11s 6d premio of assureance of £200 in the ship *Betty* to *Cadiz*, which hee is concerned in the same *Politie*, though in my name the assureance bee made out as per said *Hemings* leter of advice February 2nd 1685	90	*2*	15	9
	To *Proffit & Losse* paid postage of leters about the assureance	105			3
1686 Aprill	To *Adventure in the ship Betty* for the neat R m proceeds of 480 doz *Wells hose* as per his acct. of sales 1675 *Ryals* plate is 209 3/8 pieces of 8 at 4s 5d the piece of 8 1795	110	*46*	4	7

				£	s	d
By *Proffit & Losse for money lost on 10 doz to Pedro Sanche per Pragmatica same acct.*	32	17	*137*		17	3
By *Marie Speed lost on 10 doz to Barnardo Sequera, & 12 doz to Roque Dias Lexada per same acct.*	131	21	*113*	3	9	10
By *Proffit & Losse lost on 11 doz to Don Rodrigo Muños per same account*	60	17	*137*	1	12	2
By *Ditto for losse on 19 doz to Don Rodrigo Muños Velasco per Pragmatica*	104	17	*137*	2	15	6
By *Ditto for cost & charges of 228½ pieces of 8 in the Eagle per same acct. Oct. 21th 1687*	1952	29	*137*	51	17	5
By *Adventure in the Citie of Cadiz for charges on Trunck hose per acct. Oct. 13th 1687*	638	22	*122*	16	19	2½
By *Adventure in the Dilligence for charges on Trunck hose per same date acct.*	560	20	*124*	14	17	9
By *Adventure in the Sivillia merchant for charges on Trunck hose per acct. Oct. 14th 1687*	589	12	*124*	15	13	1
By *Proffit & Losse for charges on Edward Crofts bill per same acct. Oct. 21th 1687*	6	20	*137*		3	5
By *Ditto for charges on Michael Whites bill per acct. Oct. 21th 1687*	16		*137*		8	6
By *Ditto for charges on Scarbrow Chapmans bill per acct. Ditto 1687*	32		*137*		17	
By *Plate in sundry ships from Cadiz for the cost & charges of 1000 pieces of 8 in the Friston being 1073 pieces of 8 at 52d per acct. closed Octo.br 21th & per Invoyce Sept. 30th 1687*	8589	17	*143*	232	12	8
By *Proffit & Losse for Port of leters to the 21th of Oct. 1687 as per acct. current from him closed that day*	100		*137*	2	13	1½
	56647	21				
By *ballance resting due from Samuel Kekewich as per his acct. closed in St Marie Port October 21th 1687 carried to his new acct. current*	5631	4	*148*			
	62278	25				

	Anno 1685				
	John Mayne per Contra is	Cr	£	s	d
January 18	By *Cash received of Joseph Earle on his bill drawne per Charles Wall from Malaga in favor of Isaac Heming , & by him assign;d to mee being 4800 Ryals plate is pieces of 8 — at 52d½ per piece of 8*	*107*	131	5	
	By *fruite 9 Barrills and 27 pieces laden in the ship Olive tree cost 1821 Ryals plate is 227 5/8 pieces of 8 at 52d½ per piece of 8 as per his acct. closed in Malaga November the 1st 1685 may appeare*	*110*	49	15	10
	By *Cash received of him*	*107*	4	3	
			185	3	10

	Anno 1685				
	John Mayne per Contra is	Cr	£	s	d
February 20	By *Cash recd. of his wife*	*107*	2	16	
1686 August 5	By *Cash received of him*	*119*	46	4	7
	By *Cash received of Tho. Day by his order*	*119*	49	19	6
	By *Cash received of him*	*119*	2	14	
September 24	By *Cash received of Tho. Day for his acct. due on theire bond*	*119*	80		
	By *Profit and Losse for Ballance*	*190* *	10		6
			191	14	7

			Dr	£	s	d
	To Ditto for 633¾ pieces of 8 made good by agreement for 65 doz Bristoll hose left in the hands of Samuel Kekewich, & 25 pieces of 8 for 5 doz Wells hose, 1st at 9¾ pieces the 2nd 5 pieces of 8 the piece of 8 at 4s 4d	5270		142	14	
				191	14	7

Anno 1685

	John Warren per Contra is	Dr	£	s	d
March	To Isaac Heming for my bill on him in favor of my Bro. in law Tho. Warren	113	37		
			37		

Anno 1685

	Anthony Owen of Bristoll Vintner is	Dr	£	s	d
August	To Wines 8 Butts in partnership with Tho. Day for 1 hogshead of Malaga	123	16		
1687 Feb. 11	To Wines my ½ of 20 Butts for 1 Butt sould him at 3 months time at	134	28		
			44		

Anno 1685

	Richard Haynes of Bristoll Gent.	£	s	d	Dr	£	s	d
December	To Wines 6 hhds for 2 doz bottles white wine at 9s 6d	00	19	00	97			
	To Proffit & Losse for 2 doz bottles	00	4	00	105	1	3	

(112)   Bristoll 1685

	Worsted Stockins are	paire	s	d	Dr	£	s	d
January 14	To Cash paid Tho. Hill for	117	1	3	107	7	6	3
	To Ditto pd. Ditto for	30	2	5¾	107	3	14	5
	To Ditto paid Ditto for	39	2	4	107	4	11	
16	To Ditto pd. Anthony Palmer for	47	2	6	107	5	17	6
	To Ditto pd. John Massinger for	40	2	8	107	5	6	8
	To Ditto paid Joseph White for fancies	71	2	6				
	To Ditto paid Ditto for sadds	36	2	8	107	13	13	6
18	To Ditto pd. John Perry for	60	2	6	107	8	4	
19	To Ditto pd. Tho. Walden for one dozen of Inkles				107		7	6
20	To Ditto pd. Tho. Hill for John Lukins	34	2	5	107	4	2	6
23	To Ditto pd. John Massinger for	36	2	8	107	4	16	
	To Ditto pd. John Day for	47	2	5	107	5	13	7
25	To Cash pd. Joseph White for	73	2	6	107	9	2	6
27	To Ditto paid Jonathan Abram for	53	2	4¾	107	6	11	6
28	To Cash paid John Perrie for	154	2	2				
	To Ditto paid Ditto for	41	2	4	107	21	9	4
February 1	To Cash paid Tho. Hill for	44	2	5¾	107	5	9	1
	To Ditto paid Ditto for sadds	32	2	5¾	107			
	To Ditto paid Ditto for fancies	43	2	3¾	107	7	18	6
	To Ditto paid Tho. Hill for	22	2	6	107	2	15	
	To Ditto paid John Massinger for	39	2	8	107	5	4	
	To Ditto paid Robert Webb for a large Trunck				107		13	
3	To Ditto paid Anthony Palmer for	47	2	6	107	5	17	6
4	To Ditto paid Andrew Creed for	80	1	5	107	5	13	4

	Anno 1685				
	John Warren sonne of my Bro. in law Tho. Warren of Musburie in the County of Devon Clothier is	Cr	£	s	d
January 26	By Cash left with mee to keepe in my custody to bee disposed per his order	107	27		
	By Proffit & Losse for a mare hee bought for mee by his Fathers order at Martock in the County of Somerset	105 *	10		
			37		

	Anno 1686				
	Anthony Owen per Contra is	Cr	£	s	d
October 2	By Cash received of him by the hands of Tho. Hill	119	16		
1688 May 30	By John Hurden Esq. for 4 doz qt bottles Xerie the bottles & 2 Panniers & Covers as per noat	151	4	2	
June 20	By the Lady Ann Powlet for 4 doz bottles Xerie, the bottles, & Panniers & Covers per noat	100	4	2	
	By Richard Wasbrow paid him in part by my order	50	19	6	9
	By Proffit & Losse for 6 bottles Claret, and 1 Gall. Xerie allowed hm for Ullage	153		9	3
			44	00	00

	Anno 1686				
	Richard Haines per Contra is	Cr	£	s	d
June 1	By Cash received of his Kinswoman in full	108	1	3	

	Bristoll 1685				
	Worsted Stockins per Contra are	Cr	£	s	d
January 9	By Ballance brought from that acct.	106	549	2	1½
	By Adventure in the Betty frigat to Cadiz for one Trunck cont. 65 doz fine Bristoll sadd hose is 780 paire at 2s 9d and 48 doz fancy colour'd Wells hose & 5 doz sad coloured Wells hose is 53 doz is 636 paire at 1s 6d per paire, consign'd to John Mayne	110	154	19	
	By Adventure in Ditto ship at same time for one Trunck cont. 30 doz fancy coloured hose Bristoll, and 62 doz sad coloured Bristoll hose 92 doz is 1104 paire at 2s 9d and 15 doz & 10 paire Wells fancy coloured hose & 4 1/2 doz Wells sadd coloured, is in all 244 paire at 1s 6d per paire, and goe consign'd to John Cooke & Sam. Kekewich	110	160	2	
March 23	By Adventure in the Lumley Castle to Cadiz Capt. Robert Dorrell for 1 Trunck cont. 78 doz Bristoll sadds, 39 doz Bristoll Fancies is 1014 paire at 3s per paire and six dozen fine Wells fancies is 72 paire at 2s & goe consign'd to Cooke & Kekewich	114	217	16	
			1081	19	1½

	To Ditto paid Jonathan Abram for	38	2	4				
	To Ditto paid Ditto for	16	2	5¾	107	6	8	4
5	To Ditto paid Elizabeth Dyer for	8	2	4	107		18	8
	To Ditto paid Ditto for	26	2	5	107	3	2	10
8	To Ditto paid John Massinger for	34	2	8				
	To Ditto paid Ditto for	5	2	6	107	5	3	6
9	To Ditto paid Wm. Thiery for	39	2	3	107	4	7	9
	To Ditto paid John Rudduck for	40	2	5	107	6	10	6
10	To Cash paid Tho. Hill for	63	2	5	107	7	12	3
	To Ditto paid him for an error in payment for a parcell hose the 1st instant				107	1		
	To Ditto paid Joseph White for	61	2	6	107	7	12	6
11	To Ditto paid John Perry for	53	2	2				
	To Ditto paid Ditto for	36	2	4	107	9	19	
	To Cash paid Joane White for	44	2	4½				
	To Ditto paid Ditto for	22	2	5½	107	7	18	7
12	To Ditto paid Edward Iffe in full for hot pressing stockins				107	1	10	4
	To Ditto paid Tho. Hill for	43	2	5½	107	5	5	9
	To Ditto paid John Day for	24	2	5	107	2	18	
13	To Ditto paid John Massinger for							
	1 paire womens & worsted	32	2	8	107	4	9	3
	To Ditto paid Anthony Palmer for	48	2	5¾				
	To Ditto paid Ditto for Pearles	10	2	5	107	7	3	6
15	To Ditto paid Tho. Walden for a piece of Inkle				107		7	6
	To Ditto paid Henry Britten for	65	2	5	107	7	17	
						224	11	11
17	To Ditto paid Tho. Hill for	34	2	5	107	4	2	2
	To Cash paid John Brady for	28	2	5¾	107	3	9	5
	To Ditto paid Jonathan Abram for	30	2	5½				
	To Ditto paid Ditto for	31	2	4	107	7	6	1
20	To Ditto paid John Massinger for	39	2	8	107	5	4	
	To Ditto paid Jos. White for	53	2	8				
	To Ditto paid Ditto for	60	2	6	107	14	11	4
	To Ditto paid Tho. Hill for	31	2	4½	107	3	13	7
	To Ditto paid Ditto for	72	2	5	107	8	14	
	To Ditto paid Tho. Hill for	34	2	4	107	3	19	4
24	To Cash paid Robert Webbs Wife for a Trunck				107		13	
25	To Ditto paid Jonathan Abram for							
	sadds	21	2	5				
	To Ditto paid Ditto for fancies	18	2	3½	107	4	12	
	To Ditto paid James Wollen for	34	2	5	107	4	2	2
26	To Ditto paid Henry Britten for fancies	33	2	5				
	To Ditto paid Ditto for sadds	26	2	4½	107	7	1	6
27	To Ditto paid John Massinger for	42	2	8	107	5	12	
March 1	To Cash paid John Day for	31	2	4¾	108	3	15	
2	To Ditto paid John Perry for	30	2	5	108	3	12	6
4	To Ditto paid Wm. Thiery for	68	2	4	108	7	18	8
	To Ditto paid Tho. Hill for fancies	132	1	4	108	8	16	
	To Ditto paid Ditto for	26	2	5	108	3	2	10
6	To Ditto paid Wm. Turley for	39	2	4	108	4	13	4
	To Ditto paid John Massinger for	34	2	8	108	4	10	8
	To Ditto paid Joseph White for	58	2	7¾	108	7	13	6
	To Ditto paid Edward Iffe in full for hot pressing stockins				108	1	2	3
8	To Ditto paid Tho. Hill for sadds	40	2	4¾	108	4	15	10
10	To Ditto paid Tho. Hill for Fancies	17	2	5	108	2	1	1
11	To Ditto paid John Massinger for	39	2	8	108	5	4	
	To Ditto paid John Brady for sadds	20	2	5¾				
	To Ditto paid him for	34	3	2	108	6	5	8
12	To Ditto paid Tho. Hill for sadds	34	2	4	108	3	19	4
	To Ditto paid Ditto for sadds	31	2	5	108	3	14	11

						£	s	d
13	To Cash paid John Day for sadds	21	2	4¾	108	2	10	3
	To Ditto paid Joseph White for Fancies	74	2	5¾	108	9	3	5½
	To Ditto paid Tho. Hill for sadds	84	2	5	108	10	3	
	To Ditto paid Ditto for Pearles	70	2	4½	108	8	6	3
	To Ditto paid Jonathan Abram for sadds	42	2	5	108	5	1	6
18	To Ditto paid Anthony Palmer for sadds	44	2	5¾	108	5	9	
	To Ditto paid Tho. Hill for sadds	31	2	4	108	3	12	4
	To Ditto paid Ditto for sadds	31	2	5	108	3	14	11
	To Ditto paid John Perry for sadds	52	2	5	108	6	5	8
	To Ditto paid Jonathan Abram for	43	2	5	108	5	3	11
20	To Ditto paid Robert Webb for 2 Truncks 1 at 11s tother at 13s				108	1	4	
23	To Cash paid Elizabeth Dyer for sadds	17	2	5	108	2	1	1
24	To Ditto paid John Massinger for	27	2	8	108	3	12	
						435	5	6½
	To Ballance carried to that acct.				115	646	13	7
						1081	19	1

---

(113)   **Bristoll 1685**

	Xeries wine 6 Butts imported from Cadiz in the ship Dilligence John Seward Master are	Dr	£	s	d
February	To Robert Massinger for the cost in Spaine of 4 Butts laden by him in Ditto ship in Returnes of a parcell tannd hydes sent in her consign'd to him 1402 Ryals plate is 175¼ pieces of 8 the piece of 8 at 4s 2d, as per his Invoyce Dec. 24th 1685	109	36	9	8
	To Ditto for 2 Butts & a remnant bought of him at	109	42	10	
March 9	To Cash paid John Seward for freight and averidge of 4 Butts laden for my acct.	108	7	3	8
	To Thomas Day Wine Cooper for 152 Gall. Malaga at 4s & 4 Gall. at 4s 4d and 43¾ Gall. at 5s per Gall. & whitening & forcing 1 hogshead as per noat	114	22	12	1
	To Cash paid custom fees etc. for 4 Butts	119	32	9	6½
	To Profit and Loss for Ballance	190 *	34	11	½
			175	6	

       Anno 1686

	Thomas Longman of Bristoll Grocer is	Dr	£	s	d
July	To Proffit & Losse for a barril Reisons weight neat 1 cwt 2 qr 5 lb at 26s per Cwt	127	2		

       Anno 1685

	Marie Speed my wife is	Dr	£	s	d
December	To Adventure in partnership in the Wellcom to Cadiz for her ½ cost & charges of the Trunck hose	110	73	4	3
	To Samuel Kekewich for money lost on 20 doz hose to Pedro Sanche per the Pragmattica	111	1	9	2¾
	To Ditto lost on 22 doz sould to Bernardo Sequera Roque Dias Lexara by the Pragmatica	111	3	9	10
	To Cash paid her in 2 Guinnies	141	2	3	
	To Proffit & Losse for ballance delivered her in Guinnies by her desire	153	82	10	8
			162	16	11

       Anno 1685

	Isaac Heming and John Barnard [95] of London merchants	Dr	£	s	d
February 27	To ballance of theire acct. sent mee and closed February 27th 1685 as appears	100	1628	13	9
Aprill	To Cash paid Edmond Scrope for his bill on Tho. Elliot in his favor	107	20		

Bristoll 1686

		Cr	£	s	d
	Xeries wine 6 Butts per Contra are	Cr	£	s	d
Aprill 3	*By John Blackwell for the 6 Butts Xerie sould him at £27 05s 00d per Butt payable by his bill on the 25th day of August next ensuing*	85	163	10	
	By Wines 6 Butts in partnership for 61½ Gall. Xerie at 4s per Gallon	116	12	6	
			175	16	

Anno 1686

		Cr	£	s	d
	Thomas Longman per Contra is	Cr	£	s	d
December 4	*By Cash received of him in full*	120	2		

Anno 1685

		Cr	£	s	d
	Marie Speed my wife per Contra is	Cr	£	s	d
March	*By Proffit & Losse for 68 Guinnies recd. of her at £1 1s 6d per piece*	105	73	2	
1686 Dec.	*By Isaac Heming for ½ of £67 4s 6d recd. of Wm. Atwill & Company for 300 pieces of 8 weight 262 oz imported in the James Galley in part returnes at 5s 2d¼ per oz*	130	33	12	3
1687 August 23	*By Ditto for neat proceeds of 228½ pieces of 8 weight 199 oz sould at 5s 2 3/8d per oz to Wm. Atwill etc.*	130	51	3	6
	By Proffit & Losse for ballance of the acct. of stockins taken out of Sam. Kekewich his acct. current dated Oct. 21th 1687 being 23¼ pieces of 8 & 21 mervedis the piece of 8 at 51d as per same acct.	137 *	4	19	2
			162	16	11

Anno 1686

		Cr	£	s	d
	Isaac Heming & Company per Contra	Cr	£	s	d
Aprill 10	*By Adventure in the Lumley Castle to Cadiz for charges on a Trunck stockins*	114	5	12	4
	By Proffit & Losse for money received of him in London at severall times	105	12	9	

To John Cooke & Company for money on theire bill on Richard Richards in my favor for 500 pieces of 8 at 4s 5d per piece of 8 as per said bill drawne per Richard Enys	111	110	8	4
To Plate in sundry ships from Cadiz for money of Wm. Atwill & Company for 1000 pieces of 8 in the Hannibal 600 weight 519 oz at 5s 2d¼ 400 351 oz at 5s 2 3/8d as per leter Aprill 1 1686	92	223	9	3
May To Arthur Robinson & Company for 1304 Ryals plate sent consign'd to him per the ship Angel for my acct. & sould as per his leter of 3rd August 1686 amounting to	61	33	15	1
To John Cook & Samuel Kekewich for money on theire bill on Robert Jonson assign'd to mee & by mee assign'd to him for 246 7/8 Ryals of 8 at 4s 5d the piece of 8 which hee received	111	54	10	4
July 27 To John Blackwell for John Pococks bill on Tho. Wootin in Lond. by mee assign'd to him	85	50		
To John Cooke & Sam. Kekewich for money of Atwill & Company for 500 pieces of 8 weight 434¼ oz at 5s 3d	111	112	16	3
To Sugar 3 Butts & 13 hhds in the Friendship Capt. Young from Nevis for theire neat proceeds	104	103	3	1
To Robert Richardson for 1 yeares intrest of £150 due Dec. 16th 1685	35	7	10	
To Isaac Heming & John Barnard on bond for 1 yeares intrest of £400 due 10th Nov. 1686	69	16		
To his new acct. current for the money paid Robert Henley per Contra	130	50		
To his said acct. for my 2 bills on him in favor of John Cook per Contra	130	104	4	5
		2514	10	6

Anno 1686				
John Osgood of London Linindraper is	Dr	£	s	d
February 14 To Cash paid for 2 Flitches of Bacon	120		14	4
1687 March 24 To Cash paid for 4 Flitches of Bacon	140	1	9	10
1689 May 11 To Cash paid Fra. Maynard for 4 Flitches of Bacon weight 89 lb at 3d¼ per lb	162	1	7	10
		3	12	

Anno 1687				
Arthur Hart of Bristoll merchant per Contra	Dr	£	s	d
July 21 To Cash paid him in full	121	7	4	6

(114) **Bristoll 1685/6**				
Adventure in the Lumbley Castle of London Capt. Robert Dorrell bound to Cadiz, and consign'd to John Cooke & Samuel Kekewich merchants in St Marie Port for sales and returnes	Dr	£	s	d

		£	s	d
By Wine 6 Butts in the New England merchant for what paid for 2 Butts Malaga	116	52	13	4
By Cash recd. of Tho. Day Wine Cooper for my bill on him in favor of said Day	108	54		
16 By Cash recd. of Sir Samuel Astry for which I valued my bill in his favor	108	300		
By Paul Priaulx for my bill on him in said Priaulx his favor	17	6	9	
By Adventure in the Friston to Cadiz for carriage and other charges on a Trunck of hose	116	4	7	8
By Wines 6 Butts for the first cost of 4 Butts Xerie, & charges on the whole 6 Butts	116	85	1	6
By Adventure in the Malaga merchant to Malaga for charges on a Trunck of hose	122	2		1
August By Adventure in the ship Citie of Cadiz to Cadiz for custom, carriage & other charges on Trunck hose	122	5	1	11
By Adventure in the ship Adventurers Delight for custom & charges on them for Malaga	123	2		1
By Adventure in the ship Civilia merchant the 3rd for charges on a Trunck stockins	124	5	3	7
By John Wilmer for my bill on him August 21th in favor of said Wilmer	117	9	13	6
By Jonathan Lamboll for my bill Exchange of 22th Sept. in his favor	87	50		
September 25 By Cash recd. of Robert Henley for which I valued my bill on him	119	50		
By John Cook for which I valued my bill in said Cooke's favor & Company	117	97	18	6
By Ditto for my bill which I valued on him in said Cookes favor	32	6	5	11
By Cash recd. of Wm. Jones for my bill on him Sept. 4th last	120 *	16	1	6
By John Warren for my bill on him in favor of Tho. Warren in Aprill last	111	37		
By Proffit & Losse for money pd. Richard Russell £1 & earnest for 2 places in the Coach £1	127	2		
By Martha Gay for money hee paid her on her bill obligatory in July last	32	10		
By Proffit & Losse paid for 2 doz bottles wine £1 5s 4d & a box of Wm. Russels powder £1 10s 4d	127	2	15	8
By Ditto for Port of leters to the 29th of September 1686	127	1	18	
By Ditto for money hee pd. for 40 papers Powder in March 1685	127	1		
error By Jonathan Lamboll for £50 pd. him Sept. 28th 1686				
		819	11	7
By Ballance carried to his new acct. current	130	1694	18	11
		2514	10	6

Anno 1686				
John Osgood per Contra is	Cr	£	s	d
By Cash recd. of him in full	120		14	4
1688 March 28 By Cash recd. of him	140	1	9	10
By his new acct. Current for the cost of 4 Flitches Bacon per Contra	178	1	7	10
		3	12	

Anno 1687				
Arthur Hart of Bristoll merchant is	Cr	£	s	d
By French wines 4 hhds for 1 hogshead of Cognac wine bought of him	133	7	4	6

Bristoll 1687				
Adventure in the Lumbly Castle per Contra is	Cr	£	s	d
By Samuel Kekewich for 478 Ryals is 59¾ pieces of 8 at 51d as per acct. sales closed Octo.br 14 1687 being for part of the Trunck of Stockins per Contra	111	12	13	11

Date	Description	ref	£	s	d
1March 23	To Stockins for 1 Trunck cont. 78 doz fine Bristoll sad hose)				
	To Ditto for 39 dozen fine Bristoll fancy coloured hose)				
	117 doz is 1014 paire at 3s	112	210	12	
	To Ditto for 6 doz fine fancy coloured Wells hose at 2s	112	7	4	
	To Proffit & Losse for 1 Trunck to put the stockins in with cord				
	& matting	105		14	
	To Isaac Heming for carriage to London, custom & other				
	charges per leter Aprill 10th 1686	113	5	12	4
	To Samuel Kekewich for charges on the hose 1238 Ryals is				
	154¾ pieces of 8 at 51d as by his acct. of charges closed Sept.				
	1686	111	32	18	1
			257	00	5
	To Profit and Loss, for Ballance	190 *	32	16	4½
			289	16	9½

Anno 1686

Date	Description	Dr	£	s	d
	Ann Challenor Widow Inholder at the Rose without Temple Gate	Dr	£	s	d
May 28	To Cash paid her in part	108	2		
29	To Cash paid her in full	108	4	18	6
			6	18	6

Anno 1686

Date	Description	Dr	£	s	d
	Whalebone for acct. of Robert Symes of Cerne consign'd to Jahzeel Speed	Dr	£	s	d
	To Cash paid fileing a certifficate & 1 ball of Twine to ty it	120		1	2

Anno 1686

Date	Description	Dr	£	s	d
	John Miles Seniior of Reading in the County of Berks Inholder is	Dr	£	s	d
	To John Blackwell for 2 doz bottles				
	Xerie at 18s & 2 doz bottles 4s and £ s d				
May 20	1 Panniers & covers 1s in all 2 1	85			
	To Proffit & Losse for port of a letter 3	105	2	1	3
1688 October 22	To Cash paid Robert Hodges for 2 Casks Butter with				
	Cooperidge etc.	157	2	8	3
			4	9	6

Anno 1686

Date	Description	Dr	£	s	d
	Thomas Day of Bristoll Wine Cooper	Dr	£	s	d
	To Xerie wine out of sundry ships from Cadiz for 14 Gall.				
	Rhenish & the hogshead by his own measure	101	1	15	
Aprill 14	To Cash paid him in full	108	20	17	1
May 18	To Cash paid him in full	108	20		
June	To Proffit & Losse for ½ cost & charges of 2000 of Fossets				
	from Reading	105		11	
	To John Jayn for the other ½ of the Fossets hee taking them all				
	to himselfe	116		11	
	To his new acct. current for the 124 Gall. Xerie & his noat of				
	disbursements as per Contra	123	3	14	8
			47	8	9

Anno 1686

Date	Description	Dr	£	s	d
	Edward Thornhull of Bristoll Grocer is	Dr	£	s	d
March 25	To Sugar 3 Cask in the Olive tree from Barbadoes for the 3				
	Cask sould him weight neat 14 cwt 1qr 25lbs at 21s per Cwt to				
	pay July 26th next	92	15	3	6

Anno 1686

Date	Description	Dr	£	s	d
	Marie Thring Widow, Bridget Wallis Spinster, & Samuel	Dr	£	s	d
	Thring Shipwright all of Portburie in the County of Somerset				
Aprill 8	To Cash lent them on theire bond dated Aprill 1st past	108	20		
January 22	To Cash lent them on theire bond for 3 months with intrest	120	6		
			26		

By *Samuel Kekwich his acct. of time for the value of 110 doz*
Bristoll and 6 dozen Wells hose hee took to hmselfe at 10½
pieces of 8 the Bristoll, & 7 pieces of 8 the Wells hose, sent in
the flota as per his leter of 4th August 1687 & his acct. of Sales
closed 14th Octo.br 1687 being 1304 5/8 merd 17 the piece of

8 at 51d	143	277	2	10½
	289	16	9½

	Anno 1686				
	Ann Challenor Widow	*Cr*	*£*	*s*	*d*
May	*By Proffit & Losse for keeping my two mares as per noat to 27ᵗʰ*				
	May 1686	105	6	18	6

	Anno 1690@				
	Per Contra	*Cr*	*£*	*s*	*d*
	By Profit & Loss, for Ballance	190 *		1	2

	Anno 1686				
	John Miles per Contra is	*Cr*	*£*	*s*	*d*
June	*By Jonathan Lamboll for money received of him by my order*	87	2	1	6
	By Tho. Curtis for money recd. of John Miles for the Caske of				
	Butter per Contra	169	2	8	
		4	9	6

	Anno 1685/6				
	Thomas Day per Contra is	*Cr*	*£*	*s*	*d*
February 6	*By Xeries wine 6 Butts in the Dilligence from Cadiz for 2 qtr*				
	Cask of Malaga each 26 Gall. at 4s & 4 Gall. more at 4s 4d				
	per Gallon	113	11	7	4
1686	*By Ditto for whitning and forcing one hogshead of Malaga*	113		6	
23	*By Ditto for 43 Gall. 3 qts of Malaga at 5s per Gallon*	113	10	18	9
May 15	*By Cash borrowed and received of him by my daughter Martha in*				
	my absence	108	20		
June 23	*By Cash received of him in full*	108	1	2	
	By Wines in partnership for 12¼ Gall. Xerie & his				
	disbursements as per noat	116	3	14	8
		47	8	9

	Anno 1686				
	Edward Thornhull per Contra	*Cr*	*£*	*s*	*d*
August	*By Cash recd. of him at twice*	119 *	15	3	6

	Anno 1686				
	Marie Thring & Company per Contra are	*Cr*	*£*	*s*	*d*
October 28	*By Marie Thring & Company theire acct. current transferred hence*				
	on making up an acct. with them to theire acct. of debt in that acct.	7	20		
	By Acct. of Ballances, for Ballance	190 *	6		
		26		

(115)	Bristoll 1686							
	Worsted Stockins are				Dr	£	s	d
		paire	s	d				
March 25	*To Cash for money to John Day for*	13	2	4¾	108	1	11	1
	To Ditto paid Tho. Hill for	39	2	5	108	4	14	3
27	*To Ditto paid Joseph White for*	52	2	7¾	108	6	17	7
	To Ditto paid John Brady for	27	2	4½	108	3	6	4½
	To Ditto paid Tho. Hill for	44	2	4	108	5	2	8
	To Ditto paid Ditto for	59	2	5	108	7	2	7
31	*To Ditto paid John Massinger for*							
	38 paire	37	2	8				
		1	2	6	108	5	1	2
	To Ditto paid Edward Iffe in full for hot pressing hose				108	1		
Aprill 1	*To Ditto paid Tho. Hill for*	42	2	4	108	4	18	
	To Ditto paid Ditto for	34	2	5	108	4	2	2
	To Ditto paid Ditto for	22	2	4	108	2	11	4
2	*To Ditto paid Anthony Perrie for John*							
	Perry for	71	2	4¾	108	8	10	1
3	*To Ditto paid John Rudduck for*	55	2	4½	108	6	10	7
	To Ditto paid Henry Britten for	52	2	5	108	6	5	8
	To Ditto paid John Lukins for	43	2	4¾	108	5	3	
9	*To Cash paid Elizabeth Dyer for*	9	2	5	108	1	1	8
	To Ditto paid Anthony Palmer for	42	2	5¾	108	5	4	
10	*To Ditto paid Joseph White for*	58	2	7¾	108	7	13	5
	To Ditto paid John Massinger for	39	2	8	108	5	4	
	To Ditto paid Jonathan Abram for	36	2	5	108	4	7	
12	*To Ditto paid James Wollen for*	35	2	5	108	4	4	7
	To Ditto paid Tho.Hill for	19	2	4	108	2	4	4
14	*To Cash paid John Perrie for*	60	2	4	108	7	1	6
16	*To Ditto paid John Massinger for*	38	2	8	108	5	1	4
17	*To Ditto paid Wm. Turley for*	17	2	4	108	1	19	8
21	*To Ditto paid John Day for*	11	2	4	108	1	6	4
	To Ditto paid Elizabeth Dyer for	6	2	5	108		14	6
22	*To Ditto paid Joseph White for*	52	2	7¾	108	6	17	7
	To Ditto paid John Rudduck for	33	2	5½	108	3	18	4½
	To Ditto paid James Woollen for	41	2	5	108	4	19	1
23	*To Ditto paid John Brady for*	16	2	5½	108	1	19	4
	To Ditto paid John Massinger for	39	2	8	108	5	1	4
26	*To Ditto paid Edward Iffe for hotpressing to this day*				108		16	9
	To Ditto paid Jonathan Abram for	28	2	5	108	4	11	10
29	*To Ditto paid Joseph White for*	42	2	7¾	108	6	16	2
	To Ditto paid John Lukins for	29	2	4¾	108	3	9	6
30	*To Ditto paid Henry Britten for*	63	2	5	108	7	12	3
	To Ditto paid James Wollen for	41	2	4	108	4	19	1
May 1	*To Cash paid John Massinger for*	44	2	8	108	5	17	4
	To Ditto paid Anthony Palmer for	39	2	4¾	108	4	17	6
	To Ditto paid John Perry for	53	2	4¼	108	6	5	
	To Ditto paid John Day for	20	2	5	108	2	17	11
4	*To Ditto paid Joseph White for sadds*	40	2	7¾	108			
	To Ditto paid Ditto for Pearles	13	2	6	108	6	18	4
6	*To Cash paid Elizabeth Dyer for*	10	2	5	108	1	4	
	To Ditto paid John Massinger for	45	2	8	108	6		
	To Ditto paid John Rudduck for	35	2	4½	108	4	7	10
						208	8	1
	To Cash paid Joane White for	25	2	5	108	3		
	To Ditto paid Jonathan Abram for	41	2	5	108	4	19	1
8	*To Ditto paid John Perry for*	38	2	4¼	108	4	9	6
	To Ditto paid Anthony Palmer for	48	2	5½	108	5	18	
	To Ditto paid James Wollen for	38	2	5	108	4	11	10
	To Ditto paid Henry Britten for	24	2	5	108	2	18	

Bristoll 1686

		Cr	£	s	d
	Worsted stockins per Contra				
March 24	By ballance brought from that acct.	112	646	13	7
May	By Adventure in the Friston for Cadiz for 1 Trunck laden in her containing 65 dozen is 780 paire sad colour'd Bristoll hose, & 20 doz is 240 paire of Bristoll fancy colour'd hose, is in all 1020 paire at 2s 9d & 11 doz is 132 paire Fancy colour'd Wells hose at 1s 9d is in all	116	151	16	
			798	9	7

	To Ditto paid John Brady for	24	2	5½	108	2	19	
10	To Ditto paid Joseph White for	53	2	7	108	6	16	
	To Ditto paid John Massinger for	39	2	8	108	5	4	
14	To Ditto paid James Wollen for	50	2	5	108	6	1	
15	To Ditto paid John Perry for	64	2	4½	108	7	10	6
	To Ditto paid Henry Britten for	53	2	5	108	6	8	
21	To Ditto paid Henry Britten for	41	2	5	108	4	19	1
	To Cash paid John Day for	20	2	4½	108	2	7	6
	To Ditto paid John Lukins for	36	2	4½	108	4	6	3
	To Ditto paid Jonathan Abram for	47	2	5	108	5	13	6
	To Ditto paid John Massinger for	38	2	8	108	5	1	4
22	To Cash paid Eliza. Dyer for	5	2	5	108		12	1
	To Ditto paid Joseph White for sadds	55	2	7	108			
	To Ditto paid Ditto for Pearles	14	2	6	108	9	5	
	To Ditto paid John Brady for	30	2	5	108	3	12	6
	To Ditto paid Tho. Hill for	49	2	4	108	5	14	4
	To Ditto paid Ditto for	14	2	4	108	1	13	3
	To Ditto paid Ditto for	40	2	5	108	4	16	8
25	To Cash paid Tho. Walden for 3 dozen of Inkles				108	1	4	
31	To Ditto paid John Massinger for	37	2	8	108	4	18	8
	To Ditto paid Jonathan Abram for	38	2	5	108	4	11	10
June 1	To Cash paid John Perry for	60	2	4¼	108	7	1	3
	To Cash paid Tho. Walden for 1 dozen of Inkles				108		7	6
2	To Cash paid Elizabeth Dyer for							
	& 8d over	10	2	4	108	1	4	
3	To Cash paid John Rudduck for	22	2	4½	108	2	12	3
	To Cash paid Anthony Palmer for	6	2	5½	108		14	9
7	To Cash paid Eliza Dyer for	20	2	4	108	2	6	4
8	To Ditto paid Thomas Walden for 3 dozen of Inkles				108	1	2	
9	To Ditto paid Henry Britten for	35	2	5	108	4	4	7
	To Ditto John Perry for John Day for	14	2	4¾	108	1	13	3
10	To Cash paid Joane White per Tho.							
	Hill for	35	2	4½	108	4	4	7
	To Ditto paid John Lukins for	29	2	4¾	108	3	9	3
	To Ditto paid James Wollen for	40	2	5	108	4	16	8
12	To Cash paid John Massinger for	38	2	8	108	4		
	To Ditto paid Henry Britten for	41	2	5	108	4	19	1
	To Ditto paid Tho. Hill for	32	2	5	108	3	16	
14	To Ditto paid Joseph White for sadds	38	2	7	108			
	To Ditto paid Ditto for Pearles	7	2	6	108	5	15	8
15	To Ditto paid John Perry for	61	2	4¼	108	7	3	7½
						179	1	8
						387	9	9
	By balance carried to that acct.				118	400	19	10
						798	9	7

        Bristoll 1686

				s	d
	Land in Clevedon purchased of the Earle of Bristoll (viz) my	Dr	£	s	d
	Tenement called Newlands Tenement, & t'other cal'd Insolds				
	To ballance brought from that acct. to the 2nd Feb. 1685	32	181	15	10
Aprill	To John Stretten for ½ yeares Lords rent hee paid due Sept.				
	29th 1685	57		16	
	To Ditto for 2s I gave him out of his ½ yeares rent	57		2	
July	To Richard Merrick alias Reece for poores money, & militia				
	money	92	1	4	7
	To Ditto for ½ yeares Lords rent hee paid ending 29th				
	September 1686	92		16	
	To Ditto for ½ yeares Lords rent due 25th March last 1686	92		16	
	To Ditto for mending Seawall	92		2	
1689 May	To John Stretten what hee paid Lords rent for ½ yeare ending				
	25th March 89	57		16	

Bristoll 1686

		Cr	£	s	d
	My Land in Clevedon per Contra is	Cr	£	s	d
January	By John Stretten for ½ yeares rent for insolds ending 29th September 1686	57	6		
November	By Richard Merrick for ½ yeares rent for Newlands Tenement ending September 29th 1686	92	6	10	
1687 June 7	By John Stretten for ½ yeares rent for insolds due Feb. 2nd 1686	57	6		
	By Richard Merrick for ½ yeares rent due 1st March 1686	92	6	10	
September 29	By John Stretten for ½ yeares rent due September 29th 1687	57	6		
	By John Stretten for ½ yeares rent due March 1st 1687	57	6		
1688	By Richard Merrick for 1 yeares rent due 1st March 1687	92	13		
	By John Stretten for ½ yeares rent due August 2nd for insolds	57	6		
1689 June	By Richard Merrick for 1 yeares rent ending March 1st 1688	92	13		
	By John Stretten for ½ yeares rent for insolds due March1st 1688	57	6		

October	To Richard Merrick for his two noates of Disbursments	92	6	19	
1690 April	To Ditto for what he paid the Lords Rent	174		14	3
			194	1	8

Anno 1686					
	Simon Hurle of Bristoll Soapmaker is	Dr	£	s	d
May 28	To Oyles Ten pipes for acct. of John Cooke & Samuel Kekewich weight neat 4¾ tons 2¼ Gallons at £26 per tonne to pay for them August 28th as per his noat	117	123	15	3

Anno 1686					
	Wines (viz) 2 Butts Malaga & 4 Butts of Xerie bought in London and ship'd in the ship New England merchant for Bristoll and one Butt of Xerie imported in the Betty from Cadiz	Dr	£	s	d
May 11	To Isaac Heming for what hee paid for the 2 Butts Malaga Wine 1 Butt of Xerie laden per Cook & Kekewich in the Betty Tho. Bagg Mr from Cadiz is debtor to said Cook & Kekewich	113	52	13	4
	40 pieces of 8 its first cost at 52d½ is 320 Ryals	111	9		
	To Cash paid custom, fees, bills, wharfage, freight, Prisage, & Coynage as per particulars in booke of charges on merchandises	108	10	15	7
June	To Isaac Heming for the first cost of the 4 Butts Xerie at £20 15s 00d per Butt	113	83		
	To Ditto for Cooperidge, hooping, racking, & cartage & boathire aboard	113	2	1	6
	To Cash paid landing them 1s 6d & £ s d wharfage 2s 3 6	11 ⁹⁶		3	6
	To Proffit & Losse for port of leters 1s 6d & halling them 3s 4 6				
	To Ditto for 5 Gallons milk to whiten the hogshead Malaga 1 8				
	To Ditto for cooperidge to the Widow Washrow 4 6	105		10	8
	To Cash paid Francis Plomer for freight of the 6 Butts landing chargd before	119	2	5	
	To Tho. Day for 12¼ Gall. Xerie at 4s and other charges per noat	114	3	14	8
	To Xeries wine 6 Butts in the Dilligence for 61½ Galls Xerie at 4s	113	12	6	
			176	10	3

Anno 1686					
	Adventure in the ship Friston Capt. — Gutheridge Commander from London to Cadiz, & consign'd to John Cooke & Samuel Kekewich in St Marie Port	Dr	£	s	d
May	To one Trunck of Worsted stockins cont. viz 65 Doz is 780 paire sad Bristoll hose) 20 doz is 240 paire fancy colour'd Ditto)				
	1020 paires at 2s 9d per paire	115	140	5	
	11doz is 132 paire fancy coloured Wells hose at 1s 9d per paire	115	11	11	
	£ s d				
	To a Trunck, cord & matting 16	105			
	To Isaac Heming for carriage to London, custom & petty charges 4 7 8	113	4	7	8
	To Profitt & Loss for ballance	190 *	25	00	6
			181	4	2

			£	s	d
	By John Stretten for ½ yeares rent due August 2nd 1689	57 .	6		
	By Cornelius Stretten for one year's rent of Newlands ending 2nd March 1689	62	8		
1690 Nov	By Tho. Philips and Comp.a for ½ yeares rent of insolds ending 29th September past	188 *	6		
			95		
	By Acct. of Ballances, for Ballance	194 *	99	1	8
			194	1	8

Anno 1686					
	Simon Hurle per Contra is	Cr	£	s	d
September 27	By Tobacco 26 hhds for Lawrence Washington paid Wm. Nicklus in part freight for 20 hhds	126	30		
October 2	By Cash received of him	119	93	15	3
			123	15	3

Anno 1686					
	Wines in partnership with Tho. Day (viz) 1/2 for my acct. & 1/2 for his which I spared to him by agreement made betwixt us in writing	Cr	£	s	d
August	By Wines in Partnership theire new acct. current carried for want of roome on the other syde to that acct. of debt, this 30th of August 1686	123	176	10	3
			176	10	3

Anno 1687					
Adventure in the Friston to Cadiz per Contra is	Cr	£	s	d
By Samuel Kekewich for the neat proceeds of the Trunck of stockins per Contra being 6822½ Ryals is 852¾ pieces of 8 the piece of 8 at 51d as per acct. of sales closed Octo. 14th 1687	111	181	4	2

Anno 1686		Dr	£	s	d
	John Jayne per Contra is Debtor				
June	To Proffit & Losse for ½ cost & charges of 2000 Fossets twixt Tho. Day & him	105		11	
August	To Cash paid him in full	119	1	1	1
			1	12	1

(117)

Bristoll 1686		Dr	£	s	d
	Humphrey Corsley of Bristoll Goldsmith is				
Aprill 3	To Cash for these following summes brought from that acct. of debt	1			
	To that acct. for money hee received of John Olliffe by my order	1	50		
17	To same acct. for money hee received of mee as per noat	1	100		
August 4	To Mathew Walter & Company received of the widow Beaton	103	38	7	10
	To John Olliffe for money of him by my order	98	86	10	
			274	17	10

Anno 1686		Dr	£	s	d
	John Cook & Samuel Kekewich theire acct. of Oyles				
October 4	To Isaac Heming for my bill on him for the neat proceeds of the Oyles per Contra, in favor of said Cooke per Sam. Kekewich his order	113	97	18	6
	To Profit and Loss, for Ballance	190 *		1	4
			97	19	10

Anno 1686		Dr	£	s	d
	Richard Speed the sone of Richard Speed of Bristoll marriner deceased is				
June 12	To Cash paid his uncle Richd. Miller to helpe bind him apprentice to Caleb Shuter marriner	108	6		

Anno 1686		Dr	£	s	d
	Richard Miller of Sherborne in the County of Dorset Buttonmaker is				
June 12	To Cash lent him on his noat payable 25th July next	108	4		
March 21	To Cash lent him on his bond	121	10		
			14		

Anno 1686		Dr	£	s	d
	Oyles 10 Pipes imported in the ship Betty from Cadiz Tho. Bagge master for acct. of John Cook & Sam. Kekewich and by them sent consign'd to mee £ s d				
May 27	To Cash paid custom, Fees, bills & wharfage 7 3 11				
	To Ditto paid weighing when sould 3 2				
	To Ditto paid Tho. Bagge for freight & averidge at 3s 6d per Cwt 15 12 6	108			
	To Proffit & Losse for halling to weighing place & portridge 6 5	105			
	To Ditto for my Commission for Sales at £2 per Cent 02 9 5	127	25	15	5
	To John Cooke & Company theire acct. of Oyles for theire neat proceeds	117	97	19	10
			123	15	3

Anno 1686		Dr	£	s	d
	Lincloth 4 Rolls Canvas imported from St Mallo in the ship St Mallo merchant for acct. of William Brice late of Dorsetshire now of Cork merchant				
July 17	To Cash paid custom, fees, bills, landing halling etc. £ s d 3 8 2	119			
	To Cash paid Tho. Hallet for freight & averidge at 3s 6d per Cwt 14 00	119			

	Anno 1686				
	John Jayne of Bristoll Wine Cooper is	*Cr*	*£*	*s*	*d*
June	*By Doc.t Francis Hungerford for 1½ doz Pints & 1 doz qts*				
	white wine bottles etc.	*87*	*1*	*1*	*1*
	By Tho. Day for the ½ of 2000 fossets, said Day paying mee for				
	the whole 2000	*114*		*11*	
			1	*12*	*1*

	Bristoll 1686				
	Humphrey Corsley per Contra is	*Cr*	*£*	*s*	*d*
November 25	*By Cash received of him*	*120*	*124*	*17*	*10*
December 31	*By Cash received of him at the house of Peter Wadden in the*				
	Marsh	*120*	*150*		
			274	*17*	*10*

	Anno 1686				
	John Cook & Company theire acct. of Oyles	*Cr*	*£*	*s*	*d*
August 28	*By Oyles 10 Pipes sent consign'd to mee per Sam. Kekewich in*				
	the ship Betty to bee sould for acct. of John Cooke & himselfe, for				
	theire neat proceeds which by his order were to bee remitted to said				
	Cooke in London as per acct. of sales	*117*	*97*	*19*	*10*

	Anno 1690				
	Per Contra is	*Cr*	*£*	*s*	*d*
	By Acct. of Ballances, for Ballance	*194*	*6*	*00*	*00*

	Anno 1686				
	Richard Miller per Contra is	*Cr*	*£*	*s*	*d*
August	*By Cash recd. of him in full*	*119*	*4*		
1688 August 7	*By Cash recd. of him*	*141*	*10*		
			14		

	Anno 1686				
	Oyles 10 Pipes per Contra are	*Cr*	*£*	*s*	*d*
May 28	*By Simon Hurle for said 10 Pipes cont. neat 4¾ tons 2¼*				
	Gallons sould him at £26 per tonne, to pay for them the 28th of				
	August next	*116*	*123*	*15*	*3*

	Anno 1686				
	Lincloth for acct. of Wm. Brice per Contra	*Cr*	*£*	*s*	*d*
July	*By John Bubb for the 4 Rolls cont. 448 @ cost 10s 4d½ per @*				
	at 1s 6d off is 8s 10d½ per @	*45*	*19*	*17*	*7*

To *Proffit & Losse for warehouse roome*			1	04	127		
To *Ditto for my Commission at £2 per Cent*			7	9	127	4	11	3
To *Wm. Brice for its neat proceeds carried to his acct. current*					122	15	6	4
						19	17	7

Anno 1686

	John Wilmer of London merchant is				Dr	£	s	d
1687 July 30	To *Cash paid Sam. Whiben for leading his mare to Branford*	£	s	d 4				
	To *Ditto paid James Swetnam for a new snaffle bridle*			2	119		6	
	To *Proffit & Losse for my new Bay mare that came out of Devonshire sould him here in Bristoll & sent to the red Lyon in Branford per his orders*				105	17		
August 21	To *Isaac for my bill on him in favor of John Wilmer*				105	9	13	6
	To *Isaac Heming for my bill on him in his favor*				130	13		
1687 March	To *Isaac Heming for money hee recd. of him*				152	50		
1689 June 25	To *sundry accts for 2 Panniers cont. 4 doz Xerie with bottles, Pannier etc.*				150, 164	4	3	
November 29	To *sundry accts for 2 Panniers cont. 6 doz parts Xerie, with 2 Panniers, bottles etc.*				169, 164	3	4	11
December 12	To *Cash paid Abraham Hill for 2 Firkins Butter weight 180lb at 3d¾ & 6d the Cask*				168	2	18	9
						100	6	2

Anno 1686

	John Perrie near Pensford Stockin maker is	Dr	£	s	d
November 19	To *Cash paid lent him on 60 paire of stockins*	120	5	
1688 May 28	To *Cash paid lent him on his noat*	121	4	
1688 Oct. 26	To *Ditto paid lent him on his noat*	157	4	
			9	

(118)   Bristoll 1686

	Worsted Stockins are				Dr	£	s	d
June 16	To *Cash paid for 3 Cords for 3 Truncks*				108		3	
	To *Ditto paid Robert Webb for 3 Truncks*				108	1	7	
	To *Ditto paid Jonathan Abram for*	38	2	5	108	4	11	10
18	To *Ditto paid Anthony Palmer for*	25	2	5½	108	3	1	6
	To *Ditto paid John Massinger for*	36	2	8	108	4	16	
	To *Ditto paid Peter Hinton for 1620 Seales is 133 1/3 dozen at 3d per dozen*				108	1	14	
21	To *Ditto paid Joseph White for sadds*	39	2	7				
	& Pearles	6	2	6	108	5	15	9
24	To *Ditto paid Tho. Hill for*	44	2	5	108	5	6	4
	To *Ditto paid Ditto for James Wollen for*	44	2	5	108 *	6	10	6
	To *Ditto paid John Massinger for*	35	2	8	108 *	4	13	4
26	To *Cash paid John Brady for*	50	2	5	108	6	10	
	To *Ditto paid Jonathan Abram for*	41	2	5	108	4	19	1
	To *Ditto pd. Tho. Hill for Richd. Forster for*	52	2	4	119 *	6	1	4
28	To *Ditto paid Joseph White for*	36	2	7				
		12	2	6	119	6	3	
29	To *Ditto paid John Lukins for*	43	2	4¾	119	5	3	
30	To *Cash paid Tho. Browning for*	78	1	4	119	5	4	
July 2	To *Ditto paid John Massinger for*	33	2	8	119	4	8	
3	To *Ditto paid Robert Webb for a large Trunck*				119		13	
	To *Ditto paid Tho. Hill for Henry Britten for*	50	2	5	119	6		10
6	To *Ditto paid Tho. Hill for*	42	1	4	119	2	16	
	To *Ditto paid Jonathan Abram for*	37	2	5	119	4	9	5

	Anno 1686				
	John Wilmer per Contra is	*Cr*	*£*	*s*	*d*
July 29	By Cash received of him, being 6d lesse than hee told it for by 6d on french Ecu	*119*	24	19	6
	By Proffit & Losse for money I freely abated him on the mare	*105*	2		
1687 July 27	By Cash recd. of Lewis Cox of Cardiffe for his acct.	*121*	13		
1688 Feb. 4	By Cash recd. of Henry Parsons on his bill assign'd on him in my favor	*157*	50		
1689 Sept. 7	By Cash recd. of him in full in Bristoll	*168*	4	3	
	By his new acct. current for the 2 panniers of Xerie per Contra	*174*	3	4	11
	By Ditto for the first cost of the 2 Firkins of Butter per Contra	*174*	2	18	9
			100	6	2

	Anno 1687				
	John Perrie per Contra is	*Cr*	*£*	*s*	*d*
Aprill 2	By Cash recd. of him	*121*	5		
June 3	By Cash recd. of him	*121*	4		
1688 Nov. 2	By Cash received of him	*157*	4		
			9		

Bristoll 1686

		Cr	*£*	*s*	*d*
	Stockins per Contra are				
June 16	By ballance brought from that acct.	*115*	400	19	10
July 24	By Adventure in the Malaga merchant to Malaga for 1 Trunck cont. 42 doz is 504 paire fine Bristoll hose at 2s 9d per paire	*122*	69	6	
August 3	By Adventure in the ship City of Cadiz Capt. Thomas Fyres for one Trunck laden in her for Cadiz cont. 108 doz is 1296 paire Bristoll hose at 2s 9d per paire, and 10 doz is 120 paire Wells hose at 1s 8d per paire conssign'd to Samuel Kekewich	*122*	188	4	
	By Adventure in the ship Adventurers Delight John Hardham Master for 1 Trunck shipd in her containing 42 doz is 504 paire Bristoll hose from London to Malaga consign'd to Tho. Strode merchant at 2s 9d per paire	*123*	69	6	
September 6	By Adventure 2nd in the ship Dilligence to Cadiz, for one Trunck cont. 94 doz is 1128 paire Bristoll hose at 2s 9d & 26 doz is 312 paire Wells hose at 1s 8d consigned to Samuel Kekewich merchant in St Marie Port	*124*	181	2	
25	By Adventure 3rd in the Civilia merchant to Cadiz for 1 Trunck No S 19 cont. 110 Doz is 1320 paire at 2s 9d & 12 doz Wells is 144 paire at 1s 8d per paire laden in said ship & consign'd to Samuel Kekewich merchant in St Marie Port	*124*	193	10	
			1102	7	10

Date	Description							
	To Ditto paid James Woollen for	35	2	5	119	4	4	7
9	To Cash paid John Massinger for	42	2	8	119	5	12	
12	To Ditto paid John Perry for	73	2	4¼	119	8	11	10
	To Ditto paid Henry Britten for	27	2	5	119	3	5	3
14	To Ditto paid John Day for	15	2	4	119	1	15	7½
15	To Ditto paid John Rudduck for	45	2	4½	119	5	6	10
16	To Ditto paid Anthony Palmer for	39	2	5½	119	4	16	
19	To Ditto paid Joseph White for	42	2	7	119	5	8	
20	To Ditto paid John Massinger for	47	2	8	119	6	5	4
21	To Ditto paid John Perrie for	36	2	4¼	119	4	4	9
22	To Cash paid Tho. Hill for	30	2	4½	119	3	11	3
23	To Ditto paid Tho. Hill for 42 paire	42	2	5	119	5	1	6
24	To Ditto paid Joseph White for	31	2	7				
		6	2	6	119	4	15	1
	To Ditto paid Edward Iffe in full for hotpressing stockins				119		17	4
	To Ditto paid John Brady for	35	2	5	119	4	4	7
29	To Ditto paid Jos. George for	48	1	4	119	3	4	
30	To Ditto paid John Holiman for	67	1	3	119	4	3	9
31	To Ditto paid Jonathan Abram for	40	2	5	119	4	16	8
August 3	To Cash paid John Perry for	58	2	4				
		30	2	2	119	10		4
7	To Ditto paid John Massinger for	24	2	8	119	3	4	
9	To Ditto paid Tho. Hill for	100	1	2	119	5	16	8
	To Ditto paid Joseph White for sadds	41	2	7				
	pearles	9	2	6	119	5	16	8
	To Ditto paid James Wollen for	39	2	5	119	4	14	3
13	To Cash paid Jonathan Abram for	41	2	5	119	4	19	1
24	To Ditto paid John Rudduck for	20	2	4½	119	2	7	6
	To Ditto paid John Massinger for	40	2	8	119	5	6	8
	To Ditto paid John Lukins for	20	2	4¾	119	2	7	11
	To Ditto paid John Perrie for	24	2	4¼	119	2	16	6
	To Ditto paid John Brady for	25	2	5	119	3		5
						221	1	3½
28	To Cash paid John Massinger for	35	2	8	119	4	13	4
	To Ditto paid Edward Iffe in full for hot pressing				119		12	
30	To Cash paid Jonathan Abram for	33	2	5	119	3	19	9
	To Ditto paid Joseph George for	72	1	4	119	4	16	
September 2	To Ditto paid James Wollen for	32	2	5	119	3	17	4
	To Ditto paid Tho. Hill for	72	1	3	119	4	10	
	To Ditto paid Samuel Dyer for	29	2	5	119	3	10	1
4	To Ditto paid John Massinger for	21	2	8	119	2	16	
	To Ditto paid Tho. Hill for Browning & Creed for	223	1	4	119	14	17	4
6	To Ditto paid Elizabeth Webb for a Trunck & a board for the window				119		13	6
10	To Cash paid Tho. Hill for John Lukins for	34	2	4¾	119	4	1	6
	To Ditto paid Jos. White for sadds	46	2	7				
	pearles	18	2	6	119	8	3	10
	To Ditto paid John Massinger for	40	2	8	119	5	6	8
13	To Ditto paid Jonathan Abram for	44	2	5	119	5	6	4
	To Ditto paid Joseph George for	40	1	4	119	2	13	4
	To Cash paid James Wollen for	35	2	5	119	4	4	7
	To Ditto paid Sam. Dyer for	39	2	5	119	4	14	3
	To Ditto paid Richard George for	48	1	3½	119	3	3	
	To Cash paid John Perrie for	47	2	5½	119	5	12	½
	To Cash paid Henry Britten for	23	2	5	119	2	15	7
18	To Cash paid John Rudduck for	39	2	4½	119	4	12	8
	To Cash paid John Massinger for	20	2	8	119	2	13	4
	To Cash paid John Brady for	22	2	5	119	2	13	2

					ref	£	s	d
20	To Cash paid John Lukins for	19	2	4¾	119	2	5	¼
	To Cash paid James Wollen for	31	2	5	119	3	14	11
	To Cash paid Jonathan Abram for	44	2	5	119	5	6	4
24	To Cash paid Edward Iffe in full for hot pressingg				119	1	2	
25	To Cash paid John Massinger for	25	2	8	119	3	6	8
	To Cash paid Jos. White for	51	2	7	119	6	11	9
	To Cash paid Tho. Hill for Henry Britten for	46	2	5	119	5	11	2
29	To Cash paid Jos. George for	47	1	4	119	3	2	8
	To Cash paid Tho. Browning for	100	1	4				
		11	1	6	119	7	9	10
30	To Cash paid Tho. Hill for	80	1	2	119	4	13	4
October 2	To Cash paid Sam. Dyer for	34	2	5	119	4	2	2
	To Cash paid Wm. Thiery for	20	2	4	119	2	6	8
	To Cash paid John Massinger for	34	2	8	119	4	10	8
	To Cash paid Jos. White for sadds	48	2	7				
	pearles	16	2	6	119	8	4	
	To Cash paid Jonathan Abram for	36	2	5	119	3	12	6
	To Cash paid Tho. Hill for	28	2	4½	119	3	6	6
	To Cash paid Tho. Hill for	38	2	5	119	4	11	10
	To Cash paid Tho. Hill for	28	2	5	119	2	15	7
7	To Cash pd. Tho. Walden for 2 dozen Inkle				119		13	
	To Cash pd. John Lukins for	29	2	4¾	119	3	9	5
	To Cash paid Tho. Hill for	35	1	4	119	2	6	8
	To Cash pd. John Perrie for	24	2	4¾	119	2	17	6
	To Cash pd. John Massinger for	33	2	8	119	4	8	
						190	13	9¾
						411	15	1¼
	By ballance of this acct. carryed to that acct.				128	690	12	8¾
						1102	7	10

(119)   **Bristoll 1686**

	Cash is	Dr	£	s	d
June 26	To ballance brought from that acct.	108	1315	3	
July 5	To Wm. Dawson received of his Sonne William in full	94	2	6	
7	To John Winpenny received of him	101	72		
	To Richard Holbrook received of him	98	1	10	3
12	To Thmas. Jordan received of him	95	56	15	
14	To Ralph Grant received of him	88	16	10	
24	To Richard Merrick alias Reece received of him	92	5	17	
29	To John Wilmer received of him	117	24	19	6
August 5	To Alexander Doleman received of him in full	48	19	7	
	To John Mayne received of him for ballance of his Spanish acct.	111	46	4	7
	To Charles Stubbs & John Mayne received of John Mayne for the intrest of £100 for 4 months & of one other £100 for 8 months	123	6		
6	To Wm. Rogers received of him in full	93	10	10	
	To Richard Holbrook recd. of him in part	98	2		
16	To Sir George Strode recd. of him	24	4	10	
	To Tho. Day Wine Cooper recd. of him	123	39	13	
	To John Blackwell recd. of him	85	100		
28	To Jacob Beele recd. of him	21	1	5	
	To Tho. Day recd. of him at twice	123	47	17	1
	To Richard Miller recd. of him	117	4		
	To John Mayne recd. of Tho. Day by his order	111	49	19	6
September 8	To John Olliffe recd. of him	98	80		
	To John Maine recd. of him	111	2	14	
10	To Samuel Davis recd. of his Widow	63	4	9	
	To John Hartnell Junior recd. of him in full	38	1	15	
23	To Fra. Whitchurch & Company recd. of him	103	15	17	6
	To Pendock Warren recd. of him in part	126	40		

Bristoll 1686

		Cr	£	s	d
	Cash per Contra is				
June 28	*By Stockins paid Joseph White & John Lukins*	*118*	11	6	
	By Proffit & Losse paid Charles Stubbs towards releife of the poore protestants	*105*	1	10	
30	*By Stockins paid Tho. Browning for 78 paire*	*118*	5	4	
July 1	*By Proffit & Losse paid John Pretty & Richard Cope*	*105*	1	1	
2, 3	*By Stockins paid John Massinger, Robert Webb & Tho. Hill*	*118*	11	1	10
6	*By Ditto paid Tho. Hill, Jonathan Abram & James Woollen*	*118*	11	10	
	By Proffit & Losse paid Abraham Hill	*105*		16	6
9	*By Ditto paid Joane Darracot for butter 8s 9d & to Wm. Clark for bottles £1 1s 6d*	*105*	1	10	3
	By Stockins paid John Massinger	*118*	5	12	
	By Ditto paid John Perry & Henry Britten	*118*	11	17	1
14	*By Stockins paid John Day*	*118*	1	15	7½
	By Proffit & Losse paid houshold expences 31 6 4¼ & John Hardiman 10s	*105*	31	16	4¼
15	*By Stockins paid John Rudduck*	*118*	5	6	10
16	*By Ditto paid Antho. Palmer £4 16s 0d, Jos. White £5 8s 0d, John Massinger £6 5s 4d & John Perry £4 4s 9d*	*118*	20	14	1
22	*By Proffit & Losse paid Tho. Bourne*	*105*		4	6
	By Elizabeth Tayler paid lent her	*88*		5	
	By Stockins paid Tho. Tayler alias Hill	*118*	3	11	3
23	*By house in which I live paid the Deputy Chamberlaine for 3 yeares rent for back house*	*23*	1	4	
	By Stockins paid Tho. Hill, Ed. Iffe, Joseph White & John Brady	*118*	14	18	6
29	*By Ditto paid Joseph George*	*118*	3	4	
	By Wines 6 Butts out of the New England merchant paid freight & landing	*116*	2	6	6

	To *John Mayne recd. of Tho. Day*	*111*	80		
25	To *Isaac Heming recd. of Robert Henley*	*113*	50		
27	To *Edward Crofts received of him*	*96*	12		
30	To *David Dorvele recd. of him*	*126*	50		
	To *Wm. Godwin recd. of him*	*64*	3		
October 2	To *Tobacco 26 hhds received of the Custom house*	*126*		19	9
	To *Simon Hurle recd. of him*	*116*	93	15	
	To *Wm. Prichard recd. of him*	*63*	50		
	To *Anthony Owen recd. of him*	*111*	16		
			2326	17	2

30	By Stockins paid John Holiman	118	4	3	9
	By John Wilmer paid Samuel Whiben Carrier & James Swetnam Sadler	117		6	
31	By Stockins paid Jonathan Abram	118	4	16	8
August 3	By Ditto paid John Perry	118	10		4
	By Joseph Drew paid lent him on his bond	31	4		
5	By George Cabbell paid him for mending the Pump	105		3	
	By Charles Stubbs & John Mayne lent them on theire two bonds for £100 each	123	200		
	By Nicholas Baker paid him in full	103	3		
7	By Stockins paid John Massinger	118	3	4	
	By Elizabeth Tayler lent her	88		5	
	By Proffit & Losse paid for a permit, & by John Jones paid him in full	105, 99	21	15	6
9	By Stockins paid Tho. Hill, Jos. White, and James Wollen	118	16	19	4
13	By Stockins paid Jonathan Abram	118	4	19	1
	By Proffit & Losse paid James Freeman	105		1	3
24	By Sugar 8 Butts in the Olivetree paid James Porter for freight & averidge	125	20	16	
	By Stockins paid John Rudduck, John Massinger & John Lukins	118	10	2	1
	By house in which I live paid David Roynon	23	1	6	
	By Stockind paid John Perry & John Brady	118	5	16	11
	By John Jane paid him in full	116	1	1	1
26	By Proffit & Losse paid Jacob Beele	127		17	6
28	By Stockins paid John Massinger & Edward Iffe	118	5	5	4
	By Lawrence Washington paid port of leters	30		1	6
30	By Stockins paid Jon. Abram & Joseph George	118	8	15	9
	By Sugar 1 Butt paid Tho. Walden	103	6	10	3
September 2	By Stockins paid James Wollen, Tho. Hill, & Sam. Dyer	118	11	17	5
4	By Proffit & Losse paid John Morgan for keeping my mare	127		3	
	By Stockins paid John Massinger	118	2	16	
	By Elizabeth Tayler paid her	88	1		
	By Stockins paid Tho. Hill for 223 paire	118	14	17	4
	By Adventure in the Dilligence paid custom etc. of a Trunck stockins	124	3	16	8
6	By Proffit & Losse paid Elizabeth Smith for Cheese	127	1	4	6
			516	16	6¾
	By Stockins paid Elizabeth Webb for a Trunck	118		13	6
10	By John Mayne paid him	125	20		
	By Stockins paid Tho. Hill	118	4	1	6
	By Mathew Walter paid them in full	103		19	
11	By Proffit & Losse paid John Hardiman in full	127	2		
	By Stockins paid Jos. White & John Massinger	118	13	10	6
	By Sugar 8 Butts & 1 Butt pd. weighing them at back hall	103, 125		7	2
	By Stockins paid Jonathan Abram & Joseph George	118	7	19	8
	By Tobacco 26 hhds for Lawrence Washington for pd. Ed. Watts freight 6 hhds in the John	126	9	19	6
18	By Stockins paid James Wollen, Samuel Dyer, Richard d George & John Perrie	118	17	13	10½
	By Ditto paid Henry Britten, John Rudduck, John Massinger, & John Brady	118	12	14	9
	By Sugar 8 Butts paid Fra. Challenour for 5 weeks 4 daies Celleridge	125		11	4
	By Proffit & Losse paid James Swetenham	127		15	
	By Stockins paid John Lukins	118	2	5	¼
23	By Wines in partnership paid Jos. Berry	123	1		
	By Stockins paid James Wollen & Jonathan Abram	118	9	1	3
24	By Tho. Day paid him in part	123	20		
	By Stockins paid Ed. Iffe, John Massinger & Joseph White	118	11		5

(120)	**Bristoll 1686**	Dr	£	s	d
	Cash is				
October 9	To ballance brought from that acct.	119	1313	16	5
	To John Blackwell recd. of him	85	100		
	To John Bubb recd. of him	45	19	17	6
14	To Wm. Prichard & Company recd. of Wm. Prichard	63	5	5	
	To Marie Beard recd. of her	125	3	10	
	To John Earle of Bristoll recd. of Serieant Hodges at Clevedon	80	21	18	11
	To Robert Dowding & Company received of Ozziel Browne	100	6		
27	To Pendock Warren recd. of him	126	50		
	To Marie Beard recd. of her	125	1		
30	To John Brady received of him	20	4		
November 1	To Marie Beard recd. of her by the hands of John Gore for 4				
	Cowes	125	17	7	
3	To the Lady Ann Powlet recd. of Barnard Wilkins	100	10	14	
3	To Pendock Warren recd. of him	126	10		
4	To Marie Beard recd. of her in part	125	2		
6	To Nathanael Haggatt received of him	19	100		
10	To Henry Howard & Company, recd. of Oz. Browne for ½				
	yeares intrest	92	3		
11	To David Dorvele recd. of him in part	126	65		
13	To Richard Holbrook recd. of him in part	98	2		
25	To Humphry Corsley received of him	117	124	17	10
29	To Isaac Heming recd. of Samuel Spencer	130	18	4	

			£	s	d
	By Tobacco 26 hhds paid weighing 10 hhds	126		2	6
	By Stockins paid Tho. Hill	118	5	11	2
27	By House at the lower end of Small Streat paid Ed. Croft	22	2		
29	By Stockins paid Tho. Browning & Jos. George	118	10	12	6
	By Ditto paid Tho. Hill	118	4	13	4
	By Wm. Plydall paid him	46		2	6
	By Tobacco 26 hhds paid Wm. Nicklus in full	126	2	15	
	By Proffit & Losse paid soleing shooes & port of leters	127		12	9
	By Merchandizes for Lawrence Wahington port of a leter & Wm. Belcher	124	2	15	6
October 2	By Elizabeth Tayler paid her	88	7		
	By Stockins paid Sam. Dyer, Wm. Thiery, & John Massinger	118	10	19	6
	By Marie Beard paid Ozziel Browne	125	2	10	
	By Stockins paid Joseph White for a parcell	118	8	4	
	By Tobacco 26 hhds paid Edward Watts for country duties of 6 hhds	126		12	
	By Proffit & Losse paid for a parcell of Cheese to Joane Smith	127	1	1	6
	By Stockin paid Jonathan Abram	118	3	12	6
	By Andrew Stuckey paid port of a leter to him	55		1	
	By Stockins paid Tho. Hill for 3 parcells	118	10	13	11
7	By Adventure in the Olive tree paid custom etc. on a Trunck stockins	124	2	6	7
	By stockins paid Tho. Walden, John Lukins, Tho. Hill, John Perry & John Massinger	118	15	14	7
	By Adventure in the Betty pd. custom etc. on 2 Truncks of stockins	110	7	9	6
	By Merchandizes for Law. Washington in the John paid Wm. Rogers for 2 doz shooes	124	2	12	
	By Wines 4 Butts in the Dilligence pd. custom etc. & Canvas 4 Rolls custom as per particulars	113, 117	36	11	8½
	By Sugar 8 Butts for John Swimsted paid custom etc.	125	21	4	1
	By sundry accts paid custom fees etc. for 20 hhds of Tobacco in the Fra. & Marie & 6 in the John	126	201	13	7
			1013		9
	By Ballance carried to a new acct. of Cash	120	1313	16	5
			2326	17	2

Bristoll 1686

	Cash per Contra is	Cr	£	s	d
October 9	By Stockins pd. Tho. Hill, Jos. White & Tho. Hill & John Brady	128	18	14	10
	By John Brady paid lent him	20	4		
13	By Proffit & Losse paid Henry Gibbes for ½ a piece Dowlas	127	5	17	
	By Stockins paid Jos. George & Edward Iffe	128	6	3	8
14	By Ditto paid John Rudduck, James Wollen, & Sam. Dyer	128	11	10	3
	By Joane Darracot & Welthian Ruther paid each of them ½ ¼ yeares wages	98, 94	2		
16	By Stockins pd. Jona. Abram, John Massinger, Tho. Hill & Robert Webb	128	12	9	
19	By George White pd. him	125	6	1	10
	By Proffit & Losse paid said White	127	1	16	
21, 22	By Stockins pd. Tho. Hill John Massinger & John Perry	128	16	11	10
23	By Ditto pd. Tho. Hill Jona. Abram & Joseph White	128	29	10	10
26	By Andrew Stuckey paid John England for 30 paire stockins	55	4	17	6
	By Stockins paid Joseph George for 80 paire at 1s 4d	128	5	6	8
28	By Ditto paid Tho. Hill & James Wollen	128	7		
	By House at the lower end of Small Streat paid 1 yeares Kings rent due Sept. 29th 1686	22		2	8
30	By Stockins paid John Massinger & John Brady	128	10	12	3
	By Ditto paid Jos. White & Henry Britten	128	10	2	
November 1	By Proffit & Losse paid John Morgan for keeping my mare	127		3	

Date		Folio	£	s	d
	To John Blackwell recd. of him in part	85	100		
Dec. 1	To Edward Gorges recd. of him in full	34	67	16	6
3	To John Blackwell recd. of him in full	85	9		
4	To Tho. Longman recd. of him	113	2		
8	To John Olliffe recd. of him by the hands of Humphry Corsley	98	100		
	To Isaac Hemming received of Humphrey Corsley for my bill on him	130	100		
11	To Marie Beard recd. of her in part	125	4		
	To Proffit & Losse recd. of Ann Davis	127	10		
	To Isaac Heming received of Elizabeth Tayler on my bill on him	130	12		
15	To William Brice of Fra. Edwards per the order of Daniel Cox	122	20		
28	To John Love recd. of him in full	55	1	3	
31	To Humphry Corsley received of him	117	150		
	To Robert Yate received of him in November last then omitted	39	5	17	
January 8	To David Dorvele for money of him in full	126	10	7	
13	To John Stretten received of him	57	6		
February 2	To Richard Merrick recd. of him in part	92	5	13	
	To John Whiting & Company recd. of John Whiting in part	126	122	4	
			2604	11	2
2	To Isaac Heming recd. of John Blackwell in part of a bill Exchange assign'd mee	130	74	7	
	To Richard Gotley & Company recd. of Richard Gotley & Company	16	27	5	
8	To Pendock Warren received of him in part	126	30		
10	To Edward Crofts for money recd. of him	96	17	13	4
14	To Scarbrow Chapman received of him	132	11	10	
	To Michael White received of him in full	132	44	3	4
15	To Isaac Heming received of John Blackwell in full of his Spanish bill	130	58	3	
	To John Osgood recd. of him in full	113		14	4
22	To Arthur Hobbs recd. of Marie Beard	125		10	
23	To Charles Stubbs recd. of him	133	81	10	9
26	To Pendock Warren recd. of him & Thorton Jones	126	20		
March 3	To Tho. Day Soapmaker recd. of him in full	94	101	11	
5	To Marie Beard received of her in part	125	4		
9	To Doctor Fra. Hungerford received of Tho. Hungerford	87	2	5	
10	To Tho. Scrope received of Robert Yate by order & consent of Henry Gibbes & by consent of Tho. Edwards	75	340	10	
			3418	13	11

	By Marie Thring & Bridget Wallis paid them & Ed. Freeman per order	7	77	1	3
3	*By Stockins paid John Rudduck*	128	4	10	3
	By house in which I live paid ½ a yeares Chimney money	130		8	
	By Proffit & Losse paid for mustering	127		3	6
4	*By Stockins pd. Tho. Hill for Richd. Forster, John Lukins, & Samuel Dyer*	128	10	16	9
6	*By Ditto pd. John Massinger, Edward Iffe & Jonathan Abram*	128	10	13	10
8	*By Ditto pd. James Wollen & Tho. Hill*	128	5	1	3
	By Proffit & Losse pd. Francis Maynard for a Flitch Bacon	127		7	6
9	*By Stockins pd. John Brady*	128	3	7	8
	By Proffit & Losse pd. Alexander Doleman in full	127	4	5	
10	*By Stockins pd. Richard George*	128	2	13	4
12	*By Ditto pd. Tho. Hill & John Perrie*	128	14	9	10
13	*By Ditto pd. John Massinger, Elizabeth Dyer, Thomas Hill & Joseph George*	128	16	1	5
18	*By John Cullimor pd. him*	130		5	
19	*By Stockins pd. John Massinger*	128	3	12	4
	By John Perrie paid lent him on 60 paire of stockins	117	5		
	By Proffit & Losse paid Alexander Doleman	127	3		
20	*By Stockins pd. Joseph White*	128	8	7	
	By Jonathan Abram pd. lent him	123	5		
	By Proffit & Losse pd. houshold expences	127	52	17	8
23	*By Stockins pd. Tho. Hill & Robert Webb*	128	10	9	5¼
27	*By Ditto pd. John Massinger for 31 paire at 2s 7d*	128	4		1
	By Tho. Walden paid lent him	87	5		
30	*By Stockins paid Tho. Hill for Richard George*	128	3	7	2
December 3	*By Proffit & Losse pd. John Hardiman*	127		5	
	By Stockins pd. John Massinger	128	4	5	3
	By Ditto paid Ed. Iffe & Andrew Creed	128	8	2	5½
			416	10	3¾
6	*By Tobacco 26 hhds weighing 16 hhds*	126		3	6
7	*By Stockins pd. Joseph George*	128	5	3	4
9	*By Anthony Tyler paid him in full of his noat, & lent him on his noat*	129	2		
10	*By Proffit & Losse paid the Widow Challoner in full for keeping my mare*	127		5	2
11	*By Stockins paid John Massinger & Tho. Hill*	128	10	19	6
	By Estate at Clapton pd. Ozziel Browne	72		6	
16	*By Stockins pd. John Massinger*	128	4	2	8
	By John Cullimor pd. him per the hands of Edmond Beales	130		5	
	By Tobacco 26 hogsheaddds pd. Edward Hollister for Celleridge	126	1	14	
	By Proffit & Losse pd. — Webb for drums & Colours	127		2	6
21	*By Ditto pd. Tho. Bourne for 17 weeks hay & stable roome*	127	2	1	4
22	*By Stockins pd. John Massinger for 36 paire*	128	4	13	
23	*By Ditto pd. Joseph George for 104 paire*	128	6	10	
	By Proffit & Losse pd. Jane Shepheard for a firkin of Butter	127		17	
	By Stockins pd. Tho. Hill for Tho. Browning	128	8	15	
28	*By Henry Wynter paid him for 1 yeares reserved rent of Clapton farme*	131	1	12	
	By William Brice pd. John Davis by his order	122	15	6	
30	*By Stockins pd. John Massinger*	128	3	4	7
January 3	*By Marie Washrow paid her in full*	75	2	5	6
8	*By Stockins pd. Joseph George & John Massinger*	128	7	2	3
	By Abraham Hill paid him in part	131	1		
11	*By Proffit & Losse pd. David Roynon in full*	127		4	6
14	*By Proffit & Losse pd. John Patrick for 6 Trees*	127		3	6
18	*By Stockins pd. John Massinger & Tho. Hill*	128	11	10	11
22	*By Ditto pd. Joseph George & John Massinger*	128	6	18	4
	By Samuel Thring & Company lent them on bond	114	6		

Bristoll 1686/7

		Cash is	Dr	£	s	d
March 11		To ballance from that acct.	120	2726	9	3¼
		To Richard Holebrooke received of him in part for rent	98	2		
	30	To Marie Beard recd. of severalls for 28 Cheeses	125	1	18	
Aprill 1		To Tho. Day recd. of him	123	50		
	2	To John Perrie recd. of him	117	5		
		To Marie Beard recd. of Elizabeth Pearce for 28 Cheeses	125	1	19	6
		To John Earle of Bristoll recd. of Roger Stone	132	7	17	4
	6	To Marie Beard recd. of her in part	125	3		
		To Stephen Stringer recd. of him in full	133	23		
	13	To Wm. Snellgrove recd. of his wife	134	2		
	16	To Marie Beard recd. of 3 women for 40 Cheeses weight 3 cwt 0qr 3lb	125	2	17	6
		To Charles Stubbs & Company recd. of Charles Stubbs	123	100		
		To James Webb recd. of him	16	27	5	
	18	To Wm. Rogers recd. of his wife	93		19	2
	20	To Marie Beard recd. of Elizabeth Pierce for 1 cwt 0qr 20lb Cheeses 14	125	1	2	4
	21	To Marie Beard for money of her in part	125	4	10	
	27	To Pendock Warren recd. of him	126	16		
	28	To Marie Beard recd. of her in part	125	14		
	30	To Dr. Fra. Hungerford recd. of Tho. Hungerford	87	2	1	2
May 5		To Jonathan Abram received of him	123	8		
	13	To Proffit & Losse for 53 pcs Gold sould Humphry Corsley, recd. of him	127	49	15	
	18	To sundry accts recd. of Simon Clements for overplus averidge	124, 134		7	
	21	To Anthony Tyler recd. of him	129		10	
June 1		To Tho. Walden recd. of him	87	5		
		To Proffit & Losse recd. of John Browne	127	6		
	3	To John Perrie recd. of him	117	4		
		To Richard Cope. of him	97		15	
	22	To Pendock Warren recd. of him	126	20		
		To Isaac Heming recd. of Ed. Baily on John Cox Bill from London	130	12		
		To Ditto received of him in 21 Guinnies	130	22	12	9
July 12		To John Hellier recd. of him	101	15		
		To Wm. Spoore Senior & company recd. of him in part	30	42		

			£	s	d
29	By Stockins pd. John Massinger	128	4	10	5
31	By Proffit & Losse pd. Edward Jones at twice viz. 29 & 31th present	127		18	
February 3	By Thomas Day paid him	123	80		
5	By Stockins paid John Massinger	128	4	2	8
10	By Ditto paid Tho. Hill for Tho. Browning	128	7	6	3
12	By Anthony Tyler paid him	129	1	12	
	By Stockins paid John Massinger	128	3	4	7
	By Proffit & Losse paid houshold expences to the 12th instant	127	37	11	2
14	By John Osgood for a Flitch bacon	113		14	4
	By Whalebone for acct. of Robert Symes	114		1	2
19	By Stockins paid John Massinger	128	3	14	11
26	By Ditto paid Ditto	128	4		1
March 4	By Ditto pd. John Massinger for 30 paire	128	3	17	6
9	By Ditto pd. Tho. Hill for Tho. Browning for 108 paire	128	6	15	
	By Proffit & Losse paid Charles Stubbs	127	3	5	
10	By Stockins paid John Massinger	128	3	7	2
11	By John Blackwell paid him	132	4	8	6
	By Jonathan Abram paid lent his Sonne Samuel	123	3		
			692	4	7¾
	By ballance carried to a new acct. of debt	121	2726	9	3¼
			3418	13	11

Bristoll 1686/7

	Cash per Contra is	Cr	£	s	d
March 18	By Stockins paid John Massinger	128	4	15	7
	By James Swetnam paid lent him on his bond	133	50		
21	By Richard Miller paid lent him on his bond	117	10		
22	By John Blackwell paid him	132	7	2	6
23	By Edward & John Jacob lent them on theire bond	134	20		
	By Stockins pd. John Massinger	128	3	12	4
31	By Ditto paid Ditto	128	5	8	6
Aprill 1	By Estate at Clapton paid Ann Smith	72		5	4
2	By Stockins pd. Tho. Hill & John Perrie	128	23	5	8
	By Jahzeel Speed paid Alexander Doleman	122		10	6
	By John Blackwell paid himselfe	132	7	16	6
7	By Wm. Snelgrove paid lent his wife	134	2		
8	By Stockins paid John Massinger	128	3	14	11
	By Proffit & Losse pd. John Gandy in full	127		14	6
	By Jahzeel Speed pd. John Brady	122		6	6
	By sundry acct. pd. Fra. Maynard for a Flitch of Bacon	123,127		9	
12	By Jahzeel Speed paid John Massinger & John Hardiman	122		13	7
13	By Proffit & Losse pd. Fra. Maynard	127		7	4
	By Abram Hill paid him in part	131	2	10	
16	By Jahzeel Speed paid Clement Webb & Alexander Doleman	122	1	10	3
19	By Stockins paid John Massinger	128	5		9
	By Jahzeel Speed paid John Hardiman	122		6	6
20	By Ditto paid Tho. Walden	122		2	6
	By Simon Clement paid him	103	8	10	
23	By Stockins paid John Massinger	128	5	3	4
27	By Wm. Brice delivered James Porter to carry to him in Cork 18 Guinnies & 10s 6d silver	122	19	19	
	By Jahzeel Speed sent him in his Trunck to Musburie	122	3		
	By John Warren sent him in the same Trunck to Musburie	134	6	16	
30	By Stockins pd. John Massinger	128	4	13	
	By sundry accts paid for James Swetnam & to John Blackwell	132,133	2	1	2
May 3	By Proffit & Losse pd. Joane Smith & to French Protestants	127		16	2
	By Jahzeel Speed paid him at his going to Musburie	122	1		
	By Stockins paid Jonathan Abram	135	12	1	6
	By Proffit & Losse pd. Wm. Burgesse for cloth	127	1		3
6	By Stockins paid John Massinger	135	4	10	5

			£	s	d
16	To Richard Holbrooke received of him by the hands of Susan Cope	98	1	10	
	To Jonathan Abram received of him in full	123	5		
	To Wm. Spoore Senior recd. of him in part of his bond	52	8		
19	To Ditto recd. of him in full	52	2	12	
	To Wm. Spoore Senior & Company recd. of him for 1 yeares intrest of £50	30	3		
25	To Marie Beard & Company received of Marie Beard & Geo. Collet	134	18		
27	To John Wilmer received of Lewis Cox of Cardiff	117	13		
	To Isaac Heming recd. of John Wilmer	130	20		
August 1	To Ditto recd. of severalls for what I value my bills on him	130	452		
			3701	1	¼
1	To Henry Gibbes recd. of Joseph Burgesse	79	50		
	To Isaac Heming recd. of severalls for which I valued my bills	130	200		
	To Pendock Warren recd. of him in full	126	13	17	3
4	To Ralph Grant received of John Hawkins by his order in full	88	324	15	
9	To Isaac Heming recd. of Sgt Tho. Strode	130	50		
	To the Lady Ann Powlet recd. of Christopher Parker	100	9	17	
	To Sir George Strode received of himselfe in Bristoll	24	7		
12	To Tho. Lutterell & Company recd. of Tho. Lutterell	97	2	8	
			4358	18	3½

Date					
	By Nathanael Haggatt for money lent him July 19th 1686 on a deposit as per Cashbook as per Cashbook folio (69) but was then omitted to bee brought into the Journal	19	100		
	By Proffit & Losse paid Tho. Goldney Junior for my daughter Martha's marriage portion [97]	127	800		
11	By John Love pd. him on his bill of Exchange	55	100		
12, 13	By Stockins pd. Joseph White, Henry Britten & John Massinger	135	24	4	1½
	By Jahzeel Speed paid George Popley	122		7	
	By Proffit & Losse pd. John Hardiman	127	1		
19	By Proffit & Losse pd. for 2 Panniers, & postage of a Spanish leter	127		4	
	By Edward Jacob paid lent him	134	1	10	
20	By Stockins pd. John Massinger, & John Perrie	135	7	2	8
21	By Proffit & Losse pd. Anthony Tyler in full	127	2	6	6
	By Stockins paid Jonathan Abram & Joseph White	135	12	10	9¼
	By Proffit & Losse paid Humphry Richard & Fra. Maynard	127		7	2
			469	15	9¾
23	By Proffit & Losse paid Peter Hinton	127		3	
24	By Richard Speed paid Christian Richards for a firkin of Butter	94		17	1
26	By Proffit & Losse paid Tho. Wall	127			7
28	By Stockins paid Joseph White	135	9	5	
	By John Perry paid lent him	117	4		
	By Stockins pd. John Massinger	135	4	5	3
31	By Proffit & Losse paid — for Panniers & covers	127		10	
June 2	By Edward Jacob paid lent him	134	1	10	
	By Stockins paid John Massinger & John Perrie	135	10	6	1
4	By Ditto pd. Edward Iffe	135	1	11	9
	By Lawrence Washington paid Wm. Jones	132	1		
	By John Hellier paid lent him	101	15		
	By Stockins pd. John Massinger & Joseph White	135	19	4	7¾
23	By Ditto paid Ditto	135	4	15	7
	By Jonathan Abram paid lent him	123	5		
	By Proffit & Losse paid Jane Shepheard	127		18	6
29	By Abraham Hill paid him in part	131	1		
July 1	By Stockins pd. John Massinger & John Rudduck	135	8	6	6¼
8	By Proffit & Losse paid houshold expences	127	23	7	11
9	By Stockins paid Eliza. Webb, Henry Britten, & John Massinger	135	9	3	9
15	By Malaga Wines 4 Butts pd. Joseph Berrie for Brokeridge	134		10	
16	By Stockins paid Jonathan Abram for 86 paire	135	10		8
19	By Wm. Spoore & Company paid Wm. Spoore Senior	30	42		
	By Stockins paid Anthony Palmer for 37 paire	135	4	6	4
	By Isaac Heming pd. Dennis Tayler	130	5		
20	By Stockins pd. John Massinger	135	5	11	1
21	By Arthur Hart paid him	113	7	4	6
	By Stockins pd. James Wollen & Tho. Hill	135	13	5	7
25	By Henry Gibbes paid lent him	79	50		
	By Nathanael Haggatt paid lent him	138	120		
	By Copie hold Tenement in Portburie paid Tho. Stephens	20		8	
26	By Jahzeel Speed paid sent per John Warren for his Dyet etc.	122	5		
27	By John Earle of Bristoll paid charges on a piece of Freeze	132		3	9
28	By Proffit & Losse paid given John Stretten	137		2	
29	By Estate at Clapton paid John Cullimer	72		5	
30	By Stockins paid Jonathan Abram	135	4	4	
August 4	By Richard Godwin paid lent him	23	2		
	By Proffit paid Jane Flower & Sam. Jonson for 6 baskets	137	1	9	
6	By Stockins paid Joseph White	135	9	8	5
	By Edward Jones paid him in part	25		10	
11	By Copie hold Tenement in Portburie paid Tho. Morrice	20		5	

(122)	Bristoll 1686				
	Jahzeel Speed my sonne is	Dr	£	s	d
	To ballance of his former acct. brought from folio	69	492	16	5
	To Proffit & Losse for money hee took up at several times of Robert Summers	105		13	6
	To Ditto paid Alderman Olliffe for Potts of wine as per Cashbook No. E folio 29	105	2	3	1
	To Ditto paid John Sandford for old scores as in Ditto folio of Cashbooke	105		17	
	To Proffit & Losse for money hee paid Lewis Adams for Potts of wine in folio 9 of this book	105	1	10	6
	To Ditto for money he caus'd my servant Henry Dighton privatly to deliver him out of Cash at severall times, as per particcular noat, charg'd in folio 30 of Cashbook no. E	105	21	7	11
	To Ditto for severall couple of northsea Codd hee recd. money for privatly & kept it	105	1	12	
	To John Pitts for money hee spent at severall times in wine	55	1	15	
	To Henry Priest for money hee received of him for 3 Piggs & never brought it into Cash, but kept it and spent it	52	3	1	
	To Proffit & Losse for money hee received & tooke at severall times out of Cash from May 1682 to January 1685, besydes the severall timjes mentioned in this and his former acct., as per book of Petty disbursements & Cashbook appears	105	21		
	To Henry Whitwood for money recd. of him and never brought into Cash	98	4	12	9
	To Alexander Caduggen for money received of him and never brought to acct. of Cash	48	41		
	To Proffit & Losse for money hee spent mee in Spaine in about 7 months time	127	112		
1687 Aprill 2	To Cash pd. Alexander Doleman for muzling for his Cravats	121		10	6
9	To Ditto pd. John Brady for 2 paire stockins	121		6	6
	To Ditto pd. John Massinger for new making a paire stockins	121		1	4
12	To Ditto pd. John Hardiman for repaireing his clothes	121		12	6
16	To Cash pd. Clement Webb for a paire Spurres	121			9
	To Ditto pd. Alexander Doleman for stuff, lining etc. for his coat	121	1	9	6
19	To Ditto pd. John Hardiman for making his clothes	121		6	6
20	To Cash paid Tho. Walden for thred stockins & a comb	121		2	6
27	To Cash paid sent him in his Trunck to Musburie on 18th instant	121	3		
	To Ditto paid him at his going to Musburie	121	1		
May 14	To Cash pd. George Popley for 2 paire of Shoes	121		7	
July 26	To Cash sent him by John Warren	121	1		
	To Ditto sent per John Warren to pay his monther for ¼ yeares dyet	121	4		
August 18	To Cash sent him per Henry Stover in a box Tobacco 2½ guinies & 6s 3d in silver	139	3		
September 23	To Cash paid Pendock Warren for left to pay for wine and borrowed	139		6	8
October 13	To Ditto pd. Stephen Stringer for potts of wine & money lent him	139		8	6
	To Ditto pd. John Winpenny in full for wine & money lent	139		7	4½

	By House in which I live paid John Robbins	130		16	
12	By Stockins pd. John Massinger	135	4	10	5
13	By Stockins paid Edward Iffe & James Wollen	135	3	19	2
	By Edward Jones paid him in full	25	1	3	
15	By Stockins paid Tho. Hill	135	3	14	3
	By Sugar 8 hhds pd. custom fees bills etc.	138	12	17	6
			896	13	4¼
	By acct. of it selfe carried to that acct. of debt	139	3462	4	11
			4358	18	3¾

Bristoll 1688

Jahzeel Speed per Contra	Cr	£	s	d
By his new acct. current carried to his acct. of debt	154	742	13	½

Date	Description		£	s	d
November 9	To Cash pd. Edward Woodhouse in full for potts of wine & money lent	139	1	14	
25	To Ditto pd. Alexander Doleman for 6 Cravatts	139		17	6
December 19	To Cash pd. Tho. Walden for 2 paire thred hose	140		4	6
	To Cash pd. Anthony Sanders for his bill on Abraham Clark in Axminster	140	9		
January 7	To Ditto pd. Wm. Rogers for a paire of shoes	140		3	6
27	To Cash pd. John Warren to pay his monther for ¼ yeares Dyet	140	4		
	To Cash pd. Henry Gibbes which hee received of John Burrage of Lime	141	5	5	
1688	To his new acct. current for ballance carried to that acct. of debt.	154			
			742	13	½

Anno 1686

Date	Description		Dr	£	s	d
	Adventure in the ship Malaga Merchant Simon Jays Master from London to Malaga & goe consign'd to John Aylward merchant there for sales & returnes (viz)		Dr	£	s	d
July	To Stockins for one Trunck cont. 42 dozen (is 504 paire) of fine Bristoll hose at 2s 9d per paire £ s d		118	69	6	
	To Isaac Heming for custom, Coquet, & fees 1 10					
	To Ditto for Portridge, Wharfige, & Watridge 2 6					
	To Ditto for Carriage from Bristoll, and Cartage as per leter 7 7		113	2		1
	To Proffit & Losse for a cord Trunck and matting		105		11	
				71	17	1
	To Profit and Loss, for Ballance		190 *	20	12	11
				92	10	

Anno 1686

Date	Description		Dr	£	s	d
	Adventure in the ship Citie of Cadiz Capt. Tho. Ayres to Cadiz, and consign'd for my propper acct. to Samuel Kekewich merchant in St Marie Port		Dr	£	s	d
August	To Stockins for one Trunck cont. 108 doz is 1296 paire at 2s 9d per paire		118	178	4	
	To Ditto for 10 dozen is 120 paire sad Wells hose at 1s 8d per paire		118	10		
	To Isaac Heming for custom, carriage to London & other charges there		113	5	1	11
	To Samuel Kekewich for the charges in Cadiz on said Trunck per acct. Oct. 13th 1687		111	16	19	2.5
	To Profit and Loss, for Ballance		190 *	21	19	6½
				232	4	8

Anno 1686

Date	Description		Dr	£	s	d
	William Brice late of Dorsetshire now of Cork in Ireland		Dr	£	s	d
October 8	To Cash pd. sent him to Cork by John Davis in 14 Guinnies of gold and 3s 3d in Silver as per said Brices order & said Davis his receit		120	15	6	
	To Proffit & Losse for portridge of leters from & to Dorsetshire & Ireland		127		1	
1687 Aprill 27	To Cash delivered to James Porter in 18 Guinnies & 10s 6d Silver to carry to Cork		121	19	19	
	To Profit and Loss, for Ballance		190 *			4
				35	6	4

(123)   **Bristoll 1686**

Date	Description		Dr	£	s	d
	Charles Stubbs of Bristoll merchant and John Mayne of St Georges merchant		Dr	£	s	d
July 28	To Cash lent them on theire bond payable 29th of November next £ s d 100					

Anno 1686	Cr	£	s	d
Adventure in the ship Malaga merchant per Contra				
November *By John Aylward for the neat proceeds of the Trunck of stockins*				
per Contra being 4527 Ryals Velloone at 12 Ryals the piece of				
8 is 441 pieces of 8 at 4s 2d the piece of 8 as per his acct. closed				
in Malaga Oct. 18th 1686	*131*	*92*	*10*	

Anno 1688/9	Cr	£	s	d
Adventure in the ship Citie of Cadiz per Contra is				
By Samuel Kekewich for the neat proceeds of the Trunck stockins				
per Contra 8573 Ryals plate and is 1071 5/8 pieces of 8 the				
piece of 8 at 52d as per his acct. of sales and his acct. current				
closed in St Marie Port March 16th 1688/9	*148*	*232*	*4*	*8*

Anno 1686	Cr	£	s	d
William Brice per Contra is				
July *By Lincloth 4 Rolls Canvas for theire neat proceeds brought from*				
that acct.	*117*	*15*	*6*	*4*
December 15 *By Cash recd. of Fra. Edwards Carrier sent per Daniel Cox*				
from Bemminster for him	*120*	*20*		
		35	*6*	*4*

Bristoll 1686	Cr	£	s	d
Charles Stubbs & John Mayne per Contra are				
August 5 *By Cash received for the 4 months intrest and the 8 months*				
intrest per Contra	*119*	*6*		
Aprill 16 *By Cash recd. of Charles Stubbs per the hands of Tho. Walden*	*121*	*100*		

			£	s	d
	To Ditto lent them on theire bond payable 29th March next 100	119	200		
	To Proffit & Losse for 4 months intrest of the 1st £100 2				
	To Ditto for 8 months intrest of the 2nd £100 4	119 *	6		
1687 Aprill 16	To Ditto for 4½ months intrest of the 1st £100 from the 29th Nov. 1686 to the 16th Aprill 1687	127	2	5	
	To Ditto for 7 months intrest of the 2nd £100 from 29th March to the 30th of Oct. 1687	137	3	10	
			211	15	

Anno 1686

		Dr	£	s	d
	Adventure in the ship Adventurers Delight John Hardham Master from London to Malaga, consign'd there under the mark in the margent to Tho. Strode merchant				
August	To Stockins for one Trunck cont. 42 doz is 504 paire of fine Bristoll hose laden in said ship for my acct. at 2s 9d per paire	118	69	6	
	To Isaac Heming for carriage to London, custom & other charges there	113	2		1
	To Proffit & Losse for a Cord Trunck and matting	105		11	
			71	17	1
	To Profit and Loss, for Ballance	190 *	6	7	11
			78	5	

Anno 1686

		Dr	£	s	d
	Jonathan Abram of Blagen [98] is				
November 20	To Cash paid lent him on 60 paire of stockins	120	5		
March 11	To Cash paid lent him to his sonne Samuel on his noat	120	3		
1687 June 25	To Cash paid lent him on his noat	121	5		
1688 June 18	To Cash paid lent him on 50 paire of stockins	141	4	5	
			17	5	

Anno 1686

		Dr	£	s	d
	Thomas Day of Bristoll Wine Cooper is				
	To Proffit & Losse for the halfe of £179 2s 3d being the first cost and charges of 8 Butts of wine bought, & disposed of in equall halves twixt us	123	89	11	1½
September 24	To Cash paid him in part being ½ of £40 of Pendock Warren	119	20		
January	To Adventure in the ship Olive tree to Cadiz for Simon Clements bill on him for 260 pieces of 8 furnished him there at 52d¾ the piece of 8 in my favor	124	57	2	11
February 3	To Cash paid him	120	80		
	To Isaac Heming for what hee pd. John Wilmot on Simon Clements bill for 200 pieces of 8	130	43	19	2
	To Proffit & Losse for 2 Guinnies by agreement due to mee for sparing ½ of 6 Butts wine	127	2	3	
1687 Aprill	To Ditto for the ½ of £5 4s 8d the 2 noates per Contra pd. him as per his receit 30th August 86	127	2	12	4
	To Cash pd. Fra. Maynard for ½ a flitch of Bacon sent to Tho. Cox	121		4	6
	To Isaac Heming for a French bill said Heming paid for him in London	130	62	11	7
	To Xeries wine my ½ of 20 Butts in partnership for ½ £20 3s 4d recd. for returnes on bad wines	134	10	1	8
August	To Ditto for ½ a hogshead Rhenish wine hee sould to — for £10	134	5		
	To Malaga wines 4 Butts for one Butt sould him at	134	28		
	To his new acct. current for ballance	149	12	18	9½
			414	5	1

1687 Nov.	By Charles Stubbs for 2 hhds French wine of him	*133*	15		
2	By Cash recd. of Charles Stubbs	*139*	90	15	
			211	15	

Anno 1687					
Adventure in the ship Adventurers Delight per Contra		*Cr*	*£*	*s*	*d*
By Tho. Strode for the neat proceeds of the stockins per Contra					
5417 Ryals Velloone at 15 Ryals the piece of 8 is 361¼					
piecesat 52d the piece of 8 as per his acct. sales May 7th 1687		*136*	78	5	

Anno 1687					
	Jonathan Abram per Contra is	*Cr*	*£*	*s*	*d*
May 5	By Cash received of him in full	*121*	8		
July 16	By Cash recd. of him in full	*121*	5		
30	By Cash recd. of him in full	*141*	4	5	
			17	5	

Anno 1686					
	Thomas Day per Contra is	*Cr*	*£*	*s*	*d*
July 3	By his former acct. current for 12¼ Gall.s Xerie & his noat of				
	disbursments	*114*	3	14	8
August 30	By Wines in partnership for his noat for forcing 6 Butts Xerie	*123*	1	10	
	By money in Cash received of him in part for his ½ of the wines	*119*	39	13	
	By Cash received of him more at twice	*119*	47	17	1
	By Proffit & Losse for ½ of £226 00s 00d for 7 Butts & 1				
	hogshead wine sould to severalls in equall halves betwixtr him &				
	my selfe as may appeare	*123*	113		
Aprill 1	By Cash recd. of him	*121*	50		
	By Isaac Heming received on his bill on George Long	*130*	50		
	By Cash recd. of Simon Clement for averidge overpaid on 11				
	Butts wine	*121*		3	8
	By Xeries wines 20 Butts in partnership for my ½ £200 17s				
	00d his disbursments on said wines	*134*	100	8	6
	By Malaga wines 4 Butts in partnership with him for what hee				
	pd. landing them	*134*		1	4
1687 August 25	By Wines my ½ 20 Butts in partnership for ½ cost of hogshead				
	of Rhenish wine hee bought of Joseph Davis	*134*	5	15	10
December 27	By Dr. Fra. Hungerford for 2 doz Xerie bottles & Pannier	*87*	2	1	
			414	5	1

Anno 1686

			£	s	d
	Wines 8 Butts in partnership with Tho. Day are	Dr			
August	To ballance of theire last acct. current for theire cost & charges	116	176	10	3
30	To Tho. Day for his 2nd noat for forcing 6 Butts of Xerie	123	1	10	
	To Cash paid Joseph Berrie for brokridge of 7 Butts	119	1		
	To Proffit & Losse for money spent in Guinnies at severall times	127		2	
	To Ditto for 13 weekes Celleridge	137		12	
	To Profit and Loss, for Ballance	190 *	46	5	9
			226		

Anno 1686

			£	s	d
	Feathers one bagge of musty ones, sent to Jahzeel Speed for sales	Dr			
	by Philip Stansly of Dorchester for sales, which lay long for want				
	of a market				
	To Proffit and Losse for halling into £ s d				
	Celler, portridge & weighing 8				
	To Ditto for Celleridge 4s 6d &				
	Commission for sales 1s 9d 6 3	137		6	11
	To Tho. Shepheard Executor in right of his wife for Philip Stansly				
	deceased his Will for the neat proceeds of said bagge of feathers	129	4	2	1
			4	9	

Anno 1687

			£	s	d
	John Morgan of Bristoll Upholsterer is	Dr			
	To Feathers one bage for theire value weight neate 1 cwt 2qr				
	10lb½ at 6d per pound	123	4	9	

(124)   **Bristoll 1686**

			£	s	d
	Wines my ½ of 6 Butts Xerie & 2 Butts Malaga in partnership	Dr			
	with Tho. Day Wine Cooper is				
	To Proffit & Losse for ½ £179 2s 3d theire first cost and charges	123	89	11	1½

Anno 1686

			£	s	d
	Adventure 2nd in the ship Dilligence of Bristoll, John Seward	Dr			
	Master to Cadiz consign'd to Samuel Kekewich merchant in St				
	Marie Port				
September 6	To Worsted stockins for one Trunck cont. viz				
	94 dozen fine Bristoll hose 1128 paire at 2s 9d per paire	118	155	2	
	26 doz is 312 paire Wells sad hose at 1s 8d per paire	118	26		
	To Cash paid custom fees bills etc. for the stockins	119	3	16	8
	To Samuel Kekewich for charges on the stockins per acct. closed				
	Oct. 14th 1687	111	14	17	9
	To Profit and Loss, for Ballance	190 *	31	2	1
			230	18	6

Anno 1686

			£	s	d
	Adventure in the ship Olive tree James Porter Master to Cadiz	Dr			
	& consign'd to Simon Clement merchant Supra Cargo on her				
October	To Stockins for one Trunck laden in her cont. (viz)				
	64 dozen Bristoll hose is 768 paire at 2s 9d per paire	128	105	12	
	16 doz is 192 paire Wells hose at 1s 7d per paire	128	15	4	
	To Cash paid custom fees bills etc. of the stockins	119	2	6	7
	To Stockins paid for a Trunck, cord & matting	128		12	
	To Profit and Loss, for Ballance	190 *	19	13	11
			143	8	6

Anno 1686

			£	s	d
	Adventure 3rd in the ship Civilia merchant Capt. John Bradyll	Dr			
	from London to Cadiz, & consign'd to Samuel Kekewich				
	merchant in St Marie Port				
September 26	To Stockins for one Trunck laden in said ship Civilia merchant				
	cont. viz				

Anno 1686				
Wines in partnership with Tho. Day per Contra are	Cr	£	s	d
By 1 hogshead of Malaga spent among & to make up 8 full Butts				
By Anthony Owen for 1 hogshead Malaga wine sould him at	111	16		
By Pendock Warren for 6 Butts Xerie & 1 Butt of point Malaga wine sould him at £30 per Butt	126	210		
		226		

Dates in left margin: *August*, *September 22*

Anno 1687				
Feathers one bagge per Contra	Cr	£	s	d
By John Morgan for 178½ pound sould him at 6d per pound	123	4	9	

Anno 1687				
John Morgan per Contra is	Cr	£	s	d
By Cash received of him	123	4	9	

Bristoll 1690@				
Per Contra	Cr	£	s	d
By Xeries wines 23 Butts, for Ballance	169	89	11	1½

Anno 1688/9				
Adventure 2nd in the Dilligence per Contra	Cr	£	s	d
By Samuel Kekewich for the neat proceeds of the Trunck of hose per Contra being 8526½ Ryals plate, and is 1065 6/8 pieces of 8 at 52d as per his acct. of sales and his acct. current closed in St Marie Port March 16th 1688/9	148	230	18	6

Anno 1686				
Adventure in the Olive tree per Contra is	Cr	£	s	d
By Tho. Day for Simon Clements bill on him for 260 pieces of 8 in my favor at 52d¾ the piece of 8	123	57	2	11
By Xeries wines my ½ of 20 Butts laden per Simon Clements in Ditto ship in equall halves twixt Tho. Day & my selfe for ½ 392½ & 1/16 pieces of 8 being theire first cost as per Simon Clements Invoyce, the piece of 8 at 52d¾	134	86	5	7
		143	8	6

Date in left margin: *January*

Anno 1689				
Adventure in the Civilia merchant per Contra	Cr	£	s	d
By Samuel Kekewich for the neat proceeds of the Trunck of stockins per Contra as per his acct. of sales, & his act current closed in St Marie Port March 16th 1688/9 being 9252 Ryals plate is 1156 pieces of 8 at 52d	148	250	11	6

110 dozen of fine Bristoll sad hose is 1320 paire at 2s 9d per paire	118	181	10	
12 dozen Wells sadds is 144 paire at 1s 8d per paire	118	12		
To Isaac Heming for Custom, carriage from Bristoll & other charges	113	5	3	7
To Samuel Kekewich for charges on a Trunck of hose per acct. Oct. 21th 1687	111	15	13	1
To Profit and Loss, for Ballance	190 *	36	4	10
		250	11	6

Anno 1686

		Dr	£	s	d
	Merchandizes in the ship John Edmund Watts Master for acct. of Lawrence Washington to Virginea and to himselfe consign'd	Dr	£	s	d
September	To George White for 97½ yards of grey cloth to make 18 Garments for servants at 15d per yard as per noat	125	6	1	10½
	To Cash paid port of a leter from Exon	119			6
	To Cash paid Wm. Belcher for making 11 mens & 7 womens suites	119	2	15	
	To Cash paid Wm. Rogers for 2 dozen mens plaine shooes at 26s per dozen	119	2	12	
	To Proffit & Losse for custom,fees, etc.,hallidge, Lyteridge & portridge	127		5	2
	To the widow Wasbrow for a brandy Cask to pack the Goods in	75		3	6
	To Proffit & Losse for my Commission	127		4	6½
			12	2	7

Anno 1686

		Dr	£	s	d
	Bethshuah the daughter of Daniel Wastfield, now living with her sister Deborah Binfield in Reading is	Dr	£	s	d
September	To Jonathan Lamboll for money hee paid Tho. Curtis by my order, towards the advancement of the portion of the said Bethshuah	87	5		

(125)

Bristoll 1686

		Dr	£	s	d
	George White per Contra	Dr	£	s	d
October 19	To Cash paid him in full	120	6	1	10½

Anno 1686

		Dr	£	s	d
	Marie Beard of Clapton Widow, the relict and Administratrix of the Goods & Chattles of James Beard her late deceased husband	Dr	£	s	d
September	To the ballance of her husbands acct. of rent for the farme in Clapton, and money due on bill unpaid when hee dyed, for which shee hath made over to mee by bill of sale all his goods & chattles by bill of sale	76	70	4	
	To Cash paid Ozziel Browne for charges on the Letters of Administration, drawing the 2 bills of sale & his journy to Wells	119	2	10	
1687	To Estate at Clapton for ½ yeares rent for the farme ending 1st March 86	72	32	10	
Aprill	To Proffit & Losse for 7 months intrest of £10 from 21th Sept. to the 21th of Aprill 1687	127		7	
			105	11	

Anno 1686	Cr	£	s	d
Merchandizes in the John per Contra are	Cr	£	s	d
By Lawrence Washington his acct. current for the cost and				
charges of the merchandizes per Contra	132	12	2	7

Anno 1690@	Cr	£	s	d
Per Contra is	Cr	£	s	d
By Acct. of Ballances, for Ballance	194 *	5		

Bristoll 1686	Cr	£	s	d
George White of Bristoll Woollen draper is	Cr	£	s	d
By Merchandizes in the John for acct. Lawrence Washington for				
97½ yards of Grey cloth at 15d per yard	124	6	1	10½

Anno 1686		Cr	£	s	d
	Marie Beard per Contra is	Cr	£	s	d
October	*By Cash received of her in part*	120	3	10	
28	*By Cash received of her*	120	1		
November 1	*By Cash recd. of John Gore for 4 Cowes & Calves sould him by*				
	her	120	17	7	
4	*By Cash recd. of her in part*	120	2		
December 11	*By Cash recd. of her in part*	120	4		
March 5	*By Cash received of her in part*	120	4		
30	*By Cash recd. of severalls for 28 Cheeses weight 2 cwt 0qr 0lb at*				
	19s per Cwt	121	1	18	
Aprill 2	*By Cash received of Elizabeth Pierce for 28 Cheeses weight 2 cwt*				
	0qr 9lb at 19s per Cwt	121	1	19	6
6	*By Wm. Rogers for 1 cwt 0qr 1lb of Cheese at 19s per Cwt*				
	sould his wife	93		19	2
	By Cash recd. of her in part	121	3		
16	*By Cash recd. of Eliza. Pierce, Eliz. Richards & Marie Thorp*				
	for 40 Cheeses weight 3 cwt 0qr 3lb at 19s per Cwt	121	2	17	6
20	*By Ditto recd. of Eliza. Pierce for 14 Cheeses weight 1 cwt 0qr*				
	20lb at 19s	121	1	2	4
21	*By Ditto recd. of her in part*	121	4	10	
	By Estate at Clapton for her noat of disbursments	72	2	16	2
28	*By Cash recd. of her in part*	121	14		
	By Estate at Clapton for money abated her on the last ½ yeares				
	rent by agreement	72	2	10	

Anno 1686		Dr	£	s	d
	John Mayne of St Georges at the Pill merchant				
September 9	To Cash paid him on his bill of Exchange on Samuel Kekewich merchant in St Marie Port for 100 pieces of 8 in my favor	119	20		
1687 September 29	To my Copie hold Tenement in Portbury for 1 yeares rent (lowered at his request) with promise of Punctuall payment to 40s per Annum due Sept. 29th 1687	20 *	2		
			22		

Anno 1686		Dr	£	s	d
	Arthur Hobbs of Gigly hill in the parish of Portburie in County Somerset Husbandman				
October 2	To the ballance of his former acct. current for rent due for which I tooke his bill of this date payable on demand	29	6	8	
1687 September 29	To my Copie hold Tenement in Portbury for one yeares rent (brought by his request from 50s to 40s per Annum) with promise of punctuall payment to 40s per Annum due Sept. 29th 1687	20	2		
1688 September	To Ditto for one yeares rent due September 29th 1688	20	2		
December	To Ditto for ½ yeares rent due March 25th 1688	160	1		
			11	8	

Anno 1686		£	s	d	Dr	£	s	d
	Sugar 8 Butts sent consign'd to mee by the ship Olive tree James Porter Master from Barbadoes by John Swimsted Senior merchant there, to bee sould for his own acct. & theire neate proceeds per his order to bee paid to John Eyles of London merchant							
July & August 12	To Cash paid Custom, fees bills etc. with wharfage	21	4	01				
	To Proffit & Losse pd. halling them to Cellar & thence to weighing		8	00				
August 16	To Cash paid James Porter for freight & averidge	20	16	00	119			
	To Cash paid weighing them & portridge into & out of Celler when weighed		6	8	119			
September	To Cash paid Francis Challenour for 5 weeks & 4 daies Celleridge		11	4	119			
	To Proffit & Losse for my Commission at £2 per Cent	2	8	11	127⁹⁹	45	15	
	To John Swimsted his acct. current for theire neat proceeds				132	76	18	2
						122	13	2

Bristoll 1686		Dr	£	s	d
	Tobacco 26 hhds (viz) 20 in the Francis & Marie, and 6 hhds in the John From Potomak river in Virginea, for acct. of Lawrence Washington merchant of Upper Macholick in said river				
July 22)	To Cash paid custom fees bills & wharfage of 20 hhds in the Fra. & Marie	119	152	16	5½
August 7) & 17)	To Cash paid custom fees bills wharfage etc. of 6 hhds in the John both which appear by the particulars in fol. 125) & 126) book petty disbursments	119	48	17	2

			£	s	d
	By Ditto for money abated her on the Charges disbursd by Ozziel Brown about the Administration	72		15	4
May 2	By Ballance for which shee and George Collett have given theire 2 Bonds	134	37	6	
			105	11	

Anno 1686					
	John Mayne per Contra is Creditor	Cr	£	s	d
	By Samuel Kekewich for his bill on said Kekewich in my favor For 100 pieces of 8 which hee accepted to pay us per his leter Oct. 28th 1686	111	21	5	
	By Profit and Loss, for Ballance	190 *		15	
			22		

Anno 1686					
	Arthur Hobbs per Contra is	Cr	£	s	d
February 22	By Cash recd. of Marie Beard for work hee did at Clapton	120		10	
1688 May 26	By Cash recd. of Edward Jacob for him	141		4	
	By Estate at Clapton for his part of money due for making Ditches with Abraham White	151		8	8
	By Ditto for work done at severall times	151	2	2	4
	By Cash formerly recd. of him but not charge'd	162		5	
	By Cash recd. of Edward Jacob	162		2	
1689 May	By Estate at Clapton for his part of grubbing and rooting up with Rich. Godwin as per noat	151		17	4½
			4	9	4½
	By Acct. of Ballances, for Ballance	190 *	6	18	7½
			11	8	

Anno 1686					
	Sugar 8 Butts per Contra are	Cr	£	s	d
September 13	By John Whiting & Michael Pope for said 8 Butts soiuld them weight neat 122 cwt 2qr 18lb at 20s per Cwt to bee paid 13th January next	126	122	13	2

Bristoll 1686					
	Tobacco 26 hhds for acct. of Lawrence Washington per Contra	Cr	£	s	d
September	By David Dorvele for 10 hhds sould him weight Groce 45 cwt 1qr 17lb, tare 93½ lb per hogsheadd, is 8 cwt 1qr 11lb neat 37 cwt 0qr 6lb is 4150 lb subtle at 7d¼ per pound is	126	125	7	3½
	By Cash received on Certifficate at the Custom house for Tobacco overchargd	119		19	9
December 6	By Tho. Day for 16 hhds sould him weight neat 6694lb at 7d¼ per pound	94	201	11	
			327	18	½

			£	s	d
	To Proffit & Losse for halling of them	127		7	3
	To Ditto paid the Widow Wasbrow for cooperige, for landing, stoning, opening etc.	127		17	4
	To Cash paid Edmund Watts for freight & averidge of 6 hhds in the John	119	9	19	6
	To Ditto paid him afterwards for country duties of 6 hhds in the John	119		12	
September 27	To Simon Hurle for money pd. Wm. Nicklus in part for freight of the 20 hhds in the Francis & Marie	116	30		
	To Cash paid Wm. Niclus in full for freight, averidge & country duties of 20 hhds	119	2	15	
	To Cash paid Fra. Challenor for weighing 10 hhds	119		2	6
December 6	To Cash paid portridge & weighing of 16 hhds to Tho. Day	120		3	6
17	To Ditto paid Edward Hollister for 19 weeks Celleridge	120	1	14	
	To Proffit & Losse for my Commission at 2½ per Cent	127 *	8	3	11
	To Lawrence Washington his acct. current for the neat proceeds of the above 26 hhds of Tobacco	132	71	9	5
			327	18	½

Anno 1686					
	David Dorvele of Bristoll merchant is	Dr	£	s	d
	To Tobacco 26 hhds for acct. Lawrence Washington for 10 hhds sould him to ship off weight neate 4150lb at 7d¼ per pound	126	125	7	3½

Anno 1686					
	John Whiting & Michael Pope of Bristoll Sugar Bakers	Dr	£	s	d
September 14	To Sugar 8 Butts for acct. of John Swimsted sould them at 20s per Cwt to bee paid the 13th day of January weight neat 122 cwt 2qr 18lb come to	125	122	13	2

Anno 1686					
	Pendock Warren of Bristoll Vintner is	Dr	£	s	d
	To Wines in partnership with Tho. Day for 6 Butts Xerie and one Butt of Malaga sould him at £30 per Butt to pay £50 in hand £50 more in a moneth, & the remainer at the faire Jan. 25th	116 ¹⁰⁰	210		

Anno 1686					
	Adventure in the ship Nevis merchant Timothy Clark Master from Boston in New England to Nevis consign'd to John Streater & Company	Dr	£	s	d
October	To Edward Shippen for sundry merchandizes by him ship'd & sent consignd for my acct. to John Streater & Company in Nevis being the foure barrills of Pork, 11 cwt 2qr 16lb bread 45½ Bushels of pease, 4 halfe barrills flower, with charges of commission etc. amounting to as per his Invoyce in folio 11 of Book of Invoyces No E & per his acct. 14th Sept. month 1686	87	37	13	5

Anno 1686		Cr	£ ·	s	d
	David Dorvele per Contra is	Cr	£ ·	s	d
September 30	By Cash recd. of him in part	119	50		
November 11	By Cash recd. of him	120	65		
January 8	By Cash recd. of him in full abating 3d	120	10	7	3½
			125	7	3½

Anno 1686		Cr	£	s	d
	John Whiting & Company per Contra are	Cr	£	s	d
February 2	By Cash received of John Whiting	120	122	4	
	By Proffit & Losse for 3 Sugar loaves	127		9	2
			122	13	2

Anno 1686		Cr	£	s	d
	Pendock Warren per Contra	Cr	£	s	d
September 23	By Cash recd. of him in part	119	40		
	By the Lady Ann Powlet for 6 doz bottles Xerie, the bottles, Panniers & Covers as per noat	100	6	3	
October 27	By Cash recd. of him	120	50		
November 3	By Cash received of him	120	10		
23	By Sergt. Tho. Strode for 12½ 1/8 Xerie with the Cask & charges, & Certificate	65	3	18	9
Feruary 8	By Cash received of him in part	120	30		
26	By Cash recd. of himselfe £13 17s 00d & of Thorton Jones £6 3s 00d is in all	120	20		
1687 Aprill 27	By Cash recd. of him by the hands of Simon Clement	121	16		
	By Proffit & Losse for 1 Pint of Malaga	127		1	
	By Cash recd. of him in part	121	20		
August 3	By Cash recd. of him in full	121	13	17	3
			210		

Anno 1687		Cr	£	s	d
	Adventure in the Nevis merchant per Contra	Cr	£	s	d
May	By Edmond Scrope & Company for 7096lb Sugar the neat proceeds of the goods per Contra as per acct. Sales March 10th 1686 Sugar at 10s per 100lb	33	35	9	4½
	By Profit and Loss, for Ballance	190	2	4	½
			37	13	5

(127)	Bristoll 1686				
	Proffit & Losse is	Dr	£	s	d
August	To Ballance of the former acct. brought from that acct.	105	578	5	
	To sundry accts for 79 Chests of Soape sould Fra. Whitchurch, Charles Herbert, Wm. Burges & Tho. Richard as may appeare recd. per a friend	53	234	2	2
	To Cash paid Jacob Beele for a small bill of Exchange from John Broking in Leghorne	119		17	6
4	To Cash given John Morgan for 6 weeks keeping my mare	119		3	
6	To Cash paid Elizabeth Smith for 113lb of Cheese	119	1	4	6
	To John Hurtnell Junior for money abated him for ballance	38		17	9
September 11	To Cash paid John Hardiman in full	119	2		
18	To Cash paid James Swetnam in full	119		15	
30	To Cash paid soleing 2 paire shooes	119		3	2
	To Cash paid port of severall leters from Spaine & London	119		9	6
October 2	To Cash paid Joane Smith for 125 of Cheese	119	1	1	6
	To Jonathan Lamboll for money hee paid Dr. Hungerford	87			6
13	To Cash paid Henry Gibbs for ½ a piece of Dowlas	120	5	17	
19	To Cash paid George White for cloth for Jahzeel Speed	120	1	16	
November 1	To Ditto paid John Morgan for keeping my mare to this day	120		3	
	To Isaac Heming pd. Richd. Russell, & for earnest in the Coach	113	2		
	To Ditto for 2 doz Claret, a box of Powder & port of leters to 29th Sept. 1686	113	4	13	8
	To Ditto for money pd. for 40 papers of powder in March 1685	113	1		
3	To Cash paid the souldier for the muster master etc.	120		3	6
8	To Cash paid Fra. Maynard for a Flitch of Bacon	120		7	6
9	To Cash pd. Alexander Doleman in full	120	4	5	
19	To Cash paid Alexander Doleman for 24 Ells Dowlas	120	3		
22	To Ditto paid houshold expences from July 17th to Novem.r 6th	120	52	17	8
December 3	To Cash paid John Hardiman in full	120		5	
	To John Blackwell for severall small parcells of wine of him	85		16	7
10	To Cash paid the widow Challoner in full for keeping my mare	120		5	2
17	To Cash paid — Webb for Drumms & Collors	120		2	6
21	To Ditto paid Tho. Bourne for 17 weeks hay & stable roome for my mare	120	2	1	4
23	To Cash pd. Jane Shepeheard for a firkin of Butter	120		17	
	To Marie Wasbrowe for severall noates for hooping racking of wines & other work done	75	30	17	5
	To Lawrence Washington for part ballance of a former ballance due to mee	30	3	15	
January 11	To Cash pd. David Roynon in full to this day	120		4	6
17	To Cash pd. John Patrick for 6 trees to plant at Clapton	120		3	6
29, 31	To Cash pd. Edward Jones at twice in full	120		18	
	To Richard Merrick for money abated him on ½ yeares rent	92		1	
February 2	To John Whiting & Company for 3 Sugar loafes	126		9	
12	To Cash paid houshold expences to the 12th instant	120	37	11	2
14	To Anthony Tyler for his noat for shooing, bleeding etc. my mare	129		6	
			974	16	1
	To Ant. Tyler for 8 weeks keeping my mare to the 14th Dec.	129	1	4	
	To Ditto for shooing, & 10 weeks keeping my mare to the 21th Feb. 1686	129	1	12	
	To Tho. Tayler for his noat of what I owed him	4	2	1	
	To Isaac Heming for a Kegge of sturgeon hee bought & sent me	130	1		
March 9	To John Blackwell for 9½ 1/8 Gall. Xerie	132	2	8	1½
	To Cash pd. Charles Stubbs for 1 yeares poore money ending 25th March	120	3	5	
	To Thomas Scrope for 23 particulars charg'd to his acct. of Credit as may appeare in that acct.	75	196	12	11½
Aprill 6	To Tho. Day for the proceeds of 8 Buttts sack in partnership betwixt us	123	113		

	Bristoll 1686	Cr	£	s	d
	Proffit & Losse per Contra is				
October	By Edward Gorges for intrest of £60 to 2nd August 1686	34	4	16	6
	By Oyles 10 Pipes for acct. of John Cooke & Company for my Commission for Sales	117	2	9	5
	By Houses in Reading for theire estimated value	129	450		
	By Marie Thring & Company for intrest of severall parcells of money lent them	7	3	18	9
	By Wm. Spoore Junior & Senior for 1 yeares intrest of £40 due June 5th 1686	69	2	8	
	By the Lady Ann Powlet for port of leters	100		1	
	By Tho. Longman for a small barrill reisons sould him	113	2		
	By Robert Yate for 39 weeks Celleridge of the vault under my lower house in Small Streat	39	5	17	
error	By Isaac Heming for pd. Richard Russell, Coach hire, 2 doz wine				
	By Isaac Heming & co. for 1 yeares intrest of £400	69	16		
	By Henry Howard & Company for ½ yeares intrest of £100 due Sept. 12th 1686	92	3		
	By Tobacco 20 hhds for Lawrence Washington & his friend for my commission for sales	101	3	5	
	By Ditto for 300 lb out of Tobacco due to mee for ballance of a former acct.	101	3	15	
December 11	By Cash recd. of Ann Davis for my Legacy her husband gave mee	120	10		
	By Richard Gotley & Company for 3½ yeares intrest of £50	16	10	10	
	By Lincloth for acct. Wm. Price for Warehouse roome and my Commission	117		9	1
23	By Sgt Tho. Strode for charges on wine	65			9
	By Marie Wasbrow for a parcell of empty Butts, Iron hoops & hhds etc.	75	6	18	11
	By Tobacco 26 hhds for halling them 7s 3d and for Cooperidge at 8d per hogshead paid Marie Wasbrow on her acct. being 17s 4d is in all	126	1	4	7
	By Merchandizes for my acct. in the Francis & Marie for assureance, Commission etc. on said goods	104	4		4¾
	By Sugar 8 Butts for acct. of John Swimsted for my Commission for theire sales	125	2	8	11
	By John Swinsted for Port of leters to & from Barbados	132			4
	By John Earle of Bristoll for ballance of his acct.	37		8	10
	By Ditto for portridge of leters etc.	132			6
	By Richard Gotley & Company for ½ yeares intrest of £50	16	1	10	
	By John Swimsted for Port of leters & abated in receit of the sugar money	132		1	2
February	By Dr. Francis Hungerford for portridge etc.	87			6
	By Robert Richardson for ½ yeares intrest of £150 due Dec. 16th 1686	35	3	15	
	By Merchandizes in the Francis & Marie for acct. of Lawrence Washington for severall particular goods, charges & commission	104	2	18	2
	By Tho. Day for 2 Guinnies due to mee by agreement	123	2	3	
	By Jahzeel Speed for money hee spent in Spaine	122	112		
	By Tho. Scrope for money that by agreement I was to have with his Brother Edmond Scrope when I took him an apprentice	75	100		
	By Ditto for freight formerly paid for 6 tons freight on acct., & charg'd by error	75	16	10	
	By Ditto for money charg'd short on a parcell of Pitch & Resin	75		11	10
	By Ditto for my 1/3 part of a parcell of paper	75	43	11	3
	By Ditto for the proceeds of severall small Cask of Brandy	75	23	8	5
	By Ditto for money due to mee on the Isabellas book	75		9	6
	By Ditto for ¾ parts cost & charges of Brandy & Wine on the Tho. & Francis	75	83	3	4
			923	15	1¼

			£	s	d
	To John Gore for 1¾ Bushells of Beanes at 3s 4d	31		5	10
8	To Cash pd. John Gandy	121		14	6
9	To Ditto pd. Fra. Maynard for ½ Flitch of Bacon	121		4	6
	To Nath. Haggatt for money charg'd to his acct. which I recd. of James Webb	19*	6		
13	To Cash paid Frances Maynard for a flitch of Bacon	121		7	4
	To Isaac Heming for money to his wife £3 & postage of leters 17s 6d	130	3	17	6
	To Simon Clement for 2 Quarter Cask of Xerie	103	8	10	
	To Dr. Fra. Hungerford for money abated him on acct.	87	2		2
	To Pendock Warren for 1 part of Malaga wine	126		1	
May 3	To Cash paid Joane Smith for 9 cwt 2qr 2lb Cheese at 22s per Cwt	121		11	5
	To Ditto given to French Protestants	121		4	9
5	To Cash paid Wm. Burgesse for 1½ yard of Cloth	121	1		3
13	To Nathanael Haggatt for money of Humphry Corsley for 53 pieces Gold	19	49	15	
	To Cash paid Tho. Goldney for my Daughter Martha's marriage portion [101]	121	800		
14	To Ditto pd. John Hardiman in part of his noat	121	1		
19	To Ditto pd. for 2 Panniers Covers & portidge	121		2	
	To Ditto pd. for portidge of a Spannish leter	121		2	
21	To Cash paid Anthony Tyler in full for keeping shooing etc. my mare	121	2	6	6
	To Ditto pd. Humphry Rickerd for watching	121			6
	To Ditto paid Fra. Maynard for a flitch of Bacon	121		6	8
23	To Ditto pd. Peter Hinton for 2 bottles	121		3	
25	To John Bvlackwell for 6 qt bottles Xerie	132		7	6
26	To Cash pd. Tho. Wall for Penns & Inke	121			7
31	To Ditto pd.— for 12 panniers & Covers	121		10	
	To Tho. Scrope for freight of a parcelll of Ginger & Bottoms to & from Hambrow	75	7		
June 28	To Cash paid Jane Shepheard for a Cask of Butter	121		18	6
	To Cash paid Houshold expences to the 27th of June	121	23	7	11
	To Isaac Heming for money of him in London at severall times	130	5	10	
	To Ditto for 2 Stone Juggs Oyle a ham, etc. paid John Pott	127	1	2	10
			2212	9	5

(128)

Bristoll 1686

	Worsted Stockins bought of severalls are	paire	s	d	Dr	£	s	d
October 9	To Cash pd. Tho. Hill for Henry Britten for	43	2	5	120	5	3	11
	To Cash pd. Ditto for John Brady for	34	2	5	120	4	2	2
	To Cash paid Joseph White for sadds	39	2	7	120			
	pearles	10	2	6	120	6	5	9
	To Ditto pd. Tho. Hill for Richard Forster for	27	2	4	120	3	3	
13	To Cash pd. Joseph George for	80	1	4	120	5	6	8
	To Ditto pd. Fra. Rottenburie for hot pressing to this day				120		17	
14	To Ditto pd. John Rudduck for	41	2	4½	120	4	17	4
	To Ditto pd. James Wollen for	27	2	5	120	3	5	3
	To Ditto paid Samuel Dyer for	28	2	5	120	3	7	8
16	To Cash paid Jona. Abram for	39	2	5	120	4	14	3
	To Ditto pd. John Massinger for	28	2	8	120	3	14	8
	To Ditto pd. Tho. Hill for	29	2	5	120	3	10	1
	To Ditto pd. Robert Webb for a Trunck				120		10	

By Tho. Scrope for money paid David Phillips & Robert Bound	75	15	17	10
By Ditto for money due for his part of Whistons Avizoes	75 *		7	6
By Tho. Scrope & Company viz. Henry Gibbes for 4½ yeares 1 month 4 daies intrest £300	28	82	10	
By Tho. Scrope & Marie Aldworth for 5 yeares & 2 months less 3 daies intrest 200	14	61	18	
By Tho. Day for ½ £5 4s 8d paid him & omitted to bee charged	123	2	12	4
By Xeries wine 8 Butts in partnership for Guinns in receiving of money	123		2	
By sundry accts for the Cost & charges of 8 Butts wine in partnership with Tho. Day	123, 124	179	2	3
By Charles Stubbs & Company for 4½ months intrest of £100	123	2	5	
By James Webb for 7 yeares 1 month intrest of £50	16	21	5	
By Wm. Brice for portridge of Leters	122		1	
By Merchandizes in the John for Lawrence Washington for severall charges	124		9	8½
By Simon Clement & Company for money by error charg'd to theire acct.	133	8	10	
By Dr. Fra. Hungerford for 2 paire Styrrups bought of James Swetnam & sent him	87		3	6
By Ditto for postage of a leter	87			2
By Marie Beard for 7 months intrest of £10	125		7	
By Nathanael Haggatt for 4½ yeares intrest of £100	19	27		
By Ditto for 3½ months intrest of £100 and 2 months intrest of £50	19	2	5	
By Cash recd. of Humphry Corsley for 53 piecesGold	121	49	15	
By the Lady Ann Powlet for 4 doz bottles, Panniers & portridge	100		10	6
By Cash recd. of John Browne in full	121	6		
By Sir George Strode for 2 doz bottles Pannier & cover etc.	24		5	4
By the Earle Bristoll for 10 doz bottles, Panniers covers etc.	132	1	6	4
By Malaga Wines 4 Butts for halling them to Cellar	134		2	
By Tho. Goldney Senior for a bottle or stone Jugge of oyle	132		7	10
By John Earle Bristoll for 10 dozen bottles, Panniers & covers etc.	132	1	7	
By Jonathan Lamboll on Mortgage for ½ intrest of £450 due March 25th 1687	109	11	5	
		1399	10	5¼
By ballance carried to that acct. of Debt	137	812	18	11¾
		2212	9	5

The first numeric column dates on the left margin:
1687 Aprill 16; May 13; June 1; 3; 23

Bristoll 1686

	Cr	£	s	d
Worsted Stockins per Contra are				
By ballance brought from that acct.	118	690	12	8¾
By Adventure in the Spanish merchant Capt. Blowers for Cadiz for one Trunck cont. 64 dozen is 768 paire fine Bristoll hose sent from London consigned to Samuel Kekewich merchant in St Marie Port at 2s 9d per paire	131	105	12	
By Adventure in the ship Olive tree to Cadiz for one Trunck cont. 64 doz is 768 paire Bristoll hose, & 16 doz is 192 paire Wells hose, the Bristoll at 2s 9d the Wells at 1s 7d per paire, the trunck cord etc. 12s, consign'd to Simon Clement Supra Cargo	124	121	8	
		917	12	8¾

Date column on left: October 7; December

19	To Cash pd. Tho. Hill for	43	2	1	120	5	0	4
	To Ditto pd. Ditto for	29	2	5	120	3	10	1
22	To Ditto paid Tho. Hill for	158	1	4	120	10	10	
	To Ditto pd. John Massinger for	30	2	8	120	4		
	To Ditto pd. John Perry for	34	2	4¾	120	4	1	5
23	To Ditto pd. Tho. Hill for	60	2	5	120	7	5	
	To Ditto pd. Jona. Abram for	40	2	5	120	4	16	8
	To Cash pd. Joseph White for sadds	42	2	7				
	pearles	12	2	6	120	6	18	6
26	To Ditto paid Joseph George for	80	1	4	120	5	6	2
28	To Cash paid Tho. Hill for Sa. Dyer for	25	2	5	120	3		
	To Ditto paid James Wollen in part for	35	2	5	120	4		
30	To Ditto pd. John Massinger for	37	2	8	120	4	18	8
	To Ditto pd. John Brady for	47	2	5	120	5	13	7
	To Ditto pd. Jos. White for sadds	46	2	7				
	pearles	12	2	6	120	7	8	10
	To Ditto pd. Henry Britten for	22	2	5	120	2	13	2
November 3	To Cash pd. John Rudduck for	38	2	4½	120	4	10	3
4	To Cash pd. Tho. Hill for Richard Forster for	29	2	4	120	3	7	8
	To Ditto pd. Tho. Hill for John Lukins for	38	2	4¾	120	4	3	10
	To Ditto pd. Ditto for Samuel Dyer for	27	2	5	120	3	5	3
6	To Ditto pd. John Massinger for	31	2	8	120	4	2	8
	To Ditto pd. Edward Iffe For hot pressing to this day				120	1		
	To Ditto pd. Jonathan Abram for	46	2	5	120	5	11	2
8	To Cash pd. James Wollen in full £4 being paid before, for	35			120		4	7
	To Ditto pd. Tho. Hill for Hen. Britten for	40	2	5	120	4	16	8
9	To Ditto pd. John Brady for	28	2	5	120	3	7	8
10	To Cash pd. Richard George for	40	1	4	120	2	13	1
12	To Cash pd. Tho. Hill for Tho. Browning	113	1	4	120	8	17	4
	To Ditto pd. John Perry for	47	2	4¾	120	5	12	6
13	To Cash pd. John Massinger for	28	2	7	120	3	12	5
	To Ditto pd. Elizabeth Dyer for	7	2	4½	120		16	8
15	To Ditto paid Tho. Hill for Joane White for	35	2	4	120	4	1	8
						188	4	1
	To Cash paid Joseph George for	113	1	4	120	7	10	8
19	To Ditto pd. John Massinger for	28	2	7	120	3	12	4
20	To Ditto pd. Joseph White for sadds	40	2	6½				
	pearles	18	2	6	120	8	7	
23	To Ditto pd. Tho. Hill for John Lukins for	35	2	4¾	120	4	3	10¼
	To Ditto pd. Robert Webb for a large Trunck				120		13	
	To Ditto pd. Tho. Hill for Hen. Britten for	47	2	4¾	120	5	12	7
27	To Cash pd. John Massinger for	31	2	7	120	4		1
30	To Cash pd. Tho. Hill for Richd. George for	52	1	3½	120	3	7	2
December 3	To Ditto pd. John Massinger for	33	2	7	120	4	5	3
4	To Ditto pd. Ed. Iffe for hot pressing stockins				120		12	7½
	To Ditto pd. Andrew Creed for	116	1	3½	120	7	9	10
7	To Ditto paid Joseph George for	80		15½	120	5	3	4
11	To Cash paid John Massinger for	31	2	7	120	4		
	To Ditto pd. Tho. Hill for Tho. Browning for	108		15½	120	6	19	6
16	To Ditto pd. John Massinger for	32	2	7	120	4	2	8

Date	Description							
22	To Ditto pd. John Massinger for	36	2	7	120	4	13	
23	To Cash pd. Joseph George for	104	1	3	120	6	10	
24	To Cash pd. Tho. Hill for Tho. Browning	140	1	3	120	8	15	
30	To Ditto pd. John Massinger for	25	2	7	120	3	4	7
January 8	To Ditto pd. Joseph George for	58	1	3	120	3	12	6
	To Ditto pd. John Massinger for	27	2	7	120	3	9	9
14	To Ditto pd. John Massinger for	26	2	7	120	3	7	2
18	To Ditto pd. Tho. Hill for Tho. Browning	131		15	120	8	3	9
22	To Cash pd. Joseph George for	59		15	120	3	13	9
	To Ditto pd. John Massinger for	25	2	7	120	3	4	7
29	To Cash paid John Massinger for	35	2	7	120	4	10	5
February 5	To Ditto paid John Massinger for	32	2	7	120	4	2	8
10	To Ditto paid Tho. Hill for Tho. Browning for	117		15	120	7	6	3
12	To Ditto paid John Massinger for	25	2	7	120	3	4	7
19	To Cash paid John Massinger for	29	2	7	120	3	14	11
26	To Ditto pd. John Massinger for	31	2	7	120	4		1
March 4	To Ditto paid John Massinger for	30	2	7	120	3	17	6
9	To Ditto paid Tho. Hill for Tho. Browning	108	1	3	120	6	15	
10	To Ditto John Massinger for	26	2	7	120	3	7	2
18	To Cash pd. John Massinger for	37	2	7	121	4	15	7
24	To Ditto pd. John Massinger for	28	2	7	121	3	12	4
31	To Ditto pd. John Massinger for	42	2	7	121	5	8	6
Aprill 2	To Ditto pd. Tho. Hill for Tho. Browning	104	1	3	121	6	10	
	To Ditto pd. John Perrie for	152	2	2½	121	16	15	8
7	To Cash pd. John Massinger for	29	2	7	121	3	14	11
19	To Ditto pd. John Massinger for	39	2	7	121	5		9
23	To Ditto paid John Massinger for	40	2	7	121	5	3	4
30	To Ditto pd. John Massinger for	36	2	7	121	4	13	
						403	11	8¾
	To Ballance carried to that acct. of Credit				135	514	2	
						917	12	8¾

(129)   **Bristoll 1686**

Date	Description	Dr	£	s	d
	Severall houses situate in Fryerstreat in the Towne of Reading in the County of Barks, given to Ann [102] my now Wife by the last Will & Testament of George Lamboll her father deceased, on condition to pay out of them twenty foure pound per annum to Sarah Lamboll her mother during her life				
Aprill 1	To Proffit & Losse for theire estimated value being held by 3 Lives and to yeald about £44 per Annum out of which is paid to John Blagrave £4 per Annum	127	450		
June 24	To Sarah Lamboll for ¼ of £24 Annuity payable to her out of the houses June 24 86	129	6		
September 29	To Ditto for ¼ yeares annuity due to her Sept. 29th 1686	129	6		
1687 March 25	To Ditto for ¼ yeares annuity due March 25th 1687 & Dec. 25th 1686	129	12		
	To Ditto for ¼ yeares annuity due 24th June 1687	129	6		
	To Jonathan Lamboll paid for Locks & Bolts 16s and lost by Wm. Russell ¼ rent 6s	131	1	2	
1688, 1689	To Tho. Curtis for 1yeare Lords rent ending December 1688	169	4	8	
	To Ditto for what hee paid for masons work and for nailes	169		15	2
	To Ditto for what hee paid Wm. Cole Carpenter as per noat	169		1	
	To what hee pd. Jeffery Pinnell for repaire of a well	169		15	
			487	1	2

Bristoll 1686

	Houses in Fryerstreat in Reading per Contra are	Cr	£	s	d
July 1	By Jonathan Lamboll for ¼ yeares rent hee recd. Due June 24th 1686	87	11	3	6
September 30	By Ditto for ¼ yeares rent due Sept. 29th 1686	87	11	3	6
December	By Ditto for ¼ yeares rent due December 25 1686	131	11	3	6
1687	By Ditto for ¼ yeares rent for said houses due 25th March 1687	131	11	3	6
June 24	By Ditto for ¼ yeares rent for said houses due June 24th 1687	131	11	3	6
December 25	By Ditto for 2/4 yeares rent for said houses ending 25th December 1687	131	22	7	
1688 March 27	By Ditto for ¼ yeares rent for said houses ending March 25th	147	11	3	6
June 24	By Jonathan Lamboll for ¼ yeares rent of said houses ending June 24th 1688	147	11	3	6
1689 Oct.	By Tho. Curtis for ¼ yeares rent ending Sept. 29th 1689	169	11	3	6
	By Ditto for 1 yeares rent ending September 29th 1689	169	44	14	
	By Ditto, for one year's rent, ending the 29th of Sept. past	169	44	14	
			201	3	
	By Acct. of Ballances, for Ballance	194 *	285	18	2
			487	1	2

	Anno 1686				
	Sarah Lamboll of Reading widow my Wives monther is	Dr	£	s	d
June 24	*To Jonathan Lamboll for money bee paid her for ¼ yeares Annuity due June 24*	87	6		
September 30	*To Ditto for ¼ yeares Annuity bee paid her due September 29th 1686*	87	6		
December 25	*To Ditto for ¼ bee paid her due December 25th 1687*	131	6		
1687 March 25	*To Ditto for ¼ bee paid her due March 25th 1687*	131	6		
June	*To Ditto for ¼ bee paid her due June 24th 1687*	131	6		
September 29	*To Ditto for ¼ though not due yet allowed Jonathan Lamboll although shee dyed before the Quarter day as per acct. sent him*	131	6		
			36		

	Anno 1687				
	Thomas Shepheard of Dorchester Executor to Philip Stansly of the same place deceased in right of his wife the Daughter of the said Stansly & Executrix to his Will	Dr	£	s	d
	To Cash paid John Hine by his order in full as per his order & receit	139	4	2	1

	Anno 1686				
	Anthony Tyler of Bristoll Smith & Farrier	Dr	£	s	d
December 9	*To Cash paid himselfe*	120	1	10	
	To Ditto paid lent him on his noat payable at demand	120		10	
February 12	*To Cash paid him*	120	1	12	
1687 Oct. 25	*To Cash pd. him in full for keeping and shooing my mare to 13th Oct. 1687*	139	3	1	
December 20	*To Ditto paid him in full for keeping & shooing my 2 mares*	140	1	6	
			7	19	

(130)	**Bristoll 1686**				
	Isaac Heming of London Merchant my Sonne in law is	Dr	£	s	d
September 29	*To his former acct. current brought from that acct. for ballance*	113	1694	18	11
December	*To Plate in sundry ships from Cadiz for 1000 pieces of 8 sould Wm. Atwill & Company imported in the ship James Galley weight 877¼ oz at 5s 2d¼ per oz*	92	225	2	2
	To Arthur Robinson & Company recd. of Ditto for 98 pieces of 8 weight 84½ oz at 5s 2d¼	61	21	13	10
	To Marie Speed ½ £67 4s 6d recd. of them for 300 pieces of 8 weight 262 oz at 5s 2¼	113	33	12	3
January	*To Sergt. Tho. Strode for money recd. of his Brother Hugh Strode*	65	3	18	6
February 12	*To Scarbrow Chapman for his bill on Robert Chapman by mee assign'd him*	132	76	16	8
March 1s	*To Robert Richardson for money of him for 1 yeares intrest of £150 10s 10d*	35	7	10	
	To Peter Bishop of Winchester for money by his order as per his leter of 8th March 1686	78	50		
1687 April 20	*To John Warren for money of Nath. Wheatly as per his leter April 16th 1687*	134	6	16	
	To Tho. Day for money of George Long recd. of him	123	50		
			2170	8	4

Anno 1686		Cr	£	s	d
	Sarah Lamboll my monther in law per Contra is	Cr	£	s	d
June 24	By Houses in Fryer streat for ¼ of £24 being an Annuity given her by the Will of her Husband George Lamboll issuing out of said houses payable quarterly	129	6		
September 29	By Ditto for ¼ yeares Annuity due September 29th 1686	129	6		
	By ½ yeares Annuity due March 25th 1687	129	12		
1687 June 24	By ¼ yeares Annuity due June 24th 1687	129	6		
			30		
	By Profit and Loss, for Ballance	190 *	6		
			36		

Anno 1687		Cr	£	s	d
	Thomas Shepheard per Contra	Cr	£	s	d
	By Feathers one Bagge sent per Philip Stansly deceased to Jahzeel Speed for sales for theire neat proceeds, being his Executor as per Contra	123	4	2	1

Anno 1686		Cr	£	s	d
	Anthony Tyler per Contra is	Cr	£	s	d
December	By Proffit & Losse for his noate for shooing my mares & 8 weeks keeping at 3s per week	127	1	10	
February	By Ditto for his noate for shooing 2s & for 10 weeks keeping my mare to the 21th February	127	1	12	
May 1687 21	By Cash recd. of him on acct.	121		10	
1687 October 25	By Proffit & Losse for shooing my mare, and for keeping her until the 31th instant	137	3	1	
			6	13	
	By Proffit & Loss for Ballance	190 *	1	6	
			7	19	

Bristoll 1686

		Cr	£	s	d
	Isaac Heming per Contra is	Cr	£	s	d
September 30	By his former acct. current for my bill on him in favor of Robert Henley	113	50		
	By Ditto for my bill on him in favor of John Cooke	113	97	18	6
	By Ditto for my bill in favor of said Cooke at the same time	113	6	5	11
November 29	By Cash recd. of Samuel Spencer by a bill sent mee	120	18	4	
December 8	By Cash received of Humphry Corsley for which I valued my bill in favor Alex. Rood	120	100		
11	By Ditto recd. of Elizabeth Tayler for what I valued mybill in favor of Dennis Tayler	120	12		
February 2, 15	By Cash received of John Blackwell on Samuel Kekewich his bill assign'd to mee at twice	120	132	10	
	By John Swimsted for money hee paid John Eyles on my bill in favor of said Eyles	132	76	16	8
	By Tho. Day for Simon Clements bill on him which hee paid to John Wilmot	123	43	19	2
	By Proffit & Losse for a Kegge of Sturgeon bought & sent mee	127	1		
1687 Aprill 13	By Malaga Wines 4 Butts bought of Tho. Cox & sent in the Dilligence to Bristoll	134	99	10	2
	By Adventure in the Spanish merchant to Cadiz for charges on a Trunck stockins	131	2	17	8
	By Proffit & Losse for money furnish'd his wife for Babby Clouts by my order	127	3		
	By Ditto paid port of leters to the 25th March 1687	127		17	6
	By Wine 4 Butts Malaga from London for Brokeridge on them pd. Tho. Cox	134		5	

Anno 1687		Dr	£	s	d
	Isaac Heming merchant is	Dr	£	s	d
Aprill 20	To the ballance of his former acct. current	130	1518	7	9
	To Ditto for money hee recd. of Nath. Wheatly after the closing his last acct.	130	6	16	
	To John Love recd. of Ralph Swinson on a bill of Exchange assign'd by said Love	55	100		
	To Robert Richardson on mortgage recd. of him in full				
July 19	To Cash pd. Dennis Tayler on his bill in said Taylers favor	121	5		
August	To Marie Speed for the neat proceeds of 228½ pieces of 8 weight 199 oz at 5s 2 3/8d	113	51	3	6
	To Robert Richardson recd. of him	35	153	15	
September 28	To Isaac Heming & Company for ballance brought here by his consent as per his acct. closed Nov. 12th 1687	69	416		
			2251	2	3

Anno 1686		Dr	£	s	d
	House in Small Streat in which I now live is	Dr	£	s	d
	To ballance of the former acct. brought from that acct.	23	664	18	9
November 3	To Cash paid 1/2 yeares Chimney money due Sept. 29th 1686	120		8	
1687 August 11	To Ditto paid John Robbins for 800 of Tyles at twice	121		16	
September 5	To Cash paid John Pierce Chimney doctor for mending the Dining roome Chimny	139		8	
	To Cash paid Edward Jones for work done on the house	139		4	
January 4	To Ditto paid John Strode for ½ yeares Chimney money ending 29th Sept. 1687	140		8	
1688 Aprill 24	To Cash pd. Edward Jones for 2000 of Tyles	141		19	
	To Cash paid Caleb Kippin for ½ yeares hearth money ending March 25th 1688	141		8	
August 21	To Cash pd. Hnery Bradley for nailes to mend the Turret	141		13	1
November 3	To Cash paid Caleb Kippen for 1/2 yeares Chimney money	157		8	
10	To Ditto pd. John Cheshire in full	157		18	
February 6	To Cash pd. Bartholmew Willliams Deputy Chamberlaine for 2½ yeares rent due Dec. 25th 1688	157	1		
			671	8	10

By his new acct. current for money hee received after hee had closed his last acct. of 25th March 1687, as per said acct. may appeare	130	6	16	
By his new acct. current for ballance	130	1518	7	9
		2170	8	4

Anno 1687					
Isaac Heming merchant per Contra is		Cr	£	s	d
June By Tho. Day for what hee paid for said Day on a french bill		123	62	11	7
By Cash for money received of Edward Baily by bill from John Cox		121	12		
By Cash recd. of him in 21 Guinnies		121	22	12	9
By Proffit & Losse recd. of him at severall times in London		127	5	10	
By Adventure in the Cadiz merchant to Cadiz for charges on a Trunck of stockins		136	5	10	11
By Proffit & Losse paid John Potts his noat for 2 Juggs oyle & ham etc.		127	1	2	6
July 27 By Cash recd. of John Wilmer for which I valued my bill		121	20		
By Reisons solis 27 barrils for his disbursments of freight custom etc.		136	17	5	3
August 1 By Cash recd. of Joshuah Monger for which I valued my bill on him		121	82		
By Cash recd. of Samuel Crisp for which I valued my bill		121	170		
By Cash recd. of Tho. Lane for which I valued my bill on him		121	200		
3 By Cash recd. of Tho. Lane for which I valued my bill		121	100		
By Ditto recd. of John Plane for which I valued my bill		121	100		
9 By Cash recd. of Sgt. Tho. Strode for which I valued my bill on him		121	50		
By Proffit & Losse for money overcharg'd on Robert Richardsons money per Contra		137		10	
September 28 By Cash recd. of John Stubbs for which I valued my bill in favor of Mannering Davis		139	50		
By Adventure in the Greyhound to Alicant for charges on a box of stockins		142	1	10	
By Proffit & Losse pd. for 2 places in the Coach from London		137	1		
By Ditto paid him for the use of his Children		137	80		
By Ditto for money lost on sales of 700 Guinnies		137		14	7
By Ditto pd. the Widow Russell for papers of powder		137		16	
By Ditto paid Tho. Cox for wine sent to Reading		137	1		6
By Ditto paid port of leters		137		17	3
By John Wilmer for money paid him on my bill Sept. 5th 1687		117	13		
By Ballance carried to his new acct. current in that acct.		143	1253		11
			2251	2	3

Anno 1690@					
Per Contra is Creditor		Cr	£	s	d
By Acct. of Ballances, for Ballance		194 *	671	8	10

Anno 1686					
	John Cullimor of Portshead in the County of Somerset Tyler	Dr	£	s	d
November 18	To Cash paid him	120		5	
December 16	To Cash pd. Edmond Beakes, which hee pd. said Cullimore in Portshead	120		5	
1687 July 29	To Proffit & Losse for money paid him, by error charg'd to Estate at Clapton	137		5	
March 5	To Cash paid him at Clapton	140		2	
1690 April 2	To Ditto paid him	175		1	
				18	

(131)	Bristoll 1686				
	Jonathan Lamboll of Reading Maultster my Bro. in law is	Dr	£	s	d
November 1	To ballance of his former acct. adjusted betwixt us in Bristoll Nov. 1st 1686	87	8	1	3
	To Natha. Haggatt for drawing the Articles of partnership in Maulting	19	3		
	To Ditto for drawing the mortgage, and procurring the Statute etc.	19	3		
	To Houses in Reading for ¼ yeares rent due 25th of December 1686	129	11	3	6
1687 March	To Ditto for ¼ yeares rent due 25th March 1687	129	11	3	6
	To Ditto for ¼ yeares rent due June 24th 1687	129	11	3	6
December 25	To Ditto for 2/4 yeares rent due the 25th of this instant December 1687	129	22	7	
	To his acct. of money on Mortgage for 1 yeares intrest of £450 due Sept. 29th 1687	109	22	10	
			92	8	9

Anno 1686					
	John Aylward merchant a factor resident in Malaga in Spaine	Dr	£	s	d
November	To Advnture in the ship Malaga merchant for the neat proceeds of one Trunck cont. 42 doz Bristoll hose 4527 Ryals Velloone is 441 pieces of 8½ at 12 Ryals Velloone per piece of 8 & piece of 8 at 4s 2d per piece as per his acct. sales closed Malaga Oct. 18th RV 1686 4527	122	92	10	

Anno 1686					
	Adventure in the ship Spanish merchant Capt. Arthur Blowers to Cadiz	Dr	£	s	d
	To sundry accts, being the cost & charges of one Trunck of stockins laden in her per Isaac Heming in London for my acct., and goe consign'd to Samuel Kekewich merchant in St Marie Port (viz)				

Anno 1690	Cr	£	s	d
Per Contra is				
By Acct. of Ballances, for Ballance	190 *	0	18	

Bristoll 1686/7		Cr	£	s	d
	Jonathan Lamboll per Contra is	Cr	£	s	d
January	By my houses in Reading for one yeares Lords rent hee paid to				
	Nicholas Round for John Blagrove	129 *	4	8	
	By Sarah Lamboll his monther pd. her ¼ yeares Annuity ending				
	25th of Dec. 1686	129	6		
1687	By Ditto for ¼ Annuity due & paid her March 25th 1687	129	6		
	By Ditto for ¼ Annuity due 24th June 1687	129	6		
	By Ditto paid for Locks & Bolts as per acct.	129		16	
	By Reading houses for money lost ¼ rent of Wm. Russell	129		6	
	By Proffit & Losse for a messenger to Farnham and the Dyers				
	man for a leter	137		3	6
	By Ditto for money paid my wife at severall times in Reading	137	10		
July 4	By Proffit & Losse for money of him when I came from Reading	137	2		
	By Ditto for what more hee furnished my wife with in Reading	137	3		
	By Ditto paid Tho. Connick for haire plush	137		14	6
	By Ditto for 3 doz bottles beere bought & sent to Isaac Heming				
	in London	137		4	
	By Ditto for severall pieces of houshold goods as brasse, pewter,				
	severall pieces of plate etc. as per particulars in his acct. thereof				
	Oct. 31th 1687 bought of him by my wife	137	42	8	
	By Proffit & Losse for money pd. Ed. Piercy in Oct. 1686 as				
	per his acct. sent mee	137		5	
September	By Ditto pd. to John Bisley for nailes etc. in June 1687 as per				
	same acct. August 4th 1687	137		11	
	By Sarah Lamboll for ¼ yeares annuity allowed him though not				
	due because shee dyed sometime before the expiration of the				
	quarter	129	6		
			88	16	
	By ballance carried to his new acct. Current	147	3	12	9
			92	8	9

Anno 1687	Cr	£	s	d
Johnn Aylward per Contra is	Cr	£	s	d
By Reisons solis 27 Barrills in the Abraham & Robert consignd				
to Isaac Heming merchant in London for theire cost & charges				
as per Invoyce dated Feb. 11th 1687 amounting to 4520 Ryals				
Velloone, is 301 pieces of 8 5/8 & 19 Mervidees, the piece of 8				
at 52d	136	65	5	10
By Profit and Loss, for Loss by the fall of Velloon	190 *	27	4	2
		92	10	0

Anno 1687	Cr	£	s	d
Adventure in the ship Spanish merchant per Contra is	Cr	£	s	d
By Samuel Kekewich for the neat proceeds of the Trunck of				
stockins per Contra being 4819½ Ryals and is 602 pieces of 8				
2½ Ryals at 51d as per his acct. of sales closed Oct. 14th 1687	111	128		4

To Worsted stockins for 64 dozen is 768 paire in said Trunck at 2s 9d per paire	128	105	12	
To Isaac Heming For custom & charges pe acct. closed March 25th 1687	130	2	17	8
		108	9	8
To Profit and Loss, for Ballance	190 *	19	10	8
		128	0	4

Anno 1686

Henry Wynter of Clapton the Sonne of Henry Wynter deceased	Dr	£	s	d
December 28 — To Cash paid him for 1 yeares reserv'd rent on Clapton farme due Sept. 29th 1686	120	1	12	

Anno 1686

Abraham Hill the Sonne of Tho. Hill of Bristoll my servant	Dr	£	s	d
January 8 — To Cash paid him in part	120	1		
1687 Aprill 14 — To Cash paid him in part	121	2	10	
June 29 — To Cash paid him in part	121	1		
August 26 — To Cash pd. him in part	139	1	10	
October 27 — To Cash paid him in part	139	2	10	
November 15 — To Ditto paid him in full for one yeares service ending Nov. 15th 1687	139			
26 — To Cash paid him	139	1	10	
February 2 — To Cash paid him for a paire of boots bought	140		8	
22 — To Cash paid himselfe	140	2	10	
1688 May 18 — To Cash paid himselfe	141	2	10	
June 21 — To Cash paid himselfe	141	1		
July 26 — To Cash pd. himselfe	141	2		
September 15 — To Cash pd. him	141	1		
		19	8	

(132)   Bristoll 1686

Lawrence Washington of Virginea Merchant is	Dr	£	s	d
August — To his former acct. for Port of leters from Exon	30		1	6
To Richard Gotley & Company for his bill of May 20th 1686 on mee in theire favor	16	16		
To Ditto for his bill in favor of Johanna Pope August 27th by her assign'd to said Gotley	16	19		
To Ditto for a Post entry on goods in the ship Francis & Marie paid by said Gotley	16		5	7
To merchandizes laden for his acct. in the ship Francis & Marie October 1685 To theire cost & charges as per Invoyce	104	23	14	
To Merchandizes in same ship for acct. of his nameless friend for theire cost & charges	104	9	2	6
To Merchandizes in the Francis & Marie laden under my mark as per margent, but by agreement taken to himselfe	104	42	3	1¼
To Merchandizes in the John under the mark LS for theire cost & charges	124	12	2	7
1687 June 4 — To Cash paid Wm. Jones — on his bill on mee in his favor	121	1		
August 18 — To Cash paid Wm. Clark on his bill in favor of Francis Sexton	139	5		
To Merchandizes in the John Ed. Watts Master for theire cost & charges	145	31	13	3
1688 August 11 — To Cash paid Tho. Atkinson his bill in favor of Arthur Spicer	141	5		
December 19 — To Cash pd. postage of a Pacquet of leters etc.	157		3	6
To Merchandizes in the Comfort sent by his order for theire cost & charges	160	12	19	3½
To Merchandizes in the John for his Friend Dr. Warcupp sent by his order	160	9	1	6
		187	6	9¾
To his new acct. current for ballance carried to that acct.	167	8	18	2¼
		196	5	

Anno 1690@				
Henry Winter per Contra is	*Cr*	*£*	*s*	*d*
By Profit and Loss, for Ballance	*190 **	1	12	

Anno 1687				
Abraham Hill per Contra	*Cr*	*£*	*s*	*d*
November 15 By Proffit & Losse for 1 yeares sallary due to him Nov. 15th				
1687	*137*	10		
1688 Nov. 15 By Proffit and Losse				
By Ballance carried to his new acct. current	*156*	9	8	
		19	8	

Bristoll 1686				
Lawrence Washington per Contra is	*Cr*	*£*	*s*	*d*
By Tobacco 20 hhds in the ship John for his own acct. for theire				
neat proceeds	*101*	93	15	
To Tobacco 6 hhds in same ship, by him said to bee for acct. of				
his nameless friend, for theire neat proceeds	*101*	29	5	
By Tobacco 20 hhds in the Francis & Marie, and 6 hhds in the				
John for theire neat proceeds	*126*	71	9	5
By Tobacco 4 hhds in the Comfort for theire neat proceeds ·				
brought from that acct.	*147*	1	15	7
		196	5	

Anno 1686				
John Swimsted Senior of Barbadoes merchant is per Contra	Dr	£	s	d
To Proffit & Losse for portridge of 4 letters to and from Barbadoes	127			4
To Ditto for postage of 4 leters to & from London about these sugars	127		1	
To Ditto abated on receit of the money for the sugar	127			2
February To Isaac Heming for money hee paid to John Eyles on my bill on him in said Eyles his favour	130	76	16	8
		76	18	2

Anno 1687				
Thomas Goldney Senior of Bristoll Grocer is	Dr	£	s	d
July To Proffit & Losse for a Stoning Jugge 3 qr ½ a pint oyle, Jugge, & carriage	127		7	10

Anno 1686				
Scarbrow Chapman of Bristoll Vintner & Merchant	Dr	£	s	d
January To John Cook & Sam. Kekewich for theire bill on him for 400 pieces of 8 at 53d	111	88	6	8
1688 Aprill To Samuel Kekewich for his bill of 360 pieces of 8 in my favor the piece of 8 at 52d as may appeare	148	78		
		166	6	8

Anno 1686				
Michael White of Bristoll Wine Cooper is	Dr	£	s	d
January To John Cooke & Samuel Kekewich for Simon Clements bill for 200 pieces of 8 at 53d	111	44	3	4
1688 Aprill To Samuel Kekewich for Simon Clements bill for 200 pieces of 8 assign'd in my favor at 52d pieces of 8	148	47	13	4
		91	16	8

Anno 1686				
John Earle of Bristoll living at Sherborne is	Dr	£	s	d
January 25 To sundry accts for the cost & charges of 2 Rundlets Xerie sent him per Esaw White	132, 127	7	17	4
1687 May 14 To John Blackwell for five Rundlets of Xerie sent per Esaw White	132	19	9	2
1687 June 3 To sundry accts for 5 Panniers cont. 10 doz White wine with bottles etc. sent per Esaw White	133, 127	6	6	4
July 13 To sundry accts for 5 Panniers cont. 10 doz Claret, bottles, Panniers etc. sent per Esaw White	133, 127	6	7	
27 To Cash paid custom fraight from Dublin fees & portridge	121		3	9
October 8 To Stephen Stringer for 6 doz Claret Panniers Covers & Bottles	133	3	15	
December 20 To John Blackwell for 13 Gall. lesse & part ½ Sack, & Proffit & Losse for portridge	132, 137	3	17	6
March 17 To Cash pd. Richard Chamneys for 12¾ Gall. Vinegar and Rundlet	140	1	8	6
		49	4	3

Anno 1686				
John Blackwell per Contra is	Dr	£	s	d
March 11 To Cash paid him	120	4	8	6
22 To Cash paid himselfe	121	7	2	6
1687 Aprill 2 To Cash paid himselfe for the Earle of Bristoll	121	7	16	6
October 30 To Cash paid himselfe in full	121	2	1	
To Proffit & Losse for 6 Panniers & Covers to his servant George	137		5	
To Ditto for 2 yeares & 10 daies rent for my vault from Nov. 20th 1685 to 1st of Dec. 1687	137	20	6	
February 23 To Cash paid him in full as per receit	140	29	11	
		71	10	

	Anno 1686				
	John Swinsted Senir of Barbadoes merchant is	Cr	£	s	d
	By Sugar 8 Butts imported in the Olive tree James Porter Master				
	from Barbadoes for theire neat proceeds	125	76	18	2

	Anno 1687				
	Thomas Goldney Senior per Contra is	Cr	£	s	d
September	By Tho. Goldney Junior my Sonne in law for the money per				
	Contra carried to that acct.	136		7	10

	Anno 1686				
	Scarbrow Chapman per Contra is	Cr	£	s	d
February 12	By Isaac Heming for his bill on Robert Chapman by mee				
	assign'd to him	130	76	16	8
14	By Cash received of him in full of the bill per Contra	120	11	10	
1688 May 19	By Cash recd. of him	141	78		
			166	6	8

	Anno 1686				
	Michael White per Contra	Cr	£	s	d
February 14	By Cash received of him in full	120	44	3	4
1688 May 19	By Cash recd. of him	141	47	13	4
			91	16	8

	Anno 1687				
	John Earle of Bristoll per Contra	Cr	£	s	d
Aprill 2	By Cash recd. of John Bullock by the hands of his Father in law				
	Roger Stone	121	7	17	4
October 8	By Cash received of Sgt. Hugh Hodges by his order at Clevedon	139	32	6	
	By Proffit & Losse abated the poore man by desire of Sergeant				
	Hodges	137			3
	By ballance carried to his new acct. current in the last 3				
	particular summes per Contra viz. £3 15s 00d £3 17s 6d and				
	£1 8 6 in all	150	9	1	
			49	4	7

	Anno 1686				
	John Blackwell of Bristoll Vintner is	Cr	£	s	d
January 25	By John Earle of Bristoll for 2 Rundlets cont. 25 Gall. 2½				
	parts at 6s & the Rundlets	132	7	16	10
February 1	By Doctor Fra. Hungerford for 2 doz Xerie, Pannier, cover, &				
	bottles	87	2	1	
March 9	By Proffit & Losse for 9½ 1/8 Galls Xerie at 5s per Gall	127	2	8	
22	By French wines 4 hhds for 1 hogshead of claret bought of him at	133	7	2	6
1687 Aprill	By Dr. Fra. Hungerford for 2 doz bottles Xerie, bottles &				
	Pannier	87	2	1	
May 14	By John Earle of Bristoll for 5 Rundlets Xerie	132	19	9	2

			£	s	d
	To ballance resting due to him from the Earle of Bristoll per Contra	148	3	17	
			75	7	6

(133)	**Bristoll 1686**				
	Charles Stubbs of Bristoll merchant is	Dr	£	s	d
January	To Samuel Kekewich for his bill on him for 372¼ pieces of 8 in my favor at 52d½	111	81	10	9¼
	To himselfe & Company for the 2 hhds French wine per Contra	123	15		
1688 Aprill 19	To Cash paid him in full for a Pipe of Canarie	140	28	10	
	To Samuel Kekewich for his bill for 200¼ pieces of 8 asssign'd in my favor at 52d	148	43	6	8
			168	7	5¼

	Anno 1687				
	William Powlet Counsellor at law is	Dr	£	s	d
Sept. 3	To French wine 4 hhds for 7 doz bottles white wine at 11s & bottles due to Proffit & Losse 14s	133,137	4	10	
October 20	To sundry accts for 1 hogshead white wine and 14 doz & 3 bottles etc.	151,153	9	15	6
			14	5	6

	Anno 1686				
	Simon Clement of Bristoll merchant & Michael White Wine Cooper	Dr	£	s	d
February 4	To Thomas Day Soapmaker for money of him by my order which I lent them on theire bond payable with intrest May 5th next	94	100		
	To Proffit & Losse for the £8 10s 0d per Contra charg'd them by error	127	8	10	
1687 Feb.	To Proffit & Losse for 8 months & 17 daies intrest of £100 from Feb. 86 to Oct. 22th 1687	137	4	5	8
1689 Aprill 22	To Ditto for ½ yeares intrest of £50 from the 22th Oct. 1687 to 22th Aprill 1688	137	1	10	
	To Ditto for one yeares intrest from the 22th Aprill 1688 to 22th Aprill 1689	164	3		
	To Ditto for ½ yeares intrest of £50 from 22th Aprill 1689 to the 22th October 1689	164	1	10	
1690 Oct.	To Ditto for one yeares intrest ending Oct. 22th 1690	180	3		
			121	15	8

	Anno 1686				
	Stephen Stringer of Bristoll Vintner is	Dr	£	s	d
March 15	To French wine 4 hogsheadogsheads for 3 hhds sould him at	133	23		
1687 Nov. 24	To Xeries wine my ½ of 20 Butts for 6 Butts at £25 per Butt payable — March	134	150		
1688 Aprill 5	To Cash paid him in full	140	5	16	
			178	16	
	To Profit and Loss, for Ballance	190 *		4	
			179		

	Anno 1686/7				
	French Wines 4 hogsheads are	Dr	£	s	d
March	To Henry Gibbes for the ½ of £26 12s 00d the cost and charges of one Tonne white wine twixt him &my selfe in the Patience from Bordeaux the ½ is	79	13	6	

			£	s	d
25	By Proffit & Losse for 6 qrt bottles Xerie for my owne use at 5s per Gallon	127		7	6
November 20	By John Earle of Bristoll for 13 Gall. lesse & part ½ & 2d mending the cask	132	3	17	
February	By Wines of severall sorts bought of severalls for 1 Pipe of Canary at	149	29		
23	By Proffit & Losse for severall small parcells of Wine at severall times	137	1	4	6
			75	7	6

Bristoll 1686

	Charles Stubbs per Contra is	Cr	£	s	d
February 23	By Cash recd. of him in full of his bill of Exchange	120	81	10	9¼
March 15	By French wine 4 hhds for 2 hhds bought of him at	133	15		
	By Wines bought of severalls for 1 Pipe of Canary bought of him at	149	28	10	
1688 May 23	By Cash recd. of him in full	141	43	6	8
			168	7	5¼

Anno 1687

	Wm. Powlet per Contra is	Cr	£	s	d
September 8	By Cash recd. of him in full	139	4	10	
1688 October 19	By Cash received of him in full	157	6	17	4
	By French wine 3 hhds for 7 doz & 9 bottles part of his hhd of White wine	151	2	18	2
			14	5	6

Anno 1686

	Simon Clement per Contra is	Cr	£	s	d
March 24	By Xeries wine 2 Quarter Cask for said Cask bought of him at	133	8	10	
1687 Oct. 22	By Cash recd. of Simon Clement in part	139	50		
			58	10	
	By Acct. of Ballances, for Ballance	194 *	63	5	8
			121	15	8

Anno 1687

	Stephen Stringer per Contra is	Cr	£	s	d
Aprill 6	By Cash recd. of him in full	121	23		
November 24	By John Earle of Bristoll for 6 doz Claret, Panniers covers & bottles as per noat.	132	3	15	
February 27	By the Lady Ann Powlett for 2 dozen Xerie Pannier, bottles etc.	100	2	1	
1688 Aprill 5	By Cash recd. of himselfe	140	128	4	
	By Cash received of Humphry Watmoore	141	22		
			179	0	0

Anno 1686/7

	French Wines 4 hhds per Contra are	Cr	£	s	d
March 15	By Stephen Stringer for 3 hhds sould him at	133	23		
1687 June 1	By Sir George Strode for 2 doz bottles at 10s per dozen	24	1		
3	By John Earle of Bristoll for 5 Panniers cont. 10 dozen bottles White at 20s per dozen	132	5		

To Charles Stubbs for 2 hhds white wine bought of him at £30 per tonne	133	15		
To John Blackwell for 1 hogshead of Claret bought of him at	132	7	2	6
To Arthur Hart for one hogshead of Cognac Wine bought of him	113	7	4	6
		42	13	

Anno 1686/7				
James Swetnam of Bristoll Sadler is	Dr	£	s	d
March 18 To Cash for money paid lent him on 3 hhds sadlers wares & his bond	121	50		
Aprill To Cash paid storing his 3 hhds from the hall to the backhouse	121			2
To Proffit & Losse for intrest of £50 from 17th March 86 to the 3rd Sept. 1687	153	1	7	6
To Ditto for the intrest of £10 from 3rd Sept. 1687 to the 30th August 1688	153		12	9
22 To Cash pd. him in full	162		6	
		52	6	5

Anno 1686				
Xeries Wine 2 Quarter Cask are	Dr	£	s	d
March 24 To Simon Clement for the two Quarter Cask bought of him at	133	8	10	
To Tho. Day for 1½ Gall. Malaga & 1 Gall. Rhenish to amend them	149		10	6
		9	0	6
To Profit and Loss, for Ballance	190 *	4	6	6
		13	7	

(134)   **Bristoll 1686/7**

Edward Jacob of Clapton & John Jacob of Kenne in the County Somerset	Dr	£	s	d
March 23 To Cash pd. lent them on theire bond payable by the said bond (through mistake) on the 23th of August but should have been Sept. 23th following	121	20		
May 19 To Cash paid lent him on his noat	121	1	10	
June 2 To Cash paid lent him	121	1	10	
1688 March 25 To Proffit & Losse for 1 yeares intrest of £20 ending March 23th 1687	137	1	4	
1689 March To Ditto for 2 yeares Intrest of 20s ending March 23th 1689	164	2	8	
1690 Oct. To Ditto for ½ yeares intrest ending Sept. 23th 1690	180		12	
		27	4	

Anno 1687				
John Warren of Musburie in the County of Devon Clothier is	Dr	£	s	d
Aprill 27 To Cash sent him to Musburie in Jahzeels Speed's Trunck	121	6	16	
1690 July 26 To Ditto pd. lent him on bond payable October 27th 1690	181	30		
		36	16	

Anno 1687				
Malaga Wines 4 Butts from London in partnership (viz) equal halves with Tho. Day Wine Cooper	Dr	£	s	d
Aprill 13 To Isaac Heming for theire cost & charges in London as per his acct.	130	99	10	2
To Isaac Heming for Brokeridge paid on buying said Butts	130		5	
To Tho. Day for what hee paid landing them at the Key	123		1	4
To Sidrick Seager for freight from London	134	2		
To Proffit & Losse for halling them to Cellar	127		1	6

July 13	By Ditto for 5 Panniers cont. 10 doz bottles Claret at 10s per dozen	132	5		
26	By Lady Ann Powlet for 1 doz 2 bottles white wine at 10s per dozen	100		11	8
August 11	By Dr. Fra. Hungerford for 1 doz bottles white wine at 10s	87		10	
17	By Sir George Strode for 2 doz 4 bottles white wine at 10s	24	1	3	4
Sept. 3	By Wm. Powlet for 7 doz bottles white wine at 11s	133	3	17	
			40	2	
	By Profit and Loss, for Ballance	190 *	2	11	
			42	13	

	Anno 1687				
	James Swetnam per Contra	Cr	£	s	d
September 3	By Cash recd. of him in part	139	40		
	By Proffit & Losse for his noat of severall things had of him	153	5	2	5
	By Tho. Goldney Junior for money hee paid James Swetnam for which said Goldney gave mee his obligation	136	6	18	
	By horses 2 for his after noat for small things	156		6	
			52	6	5

	Anno 1687				
	Xeries Wine 2 Quarter Cask per Contra are	Cr	£	s	d
May 18	By the Lady Ann Powlet for 4 doz bottles at 18s per dozen	100	3	12	
July 20	By Sir George Strode for 4 doz at 18s per dozen	24	3	12	
26	By the Lady Ann Powlet for 4 doz 10 bottles at 18s	100	4	7	
August 11	By Dr. Fra. Hungerford for 1 doz bottles at	87		18	
Spetember 2	By Cash recd. of Esaw White for 1 doz quarts at	139		18	
	By Wm. Pow		13	7	

Bristoll 1687

	Edward Jacob etc. per Contra	Cr	£	s	d
December 3	By Cash received of Edward Jacob in full of the £3 lent per Contra	139	3		
1685	By Edward Jacob his particular acct. for 1½ yeares intrest of £20 ending 23th September 1688	150	1	16	
1690 May 10	By Cash recd. of Edw. Jacob	181	1	16	
			6	12	
	By Acct. of Ballances, for Ballance	194 *	20	12	
			27	4	

	Anno 1687				
	John Warren per Contra is	Cr	£	s	d
Aprill 20	By Isaac Heming for money recd. of Nath. Wheatley of Banbury as per his leter Aprill 16th 87	130	6	16	
	By Acct. of Ballances, for Ballance	194 *	30		
			36	16	

	Anno 1687				
	Malaga Wines per Contra	Cr	£	s	d
	By Richard Chamneys for 1 Butt sould him payable the 25th July	45	31		
	By Nicholas Baker for 1 Butt sould him payable 20th of October	103	31		
	By Tho. Day for one Butt hee tooke to himselfe at	123	28		
	By an acct. of Losse to both for 1 Butt spent on our 20 Butts Xerie in the olive tree				

			£	s	d
July 15	To Cash pd. Joseph Berrie for Brokridge of 2 Butts	121		10	
	To Proffit & Losse for striking downe and storing 3 Butts in the vault	137		1	6
	To Ditto for hooping & racking 2 Butts of this Malaga	137		6	
	To Ditto for 13 weeks celleridge	137		5	
			103	0	6

Anno 1687					
	William Snellgrove of Bristoll Pewterer is	Dr	£	s	d
Aprill 7	To Cash paid lent his wife	121	2		

Anno 1687					
	Marie Beard Widow, & George Collett of Seymers Court of Portburie	Dr	£	s	d
May 2	To Marie Beard her acct. current for money payable on theire joint Bond on the 25th July next £ 18 s 13 d 00				
	To Ditto for money payable on theire bond 29th September 18 13 0	125	37	6	

Anno 1687					
	Xeries Wines my ½ of 20 Butts laden in Cadiz by Simon Clements in The ship olive tree James Porter Master in equall halves twixt Tho. Day wine Cooper & mee	Dr	£	s	d
	To Adventure in the ship Olive tree to Cadiz for ½ 6281 Ryals plate theire first cost	124	86	5	7
	To Thomas Day for ½ £200 17s 00d hee paid for custom freight etc. per acct.	123	100	8	6
August 25	To Ditto for ½ the cost & charges of a hogshead Rhenish wine bought of Jos. Davis	123	5	15	10
	To Cash pd. Joseph Burry in part brokeridge for sales of 6 Butts	139	1		
	To Thomas Day for my halfe of £69 17s 10d½, being after charges on said 20 Butts of Wine as per Copie of his acct. and in folio 41 of my booke of accts will appeare No. C	149	34	18	11½
	To Cash paid Joseph Berrie for Brokeridge	140		5	
	To Henry Gibbes for 6 Gall. Madera Wine to fill one Butt of my 7	79	1	4	
1688 August 30	To Cash pd. John Shute to buy him a paire of Gloves	141		8	
			230	5	10½
	To Profit and loss, for balance	190	35	19	1½
			266	5	

Anno 1687					
	Sydrick Seager per Contra is	Dr	£	s	d
	To Cash paid Samuel Tipton by his order left with said Tipton	139	2		

(135)   **Bristoll 1687**

	Worsted Stockins bought of severalls are				Dr	£	s	d
		paire	s	d				
May 5	To Cash pd. Jonathan Abram for	80	2	4¼	121	9	8	4
6	To Ditto pd. Ditto for	22	2	5	121	2	13	2
	To Ditto pd. John Massinger for	35	2	7	121	4	10	5
11	To Ditto pd. Jos. White for	90	2	6	121	11	5	
	To Ditto pd. Henry Britten for	78	2	2¾	121	8	13	10½
	To Ditto pd. John Massinger for	33	2	7	121	4	5	3
20	To Ditto pd. John Massinger for	35	2	7	121	4	10	5
	To Cash pd. John Perrie for	23	2	3¼	121	2	12	3
21	To Ditto pd. Jonathan Abram for	29	2	4¼	121	3	8	3¼
	To Ditto pd. Joseph White for	73	2	6	121	9	2	6

		90		
By Profit and Loss, for Ballance	190 *	13	0	6
		103	0	6

Anno 1687					
William Snellgrove per Contra is		Cr	£	s	d
Aprill 13	By Cash recd. of his wife in full	121	2		

Anno 1687					
Marie Beard & Company per Contra		Cr	£	s	d
July 25	By Cash recd. of them both	121	18		
September 28	By Cash recd. of Marie Beard	139	8	19	6
March 17	By Cash recd. of Marie Beard	140	3		
1689 June 1	By Cash recd. of Marie Beard & George Collet	162	6	15	
			36	14	6
	By Profit and Loss, for Ballance	190 *		11	6
			37	6	0

Anno 1687					
Xeries Wines my ½ of 20 Butts in partnership with Tho. Day		Cr	£	s	d
May 19	By Cash recd. of Simon Clement for overplus averidge pd. James Porter	121		3	4
	By Tho. Day for ½ £20 3s 4d hee recd. for returnes on corrupts in the Custom House as per his acct. given in to mee	123	10	1	8
August	By Ditto for ½ £10 for which hee sould the hogshead of Rhenish wine mentioned per Contra	123	5		
November	By Stephen Stringer for 6 Butts sould him at £25 per Butt to pay at 4 moneths	133	150		
February 11	By Anthony Owen for 1 Butt sould him at 3 months time price as per bill	111	28		
	By Tho. Day for ballance of the acct. of said wines resting due to mee	149	73		
			266	5	0

Anno 1687					
Sidrick Seager Seager Coaster betwixt London & Bristoll is		Cr	£	s	d
Aprill	By Malaga Wines 4 Butts for theire fraight in the Dilligence from London to Bristoll as per Bil of Lading	134	2		

Bristoll 1687					
Stockins per Contra are		Cr	£	s	d
Aprill 30	By ballance of theire last acct.	128	514	2	
	By Adventure 2nd in the Cadiz merchant to Cadiz for 1 Trunck cont. 1344 paire Bristoll hose at 2s 9d, and 164 paire Wells hose at 1s 9d laden in said ship James Clark Master, and consign'd to Samuel Kekewich in St Marie Port	136	199	3	
September	By Adventure 3rd in the Ship Dilligence to Cadiz for one Trunck cont. 960 paire Bristoll hose at 2s 9d & 528 paire Wells hose at 1s 8d per paire, laden in her consignd to Samuel Kekewich merchant, with 17s for Trunck Cords etc.	142	176	17	

Date	Description							
28	To Ditto pd. Joseph White for	74	2	6	121	9	5	
	To Ditto pd. John Massinger for	33	2	7	121	4	5	3
June 3	To Cash pd. John Massinger for	31	2	7	121	4		1
	To Ditto pd. John Perrie for	56	2	3	121	6	6	
4	To Ditto pd. Edward Iffe in full for hotpressing stockins to this day				121	1	11	9
	To Ditto pd. John Massinger for	35	2	7	121	4	10	5
	To Ditto pd. Ditto for	40	2	7	121	5	3	4
	To Ditto pd. Joseph White for	77	2	5¾	121	9	10	10¾
23	To Ditto pd. John Massinger for	37	2	7	121	4	15	7
July 1	To Cash pd. John Massinger for	36	2	7	121	4	13	
	To Ditto pd. John Rudduck for	33	2	2¾	121	3	13	6¾
9	To Ditto pd. Elizabeth Webb for a Trunck				121		13	
	To Ditto pd. Henry Britten for and something over	45	2	2¾	121	5	1	
11	To Ditto pd. John Massinger	27	2	7	121	3	9	9
16	To Ditto pd. Jonathan Abram for	86	2	4	121	10		8
19	To Cash pd. Anthony Palmer for	37	2	4	121	4	6	4
20	To Ditto pd. John Massinger for	43	2	7	121	5	11	1
21	To Ditto pd. James Wollen for	82	2	4	121	9	11	4
	To Ditto pd. Tho. Hill for John Lukins for	33	2	3	121	3	14	3
30	To Ditto pd. for Jonathan Abram for	36	2	4	121	4	4	
August 6	To Cash pd. Joseph White for	76	2	5¾	121	9	8	5
12	To Ditto pd. John Massinger for	35	2	7	121	4	10	5
13	To Ditto pd. Edward Iffe in full for hotpressing				121		13	10
	To Ditto pd. James Wollen for	28	2	4	121	3	5	4
15	To Ditto pd. Tho. Hill for John Lukins for	33	2	3	121	3	14	3
16	To Ditto pd. Anthony Palmer for	22	2	4	139	2	11	4
19	To Cash pd. Elizabeth Webb for a Trunck				139		13	
20	To Ditto pd. Joseph White for	60	2	5¾	139	7	8	9
	To Ditto pd. John Perry for	27	2	3	139	3		9
22	To Ditto pd. Jonathan Abram for	34	2	4	139	3	19	4
	To Ditto pd. Tho. Walden for one dozen of Inkle				139		7	6
	To Ditto pd. Eliza. Messenger for	32	2	7	139	4	2	8
29	To Cash pd. John Massinger for	37	2	7	139	4	15	7
September 2	To Ditto pd. John Perrie for	40	2	3	139	4	10	
	To Ditto pd. Robert Webb for a box to send stockins to Alicant				139		3	6
5	To Ditto pd. John Rudduck for	43	2	3	139	4	16	9
8	To Ditto pd. James Wollen for	29	2	4	139	3	7	8
						226	4	10¼
10	To Cash pd. Henry Britten for	58	2	3	139	6	16	6
	To Cash pd. Joseph White for	60	2	5¾	139	7	8	9
15	To Ditto pd. Jonathan Abram for	40	2	4	139	4	13	4
17	To Ditto pd. John Massinger for in contention	33	2	7	139	4	5	3
	To Ditto pd. John Massinger for	35	2	7	139	4	9	8¼
22	To Ditto pd. Tho. Hill for	37	2	3	139	4	3	3
23	To Cash pd. John Perrie for	48	2	3	139	5	8	
24	To Ditto pd. John Massinger for	28	2	7	139	3	12	4
28	To Ditto pd. Edward Iffe in full for hotpressing				139		12	4¾
29	To Ditto pd. James Wollen for	32	2	4	139	3	14	8
October 1	To Ditto pd. John Massinger for	31	2	7	139	4		1
5	To Ditto pd. Joseph Georges for	12	1	3	139		15	
8	To Cash pd. John Massinger for	30	2	7	139	3	17	6
15	To Ditto pd. Jonathan Abram for	39	2	4	139	4	11	
	To Ditto pd. John Massinger for	37	2	7	139	4	15	7
19	To Ditto paid Elizabeth Webb for a Trunck				139		13	
25	To Cash paid John Massinger for	39	2	7	139	5	9	

	By Adventure in the Greyhound to Alicant for 1 Box cont. 300 paire Bristoll hose at 2s 9d & 60 paire Wells hose at 1s 8d laden in her & consign'd to Heneage Featherstone, with the Box 3s 6d, and charges etc.	*142*	46	8	6
November	*By Adventure in the Tygre to Cadiz for 1 Trunck laden in her cont. 70 doz Bristoll and 48 doza Wells hose, the Bristoll at 2s 9d per paire & the Wells at 1s 8d per paire*	*144*	164	7	
	By Ditto for one other Trunck laden in same ship at same time, cont. 100 doz Bristoll and 12 doz Wells, the prices the same with the foregoing, & both Truncks consigned to Samuel Kekewich merchant in St Marie Port	*144*	177	17	
	By Adventure in the Tygre to Cadiz for one Trunck cont. 41 doz Bristoll and 15 doz Wells hose, the Bristoll at 2s 9d the Wells at 1s 8d laden in her consigned to Simon Clements Supra Cargo as may appeare	*144*	83	2	
			1361	16	6

26	To Ditto paid James Wollen for	30	2	4	139	3	10	
	To Ditto pd. Sam. Dyer for	28	2	3	139	3	3	
29	To Ditto pd. John Perrie for	23	2	3½	139	2	12	8½
	To Ditto pd. Jonathan Abram for	45	2	4	139	5	5	
November 2	To Cash pd. John Rudduck for	56	2	3	139	6	6	
3	To Ditto pd. John Massinger for	40	2	7	139	5	3	4
4	To Ditto pd. John Perry for	54	2	3½	139	6	3	9
9	To Ditto paid Robert Webb for a Trunck				139		9	
10	To Cash pd. Samuel Dyer for	39	2	3½	139	4	9	4½
	To Ditto pd. JamesWollen for	24	2	4	139	2	16	
11	To Ditto pd. John Perry for	30	2	3½	139	3	8	9
12	To Ditto pd. Jonathan Abram for	40	2	4	139	4	13	4
15	To Ditto pd. John Greene for six Cords for Truncks				139		5	6
	To Ditto pd. John Massinger for	38	2	7	139	4	18	2
18	To Ditto pd. Edward Iffe for hotpressing				139		11	
19	To Ditto pd. Henry Britten for	71	2	3	139	7	19	9
23	To Cash pd. John Massinger for	30	2	7	139	3	17	6
24	To Ditto pd. Samuel Abram for	40	2	3½	139	4	11	8
25	To Cash pd. John Perrie for	27	2	3	139	3		4
	To Ditto pd. Tho. Hill for Joseph George	24	1	3	139	1	10	
December 1	To Ditto pd. John Massinger for	42	2	6	139	5	5	
2	To Ditto pd. John Perrie for	54	2	3	139	6	1	6
	To Ditto pd. Tho. Hill for Sam. Dyer for	48	2	3	139	5	8	
8	To Ditto pd. Sam. Dyer for	36	2	3	139	4	1	
						390	19	10¼
	By Ballance carried to that acct.				146	970	16	7¾
						1361	16	6

---

(136)   **Bristoll 1687**

		Dr	£	s	d
	Thomas Strode merchant factor resident in Malaga in Spaine To Adventure in the ship Adventurers delight from London to Malaga for the neat proceeds of 42 doz Bristoll Hose £78 5s 00d for 5417 Ryals Velloone, being 361¼ pieces of 8 the piece of 8 at 52d as per his account sales closed in Malaga May 17th 1687	123	78	5	
1688 April 7	To Isaac Heming for money hee paid on my bill to Hugh Strode per his own order	143	54		9½
1689 Oct.	To Adventure in the Oliffe branch for the neat proceeds of 1 Trunck stockins being 5131 Ryals Velloone & 8 mervidees. Which is 342 1/15 pieces of 8 (at 52d) & 8 Maravedis as per acct. of sales closed in Malaga in May last	158	74	2	4
1690 July	To Isaac Heming for mony pd. Hugh Strode on my bill in his favour being in part of the neat proceeds of 60 Barrills and 60 Carge of Raisons	177	200		
	To Ditto pd. Hugh Strode in full of the neat proceeds of 60 Barrills and 60 Carge of Raisons	177	53	6	7¼
	To Profit and Loss, for Ballance	190 *		3	9½
			459	18	6¼

Bristoll 1687

		Cr	£	s	d
	Thomas Strode per Contra is				
	By Reisons Solis my 1/3 part of the cost & charges of 65 Barrills laden in the ship Olive branch being 2720 9 meridees Velloone & is 248 pieces of 8 9 meridees plate at 51d½ the piece of 8	149	53	4	5
March 1688	By Hugh Strode for ballance drawne on him per Tho. Strode in my favor being for 1680 Ryals Velloone, & are pieces of 8 112 at 51d½ the piece of 8	149	24		8
	By Reisons Solis 65 Barrills for his 1/3 of theire neat proceeds £162 3s 5d as may appeare	145	54	1	2
	By Proffit & Losse for Ballance	153		19	6½
1690	By Fruit my 1/4 part of 60 Barrills and 60 Carge Raisons for 3360 Ryals Velloon 30 M.dees making 224 pieces of 8 (at 52d per piece) and 30 Maravedis, being the first cost of said fruit in Malaga as per Invoice of 19th Dec. 1689	183	48	10	11
	By Ditto for my ¼ part of charges in ensuring 1000 pieces of 8 on 60 Barrills and 60 Carge Raisons being (as per his leter of 15th March 1690) 330 Ryals Velloon 16 Maravedis which make 22 pieces of 8 (at 52d per piece) and 16 Maravedis	183	4	15	5
	By Adventure in the Olive branch for 1365 Ryals Velloon which make 91 pieces of 8 at 52d per ps, being so much lost (as per said Leter of 15th March 1690) by the sale of 15 doz hose to Don Nich. Merida, he failing	158	19	14	4
	By Reisons 60 Barrills and 60 Large for ¾ parts of £339 9s 4d¾ the neat proceeds	177	254	12	¾
			459	18	6¼

	Dr	£	s	d
Anno 1687				
Reisons Solis 27 Barrills laden per John Aylward in Malaga in the ship Abram and Robert Capt. Purton, consign'd to Isaac Heming merchant in London, & by him ship'd in the ship John Robt. Deane Master, for Bristoll to my selfe				
To John Aylward for theire cost & charges in Malaga being 4520 Ryals Vell & 19 mervidees at 15 Ryals to the piece of 8 is 301 pieces of 8 & 5 Ryals 19 meri.ds at 52d the piece of 8	131	65	5	10
July To Isaac Heming for custom fraight & other charges on them	130	17	5	3
To Ditto for freight from London to Bristoll which hee paid James Deane	143	2	14	
To Cash pd. sundry Disbursments on them	175		4	
To Profit and Loss, for Ballance	190 *	2	11	11
		88	1	

	Dr	£	s	d
Anno 1687				
Reisons Solis one small Cask bought and sent by order of Hugh Strode of London merchant to Serjeant John Windham at Dunvaron Castle				
December 2 To Cash pd. Mark Jacob for 1 Cask weight groce - Cwt 3qr 22lb tare at £12 per Cent at 23[?] [103] per lb	139		19	6
To Proffit & Losse for weighing at Backhall, mending the Cask & Portridge	137			6
		1		

	Dr	£	s	d
Anno 1688				
Richard Day of Bristoll Hosier is				
Aprill To Samuel Kekewich for Simon Clements bill for 100 pieces of 8 assignd in my favor the piece of 8 at 52d	148	21	13	4

	Dr	£	s	d
Anno 1687				
Adventure the 2nd in the Cadiz merchant to Cadiz Capt. James Clarke				
To sundry accts 204 13 11 the cost and charges of 1 Trunck stockins laden in said ship, consign'd to Samuel Kekewich in St Marie Port viz £ s d				
To Stockins for 1344 paire at 2s 9d per paire 184 16 00				
To Ditto for 164 paire Wells hose at 1s 9d per paire 14 07 00	135	199	3	
To Isaac Heming for carriage to London, Custom & other charges	130	5	10	11
		204	13	11
To Profit and Loss, for Ballance	190 *	40	8	6¾
		245	2	5¾

	Dr	£	s	d
Anno 1687				
Thomas Goldney Junior my Sonne in law, of Bristoll Grocer is				
July 19 To Reisons Solis for 4 Barrills neat 19 cwt 2qr 23lb at 24s due Oct. 25th 1687	136	12	16	11
To Edward Crofts for money payable to mee by his noat of 3rd Sept. for acct. of said Crofts	96	16	9	
Sept. To Tho. Goldney his father for the cost & charges of a Stone-Jugge oyle from London	132		7	10
November 7 To Reisons solis 65 barrills for 6 barrills neat 15cwt 2qr 15lb at 24s due Feb. 7th	145	18	15	2½
1688 July 20 To french wine 3 hhds etc. for 1 doz bottles, 10s & to Proffit & Losse for bottles 2s	151, 3		12	
August 7 To sundry accts for 16 bottles Xerie at 18s 16 bottles white wine at 10s 6d, & 2 doz 8 bottles	150, 151,153	2	3	4
10 To sundry accts for 15 bottles white wine at 10s 6d and 15 bottles at 2d	151, 153		15	7½

Anno 1687				
Reisons Solis 27 Barrills per Contra	Cr	£	s	d
July 19 By sundry accts for said 27 barrills sould to John Lowe, Tho.	55, ,95			
Jordan ,Tho. Goldney Junior, Tho. Burgesse, Robert	136,			
Hawxworth, Wm. Morgan and Samuel Hollister	138, 28	88	1	

Anno 1687				
Reisons Solis per Contra	Cr	£	s	d
By Hugh Strode his acct. current for the cost & charge of the				
Cask per Contra	149	1		

Anno 1688				
Richard Day per Contra is	Cr	£	s	d
May 25 By Cash recd. of him in full	141	21	13	4

Anno 1690@				
Adventure 2nd in the Cadiz Merchant per Contra	Cr	£	s	d
May By Sam. Kekewich for the neat proceeds of said trunck of				
Stockings per contra, being 9050 Ryals 26 M.dees which make				
1131 2/8 pieces of 8 25 M.dees as per acct. of Sales closed in St				
Marie Port April 7th 1690 the piece of 8 at 52d	167	245	2	5¾

Anno 1687				
Tho. Goldney Junior per Contra	Cr	£	s	d
August 17 By Sir George Strode for a Sugar loafe weight 4 3/4 lb at 11d per pound	24		4	4
By Proffit & Losse for a Sugar loafe for myselfe weight 3lb 14oz at 11d	137		3	6½
1688 By Ditto for 2 loaves single refin'd suger weight at 10lb 1oz at 6d per lb	137		5	½
error By Ditto for money for 2 pieces of Dyaper Linnin	139	29		
November 25 By Cash received of him	137			10
By Proffit & Losse abated him	140	18	15	2
March 8 By Cash received of him and abated him	168	30		
July 5 By Cash received of him in part	168	9	5	
9 By Cash recd. of him in full				
By Proffit & Losse for ballance to this day July 9th 1689 pd. for vinegar	164		6	10

			£	s	d
30	To sundry accts for 4 bottles white wine & bottles	151,153		4	
September 17	To sundry accts for 6 bottles white wine and the bottles	151,153		6	
	To James Swetnam for money received of him for my acct. as per noat	133	6	18	
December 11	To sundry accts for 2 bottles of Xerie and the bottles, sent to the Castle	150, 153		3	4
January	To Reisons Solis 32 barrills for 9 barrills neat 23 cwt 3qr 24lb at 22s the Cwt due Aprill 1st next	158	26	7	2
	To sundry accts for 2 doz bottles Xerie £1 16s and 2 bottles white wine with the bottles 2s	150, 151	1	18	
	To sundry accts for 2 bottles Xerie and 1 bottle white wine 150,	151,153		4	4
1689 August	To sundry accts for 2 doz bottles of Xerie at 18s	164,169	2	4	
September	To Isaac Heming for money borrowed of mee and received of him in London	177	150		
			240	4	9

Anno 1687

	Paul Moone of Bristoll Currier	Dr	£	s	d
December 17	To Cash paid Wm. Dawson by his order for his bill on John Cabell of Reading	140		6	7

(137) Bristoll 1687

	Proffit & Losse is	Dr	£	s	d
	To Ballance of its former acct. from that acct.	127	812	18	11¾
	To Jonathan Lamboll for money pd. 2 messengers with leters to Farnham	131		6	6
	To Ditto for money hee paid my wife at severall times	131	10		
July 28	To Cash paid given John Stretten	121		2	
	To Ditto paid Jane Flower in full	121	1	4	
	To Cash paid for 6 Panniers & Covers	121		5	
	To Edward Jones for work done at severall times	25	8	13	
	To Jonathan Lamboll for money I recd. of him July 4th	131	2		
	To Ditto for money furnished my wife	131	3		
	To Ditto for 14s 6d pd. Tho. Connick, and 4s to James King for Isa. Hemings beere	131		18	6
August 17	To Tho. Goldney Junior for a Sugar Loafe	136		3	6½
18	To Cash pd. Wm. Clark for bottles in full	139	6		6
20	To Cash pd. Sam. Jonson for 7 Baskets	139 *		5	6
22	To Ditto pd. Richard Corsley for 6 Silver salts	139	2	2	4
	To Richard Merrick for so much abated him on his rent	92		2	6
26	To Cash pd. houshold expences to August 6th	139	9	1	7½
September 10	To Cash pd. Tho. Smith for a dimm sighted mare	139	9	17	6
14	To Cash pd. given Richard Chamneys as Charity to the Widow Palmer	139	1		
17	To Isaac Heming for money overchargd to Robert Richardson	130		10	
October 1	To Cash pd. Lot Wilkins for 2 Tubbs Butter weight 115 lb at 3d¼ per lb	139	1	11	3
	To Wm. Smart for money formerly due for painting my lower house	26	8	17	6
	To Isaac Heming for what hee pd. Earnest for 2 places in the Coach	130	1		
	To Ditto for what paid him for the use of his children	130	80		
	To Ditto for what was lost in the Exchange of Guinnies	130		14	7
	To Ditto for what paid the widow Russell for severall papers of powder	130		16	
	To Ditto for what hee paid Tho. Cox for wine sent to Reading	130	1		6
	To Ditto for port of leters to November 12th 1687	130		17	3
	To Tho. Goldney Junior for 2 Sugar loaves 5sd½ & a piece Dyaper £1 4s 0d	136	1	9	½

1689 Nov. 16	By Cash recd. of Wm. Swimmer by his order	168	100		
February 7	By Cash recd. of him	173	50		
			238		9
	By ballance carried to his new acct. current	176	2	4	
			240	4	9

	Anno 1687				
	Paul Moone per Contra is	Cr	£	s	d
January	By Jonathan Lamboll for what hee recd. in part of John Cable on the bill per Contra	147	6		
	By Cash recd. of himselfe	140		7	
			6	7	

	Bristoll 1687				
	Proffit & Losse per Contra is	Cr	£	s	d
July	By Wm. Spoore Senior for 1 yeares intrest of £10	52		12	
20	By Sir George Strode for 4 doz bottles, 2 Panniers & Covers	24		10	8
26	By Lady Ann Powlet for 3 Panniers & 6 doz bottles	100		16	
27	By James Webb for intrest of £50	16		16	8
29	By John Cullimor paid him	130		5	
August 4	By Ralph Grant for intrest of £300	88	24	15	
	By Sir Geo. Strode for 2 doz 4 bottles, 2 Panniers, port of a leter & fardle to the waggon	24		6	11
11	By Dr. Fra. Hungerford for 2 doz bottles a Pannier & Cover	87		5	2
	By Robert Richardson for ½ yeares intrest of £150	35	3	15	
September 2	By Cash recd. of Esaw White	139		2	
22	By Cash recd. of Tho. Smith back in part for his dim sighted mare	139	8	10	
	By Charles Stubbs & Company for 7 months intrest of £100	123	3	10	
	By John Sandford Linnindraper for 2 yeares intrest of £100	19	12		
	By Henry Howard & Company for 2 halfe yeares intrest of £100 ending Sept. 19th 1687	92	6		
	By Isaac Heming & Company for 1 yeares intrest of £400	69	16		
	By Samuel Kekewich overchargd on Ennys his bill as per his acct. Sept. 2nd 1687	111		10	8
	By Ditto for ½ neat proceeds of a Trunck of hose in the Wellcome 3403 Ryals per same acct.	111	85	17	10
October	By John Blackwell for 6 Panniers & covers delivered his servant George	132		5	
	By Feathers for acct. of Philip Stansly for charges of celleridge, portridge & commission	123		6	11
	By Jonathan Lamboll for ½ yeares intrest of £450 due Sept. 29th 1687	109	11	5	
December 20	By John Earle of Bristoll for portridge of a rundlet from & to the Carrier	132			6
27	By Dr. Fra. Hungerford for portridge of a pannier wine	87			2
January 7	By Wm. Godwin for ½ yeares intrest of £100 ending September 27th 1687	64	3		
	By John Gore for money due from them for hay and Cattle sould them by bond	149	127		
	By Ditto for 4 yeares intrest from 25th July 1683 to 25th July 1687	149	30	9	8

Date	Description	Folio	£	s	d
	To Samuel Kekewich for Charges on 3 Bills of Exchange from St Marie Port	111	3	6	11
	To ½ cost & charges of 300 pieces of 8 on the James Gally from Cadiz	111	33	12	4
	To Samuel Kekewich for Charges on Charles Stubbs his second bill from Cadiz 30 Ryals	111		15	11¼
	To Ditto for money lost on 10 doz hose to Pedro Sancho per Pragmatica	111		17	3
	To Ditto for losse on 11 doz to Don Rodrigo Munnos per Pragmatica	111	1	12	2
	To Ditto for losse on 19 doz to Don Rodrigo Velasco per Pragmatica	111	2	15	6
	To Ditto for the Cost and charges of 228½ pieces of 8 per the Eagle	111	51	19	6
	To Samuel Kekewich for the charges on 3 Bills of Exchange Ed. Crofts, Mich. White, Scar. Chapman	111	1	8	11
	To Ditto for port of leters to the 21th Oct. 1687	111	2	13	1½
25	To Cash paid John Massinger for footing stockins	139		1	
	To Anthony Tyler for shooing & keeping my mare to the 3th instant	129	3	1	
27	To Cash paid John Flower for a Bay Mare	139	8	5	
November 4	To Ditto pd. John Edwards Waggoner for bringing things from Reading	139	1		
	To Jonathan Lamboll for severall pieces of household goods & plate as per his noat of particulars	131	42	8	
	To Ditto for money hee pd. in Oct. 1686 to Edward Piercy, 5s & to John Bisly for nailes etc. 11s	131		16	
	To Abraham Hill for one yeares sallary due the 10th of November 1687	131	10		
			1129	10	3
	To Thomas Gouldney Junior for money abated	136			10
26	To Cash pd. Susan Keeping for a firkin of Butter	139		18	6
	To William Godwin for ½ yeares intrest for £100 recd. of him in Aprill last	64	3		
December 2	To Cash paid Richard Day for 7 Yards of freeze	139		16	3
	To Cash paid Marmaduke Boudler for a remnant of Broadcloth	139	2	7	
6	To Cash paid John Gandy for his noat	139		14	8
24	To Noah Ozborne alias Cash pd. him for a Packsaddle & Girse	140		9	6
29	To Cash pd. Marmaduke Boudler for 5 Yards Cotton	140		5	
February 2	To Cash paid John Crew for a White Rugge	140	1	18	
	To Richard Holbrook for money said to bee paid mee by his wife	98		18	
8	To Cash pd. Ann Smith for ½ Cwt Cheese	140		10	2
11	To Ditto pd. for a Groce of Corks	140			8
15	To Cash pd. Alexander Doleman in full of his noat for selfe & T. Goldney	140	5	12	2
	To Ditto pd. for sweeping 2 Chimnies	140		1	
	To Tho. Day for ½ £90 the proceeds of 4 Butts Malaga To Ditto for ½ of his	149	45		
	To Nathanael Haggatt for his Advice about Richard Hardwick's Assignment	138	1	13	
20	To Cash pd. Robert Lippyeatt in full for mault	140	4	1	
	To John Blackwell for severall small parcels of wine	132	1	4	6
	To Marie Wasbrow for work done as per her noat	144	2	8	
	To Wm. Plydall lent him at severall times & now forgiven him	46	1	7	6
	To Ditto for work done about my Vault & harths	46	1	12	
March 1	To Cash for household expences to the 14th of Nov. 1687	140	41	3	10
5	To Cash pd. John Lukins for a de[?]re colour mare	140	8	15	
	To Tho. Day Wine Cooper for ½ 11s after charges on 20 Butts Xerie	149		5	6

By Simon Clement & Company for 8 months & 17 daies intrest of £100	133	4	5	8
By Simon Clement for fourty seaven weeks Celleridge of my vault at 3s per week	103	7	1	
By John Blackwell for 2 yeares & 10 daies Celleridge of my great vault	132	20	6	
By Robert Dowding & Company for 2 yeares intrest of £100 ending August 4th 1687	100	12		
By Malaga wine 4 Butts for striking downe 3 & hooping & racking 2 Butts	134		7	6
By Wines 8 Butts in partnership with Tho. Day for Celleridge 13 weeks	123		12	
By Malaga wines 4 Butts for Celleridge	134		5	
By Jonathan Lamboll for money pd. short by John Cable, & after paid by Paul Moone	147		7	
By Tobacco 4 hhds for Law. Washington for intrest, Cooperidge, Celleridge Commission & hallidge	147	3	8	10
By Tho. Day Wine Cooper for ½ cost & charges of 4 Butts Malaga from Lond.	149	51	5	3
By Ditto for ½ of 12s the 13 weeks celleridge of 8 Butts wine	149		6	
By Nathanael Haggatt for severall months intrest of severall summes	138	6	9	5
By Marie Washbrow for 4 hhds	144		12	
By the Lady Ann Powlett for Portridge	100			4
By Reisons 1 Cask for acct. Hugh Strode pd. weighing portridge and mending the Cask	136			6
By Reisons 65 Barrills abated to the Grocers	145		3	3¾
By merchandizes in the John for acct. Lawrence Washington for sundry charges on said merchandizes as per particulars in acct.	145	1	13	8
By John Earle of Bristoll for portridge of a Rundlet of wine	150			4
By Edward Jacob & Company for 1 yeares intrest of £20	134	1	4	
By Jonathan Lamboll for ½ yeares intrest of £450 due March 25th 1688	147	11	5	
		458	12	11½
Aprill By Simon Clement & Company for ½ yeares intrest of £50	133	1	10	
By Tho. Day Soapmaker for money for ullage wine	94		2	6
May By John Sandford for ½ yeares intrest of £100 ending March 16th 1687	19	3		
By John Earle of Bristoll for portridge of wine	150			7½
By Nathanael Haggatt for ½ yeares intrest of £320	148	9	12	
By Samuel Kekewich for 10 piece of 8 hee recd. of Simon Clement at 52d the piece of 8	148	2	3	4
30 By John Hurden for portridge of wine	151			3
By Jonathan Lamboll for ¼ yeares intrest of £450 due June 24th 1688	147	5	12	6
By ballance carried to that acct. of debt	153	480	14	2½
		864	18	6¼
		1345	12	8½

8	To Cash pd. Tho. Goldney Junior in full of his noat	140		6	
	To Ditto pd. Wm. Burgesse Woollendraper in full of his noat	140	2	18	6
10	To Cash paid boushold expences to the 10th instant	140	45	10	9
23	To Cash pd. Wm. Williams for 10 Bushells Oates & 2 Bushells Beanes	140		14	7½
	To John Earle of Bristoll abated him	132			3
1688 Aprill 3rd	To Cash paid Abel Edwards for shooing, blooding etc. of my horses	141		19	
May 10	To Cash pd. Alexander Doleman in full	141	3	1	6
12	To Cash paid Tho. Nicholls for pasing & keeping my mare	141		19	6
16	To Cash pd. Robert Yate towards releife of the French protestants	141		10	
17	To Cash paid Robert Gibbons for keeping my Bay Mare	141		19	
	To John Blackwell for severall parcells of wine had of him at severall times	148	1	1	3
	To Isaac Heming for money hee paid for Coopers Bellows etc. & a silver taster	143	3	10	6
	To Ditto paid by him to Thomas Dyke in London	143	30		
	To Isaac Heming for port of leters to the 29th of May	143		9	6
			1345	12	8½

---

(138)   **Bristoll 1687**

			£	s	d
	Thomas Burgesse of Bristoll Grocer is	Dr			
July 19	To Reisons solis 27 Barrills for 4 Barrills neat 19 cwt 2qr 18¾lb at 24s due Oct. 25th 1687	136	12	16	

Anno 1688			£	s	d
	Tho. Burgesse of Bristoll Grocer and Wm. Stocker of Bristoll merchant	Dr			
August 18	To Cash paid lent them on theire bond payable Feb. 19th next	141	100		
	To Profit and Loss, for 7 moneths intrest of £100	190 *	3	10	
			103	10	

Anno 1687			£	s	d
	William Morgan of Bristoll Grocer is	Dr			
July 19	To Reisons solis 27 barrills for 4 barrils weight neat 19 cwt 2qr 26lb at 24s due Oct. 25th	136	12	17	6¾

Anno 1687			£	s	d
	Samuel Hollister of Bristoll Grocer is	Dr			
July 19	To Reisons solis 27 barrills for 3 barrils neat 8cwt 1qr 4½lb at 24s due Oct. 25th	136	9	18	11½

Anno 1687			£	s	d
	William Jones & William Clark both of Bristoll merchants are	Dr			
December 8	To Cash lent them on theire Bond payable with intrest	139	50		
1688 December 8	To Proffit & Losse for one yeares intrest ending December 8th 1688	153	3		
1689 September	To Ditto for ¾ yeares intrest due Sept. 8th 1689	164	2	5	
March	To Ditto for ½ yeares intrest ending March 8th 1689	164	1	10	
1690 Oct.	To Ditto for ½ yeares intrest ending Sept. 8th 1690@	180	1	10	
			58	5	

Anno 1687			£	s	d
	Nathanael Haggatt of Bristoll Counsellor at law is	Dr			
July 23	To himselfe for ballance of his former acct. brought from that acct.	19	116	13	7
25	To Cash paid lent him on his bond & a deposit	121	120		
September 28	To Cash paid lent him on security of a warrant for a Judgement	139	100		
	To Proffit & Losse for severall moneths intrest for the foregoing summes unto the 9th day of November 1687	137	6	9	5
			343	3	

Bristoll 1687		Cr	£	s	d
	Tho. Burgesse per Contra	Cr	£	s	d
January 16	By Cash received of him in full	140	12	16	

Anno 1688		Cr	£	s	d
	Tho. Burgesse & Wm. Stocker	Cr	£	s	d
March 28	By Cash recd. of Wm. Stocker in full	162	103	10	

Anno 1690@		Cr	£	s	d
	William Morgan per Contra	Cr	£	s	d
	By Profit and Loss, for the money per Contra, recd. but not charged to acct.	190 *	12	17	6¾

Anno 1687		Cr	£	s	d
	Samuel Hollister per Contra is	Cr	£	s	d
December 20	By Cash recd. of him in full	140	9	18	9
	By Profit and Loss, for Ballance	190 *			2½
			9	18	11½

Anno 1689		Cr	£	s	d
	Wm. Jones & William Clark per Contra	Cr	£	s	d
November	By Proffit & Losse for severall parcells of bottles recd. of W. Clark at severall times	164	6	3	5
	By Acct. of Ballances, for Ballance	190 *	52	1	7
			58	5	

Anno 1687		Cr	£	s	d
	Nathanael Haggatt per Contra is	Cr	£	s	d
	By Proffit & Losse for money formerly paid Stephen Chapman	137 *	6		
	By Ditto for money formerly paid Ed. Inketill	137 *	6		
	By Cash received of him at twice (viz) £3 & £1 10s	140	4	10	
	By Estate lately purchased at Clapton for his advice about that Purchase	142	5		

Anno 1687				
Nicholas Warren of — in the County of Devon Yeoman	Dr	£	s	d
March 21 To Cash paid Nicholas Veale for a Pendula Clock and box to put it in, sent him per Henry Stover Lime Carrier, under the mark in the margent	140	2	15	9

Anno 1687				
Sugar 8 hhds in the ship Martha & Sarah Wm. Needs Master from Nevis	Dr	£	s	d
August 15 To Cash paid custom fees & bills	121	12	17	6
To Edmund Scrope & Company for theire cost & charges in Nevis 11199 lb sugar at 10s per 100lb as per Invoyce June 4th 1687	33	55	19	7½
September 10 To Cash pd. Wm. Needs for freight & averidge	139	10	8	
		79	5	1½

Anno 1687				
Richard Lane of Bristoll Sugar baker is	Dr	£	s	d
August 15 To Sugar 8 hhds in the Martha & Sarah for them weight neat 72 cwt 3qr 14lb at 19s 6d per Cwt payable the 15th of November	138	71	1	

(139)	Bristoll 1687				
	Cash is	Dr	£	s	d
August 15	To its own acct. for ballance brought from that acct.	121	3462	4	11
22	To Henry Howard, John Thorrowgood & Company recd. of Ozziel Browne	92	3		
25	To Richard Merrick recd. of him	92	5	9	6
31	To Dr. Fra. Hungerford recd. of Tho. Hungerford	87	1	13	2
September 1	To Estate at Clapton pd. of Sir John Smith, John Piggott & Edward Gorges for 3 Closes of ground sould them	72	170		
2	To Xerie wine 4 Qtr Cask recd. of Esaw White & to proffit & Losse	133, 137	1		
3	To James Swetnam recd. of him in part	133	40		
5	To Richard Chamneys recd. of him in full	45	31		
8	To Wm. Powlet recd. of his servant	133	4	10	
21	To Edward Crofts recd. of him	96	2	11	
	To Proffit & Losse recd. of Tho. Smith	137	8	10	
28	To Isaac Heming recde of John Stubbs for which I valued my bill	130	50		
	To Marie Board & Company recd. of Marie Board in part	134	8	19	6
October 12	To John Earle of Bristoll received of Serjeant Hodges at Clevedon	132	32	6	
	To Simon Clement & Company received of Simon Clement in part	133	50		
	To Charles Stubbs & Company for money of Charles Stubbs	123	90	15	
November 3	To John Morgan recd. of him in full	123	4	9	
4	To Oliver Mosley recd. of him in full	4	2		
5	To Isaac Heming recd. of Edward Martindale Junior on my bill	143	4	4	11
	To Henry Howard & Company recd. of Ozziel Browne for ½ yeares intrest of £100	92	3		
19	To Isaac Heming recd. of Samuel Spencer & Company	143	18	4	
	To John Hardiman recd. of him in part	80	2	10	
25	To Tho. Goldney Junior recd. of him in full	136	29		
30	To John Love received of him	55	13		
December 3	To Edward Jacob recd. of him	134	3		
	To Robert Hauxworth recd. of him	28	13	8	
			4054	15	

		£	s	d
By Proffit & Losse for money allowed him for his advice about Richard Hardwicks assignment	137	1	13	
		23	3	
By Ballance lent him on a Mortgage carried to a new acct. current	148	320		

Anno 1690@				
Per Contra	Cr	£	s	d
By Profit and Loss, for Ballance	191 *	2	15	9

Anno 1687				
Sugar 8 hhds per Contra	Cr	£	s	d
August 15 By Richard Lane for the 8 hhds per Contra weight neat 72cwt 3qr 14lb at 19s 6d per Cwt	138	71	1	
By Profit and Loss, for Ballance	190 *	8	4	1½

Anno 1687				
Richard Lane per Contra	Cr	£	s	d
January 10 By Cash recd. of him in part	140	21	1	
February 1 By Cash recd. of him in full	140	50		
		71	1	

Bristoll 1687				
Cash per Contra is	Cr	£	s	d
August 16 By Stockins pd. Anthony Palmer	135	2	11	4
By Sir George Strode pd. Edward Croft & James Freeman	24		5	4
17 By Jahzeel Speed sent him per Henry Stover	122	3		
By Lawrence Washington pd. Wm. Clark on his bill	135	5		
By Proffit & Losse paid Ditto in full for bottles	137	6		6
19, 20 By Stockins pd. Eliza. Webb, John Perry & Joseph White	135	11	2	6
By Ditto pd. Jonathan Abram, Tho. Walden & Eliza. Messenger	135	8	9	6
By Estate at Clapton pd. Tho. Walden for a sparre	72		5	
By Proffit & Losse pd. Richard Corsley	137	2	2	
25 By Abraham Hill pd. him in part	131	1	10	
26 By Proffit & Losse pd. houshold expences	137	9	1	7½
By Stockins pd. John Massinger	135	4	15	7
By Lands lately Purchased in Clapton paid Bethel Walter the 18th of this moneth	142	578		
September 2 By Stockins pd. John Perrie & Robert Webb	135	4	13	6
By Wm. Powlet for 7 doz bottles	133		14	
5 By House in which I live pd. John Pierce	130		8	
By Stockins pd. John Ruddock & James Wollen	135	8	4	5
By Estate lately purchased in Clapton pd. John Long	142	4	8	
10 By Stockins pd. Henry Britten	135	6	16	6
By Sugar 8 hhds pd. Wm. Needs for freight etc.	138	10	8	
By Stockins pd. Joseph White	135	7	8	9
17 By Proffit & Losse pd. Tho. Smith & Richard Chamnyes	137	10	17	6
By Stockins pd. Jonathan Abram & John Massinger	135	13	8	3¼
By Estate at Clapton pd. Tho. Godwin	72		12	6
21 By Estate newly purchased in Clapton pd. Nath. Haggatt	142	4		
By Stockins pd. Tho. Hill	135	4	3	3
23 By Ditto pd. John Perrie	135	5	8	
By Jahzeel Speed paid Pendock Warren	122		6	8
By Stockins pd. John Massinger & Edward Iffe	135	4	4	8¾
By Nath. Haggatt paid lent him	138	100		
29 By Stockins pd. James Wollen	135	3	14	8

Date	Description				
October 1	By *Proffit & Losse pd. Lott Wilkins for 2 Tubbs Butter*	137	1	11	3
	By *Stockins pd. John Massinger*	135	4		1
5	By *Ditto pd. Joseph George for 12 paire*	135		15	
	By *Estate at Clapton pd. Henry Sydamore*	72		2	
8	By *Wm. Smart paid him in part*	26		10	
	By *Stockins paid John Massinger*	135	3	17	6
	By *Jahzeel Speed paid Stephen Stringer*	122		8	6
	By *Stockins pd. Jonathan Abram & John Massinger*	135	9	6	7
19	By *Jahzeel Speed paid John Winpenny*	122		7	4½
	By *Stockins paid Eliza. Webb for a Trunck*	135		13	
22	By *Samuel Clark & Company pd. lent them on theire Bond*	142	100		
24	By *house at lower end of Small Streat pd. Tho. Davidge for 1 yeares reserv'd rent & charges*	22		3	8
	By *Samuel Clark & Company pd. lent them on theire bond* [104]	142	100		
	By *Stockins paid John Massinger*	135	5	9	
	By *Proffit & Losse pd. Ditto for footing stockins*	137		1	
	By *Anthony Tyler paid him in full*	129	3	1	
26	By *Proffit & Losse pd. John Flower for my bay mare*	137	8	5	
			1060	11	5
	By *Abraham Hill paid him in part*	131	2	10	
	By *Stockins pd. James Wollen, Samuel Dyer, John Perrie, & Jonathan Abram*	135	14	10	8½
	By *Isaac Heming for money paid John Love by his order*	143	8	13	3
November 2	By *Stockins pd. John Rudduck*	135	6	6	
3	By *Ditto pd. John Massinger for 40 paire*	135	5	3	4
	By *Tho. Shepheard paid John Hine by his order*	129	4	2	1
4	By *Stockins pd. John Perrie*	135	6	3	9
	By *sundry accts paid Edward Jones in full*	22, 130		10	
	By *proffit & Losse paid John Edwards*	137	1		
8	By *Lands newly purchased in Clapton paid Tho. Edwards*	142	2	10	6
	By *Sidrick Seager paid Samuel Tipton by his order*	134	2		
9	By *Wm. Smart paid him in full*	26	2		
	By *Stockins paid Robert Webb*	135		9	
	By *Jahzeel Speed paid Edward Woodhouse*	122	1	14	
	By *Stockins paid Samuel Dyer*	135	4	9	4½
	By *Ditto pd. James Wollen, John Perry, & Jonathan Abram*	135	10	18	1
15	By *Stockins paid John Greene & John Massinger*	135	5	3	8
	By *Reisons solis 65 Barrills paid custom fees etc.*	145	16	19	9½
18, 19	By *Stockins paid Edward Iffe & Henry Britten*	135	8	10	9
	By *John Hardiman paid lent him*	80	5		
	By *Stockins pd. John Massinger & Samuel Abram*	135	8	9	2
	By *Welthian Ruther paid her in part*	94		10	
25	By *Xeries wine pd. Joseph Berry*	134	1		
	By *Stockins pd. John Perry & Tho. Hill for Joseph George*	135	4	10	9
	By *Jahzeel Speed paid Alexander Doleman*	122		17	6
26	By *Abraham Hill paid him in full*	131	1	10	
	By *Proffit & Losse paid Susan Keeping*	137		18	6
December 1	By *Stockins paid John Massinger*	135	5	5	
	By *Merchandizes for acct. Law. Washington pd. severalls for severall goods*	145	16	7	3
2	By *Ditto pd. Richard Day for 1½ doz Irish hose*	145		18	
	By *Proffit & Losse pd. Richard Day & Marmaduke Bowdler*	137	3	3	3
	By *Stockins paid John Perrie & Tho. Hill*	135	11	9	4
	By *reisons solis paid the weighers*	145		2	
	By *reisons 1 Cask for acct. of Hugh Strode paid Mark Jacob*	136		19	6
3	By *Proffit & Losse, & Merchandizes in the John for Law. Washington pd. John Gandy*	137, 145	3	7	
	By *reisons 65 Barrills paid Edward Dowding for freight & averidge*	145	24	17	
	By *Stockins paid Sam. Dyer for 36 paire*	135	4	1	

(140)	**Bristoll 1687**	Dr	£	s	d
	Cash is				
December	To Ballance of its former acct. brought from folio (139)	139	2742	3	10½
13	To Nicholas Baker recd. of him in part	103	15		
20	To Samuel Hollister recd. of him in full	138	9	18	9
24	To John Stretten recd. of him in part	57	4		
January 7	To Wm. Godwin recd. of him	64	3		
10	To Richard Lane recd. of him	138	21	1	
16	To Tho. Burgesse recd. of him in full	138	12	16	
23	To Nicholas Baker recd. of him in full	103	16		
27	To Robert Dowding & Company recd. of Ozziel Browne	100	6		
	To Nathanael Haggatt recd. of him	138	4	10	
28	To Isaac Heming for £200 of Tho. Edwards & £200 of Abraham Edwards	143	400		
February 1	To Richard Lane recd. of him in full	138	50		
4	To Isaac Heming recd. of Zacharie Cornock for which I valued my bill	143	15		
	To Ditto for money of Daniel Guilim for which I valued my bill	143	200		
	To Ditto for money of Tho. Day on his bill in my favor	143	80	19	2
8	To Isaac Heming for money of Henry Gibbes for which I valued my bill	143	150		
	To Paul Moone recd. of him	136	7		
11	To Dr. Fra. Hungerford recd. of Tho. Hungerford	87	2	1	2
21	To Richard Holbrook recd. of Capt. Samuel Gorges	98	3		
24	To John Love recd. of him	55	19	7	6
	To Edward Hacket recd. of him	145	18	19	
	To Henry Parsons recd. of Tho. Walden	145	26	10	
25	To Thomas Tyler recd. of him	144	19	4	
March 6	To James Fisher recd. of him	144	19	9	
	To Tho. Tayer recd. of him	144	15	16	6
	To the Lady Ann Powlett recd. of Francis Edwards	100	2	1	4
8	To Tho. Goldney for money of him	136	18	15	
9	To John Curtis received of him	145	19	9	
14	To Richard Merrick recd. of him	92	3	10	
15	To Robert Bartly recd. of him in full	144	19	1	
16	To Isaac Heming recd. of John Gore	143	15		
17	To Marie Beard & Company recd. of Marie Beard	134	3		
	To Isaac Heming recd. of Tho. Day	143	28	6	10
21	To John Stretten recd. of him	57	1	19	
23	To Tho. Jordan recd. of him	95	19	9	6
	To Tho. Day received of him in full	149	30	17	7
1688 March 28	To John Osgood recd. of him	113	1	9	10
	To Hnery Howard & Company recd. of Ozziell Browne for ½ yeares intrest	92	3		
	To Elizabeth Beaton received of Beniamin Rolston	145	10		
			4031	2	2½
Aprill 2	To John Blackwell recd. of him	148	50		
5	To Elizabeth Beaton recd. of her in full	145	9	7	
	To Stephen Stringer recd. of him	133	128	4	
			4218	13	½

			£	s	d
	By *William Jones & Company paid lent them on bond*	138	50		
9	By *Stockins pd. John Perrie in part*	146	5		
			1312	11	1½
	By *Ballance carried to that acct. of debt*	140	2742	3	10½
			4054	15	

Bristoll 1687

		Cr	£	s	d
	Cash per Contra is				
December 13	By *John Ockel paid him*	147		9	
15	By *Stockins pd. John Massinger & Tho. Hill for 3 parcells*	146	14	14	5
	By *Ditto pd. Joseph George, Tho. Hill & John Perry for 3 parcells*	146	16	8	11
17	By *Merchandizes in the John paid Jane Shepheard*	145		18	
	By *Paul Moone paid Wm. Dawson for his bill in Reading*	136	6	7	
19	By *Merchandizes in the John paid custom fees & bills*	145		11	4
	By *Jahzeel Speed paid Tho. Walden*	122		4	6
20	By *Anthony Tyler paid him in full*	129	1	6	
	By *Jahzeel Speed paid Anthony Sanders for his bill on Abraham Clark*	122	9		
23	By *Stockins pd. John Massinger*	146	4	17	6
	By *Richard Toune paid him*	147		2	6
24	*Stockins pd. Tho. Hill for Henry Britten*	146	10	12	4
	By *Proffit & Losse pd. Noah Ozburne*	137		9	6
	By *Merchandizes in the John pd. John Mathews*	145	2	5	
	By *Stockins pd. Fra. Rottenburie & Joseph White*	146	10		
	By *sundry accts pd. Joane Darracot & Welthian Ruther in full for theire wages*	94, 98	5	15	
29	By *Proffit & Losse pd. Marmaduke Boudler*	137		5	
	By *Merchandizes in the John pd. Fra. Ballard for nailes*	145	2	16	6
January 4	By *house in which I live pd. 1/2 yeares Chimney money*	130		8	
	By *Stockins pd. John Massinger*	146	5		
7	By *Merchandizes in the John paid Wm. French*	145	1		9
	By *Stockins pd. Jonathan Abram*	146	4	14	6
	By *Jahzeel Speed paid Wm. Rogers*	122		3	6
11	By *Stockins paid John Rudduck & Henry Britten*	146	8	17	8
	By *Tobacco 4 hhds for Law. Washington for Custom freight & other charges*	147	39	2	10
14	By *Stockins pd. John Massinger*	146	4	12	6
	By *Henry Gibbes paid lent him*	79	40		
19	By *Edward Jones paid lent him on his bill*	25	1		
	By *Stockins pd. John Massinger, Tho. Hill & John Perrie*	146	15	17	
23	By *Isaac Heming paid Dennis Tayler*	143	4	11	9
	By *Stockins paid Joseph White*	146	4	16	8
27	By *Jahzeel Speed pd. John Warren*	122	4		
	By *Stockins pd. John Massinger for 41 paire*	146	5	2	6
28	By *Ditto pd. John Perry*	146	8	13	4
February 2	By *Abraham Hill paid him*	131		8	
	By *Proffit & Losse pd. John Crow for a white rugge*	137	1	18	
4	By *Stockins pd. Tho. Hill for John Rudduck*	146	8	6	10
8	By *Proffit & Losse pd. Ann Smith*	137		10	2
	By *Stockins pd. John Massinger*	146	4	10	
9	By *Ditto pd. Joseph White*	146	4	4	7
	By *Proffit & Losse pd. for ½ a Groce of Corks*	137			8
15	By *Merchandizes for Law. Washington & Proffit & Losse pd. Alexander Doleman*	145, 137	7	13	
	By *Proffit & Losse for sweeping 2 Chimnyes*	137		1	
18	By *Stockins pd. John Massinger*	146	5	2	6
	By *Proffit & Losse pd. Robert Lypyeatt in full for mault*	137	4	1	
22	By *Abra. Hill paid him*	131	2	10	
	By *John Blackwell pd. him in full of all acct.s*	132	29	11	
	By *Ditto paid lent him on his bill*	148	50		

Bristoll 1688

		Dr	£	s	d
	Cash is				
Aprill 19	To Ballance of a former acct. brought from that acct.	140	3614	16	8
28	To Sir Robert Yeamans & Ed. Fox recd. of Sir Samuel Astry				
	by order of the Lady Yeamans	10	4	10	
May 8	To Tho. Day Soapmaker recd. of him in full	94	44	7	3
	To John Sandford recd. of him in full to 16th March last past	19	15		
15	To Stephen Stringer for money of Humphry Watmore	133	22		
16	To John Rudduck recd. of him	145	4		
	To Nathanael Haggatt recd. of him	148	9	12	
19	To Scarbrow Chapman recd. of him	132	78		
	To Michael White recd. of him	132	47	13	4
22	To Michael Pope recd. of him	141	34	3	4
23	To Charles Stubbs recd. of him	133	43	6	8
	To Wm. Spoore Senior & Peter Collet recd. of Wm. Spoore	30	3		

			354		3
	By Stockins pd. Tho. Hill for Jonathan Abram	146	4	19	
	By Marie Washrow pd. her in full	144	1	16	
	By Wines of several sorts pd. cooperidge etc.	149		2	4
24	By Stockins pd. John Massinger	146	4	2	2
	By Henry Parsons paid him	145	7	1	
25	By Wm. Plydall paid him in part	46	1		
	By Xeries Wine my ½ of 20 Butts pd. Joseph Berrie	134		5	
29	By Stockins pd. John Rudduck	146	6	11	6
March 1	By Wm. Plydall pd. him in full	46		12	
	By Proffit & Losse pd. houshold expences	137	41	3	10
3	By Stockins pd. John Massinger	146	3	17	4
5	By Proffit & Losse pd. John Lukins for a mare	137	8	15	
	By John Cullimer paid him	130		2	
7	By Stockins pd. Tho. Hill & Joseph White	146	10	4	2
8	By Proffit & Losse pd. Tho. Goldney & Wm. Burgesse	137	3	4	6
	By William Spoore Senior paid lent him on his bill	52	2		
9	By Stockins pd. John Massinger	146	3	17	4
10	By Proffit & Losse pd. houshold expences	137	45	10	9
	By Stockins pd. Anthony Palmer	146	4	16	6
13	By Ditto pd. Edward Iffe in full for hot pressing	146		17	8½
17	By John Earle of Bristoll pd. Richard Chamnyes	132	1	8	6
20	By Stockins pd. Jonathan Abram	146	6	17	3
	By John Massinger pd. Fra. Yeamans & John Pennington	27		5	6
21	By Stockins pd. John Massinger, & Tho. Hill for Henry Britten	146	10	9	4½
	By Nicholas Warren pd. John Veale	138	2	15	9
23	By Stockins pd. Elizabeth Webb	146		13	1
	By Proffit & Losse pd. Wm. Williams	137		14	7½
24	By John Osgood pd. Fra. Maynard for 4 Flitches of Bacon	113	1	9	10
	By Stockins pd. Joseph White	146	5	3	11
1688 March 27	By Richard Toune paid him	147		2	6
28	By Tho. Hardy paid lent him	147	10		
29	By John Rudduck paid lent him on a parcell of stockins	145	4		
	By John Massinger pd. lent him on 30 paire of stockins	27	3	5	
	By Stockins pd. Jonathan Abram	146	4	11	
Aprill 2	By Wines bought of severalls pd. John Ford	149		2	
	By Stephen Stringer pd. him in full	133	5	16	
7	By Stockins pd. Joseph White	146	5	8	9
	By John Massinger pd. lent him on a parcell of hose	27	3	5	
	By John Occell paid him	147	4		
19	By Charles Stubbs paid him in full	133	28	10	
			603	16	4½
	By Ballance carried to a new acct. of Cash	141	3614	16	8
			4218	13	½

Bristoll 1688

	Cash per Contra is	Cr	£	s	d
Aprill 12	By John Massinger paid lent him	27	4	6	8
21	By Ditto paid him	14	3	5	
	By Proffit & Losse pd. Abel Edwards	137		19	
	By House in which I live pd. Edward Jones	130		19	
30	By Dennis Tayler lent him on his Bottomree bond at returne of the Neptune from Nevis	11	5		
May 2	By John Massinger paid him on stockins deposited	27	4	6	8
	By Marie Speed paid her in 2 Guinnies	113	2	3	
	By Joseph Drew paid lent him on his bond	31	4		
8	By Tho. Day paid him in full	94	45	17	6
10	By Proffit & Losse pd. Alexander Doleman for 60 Ells of Canvas	137	3	1	6
	By John Massinger pd. lent him on 30 paire hose	27	3	5	

	To Wm. Spoore Senior recd. of him	52	2		
25	To Richard Day recd. of him	136	21	13	4
	To Arthur Hobbs recd. of Edward Jacob	125		4	
	To Isaac Heming recd. of Robert Henley	152	12		
30	To Xeries wines 23 Butts for returnes out of custom house on 7 Butts	150	17	8	10
June 9	To Richard Godwin recd. of him	23	2		
12	To Tho. Day recd. of him	150	100		
13	To John Harding recd. of Christopher Hurlston	151	4		
	To Richard Cope recd. of him	97		18	
	To Tho. Day recd. of him	150	200		
	To John Gore recd. of him formerly for which I valued my bill on my sonne Heming	31	5		
28	To Arthur Bramley & Company recd. of John Brisco	12	1	5	6
July 20	To Richard Hawksworth recd. of him	152	3	1	9
21	To Isaac Heming recd. of Wm. Phelps	152	10		
28	To Robert Pocock recd. of Godfry Harcourt	149	94		
	To Edward Jacob recd. of him in part	150	6		
	To Jonathan Abram recd. of him	123	4	5	
30	To Beniamin Cole recd. of him	147	12		
August 6	To Sir George Strode recd. of him in full	24	4	18	4
7	To Richard Miller recd. of him	117	10		
15	To Edward Crofts recd. of him in part	96	20		
	To John Stretten recd. of him in part	57	4		
	To Tho. Day Wine Cooper recd. of him	150	100		
	To Samuel Clarke & Company recd. of them	142	100		
18	To Ditto recd. of them in full for intrest	142	4	18	4
24	To Tho. Day recd. of him	150	60		
September 5	To Dr. Fra. Hungerford recd. of Tho. Hungerford in full	87	1	19	2
8	To Tho. Day recd. of him in full	150	21	15	10½
19	To Henry Howard & Company recd. of Ozziel Browne	92	3		
22	To Joseph Drew recd. of him in full	154	3		
			4749	17	4½

12	By *Welthian Ruther paid her for ½ yeares wages*	94	1	5	
	By *Proffit & Losse pd. Tho. Nicholls*	137		19	6
16	By *Ditto pd. Robert Yate towards releife of French Protestants*	137		10	
17	By *John Massinger pd. lent him on 40 prs hose*	27	4	6	8
	By *Proffit & Losse pd. Robert Gibbons*	137		19	
	By *Abraham Hill pd. him for ¼ yeares wages*	131	2	10	
24	By *John Blackwell paid him*	148	32		
	By *John Massinger pd. lent him on 32 paire hose*	27	3	9	4
	By *the house in which I live paid Caleb Kippin for ½ yeares*				
	Chimny money	130		8	
	By *Xeries wines 23 Butts paid custom fees bills etc.*	150	186	3	1½
	By *Ditto pd. Joseph Davis for 3 Awnes of Rhenish*	150	16	10	
	By *Adventure in the Neptune Sloop paid custom fees bills etc.*	143	1	17	3
31	By *Wm. Spoore Senior & Company lent them on theire bond*	151	10		
June 12	By *John Massinger pd. lent them on 30 paire hose as per noat*	27	3	5	
	By *Isaac Heming pd. Richard Baily for Foots bill*	152	100		
18	By *Jonathan Abram pd. lent him on 50 paire hose*	132	4	5	
	By *John Massinger pd. lent him on 30 paire hose*	27	3	5	
	By *Abraham Hill pd. him*	131	1		
21	By *Richard Wasbrow paid him in full*	50	6	5	3
	By *Proffit & Losse pd. Robert Lyppiatt in full*	153	3	17	
	By *Jahzeel Speed paid Henry Gibbes*	122	5	5	
26	By *Charles King paid him*	152	5		
	By *John Massinger paid lent him on 30 pair stockins*	27	3	5	
	By *Isaac Heming pd. John Bubbs order being Peter Saunders*	152	100		
	By *Estate at Clapton delivered Joseph Drew*	151	1	10	
28	By *Richarde Towne pd. him*	147		2	6
July 2	By *John Massinger pd. lent him on 33 prs of hose*	27	3	11	6
3	By *Tho. Day paid lent him on 80 pieces Gold*	150	100		
6	By *Richard Speed paid Caleb Shuter*	49	2	3	
	By *Proffit & Losse pd. Jane Shepheard*	153		15	6
	By *Wm. Pleydall pd. him*	152		4	
11	By *John Massinger pd. lent him on 30 prs hose*	27	3	5	
	By *Wm. Pleydall pd. him*	152		6	
	By *Jahzeel Speed paid him for drinking money*	154		10	
	By *Edward Dowding paid lent him*	154	120		
			805	15	11½
16	By *Joseph Drew paid him*	154		10	
18	By *John Massinger pd. lent him on 30 paire hose*	155	3	5	
19	By *Proffit & Losse pd. Sam. Jonson for a dozen of Panniers*	153		10	
21	By *Proffit & Losse pd. Anthony Tyler*	153		1	8
24	By *Jahzeel Speed Elizabeth Milner*	154	5		
26	By *Abraham Hill paid him*	131	2		
	By *John Massinger pd. lent him on 33 paire of Hose*	155	3	11	6
	By *Robert Pocock pd. lent him*	149	94		
	By *Jonathan Lamboll pd. Jane Shepheard for a Cask of Butter*	147		18	2½
	By *Proffit & Losse pd. John Warren*	153	1	16	
August 1	By *John Hardiman paid him in part*	80	2		
	By *Wm. Pleydall paid him in part*	152	1		
7	By *Jahzeel Speed paid Elizabeth Milner for severall particulars*	154	2	1	6
9	By *Richard Speed paid John Curtis for schooling*	92		3	6
	By *Proffit & Losse pd. Edward Young*	153	1	2	6
10	By *John Massinger paid lent him on 30 prs stockins*	155	3	5	
	By *Lawrence Washington pd. Tho. Atkins*	132	5		
11	By *Proffit & Losse pd. John Gandy and Edward Reece in full*	153		18	10
	By *John Occoll paid him*	147	1		6
	By *Edward Jones pd. him in part*	25	1	5	
18	By *Tho. Burges and Wm. Stocker lent them on theire bond*	138	100		
	By *John Massinger pd. lent them on 30 paire hose*	155	3	5	
21	By *house in which I live paid Henry Bradly for nailes*	130		13	1

(142)	Bristoll 1687				
	Lands in Clapton (viz) 4 Acres on Oldburie, 7 Acres in the Tynings, the great Mousty, the two little Mousties Adjoyning, and Welby Paddock acre, Two acres adjoyning to my Conncrafts [?], 4 acres adjoyning to that, and 7 acres adjoyning to that, lately purchased of Maurice Lord Fitzharding, Sir John Smith Esq. Gorges Esq. John Piggot, Henry Winter & Katherine his mother	Dr	£	s	d
August 18	To Cash paid to Bethel Walter & Katherine his wife by direction of the said Lord Fitzharding & Edward Gorges the Trustees in part of her portion & in full of my purchase money for said Lands as by theire receit on my deed of purchases endorsed may appeare	139	578		
September 8	To Cash pd. John Long which hee pd. Edward Strode for 3 Reeks of Hay	139	4	8	
21	To Ditto pd. Nath. Haggatt for Wm. Phelps for drawing writings	139	4		
November	To Cash paid Tho. Edwards for the Copies of severall writings he drew for mee	139	2	10	6
	To Nathanael Haggatt for his advice about the purchase of said lands	138	5		
			593	18	6

	Anno 1689				
	Xeries wine 10 Butts imported in the ship Wellcom from Cadiz ½ of which are for the acct. and Risgo of Thomas Day of Bristol Wine cooper	Dr	£	s	d
June 17	To Cash paid Ozziel Browne for assurance of £100 from Cadiz to Bristoll	162	13	1	
	To Samuel Kekewich for theire first cost & charges 3167 Ryals 25 mervidees is 392 7/8 pieces of 8 at 52d the piece of 8 as per his Invoyce received in July 1689 appeares	167	85	16	0
		£	s	d	
	To Cash paid custom bills etc.	78	10	2	
	To Ditto pd. Henry Gibbes towards prisage and averidge	8	00		

28	By Stockins paid John Rudduck	146	3	9	
30	By Horses pd. Stephen Sash for Oates	156		10	
	By Edward Jones paid him in full	25	1	2	
	By John Massinger pd. lent him on 40 paire hose	155	4	6	8
	By Joseph Davis pd. him in full	155	14	16	6
	By Xeries wine ½ of 20 Butts pd. John Shute	134		8	
September 4	By Proffit & Losse pd. Ann Smith	153	1	1	10
7	By Stockins pd. John Perry	146	2	5	10
	By John Massinger pd. lent him on 30 prs hose	155	3	5	
	By Proffit & Losse pd. James Shute	153		8	
12	By Jahzeel Speed paid Marmaduke Bowdler and John Mathew	154	4	1	
15	By Charles King paid him	152	5		
	By Abraham Hill pd. him	131	1		
	By John Massinger pd. lent him on 30 paire of hose	155	3	5	
	By John Hardiman pd. him in part	80	1		
19	By John Earle of Bristoll paid John Aydman for a Westphalia Ham	150		14	2
20	By horses pd. severalls for a Curricomb, cloth, Oates Beanes etc. as per particulars	156		18	10
21	By Joseph Drew formely paid him but omitted to bee charg'd	154	2	5	
	By John Hardiman pd. him in full	80	1	8	
22	By John Massinger pd. lent him on 30 paire of hose	155	3	5	
24	By John Occoll pd. him in full	147	4	5	6
	By Horses paid Abell Edwards	156		17	
			1097	15	6½
	By Ballance carried to that acct.	157	3652	1	10
			4749	17	4[½]

Bristoll 1688					
Lands in Clapton lately purchased		Cr	£	s	d
By Edward Jacob for the after Grasse of the 4 acres in Normead		150		8	
By Estate at Clapton old farme and newly purchased for the purchase money pd. the Trustees per Contra		151	578		
By the charges of Counsell and drawing writings pd. Wm. Phelps, Thomas Edwards and Nathanael Haggatt as per Contra by the particulars carried to that acct.		151	11	10	6
By Proffit & Losse for ballance		164	4		
			593	18	6

	Xeries Wine 10 Butts per Contra are	Cr	£	s	d
September 7	By Cash received at the custom house for returnes on bad wines	168	7	7	3
	By Xeries wines my Half of 10 Butts for ½ of £196 6s 5d the Cost and Charges of the 10 Butts per Contra	170	98	3	2½
	By Thomas Day for his half of £196 6s 5d the Cost & Charges of said ten Butts of Xerie	161	98	3	2½
			203	13	8

	To Ditto paid Philip Freake in full for freight		17	10	*168*	104		2
	To Proffit & Losse for halling etc. port letters 3s 6d Coopers noat 13s			16	6	*164*		16	6
						203	13	8

Anno 1687								

	Adventure 3rd In the ship Dilligence John Seward Master To Cork & Cadiz, & consign'd to Samuel Kekewich merchant in St Marie Port, is debitor to sundry accts for these particulars (viz)		*Dr*	*£*	*s*	*d*
September	To Stockins for one Trunck cont. viz) laden in her 80 dozen being 960 paire fine Bristoll hose at 2s 9d	£ 132 s 00 d 00	*135*			
	44 Doz being 528 paire Wells hose at 1s 8d	44 00 00	*135*			
	To Ditto for Trunck Cord & Matting at	17 00	*135*	176	17	
	To Cash paid Custom etc.		*175*	4	0	10
				180	17	10
	To Profit and Loss, for Ballance		*190 **	28	19	
				209	16	10

Anno 1687								

	Adventure in the ship Greyhound of London Robert Saunders Commander is debitor to sundry accts £47 18s 6d, being the Cost & Charges of one Box of stockins laden in her by Isaac Heming in London for my acct., & goe consigned to Henneach Fetherston merchant in Alicant, cont. (viz)		*Dr*	*£*	*s*	*d*
	To Stockins for these particulars following (viz) 25 dozen is 300 paire fine Bristoll hose at 2s 9d	£ 41 s 05 d	*135*			
	5 dozen is 60 paire at 1s 8d, & the box 3s 6d	5 03 6	*135*			
	To Isaac Heming for custom & all other charges in London	1 10 00	*130*	47	18	6
	To Profit and Loss, for Ballance		*190 **	9	17	1½
				57	15	7½

Anno 1687							

	Samuel Clark of Bristoll Merchant, & Isaac Hort of the same Sugar baker		*Dr*	*£*	*s*	*d*
October 22	To Cash paid lent them on theire bond Oct. 22th 1687 due Aprill 23th 1688		*139*	100		
1688 August 18	To Proffit & Losse for 10 months less 5 daies intrest of £100		*153*	4	18	4
				104	18	4

Anno 1688							

	Edward Chetwine of Bristoll Grocer is		*Dr*	*£*	*s*	*d*
1688 January	To Reisons solis 32 Barrills for 7 Barrills neat 18cwt 3qr 0lb at 22s per Cwt due Aprill 1st		*158*	20	12	6

(143)	**Bristoll 1687**						

	Isaac Heming of London Merchant my Sonne in law is		*Dr*	*£*	*s*	*d*
	To Ballance of his acct. current brought from that acct.		*130*	1253		11
Error	To Samuel Kekewich for cost & charges 1000 pieces of 8 being 1073 pieces of 8 in the Friston as per acct. current and Invoyce of 30 Sept. 1687 the piece of 8 at 52d		*111*	0000		
	To Cash paid John Love by his order		*139*	8	13	3
	To Edward Crofts for money on his bill assign'd on Edward Tayler		*96*	15		
				1276	14	2

Anno 1688/9		Cr	£	s	d
Adventure 3rd in the Dilligence per Contra		Cr	£	s	d
By Samuel Kekewich for the neat proceeds of the Trunck of stockins per Contra 7748 Ryals plate and is 968½ pieces of 8 the piece of 8 at 52d as per his acct. of sales, and his acct. current closed in St Marie Port March 16th 1688/9		148	209	16	10

Anno 1688			Cr	£	s	d
	Adventure in the ship Greyhound per Contra		Cr	£	s	d
October	By Heneage Fetherstone for theire neat proceeds being 256 Ecu 16 sous 2 denier the Liver at 4s 6d as per his acct. of sales Sept. 24th 1688		160	57	15	7½

Anno 1688			Cr	£	s	d
	Samuel Clark & Company per Contra are		Cr	£	s	d
August 18	By Cash recd. of them by the hands of Ozziel Browne		141	100		
	By Ditto received by the same hand in full for intrest		141	4	18	4
				104	18	4

Anno 1689			Cr	£	s	d
	Edward Chetwin per Contra		Cr	£	s	d
July 3	By Cash recd. of him in full		162	20	12	6

Bristoll 1687			Cr	£	s	d
	Isaac Heming per Contra is		Cr	£	s	d
November 5	By Cash recd. of Ed. Martindale Junior for which I valued my bill		139	4	4	11
	By Adventure in the Tygre to Cadiz for premio of assurance of £200		144	2	4	
	By Reisons solis 27 barrills pd. James Deane for freight of them to Bristoll from Lond.		136	2	14	
	By himselfe for Ballance carried to his new acct. underneath		143	1267	11	3
				1276	14	2

Anno 1687					
	Isaac Heming my Sonne in law of London Merchant is	*Dr*	*£*	*s*	*d*
November 12	*To Ballance of his above acct. Currant brought thence*	*143*	*1267*	*11*	*3*
December	*To Plate in sundry ships from Cadiz for 1000 pieces of 8 sould*				
	Wm. Atwill & Comp. 866 oz at 5s 3d¼ per oz	*143*	*228*	*4*	*6*
January	*To JonathanLamboll for money hee recd. of him in London*	*147*	*6*	*7*	
23	*To Cash pd. Dennis Tayler on his bill*	*140*	*4*	*11*	*9*
			1506	*14*	*6*
	To his new acct. current carried to Folio	*152*	*45*	*9*	*1*
			1552	*3*	*7*

Anno 1688								
	Adventure in the Neptune sloope Ketch Dennis Tayler master to Nevis is				*Dr*	*£*	*s*	*d*
May	*To Richard Wasbrow for 20 Boxes Candles cont. 128 dozen & 10 at 3s 10d per doz laden in the said vessell and consign'd to said Tayler for sailes and returnes as per Book of Invoyces*	*£*	*s*	*d*				
		24	*13*	*11*				
	To Ditto for 20 Boxes to put them in at 1s 5d per Box	*01*	*08*	*04*	*50*	*26*	*2*	*3*
	To Cash pd. custom fees, bills hallidge etc.				*141*	*1*	*17*	*3*
						27	*19*	*6*
	To Profit and Loss for Ballance				*190 **	*7*		*2*
						34	*19*	*8*

Anno 1689					
	William Picket of Bristoll Butcher is	*Dr*	*£*	*s*	*d*
	To Cattle two steeres for said steeres sould him by John Hurtnell	*5*	*6*	*5*	

Anno 1687					
	Plate imported on sundry ships from Cadiz in Spaine	*Dr*	*£*	*s*	*d*
	To Ballance of a former acct. brought from that acct. of Credit	*92*	*19*	*8*	*4*
October	*To Samuel Kekewich for cost & charges on 1000 pieces of 8 1073 pieces of 8 in the Friston Capt. Gutteridge, as per acct. current Oct. 21th & Invoyce Sept. 30th 1687 the piece of 8 at 52d*	*111*	*232*	*12*	*8*

	Anno 1687				
	Isaac Heming per Contra is	Cr	£	s	d
November 19	By Cash received of Samuel Spencer on his bill	139	18	4	
	By Plate in sundry ships from Cadiz for freight & other charges on the 1000 pieces of 8 per Contra	143	2	7	
January 28	By Cash recd. of Tho. Edwards for which I valued my bill on him	140	200		
	By Ditto recd. of Abraham Edwards for which I valued my bill on him	140	200		
February 4	By Cash recd. of Zacharie Cornock for which I valued my bill on him	140	15		
	By Ditto recd. of Daniel Guillim for which I valued my bill	140	200		
	By Ditto recd. of Tho. Day on his bill in my favor	140	80	19	2
8	By Cash recd. of Henry Gibbes for which I valued my bill in favor of James Hulbert	140	150		
March 16	By Cash recd. of John Gore for which I valued my bill on him	140	15		
17	By Cash recd. of Tho. Day on his bill on said Day in my favor	140	28	6	10
1688 Aprill 7	By Hugh Strode for my bill on him in favor of said Strode	149	29		1
	By Tho. Strode for my bill on him in favor of Hugh Strode for acct. of said Tho.	136	54		9
	By John Gore recd. of him for which I valued my bill	31	5		
May	By Proffit & Losse for what hee paid for a set of racking tooles	137	2	3	6
	By Ditto pd. for a Silver Taster	137	1	7	
	By Ditto pd. Tho. Dike of Bristoll	137	30		
	By wines of severall sorts bought of severalls for what hee paid for a Pipe Palme wine	149	22		
	By Tho. Day for money hee paid him on my bill	150	100		
	By Ditto for money furnished him by my order in London	150	191	6	
	By Ditto for a foreigne bill hee paid for him for which he valued his bill in my favor	150	206	19	9
	By Proffit & Losse for port of leters to the 29th of May 688 as per his acct.	137		9	6
			1552	3	7

	Anno 1688				
	Adventure in the Neptune per Contra	Cr	£	s	d
January	By Dennis Tayler for the neat proceeds of said Candles being 6997 lb as per his acct. of sales the sugar at 10s per Cwt	11	34	19	8

	Anno 1689				
	Wm. Picket per Contra is	Cr	£	s	d
	By Cash received of him per the hands of John Hurtnell	173	6	5	

	Anno 1687				
	Plate in sundry ships from Cadiz per Contra	Cr	£	s	d
November 26	By Isaac Heming for 1000 pieces of 8 per Contra sould Atwill & Company weight 866 oz at 5s 3d¹/₄ per oz	143	228	4	6
1689 July	By Isaac Heming for the neat proceeds of 12 Loggs of Silver in the Friston weight 2625 oz at 5s 4d¹/₄ per oz sould to Wm. Atwill & Company Merchants in London	152	702	14	8

		£	s	d
To Isaac Heming for freight & other charges on said 1000 pieces of 8	143	2	7	
1688 To Samuel Kekewich 3318 5/8 pieces of 8 the cost and charges				
9 of 12 Loggs of Silver laden in the ship Friston Capt. Gutteridge				
as per his acct. current closed March 16 168 7/8 and bill lading				
and Invoyce appeares the piece of 8 at 52d	148	719		8
To Ditto for 1520 7/8 1/16 pieces of 8 the cost and charges of a				
parcell of Loggs and 812 pieces of 8 ~ pieces of 8 laden in the ship				
Andaluzia Capt. Perriman as per his acct. current closed March				
16 168 8/9 and bill lading and Invoyce the piece of 8 at 52d	148	329	10	8½
To Plate ship'd in the Friston for premio of assurance of £600				
thereon	163	18	2	
To Isaac Heming for premio of assurance of £150 on plate in the				
Andaluzia	152	5	6	
To Ditto for charges on the plate in the Friston and Andaluzia	152	7	11	4
		1333	18	8½

Anno 1687

	Dr	£	s	d
Samuel Kekewich his acct. of Time merchant in St Marie Port in Spaine				
October To *Adventure* in the *Betty* to Cadiz for neat proceeds of 19 doz				
Bristoll, & 9 doz Wells hose hee sent in flota on his hazard to pay				
mee 10½ pieces of 8 for the Bristoll, & 7 pieces of 8 for the Wells				
hose in 16 moneths to commence from the 4th August 1687, or at				
returne of the flota which shall first happen, with £9 per Cent				
Premio as per his leter of that date and his acct. of sales of				
October 14th 1687 may appeare R m				
the piece of 8 at 51d 2289	110	60	16	3¼
To *Adventure* in the *Lumbly Castle* for the value of				
110 dozen Bristoll and 6 dozen Wells hose which				
hee took to himselfe at the same prices, and time of				
payment and all other terms with the foregoing				
parcell in the *Betty*, as per same acct., and same leter				
of same date may appeare, being 1304 pieces of 8				
5/8 17Mervides the piece of 8 at 51d 10437 17	114	277	4	7¾
		338		11

     Bristoll 1687

	Dr	£	s	d
Adventure in the ship *Tygre* Charles Tayler Master to Cadiz is				
November To sundry accts, being the cost and charges of Two Truncks of				
stockins laden in said ship, & consign'd to Samuel Kekewich in				
St Marie Port for sales etc.				
To Stockins for one Trunck cont. (viz) No SC 23				
70 dozen mens Bristoll hose is 840 £ s d				
paire at 2s 9d per paire 115 10 00				
48 dozen mens Wells hose is 576 paire				
at 1s 8d per paire 48 00	135	163	10	
To Ditto for the Trunck Cord & Matting	135		17	
To Simon Clement for custom & other charges hee paid	103	3	15	
To Ditto for one other Trunck No [SM] 24 cont. (viz)				
100 dozen mens Bristoll hose is 1200				
paire at 2s 9d 165 00 00				
12 dozen mens Wells hose is 144 paire				
at 1s 8d per paire 12 00 00				
To Ditto for Trunck Cord & Matting 00 17 00	135	177	17	
To Simon Clement for Custom & other charges hee paid	103	3	10	6
To Isaac Heming for premio of assurance on the 2 Truncks of				
stockins above mention'd for £200	143	2	4	
		351	13	6
To Profit and Loss, for Ballance	190 *	46	6	9¼
		398	00	3¼

By *Ditto for the neat proceeds of 812 pieces of 8 weight 699½ oz and 73 marks 5 oz 4 weight 546½ oz is in all 1245¾ oz charges £3 8s 6d deducted at 5s 3d per oz is*	*152*	323	11	8
		1254	10	10
By *Profit and Loss, for Ballance*	*190 **	79	7	10½
		1333	18	8½

Anno 1688/9				
Samuel Kekewich his acct. of time per Contra By *Samuel Kekewich his acct. current 12726½ Ryals plate which is 1590³/₄16 pieces of 8 made good to my acct. of Credit as per his acct. current closed in St Marie Port March 16th 1688/9 the piece of 8 at 51d the piece*	*Cr*	*£*	*s*	*d*
	148	338		11
		338		11

Bristoll 1690@				
Adventure in the Tigre per Contra		*Cr*	*£*	*s*	*d*
May By *Sam. Kekewich, for the neat proceeds of the Trunck of hose (No [SM] 23) per Contra being 7201 Ryals plate 9 Mer.dees which are 900 1/8 pieces of 8 9 Merd.es (as per Acct of Sales closed in St Marie Port 7th Aprill 1690) and make Sterling at 52d per piece of 8*		*167*	195	00	09
By *Ditto for the neat proceeds of the Trunck of hose (No [SM] 24) per Contra being 7494 Ryals plate 17 Mer.dees being 936 6/8 pieces of 8 17 Merd.es as per ditto Acct Sales making in all at 52d per piece of 8*		*167*	202	19	6¼
			398	00	3¼

	Anno 1687				
	Thomas Tayer of Bristoll Grocer is	Dr	£	s	d
November 7	*To Reisons 65 barrills for 5 barrills neat 13 cwt 0 qr 22lb at 24s per Cwt due Feb. 7th*	145	15	16	8½

	Anno 1687				
	Marie Wasbrow Widow is	Dr	£	s	d
	To Proffit & Losse for 4 hhds delivered her servant	137		12	
February 23	*To Cash paid her in full as per receit*	140	1	16	
			2	8	

	Anno 1687				
	Adventure in the ship Tygre to Cadiz Charles Tayler master consign'd to Simon Clement Supra Cargo is debitor to sundry accts being the Cost & Charges of one Trunck Stockins laden in her – viz.	Dr	£	s	d
November	*To Stockins for 41 doz is 492 paire* £ s d *Bristoll hose at 2s 9d* 67 13 00	135	83	2	
	To Ditto for 15 doz is 180 paire Wells hose at 1s 8d 15 00 00				
	To Ditto for the Cord Trunck and Matting				
	To Simon Clement for custom & other Charges by him disbursed	103	1	16	6
			84	18	6

	Anno 1687				
	Robert Bartly of Bristoll Grocer is	Dr	£	s	d
November 7	*To Reisons solis 65 Barrills for 6 Barrils neat 15 cwt 3qr 14lb at 24s due Feb. 7th*	145	19	1	

	Anno 1687				
	James Fisher of Bristoll Grocer is	Dr	£	s	d
November 7	*To Reisons 65 Barrills for 6 Barrils neat 16 cwt 0 qr 26¾ lb at 24s due Feb. 7th*	145	19	9	8¾
1689 January	*To Reisons 60 Barrills & 120 pieces for 6 Barrills & 12 pieces sould him*	177	45	4	7½
			64	14	4¼

	Anno 1687				
	Thomas Tyler of Bristoll Grocer is	Dr	£	s	d
November 7	*To Reisons 65 Barrills for 6 Barrils neat 16 cwt 0qr 01 lb at 24s due Feb. 7th*	145	19	4	2

(145)	**Bristoll 1687**				
	Barrills 65 Reisons Solis laden in the ship Olive branch Ed. Dowding from Malaga , by Tho. Strode , for acct. in equall 1/3 parts betwixt Hugh Strode of London merchant, the said Tho. Strode and my selfe	Dr	£	s	d
November 8	*To Cash paid first entry and Post entry* £ s d *173 cwt 3qr 20lb* 16 11 11½	139	16	19	9½
	To Ditto paid fees bills & wharfage 00 04 06	139			
	To Ditto spent on the Grocers in theire sales 00 03 04				
	To Ditto pd. weighing them 3 00	139			
December 8	*To Ditto pd. Edward Dowding for freight and averidge* 24 17 00	139			
	To Proffit & Losse abated the Grocers in odd pence 3 3¾	177	25	3	3¾
	To Ditto for my Commission at £2 per Cent	153	4	3	3½
	To Hugh Strode for 1/3 of £162 3s 5d theire neat proceeds 54 01 01½	149			
	To Tho. Strode for his 1/3 of said summe 54 01 02	136			

Anno 1687

		Cr	£	s	d
	Thomas Tayer per Contra is				
March 6	*By Cash received of him*	*140*	15	16	6
	By Profit and Loss for Ballance	*190 **			2½
			15	16	8½

Anno 1687

		Cr	£	s	d
	Marie Wasbrow per Contra				
February	*By Proffit & Losse for her noat for her work done etc. as may appeare*	*137*	2	8	

Anno 1688

		Cr	£	s	d
	Adventure in the ship Tygre per Contra is				
May	*By Simon Clement for 2983½ Ryals plate which is 372 7/8 1/16 6 pieces of 8 the neat proceeds of the Trunck of stockins per Contra as per his acct of sales of Aprill 2d 1688 the piece of 8 at 52d*	*103*	80	16	¾
	By Profit and Loss, for Ballance	*190 **	4	2	5¼
			84	8	6

Anno 1687

		Cr	£	s	d
	Rober Bartly per Contra is				
March 15	*By Cash received of him in full*	*140*	19	1	0

Anno 1687

		Cr	£	s	d
	James Fisher per Contra is				
Marcch 6	*By Cash recd. of him*	*140*	19	9	
1690 June 24	*By Ditto recd. of him per the hands of Edw. Martindale Junior*	*181*	45	4	6
	By Profit and Loss for Ballance	*190 **			10¼
			64	14	4¼

Anno 1687

		Cr	£	s	d
	Thomas Tyler per Contra				
February 25	*By Cash recd. of him*	*140*	19	4	2

Bristoll 1687

		Cr	£	s	d
	Reisons Solis 65 Barrills mention'd for acct. per Contra				
November 7	*By Tho. Tayer for 5 barrills neat 13 cwt 0 qr 22lb at 24s per Cwt to pay for them February 7th*	*144*	15	16	8½
	By John Love for 6 barrills neat 16 Cwt 0 qr 18lb at 24s per Cwt	*55*	19	7	10¼
	By Robert Bartholmew 6 barrills neat 15 Cwt 3qr 14lb at 24s per Cwt	*144*	19	1	0
	By James Fisher 6 barrills neat 16 cwt 0 qr 26¾ lb at 24s per Cwt	*144*	19	9	8¾
	By Tho. Goldney Jnr 6 barrills neat 15 Cwt 2qr 15lb at 24s per Cwt	*136*	18	15	2½
	By Tho. Tyler for 6 barrills neat 16 Cwt 0 qr 1lb at 24s per Cwt	*144*	19	4	2½
	By John Curtis for 6 barrills neat 16 Cwt 0 qr 23½ lb at 24s per Cwt	*145*	19	9	¼
	By Edward Hacket 6 barrills neat 15 cwt 3qr 5½ lb at 24s per Cwt	*145*	18	19	7¼
	By Henry Parsons 6 barrills neat 16 cwt 0qr 24lb at 24s per Cwt	*145*	19	9	1¼

		£	s	d
To Reisons solis my 1/3 of 65 Barrills for my 1/3 of said summe 54 01 01½	149	162	3	5
		208	9	9¾

	Anno 1687				
	Sundry Merchandizes laden in the ship John Edmond Watts Master for Potomack river in Virginea for acct. of Lawrence Washington merchant there and consign'd to himselfe per bill of lading	Dr	£	s	d
October 15	To Cash paid Wm. Sanders for 1½ doz broad & 1 1/2 doz narrow hoes & ½ dozen Axes	139	2	2	
	To Ditto pd. George Popley for 1½ doz plaine shooes at 27s per doz	139	2		6
November 12	To Ditto pd. George White for 83 yards Grey cloth for Garments at 1s 3d per yd	139	5	3	9
	To Ditto pd. Tho. Ridden for 4 horse harnesse	139	2	8	
18	To Ditto pd. John Hardiman making 9 mens & 6 womens suites & a Coate	139	2	10	
December 1	To Ditto pd. Walter Paine for 2 Ruggs & 4 Blankets	139	2	3	
2	To Cash pd. Richard Day for 1½ doz Irish hose	139		18	
6	To Ditto pd. John Gandy for 2 paire of Andirons weight 2 cwt 0qr 1½ lb at 26s per Cwt	139	2	12	4
17	To Cash paid Jane Shepheard for a firkin Butter weight 82lb at 2d½ & 12d over	140		18	
19	To Ditto pd. Custom Fees & bills	140		11	4
24	To Ditto pd. John Matthews for 9 Felts & 1 Castor Hatt	140	2	5	
29	To Cash pd. Fra. Ballard for 11 [m] 10d & 4 [n/m] 6d nailes & baggs [105]	140	2	16	7
January 7	To Ditto pd. Wm. French for 3 Crosscutt sawes 3 Wrists & 3 Files	140	1		9
	To Cash pd. Alexander Doleman for 96¾ yds inn 3 pieces blew Linnin at 6d ¼ per yard	140	2	10	4
	To Proffit & Losse for 1 hhd 1 Barrill, 1 Kilderkin & package	137		8	
	To Ditto for porteridge lyteridge and searchers fees	137		7	
	To Ditto for hooing a firkin of Butter	137			6
	To Ditto for my Commission at £3 per Cent	137		18	2
			31	13	3

	Anno 1687				
	John Curtis of Bristoll Grocer is	Dr	£	s	d
November 7	To Reisons 65 Barrills for 6 barrills neat 16 cwt 0 qr 23½ lb at 24s due Feb. 7th	145	19	9	

	Anno 1687				
	Edward Hacket of Bristoll Grocer is	Dr	£	s	d
November 7	To Reisons 65 Barrills for 6 barrills neat 15 cwt 3qr 5½ lb at 24s due Feb. 7th	145	18	19	2
1689 Jan..	To Reisons 60 Barrills & 120 pieces for 8 Barrills & 16 pieces sould him at 40s & 30s	177	59	11	4¾
			78	10	6¾

	Anno 1687				
	Henry Parsons of Bristoll Grocer is	Dr	£	s	d
November 7	To Reisons 65 Barrills for 6 barrills neat 16 cwt 0 qr 24 lb at 24s due Feb. 7th	145	19	9	1½
February 24	To Cash pd. him recd. of Tho. Walden on his bill more then the above summe	140	7	1	
1689 Jan..	To Reisons 60 Barrills & 120 pieces for 8 Barrills & 16 pieces sould him	177	60	1	8
1690 April	To John Bradway for money received of him per my order	70	40		
			126	11	9½

		£	s	d
By *Elizabeth Beaton 6 barrills neat 16 cwt 0 qr 17lb at 24s per Cwt*	145	19	7	7½
By *Tho. Jordan 6 barrills neat 16 cwt 0 qr 26¾ lb at 24s per Cwt*	95	19	9	8¾
		208	9	9¾

Anno 1687				
Merchandizes in the ship John per Contra	Cr	£	s	d
By *Lawrence Washington his acct. current for the cost and charges of the Goods paricularly mentioned per Contra*	132	31	13	3

Anno 1687				
John Curtis per Contra is	Cr	£	s	d
March 9 By *Cash received of him in full*	140	19	9	

Anno 1687				
Edward Hacket per Contra is	Cr	£	s	d
February 24 By *Cash recd. of him*	140	18	19	
1690 July 4 By *Ditto recd. of him*	181	59	11	
		78	10	
By *Profit and Loss for Ballance*	190 *			6¾
		78	10	6¾

Anno 1687				
Henry Parsons per Contra	Cr	£	s	d
February 24 By *Cash recd. of Tho. Walden on his Bill due to William Provis*	140	26	10	
1690 April By *Isaac Heming for his bill on Paris Sloughter for £40 in my favour assigned to him*	177	40		
July By *Tho. Goldney Junior for his bill on said Goldney in my favour*	176	60		
By *Profiit and Loss, for Ballance*	190 *		1	9½
		126	11	9½

	Anno 1687				
	Elizabeth Beaton of Bristoll Grocer is	Dr	£	s	d
November 7	To Reisons 65 Barrills for 6 barrills neat 16 cwt 0 qr 17lb at				
	24s due Feb. 7th	145	19	7	7½

	Anno 1688				
	John Rudduck of — in the County of Somerset Stocking maker	Dr	£	s	d
March 29	To Cash pd. lent him on 96 paire of stockins deposited as per his				
	noat	140	4		

(146)	**Bristoll 1687**							
	Worsted Stockins bought of severalls				Dr	£	s	d
		paire	s	d				
December 9	To Cash paid John Perrie in part for	49	2	3				
		41	2	1½	139	5		
13	To Ditto paid John Massinger for	44	2	6	140	5	10	
	To Ditto paid Tho. Hill for John							
	Rudduck for	42	2	2½	140	4	12	9
	To Ditto pd. Tho. Hill for Jona. Abram							
	for	40	2	3½	140	4	11	8
14	To Ditto pd. Joseph George for	23		14½	140	1	7	9½
15	To Ditto pd. Tho. Hill for Tho.							
	Browning for	163	1	3	140	10	3	9
17	To Ditto pd. John Perrie in full for the 90 paire first above							
	mentioned				140	4	17	4½
23	To Cash pd. John Massinger for	39	2	6	140	4	17	6
24	To Cash pd. Tho. Hill for Henry							
	Britten for	98	2	2	140	10	12	4
	To Ditto pd. Fra. Rottenburie in full for hot pressing to this day				140		11	6
26	To Ditto pd. Joseph White for	78	2	5	140	9	8	6
January 5	To Ditto pd. John Massinger for	40	2	6	140	5		
7	To Ditto pd. Jonathan Abram for	42	2	3	140	4	14	6
11	To Cash pd. John Rudduck for	42	2	2	140	4	11	
	To Ditto pd. Henry Britten for	40	2	2	140	4	6	8
14	To Ditto pd. John Massinger for	37	2	6	140	4	12	6
20	To Cash pd. John Massinger for	37	2	6	140	4	12	6
	To Ditto pd. Tho. Hill for Jonathan							
	Abram for	42	2	3	140	4	14	6
21	To Ditto pd. John Perrie for	60	2	2	140	6	10	
24	To Ditto pd. Joseph White for	40	2	5	140	4	16	8
27	To Cash pd. John Massinger for	41	2	6	140	5	2	6
28	To Ditto pd. John Perry for	80	2	2	140	8	13	4
February 4	To Ditto paid Tho. Hill for John							
	Rudduck for	77	2	2	140	8	6	10
9	To Ditto pd. John Massinger for	36	2	6	140	4	10	
	To Cash pd. Joseph White for Pearles	35	2	5	140	4	4	7
18	To Cash pd. John Massinger for	41	2	6	140	5	2	6
23	To Ditto pd. Tho. Hill for Jona.							
	Abram for	44	2	3	140	4	19	
24	To Ditto pd. John Massinger for	34	2	5	140	4	2	2
29	To Ditto pd. John Rudduck for	62	2	1½	140	6	11	6
March 3	To Ditto pd. John Massinger for	32	2	5	140	3	17	4
7	To Cash pd. Tho. Hill for John							
	Lukins for	40	2	1	140	4	3	4
	To Ditto pd. Joseph White for	50	2	5	140	6		10
9	To Ditto pd. John Massinger for	32	2	5	140	3	17	4
10	To Ditto pd. Anthony Palmer for	43	2	3	140	4	16	6
13	To Ditto pd. Edward Iffe in full for hot pressing				140		17	8½

	Anno 1688				
	Elizabeth Beaton per Contra is	*Cr*	*£*	*s*	*d*
March 29	By Cash recd. of Beniamin Rolston by her order in part	*140*	10		
Aprill 5	By Cash recd. of her in full	*140*	9	7	
			19	7	
	By Profiit and Loss, for Ballance	*190 **			7½
			19	7	7½

	Anno 1688				
	John Rudduck per Contra is	*Cr*	*£*	*s*	*d*
May 16	By Cash recd. of himselfe	*141*	4		

	Bristoll 1687				
	Worsted Stockins per Contra are	*Cr*	*£*	*s*	*d*
December 8	By Ballance brought from that acct.	*135*	970	16	7¾
1688 August	By Adventure in the ship Ruth of London John Archer Master for one Trunck cont. 1200 paire of Bristoll, and 60 paire of Wells hose consigned to Heneage Fetherston merchant in Alicant the Bristoll hose at 2s 8d & the Wells at 1s 8d	*155*	165	17	
	By Adventure in the Olive branch to Malaga consign'd to Edward Dowding for a trunck cont. 480 paire Bristoll hose at 2s 8d & 132 paire Wells at 1s 8d	*158*	89	19	
	By Ditto for 1 Trunck cont. 360 paire Bristoll hose at 2s 9d and 264 paire Wells hose at 1s 9d consign'd to Tho. Strode merchant there, with the Trunck etc.	*158*	73	2	6
January	By Adventure in the London merchant Roger Drew Master to Cadiz, for one Trunck cont. 240 paire Bristoll sadds, 420 prs Bristoll fancies at 2s 8d 300 paire finest Wells fancies at 1s 10d, 240 ordinary fancy colours, and 120 prs ordinary sadds at 1s 8d with the Trunck cord & matting consign'd to Samuel Kekewich merchant in St Marie Port	*161*	146	7	
			1446	2	1¾

Date	Description							
20	To Cash pd. Jonathan Abram for	61	2	3	*140*	6	17	3
	To Cash pd. John Massinger for	33	2	5	*140*	3	19	9
21	To Ditto pd. Tho. Hill for Henry Britten for	61	2	1½	*140*	6	9	7½
23	To Cash pd. Elizabeth Webb for a Trunck				*140*		13	
24	To Ditto pd. Joseph White for	43	2	5	*140*	5	3	11
1688 Aprill 2	To Ditto pd. Jonathan Abram for	42	2	2	*140*	4	11	
7	To Ditto pd. Joseph White for	45	2	5	*140*	5	8	9
June 1	To Cash pd. Robert Webb for a Trunck				*141 **		13	
August 28	To Cash paid John Rudduck for	33	2	1	*141*	3	9	
						218	2	3
September 7	To Cash pd. John Perrie for	22	2	1	*141*	2	5	10
October 4	To Cash pd. John Lukins for	57	2	1	*157*	5	18	9
	To Ditto pd. Tho. Hill for James George for	127	1	1	*157*	6	17	7
13	To Ditto pd. Tho. Hill for John Ashman for	69	1	5	*157*	4	17	9
22	To Ditto pd. Tho. Hill for John Ashman for	112	1	5	*157*	7	18	8
November 1	To Cash pd. John Ashman for	175	1	4	*157*	11	13	4
2	To Ditto pd. John Perrie for	92	2	1	*157*	9	11	8
3	To Ditto pd. Nath. Pinny for halfe a dozen of Inkle				*157*		6	6
16	To Ditto pd. Edward Iffe for hotpressing to this day				*157*		19	
17	To Cash pd. Fra. Rottenburie in full for hotpressing				*157*		11	4
	To Ditto pd. John Lewkins for	37	2	1	*157*	3	17	1
20	To Ditto pd. Tho. Hill for John Perrry for	25	2		*157*	2	10	
21	To Ditto pd. Tho. Hill for John Day for	16	2		*157*	1	12	
December 7	To Cash pd. John Perry for	24	2	1	*157*	2	10	
	To Ditto pd. John Lukins for	113	2	1	*157*	11	15	
11	To Ditto pd. Joseph George for	115	1	1	*157*	6	4	7
	To Ditto pd. Robert Webb for a Trunck				*157*		13	
12	To Ditto pd. John Perry for	56	2	1	*157*	5	17	1
14	To Cash pd. Tho. Hill for Wm. Thiery for	46	2		*157*	4	12	
January 5	To Cash pd. Joseph George for	150	1	1	*157*	8	2	6
	To Ditto pd. John Perry for	72	1	1	*157*	7	18	4
7	To Cash pd. Wm. Merchant for	193	1	11	*157*	18	9	11
18	To Cash pd. Joseph George for	151	1	1	*157*	8	3	7
	To Ditto pd. John Perrie for	36	2	1	*157*	3	15	
22	To Ditto pd. Tho. Hill for Wm. Thiery for	49	1	11½	*157*	4	16	
	To Ditto pd. John Ashman for	348	1	3	*157*	21	15	
30	To Cash pd. Joseph George for	109	1	1	*157*	5	18	1
February 1	To Ditto pd. Francis Rottenbury for hot pressing				*157*		9	4½
	To Cash pd. John Perry for	31	2	1	*157*	3	4	7
6	To Ditto pd. Edward Iffe in part for hot pressing				*157*	1	2	6
8	To Ditto pd. Tho. Hill for John Ashman for	231	1	3	*162*	14	18	9
	To Ditto pd. Tho. Hill for	76	1	2	*162*	4	8	8
21	To Cash pd. Robert Webb for a Trunck				*162*		12	
22	To Ditto pd. John Perrie for	19	2	1	*162*	1	19	7
	To Ditto pd. Tho. Walden for one dozen of Inkle				*162*		6	6
25	To Cash pd. John Day for	11	1	11	*162*	1	1	1
	To Ditto pd. Tho. Hill for	12	2		*162*	1	4	
March 9	To Ditto pd. John Perrie for	28	2	1	*162*	2	18	4
15	To Cash pd. John Perrie for	83	2	1	*162*	8	12	11
	To Ditto pd. John Day for	26	2		*162*	2	12	
	To Ditto pd. Tho. Hill for John Homan for	104	1	3	*162*	6	10	

	To Ditto pd. Tho. Hill for Richd. Foster for		16	2	162	1	12
17	To Cash pd. Tho. Hill for Wm. Thiery for		69	2	162	6	18
					446	2	1½
	To ballance carried to that acct.				165	1000		¼
					1446	2	1¾

---

(147)   **Bristoll 1687**

	John Ockell of Bristoll Groome is	Dr	£	s	d
December 13	To Cash paid him for keeping my Bay mare to the 6th of Dec. 1687	140		9	
1688 Aprill 9	To Cash paid him in part	140	4		
June 2	To Cash paid him in full to 24th of May	141 *	2	8	6
August 11	To Cash paid him in full to 8th of August	141	1		6
September 24	To Cash paid him in full	141	4	5	6
			12	3	6

Anno 1688

	Beniamin Cole of Reading in the County of Birks Silkweaver is	Dr	£	s	d
	To Jonathan Lamboll for money hee received of him out of my rents in Reading	147	12		
1689 March	To Isaac Heming, Received of him on my Bill in his favour	177	8		
			20		

Anno 1687

	Richard Towne of Bristoll Cleark of Backhall is	Dr	£	s	d
December 23	To Cash pd. him for ¼ yeares Custom house presentments ending Dec. 25th 1687	140		2	6
1688 March 27	To Cash pd. him for ¼ yeares Presentments ending March 25th 1688	140		2	6
June 28	To Cash pd. him for ¼ yeares Presentments ending June 24th 1688	141		2	6
1689 Aprill 5	To Cash pd. him for ¾ yeares Custom house Presentments ending March 25th 1689	162		7	6
July 29	To Cash pd. for ¼ yeares presentments ending June 24th 89	168		2	6
October 4	To Cash paid him in full for ¼ ending Sept. 29th 1689	168		2	6
			1		

Anno 1688

	Thomas Hardy of Litton in the county of Dorset Yeoman & Schoolmaster	Dr	£	s	d
March 28	To Cash paid lent him on his bill on the score of Charity	140	10		

Anno 1687

	Tobacco 4 hhds imported in the ship Comfort Wm. Brisoe Master from Potomack river in Virginea for acct. of Lawrence Washington		£	s	d	Dr	£	s	d
July	To Cash pd. custom fees & bills for 1675lb		31	00	10				
	To Ditto pd. Abraham Hook freight, averidge & Country duties		8	01	00	140			
	To Ditto pd. weighing & portridge		00	01	00				
	To Proffit & Losse for intrest of money pd. at Custom house		01	11	08				
	To Ditto for cooperidge and halling		00	5	00				
	To Ditto for 20 Weeks Celleridge		00	10	00	137			
	To my Commission at £2½ per Cent		01	02	02		42	11	8
	To Lawrence Washington his acct. current for theire neat proceeds					132	1	15	7
							44	7	3

Bristoll 1688

		Cr	£	s	d
John Ockoll per Contra is					
By sundry accts for a Reeke of hay 50s for keeping my two mares		153			
to 17th of Sept. 1688 and for a mare Come etc. as per particulars		156	4	5	6
By Profit and Loss for keeping my horses		190 *	7	18	
			12	3	6

Anno 1688

		Cr	£	s	d
	Beniamin Cole per Contra is				
July 30	By money in Cash recd. of him for which I gave him my noat on Jonathan Lamboll	141	12		
1689 Feb. 3	By Cash recd. of him for which I gave him my bill on Isaac Heming	173	8		
			20		

Anno 1689

	Cr	£	s	d
Richard Towne per Contra				
By Proffit & Losse for Presentments in Custom house 1½ yeare ending March 25th 1689	164		15	
By Ditto for ½ a year's presentments	190 *		5	
		1		

Anno 1690@

	Cr	£	s	d
Thomas Hardy per Contra is	194 *	10		
By Acct. of Ballances, for Ballance				

Anno 1687

		Cr	£	s	d
	Tobacco 4 hhds for acct. Lawrence Washington per Contra				
December 30	By Tho. Day Soapmaker for the 4 hhds weight neat 1638lb at 6d½ per lb is	94	44	7	3

		Dr	£	s	d
	Anno 1687				
	Jonathan Lamboll of Reading Maultster my Bro. in law is				
December 25	To ballance of hogsheadis acct. current brought from that acct.	131	3	12	9
January	To Paul Moone received of John Cable in Reading on said Moone's bill	136	6		
	To proffit & Losse for the 7s per Contra, which afterwards Paul Moone paid	137		7	
1688 March 27	To Ditto for ½ yeares intrest of £450 due 25th March 1688	137	11	5	
	To Howses in Reading for ¼ yeares rent due 25th Ditto	129	11	3	6
June 24	To Ditto for ¼ yeares rent for said Houses ending June 24th 1688	129	11	3	6
	To his acct. on mortgage ¼ yeares intrest of £450 due June 24th 1688	109	5	12	6
July 25	To Cash pd. Jane Shepheard for a Cask of Butter sent to Reading	141		18	2½
September	To Cash for ½ a Guinny return'd to him being suspicious	157		10	9
January	To Cash paid lent him	157	8		
	To James Freeman for powder, Pills & other Physick as per noat	21		10	6
1689	To Richard Langsworth for a paire of wax'd leather shooes	163		4	6
Sept. 2	To Isaac Heming for money hee paid John Wilmer at his request to helpe pay his composition money, as per receit	152	116		
	To Nathanael Haggatt for his advice at severall times about his buisness	148	2		
	To Cash paid Philip Higgenbotton for his dyet 34 Weeks	168	8	10	
November 4	To Ditto pd. lent him on his noat	168	1	15	
	To Cash pd. Abra. Hills expences to Reading	168		12	
	To his acct. of money on Mortgage for 1 yeares intrest £450, ending June 24th 89	109	22	10	
	To Ditto for ½ yeares intrest due December 25th 1689	109	11	5	
	To Ditto for 1 months intrest of £450 fromDec. 25th 1689 to Jan. 25th 1689	109	1	17	6
	To his Acct. of Mortgage for Ballance of the Acct.	109	450		
			673	17	8½
	To Profit and Loss, for Ballance	191 *	3	11	3½
			677	9	

(148)	**Bristoll 1688/9**		Dr	£	s	d
	Samuel Kekewich merchant residing in St Marie Port as a Factor in Spaine to as acct. current is		Dr			
October 21	To ballance of his former acct. current closed in St Marie Port October 21th 1687 as by the same may appeare 703 7/8 pieces of 8 at 51d	R m	111	149	11	6
		5631				
March Error	To Proffit & Losse for 10 pieces of 8 hee received of Simon Clement per his own leter					
	To Adventure the 3rd in the Sevilia merchant for the neat proceeds of one Trunck of stockins in her amounting to 1956½ pieces of 8 the piece of 8 at 52d as per his acct. sales & acct. current closed March 16th 8 8/9	9252	124	250	11	6
	To Adventure 2d in the Dilligence for the neat proceeds of one Trunck of stockins in her amounting to 1065¾ pieces of 8 the piece of 8 at 52d as per his acct. of sales and acct. current closed March 16th 1688/9	8526 17	124	230	18	6
	To Xeries wine 23 Butts for 10 pieces of 8 hee recd. of Simon Clement allowed mee on my freight in the Tygre, as per acct. March 16th 1688/9 the piece of 8 at 52d	80	150	2	3	4

	Anno 1687				
	Jonathan Lamboll per Contra is	Cr	£	s	d
January	By Isaac Heming for money hee paid said Heming in London	143	6	7	
1688 July 25	By Cash recd. of him	141 *	4		
	By Isaac Heming for money pd. him in London out of my rents	152	10		
	By Beniamin Cole for money hee pd. out of my rents of my houses in Fryer Streat	147	12		
October 6	By Cash recd. of him	157	5		
	By Proffit & Losse for the money charg'd per Contra for Abra. Hills expences to Reading	164		12	
1689 May	By Isaac Heming for money recd. of Edw. Clarke and John Miles	177	639	10	
			677	9	

Bristoll 1688				Cr	£	s	d
Aprill	By Scarbrow Chapman for 360 pieces of 8 on Simon Clements bill furnished Robert Wilmot at 52d the piece of 8 assign'd per said Wilmot in my favor, value of Sam. Kekewich	R	m				
		2880		132	78		
	By Michael White for £220 pieces of 8 on Simon Clements bill furnished Rob. Wilmot at 52d	1760		132	47	13	4
	By Charles Stubbs for 200 pieces of 8 on Simon Clements bill furnished Rob. Wilmot at 52d	1600		133	43	6	8
	By Michael Pope for 160 pieces of 8 on Simon Clements bill furnished R. Wilmot at 52d	1280		48	34	13	4
	By Richard Day for 100 pieces of 8 on Sim Clements bill furnished Robt. Wilmot at 52d	800		136	21	13	4
May	By Xeries wine 23 Butts for 675 1/8 1/16 pieces of 8 the cost of 17 Butts in the Tygre the piece of 8 at 52d	5401		150	146	9	1¾
	By Adventure 3rd in the Civilia	0	17				
1688/9	By Proffit & Losse for 12 3/4 pieces of 8 charges of commission etc. on the bills of Exchange abovementioned, as per his acct. current closed March 16th 1688/9 the piece of 8 at 52d	99		164	2	13	7½

To *Adventure 3rd in the Dilligence for the neat proceeds of one Trunck of hose* 968½ *pieces of 8 the piece of 8 at 52d as per his acct. of sales and his acct. current closed March 16th 1688/9*	7748		142	209	16	10
To *Adventure in the Citie of Cadiz for the neat proceeds of one Trunck of hose* 1071 5/8 *pieces of 8 at 52d the piece of 8 as per his acct. of sales and acct. current closed March 16th 1688/9*	8573		122	232	4	8
To *his acct. of time for 2 parcells of stockins hee tooke to him selfe by agreement, made good to my acct. of Credit, as per his acct. Current closed in St Marie Port March 16th 1688/9 being* 1590¾ *pieces of 8 the piece of 8 at 51d*	12726	17	143	338		11
	52537			1413	7	3
To *Proffit and Losse for the ballance of the acct. Sterling which is occasion'd only by the different estimates on the piece of 8*			164	9	13	7¼
				1423		10¼

Anno 1687				
Nathanael Haggatt Counseler at Law in Bristoll	Dr	£	s	d

			£	s	d
November 9	To *Ballance of his acct. Current lent him on a Mortgage of severall lands in Mark & in Bristoll as by the Writings Wm. more particularly appeare*	138	320		
1688 May 9	To *Proffit & Losse for* ½ *yeares intrest of* £320 *due May 9th 1688*	137	9	12	
November 9	To *Ditto for* ½ *yeares intrest due November 9th 1688*	153	9	12	
1689 May 9	To *Ditto for* ½ *yeares intrest due May 9th 1689*	164	9	12	
November 9	To *Ditto for* ½ *yeares intrest due November 9th 1689*	164	9	12	
Oct.	To *Ditto for* ¾ *year's intrest ending August 9th 1690*	180	14	8	
			372	16	

Anno 1687				
John Blackwell of Bristoll Vintner is per Contra	Dr	£	s	d

			£	s	d
February 23	To *Cash paid lent him on his bill payable on demand*	140	50		
1688 May 24	To *Cash paid him in full of all money due from my selfe*	141	32		
October 10	To *Cash paid him in full*	157 *	29	10	
December	To *french wines 3 hhds etc. for a hogshead of white wine sould him*	151	8	5	
1689 July 18	To *Cash pd. him in full as per his receit*	168	4	1	
			123	16	

(149)   **Bristoll Anno 1687**

			£	s	d
John Gore of Bristoll Grasier, & John Hurtnell of the same Citie merchant		Dr	£	s	d
To *Proffit & Losse for Cattle and hay sould them at Clapton due on theire bond July 25th 1683 as per bond appeareth*		137	127		
To *Ditto for one yeares intrest due July 25th 1684*		137	7	12	5

By *Plate imported in sundry ships from Cadiz for 3318 5/8 pieces of 8 the cost and charge of 12 Loggs of Silver laden in the Friston Capt. Gutteridge as per his acct. current closed March 16th 1688/9 and Invoyce the piece of 8 at 52d*	26549		143	719		8½
By *Ditto for 1520 7/8 1/16ps of 8 the cost and charge of Loggs of Silver and pieces of 8 laden in the Andaluzia Capt. Perriman as per his acct. current closed March 16th 1688/9 and Invoyce may appeare the piece of 8 at 52d*	12167	17	143	329	10	8½
	52537			1423		10¼

	Anno 1688				
	Nathanael Haggatt per Contra is	*Cr*	*£*	*s*	*d*
May 16	By *Cash recd. of him for ½ yeares intrest of £320 ending May 10th 1688*	141	9	12	
1689	By *Jonathan Lamboll for his advice about his buisnesse in Reading*	147	2		
			11	12	
	By *Acct. of Ballances, for Ballance*	194 *	361	4	
			372	16	

	Anno 1687				
	John Blackwell his acct. with John Earle of Bristoll	*Cr*	*£*	*s*	*d*
February 23	By *Ballance resting due to him from the Earle of Bristoll*	132	3	17	
1688 Aprill 2	By *Cash recd. of him*	140	50		
11	By *John Earle of Bristoll for 13 Gall. Xerie and the Rundlet*	150	4		6
May 11	By *Ditto for 4 Rundlets cont. 51 Gallons of Xerie*	150	15	11	6½
	By *Tho. Day for 3 1/8 Gall. Canary at 6s*	150		18	9
	By *french wine 3 hhds etc. for 3 Tierces Claret & 1 hogshead white wine at*	151	30		
	By *Proffit & Losse for severall small parcells of wine at severall times*	137	1	1	3
July 2	By *Richard Hawksworth for 3 doz bottles Xerie, the bottles, Panniers & Covers per note*	152	3	1	6
Sepember 19	By *the Lady Ann Powlet for 2 doz Xerie the Panniers and cover*	155	2	1	
	By *Proffit & Losse for severall small parcells of wine at severall times*	153		18	5½
October 12	By *John Earle of Bristol for1 Rundllet cont. 13 Gall. 2qt Gallons Xerie at 6s*	150	4	1	
	By *Proffit & Losse for a hogshead white wine of him*	164	8	5	
			123	16	

	Bristoll 1688				
	John Gore & John Hurtnell per Contra	*Cr*	*£*	*s*	*d*
November 17	By *Cash recd. of John Gore in part*	157	48	13	6
	By *Acct. of Ballances, for Ballance*	194 *	133	11	4
			182	4	10

				s	d
	To Ditto for one yeares intrest due July 25th 1685	*137*	7	12	5
	To Ditto for one yeares intrest due July 25th 1686	*137*	7	12	5
	To Ditto for one yeares intrest due July 25th 1687	*137*	7	12	5
1689 Jan	To Ditto for 2½ years intrest due Jan. 25th 1689	*164*	19		10
1690 Oct.	To Ditto for ¾ year's intrest due Oct. 25th 1690	*180*	5	14	4
			182	4	10

				s	d
	Anno 1687/8				
	Reisons Solis my 1/3 of 65 Barrills in partnership with Hugh Strode of London & Thomas Strode of Malaga merchants	Dr	£	s	d
	To Thomas Strode for the value of 2720 Ryals Velloone 9 merridees and is 248 pieces of 8 9 merridees the cost & charges of my said 1/3 part in Malaga, the piece of 8 at 15 Ryals Velloonne, valued at 51d½ the piece of 8 as per his acct. in Invoyce	*136*	53	4	5
	To Profit and Loss, for Ballance	*191 **		16	8½
			54	1	1½

				s	d
	Anno 1687				
	Hugh Strode of London merchant is	Dr	£	s	d
December	To Reisons 1 small Cask sent to Dunraven Castle per his order for its cost & charge	*136*	1		
	To Tho. Strode for his bill drawne on Hugh Strode in my favor for ballance	*136*	24		8
1688 Aprill 7	To Isaac Heming for money for which I valued my bill on said Heming	*143*	29		1½
	To Profit and Loss, for Ballance	*191 **			4
			54	1	1½

				s	d
	Anno 1687				
	Thomas Day of Bristoll Wine Cooper is	Dr	£	s	d
	To Proffit & Losse for ½ cost & charges of 4 Butts Malaga in partnership	*137*	51	5	3
	To Ditto for ½ of 12s pd. celleridge on 8 Butts wine in partnership	*137*		6	
	To Wines my ½ of 20 Butts for ballance of the acct. of said wines	*134*	73		
			124	11	3

				s	d
	Anno 1688				
	Robert Pocock of Reading in the County of Berks Woollen draper	Dr	£	s	d
July 26	To Cash paid lent him on his noat	*141*	94		
1689 January 27	To Cash paid Robert Bult per his order as per his own receit	*173*	40		
			134		

				s	d
	Anno 1687				
	Wines bought of severall & of severall sorts	Dr	£	s	d
February18	To John Blackwell for 1 Pipe of Canary bought of him at	*132*	29		
19	To Tho. Day Soapmaker for 2 Butts Malaga bought of him at £23 per Butt	*94*	46		
	To Cash pd. cooperidge & halling 2 Pipes Canarie	*140*		2	4
1688 Aprill 2	To Ditto pd. John Ford for 7 Gallons milk to whiten a Butt of Malaga	*140*		2	
	To Charles Stubbs for 1 Pipe of Canarie bought of him at	*133*	28	10	

Anno 1688				
Reisons Solis my 1/3 part etc.	*Cr*	*£*	*s*	*d*
By Reisons solis 65 Barrills in partnership for my 1/3 of £162				
3s 5d theire neat proceeds as may appeare	*145*	54	1	1½

Anno 1688				
	Cr	*£*	*s*	*d*
By Reisons solis 65 Barrills in partnership with Tho. Strode				
himselfe & mee for 1/3 of £162 3s 5d theire neat proceeds as				
may appeare	*145*	54	1	1½

Anno 1687				
Thomas Day per Contra is	*Cr*	*£*	*s*	*d*
By ballance of his former acct. current brought from that acct.	*123*	12	18	9
By Xeries wine 2 Qtr Cask for 1½ Gall. Malaga & one				
Gallon Rhenish wine	*133*		10	6
By Proffit & Losse for ½ of £90 the proceeds of 4 Butts of				
Malaga	*137*	45		
By ½ 20 Butts for my part of after charges, which with money				
already charg'd to his Credit in folio (123) of this book, is in full				
for my ½ of all his disbursments on 20 Butts of Xeries in				
partnership betwixt us the whole of the disbursements £270 14s				
10d½	*134*	34	18	11
By my ½ 20 Butts Xerie for ½ of 11s after charges on said 20				
Butts	*137*		5	6
By Cash received of him for Ballance	*140*	30	17	7
		124	11	3

Anno 1688					
	Robert Pocock per Contra	*Cr*	*£*	*s*	*d*
July 28	*By Cash recd. of Godfry Harcourt on a bond left in my custody*	*141*	94		
1689 Dec. 28	*By Cash recd. of Stephen Wellsted by the hands of Katherine*				
	Bisse of Wells	*173*	40		
			134		

Anno 1688				
Wines bought of severalls per Contra	*Cr*	*£*	*s*	*d*
By Xeries wines 23 Butts for the cost & charges of the wine per				
Contra carried to that acct. of debt to make but one acct. of all				
my Xeries	*150*	280	9	9½

			£	s	d
	To Isaac Heming for what hee paid for 1 Pipe of Palme wine	143	22		
	To Ditto paid charges on a parcell of wines part mine part Tho.				
	Day's	152	3	5	6
	To Isaac Heming for a Butt of Malaga hee paid for	152	23		
	To Tho. Day for ½ cost of 12 Butts of Xerie bought in London	150	124	10	
	To Ditto for ½ charges on said wine in London and here	150	3	19	11½
			280	9	9½

Anno 1689					
	John Clarke of Bristoll Junior Wine Cooper	Dr	£	s	d
March 4	To Xeries wine 23 Butts for 1 Butt sould him payable Aprill 24th	169	31		

(150)   **Bristoll 1688**

			£	s	d
	John Earle of Bristoll is	Dr	£	s	d
Aprill	To Ballance of his former acct. current for 2 parcells wine &				
	one of Vinegar	132	9	1	
11	To John Blackwell & Proffit & Losse for 13 Gall. Xerie, the	137,			
	Rundlet etc. sent per order per Es. White	148	4		10
May 11	To Ditto for 4 Rundlets cont. 51 Gall. Xerie, & to Proffit &	148,			
	Losse 7½ portridge	137	15	12	2
	To sundry accts for 6 Panniers cont. 10 doz Claret, 2 doz	151,			
	whitewine bottles Panniers and covers, as per particulars	153	7	17	
September 19	To sundry accts for 2 Pannier cont. 2 doz Claret 1 doz	151,			
	whitewine & bottles & Panniers & per white	153	2	1	
	To Cash pd. John Aydman for a Westphalia Ham weight				
	17lb at 10d for his Countesse	141		14	2
October 12	To John Blackwell for a Rundlet of Xerie cont. — Gallons	148	4	1	
	To sundry accts for 4 doz bottles of Claret the bottles &	151,			
	Pannier etc.	153	2	10	6
December 19	To sundry accts for 2 Rundlets Xerie cont. 26 Gall. wiith	150,			
	cooperidge, portridge etc.	153	7	17	
February	To sundry accts for 2 Rundlets cont. 24 3/8 Gall. sent to	150,			
	Lond. & 2 qt. bottles to Sherborne & the bottles	153	7	18	3
March 22	To sundry accts for 10 doz Claret, bottles, Panniers etc.	160,			
		164	6	10	10
1689 June 15	To sundry accts for 4 doz bottles Xerie, bottles Panniers etc.	150,			
	sent to Lond. per Mooreman	164	4	2	6
August 28	To sundry accts for 2 Rundlets cont. 25 5/8 Gall. Xerie at 6s	169,			
	per Gall. & 9d charges	164	7	14	6
31	To sundry accts for 6 doz bottles White wine, bottles, Panniers	160,			
	etc.	164	4	7	8
January 14	To sundry accts for 2 Rundlets cont. 25½ Gall. Xerie sent	169,			
	him per Esaw White	164	7	14	5
February 18	To sundry accts for the cost & charges of 2 Rundlets cont.	169,			
	24¾ Gall. Xerie, with the 2 Rundlets etc. sent to London by	164,			
	Wm. Tarrants Waggon as per particulars in Journall	175	7	15	10
1690 July 4	To sundry accts for the Cost and charges of 1 Rundlett and 2	56,			
	qts bottle Xerie sent him	180	4	11	8
			104	10	4

Anno 1688					
	Xeries Wines 23 Butts, viz. 17 laden per Samuel Kekewich and	Dr	£	s	d
	6 Butts laden per Simon Clement in the ship Tygre Charles				
	Tayler Master from Cadiz				
May	To Samuel Kekewich for 675 1/8 1/16 pieces of 8 the cost &				
	charges of 17 Butts the piece of 8 at 52d	148	146	9	1¾
	To Simon Clement for 278¼ pieces of 8 the cost of 6 Butts the				
	piece of 8 at 52d	103	60	5	9
	To Cash paid custom, fees, bills & wharfage	141	186	3	1½
	To Ditto pd. Joseph Davis for 3 Cask of Rhenish wine being				
	Funes	141	16	10	

	Anno 1690@				
	John Clark per Contra	*Cr*	*£*	*s*	*d*
June 30	*By Cash recd. of him*	*181*	31		

	Bristoll 1688				
	John Earle of Bristoll per Contra	*Cr*	*£*	*s*	*d*
October 3	*By Cash received in money of Esaw White £2 14s 00d & 1s*				
	2d short paid	*157*	2	15	2
10	*By Cash recd. of Serjeant Hodges in full*	*157*	36	11	
1689 March 25	*By Cash recd. of Edward Bryar by his order in full*	*162*	28	17	6
October 16	*By Cash recd. of his Steward at Clevedon Court*	*168*	16	4	6
1690 April 16	*By Ditto received of Serjeant Hodges at Clevedon Court*	*175*	15	10	
			99	18	2
	By Acct. of Ballances, for Ballance	*194 **	4	12	2
			104	10	4

	Anno 1688				
	Xeries Wine 23 Butts per Contra	*Cr*	*£*	*s*	*d*
May 30	*By Cash received for returnes on 7 Butts of wine*	*141*	17	8	10
	By Simon Clement for an error on 6 Butts of Xerie &				
	overcharge in averidge	*103*	4	16	9
July 18	*By Sir George Strode for 2 doz bottles at 18s per dozen*	*24*	1	16	
August 7	*By Tho. Goldney Junior for 16 bottles Xerie at 18d*	*136*	1	4	
23	*By Dr. Francis Hungerford for 2 doz bottles Xerie 1 doz at 18s*				
	1 doz at 16s	*87*	1	14	
September 19	*By the Lady Ann Powlett for 2 doz bottles at 18s per dozen*	*155*	1	16	
December 11	*By Tho. Goldney Junior for 2 bottles at*	*136*		3	

			£	s	d
June 7	To Cash pd. Charles Tayler in full for freight & averidge of 23 Butts	141 *	41	11	10
August	To Joseph Davis for ½ cost and charges of 2 hhds Rhenish wine	155	7	8	3
	To Tho. Day for 2 Gall. Rhenish and 2 pound of Isinglasse	150		15	2
December 19	To Cash paid for milk	157		1	8
January	To Ditto pd. Charles King	157		8	
	To Wines bought of severalls for theire cost and charges brought from that acct.	149	280	9	9½
			740	2	8¾

Anno 1688					
Edward Jacob of Clapton Yeoman my present Tennant is		Dr	£	s	d
To my Estate in Clapton for 1 yeares rent for my Farme purchased of Marie Thring and Bridget Wallis, ending March 2nd 1687		151	55		
To my Estate lately purchased in Clapton for the Yeamonth of the 4 Acres		142		8	
To Cash pd. Arthur Hobbs for work hee did for him		157		5	1
To Edward Jacob & Company for 1½ yeares intrest of £20 ending Sept. 23th 1688		134	1	16	
To Edward Jacob his new acct. current for ballance towards the next halfe yeares rent ending the 2nd of September 1688		156	2	4	3
			59	13	4

Anno 1688					
Tho. Day of Bristoll Soapmaker is		Dr	£	s	d
October	To sundry accts for 5½ dozen of Claret & Bottles	151,153	3		
1689 August	To sundry accts for 1 doz qt bottles of Xerie & the bottles	150,164	1		
			4		

Anno 1688					
Tho. Day of Bristoll Wine Cooper is		Dr	£	s	d
May	To John Blackwell for 3 Gall. 1/8 of Canary at 6d per Gallon I bought for him	148		18	9
	To Isaac Heming for my bill on him in his favor	143	100		
	To Ditto for money hee recd. of him in London	143	191	6	
	To Ditto for money hee paid on his forreigne bill, for which hee drew a bill in my favor	143	206	19	9
June 12	To Cash pd. lent him on 80 pieces broad Gold	141	100		
	To Isaac Heming for his part of charges on severall parcells of wine and Mum	152	4	6	
August	To Ditto for money hee paid Tho. Cox for 2 Brasse Cocks	152		4	
	To Joseph Davis for 1/2 cost and charges of 2 hhds Rhenish Wine	155	7	8	3
			611	2	9

19	*By John Earle of Bristoll for 2 Rundlets cont. 26 Gallons at 6s per Gallon*	*150*	7	16	
January 2	*By Lewis Adams for 10 Butts sould him at £26 per Butt*	*56*	260		
	By John Bradway for 8 Butts at £26 5s 00d per Butt	*70*	210		
29	*By Tho. Goldney Junior for 2 doz bottles at 18s*	*136*	1	16	
February 4	*By John Earle of Bristoll for 2 Rundlets and 2 bottles cont. 24 Gall. ¾ Xerie at 6s*	*150*	7	9	3
6	*By John Hurding for 2 doz bottles at 6s sent per Bernard Wilkins*	*151*	1	16	
11	*By the Lady Ann Powlett for 4 Panniers cont. 8 dozen at 18s per dozen*	*155*	7	4	
18	*By Tho. Goldney Junior for 2 bottles Xerie wt.*	*136*		3	
March 22	*By John Eastmont for 3 Rundlets cont. 40 3/4 Gallon at 6s*	*163*	12	4	6
1688/9	*By Samuel Kekewich for 80 Ryals plate hee recd. of Simon Clement abated on freight*	*148*	2	3	4
1689 June 15	*By John Earle of Bristoll for 4 doz bottles Xerie at 18s per dozen*	*150*	3	12	
	By Dr. Fra. Hungerford for 1 doz qrts & 1 doz pints at 18s	*87*	1	16	
	By Cash recd. of Wm. Whitwood & Beniamin Smith for 2 Butts of Lees	*162*	6	3	8
25	*By John Wilmer for 4 doz bottles Xerie at 18s per dozen*	*117*	3	12	
	By Tho. Day for 4 Butts sould him at £24 per Butt to bee paid May 10th 1689	*161*	104		
	By Tho. Day Soapmaker for 1 doz qt bottles Xerie at	*150*		18	
	By Ballance carried to that acct.	*169*	80	10	4¾
			740	2	8¾

	Anno 1688				
	Edward Jacob per Contra is	*Cr*	*£*	*s*	*d*
July 28	*By Cash recd. of him in part for one yeares rent for the old farme due March 2nd 1687*	*141*	6		
	By Wm. Pleydall paid him by my order	*152*	1		
October 20	*By Cash recd. of him*	*157*	4	10	
	By Proffit & Losse for severall things received of him as per noat	*153*	5	18	
	By Estate at Clapton for £9 allowed him towards plowing of 7 acres	*151*	9		
	By Ditto for money abated in consideration of the yearely advance £5 on the rent	*151*	20		
	By Estate at Clapton for his noat of disbursments as per noat	*151*	13	5	4
			59	13	4

	Anno 1688				
	Tho. Day per Contra is	*Cr*	*£*	*s*	*d*
October 26	*By Cash recd. of him in full*	*157*	3		
1689 September 25	*By Cash recd. of him in full*	*168*	1		
			4		

	Anno 1688				
	Tho. Day per Contra is	*Cr*	*£*	*s*	*d*
June 12	*By Cash recd. of him*	*141*	100		
16	*By Cash recd. of him*	*141*	200		
August 16	*By Cash recd. of him*	*141*	100		
24	*By Cash recd. of him in part*	*141*	60		
	By sundry accts for 2 Gall. Rhenish, 2 pound Isinglasse, & 4 Iron hoops	*150, 153*		17	
September 8	*By Cash recd. of him in full*	*141*	21	15	10
	By Wines of severall sorts for ½ cost of 12 Butts of Xerie bought in London	*149*	124	10	
	By Ditto for ½ charges on them in London & here as per particulars	*149*	3	19	11
			611	2	9

Anno 1688				
Sailecloth 20 pieces deposited by Henry Gibbes as security for £40 in my hands To Henry Gibbes his acct. current for the money per Contra, saveing that hee resteth one dozen bottle whitewine in my debt for my Commission for sales, and for Celleridge	Dr	£	s	d
	151	44		

(151)   **Bristoll 1688**

My Estate in Clapton consisting of the farme I formerly purchased of Marie Thring and Bridget Wallis, and of severall Grounds (viz) 4 Acres on Oldburie, 7 Acres in the Great Tinings, 6 Acres the great Mousty and the Strap, 3 acres & 2 acres adjoyning, and Welby Paddock acre, and 7 acres in Normead late Ed. Stroods, 4 acres there late Richard Hardwicks, & 2 acres late Ed. Willlin his, purchased of the Ld. Fitzharding, Ed. Gorges Esq. & others	Dr	£	s	d
To Estate at Clapton for ballance brought from that acct.	38	1422	2	3
To Estate at Clapton for the cost & charges of the particular lands beforemention'd	142	589	10	6
June 28 To Cash pd. Joseph Drew to buy deale boards etc.	141	1	10	
To Edward Jacob for £9 allowed him towrds charges of plowing the 7 acres	150	9		
To money abated him by agreement for his advance of £5 per Annum rent	150	20		
To Ditto for his noat of Disbursments for the yeare 1687	150	13	5	4
To Edward Jacob for what pd. Abraham White and Co. for making Ditches	150	2	4	5
To Arthur Hobbs for his share of money for making those Ditches	125		8	8
January To Edward Jacob for what pd. Abra. White etc. for planting the hedges, & Rog. Sydmoore for rooting hedges	156	1	12	3
To Ditto for what the Widow Cotterell pd. John Holiman for the poores money	156	1	16	6
To Arthur Hobbs for work done at severall times	125	2	2	4
1689 May To sundry accts for rooting up trash on the brow of the new Tynings and faggotting	125	1	13	9
		2065	6	2

Anno 1688				
John Hurding of Litton in the County of Dorset Counsellor at Law	Dr	£	s	d
May 30 To Anthony Owen for 12 Gall. Xerie 4 doz. bottles, 2 Panniers & Covers	111	4	2	
To Proffit & Losse for Portridge etc.	137			3
February 6 To sundry accts for 1 Pannier cont. 2 doz bottles Xerie, with bottles etc. sent per Bernard Wilkins	150, 153	2	1	6
		6	3	9

Anno 1688				
French Wine 3 hhds & 3 Tierces bought of severalls are	Dr	£	s	d
May To John Blackwell for 3 Tierces Claret & 2 hhds whitewine at £30 per tonne	148	30		
To Henry Gibbes for 1 hogshead Cognac wine bought of him	79	7		
To Wm. Powlet for 7 doz & 9 bottles of white wine	133	2	18	1½
		39	18	1½

	Anno 1688	Cr	£	s	d
	Saile Cloth 20 Pieces per Contra are				
October 18	By John Bubb for the value of said saile cloth sould him at 44s per piece	45	44		

	Bristoll 1688	Cr	£	s	d
	My Estate in Clapton consisting of my old farme, and Lands lately purchased				
	By Edward Jacob for 1 yeares rent for the old farme ending March 2nd 1687	150	55		
October	By Ditto for ½ a yeares rent for the whole farme ending September 2nd 1688	150	40		
	By Estate at Clapton for money recd. of Sir John Smith Edward Gorges etc. for the piece of ground sould them in Clapton, charg'd there by Error to that acct. of credit	72	170		
	By Edward Jacob for ½ yeares rent due March 2nd 1688	156	40		
1689 March	By Ditto for 1 year's rent due March 2nd 1689	156	80		
			385		
	By Acct. of Ballances, for Ballance	194 *	1680	6	2
			2065	6	2

	Anno 1688	Cr	£	s	d
	John Hurding per Contra is				
June 13	By Cash recd. of Christopher Hurlstone the Carrier in part	141	4		
March 6	By Cash recd. of Bernard Wilkins	162	2	1	6
			6	1	6
	By Profit and Loss, for Ballance	191 *		2	3
			6	3	9

	Anno 1688	Cr	£	s	d
	French wine per Contra is				
July 18	By Sir George Strode for 4 doz of whitewine at 10 6d	24	2	2	
20	By John Earle of Bristoll for 10 doz Claret & 2 doz whitewine at 10s 6d	150	6	6	
	By Simon Clement for 1 doz Claret and 1 doz whitewine at 10s	103	1		
	By Tho. Goldney Junior for 1 doz whitewine at	136		10	
August 3	By Edward Gorges for 6 bottles white and 6 bottles Claret at 10s 6d	34		10	6
7	By Tho. Goldney Junior for 16 Bottles of Whitewine at 10s 6d	136		14	
10	By Ditto for 15 bottles whitewine at 10s 6d	136		13	1½
28	By Simon Clement for 1 doz whitewine sent to Charles Jones by his order	103		10	6
	By Ditto for 6 bottles white wine	103		5	
	By Tho. Day Soapmaker for 12 bottles pints Claret at 10s	155		5	

	Anno 1688				
	Wm. Spoore Senior of Ashton, & Tho. Tuckey of the same Parish Yeoman	Dr	£	s	d
May 31	*To Cash lent them on theire bond payable August 30th next*	141	10		
	To Proffit & Losse for 7 months intrest ending 31 December 1688	153		7	

	Anno 1688				
	Henry Gibbes of Bristoll merchant is	Dr	£	s	d
	To Ballance of his former acct. current brought from that acct.	79	40	16	
	To Proffit & Losse for intrest of £40 from Jan. 16th 1688 to Feb. 8th 1688/9	164	2	10	
	To Cash paid himselfe	162		14	
February 25	*To Cash paid himselfe for Ballance*	162		16	
1689 March 25	*To Cash pd. lent him in his Bond and 15 Packets Dowlas for Collateral security*	162	150		
July 25	*To Cash pd. lent him in his bill on John Blackwell accepted to bee paid August 25th 1689*	168	100		
October	*To Proffit & Losse for ½ yeares intrest of £150 ending Sept. 25th 1689*	164	4	10	
	To Ditto for 2 months 16 daies intrest of £100 ending October 12th 1689	164	1	5	4
February 15	*To Cash paid lent him on his noat payable on demand*	175	30		
1690 April 2nd	*To Cash paid Lent him on his Noat*	175	21	10	
	To Profit and Loss for the Intrest of £150 from Sept. 25th 1689 to Feb. 4th 1689	164	3	3	9
	To Ditto for intrest of £50 from Feb. 4th 1689 to April 10th 1690	164		10	
	To Ballance Carried to his new Account	179	6	3	11
			361	19	00

(152)	**Bristoll 1688**				
	Isaac Heming per Contra is	Dr	£	s	d
June 12	*To Cash pd. Richard Baily for Foots Bill assign'd him*	141	100		
26	*To Cash pd. Peter Sanders for John Bubbs bill on — Hulbert*	141	100		
September	*To Jonathan Lamboll for money hee received of him part of my rents for my houses in Reading*	147	10		
March	*To Dr. Henry Jones for money hee received of James King by bill of Exchange in his favor*	161	200		
	To Tho. Curtis for money recd. of him	58	25		
1689 July	*To Sugar 4 hhds out of the Nathanael from Nevis for theire neat proceeds*	166	43	16	11
	To Plate out of the Friston & Andaluzia for its neat proceeds recd. of Atwill & Company	143	1026	6	4
			1505	3	3

30	By Tho. Goldney Junior for 4 bottles whitewine at	136		3	4
September 17	By Ditto for 6 bottles white wine	136		5	
19	By the Lady Ann Powlet for 4 dozen bottles whitewine at 10s	155	2		
	By John Earle of Bristoll for 2 doz Claret & one dozen whitewine for his Countesse	150	1	11	6
26	By the Lady Ann Powlet for 1 doz Claret & 1 doz whitewine at 10s	155	1		
October 12	By John Earle of Bristoll for 4 dozen Claret at	150	2		
20	By Wm. Powlet for 1 hogshead whitewine at	133	8	5	
23	By Tho. Day Soapmaker for 5½ doz Claret at	150	2	10	
	By John Blackwell for 1 hogshead of whitewine sould him	148	8	5	
January 29	By Tho. Goldney Junior for 2 bottles whitewine and the wine	136		2	
	By Ballance carried to a new acct. current	160	1		2
			39	18	1½

Anno 1688					
	Wm. Spoore & Tho. Tuckey per Contra are	Cr	£	s	d
January 2	By Cash recd. of Wm. Spoore Senior in full for the money per Contra	157	10	7	

Anno 1688					
	Henry Gibbes per Contra	Cr	£	s	d
	By Proffit & Losse for an error of omission in his last acct. current for which hee should have had Credit, being shortchargd to his acct. of Credit for Brandy	153		16	
	By Saile cloth 20 pieces deposited for theire neat proceeds save one dozen bottles whitewine which hee owed to mee for my Commsiion for sales & for warehouseroome	150	44		
1689 October 12	By Cash recd. of John Blackwell by bill on him	168	100		
1690 April	By Lincloth 15 pacquetts deposited in my Hands for their neat proceeds	171	195	13	
			340	9	
	By his new Account Current for money per Contra lent him	179	21	10	
			361	19	

Bristoll 1688					
	Isaac Heming of London merchant my Sonne in law is	Cr	£	s	d
May 29	By ballance of his former acct. currrent brought from that acct. & his owne	143	45	9	1
	By Cash recd. of Robert Henley for which I valued my bill	141	12		
July 21	By Cash recd. of Wm. Phelps on Nathanael Haggatts bill	141	10		
	By sundry accts for his disbursments on severall parcells of wine & Mumm bought by Tho. Day	149, 150	7	11	6
	By Wines bought of severalls for what hee paid for one Butt of Malaga	149	23		
	By Tho. Day paid Tho. Cox for 2 brasse Cocks	150		4	
August	By Adventure in the Ruth paid charges on a Trunck of stockins	155	4	9	4
October 31	By Cash recd. of Francis Spencer and Co. on a bill from London	157	18	3	6
November 6	By Cash recd. of Edward Baily on a bill assign'd in my favor	157	12		
December 3	By Cash for money hee pd. on my bill in favor of Tho. Goldney	157	50		
January	By Proffit & Losse for 3 Juggs Oyle, a couple of fish etc.	153		16	

Anno 1689		Dr	£	s	d
	Isaac Heming merchant is				
August 2	To ballance of his former acct. current as per his own acct. and then ballanced	152	1176	2	
	To Tho. Day Wine Cooper for money recd. by his order in London	161	46	4	
	To Tho. Curtis recd. of him	169	15		
January 7	To Cash pd. Richard Corsley for his bill on John Sutton assign'd by mee in his favor	173	300		
			1537	6	

Anno 1688		Dr	£	s	d
	Charles King of Bristol Wine Cooper now my Cooper is				
June 26	To Cash paid him in part	141	5		
September 15	To Cash paid him	141	5		
February 11	To Cash paid lent him on his obligation in Receit booke	162	5		
1689 Aprill 9	To Cash paid lent him	162	5		
October 4	To Cash paid lent him	168	5		
January 24	To Cash pd. lent him on his obligation	173	6		
1690 August 18	To Ditto pd. lent him on his bill payable Sept. 2nd 1690 @	187 *	3		
			34		

The Ledger of Thomas Speed 1681–1690423

	By *Adventure in the London merchant to Cadiz for carriage,*				
	custom etc. Trunck of stockins	*161*	4	18	7
	By *Ditto for charge of Assureance of £150 on Ditto stockins*	*161*	4	12	
February 23	By *Cash recd. of Louis Addams for a set of Racking Tooles*	*162*	2	3	3
	By *Plate shipd. in the Friston at Cadiz for assureance pd. for*				
	£600 to London	*163*	18	2	
March	By *John Wilmer for money paid him by my order*	*117*	50		
Aprill	By *Elizabeth Milner for my bill on him in her favor*	*15*	12	19	9
	By *Adventure in the Merchants Goodwill to Cadiz for charges*				
	on a Trunck of stockins	*166*	5	1	
	By *Proffit & Losse pd. for powder, a Cheese to Tho. Curtis,*				
	Port of leter etc.	*164*	2	13	7
	By *Adventure 3rd in the Wellcom for assureance of £100*	*166*	4	2	
	By *Plate in the Friston & Andaluzia as per his acct. for charges*				
	on it	*143*	12	17	4
	By *Rhenish wine 2 Aulnes for theire cost & charges*	*163*	17	2	
	By *Adventure in the Cesar to Cadiz pd. custom of 1 Trunck*				
	hose & assureance of £150 on her	*169*	10	16	4
	By *his new acct. current for ballance carried to that acct. of debt*	*152*	1176	2	
			1505	3	3

Anno 1689					
	Isaac Heming per Contra	*Cr*	*£*	*s*	*d*
August 6	By *Cash recd. of Henry Parsons for my bill in his favor*	*168*	200		
	By *Ditto recd. of Richard Baily for my bill on him in his favor*	*168*	200		
7	By *Cash recd. John Le Conti for my bill in favor of Maurice*				
	Williams	*168*	100		
8	By *Cash recd. of Richard Baily for my bill on him in his favor*	*168*	200		
9	By *Ditto recd. of Elias Osborne for my bill on him in his favor*	*168*	60		
13	By *Cash recd. Sgt Tho. Strode for my bill on him in favor of*				
	Hugh Strode	*168*	50		
	By *adventure in the ship Sarah to Cadiz for, custom, assureance*				
	etc. Trunck stockins	*169*	8	13	11
	By *Xeries wine 23 Butts for one hogsheadogshead Malaga wine*				
	sent per Waggon	*170*	13	1	
	By *Adventures in the Merchants Goodwill & Cesar to Cadiz*	*166,*			
	for assureance of £100 & £150	*169*	10	1	
September 2	By *Jonathan Lamboll pd. John Wilmer by my order*	*147*	116		
November	By *Adventure in the Sarah for carriage, cartage, custom & fees*				
	of one other trunck	*169*	3	17	4
December	By *Profit & Losse for a parcell Dr. Russells powder, a viall of*				
	his Tincture & Cordiall	*164*	1	13	
	By *Proffit & Losse for a cheese hee bought & sent to Tho. Curtis*	*164*		10	6
January 20	By *Giles Clark for money hee paid Col. Tho. Joorey on the*				
	taking up his assignment	*171*	425		
	By *Ditto for his Commission for receiving & paying said money,*				
	& his paines in taking the Assignment	*171*	1		
			1389	16	9
	By *his new acct. current for balance carried to that acct.*	*177*	147	9	3
			1537	6	

Anno 1688					
	Charles King per Contra is	*Cr*	*£*	*s*	*d*
	By *Richard Hawksworth for 24 Iron hoops at 6d per hoope*	*152*		12	
	By *Acct. of Ballances, for Ballance*	*194 **	33	8	
			34		

Anno 1688		Dr	£	s	d
	Richard Hawksworth of Alveston in the County of Glocester Atturny at the Law				
July 2	To John Blackwell for 3 doz 9 Gall. Xerie the bottles & Pannier & to Proffit & Losse for portridge, sent by Tobias Luton, consign'd to Giles Campian in Lond. per his order	148,153	3	1	9
January	To Charles King for 14 Iron hoops at 6d the hoope, sent him per Carrier	152		12	
			3	13	9

Anno 1688		Dr	£	s	d
	Wm. Plydall of Bristoll Mason is				
1688 July 6	To Cash paid him in part	141		4	
	To Ditto paid him	141		6	
August 3	To Cash paid him in part	141	1		
	To Edward Jacob received of him by my order	150	1		
November 12	To Cash paid him	157	1		
1689 January 4	To Cash paid lent him	173		3	
1690 June 25	To Ditto paid him	181		10	
			4	3	

(153)	**Bristoll 1688**	Dr	£	s	d
	Proffit & Losse is				
May 30	To Ballance brought from that acct.	137	480	14	2¼
June 1	To Cash pd. Robert Webb for mending 2 Truncks	141 *		4	
	To Anthony Owen for 6 bottles Claret & 1 Gall. Xerie for Ullage	111		9	3
21	To Cash pd. Robert Lyppiott in full for Mault	141	3	17	
July 6	To Ditto pd. Jane Shepheard for a Cask of Butter sent to Isaac Heming	141		15	6
19	To Cash for pd. Samuel Jonson for a doz of Panniers & Covers	141		10	
21	To Cash paid Anthony Tyler for shooing my lame mare	141		1	8
	To the Lady Ann Powlet for money for ballance of her acct.	100	2	1	8
27	To Cash pd. John Warren for 6 yards of Grey Cloth	141	1	16	
August 9	To Cash pd. Edward Young for keeping my two mares at Grasse	141	1	2	6
11	To Ditto pd. John Gandy in full	141		7	6
	To Cash pd. Edward Rice for 8 Groce of Corks	141		11	4
18	To Simon Clement for 2 doz & 1 bottle Xerie	103	1	7	
	To Tho. Day for 4 Iron hoops	150		2	
September 4	To Cash pd. Ann Smith for a parcell of cheese	141	1	1	10
8	To Cash pd. James Shute for Carriage of a Trunck from Reading	141		8	
	To Joseph Drew for work done as per his severall noates	154	7	15	
21	To John Hardiman for work done and severall things bought for mee per noat	80	4	13	4
22	To John Ochell for keeping my 2 mares to the 17th of September	147	1	13	
	To Tho. Strode for ballance of his acct.	136		19	6½
29	To Cash pd. Ed. Tily for new making a Quilt	157		16	9
	To Ditto pd. my wife to pay Tho. Dike for bravery [106] in the forestreat chamber	157	12	15	
October 6	To Cash pd. John Roome for 9 weeks keeping my lame mare	157		13	6
10	To Cash pd. Lott Wilkins for a Tubb of Butter	157	1	3	10
	To John Blackwell for severall small parcells of wine	148		18	5½
13	To Robert Lipyeatt for severall parcells of Mault as per noat	154	3	19	
	To Cash pd. for severall small things	157		3	
15	To Ditto pd. the Widow Flower in full for halling to this day	157	1	7	6
16	To Cash pd. Tho. Dyke for 6 Rushia Leather Chaires	157	2	5	
18	To Ditto pd. postage of severall leters	157		4	3
	To Tho. Curtis for ballance of his acct.	58	11		
22	To Cash pd. Wm. Richards for a Cask Butter sent Isaac Heming	157	1		
	To Edward Jacob for severall things had of him	150	5	18	

Anno 1688					
	Richard Hawksworth per Contra	*Cr*	*£*	*s*	*d*
July 20	*By Cash recd. of him*	*141*	3	1	9
February 2	*By Cash recd. of him*	*162*		12	
			3	13	9

Anno 1689					
	Wm. Plydall per Contra	*Cr*	*£*	*s*	*d*
	By Proffit & Losse for building my orchard wall at Clapton & other work there	*164*	3	10	
January 4	*By Ditto for Setting up a Boiler and other work*	*180*		13	
			4	3	

Bristoll 1688					
	Proffit & Losse per Contra is	*Cr*	*£*	*s*	*d*
June	*By the Lady Ann Powlett for portridge of wine*	*100*			3
	By Wm. Spoore Senior & Peter Collet for 2 yeares intrest of £50	*30*	6		
	By Richard Hauxworth for portridge of wine	*152*			3
	By Arthur Bramley & Company pd. charges on the arrest of John Brisco	*12*	1	5	6
July 18	*By Sir George Strode for 6 doz bottles 3 Panniers & covers portridge etc.*	*24*		15	8
20	*By John Earle of Bristoll for 12 doz bottles, 6 Panniers & covers & portridge*	*150*	1	11	
	By Simon Clement for 2 doz bottles	*103*		4	
24	*By Edward Crofts for 2 yeares rent for the house in which hee liveth ending June 24th 1688*	*96*	72		
	By Tho. Goldney Junior for 1 doz bottles	*136*		2	
August 3	*By Edward Gorges for 1 doz bottles*	*34*		2	
7	*By Tho. Goldney Junior for 2 doz & 8 bottles at 2s*	*136*		5	4
11	*By Ditto for 15 bottles*	*136*		2	6
	By Samuel Clarke & Company for 10 months less 5 daies intrest of £100	*142*	4	18	4
23	*By Dr. Francis Hungerford for 2 doz bottles Pannier & cover*	*87*		5	2
28	*By Simon Clement for 1 doz bottles*	*103*		2	
	By Ditto for 6 bottles	*103*		1	
30	*By Tho. Goldney Junior for 4 bottles*	*136*			8
September 17	*By Ditto for 6 bottles*	*136*		1	
	By the Lady Ann Powlet for 6 doz bottles, 3 Panniers & Covers	*155*		16	
19	*By John Earle of Bristoll for 3 doz bottles 2 Panniers covers etc.*	*150*		9	6
	By Henry Howard & co. for ½ yeares intrest of £100 due Sept. 19th 1688	*92*	3		
26	*By Proffit viz. by Lady Ann Powlet for 2 doz bottles 1 Pannier etc.*	*155*		5	3
	By Reisons solis 65 Barrills for my Commission for sales	*145*	4	3	3
October 12	*By John Earle of Bristoll for 4 doz bottles Pannier etc.*	*150*		10	6
20	*By Wm. Powlett for 14 doz & 3 bottles*	*133*	1	10	6
23	*By Tho. Day Soapmaker for 5 doz bottles*	*150*		10	
	By Marie Speed my wife for ballance of her acct.	*113*	82	10	8
	By James Swetnam for £50 5½ months and of £10 from 3rd Sept. 87 to the 30th August 88	*133*	2		3

30	To Cash pd. John Cheshire in full for bottles	157	6	9	11
November 3	To Ditto pd. Joseph Drew for work done at severall times	157		7	
	To Ditto pd. Francis Horwood for 1 day & nights mustering	157		2	6
	To James Swetnam for severall things had of him as per noat	133	5	2	7
20	To Cash paid Robert Yate for Church and poores money	157	3	12	
	To Ditto paid Edward Lloyd for Drums and colours	157		7	
	To Abraham Hill for one yeare sallary due November 15th 1688	156	10		
			578	15	7¼
	To Cash pd. for severall small things	157		19	2
21	To Ditto pd. Edward Jones for work done at severall times	157		5	
December 5	To Cash pd. Joseph Drew in full for work done	157		9	6
24	To Ditto pd. John Jenkin for bearing armes 1 day	157		1	
	To Isaac Heming for 3 bottles oyle 1 Couple Fish etc.	152		16	
	To Henry Gibbes for an error of omission in his acct. current	151		16	
February 4	To Cash pd. Tho. Hungerford in full for cloth bought of himselfe & Company	157	6	14	
	To Elizabeth Milner for severall things had of her as per noat	15		16	11
	To Olliver Mosley for Ballance	4	1	14	5
	To Reynold Williams for Ballance	10	13	6	11
	To Samuel Searle for Ballance	10	6		8
	To John Bush & Company for ballance	10	5	7	2
	To Edward Colston for Ballance	10	1	4	4
	To Robert Tyler for Ballance	10	1	5	
	To John Spoore Senior for Ballance	11	2	8	11
	To James Slaughter for Ballance	11		10	
	To Ann Hiscox for Ballance	11	1	5	
	To Edward Biddle for Ballance	12	1	17	6
	To John Dolphin for ballance	12	1		
	To Christopher Toomer for Ballance	12	6	10	3
	To Stanton Jones for Ballance	12	2	18	7
	To Voyage in the Adventure to Barbados for ballance	13	27		
	To Indigoe one Cask for Ballance	13	15	1	2
	To John Bowen for Ballance	13	1	4	6
	To Marie Russet for Ballance	13		6	6
	To Mehetabel Heming for Ballance	13	35	8	
	To Edward Payne for Ballance	14	2		
	To Tho. Wilcox for Ballance	14	6	7	3
	To Voyage in the Zant to Newfoundland for Ballance	14	52	5	7
	To Habacock Turner for Ballance	14	1		
	To George Hawes for Ballance	14	10	8	
	To Isaac Newton for Ballance	15	7	16	3
	To French wines in the Pheenix for Ballance	15	319		11
	To Adventure in the Fortune to Nevis for Ballance	15	27	18	4
	To John Rumsey for Ballance	16		18	
	To Hugh Tynt for Ballance	17		12	5
	To Elizabeth Seward for Ballance	18	1		3
	To Adventure in the Nathanael for Ballance	18	16	11	10
	To Adventure in the Hope for Ballance	19	15	9	9
	To Kersies for Ballance	19	30	7	9
	To Tho. Shewell for Ballance	19		15	
	To Wm. Coles for Ballance	19		7	1
	To house at the lowe end of Small Streat for money charg'd to square that acct.	22	10	19	7½
			1193		1¾

(154)	**Bristoll 1688**				
	Jahzeel Speed my Sonne is	Dr	£	s	d
	To ballance of his former acct. current brought from that acct.	122	742	13	½
July 11	To Cash pd. him for drinking money	141		10	
24	To Cash paid Elizabeth Milner for ¼ yeares tabling ending	141	5		
August 7	To Cash paid Elizabeth Milner for stockins etc.	141	1	16	6

			£	s	d
	By Wm. Godwin for 1 yeares intrest of £100 ending Sept. 27th 1688	64	6		
	By sundry accts for severall summes due for intrest from severall persons	154,100,138, 92,97,148	28	4	
December	By Tho. Goldney Junior for 2 bottles	136			4 ⸗
	By John Earle of Bristoll for cooperidge, portridge etc.	150		1	
	By Merchandizes in the Comfort for acct. Law: Washington for a lyghteridge & commission	160		6	10
	By Wm. Spoore Senior & Company for 7 months intrest of £10	151		7	
February	By John Earle of Bristoll for 2 Rundlets, Certifficate, etc.	150		9	
7	By John Hurding for 2 doz bottles Pannier and portridge	151		5	· 2
	By Merchandizes in the John for Law. Washington for my commission	160		4	5
11	By the Lady Ann Powlet for 8 doz bottles 4 Panniers covers etc.	155	1	1	
	By Tho. Goldney Junior for 3 bottles	136			6
	By Wm. Spoore Junior & Senior for intrest due	69	6		
	By Wm. Spoore Junior & Senior for 2½ yeares intrest of £10 due Oct. 16th 1688	31	1	10	
	By Adventure in the Zant for Ballance	4	10	13	
	By Tobacco 9 hhds for Ballance	5	47		
	By Cattle for Ballance	5	58	5	½
	By Bartholmew Reece for Ballance	6		9	2
			344	9	6½
	By Jahzeel Speed & Company for Ballance	6	5	7	3
	By William Emblen for Ballance	6	7	16	9
	By Sir Robert Yeamans & Company for intrest long due	10	3		
	By Ginger for Ballance of that acct.	17	5	16	11
	By Adventure in the Dyamond Ketch for Ballance	18	27	1	8
	By Tho. Gibson for Ballance	1	3	14	11
	By Fra. Ballard for ballance	2		8	4
	By Sam. Hale for Ballance				
	By Adventure in the Dyamond Ketch to Nevis for Ballance	21	43	12	9
	By James Freeman for ballance	21		1	
	By my Copiehold Tenement in Portburie for intrest of £100 6 yeares	20	36		
	By my house at the Lower end of Small Streat for money charg'd by error	22	132	17	
			610	6	1½
	By ballance carried to a new acct. current	164	582	14	¼
			1193		1¾

Bristoll 1690@		Cr	£	s	d
Jahzeel Speed per Contra					
By Jahzeel Speed for all the Severall Sums of mony per Contra which are Carried to his debt in his new acct. as may appear		178	826	3	11

Date	Description				
	To *Ditto* paid her for money shee furnished him	141		5	
September 12	To Cash pd. Marmaduke Bowdler for 3½ yrds cloth to make him a coate	141	2	16	
14	To *Ditto* pd. John Mathews for a hat and Gold band	141	1	5	
21	To John Hardiman for making severall Garments for him as per noat	80	2	4	3
29	To Cash paid for cloth for sleeves	157		5	
November 17	To Cash pd. John Hardiman for making his clothes	157	1	1	
21	To *Ditto* pd. Richard Day for a piece of Freeze for a coate & breeches	157	1		
December 12	To Cash pd. John Hardiman for work done	157		3	
26	To Cash pd. Louis Addams in full for potts of wine	157	1	18	6
February 8	To Cash pd. Tho. Hungerford for 30 Ells cloth for shirts	162	2	10	
11	To Elizabeth Milner pd. her for ¼ yeares dyet ending	15	5		
	To *Ditto* for money furnished him at severall times	15	2	18	
27	To Cash pd. Henry Stover for carriage of his Trunck to Musburie	162		4	6
1689 June	To Elizabeth Milner for ½ yeares dyet ending the 7th March 1688	15	10		
4	To Cash pd. Nicholas Baker his noat for pots of wine	162	1	6	
7	To *Ditto* pd. John Jones for severall things for him	162		16	
27	To Cash pd. Alexander Caduggan in full of his noat for potts of wine	162	1	10	
July 13	To Elizabeth Milner for ¼ yeares dyet ending June 7th 1689	15	5		
	To *Ditto* for a cap, gloves, & dressing a hatt 10s 10d	15		10	10
	To *Ditto* for money delivered him for drinking money	15	1	13	
23	To Cash pd. Wm. Rogers for 4 paire of shooes	168		13	6
August 5	To *Ditto* pd. Tho. Walden for 2 paire thred stockins	168		4	
24	to *Ditto* pd. John Crindall in full of his noat for potts of wine	168	1	10	
September 19	To *Ditto* pd. Eliza. Milner for ¼ yeares dyet ending 7th Sept. 1689	168	5		
	To *Ditto* pd. her for spending money	168	1	17	
	To Richard Langsworth for a paire of shooes etc.	163		4	6
November	To Cash pd. John Mathews for a new hatt	168	1	5	
	To John Hardiman for making & repaireing clothes for him	80	2	4	5½
January	To Elizabeth Milner for ¼ yeares dyet ending Dec. 7th 1689	15	5		
	To *Ditto* for money shee furnished him for liquor, stockins, physick etc.	15	2	9	2½
March 4	To Cash pd. Tho. Bourne in full of his noat for physick	175	1	11	9
	To Elizabeth Milner for ¼ year's Dyet ending March 7th 1689	15	5		
	To *Ditto* for money furnished him with etc. pd. by her for necessaries for him	15	2	5	2
1690 25	To Cash paid Richard Sandford in full for Trimming him letting blood etc. to this day	175	3		
April 14	To *Ditto* paid Dr. Bourne as a Fee	175		10	
	To *Ditto* paid his Expences at Bath	175	1	3	8½
			826	3	11

	Anno 1688				
	Edward Dowding late of Bristoll now of Westburie Marriner	Dr	£	s	d
July 7	To Cash lent him on his bond and Collaterall security payable with lawfull intrest January 9th 1688	141	120		
	To Proffit & Losse for ½ yeares intrest due January 9th 1688	153	3	12	
	To Adventure in the Olive branch for 3588 Ryals plate 448½ pieces of 8 at 52d for stockins	158	97	3	6
1689 July 9	To Proffit & Losse for ½ yeares intrest ending July 9th 1689	164	3	12	
October	To Proffit & Losse for ¼ yeares intrest of £120 ending Oct. 9th 1689	164	1	16	
1690 April	To *Ditto* for ½ years intrest of £120 due April 9th 1690	164	3	12	
1690 October	To *Ditto* for ½ year's intrest ending October 9th 1690 @	180	3	12	
			233	7	6

Anno 1688				
Edward Dowding per Contra is	*Cr*	*£*	*s*	*d*
By Reisons solis 32 barrills for 3390 Ryals is 423¾ pieces of 8				
at 52d theire cost in Malaga	*158*	91	16	3
By Ditto for the freight & averidge of said Barrills	*158*	12	6	8¾
By Cash recd. of him	*168*		4	6¼
		104	7	6
By Acct. of Ballances, for Ballance	*194 **	129		
		233	7	6

	Anno 1688				
	Joseph Drew of Bristoll house Carpenter is	Dr	£	s	d
	To Cash in his former acct. current lent him on his Bond August				
	5th 86	31	4		
	To Ditto lent him on his bond May 3rd 1688	31	4		
July 16	To Cash paid him	141		10	
	To Cash formerly paid him, & omitted to bee charge'd as per his				
	noate	141	2	5	
			10	15	

	Anno 1688				
	William Spoore Senior of Long Ashton in the County of				
	Somerset Gent.	Dr	£	s	d
October 4	To Cash paid lent him on his bill	157	2	10	
1689 March 28	To Cash pd. lent him on his bill payable on the 29th June next				
	1689	162	5		
			7	10	

	Anno 1688				
	Robert Lipyeatt of Bristoll Maultster & distiller is	Dr	£	s	d
October 18	To Cash paid him in full	157	3	19	
1689 June 7	To Cash paid him in full	162	7		
			10	19	

(155)	**Bristoll 1688**				
	John Massinger of Bristoll Hosier is	Dr	£	s	d
	To his former acct. current for money lent him Sept. 25th 1684				
	on bond	27	10		
	To Ditto for money lent him at severall times on parcells stockins				
	as per his noats	27	49	11	4
July 18	To Cash paid lent him on 30 paire of stockins as per noat	141	3	5	
26	To Cash pd. lent him on 33 paire of hose as per noat	141	3	11	6
August 10	To Cash pd. lent him on 30 pre of hose as per noat	141	3	5	
21	To Cash pd. lent him on 30 prs hose as per noat	141	3	5	
30	To Ditto pd. lent him on 40 paire of hose as per noat	141	4	6	8
September 8	To Ditto pd. lent him on 30 prs hose as per noat	141	3	5	
15	To Cash pd. lent him on 30 prs hose as per noat	141	3	5	
22	To Ditto pd. lent him on 30 prs hose as per noat	141	3	5	
October 2	To Cash pd. lent him on 40 prs hose as per noat	157	4	6	8
13	To Ditto pd. lent him on 50 paire of hose as per noat	157	3	5	
20	To Ditto pd. lent him on 27 paire as per noat	157	2	18	6
26	To Cash pd. lent him on 32 paire as per noat	157	3	9	4
November 12	To Cash pd. lent him on 48 paire as per noat	157	5	4	
20	To Ditto pd. lent him on 31paire as per noat	157	3	7	2
30	To Ditto pd. lent him on 29 paire as per noat	157	3	2	10
December 12	To Cash pd. lent him on 33 paire as per noat	157	3	11	6
	To Fra. Yeamans for his note of charges on the suite with George				
	Freeman	160	2	1	4
	To Cash pd. Counsellor Haggatt his fee to manage said suite				
18	To Ditto pd. lent him on 37 paire as per noat	157	4		2
26	To Ditto pd. lent him on 33 paire as per noat	157	3	11	6
January 14	To Cash pd. lent him on 32 paire as per noat	157	3	9	4
18	To Ditto pd. lent him on 44 paire as per noat	157	4	15	4
28	To Ditto pd. lent him on 51 paire as per noat	157	5	10	6
			139	12	8

Anno 1688				
Joseph Drew per Contra is	Cr	£	s	d
September By Proffit & Losse for work done as per his noates	153	7	15	
22 By Cash recd. of him in full	141	3	15	
		10	15	

Anno 1688				
William Spoore Senior per Contra is	Cr	£	s	d
October 27 By Cash recd. of him	157	2	10	
1689 June 25 By Cash recd. of him	162	5		
		7	10	

Anno 1688				
Robert Lypyeat per Contra	Cr	£	s	d
October 13 By Proffit & Losse for severall parcells of Mault as per noat	153	3	19	
1689 June 7 By Ditto for severall parcells of Mault had to this 7th of June 1689	164	7		
		10	19	

Bristoll 1688				
John Massinger per Contra	Cr	£	s	d
By his new acct. current for the money per Contra carried to his acct.	163	139	12	8

	Anno 1688		£	s	d
	Adventure in the ship Ruth of London John Archer Master to Alicant	Dr			
	To Worsted stockins for one Trunck laden in her by Isaac Heming for my acct. consign'd to Heneage Fetherston merchant there cont. (viz) £ s d				
	100 dozen fine Bristoll hose is 1200 paire at 2s 8d 160 00 00				
	5 dozen fine Wells hose is 60 paire at 1s 8d 5	146	165	17	
	To Ditto for Trunck cord and matting 17				
August	To Isaac Heming pd. carriage to London, custom and other charges	152	4	9	4
			170	6	4

	Anno 1688		£	s	d
	Joseph Davis per Contra is	Dr			
August 30	To Cash paid him in full	141	14	16	6

	Anno 1688		£	s	d
	Thomas Day Soapemaker now Mayor of Bristoll [107]	Dr			
	To French wines 3 hhds etc. for 6 pint bottles Claret	151 *		2	6
August 28	To Ditto for 1 dozen pint bottles of my own mark Claret at 10s	151		5	
				7	6

	Anno 1688		£	s	d
	The Lady Ann Powlett of Chantmarle in the County of Dorset Widow	Dr			
September 19	To sundry accts for 4 dozen Xerie, 4 doz white wine with the Panniers, Covers and bottles sent per Francis Edwards	150,151, 148,153	6	13	
26	To sundry accts for 1 Pannier cont. 1 doz white, & 1 doz Claret with bottles & Pannier	151,153	1	5	3
February 11	To sundry accts for 4 Panniers cont. 8 doz Xerie with bottles Panniers etc. sent per Francis Edwards	150,153	8	5	
1689 August 28	To sundry accts for 8 doz Xerie, bottles, Panniers etc.	169,164	8	5	
31	To sundry accts for 4 doz white wine bottles panniers etc.	160,164	2	18	6
October					
December	To sundry accts for 4 dozs Xerie, 2 Panniers, 4 doz bottles, sent per Wilkins	169,164	4	2	8
1690 June 18	To Sundry accts for 4 doz Xerie sent her per Bernard Wilkins	56,180	4	8	8
Sept. 30	To Sundry accts for 6 doz of Xerie, 3 Panniers, 6 doz Bottles etc. sent per Ditto	186,180	6	15	9
			42	13	10
	To Profit and Loss for Ballance	191 *			9
			42	14	7

(156)	**Bristoll 1688**		£	s	d
	Horses my Two Mares 1 black the other Bay are	Dr			
August 30	To Cash paid Stephen Sash for 11 Bushells Oates	141		10	
September 20	To Ditto pd. severalls for a Drench, a Curricombe & horse haire cloth	141		1	9
	To Ditto pd. Tho. Day for what hee pd. for ½ score Oates & 5 Bushells beanes	141		17	1
	To John Occoll for a mane come and a Reeke of hay bought of him	147	2	12	6
22	To Cash paid Abell Edwards in full to this 22th Sept. 1688	141		17	
29	To Cash pd. for 2 doz Straw carriage of oates etc.	157		2	2
October 18	To Cash pd. John Jenkin for keeping them to the 17th instant October	157		4	6
November 16	To Ditto pd. John Jenkin for keeping them to the 17th November	157		4	8

Anno 1690@				
Adventure in the Ruth per Contra	Cr	£	s	d
By Acct. of Ballances, for Ballance	194 *	170	6	4

Anno 1688				
Joseph Davis of Bristoll merchant is	Cr	£	s	d
August To sundry accts for the cost & charges of 2 hhds Rhenish wine				
sent per Isaac Davis from Holland	150	14	16	6

Anno 1690@				
Thomas Day per Contra	Cr	£	s	d
By Profit and Loss, for Ballance	191 *		7	6

Anno 1688				
The Lady Ann Powlet per Contra	Cr	£	s	d
October 2 By Cash recd. of Francis Edwards	157	7	19	3
February 18 By Cash received of Fra. Edwards	162	8	5	
1689 October 2 By Cash recd. of Fra. Edwards in part	168	8		
23 By Ditto recd. of Ditto in part	168	2		
November 13 By Cash received of Fra. Edwards in full	168	1	3	6
January 8 By Cash recd. of Bernard Wilkins by her order in full	173	4	2	8
1690 June 24 By Ditto, recd. of Ditto in full	181	4	8	8
Sept. 30 By Ditto recd. of Christopher Barker by her order in full	187 *	6	15	6
		42	14	7

Bristoll 1688 1689				
Horses Two per Contra are	Cr	£	s	d
By Proffit & Losse for all the charges and disbursments per				
Contra	164 *	32	11	11

Date	Description	Fol.	£	s	d
21	To Ditto pd. for 2 dozen straw	157		2	
December 24	To Cash pd. John Jenkin for keeping the 2 mares to the 17th December	157		4	6
January 2	To Cash pd. for 5 Bushells Oates	157		5	6
14	To Ditto pd. for 3 dozen of Straw	157		3	
18	To Ditto pd. John Jenkin for keeping the 2 mares to the 17th January 1688	157		4	8
	To Cash pd. Abel Edwards in full for shooing etc. to this day	157		9	3
26	To Ditto pd. John Wickham & Edward Tibbet for hay	157	3	5	
February 13	To Cash pd. John Jenkyn for keeping them to the 17th instant	162		4	8
20	To Cash pd. Wm. Williams for 11 Bushells of Oates	162		9	2
March 13	To Ditto pd. John Jenkin for keeping the 2 mares to the 17th March	162		4	8
	To Wm. Spoore Junior for 1 Tonne of Hay put into the Loft at Clapton	31	1	10	
1689 Aprill 9	To Cash pd. John Jenkyn for keeping the 2 mares to this day	162		6	8
	To James Swetnam for 2 Saddles and other things as per noat	133		6	
27	To Cash pd. Tho. Lewis for ½ a Score of Oates	162		9	2
May 7	To Cash pd. John Jenkyn for keeping my mares to the 7th instant	162		5	
June 3	To Cash pd. Jonathan Perkyn for a Tonne of Hay	162	1	10	
9	To Ditto pd. John Jenkin in part	162		3	
15	To Ditto pd. for 2 Bushells of Beanes	162		4	
29	To Cash pd. Abel Edwards for shooing etc. per noat	162		14	
July 9	To Ditto pd. John Brewer for 10 Bushells Oates	168		8	10
16	To Ditto pd. John Jenkin in part	168		2	6
25	To Cash pd. Ezekiel Powell for a Reeke of hay standing in a ground neare his house	168	5		
August 9	To Cash pd. John Jenkin in part	168		2	
14	To Cash pd. Wm. Dawson for 1 months Grasse for my bay mare	168		10	
23	To Ditto pd. Anthony Spicket for 1 Tonne & 1/3 of a tonne of hay	168	2	13	4
	To John Gore for a Stack of Hay bought of him	31	4	10	
September 20	To Cash pd. John Jenkyn for keeping my mares in full to the 20th instant	168		6	8
25	To Ditto pd. John Jenkyn in full for keeping my mares to the 23th instant	168		2	9
November 2	To Cash pd. Anthony Picket for bringing in a Reeke of hay	168		12	
26	To Cash pd. John Little for 2 dozen of Straw	168		2	4
December 2	To Ditto pd. Henry Lloyd for 1 month & 4 daies Grasse for my mare	168		11	6
20	To Cash pd. Abel Edwards in full for shooing my mares to this day	173		15	
24	To Ditto pd. Jacob Lloyd in full for keeping them to the 24th Dec. 1689	173		5	4
			32	11	11

Anno 1688					
	Edward Jacob of Clapton in the County Somerset my Tenant	Dr	£	s	d
October	To my Estate formerly & lately purchasd in Clapton for ½ a yeares rent of the whole ending September 2nd 1688	151	40		
	To Ditto for ½ years rent due March 2nd 1688	151	40		
1689 March	Tp Ditto for one years rent due March 2nd 1689	151	80		
			160		

	Anno 1688				
		Cr	£	s	d
	Edward Jacob per Contra				
October 20	By ballance of his former acct. in part of the 1/2 yeares rent due				
	Sept. 2nd 1688	150	2	5	9
January	By Estate at Clapton for what hee paid Abra. White &				
	Company for making Ditches	151	2	4	5
	By Ditto pd. Ditto for planting a hedge	151	1	1	
	By Ditto for what hee pd. Roger Skydmore for rooting up a hedge				
	and levelling the ditch	151		11	3
	By Ditto for what the Widow Cotterell pd. John Holliman				
	poores money in part of her 1/2 yeares rent	151	1	16	6
	By Ditto recd. of Ditto in full for 1/2 yeares rent due for the				
	Tynings 7 acres & great Mousty	157	4	3	6

	Anno 1688				
	Abraham Hill is	Dr	£	s	d
	To Ballance of his former acct. for what pd. him in part for a yeares service due Nov. 15 88	131	9	8	
November 21	To Cash paid him	157 *	1	10	
January 5	To Ditto paid him	157	1		
February 6	To Ditto paid him	157	1	10	
1689 May 2	To Cash paid him	162	2	10	
July 8	To Cash pd. Edward Pruet for his pole	168		2	6
August 13	To Ditto pd. him per receit	168	1		
21	To Cash paid him	168	1		
November 25	To Ditto paid him in full	168	2	10	
			20	10	6

(157)	*Bristoll 1688*				
	Cash is	Dr	£	s	d
	To Ballance of the former account brought from that acct.	141	3652	1	10
October 2	To the Lady Ann Powlet recd. of Francis Edwards	155	7	19	3
3	To John Earle of Bristoll recd. of Esaw White	150	2	15	2
6	To Jonathan Lamboll recd. of him	147	5		
10	To John Earle of Bristoll recd. of Sergeant Hodges in full	150	36	11	
19	To Wm. Powlet recd. of him	133	6	17	4
20	To Edward Jacob recd. of him	150	4	10	
23	To Edward Crofts recd. of him	96	16		
26	To Tho. Day Soapmaker recd. of him	150	3		
27	To Wm. Spoore Senior recd. of him	154	2	10	
31	To Arthur Bramley & Company recd. of John Brisco	12	10	1	
	To Isaac Heming recd. of Samuel Spencer	152	18	3	6
November 2	To John Perrie recd. of him	117	4		
6	To Isaac Heming received of Edward Baily on a bill assign'd in my favor	152	12		
21	To John Stretten received of him in Full for rent to 2nd Feb. 1687	57	2		
December 3	To Isaac Heming for money hee pd. on my bill assign'd in favor of Tho. Goldney	152	50		
January 2	To Wm. Spoore Senior & Tho. Tuckey recd. of Wm. Spoore	151	10	7	
	To John Gore & John Hurtnell recd. of John Gore November 17th past	149	48	13	6
18	To Edward Jacob received of the Widow Cotterell in full for ½ a yeares rent	156	4	3	6
26	To Joane Darracott recd. of her	98	2		
February 4	To John Wilmer recd. on his assign'd bill on Henry Parsons in my favor	117	50		
6	To John Bubb recd. of him in full	45	44		
			3992	13	1

1689 June 15	By Cash recd. of Edward Jacob in part	*162*	20		
18	By Cash recd. more of the Widow Cotterell in part	*162*	3	10	
July 20	By Ditto recd. of the Widow Cotterell in part	*168*	1	10	
August 31	By Cash recd. of the Widow Cotterell	*168*	1		
1690 May 8	By Ditto recd. of him	*181*	14	7	7
	By Profit and Loss, for what allowed him in full of all his noats				
	of Disbursements and things had of him to this 8th of May 1690	*180*	27	10	00
			80	00	00
	To his new Acct. Current for Ballance carried to that Acct.	*183*	80	00	00
			160	00	00

	Anno 1688				
	Abraham Hill per Contra is	*Cr*	£	s	d
November 15	By Proffit & Losse for one yeares sallary due Nov. 15th 1688	*153*	10		
1689 Nov.	By Ditto for 1 yeares sallary ending in November 1689	*161*	10		
	By Proffit & Losse for a paire of Boots I bought for him	*164*		8	
	By Ditto for his Pole money which I freely give him	*164*		2	6
			20	10	6

	Bristoll 1688				
	Cash per Contra is	*Cr*	£	s	d
September	By Jonathan Lamboll for ½ a Guinny returned back to him	*147*		10	9
29	By Jahzeel Speed pd. for cloth for sleeves	*154*		5	
	By Hugh Strode pd. postage of a pacquet from him to my selfe &				
	Capt. Liston	*149 **		1	3
	By Horses two paid for straw etc.	*156*		2	2½
	By Proffit pd. my wife & Edward Tily	*153*	13	11	9
October 2	By John Massinger paid lent him on 40 prs hose per noat	*155*	4	6	8
4	By Wm. Spoore Senior pd. lent him	*154*	2	10	
6	By Stockins pd. John Lukins & Tho. Hill	*146*	12	16	4
	By Proffit & Losse pd. John Roome	*153*		13	6
10	By Proffit & Losse pd. Lot Wilkins for Butter	*153*	1	3	10
13	By John Massinger pd. lent him on 30 paire of stockins	*155*	3	5	
	By Proffit & Losse pd. severall small things	*153*		3	
	By Stockins pd. Tho. Hill for John Ashman	*146*	4	17	9
15	By Proffit & Losse pd. the Widow Flower & Tho. Dyke	*153*	3	12	6
18	By Horses 2 pd. John Jenkyn	*156*		4	6
	By Proffit & Losse pd. postage of leters	*153*		4	3
	By Robert Lypyeatt pd. him in full	*154*	3	19	
20	By John Massinger pd. lent him on 27 paire stockins	*155*	2	18	6
	By Stockins pd. Tho. Hill	*146*	7	18	8
	By sundry accts for 10 Cask Butter with charges	*58,114,153*	11	3	9½
	By Edward Jacob pd. Arthur Hobbs for work hee did for him	*150*		5	
23	By Edward Crofts pd. him	*96*	2		
	By house at the lower end of Small Streat pd. Ed. Crofts for				
	repaire of a furnace	*22*		10	
26	By John Perrie pd. lent him	*117*	4		
	By John Massinger pd. lent him on 32 paire hose	*155*	3	9	4
30	By Proffit & Losse pd. John Cheshire in full for bottles	*153*	6	9	11
31	By Stockins pd. John Ashman for 175 paire	*146*	11	13	4
November 2	By Joseph Berrie paid him	*62*		5	
	By Stockins pd. John Perrie	*146*	9	11	8
3	By house in which I live pd. Caleb Kippin Chimney money	*130*		8	
	By Proffit & Losse pd. Joseph Drew and Francis Horwood	*153*		9	6
	By Stockins pd. Nath. Pinny for Inkle	*146*		6	6

10	By house in which I live pd. John Cheshire	*130*		18	
12	By Wm. Plydalll paid him	*152*	1		
	By John Massinger pd. lent him on 48 paire hose	*155*	5	4	
	By Horses pd. John Jenkin	*156*		4	8
	By Stockins pd. Ed. Iffe & Fra. Rottenburie in full for hotpressing	*146*	1	10	4
	By Ditto pd. John Lukins	*146*	3	17	1
	By Jahzeel Speed paid John Hardiman	*154*	1	1	
20	By Stockins pd. Tho. Hill for John Perry	*146*	2	10	
	By Proffit & Losse pd. Robert Yate poore money	*153*	3	12	
	By Ditto pd. Edward Lloyd for Drumms & Colours	*153*		7	
	By Ditto pd. Edward Lloyd for a parcell of Xerie	*158*	3	3	
	By John Massinger pd. lent him on 31 paire stockins	*155*	3	7	2
21	By Proffit & Losse pd. severall small things	*153*		19	2
	By Horses two pd. for straw	*156*		2	
			141	11	11
	By house at lower end of Small Streat pd. Proffit & Losse pd. Edward Jones	*22, 153*		11	
	By Jahzeel Speed pd. Richard Day	*154*	1		
	By Stockins pd. Tho. Hill for John Day	*146*	1	12	
	By Adventure in the Olive branch to Malaga consign'd to Ed. Dowding	*158*	2		
	By Adventure Ditto for custome of a Trunck of stockins consign'd to Tho. Strode	*158*	1	14	6
30	By John Massinger pd. lent him on 29 paire hose	*155*	3	2	10
December 5	By Proffit & Losse pd. Joseph Drew in full	*153*		9	6
7, 11	By Stockins pd. John Perry, John Lukins, & Joseph George	*146*	20	9	7
11	By Ditto pd. Robert Webb, John Perry, & Wm. Thiery	*146*	11	2	1
12	By John Massinger pd. lent him on 33 paire hose	*155*	3	11	6
	By Jahzeel Speed pd. John Hardiman	*154*	3		
19	By Lawrence Washington pd. postage of a Pacquet	*132*		3	6
	By Xeries wine 23 Butts pd. for milke	*150*		1	8
	By John Massinger for money lent him on 37 paire hose	*155*	4		2
24	By Horses 2 pd. John Jenkin for 1 moneths keeping them	*156*		4	6
	By Proffit & Losse pd. him for mustering	*153*		1	
26	By John Massinger pd. lent on 33 paire hose	*155*	3	11	6
	By Jahzeel Speed paid Lewis Adams his noat	*154*	1	18	6
January 2	By Horses 2 pd. for 5 bushells Oates	*156*		5	6
	By Wm. Spoore Senior & Junior lent them on theire bond	*158*	30		
	By Tho. Day pd. lent him on 50 Guinnies	*161*	50		
5	By Stockins pd. Jos. George & John Perry	*146*	16		10
	By Abraham Hill pd. him	*156*	1		
	By Xeries wine 23 Butts pd. Charles King	*150*		8	
7	By Stockins pd. Wm. Merchant	*146*	18	9	11
	By Horses 2 for 3 dozen straw	*156*		3	
14	By John Massinger pd. lent him on 32 paire hose	*155*	3	9	4
18	By Stockins pd. Joseph George and John Perrie	*146*	11	18	7
	By John Massinger pd. lent him on 44 paire	*155*	4	15	4
	By Joseph Berrie pd. him	*62*	4		
	By horses 2 pd. John Jenkin	*156*		4	8
	By Reisons solis pd. custom etc.	*158*	8	8	6
	By Joane Darracott pd. lent her	*98*	2		
	By horses 2 pd. Abel Edwards in full	*156*		9	3
22	By Stockins pd. Tho. Hill & John Ashman	*146*	26	11	
	By Jonathan Lamboll pd. lent him	*147*	8		
26	By horses 2 pd. John Wickham and Edward Tibbot for hay	*156*	3	5	
28	By John Massinger pd. lent him on 51 paire hose	*155*	5	10	6
30	By Stockins pd. Jos. George, Fra. Rottenburie, & John Perrie	*146*	9	12	½
February 4	By sundry accts pd. Tho. Hungerford	*153,161*	19	6	

(158)	Bristoll 1688				
	Adventure in the Olive branch Edward Dowding Master to Malaga	Dr	£	s	d
July	*To sundry accts, being the cost and charges of one Trunck of stockins laden in her & consgn'd to said Ed. Dowding for sales & returnes*				
		£	s	d	
	To Stockins for 40 doz is 480 paire Bristoll hose at 2s 8d	78	08	00	
	To Ditto for 11 doz is 132 paire at 1s 8d being Wells hose	11	00	00	146	89	8
	To Ditto for Trunck Cord and Matting				146		11
	To Cash pd. Custom fees and bills				157	2	
	To Profit and Loss, for Ballance				191 *	5	4	6
						97	3	6

(158)	Bristoll 1688	Dr	£	s	d
July	*Adventure in the Olive branch Edward Dowding Master to Malaga* *To sundry accts, being the cost and charges of one Trunck of stockins laden in her & consgn'd to said Ed. Dowding for sales & returnes*				
	To Stockins for 40 doz is 480 paire Bristoll hose at 2s 8d — 78 08 00				
	To Ditto for 11 doz is 132 paire at 1s 8d being Wells hose — 11 00 00	146	89	8	
	To Ditto for Trunck Cord and Matting	146		11	
	To Cash pd. Custom fees and bills	157	2		
	To Profit and Loss, for Ballance	191 *	5	4	6
			97	3	6

	Anno 1688	Dr	£	s	d
	Peter Hinton of Bristoll Turner is				
March 15	*To Cash pd. lent him on his Bill and a Deposite*	162	2		

	Anno 1688	Dr	£	s	d
July	*Adventure in the Olive branch to Malaga Ed. Dowding Master* *To sundry accts, being the cost and charges of one Trunck of stockins laden in her consgn'd to Tho. Strode merchant resident there*				
	To Stockins for 30 doz is 360 prs Bristoll hose at 2s 9d — 49 10 00				
	To Ditto for 22 doz is 264 prs Wells hose at 1s 9d — 23 02 00	146	73	2	6
	To Ditto for Trunck Cord and Matting at — 00 10 06				
	To Cash pd. custom bills etc. — 01 14 06	157	1	14	6
1690	*To Thomas Strode for a bad debt contracted by him on the Sales of 15 doz of stockins to Don Nich. Merrida, being (as per his leter of 15th March 1690) 1365 Ryals Velloon which make 91 pieces of 8 at 52d per ps*	136	19	14	4
			94	11	4

	Anno 1688	Dr	£	s	d
	Reisons Solis 32 Barrills laden per Ed. Dowding in the Olive branch from Malaga of which himselfe was master				
December	*To Edward Dowding for theire cost & charges in Malage 3390 Ryals plate is 423 pieces of 8¾ at 52d the piece of 8 as per acct.*	154	84	15	
	To Cash pd. Custom fees bills etc.	157	8	8	6
	To Edward Dowding for the freight & averidge of said fruite	154	12	6	8¾
			105	10	2¾

	Anno 1688	Dr	£	s	d
	Wm. Spoore Senior of Ashton, & Wm. Spoore Junior of Portburie his sone are				
January 2	*To Cash lent them on theire bond payable with intrest July 3rd 1689*	157	30		
	To Proffit & Losse for ½ yeares intrest of £30 ending July 3rd 1689	164		18	
1689 Jan.	*To Ditto for ½ year's intrest of £30 due Jan. 3rd 1689*	164		18	
1690 Oct.	*To Ditto for 1 year's intrest of £30 due Jan. 3rd 1690*	180	1	16	
			33	12	

6	By sundry accts pd. Abra. Hill & Bartholmew Williams vice Chamberlaine	156, 130	2	10	
	By Stockins pd. Edward Iffe	146	1	2	6
		424	18	8½	
	By Ballance carried to that acct. of debt	162	3567	14	4½
		3992	13	1	

Bristoll 1688

		Cr	£	s	d
	Adventure in the Olive branch per Contra is				
December	By Edward Dowding for 3588 pieces of 8 the neat proceeds of the stockins per Contra being 448½ pieces of 8 at 52d the piece of 8 as per his acct. of sales may appeare	154	97	3	6

	Anno 1689				
	Peter Hinton per Contra is	Cr	£	s	d
July 24	By Cash recd. of him in part	168	1		
1690 April 11	By Ditto Received of him in full	175	1		

	Anno 1689@				
	Adventure in the Olive branch per Contra	Cr	£	s	d
October	By Tho. Strode for the neat proceeds of the trunck of stockins per Contra, being (as) per acct. Sales Closed in Malaga in May last 5131 Ryals Velloon 8 Mer.dees which make 342 1/15 pieces of 8 8 Mer.dees the piece of 8 at 52d	136	74	2	4
	By Profit and Loss, for Ballance	191 *	20	9	
			94	11	4

	Anno 1688				
	Reisons Solis 32 Barrills per Contra	Cr	£	s	d
	By theire sales to Onesiphorus Tyndall, Wm. Burges, Tho. Goldney Junior and Edward Chetwine neat 85cwt 2qr 14lb at 22s per Cwt payable Aprill 1st	95, 53, 130,142	94	3	8
	By Profit and Loss for Ballance	191 *	11	6	6¾
			105	10	2¾

	Anno 1690@				
	William Spoore Senior & Junior per Contra	Cr	£	s	d
	By Acct. of Ballances, for Ballance	194 *	33	12	

Anno 1688/9				
Robert Berrow of Portburie in the County of Somerset Yeoman my Tenant	Dr	£	s	d
To my Copiehold Tenement in Portburie for ½ yeares rent for the 5 acres due August 2nd 1688	160	1	12	6
To Ditto for ½ yeares rent due & ending February 2nd 1688	160	1	12	6
		3	5	

(159)	**Bristoll 1688**				
	Houses in the Castle lately purchased of Joseph Drew house Carpenter, and of the Citie (viz) of the Maior, Aldermen etc. to sundry accts are	Dr	£	s	d
August 22	To Joseph Drew for Three Tenements there held by him by the last Will and Testement of Robt. Drew his father deceased, for foure lives, three of which are now in being , viz. his own life, his sister Elizabeth Horwood, & his sister Marie Page, paying to the Citie the yearly rent of £4 per Annum	159	137		
	To John Cooke Chamberlaine of said Citie for the purchase money of the reversion in Fee of severall Tenements after 3 lives in said Castle now or late in the possession of the said Joseph Drew, William Horwood and Francis Page, theire under Tenants or assignes, paying out of the whole to the Maior Burgessess & Commonalty of the said Citie the yearely reserved rent of £6 10s 00d per Annum, payable halfe yearely in equall portions, as per my deed of Purchase may appeare	159	120		
	To Fra. Yeamans for abstracting writings, drawing Contract with Jos. Drew, engrossing the deed of Assignement, & soliciting the bargaine with the Citie	160	1	4	2
	To Cash pd. Richard Yeamans for drawing writings, fees & his owne care	162	4		8
1689 June 15	To Cash pd. Wm. Plydall for work done about the backhouse there	162		3	
24	To Joane Bryan for chimny money & aid money paid by her	167		6	3
July 29	To Cash pd. John Cheshire Junior for glasing the windows of Richd. Langsworths house	168		13	
August 24	To Ditto pd. Joseph Drew for work done there	168	1		
September 14	To Cash paid Edward Jones for work done there	168		16	
October 3	To Ditto pd. James Rodman for a new Pump in the lower house	168		17	
	To Joane Bryan for Chimny money, poore & aid money	167		6	
	To Richard Langsworth for poore money, harth money & Royall ayds etc.	163		14	
	To Josph Drew for money I freely give him in consideration of his poverty, over and above the purchase money contracted for, that is to say Eleaven shillings & sixpence I paid Fra. Yeamns for him, and Twenty foure pound eleaven shillings & sixpence I paid himselfe as by his receit under his hand and seale dated June 17th 1689 both which summes are express'd in his acct. current underneath	159	25	3	
November	To John Cooke Chamberlaine for 1 yeares reserved rent ending Sept. 29th 1689	159	6	10	
25	To Cash pd. Joseph Drew for flooring a kitchen, & new windows etc.	168	3	6	3
26	To Ditto pd. John Cheshire for glazing the windows of the back house	168		12	6
December 27	To Richard Langsworth for severall disbursments on his house	163		11	1½
	To Cash pd. Chimney money formerly for the little house	175		2	
1690 April	To Joan Bryan for Sundry Disbursements pd. by her for the house in which she Lives	167		16	3
June 21	To Cash pd. John Dole & Hen. Stanckham for ¼ years tax on the act of 3s per pound for the forehouse	181		7	6
	To Richd. Langsworth for his noat of disbursments on the fore house	163		13	6

	Anno 1688				
	Robert Berrow per Contra	*Cr*	*£*	*s*	*d*
February 23	*By Cash recd. of him for ½ yeares rent ending August 2nd 1688*	*162*	1	12	6
1689 Oct. 22	*By Cash recd. of him in part*	*168*		10	
November 30	*By Cash recd. of him in part*	*168*		10	
January 11	*By Cash recd. of him in full*	*173*		12	6
			3	5	

	Bristoll 1689				
	Houses in the Castle per Contra	*Cr*	*£*	*s*	*d*
June	*By Richard Langsworth for ½ a yeares rent of his house ending March 25th 1689*	*163*	5		
	By Joane Bryan for ¼ yeares rent due June 24th 1689	*167*	2		
October 7	*By Ditto for ¼ yeares rent due Sept. 29th 1689*	*167*	2		
	By Richard Langsworth for ½ a yeares rent due Sept. 29th 1689	*163*	5		
	By Francis Page for 1 yeares reserved rent on his 2 houses ending Sept. 29th 1689	*170*		10	
	By Wm. Horwood for 1 yeares reserv'd rent ending the 29th of Sept. 1689	*170*	2		
December 27	*By Richard Langsworth for ¼ yeares rent due Dec. 25th 1689*	*163*	2	10	
	By Joane Bryan for ¼ yeares rent ending Dec. 25th 1689	*167*	2		
March	*By Ditto for ¼ year's rent due March 22th 1689*	*167*	2		
	By Richard Langsworth for ¼ year's rent due March 25th 1690	*163*	2	10	
1690 June	*By Joan Bryan for ¼ year's rent due June 24th 1690*	*167*	2		
Oct.	*By Joan Bryan for ¼ year's rent due the 29th of Sept. 1690@*	*167*	2	6	3
			29	16	3
	By Acct. of Ballances, for Ballance	*194 **	281	9	8½
			311	5	11½

To Joan Bryan for Taxes etc. on the back house	167		7	1
To Cash pd. Wm. Roynon for Lead & work on the fore-house as per noat	187 *	5	16	8
		311	5	11½

Anno 1688

Joseph Drew per Contra is	Dr	£	s	d
To Francis Yeamans for manageing his buisnesse with his Creditors whilst in Prison, release from Walton Short, bond to Rich. Haines & release from Wm. Turner	160		11	6
To Cash paid him at severall times in full of the purchase money as per receits	168	137		
To Ditto paid him over & above the purchase in consideration of his poverty etc.	168	24	11	6
1689 February 20 To Cash paid lent him on his noat payable on demand	175	2		
		164	3	

Anno 1688

John Cooke Chambelaine per Contra is	Dr	£	s	d
October 24 To Cash paid him in full for the purchase money of the houses per Contra as per his receit on the backsyde of my deed of purchase	162	120		
1689 October To Wm. Horwood for 1 yeares reserv'd rent recd. of him due Sept. 29th 1689	170	2		
To Francis Page for 1 yeares reserv'd rent recd. of him due Sept. 29th 1689	170		10	
November 21 To Cash pd. Bartholmew Williams deputy Chamberlaine for 1 yeares rent due Sept. 29th 1689	168	4		
		126	10	

(160)   **Bristoll 1688**

Heneage Fetherstone of Alicant in Spaine merchant Factor	Dr	£	s	d
To Adventure in the ship Greyhound from London for the neat proceeds of one Box stockins amounting to 256 Livers, 16 Sous, & 2 deniers, as per acct. of sakes closed Sept. 24th 1688 the Liver at 4s 6d	142	57	15	7½

Anno 1689

My Copiehold Tenement in Porthurie is	Dr	£	s	d
Aprill 1 To the former acct. current for Ballance	20	15	9	2
To Wm. Spoore Junior for part of a new Gate, 14 doz Helme, sparrs & stretc.hers, for casting a ditch, for gripeing as per his noat	31	4	1	1
To Profit and Loss, for Ballance	191 *	84	14	9
		104	5	

Anno 1689

Arthur Eastmond of Caune [108] in the County of Glocester Woollen draper	Dr	£	s	d
August 7 To Xerie wines 23 Butts for 1 doz Xerie, bottles, & Proffit & Losse	164, 169	1	1	

	Anno 1688				
	Joseph Drew of Bristoll house Carpenter is	*Cr*	*£*	*s*	*d*
August 22	*By houses in the Castle for the purchase money of his 3 Tenements there held by the lives of himselfe, his sister Elizabeth Horwood, & his sister Marie Page, taken by Assignement from himselfe and Richard Haines to Robert Henley & Thomas Walden merchants in trust for mee as by deed of purchase may appeare*	*159*	*137*		
	By Ditto for money I freely gave him in consideration of hispoverty over and above the purchase money first contracted for	*159*	*25*	*3*	
1689 March 21	*By Cash received of him*	*175*	*2*		
			164	*3*	

	Anno 1688				
	John Cooke Chamberlaine of the Citie of Bristoll is	*Cr*	*£*	*s*	*d*
September 28	*By houses in the Castle for the purchase money due to the Maior, Burgesses & Commonalty of said Citie, for the reversion of the severall Tenements there after 3 lives, under the yearely reserved rent of £6 10s 00d as per my deed of purchases*	*159*	*120*		
169 Nov.	*By houses in the Castle for 1 yeares reserved rent ending Sept. 29th 1689*	*159*	*6*	*10*	
			126	*10*	

	Bristoll 1688				
	Heneage Fetherstone per Contra	*Cr*	*£*	*s*	*d*
May	*By Alicant Soape 8 Cornes laden by him in the ship Saphire John Price Master for theire cost and charges, as per Invoyce Aprill 8th 1689 181 Livers & 7 deniers, the Liver at 4s 6d*	*167*	*40*	*14*	*7½*
	By Acct. of Ballances, for Ballance	*194 **	*17*	*1*	
			57	*15*	*7½*

	Anno 1688/9				
	My Copiehold Tenement in Portburie per Contra is	*Cr*	*£*	*s*	*d*
February 18	*By Robert Berrow for ½ yeares rent of 5 Acres ending the 2nd of August 1688*	*158*	*1*	*12*	*6*
March	*By Wm. Spoore Junior for 1 yeares rent of the 2 acres and 2 halfe acres due 25th March 88*	*31*	*3*		
1689 Aprill 13	*By John Corant for the purchase money for which I sould him my said Tenement*	*166*	*90*		
	By Richard Cope for 2 yeares rent ending March 24th 1688	*97*	*7*		
	By Arthur Hobbs for ½ yeares rent due March 25th 1688	*125*	*1*		
	By Robert Berrow for ½ yeares rent for the 5 acres due Feb. 2nd 1688	*158*	*1*	*12*	*6*
			104	*5*	

	Anno 1689				
	Arthur Eastmond per Contra	*Cr*	*£*	*s*	*d*
August 2	*By Cash recd. of him*	*168*	*1*	*1*	

Anno 1688				
Francis Yeamans per Contra is	Dr	£	s	d
To Proffit & Losse for a fee delivered him for Counsellor Robbins but not given	155		10	
To John Massinger for money for a fee charg'd in acct. but was before paid him	163		3	4
To Ditto for money hee received out of Court on Geo. Freemans triall	163	2	7	
To Cash paid him in full	162		16	8
		3	17	

	Anno 1688				
	Merchandizes in the ship Comfort Wm. Brisco Master for acct. Law. Washington to Virginea are debitors £12 19s 3d 1/2 being theire cost and charges	Dr	£	s	d
December	To Abraham Edwards & Tho. Hungerford for 2 boxes cont. 1 piece fine dowlas, at £10 and 4 piecesblew linnin 88¾ yards of blew Linnin at 6d¼ £2 6s 2d½ in all	161	12	6	2½
	To Ditto for a box and cord 2s 8d a custom house permitt & Tydeman 6d	161		6	3
	To Proffit & Losse for lyteridge	153			7
	To Ditto for my Commission	153		6	3
February 7			12	19	3½
	Merchandizes in the John Edward Watts Master for acct. Law. Washington	Dr			
February 7	To James Freeman for 2 Boxes medicines sent by his order for Dr. Warcupp	21	8	17	1
	To Proffit & Losse for my commission	153		4	5
			9	1	6

Anno 1688				
French wine 3 hhds and 3 Tierces are	Dr	£	s	d
To a former acct. current for Ballance brought from that acct.	151	1		2
To Profit and Loss for Ballance	191 *	11	9	8
		12	9	10

(161)	**Bristoll 1688**				
	Abraham Edwards and Company per Contra	Dr	£	s	d
February 4	To Cash paid Tho. Hungerford in full	157	12	12	
	To Profit and Loss, for Ballance	191 *			5½
			12	12	5½

	Anno 1688				
	Tho. Day of Bristoll Wine Cooper is	Dr	£	s	d
January 2	To Cash paid lent him on 50 Guinnies	157	50		
	To Proffit & Losse for intrest from 2nd January 1688 to 2nd August 1689	164	1	15	
10	To Xeries wine 23 Butts for 4 Butts sould him at £26 per Butt payable May 10th 1689	150	104		
1690 April	To Horses two for ½ Ton of Hay sold him at the rate of £2 15s 00d per Ton	174	1	7	6
	To Xeries wines 10 Butts for half their Cost , and charges being £196 6s 5d	142	98	3	2½
	To Rhenish wines 2 Aulns in partnership for ½ their Cost and Charges	163	9	8	2

Anno 1688				
Francis Yeamans of Bristoll Atturney at the Law is	Cr	£	s	d
By Joseph Drew for manageing his buisnesse with his Creditors etc. as per acct.	159		11	6
By Houses in the Castle for drawing writings etc. as per acct.	159	1	4	2
By John Massinger for charges on the Suite with George Freeman	155	2	1	4
		3	17	

Merchandizes in the Comfort per Contra	Cr	£	s	d
By Lawrence Washington his acct. current for the Merchandizes per Contra theire cost and charges	132	12	19	3½
		12	19	3½

Merchandizes in the John per Contra	Cr			
By Lawrence Washington his acct. current for theire cost and charges as per Contra	132	9	1	6
		9	1	6

Anno 1688					
	French wine per Contra	Cr	£	s	d
Feb. 18	By Tho. Goldney Junior for 1 bottle white wine	136			10
March 22	By John Earle of Bristoll for 10 doz of Claret at 10s 6d	150	5	5	
1689 August 31	By the Lady Ann Powlett for 4 doz whitewine at 12s	155	2	8	
	By John Earle of Bristoll for 6 doz whitewine at 12s	150	3	12	
	By Sir George Strode for 2 doz whitewine at 12s	24	1	4	
			12	9	10

Bristoll 1688					
	Abraham Edwards and Tho. Hungerford of Bristoll Linin drapers are	Cr	£	s	d
December	By Merchandizes in the Comfort for Law. Washington for 1 piece Dowlas, 4 pieces blew Linnin, the box etc. as per noat of particulars	160	12	12	5½

Anno 1689					
	Thomas Day per Contra is	Cr	£	s	d
May 6	By Tho. Walden for 1 doz qrt bottles Claret & the bottles	87		14	
	By Proffit & Losse for 5½ Gall. Claret to fill a Cask at 3s per Gall. per noat	164		16	6
June 17	By Cash recd. of him in 6 Guinnies at £1 1s 6d per piece	162	6	9	
July 29	By Cash recd. of him	168	100		
August 7	By Cash recd. of Humphry Corsley by his order	168	50		
	By Isaac Heming for money hee recd. of his order in London	152	46	4	
	By Xeries wine 23 Butts for one Aune of Rhenish recd. of him	169	6		
October 16	By Cash recd. of Esaw White for a parcell of sack whitewine & Claret he had of him	168	1	12	
	By Xeries wine 23 Butts for severall small parcells of Rhenish etc.	169	1	15	8
November	By Cash recd. of him in 3 halfe Crownes	168		7	6

To Samuel Kekewich for ½ the Cost and Charges in Cadiz of 19 Butts Xerie and one Butt of Tent imported in the Rachel and Olive-branch being (as per invoice dated in St Mary Port May 10th 1690) 3507 Ryals Plate 17 Mer.des which make 438 3/8 pieces of 8 and 17 mer.des at 53d per pieces of 8	185	96	16	5
		361	10	3½

Anno 1688

	Adventure in the ship London merchant Roger Drew Master to Cadiz	Dr	£	s	d
January	To sundry accts £155 17s 7d being the cost and charges of a Trunck hose containing as underneath, & goe consign'd to Samuel Kekewich merchant in St Marie Port viz.				

	£	s	d
20 Dozen Bristoll sad hose is 240 paire)			
35 Dozen Ditto fancy colours is 420 paire)			
660 paire at 2s 8d	88	00	00
25 Doz fine Wells folded Bristoll fashion, 300 paire at 1s 10d	27	10	00
20 Doz Wells fancies made up at length is 240)			
10 Doz Ditto sadds at length made up is 120)			
360 paire at 1s 8d	30	00	00
To Ditto for Trunck cord and matting	00	17	00
To Isaac Heming for carriage to London custom etc.	4	18	07
To Ditto for assureance of £150 on said stockins	4	12	00

		Dr	£	s	d
		146	146	7	
		152	9	10	7
			155	17	7
To Profit and Loss, for Ballance		191 *	15	1	5
			170	19	

1689

	My house at the lower end of Small streat in which Ed. Croft liveth	Dr	£	s	d
Aprill 1	To Ballance of a former acct., being the first cost and charge of alltering, repaireing and fitting it for a Tenant	22	718	19	4
	To Ed. Croft for the rent of 2 roomes reserv'd in his house ending June 24th 89	96	1		
	To Ditto for aid money hee paid there	96		11	3
January 24	To Cash pd. Ed. Jones for keeping the roofe 1 yeare ending Sept. 29th 1689	173		6	
	To Edward Croft for ½ year's rent of two rooms in his house ending 25th Dec. 1689	96	1		
	To Ditto for severall disbursments pd. on said house	96	1	5	
			723	1	7

Anno 1688

	Henry Jones Chancellor to the Bishop of Bristoll	Dr	£	s	d
March 21	To Cash paid himselfe as per receit	162	200		

	By *Proffit & Losse for the intrest of the £50 per Contra which I remitt to him*	164	1	15	
January 27	By *Cash recd. of him*	173	48		
1690 June	By *Dr. Fra. Hungerford fpr 18 qts and 12 pints Xerie £2 00s 00d and bottles £00 04s 04d*	184	2	4	4
	By *Xeries wines 23 Butts for 4¼ Gall. Rhenish, and ¼ pound Isinglass*	169		15	10½
	By *Profit and Loss, for 4 doz parts of white-wine, and a qt of Rhenish*	180	1	6	10
July	By *Ditto for money abated him on account*	180		3	1
8	By *Cash recd. of him*	181	93	6	6
			361	10	3½

Anno 1688				
Adventure in the ship London merchant to Cadiz per Contra	Cr	£	s	d
By *Samuel Kekewich for neat proceeds of the stockins per Contra 6312 Ryals plate is 789 pieces of 8 the piece of 8 at 52d as per his acct. of Sales dated in Aprill 1689 may appeare*	167	170	19	00

Anno 1689				
My house at the Lower end of Small Street per Contra is	Cr	£	s	d
Dec. 21 By *Edward Croft for ½ year's rent due Dec. 21th 1689*	96	18		
By *Acct. of Ballances, for Ballance*	191 *	705	1	7
		723	1	7

Anno 1688				
Henry Jones	Cr	£	s	d
February 27 By *Isaac Heming for his bill on James King in favor of said Heming*	152	200		

(162)	**Bristoll 1688/9**				
	Cash is	Dr	£	s	d
	To Ballance of its former acct. brought from that acct.	157	3567	14	4½
February 11	To Richard Merrick recd. of him in part	92	4	10	6
16	To Ditto recd. more of him in part	92		9	6
	To the Lady Ann Powlet recd. of Fra. Edwards	155	8	5	
22	To Richard Hauxworth recd. of him	152		12	
	To Arthur Hobbs recd. of himselfe 5s & of Ed. Jacob 2s	125		7	
23	To Isaac Heming recd. of Lewis Adams	152	2	3	4
	To Proffit & Losse recd. of said Adams	164		3	2
	To Robert Berrow recd. of him for 1/2 yeares rent	158	1	12	6
March 6	To John Harding recd. of Bernard Wilkins	151	2	1	6
14	To Wm. Godwin recd. of him	64	6		
1689 March 28	To Henry Howard & Company recd. of Ozziell Browne	92	3		
	To Tho. Burgesse & Company recd. of Wm. Stocker	138	103	10	
29	To John Eastmont Esquire recd. of Esaw White	163	12	13	
	To John Earle of Bristoll recd. of Edward Bryer	150	28	17	6
Aprill 11	To Edward Crofts for money recd. of him	96	20		
13	To Wm. Godwin recd. of him	166	3		
15	To Richard Langsworth recd. of him	163	4	9	4
16	To John Corant recd. of him in part	166	83		
	To Simon Clement recd. of him £30 of August last, and then omitted to bee charg'd	103	30		
25	To Elizabeth Milner received of her	15	7		
29	To Lewis Adams for money recd. of him in part	56	50		
May 7	To Arthur Bramley & John Brisco recd. of John Brisco	12		6	
8	To Tho. Walden recd. of him	87		14	
11	To John Stretten recd. of him	57	5	4	
15	To Edward Crofts recd. of him by the hands of his Daughter Elizabeth	96	18		
18	To Richard Merrick recd. of him in part	92	5		
25	To Wm. Burges for money of Wm. Louis	53	10		
31	To Ditto recd. of himselfe in full	53	13	10	
June 1	To Onesiphorus Tyndall recd. of him	95	23	13	6
	To Marie Beard & George Collet recd. of them	134	6	15	
15	To Edward Jacob recd. of him	156	20		
17	To Tho. Day recd. of him	161	6	9	
18	To Edward Jacob recd. of the widow Cotterell	156	3	10	
21	To Walter Stephens recd. of him	53	13		
	To Xeries wines 23 Butts recd. of Wm. Whitwood & Ben Smith	150	6	3	8
25	To Richard Chamnyes recd. of him	45	8	8	
	To Wm. Spoore Senior recd. of him	154	5		
July 1	To Joane Bryan recd. of her by the hands of hir sisters	167	1	13	9
	To Edward Chetwine recd. of him	142	20	12	6
			4107	8	1½

	Bristoll 1688/9	Cr	£	s	d
	Cash per Contra is				
February 8	By Stockins paid Tho. Hill for 2 parcells	146	19	7	5
	By John Massinger pd. lent him on 33 paire stockins per receit	163	3	11	6
	By Jahzeel Speed pd. Tho. Hungerford for Lincloth for him	154	2	10	
11	By Charles King pd. lent him	152	5		
13	By Horses two pd. John Jenkin	156		4	8
	By John Massinger for a fee given Counsellor Haggatt	163		10	
	By houses in the Castle pd. Richard Yeamans	159	4		8
18	By James Freeman pd. him in full	21	8	17	
20	By Henry Gibbes paid him	151		14	
	By horses two paid Wm. Williams for oates	156		9	
	By Stockins pd. Robert Webb, John Perry, & Tho. Walden	146	2	18	1
21	By John Massinger pd. lent him on 33 paire of hose	163	3	11	6
	By Elizabeth Milner paid her	15	8		
23	By Proffit & Losse pd. charges on racking tooles and houshold expences to January 5th 88	164	75	12	1½
25	By Henry Gibbes paid him in full	151		16	
	By Stockins John Day & Tho. Hill	146	2	5	1
27	By Jahzeel Speed pd. Henry Stover	154		4	6
	By John Hardiman paid lent him	80	3		
28	By John Massinger pd. lent him on 31 paire hose	163	3	7	2
March 7	By Joane Darracot pd. her in full	98	3	15	
9	By John Massinger lent John Massinger on 30 paire hose	163	3	5	
	By Stockins pd. Tho. Hill for John Perrie	146	2	18	4
	By Edward Crofts pd. lent him	96	20		
13	By horses two pd. John Jenkyn	156		4	8
15	By Proffit & Losse pd. for 5 Panniers & 18 dozen Corks	164		6	2
17	By Stockins pd. John Perrie, John Day, Tho. Hill & Tho. Hill	146	26	4	11
	By Peter Hinton pd. lent him on his bill & a deposit	158	2		
	By John Massinger pd. lent him on 39 prs hose per noat	163	4	4	6
21	By Dr. Henry Jones pd. himselfe	161	200		
	By John Massinger pd. lent him on 28 prs stockins	163	3		8
22	By Stockins pd. Robert Webb, John Perry & John Greene	165	3	1	1
28	By Wm. Spoore Senior pd. lent him on his bill	154	5		
	By Proffit & Losse pd. John Greene for a Jackline	164		1	
1689 March 28	By Wm. Spoore Senior pd lent him (Error)	154	-	-	-
	By Henry Gibbes pd. lent him on his bond etc.	151	150		
Aprill 30, 1	By John Massinger pd. lent him on 49 paire hose at twice as per noat	163	5	6	2
	By Fra. Yeamans paid him in full formerly	160		16	8
5	By Richard Toune paid him	147		7	6
	By Proffit & Losse pd. pd. port of leters & to Robert Yate for Irish Protestants	164		14	
9	By Horses 2 pd. John Jenkin for keeping my 2 mares	156		6	8
	By Charles King pd. lent him	152	5		
10	By Stockins pd. Thomas Hill for John Ashman	165	13	17	6
11	By John Massinger pd. lent him on 30 paire hose per noat	163	3	5	
12	By Stockins pd. John Perrie	165	7	12	1
15	By James Freeman pd. him in full	21		10	6
16	By Stockins pd. Tho. Hill & Edward Iffe	165	2	10	2
19	By Ditto John Perrie for one parcell & Tho. Hill for John Ashman, John Day and Richd. d Forster	165	26	1	
20	By John Massinger pd. lent him on 34 paire hose per noat	163	3	13	8
22	By James Swetnam pd. him in full	133		6	
	By Simon Clement pd. returned him of his own bad money	103		17	6
			640	4	7½
24	By Stockins pd. Tho. Hill for Jonathan Abram and — Sanders	165	4	5	8
26	By Ditto pd. John Perry for 24 paire	165	2	10	
27	By Horses 2 pd. Tho. Lewis	156		9	2

(163)

(163)	**Bristoll 1688/9**				
	John Massinger of Bristoll hosier	Dr	£	s	d
February 8	To Ballance of his former acct. current brought from that acct.	155	139	12	8
	To Cash pd. lent him on 33 paire of stockins as per noat	162	3	11	6
13	To Ditto pd. lent him				
	To Cash pd. Counsellor Haggatt his fee for counsell in Geo. Freemans case	162		10	
21	To Cash pd. lent him on 33 paire hose as per noat	162	3	11	6
28	To Cash pd. lent him on 31 paire hose as per noat	162	3	7	2
March 9	To Cash pd. lent him on 30 paire hose as per noat	162	3	5	
17	To Cash pd. lent him on 39 paire hose as per noat	162	4	4	6
21	To Ditto pd. lent him on 28 paire hose per noat	162	3		8
1689 March 30	To Ditto pd. lent him on 33 paire hose per noat	162	3	11	6

Date	Description	Folio	£	s	d
30	By Stockins pd. Tho. Hill	165	11	18	9
May 2	By Proffit & Losse pd. Isaac Dighton	164		6	8
3	By Abraham Hill pd. him	156	2	10	
	By Stockins pd. John Perrie	165	2	14	2
4	By John Massinger pd. lent him on 30 paire stockins	163	3	5	
	By Proffit & Losse pd. Tho. Goldney Junior	164		2	
7	By Horses two pd. John Jenkin	156		5	
8	By Proffit & Losse pd. Edward Jones	164		5	3
	By John Massinger pd. lent him on 40 pre hose per noat	163	4	6	8
10	By Stockins pd. John Perrie and Tho. Hill for 3 parcells	165	14	4	5
11	By sundry accts pd. Fra. Maynard for 5 Flitches Bacon	113, 164	1	13	2
16	By Lawrence Washington pd. postage of a leter	167			6
	By John Massinger pd. lent him on 34 paire hose	163	3	13	4
23	By Stockins pd. John Perrie and Henry Britten	165	11	17	6
	By Proffit & Losse pd. Jonathan George for ayd money	164	1		
28	By John Massinger pd. lent him on 30 paire hose	163	3	5	
30	By Proffit & Losse pd. Susan Kippin and port of leters	164	1	4	9
31	By Stockins pd. John Perrie & Francis Rottenburie	165	9	4	
June 1	By Stockins pd. Elizabeth Webb, Fra. Rottenburie & Tho. Hill	165	4	11	3
3	By horses 2 pd. Jonathan Perkin	156	1	10	
4	By Jahzeel Speed pd. Nicholas Baker & John Jones	154	2	2	
7	By Stockins pd. Henry Britten	165	3	19	2
	By John Massinger pd. lent him on 31 paire	163	3	7	2
	By Robert Lyppiat paid him in full	154	7		
9	By horses 2 pd. John Jenkin	156		3	
	By Proffit & Losse pd. postage of leters	164		3	2
11	By Stockins paid John Perrie & Tho. Walden	165	14	1	2
14	By John Massinger paid lent him on 27 paire	163	2	18	6
15	By Proffit & Losse paid postage of leters & Panniers	164		5	3
	By houses in the Castle paid Wm. Plydall	159		3	
	By horses 2 pd. for 2 Bushells beanes	156		4	
17	By Xeries wine 10 Butts in the Welcom from Cadiz	142	13	1	
	By John Massinger paid lent him on 28 paire hose	163	3		8
	By Stockins paid John Perrie, Henry Britten & Tho. Hill	165	9	10	10
22	By Stockins pd. Tho. Hill	165	6	12	
27	By Jahzeel Speed pd. Alexander Cadduggan	154	1	10	
	By Stockins pd. Tho. Hill, Francis Rottenburie & John Perry for 5 parcells	165	13	13	3
	By Proffit & Losse pd. John Gandy	164		10	6
28	By John Massinger pd. lent him	163	4	2	4
	By horses 2 pd. Abel Edwards	156		14	
July 4	By Stockins paid Tho. Hill for 5 parcells of stockins	165	19	16	
	By John Cooke pd. him Octo.br 24th 1688 the purchase money of my houses in the Castle then omitted	162	120		
			952	3	10½
	By ballance carried a new acct. current	168	3155	4	3
			4107	8	1½

Bristoll 1688

Description	Cr	£	s	d
John Massinger per Contra				
By Francis Yeamans for a Fee overcharg'd being formerly paid as per his acct.	160		3	4
By Ditto for money hee recd. out of Court on the Tryall with George Freeman	160	2	7	
By Worsted stockins for severall parcells deposited in my hands on which I advanced money in charity at 2s 2d per paire as per Contra	165	198	13	8
By Ditto for money advanced when I tooke the stockins to my selfe 1d per paire which with 2s 2d was 2s 3d per paire, and was 2d per paire more than I then gave for the best stockins I bought of any man besydes	165	7	12	10

			£	s	d
Aprill 1	To Cash pd. lent him on 16 paire hose per noat	162	1	14	8
11	To Ditto pd. lent him on 30 paire hose per noat	162	3	5	
20	To Cash pd. lent him on 34 paire hose as per noat	162	3	13	8
May 4	To Ditto pd. lent him on 30 paire hose per noat	162	3	5	
9	To Ditto pd. lent him on 40 paire hose per noat	162	4	6	8
16	To Ditto pd. lent him on 34 paire of hose per noat	162	3	13	4
28	To Ditto pd. lent him on 30 paire as per noat	162	3	5	
June 7	To Cash pd. lent him on 31 paire as per noat	162	3	7	2
14	To Ditto pd. lent him on 27 paire as per noat	162	2	18	6
20	To Ditto pd. lent him on 28 paire stockins as per noat	162	3		8
28	To Ditto pd. lent him on 38 paire at 2s 2d per noat	162	4	2	2
July 5	To Cash pd. lent him on 21 paire as per noat	168	2	5	6
13	To Ditto pd. lent him on 35 paire as per noat	168	3	15	10
			207	7	8
	To Profit and Loss, for Ballance	191 *	1	9	2
			208	16	10

Anno 1689					
	Rhenish Wine 2 Aulnes from London for acct. of Tho. Day & myselfe in equall halves	Dr	£	s	d
July	To Isaac Heming for theire first cost & charges in London	152	17	2	
31	To Cash pd. John Edwards for carriage and halling	168	1	14	4
			18	16	4

Anno 1688					
	Plate (viz) 12 Loggs of Silver importing 3000 pieces of 8 laden per Samual Kekewich in the ship Friston Capt. Gutteridge commander at Cadiz bound to London	Dr	£	s	d
February	To Isaac Heming for assureance of £600 at £3 per Cent and charges	152	18	2	

Anno 1688					
	John Eastmont of Sherborne in the County Dorset Esq. High Sherriffe	Dr	£	s	d
March 22	To sundry accts for 3 Rundlets cont. 40¾ Gallons Xerie, the Rundlets etc.	150, 164	12	13	

Anno 1689					
	Henry Howard & Company viz. John Thorrowgood & Geo. Hurt on bond	Dr	£	s	d
	To Ballance resting due on theire bond brought from that acct.	92	100		
October	To Proffit & Losse for ½ yeares intrest due Sept. 18th 1689	164	3		
March	To Ditto for ½ year's intrest of £100 due March 16th 1689	164	3		
1690 Oct.	To Ditto for ½ year's intrest of £100 ending Sept. 16th 1690@	180	3		
			109		

Anno 1689					
	Richard Langsworth of Bristoll Shoemaker	Dr	£	s	d
Aprill	To houses in the Castle for ½ yeares rent for his house ending March 25th 1689	159	5		
October	To Ditto for ½ yeares rent due 29th of Sept. 1689	159	5		
December 27	To Ditto for ¼ yeares rent due December 25th 1689	159	2	10	
1690	To Ditto, for ¼ year's rent due 25th March 1690 @	159	2	10	
			15		

	208	16	10

Anno 1690				
Rhenish wine per Contra	Cr	£	s	d
By Rhenish wines my ½ of 10 Butts for half the Cost & Charges of the two Aulns of Rhenish er Contra	170	9	8	2
By Tho. Day for his ½ of £18 16s 4d the Cost & Charges of the 2 Aulns Rhenish per Contra	161	9	8	2

Anno 1689				
Plate in the Friston per Contra	Cr	£	s	d
By Plate imported on sundry ships from Cadiz for the money per Contra	143	18	2	

Anno 1689				
John Eastmont per Contra	Cr	£	s	d
March 29 By Cash recd. of Esaw White by his order	162	12	13	

Anno 1689				
Henry Howard & Company per Contra	Cr	£	s	d
October 26 By Cash recd. of Ozziel Browne for 1/2 yeares intrest of £100 due Sept. 18 1689	168	3		
1690 April 10 By Ditto received of Ozziel Brown for 1/2 year's intrest due March 16th 1689	175	3		
		6		
By Acct. of Ballances, for Ballance	194 *	103		
		109		

Anno 1689				
Richard Langsworth	Cr	£	s	d
By Proffit & Losse for 2 paire shooes, taxes and reparations of his house per noat	164		10	8
Aprill 15 By Cash recd. of him in full for ½ yeares rent due March 24th 1688	162	4	9	4
By sundry accts for shooes & his noat of disbursments for poore, harth money etc.	147,159, 154	1	3	
October 16 By Cash recd. of him in full for ½ yeares rent ending Sept. 29th 1689	168	3	17	
December 27 By houses in the Castle for sundry disbursments on his house	159		11	1½

(164)	Bristoll 1688/9	Dr	£	s	d
	Proffit & Losse is				
	To Ballance of a former acct. brought from that acct.	153	582	14	¼
	To Thomas Puxton for Ballance	22	6	15	
	To Joseph Speed for Ballance	24	22	12	9
	To Adventure in the Martha and Sarah for Ballance	25	19	16	4
	To Edward Jones forn severall parcells of work done	25	3	7	
	To William Smart for Ballance	26	2	10	
	To Ann Blackwell for Ballance	26		2	
	To Henry Winter for Ballance	26	6		
	To John Browne for Ballance	26		8	
February 23	To Cash pd. pd. for charges on a set of racking tooles	162		3	2
	To Ditto pd. houshold expences to the 11th of Aprill last past 1688	162	37	3	7½
	To Cash pd. houshold expences to the 5th of January 1688	162	38	5	4
March 13	To Ditto pd. for 5 Panniers and 18 dozen Corks	162		6	2
1689 March 28	To Cash pd. John Greene for a Line for the Jack	162		1	
	To Richard Toune for 1½ yeares Customhouse Presentments ending March 25th 1689	147		15	
Aprill 5	To Cash pd. port of leters	162		4	
	To Ditto pd. Robert Yate for reliefe of Irish Protestants	162		10	
	To Richard Langsworth for Shooes, Taxes on the house and reparations as per noat	163		10	8
	To John Earle of Bristoll for Ballance	80		8	5
May 2	To Cash pd. Isaac Dighton for 4 Firkins of beere	162		6	8
4	To Cash pd. Tho. Goldney for 6 Quier of paper	162		2	
6	To Tho. Day for 5½ Gall. Claret	161		16	6
	To Lands in Clapton lately purchased of the Ld. Fitzharding for ballance	142	4		
8	To Cash pd. Edward Jones for work done about my house	162		5	3
	To Samuel Kekewich 12¾ pieces of 8 at 52d as per acct. current March 16th 1688/9	148	2	13	7½
11	To Cash pd. Fra. Maynard for a Flitch Bacon	162		5	4
25	To Cash for what pd. Jonathan George for 3 months ayd money	162	1		
30	To Cash pd. Susan Kippin for a Cask of Butter	162	1		2
	To Ditto pd. port of severall leters	162		4	7
June 7	To Robert Lyppiot for severall parcells of Mault had to June 7th 1689	154	7		
9	To Cash pd. port of severall leters	162		3	2
15	To Cash pd. for 2 panniers etc.	162		3	1
	To Ditto pd. port leters	162		2	2
27	To Cash pd. John Gandy in full	162		10	6
	To John Blackwell for one hogshead of whitewine	148	8	5	
July 8	To Cash pd. Edward Pruet for Pole money	168	3	12	
9	To Cash pd. port of leters	168		1	3
	Tto Tho. Goldney Junior for ballance of his acct.	136		6	10
13	To Cash pd. port of leters	168		2	9
	To Dennis Tayler for so much abated given him	11	3	5	
18	To John Blackwell for 20 Gall. Xerie at 5s & 1 Gall. Sweet	148	5	9	
	To Isaac Heming for ½ pound of Dr. Russells powder	152		16	
	To Ditto for a cheese sent to Tho. Curtis	152		6	10
	To Isaac Heming for port of leters, books etc.	152	1	10	9
August 14	To Cash pd. — Baker for ½ Cwt & 18lb cheese	168		16	6

		£	s	d
By Cash recd. of him in full with his disbursments for ¼ yeares rent due Dec. 25	173	1	18	10½
1690 June 28 By Cash recd. of him	181	1	16	6
By Houses in the Castle for his noat of disbursments on the fore house	159		13	6
		15		

Bristoll 1688/9

	Cr	£	s	d
Proffit & Losse per Contra				
By Tobacco 6 hhds in the Victory	25	11	1	7
By Henry Gibbes for intrest of £40	151	2	10	-
By Fra. Yeamans for money design'd for Counsellor Robbins but returnd	160		10	
By Cash recd. of Lewis Addams for charges on a set of racking tooles	162		3	2
March 22 By John Earle of Bristoll for 10 doz bottles 5 panniers etc.	150	1	5	10
By John Eastmont for 3 Rundlets etc.	163		8	6
By Edward Crofts for ½ yeares rent of the house bee lives in ending December 22th 1688	96	18		
By Wm. Godwin for 1 yeares intrest of £100 ending etc. formerly omitted to bee chargd	64	6		
By Dennis Tayler for the Bottomree money for £5 on the Nathanael to and from Nevis	11	1	5	
By Estate at Clapton for ballance of that acct.	72	49	10	2
By John Brisco & Company recd. of John Brisco	12		6	
1689 May By Samuel Kekewitch for ballance of his acct. current in Sterling	148	9	13	7¼
By Nathanael Haggatt for ½ yeares intrest of £320 due May 9th 1689	148	9	12	
By sundry accts due for intrest money	100	9		
By Dr. Fra. Hungerford for 2 doz bottles a pannier etc.	87		5	8
June 25 By John Wilmer for 4 doz bottle, Pannier etc.	117		11	
By Edward Dowding for ½ yeares intrest of £120	154	3	12	
By Tho. Day Wine Cooper for 7 months intrest of £50	161	1	15	
By John Earle of Bristoll for 4 doz bottles Pannier etc.	150		10	6
By Jonathan Lamboll for 1 yeares intrest of £450 ending June 24th 1689	109	22	10	
August By Tho. Day Soapmaker for 1 doz bottles	150		2	
7 By Arthur Eastmond for 1 doz bottles Pannier etc.	160		3	
By Tho. Goldney Junior for 2 doz bottles	136		4	
28 By the Lady Ann Powlet for 8 doz bottles panniers etc.	155	1	1	
By John Earle of Bristoll for portridge of 2 Rundlets etc.	150			9
31 By the Lady Ann Powlet for 4 doz bottles 2 panniers etc.	155		10	6
By John Earle of Bristoll for 6 doz bottles 3 Panniers etc.	150		15	8
September By Sir George Strode for 4 doz bottles 2 Pannniers etc.	24		11	
October By Simon Clement and Michael White for 1 yeares intrest of £50	133	3		
By Edward Croft for ½ yeares rent of his house ending 24th June 1689	96	18		
By Xeries wines 10 Butts in the Wellcom for sundry charges on them	142		16	6
By Simon Clement & his Father 10 yeares 3 months intrest ending Sept. 24th 1689	22	36	4	4
By Ditto & Michael White for ½ yeares intrest of £50 ending Oct. 22nd 1689	133	1	10	
16 By John Sandford for 1/2 yeares intrest of £100 ending September 16th 1689	19	3		
By Robert Dowding & Company for ½ a yeares intrest of £100 due August 4th 1689	100	3		
By Henry Howard & Company for ½ a yeares intrest of £100 due Sept. 18th 1689	163	3		
By Edward Dowding for ¼ yeares intrest of £120 due Oct. 9th 1689	154	1	16	

Date	Description				
	To Cash pd. port of leters	168		3	
September 1	To Cash paid for Panniers	168		6	1
5	To Ditto pd. for Panniers	168.		4	10
14	To Ditto pd. Abraham Hill for his expences to and from Musburie	168		7	6
19	To Ditto pd. Eliza. Milner for 10 yards of Baies	168	1	10	
25	To Cash paid Charles White for royall aid money	168	1		
October 2	To Cash paid Jane Shepheard for a Cask of Butter sent to Sonne Heming	168	1	9	9
3	To Ditto pd. James Rodman for mending my Pump	168		3	
	To Edward Croft for 3 Grose of Corks	96		5	3
	To Abraham Hill for 1 yeares sallary ending Nov. 1689	156	10		
	To Ditto for a paire of Boots I gave him 8s & for his pole 2s 6d	156		10	6
26	To Cash pd. Lott Wilkins for a Tubb of Butter	168	1	6	11
November 2	To Ditto pd. John Bussle for mending of the Musket	168		1	6
15	To Cash pd. Ed. Lloyd & John Webb for 12d in the pound for personall estate & house	168	7	4	
18	To Ditto pd. John Gandy in full	168		4	4
	To John Hardiman for making & repaireing of severall garments	80	1	6	7½
	To Wm. Jones & Wm. Clark for severall parcells of bottles recd. of Wm. Clark	138	6	3	5
25	To Cash pd. John Greene for 2 cords & 2 balls of twine	168		3	2
December 6	To Cash pd. for passages at Rounham, & severall small disbursments	168			10
	To Thomas Day for the intrest of £50 remitted to him	161	1	15	
	To Isaac Heming for Dr. Russells powder, scorbutick Tincture & Cordialls	152	1	13	
24	To Cash pd. Humphry Nickins for watching	173			8
	To Isaac Heming for a Cheshire Cheese sent to Tho. Curtis	152		10	6
	To Cash pd. severall petty disbursments	173			5¾
	To Wm. Plydall for building my orchard wall, & severall pieces of work	152	3	10	
January 6	To Cash pd. John Hardiman in full	173	1	8	
7	To Ditto pd. Tho. Wall in full of his noat for a new Leadger	173	1	4	
14	To Ditto pd. Tho. Barret in full for pruning tooles	173		4	6
	To Elizabeth Milner for 8 yards of Crape at	15		10	8
	To Jonathan Lamboll for Abra. Hills expences to Reading	147		12	
25	To Cash pd. for 4 Panniers	173		2	10
28	To Cash pd. for newsleters	173			1
29	To Cash pd. for 3 Groce of Corks	173		4	3
Febraury 3	To Cash pd. postage of leters to this 3rd of February	173	1	19	1
10	To Ditto pd. John Gandy in full	173		2	6
14	To Ditto pd. Humphry Nickins for watching to this 14th day	175			8
March	To Cash pd. houshold expences to 20th July 1689	175	49	2	1
	To Ditto pd. houshold expences to the 29th of January 1689	175	55	2	5
15	To Elizabeth Milner for 16 yds of Flannel Crape at 1s 5d per yard & 8 yds Ditto at 1s 4d	15	1	13	4
19	To Cash paid Isaac Dighton (for his father Geo. Dighton) for two firkins of beer	175		3	4
1690 April 3	To Ditto paid Wm. Phelps & John Bartlett on the Act of 3d per pound for my House being ¼ of £4 10 which I am to pay on said Act	175	1	2	6
5	To Ditto pd. Humphrey Nickins for Watching to the 20th day of March 1690	175			8
	To Ditto pd. Wm. Phelps & John Bartlett on the act of 3d per pound for my personall Estate	175	18		
			937	10	8½
	To Ballance carried to a new Account	180	717	4	½
			1654	14	9

Month	Description	Folio	£	s	d
	By Henry Gibes for intrest of 2 summes of money	151	5	15	4
	By Wm. Godwin for ½ yeares intrest of £100 due Sept. 27th 1689	166	3		
	By Tho. Lutterell & Company for 1 yeares intrest of £20 due Oct. 26 1689	97	1	4	
	By Wm. Spoore Senior & Peter Collet for				
	By Wm. Spoore Junior for 1 yeares intrest of £10 ending Oct. 16 1689	31		12	
	By Wm. Spoore Junior & Senior for ½ yeares intrest of £40 due June 5th 1689	69	1	4	
	By Wm. Spoore Senior & Junior for ½ yeares intrest of £30 due July 3rd 1689	158		18	
	By Wm. Jones & Company for 3/4 yeares intrest of £50 due Sept. 8th 1689	138	2	5	
	By Wm. Spoore & Peter Collet for ½ yeares intrest of £50 due Oct. 21th 1688	30	1	10	
November	By Ditto for 1 yeares intrest of £50 ending Octo.br 21th 1689	30	3		
	By John Wilmer for 6 doz. pint bottles panniers & covers	117		10	11
	By Worsted stockins for ballance of that account	165	1338	15	2¼
	By Tho. Smith Wine Cooper for ½ yeares rent of my Vault in Small Streat	171	3	5	
December	By John Wilmer pd. hooping of 2 Firkins Butter, packing cloth etc.	174		1	7
	By Wm. Spoore Junior for 2 months intrest of £10	31		2	
	By Wm. Spoore Junior & Senior for 6 months & 12 daies intrest of £40	69	1	5	6
31	By the Lady Ann Powlet for 4 doz bottles 2 Panniers, Covers etc.	155		10	8
January 8	By Sir George Strode for 2 doz bottles a pannier & cover etc.	173		5	6
	By Jonathan Lamboll in mortgage for 7 months intrest of £450 ending Jan. 25 89	109	13	2	6
	By John Earle of Bristoll for cooperidge & portridge of 2 Rundlets Xerie	150		1	5
February 18	By Ditto for 2 new Rundlets, cooperidge, custome etc.	150		6	10
	By Nathanael Haggatt for ½ yeares intrest of £320 ending Nov. 9th 1689	148	9	12	
	By Robert Dowding & Company for ½ yeares intrest of £100 due Feb. 4th 1689	100	3		
March 16	By Henry Howard & Company for ½ year's intrest of £100 due 16th March 1689	163	3		
	By John Sandford for ½ year's intrest of £100 due 16th March 1689	19	3		
27	By William Godwin for ½ year's Intrest of £100 due March 27th 1690	166	3		
April	By Lincloth 15 Pacquets for warehouse room £0 18s 0d and my Commission £4 0s 0d	172	4	18	
	By Henry Gibbes for intrest of £150 from Sept. 25th 1689 to Feb.ry 4th 1690	151	3	3	9
	By Ditto for Intrest of £50 from Feb.ry 4th 1689 to April 10th 1690	151		10	
	By Edw. Jacob & Company for 2 years intrest of £20	134	2	8	
	By Wm. Jones & Company for ½ years intrest of £50	138	1	10	
	By John Gore & Comp.a for 2½ years intrest of £127	149	19		10
	By Will. Spoore Senior & Junior for ½ yeares intrest of £30	158		18	
	By Tho. Lutterell & Comp.a for ½ yeares intrest of £20	97		12	
	By Edw. Dowding for ½ years intrest of £120	154	3	12	
			1654	14	9

(165)	**Bristoll 1688/9**							
	Worsted Stockins bought of severalls are				Dr	£	s	d
March 22	To Cash pd. Robert Webb for a Trunck				162		13	
1689 March 28	To Cash pd. Tho. Hill for John Perrie	paire	s	d				
	for	21	2	1	162	2	3	9
Aprill 10	To Ditto pd. John Greene for 4 Trunck Cords				162		4	4
	To Ditto pd. Tho. Hill for John							
	Ashman for	222	1	3	162	13	17	6
12	To Ditto pd. John Perrie for	73	2	1	162	7	12	1
16	To Cash pd. Tho. Hill for Jonathan							
	Abram for	20	2	1	162	2	1	8
	To Ditto pd. Edward Iffe in full for hotpressing				162		8	6
19	To Cash pd. John Perrie for	48	2	1	162	5		
	To Ditto pd. Tho. Hill for John							
	Ashman for	228		15	162	14	5	
	To Ditto pd. Tho. Hill for John Day for	20	2		162	2		
20	To Ditto pd. Tho. Hill for Richard							
	Forster for	48	2		162	4	16	
24	To Cash pd. Tho. Hill for Jonathan							
	Abram for	20	2	1	162	2	1	8
	To Ditto pd. Tho. Hill for — Sanders							
	for	22	2		162	2	4	
26	To Ditto pd. John Perrie for	24	2	1	162	2	10	
30	To Ditto pd. Tho. Hill for John							
	Ashman for	191		15	162	11	18	9
May 3	To Cash pd. John Perrie for	26	2	1	162	2	14	2
10	To Ditto pd. John Perrie for	47	2	1	162	4	17	11
	To Ditto pd. Tho. Hill for Jonathan							
	Abram for	24	2	1	162	2	10	
	To Ditto pd. Tho. Hill for Joseph							
	George for	117	1	2	162	6	16	6
23	To Cash pd. John Perrie for	29	2	1	162	3		5
25	To Ditto pd. John Perrie for	61	2	1	162	6	7	1
	To Ditto pd. Henry Britten for	24	2	1	162	2	10	
31	To Ditto pd. John Perrie for	69	2	1	162	7	3	9
	To Ditto pd. Fra. Rottenburie for	21		23	162	2		3
June 1	To Cash pd. Fra. Rottenburie for hotpressing				162		15	9
	To Ditto pd. Elizabeth Webb for a Trunck				162		13	
	To Ditto pd. Tho. Hill för Jonathan							
	Abram for	30	2	1	162	3	2	6
7	To Ditto pd. Henry Britten for	38	2	1	162	3	19	2
11	To Ditto pd. John Perrie for	122	2	1	162	12	14	2
14	To Ditto pd. Tho. Walden for 4 dozen of Inkle				162	1	7	
21	To Cash pd. John Perrie for	19	2	1	162	1	19	7
	To Ditto pd. Henry Britten for	36	2	1	162	3	15	
	To Ditto pd. Tho. Hill for the Widow							
	White for	27	2	1	162	2	16	3
22	To Ditto pd. Tho. Hill for Wm.							
	Thiery for	49	2		162	4	18	
	To Ditto pd. Tho. Hill for	17	2		162	1	14	
27	To Cash pd. Tho. Hill for John Day							
	& Sam. Dyer for	20	2	1				
		32	2		162	5	5	
28	To Cash pd. John Perrie for	31	2	1	162	3	4	7
29	To Ditto pd. Fra. Rottenburie for the							
	Widow Abram for	28	1	11	162	2	13	8
	To Ditto pd. Tho. Hill for Jonathan							
	Abram for	24	2	1	162	2	10	
July 4	To Ditto pd. Tho. Hill for Richard							
	Forster for	48		23	162	4	12	

	Bristoll 1688/9	Cr	£	s	d
	Worsted Stockins per Contra are				
1689	*By Ballance of a former acct. brought from that acct.*	*146*	1000		¼
Aprill	*By Adventure 2nd in the Merchants Goodwill Ben. Morley Master to Cadiz for 1 Trunck cont. 240 paire Bristoll sadds, and 454 prs Bristoll fancies at 2s 6d and 132 prs Wells fancies folded Bristoll waies, and 558 prs Wells made up plaine, the first at 1s 7d per paire & the later at 1s 6d with the Trunck cord and matting consign'd to Samuel Kekewich merchant inn St Marie Port for sales and returnes*	*166*	142	8	
	By Adventure 3rd in the Wellcom Philip Freake Master to Cadiz for one Trunck cont. 444 paire Bristoll Fancies at 2s 6d, 264 prs Wells Fancies folded at 1s 7d & 624 prs Ditto made up plaine at 1s 6d with Trunck Cord ie& matting consgn'd to Samuel Kekewich merchant in St Marie Port	*166*	119	1	
June	*By Adventure in the ship Cesar for 2 Trunck laden in her by Isaac Heming for Cadiz cont. 150½ doz Bristoll Sades & Fancies, and 79 doz Wells fancies, the Bristoll in the whole 1806 paire at 2s 8d, Wells hose 948 paire at 1s 8d*	*169*	319	16	
August	*By Adventure in the ship Sarah Capt. John Bradill to Cadiz for 78 doz cont. 938 paire Bristol sades, & 22 doz cont. 264 paire Bristoll fancies, all at 2s 8d per paire and 10 doz 10 paire is 130 paire Wells sades at 1s 8d per paire laden in said ship and goe consign'd to Samuel Kekewich merchant in St Marie Port, and the Trunck cord & matting, all amounting to*	*169*	171	13	8
November	*By Adventure in the Sarah for one other Trunck laden in her consign'd as before cont. 44 doz 5/12 Bristoll Sadds & 22 doz ditto Fancies, 797 paire at 2s 6d & 19¼ doz Wells Fancies 231 paire at 1s 6d with Trunck cord & matting*	*169*	117	16	
			1870	14	8¼

Date	Description				Folio	£	s	d
	To Ditto pd. Tho. Hill for the Widow Abram for	36	2		*162*	3	12	
	To Ditto pd. Tho. Hill for	19	2		*162*	1	18	
	To Ditto pd. him for John Lukins & Jeremy Cook for	97	2		*162*	9	14	
5	To Cash pd. Tho. Hill for James Woollen etc. for	52	2		*168*	5	4	
	To Ditto pd. Ditto for John Aplin for	266	1	2	*168*	15	10	4
	To Ditto pd. John Perrie for	21	2	1	*168*	2	3	9
	To Ditto pd. Tho. Hill for Henry Britten for	42	2	1	*168*	4	7	6
8	To Ditto pd. Tho. Hill for John Day for	13	2		*168*	1	6	
11	To Ditto pd. Tho. Hill for Joseph George for	110		15	*168*	6	17	6
					168	216	9	1
11	To Cash paid Tho. Hill for John Rudduck for	54	2		*168*	5	8	
	To Ditto pd. Fra. Rottenburie for hotpressing to this day				*168*	1	8	4
13	To Ditto pd. Robert Webb for a Trunck				*168*		13	
22	To Ditto pd. John Lukins for	37	2		*168*	3	14	
	To Ditto pd. Henry Britten for	27	2	½	*168*	2	15	1½
23	To Ditto pd. Tho. Hill for	27		23	*168*	2	11	9
	To Ditto pd. Peter Hinton for making of seales for my stockins				*168*	2	16	
25	To Cash pd. Henry Britten for	29	2	½	*168*	2	19	2½
29	To Ditto pd. Tho. Hill for Jonathan Abram for	48	2	1	*168*	5		
31	To Ditto pd. John Perrie for	75	2	1	*168*	7	16	
August 5	To Ditto pd. John Perrie for fancies	27			*168*			
	and sadds	113	2	1	*168*	14	7	1
10	To Ditto pd. Tho. Hill for Jona.n Abram for	24	2	1	*168*	2	10	
20	To Cash pd. Robert Webb for a Trunck				*168*		13	
September 1	To Cash paid Edward Iffe in full for hotpressing Wells hose				*168*		2	11
7	To Ditto pd. Henry Britten for	34	2	½	*168*	3	9	5
17	To Ditto pd. Tho. Hill for John Ashman for	118		15	*168*	7	7	6
	To Ditto pd. Jonathan Abram for	24	2	1	*168*	2	10	
19	To Ditto pd. Tho. Hill for Joseph George for	113		15	*168*	7	1	3
20	To Cash pd. John Perry for	179	2	1	*168*	18	12	11
October 1	To Ditto pd. Fra. Rottenburie for hotpressing Bristoll hose				*168*		17	
2	To Ditto pd. Henry Britten for	62	2	½	*168*	6	6	7
4	To Ditto pd. Tho. Hill for Jonathan Abram for	20	2	1	*168*	2	1	8
	To Cash pd. Tho. Hill for the Widow White for	30	2		*168*	3		
11	To Ditto pd. John Perrie for	44	2	1	*168*	4	11	8
22	To Cash pd. Robert Webb for a Trunck				*168*		11	6
	To John Massinger for severall parcells received of him at severall times deposited in my hands for which I advanced money in charity 2s 2d per paire	1834	2	2	*163*	198	13	8
	To Ditto for 1d per paire I advanced in charity and took the stockins by agreement at 1d per paire advance				*163*	7	12	10
November 22	To Cash pd. John Perrie for [109]							
						531	19	6
	To Proffit & Losse for balance [110]				*164*	1338	15	2¼
						1870	14	8¼

(166)	**Bristoll 1689**				
	John Covant of Portburie inn the County of Somerset Marriner	Dr	£	s	d
Aprill	To my Copiehold Tenement in Portburie for the purchase money thereof sould him	160	90		

	Anno 1689				
	William Godwin of Nailsey in the County of Somerset	Dr	£	s	d
	To ballance of his former acct. current resting dueon his mortgage Sept. 7th 1688	64	100		
Aprill	To Proffit & Losse for 1/2 yeares intrest due March 27th 1689	164	3		
October	To Ditto for ½ yeares intrest of £100 ending September 27th 1689	164	3		
March 27	To Ditto for ½ year's intrest of £100 due March 27th 1690	164	3		
1690 Oct.	To Ditto for ½ year's intrest of £100 ending October (I say Sept.) 27th 1690@	180	3		
			112		

	Anno 1689				
	Sugar 4 hhds laden in the Nathanael by Dennis Tayler in Nevis and delivered over by him to Isaac Heming in London, being the returnes of 20 boxes Candles sent by him	Dr	£	s	d
	To Dennis Tayler for theire cost & charges in Nevis 7353lb as per his acct. at 10s per 100lb	11	36	15	3
	To Ditto for theire freight & averidge from Nevis to London, as per his leter May 26th 1689	11	4	12	
			41	7	3
	To Profit and Loss for Ballance	191 *	2	9	8
			43	16	11

	Anno 1689				
	Ann Morgan my Maidservant is	Dr	£	s	d
July	To Cash paid Edward Pruet for her Pole	168		2	
September 20	To Cash paid her in full of her wages	168	1	7	6
			1	9	6

	Anno 1689				
	Simon Clement per Contra	Dr	£	s	d
	To Acct. of Ballances, for Ballance	194 *	5		11½

	Anno 1689				
	Adventure in the Merchants Goodwill Ben. Morley Master to Cadiz, and consign'd to Samuel Kekewich merchant in St Marie Port for sales & returnes	Dr	£	s	d
	To Stockins for 1 Trunck cont £ s d				
Aprill	20 doz Bristoll sadds)				
	39 1/2 doz Bristoll Fancy)				
	in all 714 paire at 2s 6d per paire 89 05 00				
	To Ditto for 11 doz Wells folded as				
	Bristoll is 132 prs at 1s 7d £10 9s 0d				
	To Ditto for 46½ doz Wells made up				
	plaine way 558 prs at 1s 6d				
	£41 17s 0d 52 06 00	165	142	8	
	To Ditto for a Trunck cord & matting 00 17 00				
	To Isaac Heming for custom carriage to London & other petty charges as per leter Aprill 30th 89	152	5	1	
	To Ditto for assureance of £100 on said stockins	152	4	1	
	To Isaac Heming pd. for filing a Certificate	177		4	
			151	14	

Bristoll 1689

	John Covant per Contra is	Cr	£	s	d
Aprill 16	By Cash recd. of him in part	162	83		
	By Cash received of — by his order in full	168	7		
			90		

	Anno 1689				
	William Godwin per Contra is	Cr	£	s	d
Aprill 13	By Cash recd. of him for ½ yeares intrest due March 27th 1689	162	3		
November 9	By Cash recd. of him for ½ yeares intrest due September 29th 1689	168	3		
1690 April 26	By Cash received of him	175	3		
			9		
	By Acct. of Ballances, for Ballance	194 *	103		
			112		

	Anno 1689				
	Sugar 4 hhds per Contra are	Cr	£	s	d
July	By Isaac Heming for theire neat proceeds	152	43	16	11

Anno 1690@				
Ann Morgan per Contra	Cr	£	s	d
By Profit and Loss, for Ballance	191 *	1	9	6

Anno 1689				
Simon Clement of Bristoll merchant is	Cr	£	s	d
By Ballance of his former acct. brought from that acct.	103	5		11¼

Anno 1690@				
Adventure in the Merchant's Goodwill per Contra	Cr	£	s	d
By Acct. of Ballances, for Ballance	194 *	151	14	

	Anno 1689				
	Adventure 3rd in the Wellcome Philip Freake Master to Cadiz,	Dr	£	s	d
	consign'd to Sam. Kekewich in Port £ s d				
Aprill	To Stockins for 37 doz Bristoll fancies, is 444				
	paire at 2s 6d 55 10 00				
	To Ditto for 264 prs Wells fancies made up				
	Bristoll fashion at 1s 7d per paire 20 18 00				
	To Ditto for 624 prs Wells fancies made up				
	plaine at 1s 6d per paire 41 16 00				
	To Ditto for a Cord Trunck and Matting 00 17 00	165	119	1	
	To Isaac Heming for premio of assureance of £100 on said goods				
	to Cadiz	152	4	2	
	To Cash pd. Custom etc.	175	3	11	9
			126	14	9
	To Profit and Loss, for Ballance	191 *	42	4	5¼
			168	19	2¼

	Bristoll 1689				
	Alicant Soape eight Cernes laden per Heneach Fetherstone	Dr	£	s	d
	merchant in Alicant, & imported in the ship Saphire John Price				
	Master				
May	To Heneage Fetherstone for theire cost and charges in Alicant				
	181Livres 00 sous 7denier as per Invoyce of 8th Aprill 1689				
	the Liver at 4s 6d	160	40	14	7½
	To Cash paid Custom etc.	175	3	4	10½
			43	19	6
	To Profit and Loss, for Ballance	191 *	10	12	6
			54	12	

	Anno 1689				
	Joan Bryan of Bristoll single woman is	Dr	£	s	d
June 24	To Howses in the Castle for ¼ yeares rent for the house shee lives				
	in due June 24th 89	159	2		
October 7	To Ditto for ¼ yeares rent of her house ending 29th Sept. 1689	159	2		
December	To Ditto for ¼ yeares rent of her house ending Dec. 25th 1689	159	2		
March	To Ditto for ¼ year's Rent for the house in which she Lives due				
	March 25th 1689	159	2		
1690 June	To Houses in the Castle for ¼ year's rent for the back-house due				
	June 24th 1690	159	2		
Oct.	To Ditto for ¼ year's rent for the back-house ending Sept. 29th				
	1690	159	2	6	3
			12	6	3

	Anno 1689				
	Henry Britten of Bedminster hosier	Dr	£	s	d
September 23	To Cash paid lent him on 43 paire of stockins	168	3		

	Anno 1689				
	Lawrence Washington of Potomack river in Virginea per Contra	Dr	£	s	d
May 16	To Cash paid port of a leter per post	162			6
November 16	To Cash pd. John Sandford on his bill in favor of Nicholas				
	Spencer	168	10	15	
			10	15	6

Anno 1690@				
Adventure 3rd in the Welcome per Contra	*Cr*	*£*	*s*	*d*
By Sam. Kekewich for the neat proceeds of the Stockins per				
Contra being 6238 Ryals Plate 17 Mervides which is 779 6/8				
pieces of 8 17 Mer.dees as per acct. of Sales closed in St Mary				
Port April 7th may appear the piece of 8 at 52d make Sterling	*167*	*168*	*19*	*2¼*

Bristoll 1689				
Alicant Soape per Contra is	*Cr*	*£*	*s*	*d*
By Richard Baily for the 8 Cernes per Contra sould him weight				
neat 21 cwt 0qr 0lb at 52s per Cwt	*176*	*54*	*12*	

Anno 1689					
	Joane Bryan per Contra	*Cr*	*£*	*s*	*d*
June	*By Cash recd. of her Sister in part for 1 quarters rent*	*162*	*1*	*13*	*9*
	By houses in the Castle for chimny money and ayd money shee				
	paid, is in full	*159*		*6*	*3*
October 4	*By Cash recd. of her for part of ¼ yeares rent ending Sept. 29th*				
	1689	*168*	*1*	*14*	
	By houses in the Castle for Chimny money, poore money and				
	royall ayd money	*159*		*6*	
January 11	*By Cash recd. of her in part for ¼ yeares rent ending Dec. 25th*				
	1689	*173*	*1*	*10*	*10*
	By Houses in the Castle for money paid in sundry Disbursments				
	on her House	*159*		*16*	*3*
1690 April 21	*By Cash recd. of her*	*175*	*1*	*12*	*11*
July 2	*By Ditto recd. of her Sister Hephzibah*	*181*	*1*	*12*	*11*
Oct.	*By Houses in the Castle for sundry Disbursments on the house in*				
	which she liveth	*159*		*7*	*1*
21	*By Profit and Loss for sundry Disbursements on Ditto house @*	*180*		*8*	*9½*
	By Cash received of her Sister Hephzibah	*187 **	*1*	*17*	*5½*
			12	*6*	*3*

Anno 1689					
	Henry Britten per Contra is	*Cr*	*£*	*s*	*d*
October 2	*By Cash recd. of him*	*168*	*3*		

Anno 1689					
	Lawrence Washington of Potomack river in Virginea merchant	*Cr*	*£*	*s*	*d*
Dec. 88	*By Ballance of his former acct. current sent him per the ship John*	*132*	*8*	*18*	*2¼*
	By Acct. of Ballances, for Ballance	*194 **	*1*	*17*	*3¾*
			10	*15*	*6*

					Dr	£	s	d
		Anno 1689						
		Samuel Kekewich of St Marie Port in Spaine my Factor there is			Dr	£	s	d
		To adventure in the ship London merchant to	R	m				
July		*Cadiz for the neat proceeds of one Trunck*						
		stockins sent in her as per his acct. sales being						
		789 pieces of 8 at 52d Aprill 1689	6312		*161*	170	19	
1690 May		*To Adventure in the Ship Welcome to Cadiz*						
		for the neat proceeds of one trunck stockins						
		sent in her as per his acct. of Sales, being						
		779 6/8 pieces of 8 17 Meridees the piece of						
		8 at 52d	6238	17	*166*	168	19	2¼
		To Adventure in the Cadiz Merchant to						
		Cadiz, for the neat proceeds of one Trunck of						
		Stockins sent in her as per his acct. of Sales,						
		1131 2/8 pieces of 8 25 Meridees at 52d						
		per pieces of 8	9050	25	*136*	245	2	5¾
		To Adventure in the Tigre to Cadiz for the						
		neat proceeds of the Trunck of Stockins (No						
		S 23) beiing (as per said acct. of Sales) 900						
		1/8 pieces of 8 9 Meridees the piece of 8 at						
		52d	7201	09	*144*	195	0	9
		To Ditto for the neat proceeds of the Trunck						
		of hose (No S 24) beiing (as per Ditto acct.						
		of Sales) 936 6/8 pieces of 8 17 Meridees at						
		52d per pieces of 8	7494	17	*144*	202	19	6¼
			36297			983		11¼

(168)		**Bristoll 1689**		Dr	£	s	d
		Cash is		Dr	£	s	d
July 4		*To ballance of its former acct. brought from that acct.*		*162*	3155	4	3
	5	*To Tho. Goldney Junior recd. of him*		*136*	30		
	9	*To Ditto recd. of him in full*		*136*	9	5	
	13	*To Edward Dowding recd. of him*		*154*		4	6¼
	20	*To Edward Jacob recd. of the Widow Cotterell in part of her rent*		*156*	1	10	
	24	*To Peter Hinton recd. of him in part*		*158*	1		
	25	*To Elizabeth Milner recd. of her in part*		*15*	5		
	29	*To Tho. Day recd. of him*		*161*	100		
		To John Bradway recd. of him		*70*	50		
August 2		*To Arthur Eastmond recd. of him*		*160*	1	1	
	5	*To Isaac Heming for my bill in favor of Henry Parsons*		*152*	200		
		To Lewis Adams for money of him in part		*56*	50		
		To Isaac Heming for recd. of Richard Baily for my Bill on him in his favor		*152*	200		
	7	*To Ditto recd. of John Le Conti for my Bill on him*		*152*	100		
		To Tho. Day Wine Cooper recd. of Humphry Corsley		*161*	50		
	8	*To Isaac Heming recd. of Richard Baily £200 & Elias Osbourne £60 bills on him*		*152*	260		
	13	*To Sgt. George Strode recd. of him*		*24*	3	13	
		To Isaac Heming recd. of Sgt Tho. Strode for my Bill on him in favor of Hugh Strode		*152*	50		
	23	*To Dr. Fra.s Hungerford recd. of Tho. Hungerford*		*87*	2	1	8
	31	*To Edward Jacob recd. of the Widow Cotterell*		*156*	1		
		To Edward Jacob recd. of the Widow Cotterell		*00*	-	-	-
September 7		*To Xeries wine 10 Butts in the Welcom recd. at Customhouse for returnes*		*142*	7	7	3
		To John Wilmer recd. of him in full		*117*	4	3	
	17	*To Sir George Strode recd. of Bernard Wilkins*		*24*	1	13	
	25	*To John Bradway recd. of him in part*		*70*	30		
		To Alderman Tho. Day recd. of him		*150*	1		
	28	*To Lewis Adams received of him*		*56*	50		
October 2		*To the Lady Ann Powlet recd. of Francis Edwards in part*		*155*	8		

	Anno 1689	R	m	Cr	£	s	d
	Samuel Kekewich per Contra			Cr	£	s	d
July	By Xeries wines 10 Butts in the Welcome for theire cost & charges 3167 Ryals 25 Meridees is 395 7/8 pieces of 8, at 52d as per Invoyce appears	3167	25	142	85	15	10
March	By Isaac Heming for money recd. by him of Nathanael Maxy & John Barnard on his Bill drawn on them By Ben. Warren & Company for 8000 Ryals plate is 1000 pieces of 8 at 50d 3/8 per piecesby him assigned to me & by me to said Heming	8000	00	177	209	17	11
1690 May	By Ditto for money recd. of John Stracy per his bill in my favour, for 864 pieces of 8 2½ Ryals plate at 52d½ per pieces of 8	6914	17	177	189	1	4
	By Ditto for mony recd. on his bill on Sam. Proctor in my favour, for 1250 pieces of 8 at 52d¼ per pieces of 8	10000		177	272	2	8
		28082	8		756	17	9
	By his new acct. Current for Ballance Carried to his Debt in the Account	8214	26	185	226	3	2¼
		36297			983		11¼

Bristoll 1689

	Cash per Contra is	Cr	£	s	d
July 5	By Worsted stockins pd. Tho. Hill for James Woollen, Sam. Dyer, John Perrie, John Aply & Hen. Britten	165	27	5	7
	By John Massinger pd. lent him on 21 paire stockins	163	2	3	9
8	By Stockins pd. Tho. Hill for John Day	165	1	6	
	By Proffit & Losse pd. Edward Pruet	164	3	12	
	By sundry accts pd. Edward Pruett for my servants poles	156		6	6
9	By horses 2 pd. John Brewer for ½ score of oates	156		8	10
	By Proffit & Losse pd. port of Leters	164		1	3
11	By Stockins pd. Tho. Hill for Joseph George & John Rudduck	165	12	5	6
	By Ditto pd. Fra. Rottenburie	165	1	8	4
	By Abraham Hill paid him	156	1		
13	By Proffit & Losse pd. port of leters	164		2	9
	By Stockins pd. Robert Webb for a Trunck	165		13	
	By John Massinger pd. lent him on 35 paire hose	163	3	15	10
16	By Dennis Tayler paid his monther	11	1	5	7
	By Joseph Drew paid him at sundry times	159	161	11	6
	By Horses two pd. John Jenkin	156		2	6
	By Proffit & Losse & John Blackwell paid John Blackwell in full	164	9	10	
22, 23	By Stockins pd. John Lukins, Henry Britten, Tho. Hill & Peter Hinton	165	11	10	10½
	By Jahzeel Speed pd. Wm. Rogers	154		13	6
25	By Henry Gibbes pd. lent him on his bill on John Blackwell accepted to bee pd. August 25th 1689	151	100		
	By horses two pd. Ezekiel Powell of Bedminster for a reeke of hay	156	5		
	By Stockins pd. Henry Britten & Tho. Hill	168	7	19	2½
25	By Elizabeth Milner pd. her	15	6	19	
29	By houses in the Castle pd. John Cheshire	159		13	
	By Richard Toune paid him	147		2	6
31	By Rhenish wine two Aulnes paid carriage etc. from London	163	1	14	4
	By Stockins pd. John Perrie	165	7	16	
August 5	By Jahzeel Speed paid Tho. Walden	154		4	

	To Henry Britten recd. of him	167	3		
	To John Corent received of his order in full	166	7		
4	To Joan Bryan for part of ¼ yeares rent recd. of her	167	1	14	
11	To Robert Dowding & Company formerly recd. of Ozziel Browne	100	6		
12	To Henry Gibbes recd. of John Blackwell	151	100		
14	To Edward Croft recd. of his daughter Elizabeth	96	16	3	6
	To Richard Langsworth recd. of him	163	3	17	
16	To John Earle of Bristoll recd. of his Bailiffe	150	16	4	6
	To Tho. Day recd. of Esaw White	161	1	12	
22	To Robert Berrow recd. of him in part	158		10	
23	To the Lady Ann Powlet recd. of Fra. Edwards	155	2		
25	To Arthur Bramly & Company recd. of John Brisco	12	10	5	
26	To Henry Howard & Company recd. of Ozziell Borwne for ½ yeares intrest	163	3		
	To Wm. Spoore & Peter Collet for intrest 1½ yeares of £50 recd. of said Spoore	30	4	10	
			4547	8	8¼
November 9	To William Godwin recd. of him	166	3		
13	To the Lady Ann Powlet recd. of Fra. Edwards	155	1	3	6
16	To John Stretten recd. of him in part	57	3	10	
	To Tho. Goldney Junior recd. of Wm. Swimmer	136	100		
20	To John Bradway recd. of him in part	70	30		
	To Tho. Day recd. of him in part	161		7	6
30	To Robert Berrow recd. of him in part	158		10	
December 6	To George Shuttleworth recd. of him in full	93	1	3	8
			4687	13	4¼

Date	Description				
	By Stockins pd. John Perrie	*165*	14	7	1
7	By Horses 2 pd. John Jenkin	*156*		2	
9	By Stockins pd. Tho. Hill for Jonathan Abram	*165*	2	10	
14	By horses 2 pd. Wm. Dawson	*156*		10	
	By Proffit & Losse — Baker for Cheese and 3s for port of leters	*164*		19	6
	By Stockins pd. Robert Webb	*165*		13	
21	By Abraham Hill paid him	*156*	1		
23	By Horses 2 pd. Anthony Spicket	*156*	2	13	4
	By Houses in the Castle pd. Joseph Drew	*159*	1		
24	By Jahzeel Speed pd. John Crindall	*154*	1	10	
28	By Xeries wines 23 Butt pd. Charles King for John Cann	*169*	10	6	
September 1	By Stockins pd. Edward Iffe and Henry Britten	*165*	3	12	4
5	By Proffit & Losse pd. for Panniers	*164*		10	11
14	By houses in the Castle pd. Edward Jones	*159*		16	
	By Proffit & Losse pd. Abraham Hill	*164*		7	6
	By Stockins pd. Tho. Hill for John Ashman & for Jonathan Abram	*165*	9	17	6
19	By Ditto pd. Tho. Hill for Joseph George	*165*	7	1	3
	By sundry accts paid Elizabeth Milner	*164*	8	7	
20	By Ann Morgan paid her in full	*166*	1	7	6
	By horses 2 paid John Jenkin	*156*		6	8
	By Stockins pd. John Perry	*165*	18	12	11
	By Henry Britten pd. lent him	*167*	3		
25	By horses 2 pd. John Jenkin in full	*156*		2	9
			459	4	7
25	By Proffit & Losse pd. Charles White for royall ayd money	*164*	1		
October 1	By Xeries wines my ½ of 10 Butts for what pd. James Shute for carriage a hogshead Malaga	*170*		19	
2	By Stockins paid Fra. Rottenburie and Henry Britten	*165*	7	3	7
	By Proffit & Losse paid Jane Shepheard for a Cask of Butter	*164*	1	9	9
3	By Howses in the Castle & Proffit & Losse paid James Rodman	*164*	1		
4	By Charles King paid lent him	*152*	5		
	By Xeries wines my ½ of 10 Butts paid Ditto for Lees	*170*		15	
	By Jacob Lloyd pd. him in part	*170*		1	
	By Richard Toune paid him in full	*147*		2	6
	By Stockins pd. Tho. Hill for Jonathan Abram & the Widow White	*165*	5	1	8
11	By Stockins pd. John Perrie	*165*	4	11	8
	By Xeries wines 10 Butts pd. custom, freight, & other charges	*142*	104		2¼
	By George Shuttleworth pd. James Freemans noat	*93*		4	
22	By Stockins pd. Robert Webb for a Trunck	*165*		11	6
	By Jacob Lloyd paid him in part	*170*		4	4
26	By Ditto paid him in part	*170*			6
	By Proffit & Losse pd. Lott Wilkins for a Tubb of Butter	*164*	1	6	11
November 2	By Jonathan Lamboll pd. Philip Higginbottom £8 10s 0d, & lent him £2 on his noat	*147*	10	10	
	By horses 2 pd. Anthony Picket for bringing in a reeke of hay	*156*		12	
	By John Hardiman pd. him in full	*80*		11	
	By Proffit & Losse pd. John Bussle for mending the musket	*164*		1	6
8	By Jahzeel Speed paid John Matthews for a hatt	*154*	1	5	
	By Jonathan Lamboll pd. Abraham Hills expences to Reading	*147*		12	
	By Jacob Lloyd pd. him in part	*170*		2	6
15	By Proffit & Losse pd. Ed. Lloyd & John Webb aid money at 12d per £	*164*	7	4	
16	By Lawrence Washington pd. John Sandford on a bill in favor of Nicho.s Spencer	*167*	10	15	
	By Proffit & Losse pd. John Gandy in full	*164*		4	4
21	By Giles Clark paid lent him on a mortgage	*171*	400		
	By John Cooke pd. Bartholmew Williams in full for rent	*159*	4		
22	By Worsted stockins pd. John Perrie	*172*	10	18	9

(169)	Bristoll 1689							
	Adventure in the ship Cesar Capt. Wm. Maddison to Cadiz is				Dr	£	s	d
	To sundry accts, being the cost & charges of — Truncks of Worsted stockins laden under the mark in the margent in said ship, and consign'd to Samuel Kekewich merchant in St Marie Port (viz)							
	To Stockins for 2 Truncks cont. viz	£	s	d				
	No 29 cont. 70 doz Bristoll fancies							
	840 paire at 2s 8d	112	00	00				
	42 doz Wells Fancies at 1s 8d per paire being 504 pre	42	00	00	165	154		
	To Isaac Heming paid custom etc. in London	4	14	4				
	To Ditto pd. Assureance of £150 on said Trunck	6	02	00	152	10	16	4
	No 30 cont.							
	63½ doz Bristoll fancies is 762 paire)							
	17 doz Bristoll sadds is 204 paire)							
	966 prs at 2s 8d	128	16	00				
	37 doz Wells Fancies is 444 paire at 1s 8d is	37	00	00	165	165	16	
	To Isaac Heming for assureance of £150 on said stockins	6	00	00	152	6		
	To Ditto for filing a Certificate and Custom etc.				177	4	18	11
						341	11	3

	Anno 1689	Dr	£	s	d
	Thomas Curtis of Reading Woolendraper is	Dr	£	s	d
	To houses in Reading for ¼ rent due September 29th 1688	129	11	3	6
	To Ditto for ¼ yeares rent ending December 25th 1688	129	11	3	6
	To Ditto for ¼ yeares rent ending March 25th 1689	129	11	3	6
	To Ditto for ¼ yeares rent ending June 24th 1690	129	11	3	6
	To Ditto for ¼ yeares rent ending September 29th 1690	129	11	3	6
	To John Miles for money recd. of him for a Cask of Butter bought & sent him	114	2	8	
	To Houses in Reading, for one year's rent of them, ending 29th Sept. past	129	44	14	
			102	19	6

	Anno 1689	Dr	£	s	d
	Xeries Wine 23 Butts etc. is	Dr	£	s	d
	To ballance of a former acct.	150	80	10	4
August 23	To Cash pd. Charles King for John Cann for 1 Pipe & 22 Gallons of Canary Lees	168	10	6	

25	By houses in the Castle pd. Joseph Drew & John Cheshire	159	3	18	9
	By Abraham Hill pd. him in full	156	2	10	
	By Proffit & Losse pd. John Greene	164		3	2
26	By horses two paid Jacob Lloyd for John Little for 2 doz straw	156		2	4
	By Geo. Shuttleworth paid severall disbursments	93		19	8
	By Jacob Lloyd pd. him in full	170		3	
	By Tho. Hill & Abraham his Sonne lent them on bond	170	10		
29	By Worsted stockins pd. John Perrie	172	4	5	5
December 2	By horses two paid Henry Lloyd	156		11	6
6	By Proffit & Losse paid petty disbursments	164			10
12	By John Wilmer paid Abraham Hill	117	2	18	9
	By Worsted stockins paid John Perrie	172	10		
			1075	5	8¼
	By Ballance carried to that acct. of debt	173	3612	7	8
			4687	13	4¼

Bristoll 1690@

Adventure in the Ceesar to Cadiz per Contra	Cr	£	s	d
By Acct. of Ballances, for Ballance	194 *	341	11	3

Anno 1689					
Tho. Curtis per Contra is	Cr	£	s	d
By Ballance of his former acct. current brought from that acct.	58	14	1	6
By Isaac Heming received of him in London	152	15		
By Houses in the Reading for what hee paid Lords rent for 1 yeare ending Dec. 1688	129	4	8	
By Ditto for what hee paid for masons work and for nailes	129		15	2
By Ditto for what hee pd. Wm. Cole 1s & Jeffery Pinnell for repairng the well 15s in all	129		16	
1690 By Isaac Heming recd. of him	177	12		
		47		8
By Acct. of Ballances, for Ballance	194 *	55	18	10
		102	19	6

Anno 1689					
Xeries Wines 23 Butts per Contra	Cr	£	s	d
August 7 By Arthur Eastmond for 1 doz of Xerie at	160		18	
By Tho. Goldney Junior for 2 doz of Xerie at 18s	136	1	16	
28 By the Lady Ann Powlett for 8 doz of Xerie at 18s	155	7	4	

			£	s	d
October	To Tho. Day for one Aune of Rhenish	161	6		
	To Tho. Day for severall small parcells of Rhenish etc.	161	1	15	8
1690	To Isaac Heming for charges formerly pd. on a Butt of Malaga	177		7	
	To Charles Jones Junior for money abated him, on 3 Butts sold him	171		5	
July	To Alex. Caduggan for money abated him on 5 Butts sold him	148	1	1	6
	To Tho. Day 4¼ Gall. Rhenish, and ¼ pound Isinglass	161		15	10½
	To Wines my ½ of of 6 Butts of Xerie and 2 of Malaga, for Ballance	124	89	11	1½
			190	12	6
	To Profit and Loss, for Ballance	191 *	231	8	9
			422	1	3

	Anno 1689	Dr	£	s	d
	Adventure to Cadiz in the ship Sarah John Bradill Master is To sundry accts, being the cost & charges of Two Truncks of stockins laden in said ship mark'd as per margent consign'd to Samuel Kekewich in St Marie Port				
	To Worsted stockins for one Truncks cont. (viz)				
	78 doz Bristoll sadds)				
	22 doz Bristoll fancies)				
	are 1200 paire at 2s 8d 160 00 00				
	10 doz 10/12 of Wells sads				
	being 130 paire at 1s 8d 10 16 08				
	To a Trunck cord and matting 17 00	165	171	13	8
	To Isaac Heming for custom, Carriage to Lond etc. 4 13 11				
	To Ditto for assureance of £100 at 4 Guinnies and 2s charge Policie 4 6	152	8	19	11
	A Trunck cont.				
	44 doz 5 paire Bristoll sadds)				
	22 Ditto Fancies)				
	68 doz 5 pr 797 prs at 2s 6d 99 12 06				
	19 doz & 3 prs Wells Fancies				
	231 paire at 1s 6d 17 06 06	165	117	16	
	For a Trunck, cord and matting 17 00				
	To Isaac Heming for carriage to Lond cartage, custom, fees etc.	152	3	17	4
	To Ditto for filing a Certificate and ensurance on £100	177	4	11	
			306	17	11

---

(170)	**Bristoll 1689**	Dr	£	s	d
	Xeries Wine my halfe of 10 Butts in the Welcom Phil. Freake Master from Cadiz in equall halves betwixt Tho. Day Wine Cooper & myselfe				
	To Isaac Heming for the cost and charges of 1 hogshead of Malaga sent per waggon	152	13		
October 1	To Cash paid James Shute for John Edwards for carriage of said hogshead from London	168		19	
4	To Ditto pd. Charles King for 15 Gall.s Lees	168		15	
	To Xeries wines 10 Buttts, for ½ of £196 6s 5d their first Cost and Charges	142	98	3	2½
1690	To Rhenish wine 2 Aulns in partnership with Tho. Day for ½ their cost & Charges	163	9	8	2
			122	6	4½

	By John Earle of Bristoll for 2 Rundlets cont. 25 5/8 Gall.				
	Xerie at 18s	150	7	13	9
31	By Sir George Strode for 2 doz Xerie at 18s per doz	24	1	16	
November 29	By John Wilmer for 6 doz pints Xerie at 9s per dozen	117	2	14	
	By Charles Jones Junior for 3 Butts sould him at £28 per Butt	171	88		
	By Alexander Caduggan for 5 Butts sould him at £29 per Butt	48	145		
December 31	By the Lady Ann Powlet for 4 doz qrt bottles Xerie at 18s per				
	dozen	155	3	12	
January 8	By Sir George Strode for 2 doz bottles at 18s	173	1	16	
	By George Mason for 1 hogshead of Canary sould him at	79	16	10	
14	By John Earle of Bristoll for 25½ Gall. Xerie at 6s per Gallon	150	7	13	
February 18	By Ditto for 24¾ Xerie sent him to London at 6s per Gallon	150	7	8	6
March 3	By Joane Hancock for 2 Butts sould her at £30 per Butt	176	60		
4	By John Clark Junior for 1 Butt sould him at	149	31		
14	By Lewis Adams for one Butt sold him at	59	34		
	By Benjamin Smith for 2 Casks of Lees sold him	50	6		
			422	1	3

	Anno 1690@				
	Adventure in the Sarah per Contra is	Cr	£	s	d
	By Acct. of Ballances, for Ballance	194 *	306	17	11

	Bristoll 1690@				
	Xeries Wines per Contra	Cr	£	s	d
	By Profit and Loss, for Ballance	191 *	122	6	4½

	Anno 1689				
November	*Francis Page of Bristoll house Carpenter is*	Dr	£	s	d
	To houses in the Castle for 1 yeares reserved rent for his 2 houses due Sept. 29th 1689	159		10	

	Anno 1689				
November	*Wm. Horwood of Bristoll Feltmaker is*	Dr	£	s	d
	To houses in the Castle for 1 yeares reserved rent on his 3 houses due Sept. 29th 1689	159	2		

	Anno 1689				
	Jacob Lloyd of Bristoll Translator (alias Cobler) my Groome is	Dr	£	s	d
October 4	*To Cash paid lent him*	168		1	
22	*To Ditto paid him in part for keeping my two mares*	168		4	4
26	*To Ditto paid him in part*	168			6
November 8	*To Cash paid him in part*	168		2	6
26	*To Ditto pd. him in full for keeping my 2 mares to the 26th Nov. 1689*	168		3	
January 8	*To Cash pd. him in part*	173			6
22	*To Ditto pd. him in full for keeping the mares to the 21th January*	173		4	9
February 18	*To Cash pd. him in full for keeping them to this 18th*	175		5	1
March 18	*To Ditto pd. him in full for keeping the two mares to this 18th day of March 1689*	175		5	4
1690 April 15	*To Ditto pd. him in full for keeping the Two mares to this 15th day of April 1690*	175		5	4
May 2	*To Cash pd. him in full for keeping the two mares to this 2nd day of May 1690*	175		3	3¾
20	*To Ditto pd. him for keeping them to the 19th instant*	181		1	
			1	16	7¾

	Anno 1689				
	Thomas Hill of Bristoll Porter & Abraham his Sone are	Dr	£	s	d
November 26	*To Cash lent them on theire bond payable May 26th 1690*	168	10		
1690 Oct.	*To Profit and Loss for ¾ year's intrest of £10 ending August 26th 1690*	180		9	
			10	9	

(171)	**Bristoll 1689**				
	Giles Clark of Alveston in the County of Glocester Yeoman	Dr	£	s	d
November 21	*To Cash paid Ann Perkin, but lent to him on a mortgage of certaine lands lying at Holbrooke in the Parish of Abston in the County of Glocester at £5 per Cent per Annum as by her & her Trustees Assignement may appeare*	168	400		
January 20	*To Isaac Heming for money hee pd. Col. Tho. Joorey on his giving up the Assignement of his mortgage on certaine Lands in Alveston belonging to said Clark*	152	425		
	To Ditto for his commission for paying & receiving the said money and negotiating the taking up the said Assignment of Col. Joorey	152	1		
Feb. 5	*To Cash paid him more on his 2 mortgages as per his receit*	173	100		
	To Profit and Loss, for ½ Intrest of £1000 from 15th July 1689 to 15th Nov. 1689 at £5 per Cent	180	8	6	8
	To Ditto for whole Intrest of £400 from Nov. 15th 1689 to Feb. 2nd 1689 at £5 per Cent	180	4	8	1
	To Ditto for ½ Intrest of £600 from Nov. 15th 1689 to Feb. 2nd 1689 at £5 per Cent	180	1	10	3
	To Ditto for the whole Intrest of £525 from Dec. 2nd to Ditto 2nd Feb.	180	4	7	6
	To Ditto for port of Leters	180		1	6
1690 May 19	*To Cash pd. him*	181	55	6	
			1000		

Anno 1689				
Francis Page per Contra is	Cr	£	s	d
By John Cooke Chamberlaine for money of him recd. for 1 yeares				
reservd rent due Sept. 29th 1689	159		10	

Anno 1689				
Wm. Horwood per Contra is	Cr	£	s	d
By John Cooke Chamberlaine for money of him for 1 yeares				
reservd rent due Sept. 29th 1689	159	2		

Anno 1690@				
Per Contra	Cr	£	s	d
By Profit and Loss, for keeping my horses	191 *	1	16	7¾

Per Contra	Cr	£	s	d
By Acct. of Ballances, for Ballance	194 *	10	9	

Bristoll 1690@

Giles Clark per Contra	Cr	£	s	d
By his new Acct. Current for money lent him on his two				
Mortgages, and Intrest due from him and other monies disbursd				
for him as per particulars per Contra, amounting in all to the				
Sum of	184	1000		

		Dr	£	s	d
	Anno 1689				
	Wm. Bush of the Citie of Bristoll Linindraper is	Dr	£	s	d
November	To Lincloth 15 Pacqets Dowlas sould him at 26s per piece				
	towards charges to pay for them ½ the 1st day of Februaryu, &				
	½ the 1st day of Aprill next	171	201		
	To Profit and Loss for Ballance	191 *		3	
			201	3	

		Dr	£	s	d
	Anno 1689				
	Charles Jones Junior of Bristoll merchant is	Dr	£	s	d
December	To Xeries wine 23 Butts in the Tygre for 3 Butts at £28 per				
	Butt due 21th March 89	159	88		

		Dr	£	s	d
	Anno 1689				
	Lincloth 15 Pacqets Dowlas deposited in my hands by Henry	Dr	£	s	d
	Gibbes				
1690 April	To Wm. Bush, allowed him for Dammages on ½ piece of				
	Dowlas	171		6	
	To William Bush for money allowed him for Dammage	171		3	
	To Profit and Loss for 36 weeks warehouse room at 6d per week	164		18	
	To Ditto for my Commission for sales at £2 per Cent	164	4		
	To Henry Gibbes his Account Current for the neat proceeds				
	hereof	151	195	13	
			201		

		Dr	£	s	d
	Anno 1689				
	Thomas Smith of Bristoll Wine cooper is	Dr	£	s	d
December	To Proffit & Losse for ½ yeares rent of my Vault in Small				
	Streate due Nov. 13th	164	3	5	
1690	To Ditto for 5 months rent for my Vault at the Lower end of				
	Small Street, ending July 14th 1690	180	2	14	2
			5	19	2

(172)	**Bristoll 1689**							Dr	£	s	d
	Worsted Stockins are							Dr	£	s	d
				paire	s	d					
November 22	To Cash pd. John Perrie for			105	2	1		168	10	18	9
29	To Ditto pd. John Perrie for			41	2	1		168	4	5	5
December 12	To Ditto pd. John Perrie for			96	2	1		168	10		
14	To Ditto pd. Tho. Hill for James										
	Woollen for			17	2	1		173	1	15	5
20	To Cash pd. John Perrie for			25	2	1		173	2	12	
24	To Ditto pd. Fra. Rottenburie in full for hotpressing							173		9	2¼
30	To Ditto pd. Ed. Iffe in full for hotpressing							173		3	10
January 3	To Ditto pd. John Perrie for			37	2	1		173	3	17	
7	To Cash pd. Tho. Hill for John										
	Lukns for			80	2			173	8		
10	To Ditto pd. John Perrie for			35	2	1		173	3	12	11
14	To Cash pd. John Rudduck for			46	2			173	4	12	
	To Ditto pd. Joseph George for			98		14½		173	5	18	6
22	To Ditto pd. John Ashman for			73	1	3		173	4	11	3
	To Ditto pd. Tho. Hill for J P			52	2	1		173	5	8	4
24	To Cash pd. John Perrie for			51	2	1		173	5	6	3
27	To Cash pd. Tho. Dyer for			40	1	11		173	3	16	8
28	To Ditto pd. James Woollen for			36	2	1		173	3	15	
	To Ditto pd. Joseph George for			96	1	3		173	6		
31	To Ditto pd. John Perrie for			61	2	1		173	6	7	1
	To Ditto pd. John Rudduck for			64	2			173	6	8	
February 4	To Cash pd. Tho. Dyer in full for			22	1	11		173	2	2	2
	To Ditto pd. Tho. Hill for Jon Abram			29	2	1		173	3		5

Anno 1689				
William Bush per Contra is	Cr	£	s	d
February 4 By Cash recd. of him in part	173	100	10	
1690 April 10 By Ditto received of him in full	175	100	4	
By Lincloth 15 Pacquetts for Dammage on ½ piece of Dowlas	171		6	
By Ditto for more Dammage	171		3	
		201	3	

Anno 1690@				
Charles Jones per Contra	Cr	£	s	d
May 10 By Cash recd. of him	181	87	15	
By Xeries wine 23 Butts for money abated him	169		5	
		88		

Anno 1689				
Lincloth 15 Pacquet Dowlas per Contra	Cr	£	s	d
November By William. Bush for the 15 Paquets sould him at 26s per piece towards charges, to pay ½ 1st of February, & tother ½ the 1st of Aprill next	171	201		

Anno 1689				
Tho. Smith per Contra is	Cr	£	s	d
December 14 By Cash recd. of him for ½ yeares rent of my lower Vault ending Nov. 13th	173	3	5	
1690 By Profit and Loss, for taxes pd. on the Lower Vault	180		19	2
Sept. 24 By Cash recd. of him	187 *	1	15	
		5	19	2

Bristoll 1690@				
Worstead Stockins per Contra	Cr	£	s	d
By Worstead stockins for the severall sums of money per Contra being the cost and charges of 4505 pair Carried forward to a new Account	182	385	8	1¾

Date	Description							
5	To Ditto pd. John Ashman for	165	1	3	173	10	6	3
	To Ditto pd. Tho. Hill for John Day for	12	2		173	1	4	
7	To Ditto pd. John Rudduck for	65	2		173	6	10	
	To Ditto pd. John Perrie for	38	2	1	173	3	19	2
	To Ditto pd. Joseph George for	115		15	173	7	3	9
10	To Cash pd. Tho. Hill for Jon. Abram for	16	2	1	173	1	13	4
14	To Ditto pd. John Perrie for	31	2	1	175	3	4	7
	To Ditto pd. Tho. Hill for John Ashman for	125		15	175	7	16	3
17	To Ditto pd. Jonathan Abram for	30	2	1	175	3	2	6
18	To Ditto pd. Tho. Hill for Joseph George for	111		15	175	6	18	9
20	To Cash pd. John Rudduck for	68	2		175	6	16	
	To Ditto pd. James Woollen for	74	2	1	175	7	14	2
	To Ditto pd. John Perrie for	52	2	1	175	5	8	4
22	To Ditto pd. Fra. Rottenburie in full for hotpressing to this day				175		14	¾
27	To Ditto pd. Tho. Hill for Jona. Abram for	29	2	1	175	3		5
28	To Ditto pd. Joseph George at twice for	110		15	175	6	17	6
	To Ditto pd. John Perrie for	32	2	1	175	3	6	8
March 3	To Cash pd. Tho. Dyer for	38	1	11	175	3	13	10
5	To Ditto pd. John Day for	24	2		175	2	8	
	To Ditto pd. Tho. Hill for John Rudduck for	60	2		175	6		
	To Ditto pd. Ditto for Jona. Abram for	24	2	1	175	2	10	
8	To Ditto pd. Joseph George in part for	116		15	175	5		
	To Ditto pd. him in full for the quantity				175 *	2	5	
	To Ditto pd. Tho. Hill for John Perrie for	30	2	1	175	3	2	6
	To Ditto pd. Ditto for Jona. Abram for	29	2	1	175	3		5
11	To Cash paid Tho. Hill (for John Ashman) for	253	1	3	175	15	16	3
13	To Ditto paid James Wollen for	94	2	1	175	9	15	10
14	To Ditto paid John Perry for	67	2	1	175	6	19	7
15	To Ditto paid Thomas Dyer for	41	1	11	175	3	18	7
	To Ditto pd. Tho. Hill (for Jon Abram) for	25	2	1	175	2	12	1
17	To Ditto pd. Ditto (for John Day) for	7	2		175		14	
19	To Ditto paid John Ashman for	181	1	3	175	11	6	3
	To Ditto paid John Rudduck for	73	2		175	7	6	
	To Ditto paid Tho. Hill (for John Ashman) for	80	1	3	175	5		
21	To Ditto paid Joseph George for	141	1	3	175	8	16	3
	To Ditto paid John Perry in full for	50	2	1	175	5	4	2
22	To Ditto paid Tho. Dyer for	27	1	11	175	2	11	9
1690 25	To Cash paid Tho. Hill (for Jona. Abram) for	20	2	1	175	2	1	8
	To Ditto paid Ditto (for Tho. Browning) for	142	1	3	175	8	17	6
	To Ditto paid Edward Iff in full for Hotpressing to this day				175	1	1	
29	To Ditto paid Francis Rattenbury in full for hotpressing to this Day				175		14	7¾
April 4	To Ditto pd. John Perry for	39	2	1	175	4	1	3
	To Ditto paid Tho. Hill (for Jona. Abram) for	20	2	1	175	2	1	8
	To Ditto paid Ditto (for John Rudduck) for	67	2		175	6	14	

	To Ditto paid Joseph George £6 00s 00d & Tho. Hill (for said George) £5 15s 00d for	188	1	3	175	11	15	
5	To Ditto paid Tho. Dyer for	35	1	11	175	3	7	1
9	To Ditto pd. Tho. Hill (for Jona. Abram) for	24	2	1	175	2	10	
	To Ditto pd. Ditto (for John Massinger) for	26	2	1	175	2	14	2
10	To Ditto pd. John Ashman for	152	1	3	175	8	17	4
	To Ditto pd. John Rudduck for	51	2		175	5	2	
	To Ditto pd. John Perry for	18	2	1	175	1	7	6
17	To Cash paid Eliz. Webb for a Trunck				175		13	
	To Ditto pd. John Day for	16	2		175	1	12	
18	To Ditto pd. John Perry for	16	2	1	175	1	13	4
	To Ditto pd. Tho. Hill (for Jona. Abram) for	24	2	1	175	2	10	
19	To Cash pd. Joseph George for	36	1	3	175	2	5	
23	To Ditto paid Tho. Hill (for Joan White) for	42	2		175	4	4	
26	To Ditto paid Ditto (for John Perry) for	28	2	1	175	2	18	4
May 2	To Cash pd. John Perry for	15	2	1	175	1	11	3
		4505			182	385	8	1¾

(173)   **Bristoll 1689**

			Dr	£	s	d
	Cash is		Dr	£	s	d
December	To Ballance of a former acct. brought from that acct. of Credit		168	3612	7	8
14	To Tho. Smith recd. of him for ½ yeares rent of my Lower Vault		171	3	5	
21	To Alexander Cadduggan recd. of him in part		48	40		
27	To Richard Langsworth recd. of him		163	1	18	10½
28	To Richard Pocock recd. of Elizabeth Bisse		149	40		
	To Lewis Adams for money recd. of him in part		56	80		
January 8	To the Lady Ann Powlett recd. of her in Full		155	4	2	8
10	To Alexander Caduggan recd. of him in part		48	5		
11	To George Mason recd. in full		79	16	10	
	To Joane Bryan recd. of her in part		167	1	10	10
	To Robert Berrow recd. of him in full		158		12	6
27	To Tho. Day Wine Cooper paid mee in part		161	48		
28	To John Wilmer recd. of Lewis Cox		174	10		
	To Andrew Binfield recd. of him in full		173	50		
February 3	To John Bradway recd. of him		70	40		
	To Beniamin Cole recd. of him		147	8		
4	To Wm. Bush recd. of him in part		171	100	10	
7	To Tho. Goldney Junior received of him		136	50		
10	To Wm. Ricket recd. of him		143	6	10	
				4118	7	6½

Bristoll 1689

	Cash per Contra is	Cr	£	s	d
December 14	By John Wilmer pd. Fra. Maynard	174		16	
	By Worsted stockins pd. Tho. Hill for James Woollen	172	1	15	5
20	By horses 2 pd. Abel Edwards	156		15	
	By Worsted stockins pd. John Perrie	172	2	12	
24	By Ditto pd. Fra. Rottenburie in full	172		9	2¼
	By horses 2 pd. Jacob Lloyd in full	156		5	4
	By Proffit & Losse pd. Humphry Nickins in full for watching	164			8
30	By Worsted stockins pd. Edward Iffe	172		3	10
	By Alderman Joseph Creswick for several disbursments in repairing his stables	173	4		
January 2	By Proffit & Losse paid severall disdbursments	164			5¾
	By Worsted stockins pd. John Perrie for 37 paire	172	3	17	
4	By Wm. Plydall pd. lent him	152		3	
6	By Proffit & Losse pd. John Hardiman in full	164	1	8	
7	By Worsted stockins pd. Tho. Hill for John Lukins	172	8		
	By Isaac Heming pd. Richard Corsley for his bill on John Sutton	152	300		
	By Proffit & Losse pd. Tho. Wall in full	164	1	4	
8	By Jacob Lloyd pd. him in part	170			6
10	By Worsted stockins pd. John Perrie	172	3	12	11
14	By Ditto pd. John Rudduck and Joseph George	172	10	10	6
	By Proffit & Losse pd. Tho. Barret for pruning tooles	164		4	6
20	By horses 2 pd. James Swetnam & Robert Little	174		16	4
	By Worsted stockins pd. John Ashman and Tho. Hill for John Perry	172	9	19	7
22	By Jacob Lloyd pd. him in full to the 21th January	170		4	9
23	By Elizabeth Milner pd. her in full	15	7	19	10½
24	By Worsted stockins pd. John Perrie	172	5	6	3
	By Charles King pd. lent him on his obligation	152	6		
	By house at lower end of Small Streat pd. Ed. Jones	161		6	
25	By Proffit & Losse pd. for 2 Panniers	164		2	10
27	By Robert Pocock pd. Walter Bult	149	40		
	By Andrew Binfield pd. lent him	173	50		
	By Worsted stockins pd. Tho. Dyer for 40 paire	172	3	16	8
28	By Ditto pd. James Woollen & Joseph George £9 15s 00d & 1d for news letters	164	9	15	1
29	By Proffit & Losse pd. for 3 Grosse of Corks	164		4	3

Anno 1689				
Joseph Creswicke merchant one of the Aldermen of the Citie of Bristoll	Dr	£	s	d
To Cash for sundry disbursments on his Stable in Ducklane [111] by agreement under his hand and seale, as may appeare, being for these particulars £ s d				
To what spend on the workmen at severall times 00 01				
To what pd. John Jones Mason for new pendanting, the Stables etc. 2 4 6				
To what pd. John Gandy for a Lock & key, & rings & staples 2 6				
To what pd. Joseph Drew the Carpenter 1 12	173	4		
February 4 To Cash pd. Matthias Jones for the tax of 12d in the pound for the Stables	173		2	
1690 March 28 To Cash pd. Geo Bond & Wm. Fry for the Tax of 3s per pound for his stables	175		1	6
June 27 To Cash pd. Giles Gough and Wm. Fry ¼ years tax on the 3s act for his stable	181		1	6
August 4 To Ditto pd. Nathanael Jones and Morgan Williams for drums and colours	181			1
Sept. 23 To Ditto pd. Geo Bond for ¼ year's tax on his stable	187 *		1	6
		4	6	7

Anno 1689				
Sir George Strode of Leweston in the County Dorset Sergt. at law is	Dr	£	s	d
January 8 To sundry accts for one Pannier & Cover cont. 2 doz bottles Xerie sent per B. Wilkins	164	2	1	6
To Cash pd. James Swetnam for a paire Gambadoes for Judge Gregory	175	1	5	1
To sundry accts for one pannier cont. 2 doz Xerie	186, 180	2	5	6
		5	12	1

Anno 1689				
Andrew Binfield of Reading Salesman is	Dr	£	s	d
January 27 To Cash pd. lent him on his obligation payable the 28th instant	173	50		

(174) **Bristoll 1689**				
John Wilmer [112] of London Silkman my Bro. in law is	Dr	£	s	d
December To his former acct. current for the cost & charges of 2 Panniers Xerie sent him	117	3	4	11
To Ditto for 2 Firkins Butter sent him	117	2	18	9
14 To Cash pd. Francis Maynard for 2 Flitches Bacon weight 59lb at 3¼d per lb	173		16	
25 To Proffit & Losse for hooping the Butter, packing cloth for the Bacon & portridge	164		1	7

			£	s	d
31	By Worsted stockins pd. John Perrie and John Rudduck	172	12	15	1
February 3	By Proffit & Losse pd. postage of leters to this day	164	1	19	1
4	By Worsted Stockins pd. Tho. Hill & Tho. Dyer	172	5	2	7
	By Joseph Creswick pd. the Tax for his stable	173		2	
	By Hugh Walter & Company pd. lent them on theire bond	174	100		
5	By Worsted stockins pd. John Ashman & John Day	172	11	10	3
	By John Hardiman pd. lent him	80	2		
7	By Horses 2 pd. Ed. Tippet	174		7	
	By Worsted stockins pd. John Rudduck John Perrie & Joseph George	172	17	12	11
	By Giles Clark paid him Feb. 5th as per his receit	171	100		
10	By John Hartnell and Co. pd. lent them on theire bond	174	30		
	By Proffit & Losse pd. John Gandy in full	164		2	6
	By Worsted stockins pd. Tho. Hill for Jona. Abram	172	1	13	4
	By ballance carrried to that acct.	175	3360	12	10
			4118	7	6½

		Anno 1690@			
	Joseph Creswick per Contra	Cr	£	s	d
	By Acct. of Ballances, for Ballance	194 *	4	6	7

		Anno 1689			
	Sir George Strode per Contra is	Cr	£	s	d
March	By Isaac Heming paid him in London	177	3	6	7
1690 Sept. 30	By Cash recd. of him	187 *	2	5	6
			5	12	1

		Anno 1689			
	Andrew Binfield per Contra is	Cr	£	s	d
January 28	By Cash recd. of him in full	173	50		

		Bristoll 1689			
	John Wilmer per Contra	Cr	£	s	d
January 28	By Cash recd. of Lewis Cox of Cardiffe for his acct.	173	10		
1690 July 26	By Cash recd. of Wm. Higgins in part of his bill for £20	181	10		
28	By Ditto recd. of Lewis Cox	181		15	
31	By Cash recd. of Jane Foot of Chippenham on his bill per the hands of Tho. Goldney	181	11	2	
			31	17	

January 28					
1690 July	To Isaac Heming for money recd. of him on my Bill	177	2	18	9
August	To Ditto for money remitted per bill on him	177	21	17	
			31	17	

Anno 1689					
	Hugh Walter of Bristoll Linnindraper, Katharine his monther, and Ozziell Browne of the same Citie Attorney	Dr	£	s	d
February 4	To Cash pd. lent them on theire bond payable with intrest on 4th August 90	173	100		
1690 August 4	To Profit and Loss for ½ year's intrest of £100 ending this 4th August 1690 @	180	3		
			103		

Anno 1689					
	Richard Merrick alias Reece of Clevedon is	Dr	£	s	d
October 10	To his former acct. current for ballance thereof for which I took his bill	92	5	11	

Anno 1689					
	Horses Two my two mares are	Dr	£	s	d
January 20	To Cash paid James Swetnam in full of his noat for bridles etc.	173		14	
	To Ditto pd. Robert Little for 2 doz Straw	173		2	4
February 7	To Ditto pd. Ed. Tippet in full for bringing in a reek of Hay from Clifton	173		7	
15	To Cash pd. David Philips for a Bushell of Branne	175			6
March 1	To Ditto pd. John Wickham in full for a Reeke of Hay	175	8		
6	To Cash pd. David Philips for a Bushell of Bran	175			6
24	To Cash paid John Moon for mending Bridles etc.	175		1	8
1690 29	To Ditto paid Robert Little's wife for 2 doz of Straw at 1s 2d per doz	175		2	4
April 5	To Ditto paid Joan Fletcher for a Bushel of Bran	175			6
14	To Cash paid Thomas Lawford for 5 Bushels of Oates at 13d per Bushell and Portridg	175		5	8
17	To Cash paid Katharine Higginbottom for 2lb of Grease for the bay Mare's Heels	175			6
24	To Ditto pd. Abel Edward in full of his noat for shoeing etc. said Horses	175		9	
28	To Ditto paid Joan Fletcher for a bushell of bran	175			6
May 3	To Ditto pd. John Moon in full of his noat for mending Bridles etc.	175		1	8
June 26	To Cash pd. Tho. Harris, for one years rent for his stables ending 29th Sept. 1689	181	2		
Oct. 4	To Ditto pd. the Widow Goodman (per the hands of John Hartnell) for a reek of Hay	187 *	4		
8	To Ditto pd. Ant. Pickett for horseloads of hay	187 *		10	
11	To Ditto pd. Ed. Willliams to this day	187 *		5	4
17	To Ditto pd. John Room, for their Grazing the Last Summer	187 *	2	10	
	To Ditto pd. John Hartnell for a reek of Hay	187 *	7		
28	To Cash paid for an horseload of hay	189 *		5	
Nov.r 4	To Ditto paid Tho. James for keepng them to this day	187 *		5	4
	To Ditto paid Abr. Hill for ½ a Score of oats	187 *		10	10
			27	12	8

Anno 1689					
	John Hartnell of Bristoll merchant & William his Brother Butcher are	Dr	£	s	d
February	To Cash paid lent them on theire bond payable March 25th with intrest	173	30		
1690 Oct.	To Profit and Loss for ½ year's intrest of £30 ending August 10th 1690 @	180		18	

Anno 1690@		Cr	£	s	d
	Hugh Walter and Co. per Contra				
August 4	By Cash recd. of Ozziel Brown for ½ years intrest due this 4th August	181	3		
	By Acct. of Ballances, for Ballance	194 *	100		
			103		

Anno 1690		Cr	£	s	d
	Richard Merrick alias Reece per Contra is	116		14	3
April	By Land at Clevedon for what he paid the Lords Rent	194 *	4	16	9
	By Acct. of Ballances, for Ballance		5	11	

Anno 1690		Cr	£	s	d
	Horses two per Contra are	161	1	7	6
April 4	By Tho. Day for ½ Ton of Hay sold him	175	4	4	3
26	By Cash received of severalls for a Parcell of Hay sold them	191 *	22		11
	By Profit and Loss for Ballance		27	12	8

Anno 1690@		Cr	£	s	d
	Per Contra	194 *	30	18	
	By Acct. of Ballances, for Ballance				

(175)	Bristoll 1689				
	Cash is	Dr	£	s	d
	To ballance brought from that acct.	173	3360	12	10
February 20	To Lewis Adams received of him in full	56	30		
March 3	To Joane Hancock recd. of her in part	176	20		
	To Reisons solis 60 Barrills etc. received out of the Customhouse for dammage	177		12	5
13	To Edward Croft Received of him in full for ½ year's rent for his house due Dec. 25th 1689	96	15	15	
21	To Joseph Drew received of him	159	2		
1690 26	To Richard Baily Received of him in full	176	54	8	
28	To Benjamin Smith Received of him in full	50	6		
29	To Robert Dowding and Company received of Ozziel Brown for 1 year's intrest due August 4th 89	100	6		
April 5	To Joan Hancock received of her daughter Sarah	176	20		
10	To Henry Howard and Company received of Ozziel Brown	163	3		
	To William Bush received of him in full	171	100	4	
11	To Peter Hinton received of him in full	158	1		
14	To Alexander Caduggan received of him per the Hands of Edw. Martindale Junior	48	50		
16	To John Earl of Bristoll, received of Sarjeant Hedges at Clevedon	150	15	10	
21	To Joan Bryan received of her	167	1	12	11
26	To William Godwin Received of him	166	3		
	To Horses Two received of severalls For a parcell of Hay sold them	174	4	4	3
			3693	19	5

			Cr	£	s	d
	Bristoll 1689					
	Cash per Contra is					
February 14	By *Worsted stockins pd. John Perrie & Tho. Hill*		*172*	11		10
	By *Proffit & Losse pd. Humphry Nickins*		*164*			8
15	By *Henry Gibbes pd. lent him*		*151*	30		
	By *Horses 2 pd. for a Bushell of Branne*		*174*			6
17	By *Worsted stockins pd. Jonathan Abram for 30 paire*		*172*	3	2	6
	By *John Earle of Bristoll pd. for a custom house certificate for 2*					
	Rundlets of wine		*150*			6
18	By *Worsted stockins pd. Tho. Hill*		*172*	6	18	9
	By *Cattle 2 steeres pd. John Hurtnell in May last*		*5*	5		
	By *Jacob Lloyd paid him in full*		*170*		5	1
20	By *Worsted stockins pd. John Rudduck and James Woollen*		*172*	14	10	2
	By *Ditto pd. John Perrie for 52 paire*		*172*	5	8	4
	By *reisons of Malaga 60 barrills & 120 pieces pd. Freight ,*					
	custom & other charges		*177*	96	16	8½
	By *Joseph Drew paid lent him on his noat*		*159*	2		
22	By *Stockins pd. Fra. Rottenburie*		*172*		14	¾
27	By *Ditto pd. Tho. Hill for Jonathan Abram*		*172*	3		5
28	By *Ditto pd. Joseph George and John Perrie*		*172*	10	4	2
March 1	By *horses 2 pd. John Wickham for a Reeke of hay*		*174*	8		
3	By *Worsted stockins pd. Tho. Dyer*		*172*	3	13	10
4	By *Jahzeel Speed pd. Tho. Bourne*		*154*	1	11	9
	By *Proffit & Losse pd. household expences to the 29th of January*					
	1689		*164*	104	4	6
5	By *Worsted stockins pd. John Day & Tho. Hill*		*172*	10	18	
	By *Tho. Goldney Junior pd. lent him on his obligation*		*176*	100		
6	By *horses 2 pd. David Philips for a Bushell of Bran*		*174*			6
8	By *Worsted stockins pd. Tho. Hill & Joseph George*		*172*	11	2	11
	By *Sir George Strode pd. James Swetnam*		*173*	1	5	1
11	By *Worsted stockins paid Tho. Hill (for John Ashman)*		*172*	15	16	3
13	By *Ditto paid James Wollen*		*172*	9	15	10
	By *Raisons Solis 27 Barrils paid sundry Disbursements on them*		*136*		4	
	By *Adventure the third in the Ship Diligence paid Custom etc.*		*142*	4		10
	By *Adventure the 3rd in the ship Welcome paid Custom etc.*		*166*	3	11	9
	By *Alicant soap 8 Cerns paid Custom etc.*		*167*	3	4	10½
	By *houses in the Castle paid Chimney money for the Little house*					
	not charged in due time		*159*		2	
14	By *Worsted stockins pd. John Perry*		*172*	6	19	7
15	By *Ditto paid Thomas Hill*		*172*	2	12	1
	By *Ditto paid Ditto and Thomas Dyer*		*172*	4	12	7
	By *Elizabeth Milner paid Her*		*15*	8	18	6
19	By *Worsted stockins pd. John Ashman*		*172*	11	6	3
	By *Ditto paid John Rudduck and Tho. Hill (for John Ashman)*		*172*	12	6	
	By *Jacob Lloyd Paid him*		*170*		5	
21	By *Profit and Loss paid Isaac Dighton (for his father George*					
	Dighton)		*164*		3	4
	By *Worsted Stockins paid Joseph George & John Perry*		*172*	16	5	5
22	By *Ditto paid Tho. Dyer*		*172*	2	11	9
24	By *Horses two paid John Moon*		*174*		1	8
1690 25	By *Worsted Stockins paid Tho. Hill (for Jona. Abram & Tho.*					
	Browning) and Edw. Iff		*172*	12		
	By *Jahzeel Speed Paid Richard Sandford*		*154*	3		
28	By *Alderman Joseph Creswick paid Geo. Bond and Will. Fry*		*173*		1	6
29	By *Horses two paid Robert Littles Wife*		*174*		2	4
	By *Worsted stockins paid Francis Rottenbury*		*172*		14	7¾
April 2	By *John Cullimore paid him*		*130*		1	
	By *Henry Gibbes paid Lent him on his noat*		*151*	21	10	
3	By *Profit and Loss paid William Phelps and* [113]		*164*	1	2	6

(176)	**Bristoll 1689**	Dr	£	s	d
	William Spoore Junior of Portburie his acct. current is	Dr	£	s	d
December 17	To his former acct. current for money resting due on bond for which intrest is there charg'd to the 17th of December 1689	31	10		
	To acct. of himselfe and father on bond for intrest of £40 ending Dec. 17th 1689	69	10	17	6
			20	17	6

	Anno 1689	Dr	£	s	d
	Wm. Spoore Junior is	Dr	£	s	d
December 17	To his above acct. for money due on his bond	176	10		
	To Ditto for ballance of that acct. for which hee gave mee his Bill payable March 17th 1689	176	10	10	6
1690 @ Oct.	To Profit and Loss for ¾ year's intrest of £20 10s 6d ending Sept. 17th 1690 @	180		18	5
			21	8	11

	Anno 1689	Dr	£	s	d
	Richard Baily of Bristoll Soapemaker is	Dr	£	s	d
	To Alicant Soape 8 Cernes for the said Cernes weight 21 cwt 0 qr 0 lb neat at 52s per cwt	167	54	12	

			£	s	d
4	By Worsted stockins paid John Perry, Tho. Hill & Joseph George	172	24	11	11
5	By Profit and Loss paid Humphrey Nickins for watching to the 25th day of March last	164			6
	By Ditto paid Wm. Phelps and —— —— on the Act of 3d per pound for my personal Estate	164	18		
	By Worsted stockins pd. Tho. Dyer	172	3	7	1
	By Horses two paid Joan Fletcher for a Bushell of Bran	174			6
9	By Worsted stockins pd. Tho. Hill (for Jonathan Abram & John Massinger)	172	5	4	2
10	By Ditto pd. John Ashman John Rudduck and John Perry	172	15	16	10
14	By Horses two paid Thomas Lawford	174		5	8
	By Jahzeel Speed paid Doctor and his Expences at Bath	154	1	13	8½
15	By Jacob Lloyd paid Him in full to this 15th day of April 1690	170		5	4
17	By Worsted stockins paid Eliz. Webb and John Day	172	2	5	
	By Horses two pd. Katharine Higginbottom	174			6
18	By Worsted Stockins paid John Perry & Tho. Hill	172	4	3	4
19	By Tho. Tuthar pd. him	178	50		
	By Worsted stockins pd. Joseph George	172	2	5	
	By Jahzeel Speed pd. Welthean Ruther for him	178	1	12	2
20	By Eliz. Taylor and Co. pd. Lent them on their Bond	179	2		
23	By Worsted stockins paid Tho. Hill	172	4	4	
24	By Horses two paid Abell Edwards	174		9	
26	By Worsted stockins pd. Tho. Hill	172	2	18	4
28	By Henry Gibbes pd. him in full	179	6	3	11
	By Horses two pd. Joan Fletcher for A Bushel of Bran	174			6
	By Profit and Loss pd. Passage at Roundham	180		1	1
May 2	By Worsted stockins paid John Perry	172	1	11	3
	By Jacob Lloyd, pd. him in full to this day	170		3	3¾
3	By Horses two pd. John Moon for mending Bridles etc.	174		1	8
	By Profit and Loss pd. Frances Maynard for 27 lb Bacon at 3d½ per lb	180		7	10½
	By John Osgood paid Ditto for 108 lb of Bacon at 3d½ per lb	178	1	11	6
			720	13	7[¼]
	By Ballance Carried to a new Account	181	2973	5	9[¾]
			3693	19	5

Bristoll 1689

		Cr	£	s	d
	Wm. Spoore Junior per Contra is				
December 17	By ballance of his former acct. current brought from that acct.	31		7	
	By his new account current for the £10 per Contra resting due on his bond	176	10		
	By Ditto for ballance for which I took his bill, payable 17th March 1689	176	10	10	6
			20	17	

Anno 1690@

	Cr	£	s	d
Per Contra				
By Acct. of Ballances, for Ballance	194 *	21	8	11

Anno 1689

		Cr	£	s	d
	Richard Bayly per Contra is				
March 26	By Cash recd. of him in full	175	54	8	
	By Profit and Loss for Ballance	191 *		4	
			54	12	

Anno 1689				
	John Scandred of Bristoll Grocer is	*Dr*	*£*	*s*	*d*
January	To Reisons 60 Barrills & 120 piecesfor 6 Barrills & 12 pieces sould him	177	45		

Anno 1689				
	Tho. Goldney Junior my Sonne in law is	*Dr*	*£*	*s*	*d*
	To Ballance of his former acct. current brought from that acct. 2 doz bottles	136	2	4	
January	To Reisons 60 Barrills & 120 piecesfor 8 Barrills & 16 piecesat 40s & 30s per Cwt	177	58	9	11¾
March 5	To Cash paid lent him on his bill payable Aprill 6th	175	100		
1690 July 5	To Henry Parsons, for said Parsons his bill on him, in my favour	145	60		
			220	13	11¾

Anno 1689				
	Joane Hancock of Bristoll Widow Vintner	*Dr*	*£*	*s*	*d*
March 3	To Xeries wine 23 Butts for 2 Butts sould her at £30 per Butt payable at 3 payments	169	60		

(177)	**Bristoll 1689/90**							
	Reisons of Malaga 60 Barrills and 120 pieces laden per Thomas Strode in the ship Pellican of Biddiford ¾ parts of which are for the propper acct. of said Strode and ¼ pt for my propper acct. Philip Cade being Master	*Dr*						
			£	*s*	*d*			
Jan. 9 February 6	To Cash pd. custom, fees bills etc. for 157cwt 0 00d Reisons solis, and 84cwt 2qr 4lb of great reisons as per particulars		21	9	8½	175		
	To Ditto paid Philip Cade for the freight and averidge of said Fruite in money £73 17s 6d with £4 10s 7d hee allowed for dammage is in all £78 8s 1d as per particulars in his receit of 15th Feb. 1689		73	17	6	175		
	To Profit & Losse for halling to the Cellar			12	0	180		
	To Cash pd. portridge into & out of the Cellar, and weighing		1	6	2	175		
	To Ditto pd. John Harper for 2 weeks Celleridge			3	4	175		
	To Profit and Loss for Port of Leters			7	6	180		
	To Ditto for Cooperidg			3	6	180		
	To Ditto for charges in giving the Grocers & Nailers a Treat			16	9	180		
	To Ditto for what abated in odd pence			3	0	180	*£*	*s*	*d*
	To Ditto for my Commission at 2 per Cen.to		8	18		180	107	17	5½
	To Tho Strode for ¾ parts of the neat proceeds being £339 09s 04d ¾		254	12	0¾	136			
	To Fruit my 1/4 part of 60 Barrils and 60 Carge of Raisons for my ¼ pt of £339 09s 04d ¾ the neat proceeds		84	17	4	183	339	9	4¾
							447	6	10¼

Anno 1690@				
John Scandred per Contra	*Cr*	*£*	*s*	*d*
June 26 By Cash recd. of him per the hands of Edw. Martindale Junior	181	45		

Anno 1690				
Tho. Goldney per Contra	*Cr*	*£*	*s*	*d*
April 1 By John Cary, for money paid him per the Hands of John Corsley by my order	178	100		
July 5 By Cash, recd. of Richd. Bayly on Wm. Riddley's bill, in said Goldney's favour	181	20		
7 By Ditto recd. of John Bubb Esq. on Sam. Ingelo his servant's obligation in favour of John Hawkins, and by him assigned to said Goldney	181	66		
By Cash recd. of him	187 *	32	8	
By Sir Geo. Strode, for goods formerly had of him, & sent to said Strode	24	1	13	
		220	1	
By Acct. of Ballances, for Ballance	194 *		12	11¾
		220	13	11¾

Anno 1689				
Joane Hancock per Contra is	*Cr*	*£*	*s*	*d*
March 3 By Cash received of her in part	175	20		
1690 April 5 By Cash received of her Daughter Sarah	175	20		
July 29 By Ditto recd. per her in full	181	20		
		60		

Bristoll 1689/90							
Reisons 60 Barrills & 120 ps per Contra are				*Cr*	*£*	*s*	*d*
	cwt	*qr*	*lb*				
By John Love for 8 Barrills neat at 40s	21	0	9¾				
January &16 pieces neat at 30s	11	1	8	55	59	3	1¼
By Fra.Whitchurch							
8 Barrills neat at 40s	21	1	2¼	53	59	1	½
& 16 pieces neat at 30s	11	0	1				
By Henry Parsons							
8 Barrills neat at 40s	21	1	16½	145	60	1	8
& 16 pieces neat at 30s	11	2	3				
By Edward Hacket for							
8 Barrills neat at 40s	21	1	20	145	59	11	4¾
&16 pieces neat at 30s	11	0	16				
By John Scandred for							
6 Barrills neat at 40s	16		18¾	176	45		1¾
& 12 pieces neat at 30s	8	1	22				
By James Fisher for							
6 Barrills neat at 40s	16		18	144	45	4	7½
& 12 pieces neat at 30s	8	2	12				
By Robert Hawksworth							
Barrills neat at 40s	21	2	12¾	28	60	2	6¾
& 12 pieces neat at 30s	11	1	2				
By Tho. Goldney Junior							
for 6 Barrills neat at 40s	21	0	15	176	58	9	11¾
& 12 pieces neat at 30s	10	3	8				
March 3 By Cash recd. out of Customhouse allowed for dammage				175		12	5
					447	6	10¼

Anno 1689		Dr	£	s	d
	Isaac Heming of London merchant *my Sonne in law is*	Dr	£	s	d
January	To Ballance of his former acct. current brought from that acct.	152	147	9	3
	To Sir George Strode received of him in London	173	3	6	7
March	To Samuel Kekewich for the value of 8000 Ryals Plate is 1000 pieces of 8 received of Nathanael Maxy & John Barnard on a Bill drawn by Ben. Warren & Comp.@ on them in favour of said Kekewich and by him assigned to me, the piece of 8 at 50 3/8d per piece	167	209	17	11
April	To Henry Parsons for money recd. of Paris Sloughter on said Parsons his bill in my favour	145	40		
	To Jonathan Lamboll recd. of John Miles and Edw. Clarke in part of the Purchase money for the houses in Reading sold them	147	639	10	
	To Tho. Curtis for money formerly recd. of him, but not charg'd when recd	169	12		
			1052	3	9

Anno 1690@		Dr	£	s	d
	Isaac Heming of London Merchant	Dr	£	s	d
	To Ballance of his former acct. Currrent, which agrees with his Account sent me, Closed in London May 7th 1690	177	881	15	7
May	To Sam. Kekewich, recd. of John Stacy, on his bill in my favour, for 864 pieces of 8 and 2½ Ry.ls p.la at 52½ per pieces of 8	167	189	1	4
	To Ditto, recd. of Samuel Proctor, on his bill in my favour, for 1250 pieces of 8 at 52¼d	167	272	2	8
Oct.	To Ditto recd. of John Franck for his bill in my favour for 77¾ pieces of 8 at 52d	185	16	16	11
			1359	16	6

(178)	**Bristoll 1690**	Dr	£	s	d
	John Cary of Bristoll Merchant	Dr	£	s	d
April 1	To Thomas Goldney Junior for money recd. of him per the hands of John Corsley by my order payable (as per his bond) with Intrest on the first day of October 1690	176	100		
	To Profit and Loss for ½ years intrest of £100 ending October 1st 1690 @	180	3		
			103		

Anno 1690		Dr	£	s	d
	Thmas Tuthar of the Citie of Bristoll Plumber	Dr	£	s	d
April 19	To Cash paid him in part for Ten Tonns of Lead	175	50		
May 7	to Ditto paid him in full	181	45	8	3
			95	8	3
	To Profit and Loss, for Ballance	191 *			4¾

Anno 1689				
Isaac Heming per Contra is	*Cr*	£	*s*	*d*
March By Tho. Goldney for money pd. him in Sept. last per my order then omitted to bee chargd	*136*	150		
By Benjamin Cole for money he paid him on my Bill in favour of said Cole [114]	*147*	8		
By Adventure in the ship Sarah to Cadiz for money omitted to bee chargd on assureance made on said ship, to Cadiz, to his Credit although charged to the debt of said Adventure	*169*		6	
By Profit and Loss for port of Leters, and books etc. sent me	*180*	2	1	3
By Xeries Wines 23 Butts, for charges formerly pd. on a Butt of Malaga	*169*		7	
By Adventure in the Merchant's Goodwill, pd. for filing a Certificate	*166*		4	
By Adventure in the Caesar pd. Ditto and Custom etc.	*169*	4	18	11
By Adventure in the Sarah, pd. for filing a Certificate & ensurance on £100	*169*	4	11	
		170	8	2
To his new (under-written) Acct. Current for Ballance	*177*	881	15	7
		1052	3	9

Anno 1690@				
Isaac Heming per Contra	*Cr*	£	*s*	*d*
May By Francis Creswicke Esq. and Company pd. Tho. Callow on my bill	*184*	100		
July 16 By Cash, recd. of Wm. Higgs for my bill in favour of Castor Higgs	*181*	200		
By Thomas Strode for money pd. Hugh Strode on my Bill	*136*	200		
By John Wilmer pd. him on my Bill	*174*	2	18	9
To Tho. Day for ½ the Charges in ensuring £200 on the Rachel and Olive-branch	*186*	7	11	6
By Wines my ½ of 20 Butts for ½ the Charges in ensuring £200 on Said Ships	*186*	7	11	6
August By John Wilmer for money pd. on my bill in his favour	*174*	21	17	
7 By Cash recd. of Isaac Barnard for my Bill in his favour	*181*	100		
By Tho. Strode for mony pd. Hugh Strode for his Account	*136*	53	6	7¼
By Tho. Day pd. Tho. Lock per order of said Day	*186*	30		
Sept. 30 By Cash recd. of Serjeant Tho. Strode for my bill in favour of Hugh Strode	*187 **	30		
By Wines my ½ of 20 Butts for ½ the Cost and Charges of 2 pipes of Canary	*186*	29	14	6
By Ditto for the Cost and Charges of a Cask of Rhenish	*186*	14	15	2
By Thomas Day for ½ the Cost of 2 pipes of Canary	*186*	26	14	6
		824	9	6[¼]
By Acct. of Ballances, for Ballance	*194 **	535	6	11[¾]
		1359	16	6

Bristoll 1690@

John Cary per Contra	*Cr*	£	*s*	*d*
By Acct. of Ballances, for Ballance	*194 **	103		

Anno 1690@				
Thomas Tuthar per Contra is	*Cr*	£	*s*	*d*
May 6 By Lead bought for my propper acct. for 10 ton 9 cwt 3qr 18lb bought of him, at 9s 10d	*183*	95	8	7¾

Anno 1690					
	Jahzeel Speed	Dr	£	s	d
	To Ballance of his former Account brought from That Account	154	826	3	11
April	To Cash delivered Welthean Ruther for him at his going to Bath	175	1	12	2
June	To Eliza. Milner for ¼ years dyet ending June 7th 1690	15	5		
	To Ditto for money furnished him with, and other necessaries bought for him	15	4	5	6
			837	1	7

Anno 1690					
	John Osgood of London Linnen Draper is	Dr	£	s	d
	To his former account Current for the Cost of 4 Flitches of Bacon	113	1	7	10
May 3	To Cash pd. Frances Maynard for 108 lb Bacon at 3d½ per lb	175	1	11	6
			2	19	4

(179)   **Bristoll 1690**

	Elizabeth Taylor of the Citie of Bristoll Widow, Dennis Taylor of the same Citie Mariner & Margarett Taylor of the same Citie Spinster are	Dr	£	s	d
April 20	To Cash paid Lent them on their bond payable on demand	175	2		

Anno 1690@					
	Henry Gibbes of [Bristo]ll Merchant is	Dr	£	s	d
	To money lent as in his f[ormer A]ccount Current brought from that account	151	21	10	
April 28	To Cash pd. him in full	175	6	3	11
			27	13	11

Anno 1690					
	Henry Gibbes of Bristoll Merchant is	Dr	£	s	d
	To Ballance of his above written Account Current	179	21	10	
June 14	To Cash pd. him on his bill on Alex. Dolman & his own obligation	181	50		
	To Profit and Loss for Intrest thereof from 14 June 1690 to 2nd August 1690 when his bill on Alex. Dolman is Payable	180		8	4
			71	18	4

Anno 1690@					
	Thomas Simonds of Yate in GlocesterShire Yeoman	Dr	£	s	d
Oct. 6	To Cash pd. him on a mortgage of Lands lying in Mangottisfield in the County of Glocester	187 *	250		

(180)   **Bristoll 1690**

	Profit and Loss is	Dr	£	s	d
April 28	To Cash pd. Passage at Roundham	175		1	1
May 3	To Ditto paid Francis Maynard for 27lb Bacon to be sent to Is. Heming	175		7	10½
7	To Ditto paid Ditto for a flitch of Bacon weight 22lb qt 3d½ per pound	181		6	5
	To Eliz. Croft for ¼ year's rent of 2 rooms reserved in the house in which she liveth due March 25th 1690	183		10	
	To Ditto for money pd. in disbursments on Ditto house	183	1	1	
	To Isaac Heming for port of Leters and books etc. sent me	177	2	1	3
8	To Edw. Jacob for severall disbursments pd. and things had of him, to this 8th May 1690	156	27	10	
20	To Cash pd. Abr. Hill for a Firkin of Butter weight neat 77lb at 3d¼ & 6d Cask	181	1	1	4
	To Ditto pd. Ditto for setting out a Trainband Souldier	181		2	11
	To Ditto pd. Humphrey Nickins for watching to 19th instant	181			6
26	To Cash pd. David Philips Poor's mony	181	3	12	
	To Ditto pd. Ditto for baking for us for four years, ending this 26th May 1690	181		16	

Anno 1690@				
Jahzeel Speed per Contra	*Cr*	*£*	*s*	*d*
By Acct. of Ballances, for Ballance [115]	*194 **	*837*	*1*	*7*

Anno 1690@				
John Osgood per Contra	*Cr*	*£*	*s*	*d*
May 15 *By Cash recd. of him in full*	*181*	*2*	*19*	*4*

Bristoll 1690@				
Per Contra	*Cr*	*£*	*s*	*d*
By Acct. of Ballances, for Ballance	*194 **	*2*		

Anno 1690				
Henry Gibbes per Contra is	*Cr*	*£*	*s*	*d*
By his former Account Current for Ballance of that Account	*151*	*6*	*3*	*11*
By his now underwritten Account per contra for Ballance	*179*	*21*	*10*	
		27	*13*	*11*

Anno 1690@				
Henry Gibbes per Contra	*Cr*	*£*	*s*	*d*
May 23 *By Cash recd. of Richard Champney per Bill*	*181*	*21*	*10*	
June 14 *By Ditto recd. of him for the Intrest of the £50 per Contra,*				
though not due till 2nd Aug. 1690	*181*		*8*	*4*
August 4 *By Cash, recd. of Alexander Dolman, for said Gi[bbes] his bill*	*181*	*50*		
		71	*18*	*4*

Anno 1690@				
Thomas Simonds per Contra	*Cr*	*£*	*s*	*d*
By Acct. of Ballances, for Ballance	*194 **	*250*		

Bristoll 1690@				
Profit and Loss per Contra	*Cr*	*£*	*s*	*d*
By Ballance from a former acct.	*164*	*717*	*4*	*½*
By Elizabeth Croft for ¼ year's rent due March 25th 1690	*183*	*9*		
By Giles Clark for Intrest of Severall Summs of money etc. as				
per his acct. in fol (171) of this Leadger No E	*171*	*18*	*14*	*0*
June *By Dr. Fra. Hungerford for a pannier Corks etc. for 2 doz*				
Xerie	*184*		*2*	
14 *By Henry Gibbes for intrest of £50 from 14th June 1690 to*				
August 2nd 1690	*179*		*8*	*4*
18 *By the Lady Ann Powlett for Portridg of 4 doz Xerie*	*155*			*4*
21 *By Cash, recd. of James Shute, for a Cask of Butter said to be*				
lost in carriage to London	*181*	*1*	*2*	
July *By John Earl of Bristoll for port of leters etc.*	*150*			*4*
August 4 *By Hugh Walter and Company for ¼ year's intrest of £100*				
ending this 4th August 1690	*174*	*3*		
By Raisons 60 Barrils and 120 pieces for Hallage to the Cellar	*177*		*12*	
By Ditto for port of leters & Cooperidg	*177*		*11*	
By Ditto for a treat given the Grocers & Waiters	*177*		*16*	*9*
By Ditto abated in odd pence	*177*		*3*	

June 5	*To Ditto pd. John Webb, on a review of the Poll bill*	*181*	1		
7	*To Ditto pd. Edw.* J[one]*s for whiteliming my house*	*181*		10	
11	*To Cash pd. John Bart*[lett] *for ¼ years tax on the act of 3d per pound for my house*	*181*	1	2	6
17	*To Ditto pd. John Gandy in full of his noat*	*181*		14	6
	To Eliz. Milner for Crape etc. had of her	*15*		18	2
21	*To Cash pd. Humphrey Nickins, for watching to the 19th instant*	*181*			6
26	*To Ditto pd. Abr. Hill for a Cask of Butter weight neat 9 cwt 3qr 6lb 77lb at 3d¼*[&] *6d Cask*	*181*	1	5	
28	*To Cash pd. John Duddlestone and — Ranstrope on the Poll act*	*181*	3	13	
	To Tho. Day for 4 doz parts of Whitewine and a quart of Rhenish	*161*	1	6	10
	To Ditto for money abated him on acct.	*161*		3	1
July 9	*To Cash pd. Jona.* [Abrah]*am for a pair of stockins for my own wearing*	*181*		2	
	To Ditto pd. — [?] *on the assessment for drums and Colours*	*181*		2	1
10	*To Ditto pd. John* [Hosey] *for carriage of a Kegg of sturgeon from London*	*181*		2	11
	To Sam. Kekewi[ch for] *postage of leters to April 7th 1690 being (as per acct. Current clo*[sed at] *St Marie Port April 7th 1690) 200 Ryals Plate which make 25 pieces of 8 at 52d*	*185*	5	8	4
	To Ditto for Brokeridg and Commission, for severall Bills of Exchange sent me as per said Acct. Current, being 265 Ryals Plate which make 33 1/8 pieces of 8 at 52d per pieces of 8	*185*	7	3	6½
19	*To Cash pd. Abr. Hill for setting out a Train-band Souldier*	*181*		1	9
26	*To Cash pd. Welthean to pay for ¼ cwt 3 lb of Cheese at 22s per cwt*	*181*		6	¾
	To Wm. Pleydall for setting up a boiler and other work	*152*		13	
August 5	*To Cash pd. Abr. Hill to pay off a Trainband Souldier*	*181*		2	6
9	*To Ditto pd. Humphrey Nickins for watching to the 5th August 1690 @*	*181*			6
15	*To Ditto pd. Robert Lypyeatt, in full for malt, to this day*	*187 **	3	4	6
23	*To Cash pd. Dorcas Flay for 28 sacks of cole, deducting for grains*	*187 **		12	1
Sept. 5	*To Ditto pd. Abr. Hill to pay Off a Train-band Souldier*	*187 **		1	9
	To Ditto pd. Wm. Phelps for ¼ years tax for my house	*187 **	1	2	6
11	*To Cash pd. Abr. Hill for a Cask of Butter weight neat 92lb at 3d¼ & 12d Cask*	*187 **	1	6	
	To Ditto pd. Ditto to pay a Trainband Souldier	*187 **			6
15	*To Cash pd. John Dole & Henry Stanckham for ¼s tax for the house in the Castle*	*187 **		7	6
	To Tho. Smith for his noat of disbursments on the Lower Vault	*171*		19	2
23	*To Cash pd. John Sandford for gloves, as per noat*	*187 **		3	6
	To Ditto pd. John Coppothwright for ¼ years tax on the Lower Vault	*187 **		3	6
30	*To Ditto pd. John Hardiman in full of his noat*	*187 **		15	
	To Ditto pd. Jane Flower in full of her noat	*187 **	2	6	
Oct. 6	*To Cash pd. Tho. Moreman for Carraige of 5 boxes from London*	*187 **		8	
8	*To Ditto pd. Wm. Roynon for all lead used on my dwelling house to this day*	*187 **	1	11	4
11	*To Ditto pd. Steph. Stringer on a poor rate for the Lower Vault*	*187 **		2	2
18	*To Ditto paid Abraham Hill for a Cord of wood*	*187 **		11	6
	To Joan Bryan for her noat of Disbursements on the house in the Castle	*167*		8	9½
	To Sam. Kekewich, for 6 Ryals and 26 Meridees after the rate of 52d per pieces of 8 being for his Commission on a bill of Exchange on John Frank in my favour	*185*		3	8

	By Ditto for my Commission at 2 per Cento	*177*	8	18	
Sept.	By Tho. Smith for 5 months rent of the Lower Vault ending July 14th 1690	*171*	2	14	2
26	By Philip Frowd for 3 doz quart Bottles 6s, 2 panniers 1s 8d, and Porterage 4d	*85*		8	
30	By the Lady Ann Pawlett for 6 doz Bottles 12s, 3 panniers 3s & porteragge 9d	*155*		15	9
Oct. 8	By Sir Geo. Strode for 1 pannier & Cover, & 2 doz Bottles etc.	*173*		5	6
	By Cattle 2 Steers for Ballance of that acct.	*5*	1	5	
Dec. 5	By Debts due to the Lands at Redland for Ballance	*6*	8	18	11
	By Arthur Bramley and Comany for Ballance	*12*		6	
	By John Sandford for ½ years intrest of £100	*19*	3		
	By Simon Clement and his Father for 1 years intrest of £59 9s 6d	*22*	3	10	9
	By Wm. Spoore Senior and Peter Collet, for 1 years intrest of £50	*30*	3		
	By William Spoore Junior and Senior for 1 years intrest of £40	*69*	2	8	
	By Tho. Luttrel and Company for ½ years intrest of £[2]0	*97*		12	
	By Robt. Dowding and Co. for ½ years intrest of £100	*100*	3		
	By Simon Clement and Michael White, for 1 year's intrest of £50	*133*	3		
	By Edward Jacob and Company for ½ years intrest of £20	*134*		12	
	By Wm. Jones and Company for ½ years intrest of £50	*138*	1	10	
	By Nathanael Haggatt for ¾ year's intrest of £320	*148*	14	8	
	By John Gore and John Hartnell, for ¾ year's intrest of £127	*149*	5	14	4
	By Edw. Dowding for ½ years intrest of £120	*154*	3	12	
	By Wm. Spoore Senior and Junior for one year's intrest of £30	*158*	1	16	
	By Henry Howard and Co. for ½ years intrest of £100	*163*	3		
	By Wm. Godwin for ½ years intrest of £100	*166*	3		
	By John Hartnell and Co. for ½ years intrest of £30	*174*		18	
	By Wm. Spoore Junior for ¾ years intrest of £10 10s 6d	*176*		18	5
	By John Cary for ½ years intrest of £100	*178*	3		
	By Giles Clarke, for ½ year's intrest of £1000 at £5 per Cent	*184*	25		
	By Francis Creswick and Company for ¼ Year's intrest of £100	*184*	1	10	
	By Thomas Hill and Abraham his son for ¾ years intrest of £10	*170*		9	
			858	11	7½

To Sotherland for Ballance	10	15		
To John Scanfield for Ballance	· 11	1		
To Sam. Davis and Company for Ballance	11		18	
To Henry Moor for Ballance	11	1		6
To Thomas Fownes for Ballance	11	4		
To Lewis Mathew and Co. for Ballance	12	1	6	2
To Tho. Guinne of Boston for Ballance	12	35	8	10
To Edward Prestwitch for Ballance	13		6	8
To Nathanael Milner for Ballance	13	8	7	5
		144	1	8¼
To it's self for Ballance carried to a new acct.	189*	714	9	11¼
		858	11	7½

181   Bristoll 1690@

	Cash is	Dr	£	s	d
	To Ballance of a former Account brought from that Account	175	2973	5	9¾
May 8	To Edw. Jacob recd. of him	156	14	7	7
10	To Elizabeth Croft recd. of her in full	183	7	9	
	To Edw/ Jacob, and Company recd. of Edw. Jacob for ½ years intrest of £20	134	1	16	
	To Charles Jones Junior recd. of him in full	171	87	15	
15	To Richd. Cope recd. of him in part	97	1		
	To John Osgood recd. of him in full	178	2	19	4
	To Henry Gibbes recd. (on Wm. Hartly's bill in his favour) of Richd. Champney	179	21	10	
June 14	To Ditto recd. of him for Intrest of £50 from June 14th 1690 to 2nd Aug. 1690	179		8	4
17	To John Bradway, recd. of him in full per the Hands of Henry Parsons	70	20		
21	To James Fisher, recd. of him of him in full per the hands of Edw. Martindale Junior	144	45	4	6
	To Profit and Loss, recd. of James Shute, for a Cask of Butter lost (or so pretended) by Sam. Watts in Carriage to London	180	1	2	
24	To the Lady Ann Powlett, recd. of Bernard Wilkins in full	155	4	8	8
25	To Fra. Whitchurch recd. of him in full	53	59	1	
26	To John Love recd. of David Phillips, on his bill	55	59	3	
	To Alex. Caduggan recd. of him in full	48	48	18	6
	To John Scandred recd. of him of him in full per the hands of Edwardd Martindale	176	45		
28	To Richd. Langsworth recd. of him	163	1	16	6
30	To John Clark Junior recd. of him	149	31		
July 2	To Joan Bryan recd. of her Sister Hephzibah	167	1	12	11
4	To Edw. Hackett, recd. of him in full	145	59	11	
5	To Robt. Hawksworth recd. of him	28	40		
	To Tho. Goldney Junior recd. of Richd. Bayly on Wm. Riddley's bill said Goldney's favor	176	20		
7	To Ditto, recd. of John Bubb Esq. on his servant Sam. Ingelo's obligation to John Hawkins and by him [assi]gned to Said Goldney	176	60		
8	To Thomas Day, recd. of him	161	93	6	6
	To Dr. Fra. Hungerford recd. of Tho. Hungerford	184	2	6	4
16	To Isaac Heming recd. of Wm. Higgs, for my bill on said Heming in favour of Caster Higgs	177	200		
21	To Robert Hawksworth recd. of him	184	7	2	
21	To Edward Jacob recd. of him at Clapton	183	8	15	
24	To Robert Hawksworth recd. of Geo. Saunders	184	13		
	To Lewis Adams recd. of him in full	56	25		4
26	To John Wilmer, recd. of Wm. Higgins in part of a Bill for £20 on him	174	10		
28	To Ditto recd. of Lewis Cox of Cardiff	174		15	

	Bristoll 1690@	Cr	£	s	d
	Cash per Contra is				
May 5	By Worstead Stockins pd. Tho. Hill and Joseph George	182	10	19	7
7	By Profit and Loss pd. Frances Maynard for a Flitch of Bacon	180		6	5
	By Thomas Tuthar pd. him in full	178	45	8	3
	By Worstead Stockins pd. John Rudduck	182	4	12	
9	By Ditto pd. John Perry	182	5	3	9
13	By lead for my propper acct. pd. Tho. Blackwell for weighing	183		2	6
16	By Stockins pd. John Perry, Tho. Hill, and Tho. Dyer	181	8	15	2
19	By Giles Clarke pd. him	171	55	6	
20	By Profit and Loss, pd. Abra. Hill for a Firkin of Butter	180	1	1	4
	By Ditto pd. Ditto for setting out a Trainband souldier	180		2	11
	By Jacob Lloyd pd. him to 19th Instant	171		1	
21	By Profit and Loss, pd. Humphrey Nickins for watching to Ditto	180			6
	By Worstead Stockins pd. John Perry	182	4	5	5
26	By Profit and Loss, pd. David Phillips Poor's mony	180	3	12	
	By Ditto pd. Ditto for 4 years baking, ending this 26th May 1690	180		16	
28	By Worstead Stockins pd. Tho. Hill John Day, and John Perry	182	11	2	
June 4	By Ditto pd. Tho. Hill for Jonathan Abram	182	2		
5	By Profit and Loss, pd. John Webb, on a review of the Poll bill	180	1		
7	By D[itto p]d. Edward Jones for whiteliming my ho[use]	180		10	
11	By Ditto pd. John Bartlett 1/4 years tax, on the Act of 3[d per p]ound for my house	180	1	2	6
12	By Eliz. Milner pd. her	15	2		
14	By Henry Gibbes pd. him on his bill on Alex. Dolman	179	50		
16	By Worstead Stockins pd. Jonathan Abram	182	3	2	
17	By Profit and Loss pd. John Gandy in full	180		14	6
19	By Worstead Stockins pd. Joseph George	182	3	7	8
20	By Ditto pd. John Perry	182	4	8	
21	By Profit and Loss, pd. Humphrey Nickins f[or wa]tching	180			6
	By Houses in the Castle pd. John Dole and Hen. Sta[nkha]m on the 3s act	159		7	6
25	By Wm. Pleydall pd. him	152		10	
26	By Eliza. Milner pd. her in full	15	8	3	8
	By Profit and Loss pd. Abr. Hill for a Cask of Butter to be sent Isa. Heming	180	1	5	
	By Tho. Lutterell pd. lent him on his bill for the Earl of Bristolls use	25	10		
	By Horses two pd. Tho. Harris for a year's rent for his stable	174	2		
27	By Joseph Creswick pd. Giles Gough and Wm. Fry on [the] 3s act for his Stable	173		1	6
28	By Edward Williams pd. him for keeping the m[ares on]e week	185		1	
	By Worstead Stockins pd. Eliz. Webb for 2 [trun]cks	182	1	6	
	By Profit and Loss, pd. John Duddlestone and J Ranstrope on the Poll act etc.	180	3	13	

29	To Joan Hancock recd. of her in full	176	20		
31	To John Wilmer, recd. of James Foot of Chippenham on his bill	174	11	2	
August 2	To Thomas Day recd. out of Customs house, for returns on Corrupt wines	186	3	13	7½
	To Wines my half of 30 Butts recd. out of Custome house on a Certificate on bad wines	186	3	13	7½
4	To Henry Gibbes recd. on his bill on Alexander Dolman	179	50		
	To Hugh Walter and Co. recd. of Ozziel Brown	174	3		
7	To Isaac Heming, recd. of Isaac Barnard for my Bill on said Heming	177	100		
			4159	3	6¾

Bristoll 1690@

					Dr	£	s	d
	Worstead Stockins are To Ballance brought from a former acct. being the Cost and Charges of	paire 4505	s	d	172	385	8	1¾
May 5	To Cash pd. Tho. Hill (for Jona. Abram) for	30	2	1	181	3	4	7
	To Ditto pd. Joseph George for	124	1	3	181	7	15	
7	To Ditto paid John Rudduck for	46	2	0	181	4	12	
9	To Ditto pd. John Perry for	21	2	1	181	2	3	9
	To Ditto pd. Ditto for	30	2		181	3		
16	To Ditto pd. Ditto for	20	2	1	181	2	1	8
17	To Ditto pd. Thomas Dyer for	12	1	9	181	1	1	
19	To Ditto pd. Tho. Hill (for Jon. Abram) for	30	2	1	181	3	2	6
	To Ditto pd. Ditto (for Jos. George) for	40	1	3	181	2	[10]	
21	To Cash pd. John Perry for	41	2	1	181	4	5	5
26	To Ditto pd. Tho. Hill (for Jon. Abram) for	18	2	1	181	1	17	6
	To Ditto pd. Ditto (for Jos. George) for	38	1	3	181	2	7	6
28	To Ditto pd. John Day for	12	1	11	181	1	3	
30	To Ditto pd. John Perry for	57	2	0	181	5	14	
June 4	To Cash pd. Tho. Hill (for J. Abram) for	20	2	0	181	2		
16	To Ditto pd. Jon. Abram for	31	2	0	181	3	2	
19	To Cash pd. Joseph George for	56	1	2½	181	3	7	8

			£	s	d
	By Welthean Ruther, pd. Ditto for her Poll	*94*		1	
	By Sibyll Williams pd. Ditto for her Poll	*185*		1	
30	By Worstead Stockins pd. Joseph George, and Tho. Walden's man	*182*	4	18	2
July 5	By Ditto pd. Tho. Hill, John Perry, and John Green	*182*	3	18	
8	By Ditto pd. John Perry, and Jona. Abram	*182*	10	13	4
9	By Profit and Loss pd. Jon. Abram for a pair of stockins for my wearing	*180*		2	
	By Ditto pd. on the assessment for drums and Colours	*180*		2	1
10	By Ditto pd. John Hosey for Carriage of a Keg of sturgeon from London	*180*		2	11
12	By Worstead Stockins pd. Joseph George, Francis Rattenbury and Edward Iff	*182*	6	13	5
14	By Ditto pd. John Ashman	*182*	9		
18	By Ditto pd. John Perry	*182*	1	16	
19	By Profit and Loss pd. Abr. Hill for setting out a Train-band Souldier	*180*		1	9
	By Worstead Stockins pd. John Rudduck	*182*	6	3	9
24	By Ditto paid Joseph George	*182*	4	13	4
26	By John Warren paid lent him on bond	*132*	30		
	By Profit and Loss pd. Welthean to pay for Cheese	*180*		6	
August 1	By Worstead Stockins pd. John Perry	*182*	4	18	
2	By Wm. Pleydall paid him	*184*		10	
3	By Ditto pd. him	*184*		4	
4	By Joseph Creswick pd. Nathanael Jones and Morgan Williams	*173*			1
5	By Profit and Loss pd. Abr. Hill to pay off a Trainband Souldier	*180*		2	6
7	By Worstead Stockins pd. Jonathan Abram	*182*	3	10	
9	By Profit and Loss, pd. Humphrey Nickins for watching to 5th Instant	*180*			6
			335	5	6
	By itself for Ballance Carried to a new Account	*187 **	3823	18	
			4159	3	6

Bristoll 1690@

		Cr	£	s	d
	Per Contra				
	By Acct. of Ballances for the Cost and Charges of 7187 pair of stockins as per particulars per Contra	*194 **	623	14	9¾

Date	Description					£	s	d
20	To Ditto paid John Perry for	44	2		181	4	8	
28	To Cash pd. Elizabe[th] Webb for 2 truncks				181	1	6	
30	To Ditto pd. Joseph G[eor]ge for	76	1	2½	181	4	11	10
July 1	To Cash pd. Tho. Walde[n's man] for A doz of Inkle				181		6	4
5	To Cash pd. Tho. Hill (fo[r John Perry)] £3, and said Perry himse[lf 16s] for	38	2		181	3	16	
	To Ditto pd. John Gr[een for tw]o Trunck-cords				181		2	
8	To Ditto pd. John P[erry for]	56	1	11	181	5	7	4
9	To Cash pd. Jonathan [Abram f]or	53	2		181	5	6	
12	To Ditto pd. Joseph Geo[rge f]or	78	1	2½	181	4	14	3
	To Ditto pd. Fra. R[attenb]ury for hotpressing to this day				181		19	
	To Ditto pd. Edw. Iff [for] hotpressing to this day				181	1		2
14	To Ditto pd. John Ash[man] for	160	1	1½	181	9		
	To Samuel Kekewich for charges [m]ending and making 22 doz of motheaten hose as per Acct. Current, closed in St Marie Port Aprill 17th 1690				185	1	15	9
18	To Cash pd. John Perry for	18	2		181	1	16	
19	To Cash pd. John Rudduck for	66	1	10½	181	6	3	9
24	To Ditto paid Joseph George for	80	1	2	181	4	13	4
August 1	To Cash paid John Perry for	49	2		181	4	18	
7	To Cash pd. Jonathan Abram for	35	2		181	3	10	
14	To Ditto paid Joseph Geor[ge for]	116		14	187 *	6	15	4
16	To Cash paid John Perry [for]	23	2		187 *	2	6	
29	To Ditto pd. Ditto for	69	2		187 *	6	18	
Sept. 10	To Ditto paid Joseph George for	90	1	2	187 *	5	5	
12	To Ditto pd. John Perry for	39	2		187 *	3	18	
	To Ditto pd. Tho. Hill (for James s Wollen) for	91	2		187 *	9	2	
	To Ditto pd. Ditto (for Sam. Dyer) for	87	2		187 *	8	14	
18	To Ditto pd. James Wollen for	103	2		187 *	10	6	
	To Ditto pd. Sam. Dyer for	102	2		187 *	10	4	
19	To Ditto pd. James Wollen for	91	2		187 *	9	2	
	To Ditto pd. John Perry for	39	2		187 *	3	18	
23	To Ditto pd. Thomas Walden for 2 doz of Inkle				187 *		12	6
30	To Ditto pd. Fra. Rattenbury for Hot pressing 812 pair				187 *		13	6
Oct. 4	To Ditto pd. Sam. Dyer for	79	2		187 *	7	18	
	To Ditto pd. Tho. Hill (for John Perry) for	38	2		187 *	3	16	
7	To Cash pd. Joseph George for	78		14	187 *	4	11	
11	To Ditto paid John Perry for	27	2		187 *	2	14	
16	To Ditto pd. James Wollen for	192	2		187 *	19	4	
	To Ditto pd. Tho. Hill for	39	2		187 *	3	18	
18	To Ditto paid Robert Webb for two truncks				187 *	1	10	
		7187				623	14	9¾

183	**Bristoll 1690@**							
	Lead bought for my propper Account is				Dr	£	s	d
May 6	To Thomas Tuthar for 288 barrs and 108 Sows bought of him, at the rate of £9 10s per Ton, weight 10 Ton 9 cwt 3qr 18lb				178	95	8	7¾
13	To Cash pd. Thomas Blackwell, for weighing Ditto 288 Barrs & 108 Sows				181		2	6
						95	11	1¾

	Anno 1690@							
	Fruit my ¼ part 60 Barrils Reisons sol and 60 Carge great Reisons imported in the ship Pelican of Bidiford, Capt. Philip Cade				Dr	£	s	d

	Bristoll 1690@				
Per Contra		Cr	£	s	d
By Acct. of Ballances, for Ballances		194 *	95	11	1¾

	Anno 1690@				
Fr[uit] per Contra		Cr	£	s	d
By [Raisons 60] Barrils [and] 120 pieces for 1/4 p[t o]f the					
neat proceeds		177	84	17	4

	£	s	d
To Tho. Strode for 3360 Ryals Velloon 30 Mer.dees which make 224 pieces of 8 161 Mer.dees [(as per his] Invoice dated in Malaga Dec. 9th 1689) being the first cost of said fruit [?] the piece of 8 at 52d per pieces 136	48	10	11
To Ditto for my ¼ part charges in ensuring 1000 pieces of 8 on 60 Barrils and 60 Carge [great?] Raisons, being (as per his leter of 15 March 1690) 330 Ryals Velloon 16 Me.dees which make 22 pieces of 8 at 52d) and 16 M.dees 136	4	15	5
	53	6	4
To Profit and Loss, for Ballance 191 *	31	11	
	84	17	4

Anno 1690@

Elizabeth Croft of Bristoll Spinster is	Dr	£	s	d
To Profit and Loss for ¼ year's rent for the house in which She lives due 25th March 1690	180	9		

Anno 1690@

Edward Jacob of Clapton my Tenant is	Dr	£	s	d
To Ballance of his former Account Current, brought from that acct. being for one year's rent due 2nd March 1689	156	80		

---

184   **Bristoll 1690@**

		Dr	£	s	d
	Giles Clarke of Alveston in the county of Glocester Yeoman is	Dr	£	s	d
	To his former acct. Current, for £1000 lent him on two Mortgages of his, Intrest to commence from Feb. 2nd 1690/89	171	1000		
Oct.	To Profit and Loss for 1/2 years intrest of £1000 ending August 2nd 1690	180	25		
			1025		

Anno 1690@

	Doctor Francis Hungerford of Reading	Dr	£	s	d
June 10	To sundry acct.s, for the C[ost and C]harges of a [Panni]er of X[erie]	[161] 180	2	6	4

An[no 1690]

	Francis C[reswicke an]d Company (Viz) Thomas Stubbs, and [Allen Chapman] are	Dr	£	s	d
May 14	To Isaac Heming [for money pd. Th]o. Callow on my bill, payable (as per theire bon[d Nov. 13]th 1690	177	100		
Oct.	To Profit and Loss for ¼ y[ear's intre]st of £100 ending August 14th 1690	180	1	10	
			101	10	

Anno 1690@

Robert Hawksworth of Bristoll Grocer	Dr	£	s	d
To his former Acct. Current for Ballance of that acct.	28	20	3	2

Anno 1690@

	William Pleydall of Bristoll Mason is	Dr	£	s	d
August 2	To Cash pd. him	181		10	
3	To Ditto pd. him	181		4	
				14	

Anno 1690@				
Elizabeth Croft per C[ontra]	Cr	£	s	d
By Profit and Loss for ¼ year's [rent of 2 rooms 10s and				
T]axes £1 1s	180	1	11	
May 10 By Cash recd. of her	181	7	9	
		9		

Anno 1690@				
Edward Jacob per Contra	Cr	£	s	d
July 22 By Cash recd. of him	181	[8	15]	
Oct. 4 By Ditto recd. of him	187 *	[10]		
22 By Ditto, received of him, in part	187 *	9		
		27	15	
By Acct. of Ballances, for Ballance	194 *	52	[5]	
		80		

Bristoll 1690@				
Per Contra	Cr	£	s	d
By Acct. of Ballances, for Ballance	194 *	1025		

Anno 1690@				
[Docto]r F[rancis] H[ung]erford per Contra	Cr	£	s	d
July 8 By [Cash recd. of Tho. Hung]erford]	181	2	6	4

Ann[o 1690]				
Per Contra	Cr	£	s	d
By acct. of B[allances,] for Ballance	194 *	101	10	

Anno 1690@				
Robert Hawksworth per Contra	Cr	£	s	d
July 21 By Cash recd. of him	181	7	2	
24 By Cash recd. of Geo. Saunders	181	13		
By Profit and Loss for Ballance	191 *		1	2
		20	3	2

Anno 1690@				
Per Contra	Cr	£	s	d
By Profit and Loss for work done	191 *		14	

185 [116]	**Bristoll 1690@**				
	Edward [Willi]*ams my Groom is*	Dr	£	s	d
June 28	To Cash pd. [him fo]*r one weeks keeping the two mares*	181		1	4
August 18	To Ditto [pd. him i]*n part*	187 *		2	
21	To Ditto [pd. him in] *full*	187 *		1	6
Oct. 28	To Cash [pd. him in] *full, for keeping my two mares, to this* day	187 *		7	8
				12	6

	Sib[yll Williams my] *Maidservant is*	Dr	£	s	d
June 28	To Cash p[d John Duddlestone an]d — *Ranstorpe for her* Poll	181		1	

	Anno 1690@						
	Samuel [Ke]*kewich* [Merchant in St] *Marie Port in the* [?] *of Spain, my Fac*[tor there]			Dr	£	s	d
	To his [for]*mer Acct. Current for* [Ballance of] *that Account*	R 8214	m 26	167	226	3	2¼

	Anno 1690@						
	Samuel Kekewich Merchant in St Marie Port To Ballance of his above-written Account agreeing in Spanish money with his Acct. Current sent me, closed in St Marie Port April 7th 1690 @	R 7643	m 26	Dr 185	£ 210	s 14	d 10¾

B[ristol]*l 1690@*		*Cr*	*£*	*s*	*d*
[Per Contra]		*191* *			
[By Profit and Loss, for keeping my mares]				12	6

[Anno 1690@]		*Cr*	*£*	*s*	*d*
[per Contra]		*194* *			
[By Account of Ballances, for Ballance]				1	

Anno 1690@		R	m	[Cr	*£*	s	d]
Samuel Kekewich per Contra is							
By Profit and Loss, for Postage of Leters to	[200]	[26]					
April 7th 1690 (per acct. Currrent Closed							
in St Marie Port April 7th 1690) being							
200 Ryals plate, which mak 25 pieces of 8							
at 52d per pieces of 8			*180*	5	8	4	
By Ditto for Brokeriedge and Commission,		265					
for Severall Bills of Exchange sent me, being							
(as per said Acct. Current) 265 Ryals plate							
which make 33 1/8 pieces of 8 at 52d			*180*	7	3	6½	
By Mary Thring and Co. for charges in		40					
getting a Certificate about James Wallis,							
being (as per said acct.) 40 Ryals plate which							
make 5 pieces of 8 at 52d			*7*	1	1	8	
By Worstead Stockins, for what pd. for		66					
mending and making 22 doz moth-eaten							
hose, being (as per said acct.) 66 Ryals							
plate, which make 8 2/8 pieces of 8 at 52							
per piece			*182*	1	15	9	
		571			15	9	3½
By Ballances carried to his now underwritten							
Acct. Current		7643	26	*185*	210	14	10¾
					226	3	2¼

[Anno 1690@]		R	m	*Cr*	*£*	*s*	*d*
Samuel Kekewich per Contra							
By Tho. Day for his ½ the Cost and charges							
in Cadiz of 19 Butts Xery and one Butt							
Tent as per Invoices Closed in St Maris Port							
10th May 1690, being 3507 Ryals plate 17							
meridees making 438 3/8 pieces of 8 17							
Me,dees the piece of 8 at 53d		3507	17	*161*	96	16	5
By Wines my ½ of 20 Butts for my ½ their							
cost and Charges in Cadiz (as per said							
Invoices) being 3507 Ryals plate 17Meridees							
which make 438 3/8 pieces of 8 17							
Meridees the piece of 8 at 53d		3507	17	*186*	96	16	5
By Isaac Heming for his bill on John Frank							
for 77¼ pieces of 8 at 52d per ps		622		*177*	16	16	11
By Profit and Loss for 6 Ryals plate & 26							
Meridees his commission on Ditto bill after							
the rate of 52d per pieces of 8		6	26	*180*		3	8
		7643	26		210	13	5
By Ditto for Ballance, of the Sterling acct.				*191* *		1	5¾
					210	14	10¾

186	[Bristoll 1690@]				
	Wines *my half of 20 Butts (viz) 10 Butts of Xeries imported on the Rachel [ ] Junior and 9 Butts Xerie and* [1 butt in] *partners*[hip with] *Henry Haz*[zard] To *Samuel Kekewich for their cost and Charges in Cadiz, as per Invoices of 16th May 1690, being 3507 Ryals Plate 17Mervides which make 438 3/8 pieces of 8 17Mervides the piece of 8 at 53d*	[Dr	£	s	d]
		185	96	16	5
	To *Isaac Heming for ½ the Charges in ensuring £200 on the Rachel & Olive branch*	177	7	11	6
August 15	To *Cash paid* [for] *Carriage of a Cask of Rhenish fr*[om London?]	187 *	?	?	?
Nov.	To *Ditto* [?] *on 10 Butts in the Rachel* [?]	187 *	?	?	?
	To *Tho.* [Day] *pd. towards the making th*[?] *Olive* [branch]	186 *	?	?	9
	To *Ditto* [?] *him on 10 Butts in the Olive b*[ranch]	186 *	?	?	7
	To *Ditto for a*[? bou]*ght by him, of Arthur* [?]	186 *	?	?	9
	To *Ditto, for 48 G*[allons and ?] *pints of Rhenish at* [?]	186 *	?	?	2½
	To *Ditto for ½ pound of Isinglass*		?	2	2
	To *Ditto for 3¾* [Gallons of red Port wine ?]			18	9
	To *Isaac Heming* [for the] *Cost* [and charges of 2 pipes] *of Canary*	177	26	14	6
	To *Ditto for the* [Cost and charges of a Cask of Rhenish]	177	14	15	2
	To *Tho. Day, f*[or ½ the charges on Carriage of 2 pipes of Canary]	186 *	2	6	9
			342	2	½
	To *Profit and* [Loss ??? Bu]*tts of Xerie, and* [?]*nd Lewis Adams*	191 *	97	6	5¼
			439	8	5¾

	[Anno 1690@]				
	Tho. [Day] *of the citie of Bristoll Wine Cooper*	Dr	£	s	d
	[To *Isaac Hemin*]*g for ½ the charges in ensuring £200 on the Rachel & Olive branch*	177	7	11	6
	To *Ditto for money pd. Tho. Lock per his order*	177	30		
	To *Wines my ½ of 20 Butts for ½ the Charges on 10 Butts in the Rachell*	186 *	57	17	6
	To *Ditto for 36 5/8 Gallons of Rhenish, at 4s 6d per Gallon*	186 *	8	4	9¾
	To *Isaac Heming, for ½ the Cost and Charges, in London, of 2 pipes of Canary*	177	26	14	6
	To *Wines my ½ of 20 Butts, for ½ of £15 2s 7d recd. out of Custom house for bad wines in the Olive-branch*	186 *	7	11	3½
			137	19	7¼

The Ledger of Thomas Speed 1681–1690 511

Bristoll 1690@

	Wines my half of 20 Butts per Contra	[Cr	£	s	d]
[August?]	By Cash received out of custom-house for Corrupt [wines]	[187 *	7	11	3½]
[Sept.] 23	By Ditto red of Samuel Price for allowance on a leaky Butt of [Sack]	[187 *	1	10]	
26	By Philip Frowd for three doz of Xerie sent him at 20s [per doz]	[85	3]		
30	By the Lady Ann Pawlett for six doz of Xerie at 20s per doz	[155	6]		
[Oct.] 8	By Sir Geo. Strode for 2 doz Xerie at 20s per Doz	[173	2]		
	By John Winpenny for ½ the amountant of 9 Butts Xerie at £33 per [Butt] and 1 hogshead Tent at £18 sold him and Lewis Adams jointly	[101	157	10]	
	By Lewis Adams for his half the amountant of Ditto 9 Butts & 1 hogsheadd	[56	157	10]	
	By Tho. Day for ½ the Charges on [10 Butts in the Rachell]	[186	57	17	6]
	By Ditto for 36 5/8 Gallons of Rhe[nish etc.]	[186	[8	4	9¾]
	By Ditto for my 1/2 of what recd. [out of Custom house for bad wines etc.]	[186	7	11	3½]
			[408	14	10¾]
	By Acct. of Ballances, for a p[?]Gallon rundlett of Xerie ren[?]		[30	13	7]
			[439	8	5¾]

[Anno 1690@]

	Tho. [Day per Contra]	Cr	£	s	d
August 2	By Cash received [out of custom-house for Corrupt wines]	[187 *	15	2	7]
Sept. 23	By Ditto recd. Samuel Price for ½ allowance of £3 on a leaky Butt of Sack]	[187 *	1	10]	
	By Wines my ½ of 20 Butts [½ cost and charges on 10 But]ts				
	By Ditto for ½ Charges of [?]				
	By Ditto for money paid [?]				
	By Ditto for 48 Gallons [of Rhenish]				
	By Ditto for half a pound of Isinglass				
	By Ditto for 3¾ Gallons of red Port, 4[?]				
	By Ditto for ½ the Charges, on Carriage of 2 [Pipes of Canary]				
	By Profit and Loss, for six quarts of white [wine ?]				
	By Ditto, for a groce of Corks				
	By Acct. of Ballances, for Ballance				

Endnotes

* These counter entries will not be found. The majority of the missing matches were in the lost or badly damaged folios from 186. But there are some 126 which were simply not made where they should have been. Almost invariably the missing entry should have been posted to Profit & Loss, or Cash, or Speed's bank account with Isaac Heming; while the entry that is made ensures that dealings with others are accurately recorded. (Not surprisingly, Speed's own record of dealings with Heming is often amiss, but is simply adjusted from the account supplied by Heming – see the last entry of f. 90.1D)

[1] The accountant, Jahzeel, was going to open the new ledger with an account devoted to all the Balances carried forward from the closed Ledger D, but decided simply to open each individual account with its closing balance from D, as the start of the Ledger proper on f. 1 shows.

[2] This is very clearly written as Sr Thomas, but the counter-entry gives no title (both entries by Jahzeel). The Thomas Walden who only took freedom in 1681 was never knighted, and I can find no reference to any such knight before him – he would have been at least on the City Council. So I am inclined to put this down to Jahzeel's sense of humour: the two young men were cousins (see Appendix A Marriages 1 and 3).

[3] The counter-entry in f. 42 has the John Frigate, not the Zant, - both entries are by Jahzeel but they can hardly have been made at the same time or from a single Journal entry.

[4] The counter-entry is actually in f. 96.1C

[5] This is the first entry for a very mysterious transaction, see Introduction 3.2.4.

[6] The Cash counter-entries give no clue as to these substantial payments. They are not misappropriations by Jahzeel, for they are not included in the account which Speed opened for these. All one can say is that Speed seems not to have regarded them as either extinguishing an obligation on his side or creating one on any other. Nevertheless it is just possible that the £500 is the money advanced on the Bainham mortgage (f. 48.6) and for some reason never so designated until it was paid off.

[7] Very clearly written so. The accountant (Jahzeel) does at times use 'ffor', ie 'For' in this context but there is no other instance of 'effor' or apparent meaning in it, unless it should be a tiny phonetic pleasantry.

[8] Presumably Martha Speed, who was keeping house at this time and to whom the Household Expenses in the previous entry would have been paid.

[9] This would be the replacement of one of the lives, typically three, constituting the duration of a lease. It may have been occasioned by the death of Speed's wife Ann the previous year, perhaps replacing her with Mary Lamboll to whom he would be married two months later. The property involved cannot be identified, but Shuttleworth was Secretary to the Earl of Bristol and active in the Clevedon/ Clapton area where Speed was building up his 'estate'.

[10] This is Robert Yate the elder, the father of Speed's cousin – see Appendix A Marriages 1

[11] Very likely Speed's next-door neighbour Sara Hasell (Leech *Topography* 158)

[12] This famous Bristol figure was quite active in Bristol in the early 1680s, but the write-off may have followed his return to London.

[13] Thomas Lower was a prominent early Quaker, married to Margaret Fell's daughter Mary, amanuensis for much of George Fox's Journal and one of his literary executors.

[14] There is regrettably nothing to identify whether this was **the** Isaac Newton; but the fact that it was written off in 1690, when Newton's star was ascendant, suggests that it was not. (Or was it that Newton as, briefly, MP for Cambridge University, was exempt from proceedings for debt?)

[15] Stepsister of Jahzeel, that is - see Appendix A Marriage 1

[16] Erasmus Dole, pewterer, was an active Quaker of long standing.

[17] The Tyntes were major land-owners in North Somerset, where their name survives in Tyntesfield House (now National Trust), the Gothic extravaganza built for the Victorian guano magnate, William Gibbs.

[18] 'Then' is followed by what looks like 'v^{d}', squeezed into the end of the line.

[19] This is the only instance of an imputed, or opportunity, cost. No expenditure has been incurred: Speed is simply reckoning what the amount tied up in this property could have earned as a loan at interest. The property had earned only some £20 net over seven (not six) years. Bringing the lost interest into the account means that the property is worth less at the end of this account than at the beginning, has made a notional loss; and these calculations clearly show the reasoning behind his selling the property early in next year (f. 160.2).

[20] Joseph Jackson was a relatively undistinguished member of a leading merchant family. Miles Jackson had been one of the successful Council-sponsored candidates in the disputed election of 1654 in which Speed's brother-in-law John Haggatt and nephew George Bishop had been defeated.

[21] This is either Speed's elder brother, long since dead, or his son the mariner, also dead (c. 1678 PROB 4/11359) – whose son, the sailor lad, Speed was still assisting. The claim is not mentioned in Speed's will, and may have in the interim been converted into ownership of the tenement in Colyton which Speed ultimately bequeathed back to the surviving Speeds there.

[22] See Introduction 3.1.4

[23] This property (Nos 9 & 10 Small St: Leech *Topography* 156) had been left to the three daughters of Gabriel Sherman (see Appendix A Marriage 3). Speed had bought out the other shares.

[24] Almost certainly a mistake for Philip as in counter-entry and entry for April 30 below

[25] See Appendix A Marriage 2

[26] This is no. 18 Small Street (Leech *Topography* 158) which Speed had acquired in the late 1660s and which remained his home till his death. It was a substantial property, paying Hearth Tax on eight chimneys, backing on to the Gild Hall and leasing the cellars under it.

[27] Richard Godwin seems to have been working for Speed on the country estate at Clapton.

[28] Another member of the Devon branch whom Speed had assisted

²⁹ The Strodes were major gentry in Shepton Mallett, Somerset. Both Sir George and Thomas Strode were Sergeants-at-law

³⁰ Step-son-in-law, see Appendix A Marriage 1

³¹ Possibly William Ford sergemaker, a leading Quaker who supported William Rogers against George Fox (*MMM I* 200)

³² Probably the Quaker (*MMM I* 215)

³³ See Appendix A Marriage 2. James must be brother or other relation of Bridget Wallis, one of those from whom Speed had purchased the original holding at Clapton. A merchant, James seems to have gone to Spain, where Kekewich was asked to supply a certificate of his being alive for the benefit of his sister(s) f. 7.1

³⁴ The Winters were important landowners in north Somerset and Henry Winter was one of those from whom Speed purchased land for his Clapton estate. Winter had retained the right to Lords Rent at 32s a year and Speed disputed this at law and lost.

³⁵ These loans against stockings continue through to October 1689 (ff. 155.1, 163.1, 165.1) when Speed actually acquired the total of 1834 pairs. It is difficult to make sense of these transactions: if the actual stockings were deposited with Speed as stated, and only at the end 'taken to himself' – why not buy them outright in the first place? It would make more sense if Massinger, unable to pursue his trade by reason of his entanglement at law with George Freman as shown in the preceding entries, had merely supplied IOUs for stockings which he ultimately redeemed, but this does not go with Speed's wording.

³⁶ I cannot place this cousin.

³⁷ Grandfather of George. D Freeman *George Washington: a biography* (London 1948) 30-31.

³⁸ That is, the City Treasury. See Introduction 3.1.3

³⁹ Another indication that in the early 80s, Speed was directly engaged in farming part of his Clapton estate.

⁴⁰ It looks as though Speed had been making progress payments as the work went on, and waited for completion before crediting the entire amount to his Clapton property. £280 odd – see the credit opposite – would have built a decent house but no way a mansion.

⁴¹ See Appendix A Marriage 3 The mortgage was possibly her share in the ship Resolution, see next account.

⁴² Speed is working from accounts from his Spanish factors in Spanish currency – Appendix B Payment, currencies & bills.

⁴³ See Appendix B Payment, currencies & bills.

⁴⁴ Reproduced in the frontispiece. Note that the main amount has been carried forward from the previous ledger, and is now coolly written off to Profit & Loss. The presentation is designed impudently to advertise rather than conceal the transaction. For Speed's reaction, see f. 69.2 first line.

⁴⁵ The counter-entry is actually in f. 40.1C where it is dated 17ᵗʰ March, another example of the point that the Credit and Debit entries were often not posted at the same time.

[46] It is not clear why Massinger, a principal hosier, buys these stockings. They might be rejects on quality grounds which he takes back, but the price is well below what he commonly sells for.

[47] I cannot find this place in any atlas but Richardson is a Londoner and in f. 117.7 a man otherwise unknown is paid for taking Wilmer's mare to Branford – Wilmer being also a Londoner, so a London or Middlesex location seems indicated (there is a Bramford Rd in east Wandsworth.) f. 35.3

[48] Originally *I valued my bill* – pronouns overwritten

[49] No other reference to this person can be found in the ledger.

[50] In this single account, over just three months, Speed's nominal cash balance goes down from over £3000 to a few hundreds, where it remains for the succeeding three Cash folios. See Introduction 5.6.2.

[51] What infuriating entries! See note 6

[52] The counter-entry says Jahzeel Speed.

[53] The counter-entry is undoubtedly to the account of John Sandford, f.19.7

[54] There is no counter-entry in Wasbrow's account (f. 28.3) but this may have figured among the various notes 'evened betwixt us' in the last entry there, and all written off to Profit & Loss.

[55] Given that this is in Jahzeel's hand, the semi-pun may have been intended

[56] 'Gentleman' at this time is usually a lawyer who had studied, or at least eaten his dinners, at one of the Inns of Court.

[57] The matching P&L entry notes that the mortgage dates from April 1682, consistently with the interest calculations. This may be linked to the entry on the Profit & Loss account f.8.1, April 10-12, where over £500 is simply marked as Cash paid sundrys (the counter-entry for Cash is no more forthcoming); but it is not easy to think why this mortgage should not have entered as such from the first.

[58] In fact the counter-entry is at f. 60.4

[59] This does not add up because, as the counter-entry shows, Speed has also charged for the 20 boxes

[60] In April 1685 some copper coolers were returned to Bristol and sold back to Badger for £29 14s 2d. At the same time, Speed bought some copper taches of him for £32 3s 6d, to go at Adventure in the Joseph to Nevis. Speed in effect owed Badger £2 9s 4d.

In June, Speed showed a Cash receipt for £29 8s 11d from Badger (ie 5s 3d less than he owed) and a Cash payment of £32 3s 6d to him, a net payment of £2 14s 7d Cash. But the Cash paid was debited, incorrectly, direct to the Joseph adventure, rather than to Badger's account. This meant that Speed had Credited both Cash and Badger with the same single Debit, all for £32 3s 6d. In book-keeping practice he should have Debited Badger with the Cash paid him, and rectified the original misattribution in the Cash account by a Debit to the Joseph adventure and a matching Credit to Badger's account (or altered the original Cash Credit to show By Badger, rather than By Adventure). He should also have credited Badger's account with the Cash received and with a rebate of 5s 3d allowed him (chargeable to P&L).

Instead he saved himself time and trouble by posting neither the Cash received nor the Cash paid to Badger's account, but simply Crediting this account with the nominal difference of £2 9s 4d and charging that to P&L. This did his business, in that it correctly showed the value of stock sold from the Owners Endeavour and purchased for the Joseph; and cleared the Badger account. It also left, correctly, the net payout of £2 14s 7d from Cash. But the posting of £2 9s 4d as a credit to P&L was a nonsense, or would have been if the P&L account had held any real significance for Speed.

[61] The accountant of the third hand is in error here – the Credit side is clear and agrees with the entry in f. 33.1

[62] In fact this is credited to Scrope's account f. 75.1

[63] More of the mysterious transaction See Introduction 3.2.4

[64] This and the next three accounts are part of the mysterious affair of the soap – Introduction 3.2.4

[65] The counter-entry is actually one of several merged as Sundry accounts f. 83.1D for 3 June

[66] Benjamin Cole was a Reading Quaker and one of the leaders of the anti-Fox faction there.

[67] Actually f. 73.1D June 84

[68] See Appendix B Payment, currencies & bills.

[69] This is very plainly written but should be 157. (236 is probably the second cross reference - see Transcription notes– not here reproduced.)

[70] See note on Appendix B Payment, currencies & bills.

[71] See n. 34.

[72] Unmistakably written so but obviously wrong: the Debit total shows 10s, agreeing with the entry in Rishton's account f. 58.8

[73] This is probably Martha – see f. 60.9. There is no relevant entry for Mary.

[74] Whiston's *Remembrancer* was the proper title but Avizoe was the generic term for this sort periodical with current prices, exchange rates and commercial news

[75] See Introduction 6.3.2.

[76] Again the third accountant makes an apparently obvious error

[77] See Appendix A Marriage 1

[78] See Appendix A Marriage 2

[79] This probably a mistake for the Owners Adventure, see the counter-entry f. 80.6D

[80] The counter entries show payments to Edward. See f. 107 Credit entry between 7 and 14 January: 'Wm. alias Edward Iffe'.

[81] See Appendix A Marriage 1

[82] A coral, probably for Alice or Speed Heming to cut her teeth on (Appendix A Marriage 1)

[83] Actually f. 113.4D

[84] Port? The wines appear to be French. See OED, Port n⁷: 1691 N. LUTTRELL Diary in Brief Hist. Relation State Affairs (1857) II. 314 *English ships that went to Bourdeaux and took in wine, and after sailed to port O Porto, and then came home, pretending it to be port.*

[85] Every subsequent entry states that the person named "is debtor for". In order to match debits and credits as Speed did, but without wasting space, I have replace this phrase with a colon.

[86] Speed gives each person two lines: one for [name] per Contra, and one for By Cash etc. I have elided these two for the reasons given in the previous note.

[87] This entry is undated but made in the third hand so presumably in 1690. The accounting seems correct: Jordan is one of the buyers in the Raisins account f. 136.2C which agrees with the amounts charged to those named there. But perhaps he was mistakenly charged with a purchase made by some other person no longer to be identifed.

[88] There is some confusion here between old and new style year dating, but comparison with the Portbury account (f. 20.3) indicates that the tenancy began in September 1683 and that the last entry here is for the years to March 1688/9

[89] That is Clevedon in Somerset, not Clifton in Gloucestershire.

[90] This or a similar phrase, repeated every time the friend is mentioned, suggests that Speed was irked by the anonymity.

[91] This is the man who had been foremost in inciting informers and leading gangs of vigilantes in the enforcement of the Conventicle Act: see Introduction 3.1.3.

[92] This entry duplicates the one below, where the consignment is correctly assigned to the Rebecca

[93] There is no corresponding entry for Thiery in the Stockings account

[94] The overcorrected entry looks like 110 but this cannot be and 00 gives the correct total.

[95] John Barnard's son became Sir John Barnard, financial adviser to Robert Walpole

[96] In fact the counter-entry for the landing part of this, 1s 6d, and the charge for freight below £2 3s 6d are credited to cash on f. 119.1 July 29 and the 2s for wharfage does not seem to have been credited anywhere

[97] See Introduction 4.2.2.

[98] Blagdon, Somerset

[99] The three items above have also been posted to Cash f. 119.1, but are now included in the total posted to Profit & Loss.

[100] In fact the counter-entry is at f. 123.5, the continuation of f. 116.3 '*for want of roome*'

[101] It had not in fact been paid - see Introduction 4.2.2

[102] His now wife is actually Mary, but the previous one was Ann: a senior moment.

[103] Whether *s* or *d* I cannot relate the charge to the particulars

[104] This is a duplicate of the entry next above. Only one appears in the Clark account

[105] I cannot make out these squiggles: nails were commonly sold by the hundred retail or the hundredweight wholesale for export.

[106] i.e. decoration, not courage

[107] Thomas Day soapmaker had previously bought wine, and paid for it. But as Mayor he seems not to have volunteered payment, nor Speed to have pressed for it.

[108] Perhaps Calne in Wiltshire – I can find no likely candidate in Gloucestershire.

[109] This aborted entry appears in full as the first in the next Stocking account

[110] It is not clear why the balance of this account is written off rather than carried forward to the next as is usual with Stockins Accounts before and after.

[111] Duck Lane lies between the Pithay and Needless Gate, less than a quarter of a mile from Speed's home and in the parish of St John's.

[112] Appendix A Marriage 4

[113] The counter-entry shows that this should be John Bartlett.

[114] This entry is one of the first in the hand of the new accountant who took over and eventually closed the Ledger, the next in Speed's and the next in the accountant's again. This suggests a transitional handing over period, and the counter-entry in the Benjamin Cole account (f. 147.2) would place it around March 1689/90. But the counter-entries also afford a striking example of the irregularity of ledger posting (also f. 169.4D and f. 180.1)

[115] Jahzeel was already dead yet this account is carried forward, not closed off: see Introduction 3.2.2

[116] ff. 185 and 186 have been reconstructed from the scraps which were pasted rather haphazardly into the journal when it was restored. When Debits and Credits are matched to the same nominal accounts, much can be supplied by reference to counter entries, or by the other half in entries for 'my half' and the like.

APPENDIX A   MARRIAGES

MARRIAGE 1

William Cann = Margaret Yeamans

Robert Yeamans

William Yeamans

John Yeamans

Robert Yeamans = (1) Ann Yeamans   (2) = **THOMAS SPEED**

Elizabeth Yeamans = John Haggatt

SIR ROBERT YEAMANS

Joseph Yeamans

NATHANIEL HAGGATT

JOHN YEAMANS?

JOHN YEAMANS?

Mary
=
ROBERT YATE

Ann
=
THOMAS CURTIS

Mary
= (1)
Daniel Wastfield
= (2) JOHN HURTNELL II

ELIZABETH
=
Nathaniel Milner

Margaret
=
EDWARD MARTINDALE

Betshua
=
John Speed
(Thomas' brother)

METREDONE

MEHITABEL
=
ISAAC HEMING

JAHZEEL

DEBORAH
=
ANDREW BINFIELD

BETHSHUA

Ann
=
JOHN KENT

Mehitabel
=
John Thorpe

ALICE

SPEED
=
Joseph Smith

SMALL CAPS: PERSONS MENTIONED IN THE LEDGER   Italics: Quakers

These tables include only those mentioned in the Ledger and those through whom they are related to Speed. Siblings are orderd by convenience not seniority.

MARRIAGE 2

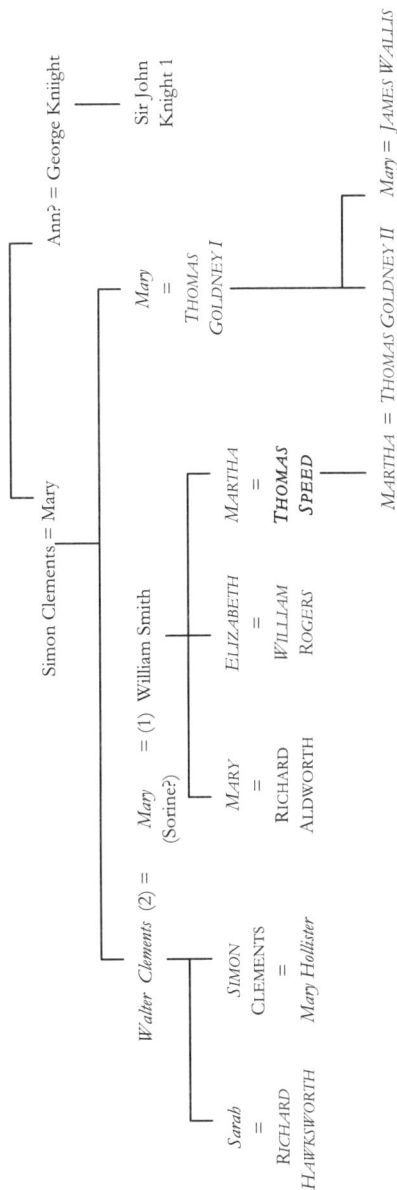

Simon Clements = Mary   Ann? = George Knight

Sir John
Knight 1

Walter Clements (2) =   *Mary*   = (1) William Smith   *Mary*
    (Sorine?)   =
    THOMAS
    GOLDNEY I

Sarah   SIMON   *MARY*   *ELIZABETH*   *MARTHA*
=   CLEMENTS   =   =   =
RICHARD   =   RICHARD   *WILLIAM*   *THOMAS*
HAWKSWORTH   Mary Hollister   ALDWORTH   ROGERS   *SPEED*

MARTHA = *THOMAS GOLDNEY II*   *Mary* = *JAMES WALLIS*

MARRIAGE 3

Gabriel Sherman

MARTHA   ANNE   Mary   =   RICHARD   THOMAS   CHARLES   JOHN
=   =   STUBBS   STUBBS   STUBBS   STUBBS
Antony   *THOMAS*
Gay   *SPEED*

Martha = THOMAS WALDEN

MARRIAGE 4

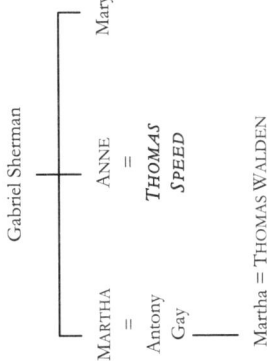

GEORGE *LAMBOLL* = *SARAH*

MARY   JONATHAN   *Sarah*
=   LAMBOLL   =
THOMAS   *JOHN*
SPEED   *WILMER*

APPENDIX B   PAYMENT, CURRENCY & BILLS

A grasp of currencies and coinages, nominal and metal values, exchange rates and methods of settlement was one of the most important parts of a merchant's training. The most useful guide I have found is McCusker *Money & Exchange in Europe & America 1600 – 1776* (Macmillan 1978).

In England, accounts were kept in Pounds, Shillings and Pence: £ or *Li, s* and *d*. The Pound was 240 *d*, or 20*s* at 12*d* per shilling. Legal tender for payments comprised Brass or Copper Farthings (¼*d*) and Halfpence; and silver Pennies, Twopences (or half groats), Threepences, Fourpences (Groats), Sixpences, Half Crowns (2*s* 6*d*) and Crowns (5*s*). Some gold coins denominated in guineas (Half, One, Two and Five) together with much older gold items (Crown, Double Crown, and Unite) still circulated but as the Ledger shows were treated as so much precious metal rather than as tender for nominal values.

The acute shortage of coins aggravated itself: those who could accumulated considerable hoards and Speed himself kept £'000s in cash on his premises. It was alleviated for the poorer sort by the private issue of farthing tokens, and for the business and landed community by the use of credit. The Bristol Fairs – St James (July 25th) or St Pauls (January 25th) were often specified as the settlement date. See for example f. 45.6, 60.4 and 126.4; though the last shows also the latitude in practice – the final settlement took place piecemeal over some seven months after the date specified. Mutiple settlements at a fair could be made by rapid circulation of rellatively small amount of cash. Cash calls were further reduced where two or more mutually indebted persons could set off debts and need only settle the outstanding differences between them.

A bill was a written acknowledgment of debt, usually with a date set for payment. A bill of exchange involved three parties: the *drawer* who ordered the *drawee* to pay a specified sum to the *payee* by a set date. It was common for landowners and business men in the country to keep credit accounts with London bankers (often merchants, goldsmiths or lawyers), drawing and accepting bills on London; and people with such accounts would often accommodate their associates by paying them cash in return for a bill on London (in effect cashing their cheques) or taking their cash in exchange for a London credit. Assuming that the drawer and drawee were men of credit, these could readily be reassigned by the payee to satisfy his own creditors, and become in themselves a currency of settlement. As with cheques and bank transfers today, the amounts settled by the drawing and exchange of bills to transfer credit many times exceeded those made in cash.

Foreign exchange rates fluctuated, as they do today, but within the narrow compass set by the intrinsic metal content of coinage plus or minus the costs of transporting specie: the french écu could not for long cost more in sterling than it would cost to send its silver equivalent to Paris.

The main French accounting units were the Livre Tournois, (20 Sous or 240 deniers to the Livre)and the Écu (3 Livres or 60 sous) (Speed occasionally mixes the two up, citing the exchange rate for the Livre when he mean the Écu.) It was with the écu that Speed made his first trial of remittance, that is paying one Jaques Gonsailes in London for a bill drawn on his, Gonsailes', correspondent or banker in Bordeaux in favour of the Kirbys (f. 64.2D, f. 90.1C). Speed calculated that he had saved against the current exchange rate (about 55*d* per écu) and continued remitting especially to France.

In Spain, there was a considerable difference between the effective metallic value of the coinage and its nominal or Vellon denomination – scarcely half as much. (See f. 131.2 where the fall in the Ryal Vellon cost Speed about 30% the sterling value of his nominal payment.) There were 8 Reales (Ryals for Speed) to the Peso or Piece of Eight, and 34 Maravedis (Mervides) to the Real; and the exchange rate in the 80s was fairly stable at 50-52*d* per Peso (metal content or plate value). As the ledger shows, Speed often took his returns from Spanish sales in Plate or silver bullion. Technically this was an illegal export but ships including those of the Royal Navy were generally happy to carry it for a fee.

The English transatlantic colonies had their own currencies but as the planters were normally in debt to English suppliers or bankers (often the same people), they could expect to pay a premium for bills of exchange on London. These would in any case only be met by the proceeds of sugar exports, at fluctuating prices. They were also short of specie. Sugar itself, used as a currency in the Caribbean, was often used (at a fixed £ sterling value) as the basis of accounting and of periodic settlement between planter and merchant as in f. 33.1D and in further transactions. (McCusker, also K. G. Davies 'Origins of the Commission System in the West India Trade' *Transactions of the Royal Historical Society* 5th series 2 (1952) 89-107, 95. For a contemporary example, see *The Letters of William Freeman* ed. David Hancock (London Record Society 2002) Letter 34 (September 19 1678)

APPENDIX C   CAPACITY MEASURES

	rundlet	barrel	Tierce*	hogshead	puncheon	butt/pipe	tun
US galls	18	31.5	42	63	84	126	252
rundlets	1	1.75	2.33	3.5	4.667	7	14
barrels		1	1.33	2	2.667	4	8
tierces			1	1.5	2	3	6
hogsheads				1	1.33	2	4
puncheons					1	1.5	3
butts						1	2
tuns							1

* also the Aum, which was only used for Rhenish wines

These are the nominal values. However 'nowhere in the Atlantic world was a pipe a pipe, or a ton a ton.' (David Hancock '"A revolution in the trade": wine distribution and the development of the infrastructure of the Atlantic market economy, 1703–1807' in J J Mccusker & K Morgan (eds) *The Early Modern Atlantic Economy* Cambridge CUP 2000, 105–153, n32, p 119)

SELECT READING & ABBREVIATIONS

Seventeenth-century businessmen: R. Grassby, *Kinship and Capitalism: Marriage, Family & Business in the English-speaking World, 1580-1740* Cambridge 2001; and *The Business Community of seventeenth-century England* Cambridge 1995, and sundry articles.

Early modern merchants: J. M Price 'What did merchants do? Reflections on British overseas trade, 1660-1790' *Journal of Economic History* 49 (1989) 267-284. For an unrivalled account of an individual merchant business, H. Roseveare (ed.) *Markets & Merchants of the Late Seventeenth Century: the Marescoe-David Letters 1668-1680* Oxford 1991. For Bristol merchants: P. McGrath (ed) *Records relating to the Society of Merchant Venturers of the city of Bristol in the Seventeenth Century* BRS XVII, 1952; and *Merchants & Merchandise in Seventeenth-Century Bristol* BRS XIX, 1955.

Seventeenth-century Bristol: J.Latimer *Annals of Bristol in the Seventeenth Century* Bristol 1900; R. Leech (ed.) *The Topography of Medieval and Early Modern Bristol I* BRS XLVIII, 1997, especially with E. Ralph & M. E. Williams (eds) *The Inhabitants of Bristol in1696* BRS XXV 1968 and Millerd's Map of 1673

Money, credit and payment systems: E. Kerridge *Trade and Banking in early modern England* Manchester 1988; C. Muldrew *The Economy of Obligation: The Culture of Credit and Social Relations in early modern England* Basingstoke 1998 and other works; J. McCusker *Money and Exchange in Europe and America, 1600-1775: a Handbook* London 1978.

Early modern accounting: B. S. Yamey 'Scientific Bookkeeping and the Rise of Capitalism' *Economic History Rvies* 2nd series 1, 2 & 3 (1949) 99-113; 'Some seventeenth and eighteenth century double-entry ledgers' *Accounting Review* XXXIV (1956) 534-546; and other articles.

Thomas Speed: J. Harlow 'The Life & Times of Thomas Speed' Ph D thesis, University of the West of England, 2008

Where these are referred to in this edition, the reference will be abbreviated to surname and short title only. Other abbreviations used are

BRO	Bristol Record Office
BRS	Bristol Record Society
ODNB	*Oxford Dictionary of National Biography* [2nd edn. 2004]
OED	*Oxford English Dictionary*
TBGAS	*Transactions of the Bristol & Gloucestershire Archaeological Society*
TNA	The National Archive
UBLSC	University of Bristol Library Special Collections

GLOSSARY

Abate	waive full value due on settlement, usually odd shillings or pence, as opposed to Discounts built into the original terms of sale especially for cloth
Aledraper	keeper of an alehouse, publican
Auln, aume, aum	a German measure, about 40 gallons: ≈ tierce – Appendix C Capacity Measures
Avisoe, avizo	advice, useful information, notice; generic name for a periodical with news of prices, exchange rates, sailings etc.
Barnstable Oven	clay bread oven made in north Devon. J S Moore *Goods & Chattels of our Forefathers* (Phillimore 1976) 291
Bottomry	money lent to the owner or master of a ship, on security of the vessel itself, repayable with interest at the conclusion of an intended voyage
Bays	baize
Colefish	coalfish (US pollock)
Cosasha grater	I can nowhere find Cosasha elsewhere but it is in company with items for a sugar mill, and given that the English sugar plantations derived their technology from Brazil, may reflect something like *que o açúcar* – that sugar.
Dowlas	a coarse linen
Drums & Colours	a standard phrase signifying a military parade, review or demonstration – eg stage directions to *King Lear* IV.iv; *Richard III* V.ii; *Titus Andronicus* I.1: here the rate for the support of the city or county militia
Eager	sour (Fr aigre)
Falls	veils or other hanging items of dress
Fossett	*OED* and Moore (*op. cit.*) have forcet, a small chest, but the quantities here make this unlikely
Frieze	coarse woollen cloth

Frock	a man's long coat, tunic, or mantle *OED*
Gambado	riding boot, gaiter or legging
Girse	girths
Inkle	tape, used for tying up bundles of stockings, probably by the dozen pairs
Reek (e) of Hay	rick
Replevin, replevan, repleven	an action at law for the recovery of property unlawfully detained
Stock-lock	a lock enclosed in a wooden case, usually fitted on an outer door
Tach	the smallest of the sugar-boiling coppers (R. Ligon *True Hist. Barbados* , 1657, 84)
Tent	dark red wine (cp *Tinto*)
Tiking	ticking, upholstery material
Trainband	the militia, meant to be manned by citizens, but they could send paid substitutes
Vitry	canvas from Vitré, France
Wrist	wrest, an instrunent for twisting, tightening, turning
Xerie, xeries	sherry, wine from Jerez

INDEX

All references are to the Ledger folio and account in which the entry occurs, so that 10.3 refers to the 3rd account on folio 10. This locates the entry more quickly than a page reference, since most accounts are less than a page long, though this advantage is lost in long accounts like Cash and Profit & Loss which run to more than a printed page. It also corresponds more closely than page referencing would to the cross-referencing in the Ledger text – see below. And it has made it possible to prepare the Index independently of the printing format, so applying equally to the digital version.

If the reference is to an account which deals mainly or extensively with the item concerned it is printed in **bold**, so, **10.3,** and applies to both the Debit and the Credit sides of that account. For incidental references within an account, the account is referenced in the same way but not in bold and is followed by D[ebit] or C[redit] indicating the side of the account concerned, with a bracketed number of entries to be found if more than one. So 10.3C(2) means that there are two entries to be found on the Credit side of account no 3 on folio 10.

This is a double-entry ledger, so every entry should have a counter entry, which the researcher may wish to consult – the two entries are often slightly different. Normally no extra index reference is needed for this, because it should be supplied in the Ledger itself. For example, if a merchant X is debited with the cost of items purchased from a consignment of wines, the Dr narrative will read To Wines, etc, and the column to the left of the £ s d will give the folio number of the particular Wines account in question, making it fairly easy to find the counter Credit entry, By Merchant X etc, with a reference back to the folio of the Merchants account. Counter-entries therefore are not given in the Index (and the method used in compiling it has meant that the reference given is usually to the Debit entry, unless there is clearly more information in the Credit.) But some counter entries are missing and the alleged cross–references in the text are marked *; and others are cross-referenced wrongly, in which case there is a note directing the reader to the correct counter entry.

All persons are indexed under the heading Persons and all vessels under Vessels. Merchandise is indexed by item or kind, except items for Household or Personal use, which are grouped under these headings. Speed's properties are grouped separately from Places, under Properties of TS.

All headwords are in today's spelling.

linen 5.4 6.1 7.6 17.5 35.1 35.4 36.2 47.5
50.3 56.2 56.5 56.6 57.2 69.4 99.5
171.2 104.1D 104.2D 160.5D
serges 32.4D 104.2D
vitry 48.1D(2) 57.2D
Clothing buckles, silver 104.1D
falls 104.1D 104.2D(2)
fan 22.4C
hats 104.1D 145.2D
hose 145.2D
millinery 104.2D
shoes 55.2D(2) 104.1D 104.2D(2) 124.5D
145.2D
suits 124.5D
Coach fares 89.1D 113.4.C 13.2C
Coal see Household fuel
Cod Fish 72.1 122.1D (coalfish) 72.1C(3)
Containers for exports are found in accounts
for the commodities concerned,
where they are typically the unit of
despatch and sales accounting: eg
boxes for Candles, Provisions and
Spirits; and trunks for Stockings.
For purchases and sales of other
containers: 8.1D 8.1C 9.1D 24.3D
31.5D 89.1D 92.4D 138.7D 153.1D
For inland Carriage of containers, see
Carriage.
Coopers equipment 75.2 28.3D(2) 65.5C
89.1D 137.1D
Copper 36.7 50.4D 75.1C
Cork 39.5D 45.5D 65.5D
Corks 24.3D 137.1D 164.1D(3)
Corn 75.1C
Customs within Import, Agency import
accounts
Deposits 75.1D 107.1D
Discount 44.3D 44.5D 44.6D 45.1D 48.7D
57.2D
Exports, Beer to Jamaica 20.2
Butter to Barbados 33.2
Cider to Nevis 97.7
Cloth to Cadiz 64.1 86.3
to New England 31.4
Ginger to Hamburg 75.1C
Herrings to Nevis 51.2
Hides to Cadiz 103.8
to La Rochelle 85.2
General Merchandizes to Barbados
46.4 55.2 60.9
to Nevis 17.1 21.7 31.6 37.4 49.5 50.5
57.5 58.6 61.6 65.4 80.6 98.3 126.5
143.3

to New England 126.5
to Virginia 104.1 104.2 124.5 145.2
160.5
Shot to Lisbon 27.4
Stockings to Alicant 142.4 155.2
to Cadiz 25.6 34.4 37.2 44.7 55.4 60.7
60.8 62.4 63.5 64.8 78.2 79.6 80.1
85.1 86.4 86.5 93.1 97.1 100.1 100.4
101.1 109.2 110.2 110.3 110.4 110.5
110.6 114.1 116.4 122.3 124.2 124.3
124.4 131.3 136.5 142.3 144.1 144.4
161.3 166.6 166.7 169.1 169.4
to La Rochelle 55.3D
to Malaga 122.2 123.2 158.1 158.3
unspecified 4.2 13.2 14.4 15.5 17.1 17.2
18.5 18.7 19.2 25.3 28.2 29.1 29.2
33.2 35.2
Exports to Alicant 142.4 155.2 -
Barbados 19.2 33.2 46.4 55.2 60.9
Cadiz 25.6 34.4 37.2 44.7 55.4 60.7 60.8
62.4 63.5 64.1 64.8 78.2 79.6 80.1
85.1 86.3 86.4 86.5 93.1 97.1 100.1
100.4 101.1 103.8 109.2 110.2 110.3
110.4 110.5 110.6 114.1 116.4 122.3
124.2 124.3 124.4 131.3 136.5 142.3
144.1 144.4 161.3 166.6 166.7 169.1
169.4
Jamaica 20.2 58.6
La Rochelle 85.2 55.3D
Lisbon 27.4
Malaga 122.2 123.2 158.1 158.3
Nevis 17.1 15.5 18.7 21.7 31.6 37.4 49.5
50.5 51.2 57.5 58.6 61.6 65.4 80.6
97.7 98.3 126.5 143.3
New England 31.4 126.5
Virginia 25.3 29.1 29.2 35.2 104.1 104.2
124.5 145.2 160.5
? 4.2 13.2 14.4 17.1 17.2 18.5 28.2
Farming 5.5 5.6 20.3 28.5 32.3 143.4 171.4
4.5D 125.2C 149.1D
Feathers 123.6 123.7
Firewood 73.1D 98.1D 180.1D(2)
Flour 18.7D 33.1D(3) 50.5D 61.6D 62.1D
65.4D 126.5D
Foreign exchange French 117.7C 160.1D
167.1D
Spanish 32.5 53.5 61.1 88.2 88.3 99.4
111.1 111.2 113.4 143.5 143.6 167.5
32.6D 47.3C 61.5C(3) 66.1D 69.7C
76.4D(5) 82.1D 86.2D 87.3D 87.4D
88.1C 88.1D(4) 88.2C 88.2D(6)
90.1D 90.2D(5) 92.3C 94.1D 96.6D
103.2D 109.3D 110.1D 110.3D

Persons (*continued*)
Cale, Thomas 82.1D
Callowhill, Thomas 83.1D 85.1D 86.1D
    86.2D 98.2D
Camborne, Thomas, wagoner 61.3D
    65.3D
Campian, Giles 152.4D
Cann, John 169.3D
Cardrow, Joseph of Dorchester 7.3 35.1
Cary, John of Bristol merchant 178.1
Cary, Nicholas of Exchange Ally,
    London goldsmith 51.4
Case, Thomas 104.1D
Chadwell, Richard 5.2D
Challenor, Ann widow innholder of the
    Rose 114.2 127.1D
Challenor, Francis 125.5D 126.1D
Chambers, Mary 2.7D
Champneys, Richard of Bristol
    merchant 45.6 53.6D 73.1D 77.1D
    77.1C 132.6D 137.1D 181.1D
Chance, John 72.1C(2)
Chapman, Allen 184.3
Chapman, Robert 130.1D
Chapman, Scarbrow of Bristol vintner
    & merchant 132.4 111.1C
Chapman, Stephen 27.5 7.1D 138.6C
Cheek, ? Colonel 35.6C
Cheldry, William 35.6D
Cheshire, John of Bristol glazier 80.5
    9.1D 59.6D 73.1D 89.1D 105.1D
    130.3D 153.1D 159.1D(2)
Chetwine, Edward of Bristol grocer
    142.6
Clark Willliam 137.1D
Clark, Abraham 122.1D
Clark, Edward 177.2D
Clark, Giles of Alveston, Glos yeoman
    171.1 184.1
Clark, James ship's captain 136.5D
Clark, Samuel of Bristol merchant
    142.5
Clark, Timothy ship's master 126.5D
Clark, William of Bristol merchant
    138.5 105.1D 132.1D 164.1D
Clarke, John of Bristol wine cooper
    149.7
Clement, Ann 89.1D
Clement, Simon of Bristol merchant
    22.3 86.1 86.2 96.1 96.2 97.2 103.2
    133.3 166.5 85.1D 94.1D 98.2D
    98.2C 103.7C 108.1D(4) 124.3D
    124.3C(2) 126.4C 132.5D(2) 134.6D

137.1C(2) 144.4D(2) 148.1D(2)
    148.1C(5) 150.2D; Walter father of
    22.3
Codner, ? 4.5D
Codrington, Richard 8.1D
Cole, Benjamin of Reading silkweaver
    147.2 58.1C(2)
Cole, William of Reading carpenter
    129.1D
Coleman, Thomas/William 58.1D
Coles, William of London merchant 3.3
    19.6
Collett, George of Seymers Court,
    Portisbury, Som 134.5 121.1D
Collett, Peter 30.3
Colston, Edward 10.8
Colston, Thomas 40.1D
Combes, Adam ship's master 85.6
Combes, Henry 50.6D
Connick, Thomas 131.1C
Cook, John Chamberlain of Bristol
    159.3 159.1D(2)
Cook, John of St Mary Port, Spain and
    London merchant 25.7 32.4 32.5
    32.6 32.7 39.1 45.5 58.3 65.5 69.1
    69.6 86.3 88.1 88.2 111.1 117.2 117.5
    39.5D 45.4D 47.1D 64.8D(2) 72.4D
    76.1D(2) 86.4D 93.1D 97.1D 99.4D
    100.1D 101.1D 109.2D 110.2D
    110.4D 110.6D 113.4D 116.4D
    132.4D 132.5D (3) C
Cook, Thomas of Exchange Ally,
    London goldsmith 51.4 76.4D(2)
Coombs, Adam 63.7D
Cooper, John of Yarmouth merchant
    63.7 72.1
Cope, Richard of Portbury, Somerset
    blacksmith 97.3 20.3D 105.1D
Cope, Susan 121.1D
Coppothright [Copperthwaite], John
    180.1D
Cornish, Henry 32.6D 76.4D
Cornock, Zacharie 143.2C
Corsley, Humphrey of Bristol
    Goldsmith 1.5 117.1 22.5D 32.6D
    35.6D 82.1D 89.1D 108.1D
    120.1D(2) 121.1D 127.1D 168.1D
Corsley, John 178.1D
Corsley, Richard of Bristol Goldsmith
    53.5 1.5D 35.6D(3) 69.7C 137.1D
    152.2D
Cotterell, ? Widow 151.1D 157.1D
    162.1D 168.1D(2)

Persons (*continued*)

Dorvele, David of Bristol merchant
126.2 73.1D

Dowding, Edward of Bristol and
Westbury ship's master 154.2
100.4D 110.1D 145.1D(2) 158.1D
158.3D 158.4D

Dowding, Robert of Bristol ropemaker
100.7 32.3D

Drake, John of Ash, Musbury, Devon
63.1; Sir William brother of 63.1
100.6

Drew, Joseph of Bristol, house
carpenter 31.3 154.3 159.2 8.1D
9.1D(2) 22.2D 73.1D 89.1D 105.1D
151.1D 153.1D(2) 159.1D(4) 173.2D

Drew, Roger ship's master 161.3D

Driver, Edmond 89.1D

Duddlestone, John 72.1C 94.5D 180.1D
185.2D

Dunning, William 46.6D

Durbin, Thomas of Bristol 47.4

Dyer, Mary 81.1D

Dyer, Samuel 118.1D(30 128.1D(3)
135.1D(4) 182.1D(3)

Dyer, Thomas of Bristol hosier 100.2
34.1D 172.1D(6) 182.1D; Elizabeth
wife of 74.1D(3) 81.1D(3) 100.2D
102.1D 107.1D 112.1D(3) 115.1D(6)
128.1D

Dyke, Thomas of Bristol 137.1D

Earle, Joseph 105.1D 111.2C

Earle, Mary 72.1D 72.1C(3)

Earle, Sir Thomas 65.6D

East, Robert of London brandy seller
62.2

Eastmond, Arthur of Calne, Wilts?
woollen draper 160.3

Eastmont, John of Sherborne Esquire
High Sheriff 163.4

Ebley, ? widow 8.1D

Edwards, Abel 137.1D 156.1D(4))
174.4D

Edwards, Abraham of Bristol
linendraper 33.4 161.1 5.3D 143.2C

Edwards, Francis carrier 100.5D(3)
122.4C 140.1D 155.5D(2) 157.1D
162.1D 168.1D(3)

Edwards, John wagoner 87.2D 137.1D
163.2D 170.1D

Edwards, Thomas of Bristol attorney
23.4 41.1D 120.1D 142.1D 142.1C
143.2C

Elliot, Thomas 77.1D 113.4D

Emblen, William 6.7

England, John 45.3D 55.3D

Enys, Richard 111.1C(2)

Everard, Phineas 43.1D

Evered, George 62.7D

Eyles, Joan 22.4C

Eyles, John of London merchant
125.5D 132.2D

Featherstone, Heneage of Alicant
merchant 160.1 142.4D 155.2D
167.1D

Finch, Henry 88.1C

Fisher, ? John Digby's steward 80.4C

Fisher, James of Bristol grocer 144.6

Fisher, William 73.1D

Fisher, William ship's master 87.3
62.4D 70.7D(2) 78.2D

Fitzharding, Lord Maurice 142.2D(2)
151.1D

Flay, Dorcas 180.1D

Fletcher, Joan 174.4D(2)

Flower,

Flower, Jane 18.4 8.1D 89.1D 105.1D
137.1D(2) 153.1D 180.1D;?
Daughter of 9.1D

Foot, ? 152.1D

Foot, James 174.1C

Ford, John of Bristol Butcher 52.4 60.1
73.1D 149.6D

Ford, William 25.5

Forrest, Joseph 1.2D

Forster, Richard 118.1D 128.1D(2)
146.1D 165.1D(2)

Foster, Richard 162.1C26

Fox, Captain Edward 10.4

Francis, Jonathan ship's master 50.5D

Franck, John 177.3D

Francklin, Richard 56.4

Frank, John 180.1D

Franklin, Richard 35.6D

Freake, Philip 142.2D

Freake, Philip ship's master 86.4D
110.2D 110.3D 166.7D 170.1D

Freaks, John 72.1C

Freeman, Edward 7.1D

Freeman, George 27.6D 155.1D 160.4D
163.1D

Freeman, James 7.5D 24.6D 105.1D
160.5D

Freeman, James apothecary 21.2D 93.7D

French, William 145.2D

Frere, John 90.2D

Horton, Hugh 35.6D
Horwood, Elizabeth [sister of Joseph Drew] 159.2C
Horwood, Francis 153.1D
Horwood, James 66.1D
Horwood, William of Bristol feltmaker **170.3** 159.1D
Hosey, John 180.1D
House, Samuel 58.1D
Howard, Henry of St Martins-in-the-Fields, London **92.6 163.5**
Hudson, John 35.6C
Hulbert, ? 152.1D
Hulbert, James 143.2C
Hulbert, John 68.1D
Hungerford, Dr Francis of Reading physician **59.4 87.2 184.2** 87.1D 127.1D
Hungerford, Thomas of Bristol linendraper **161.1** 59.4C(2) 70.6C 73.1C 120.1D 121.1D 139.1D 140.1D 141.1D 153.1D 154.1D 168.1D 181.1D
Hurding, John of Litton, Dorset, Counsellor at Law **151.2**
Hurle, Simon of Bristol Soapmaker **116.2** 7.3D 90.1C 126.1D
Hurlstone, Christopher carrier 62.7D(2) 151.2C
Hurne, John 20.7D
Hurst, Jarvis ship's master 55.4D
Iffe, Edward of Bristol hot-presser 74.1D(2) 81.1D(4) 89.1D 91.1D(4) 102.1D(4) 106.1D(4) 112.1D(2) 115.1D(2) 118.1D(3) 128.1D(2) 135.1D(4) 146.1D(3) 165.1D(2) 172.1D(2) 182.1D
Ingelo, Samuel [servant to John Bubb] 181.1D
Inketill, Edward 138.6C
Innes/Ynnys, Andrew 66.1D
Irish, George 35.6D 39.1D
Isay, Thomas 105.1D
Jackson, Joseph **21.5** 8.1D 38.1D 43.1D
Jackson, William 9.1C
Jacob, Edward of Clapton, Som. Yeoman **134.1 150.3 156.2 183.4** 72.3D 125.4C 141.1D
Jacob, James of Bristol distiller **45.7**
Jacob, John of Kenn, Somerset **134.1**
Jacob, Mark 136.3D
Jacobs, John ship's captain 86.3D(3)
Jaine, John 114.5D

James, Thomas 174.4D
Jayne, John of Bristol Wine cooper **116.5**
Jays, Simon ship's master 122.2D
Jefferies, William ship's master 85.1D 94.1D 96.1D 97.2D —-(2)
Jenkin, John 153.1D 156.1D(12)
Jones John **51.3**
Jones, Arthur 20.8D
Jones, Charles junior of Bristol merchant **171.3** 77.1D
Jones, Edward 22.2D(3) 130.3D(2) 153.1D 161.4D 164.1D
Jones, Edward of Bristol merchant **25.2 64.6** 105.1D 127.1D 180.1D
Jones, Henry Chancellor to the Bishop of Bristol **161.5**
Jones, John mason 173.2D
Jones, John of Bristol linendraper **99.6** 130.3D 154.1D
Jones, John ship's master 46.6D
Jones, Matthias 173.2D
Jones, Nathanael 173.2D
Jones, Stanton **12.8**
Jones, Thomas of Llandavenny 104.4C
Jones, Thornton 126.4C
Jones, William 113.4C 132.1D
Jones, William of Bristol merchant **138.5** 164.1D
Jonson, Robert 111.1C 113.4D
Jonson, Samuel 121.1C(2) 153.1D
Joorey, Col. Thomas 171.1D(2)
Jordan, Thomas of Bristol grocer **95.3** 86.2D(2)
Joyner, John 9.1D 67.1D
Keene, Thomas wagoner 2.3D
Keeping, Susan 137.1D
Kekewich, Cicely 68.1D
Kekewich, Peter of London haberdasher **65.6** 70.6C 73.1C
Kekewich, Samuel of St Mary Port, Cadiz [TS factor] **25.7 32.4 69.6 88.1 88.2 111.1 117.2 117.5 143.6 148.1 167.5 185.3 185.4** 7.1D(2) 61.5C 64.8D 74.1C(3) 86.3D 86.4D 87.4D 93.1D 97.1D 99.4D 100.1D 101.1D 109.2D 110.2D 110.4D 110.6D 113.3C 116.4D 120.1D(2) 122.3D 124.2D 124.4D 125.3D 131.3D 132.4D(2) 132.5D(2) 136.5D 144.1D 150.2D 161.3D 166.6D 166.7D 169.1D 169.4D 182.1D
Kent, John of Reading clothier **78.6**

Persons (*continued*)

Keyes, Grace of Virginia **31.5**

King, Charles of Bristol wine cooper **152.3** 150.2D 169.3D 170.1D

King, James 137.1D 152.1D

King, Nathanael of Bristol Clerk of Market 22.2D(2)

King, Richard 8.1D

King, William 72.1C

King, William of Bristol Surveyor of Customs **96.5**

Kippin, Caleb 130.3D(2)

Kippin, Joseph **24.1**

Kippin, Susan 164.1D

Kirby, Andrew I & II of Bordeaux merchants **48.3 64.2 64.3** 75.1C

Knight, Gabriel 71.1D 74.1D(2)

Knight, Sir John 49.5D

Lambard/Lambert, Thomas 90.2D

Lamboll, Jonathan of Reading Maltster [TS brother-in-law] **87.1 109.4 109.5 131.1 147.6** 147.2C; George, father of **129.1**; Sarah, mother of **129.2** 129.1D

Lane, Richard of Bristol sugar baker **138.9** 80.1C

Lane, Thomas 90.2D 130.2C(2)

Langsworth, Richard of Bristol shoemaker **163.6** 154.1D 159.1D(4)

Lansdown, William 83.1D 96.5D

Lapley, James 32.6D

Lawford, Thomas 174.4D

Lawhorne, James 68.1D

Le Conti, John 152.2C

Lewger, William **23.5**

Lewis, Thomas 156.1D

Lewis, William 162.1D

Lilly, Stephen 85.3C

Linch, Martha of Tockinton [TS maid-servant] **92.7**

Linckhorn, John **44.4**

Lipyeatt, Robert of Bristol maltster & distiller **154.5** 8.1D 137.1D 153.1D 180.1D

Liston, ? ship's captain —-

Little, Humphrey **27.1**

Little, John 168.1C

Little, Robert 174.4D(2)

Lloyd, ? ship's master 103.9D

Lloyd, Edward 58.1D 85.4C 153.1D 164.1D

Lloyd, Edward, overseer to W Rogers **94.4 95.4**

Lloyd, Henry 156.1D

Lloyd, Jacob 168.1C(2)

Lloyd, Jacob of Bristol cobbler [TS groom] **170.4**

Lock, Thomas 186.2D

Long, George 123.4C

Long, John 142.1D

Longman, Thomas of Bristol grocer **58.2 113.2**

Love, John of Bristol grocer **55.6** 143.1D

Lower, Thomas **14.3**

Lukins, John **112.1** 106.1D 115.1D(4) 118.1D(5) 128.1D(2) 135.1D 137.1D 146.1D(4) 165.1D(2) 172.1D

Luton, Tobias 49.6D 59.4D 65.3D 87.2D 89.1D 152.4D

Luttrell, Thomas of Clevedon, Som. yeoman **25.1 97.4** 4.5D(3) 32.3D(2) 42.1D(2) 66.1D

Lysons, Robert of Bristol butcher 46.5

Macey, Edward 5.2D

Machen, John 41.1D 42.1D

Maddison, William ship's master 60.7D 100.1D 169.1D

Maicock, Sarah 89.1D

Maison, George of Bristol soapmaker **79.1**

Mancell/Mansill, Thomas 103.8D

Mandeville, John 87.6D

Marsh, Richard of Bristol merchant **1.1**

Martin, Thomas 73.1D

Martin, Thomas of London **62.1**

Martindale, Edward I [TS stepson-in-law] **24.5 27.3 29.1 59.1** 5.1D 9.1D 23.3C 66.1D 103.7C; **Edward II** 139.1D 175.1D 181.1D 181.1D

Massinger, Elizabeth 91.1D(3) 135.1D

Massinger, John of Bristol, hosier **27.6 155.1 163.1** 8.1D(2) 34.1D(28) 40.1D(3) 54.1D(31 68.1D 71.1D(27) 74.1D(30) 81.1D(22) 91.1D(18) 102.1D(12) 106.1D(9) 112.1D(10) 115.1D(10) 118.1D(14) 122.1D 128.1D(29) 135.1D(24) 137.1D 146.1D(12) 165.1D(2) 172.1D

Massinger, Robert of Bristol merchant **109.3** 88.2C 103.3C 103.8D(2)

Maston, William 81.1D

Matthew, Lewis **12.2**

Matthews, John 69.2D 73.1D 89.1D 104.1D 145.2D 154.1D(2)

Maxy, Nathanael 177.2D

Persons (*continued*)
Tyler, Edward 89.1D
Tyler, Robert **10.9** 19.4D
Tyler, Thomas of Bristol grocer **144.7**
Tyndall, Onesiphorus of Bristol grocer
    95.2
Tynte, Hugh **17.7**
Tyte, George 41.1D
Vaughan, Herbert of Bristol gentleman
    63.8
Veale, Nicholas 138.7D
Velasco, Don Rodrigo 137.1D
Vickris, Richard 7.5D(2) 39.1D
Vincent, Francis 77.1D
Vincent, John **36.3**
Wadden, Peter of the Marsh, Bristol
    117.1C
Walden, Thomas of Bristol merchant
    2.1 2.3 87.6 9.1D(2) 23.2D 24.3D
    32.1D 35.6D 46.1D 60.9D 61.2C
    72.3D 77.1D 88.4D 89.1D 90.1C
    90.2C(2) 91.1D 103.9D 104.2D
    106.1D 112.1D(2) 115.1D(3) 118.1D
    122.1D(2) 123.1C 135.1D 145.5D
    145.5C 146.1D 154.1D 159.2C
    165.1D 182.1D(2)
Wall, Charles 111.2C
Wall, Matthew of Wexford, Ireland
    22.4
Wall, Noah 68.1C
Wall, Thomas of Bristol bookseller 8.1D
    127.1D 164.1D
Wallis, Bridget of Portbury, Somerset
    7.1 114.7 151.1D
Wallis, George **14.5**
Wallis, James of Clapton, Somerset
    26.3 7.1D(2) 72.1C
Walter, Bethel of Bristol Grocer **92.2**
    142.1D
Walter, Hugh of Bristol linendraper
    174.2
Walter, Katherine mother of Hugh
    174.2
Walter, Katherine wife of Bethel,
    mother Henry Winter 142.2D(2)
Walter, Martha family of Matthew
    107.1D
Walter, Matthew of Bristol grocer **103.7**
Warcupp, Dr ? 132.1D 160.5D
Ward, Philip of the Crown Office 73.1D
    105.1D 0
Warden, Matthias 8.1D
Warren, Benjamin 177.2D

Warren, John of Musbury, Devon
    Clothier [son of TS brother-in-law]
    111.4 134.2 43.1D 82.1D 107.1D
    122.1D(3) 153.1D
Warren, Nicholas of Devon Yeoman
    138.7 105.1D
Warren, Pendock of Bristol vintner
    126.4 122.1D 123.4D
Wasbrow John of Bristol cooper **28.3**
    8.1D 73.1D; Mary Wife of **75.2**
    144.3 28.3D 65.2D 116.3D 124.5D
    126.1D
Wasbrow, Richard **50.1** 5.5D 22.2D
    55.2D 57.5D 72.1D
Washington, Lawrence of Upper
    Macholick, Potomac, Virginia
    [George Washington's grandfather]
    **30.1 101.2 104.1 124.5 126.1 132.1
    145.2 147.5 160.5 167.4** 78.4D
    101.3D 104.2D
Wastfield, Bethshua [daughter of TS
    stepson-in-law Daniel] **124.6**
Watmore, Humphrey 141.1D
Watson, John 90.1C
Watts, Edmund, ship's master 101.2D
    124.5D 126.1D(2) 145.2D
Watts, Samuel 181.1D
Wayland, John 104.4D
Weare, John 62.7D 68.1D
Weaver, William 9.1C
Webb, James **16.4** 127.1D(2)
Webb, Joan 77.1D
Webb, John 106.1D 164.1D 180.1D
Webb, Robert of Bristol trunk-maker
    69.2C 102.1D(2) 106.1D(2) 112.1D
    118.1D(2) 128.1D(2) 135.1D(2)
    146.1D(3) 153.1D 165.1D(4)
    182.1D; Elizabeth wife of 112.1D
    118.1D 135.1D(3) 146.1D 165.1D
    172.1D 182.1D
Webb, William 90.2D
Webber, Nicholas ship's master 18.7D
    21.7D
Wedmore, Thomas **60.1**
Weekes, William 7.5D
Weeks, George 7.5D
Wellsted, Stephen 149.5C
Wheatley, Nathanael of Banbury
    130.2D 134.2C
Whetcombe, John 29.6C(2)
Whetham, Daniel 85.4D
Whiben, Samuel 117.7D
Whiston, James 73.1D